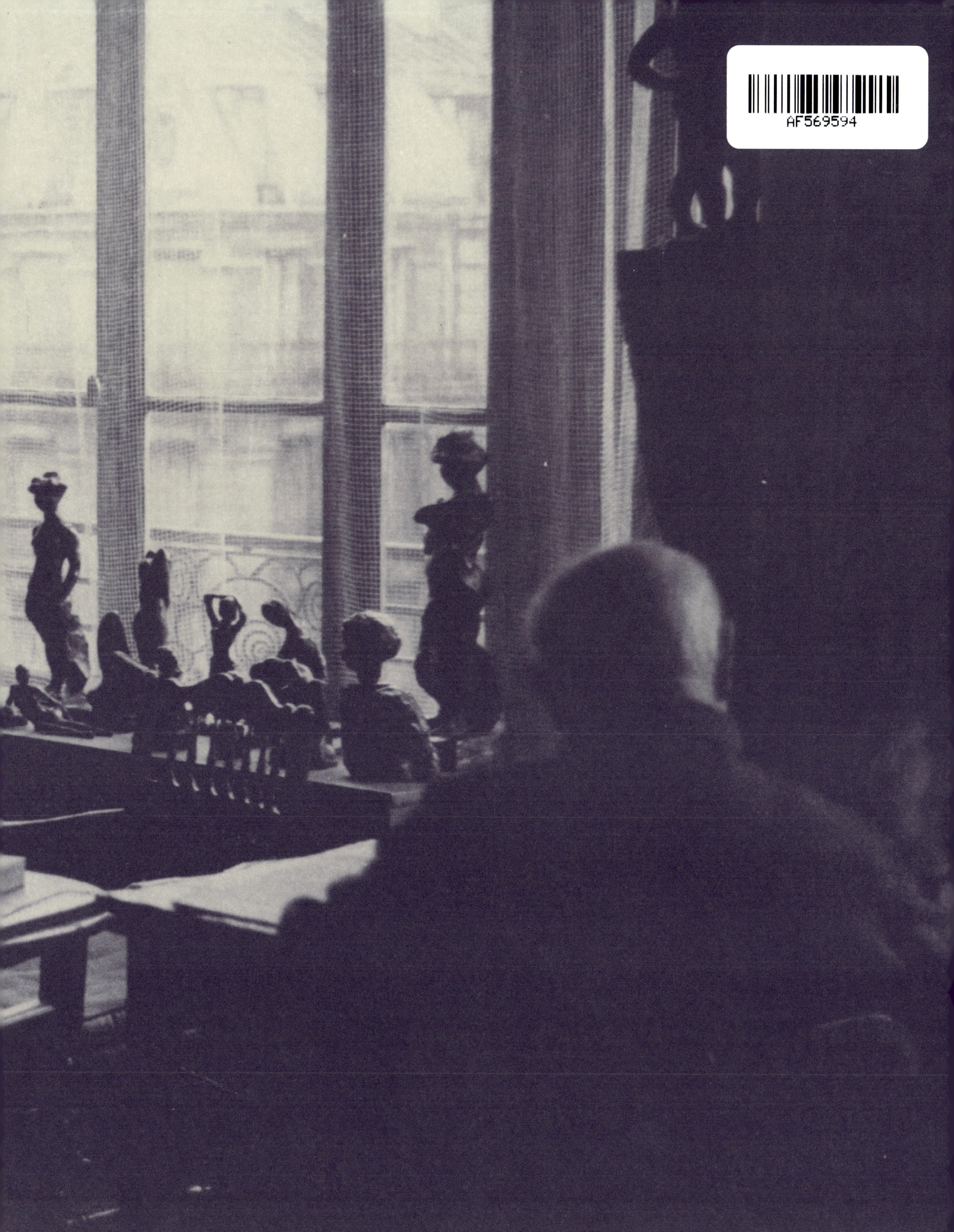

Matisse

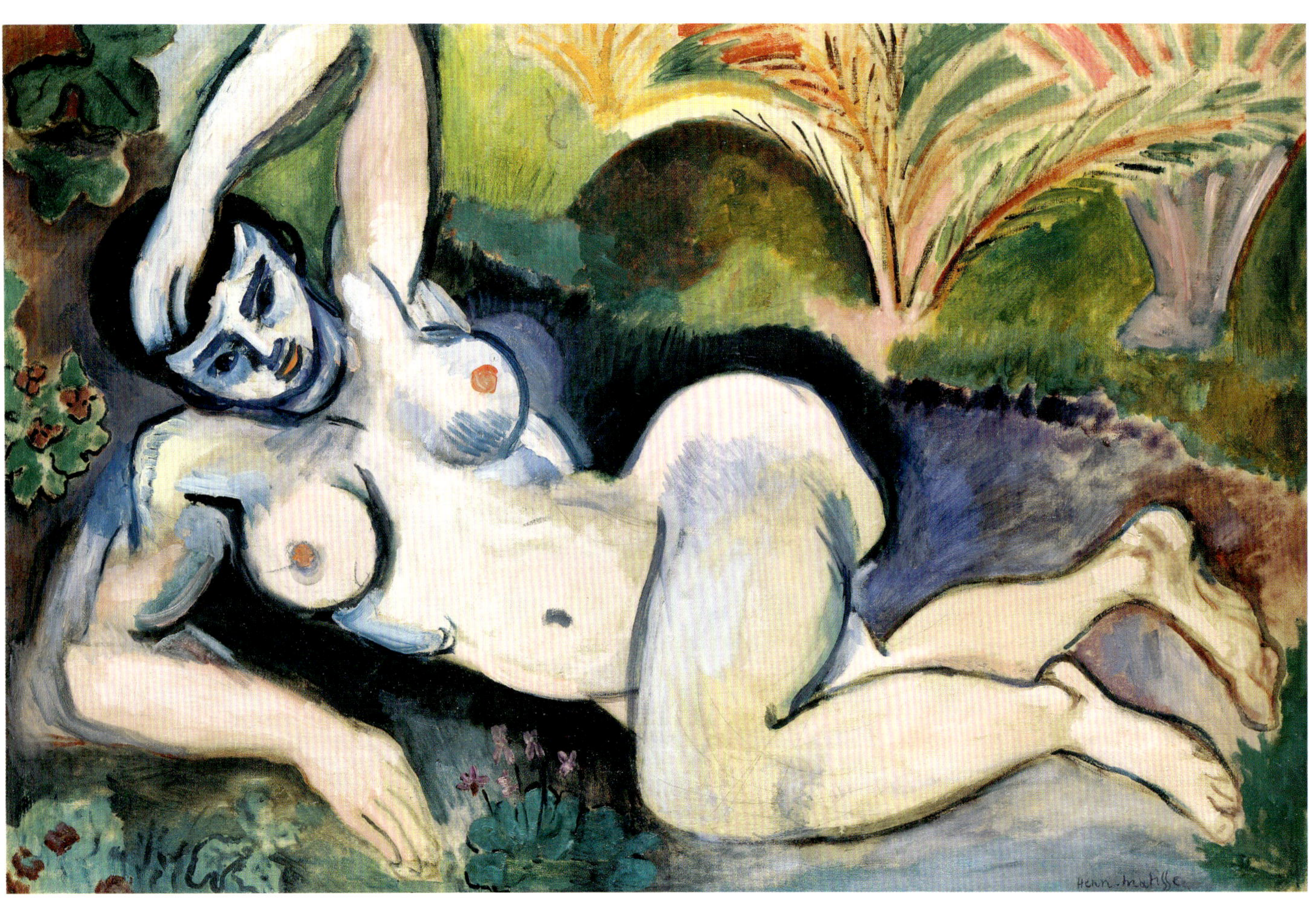

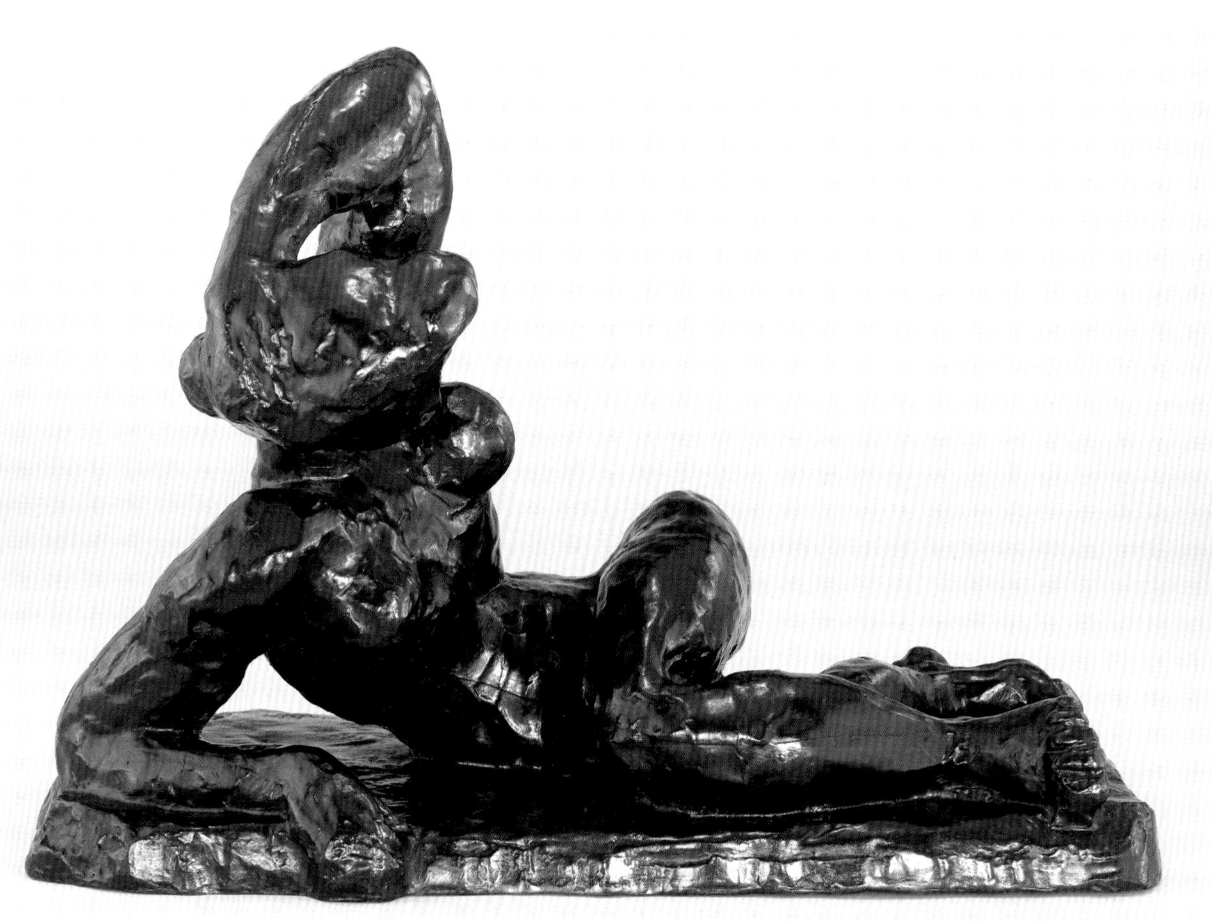

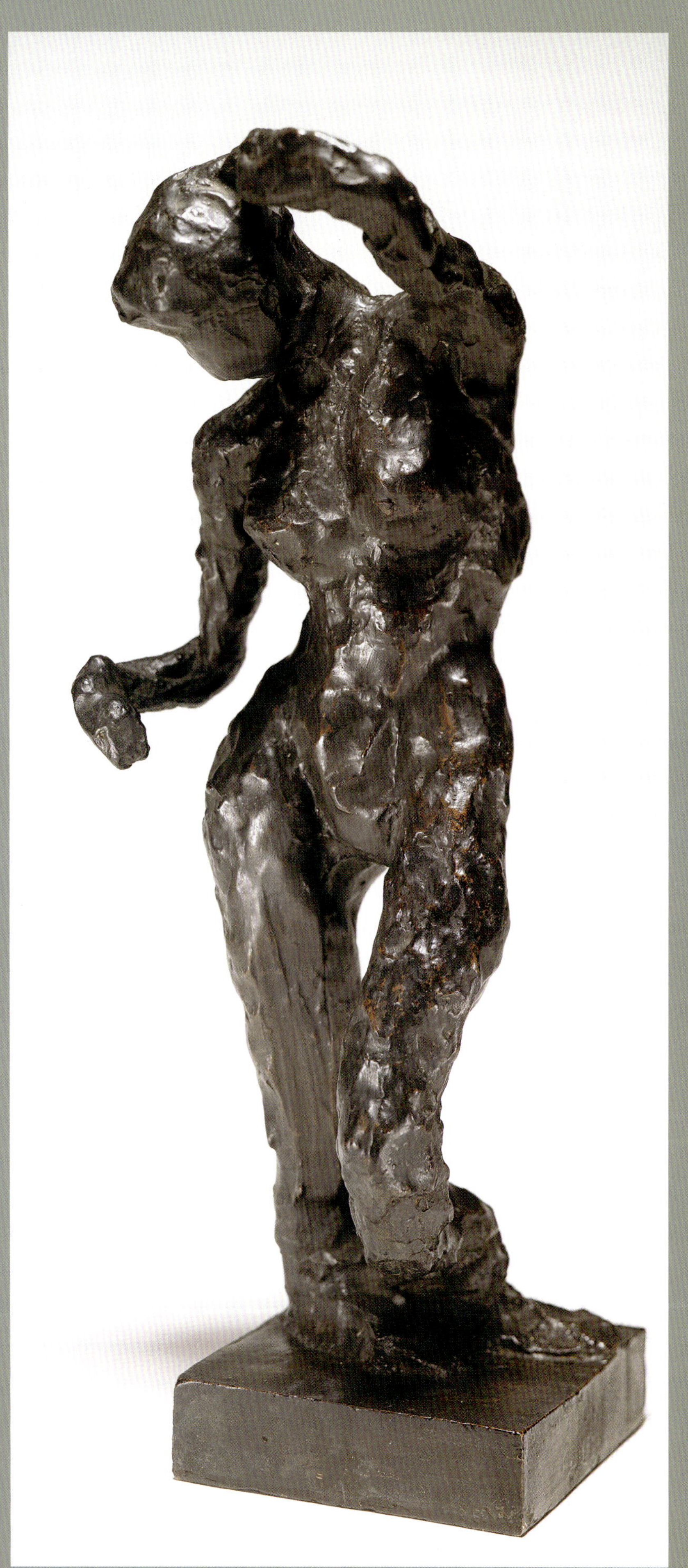

DOROTHY KOSINSKI

JAY MCKEAN FISHER

STEVEN NASH

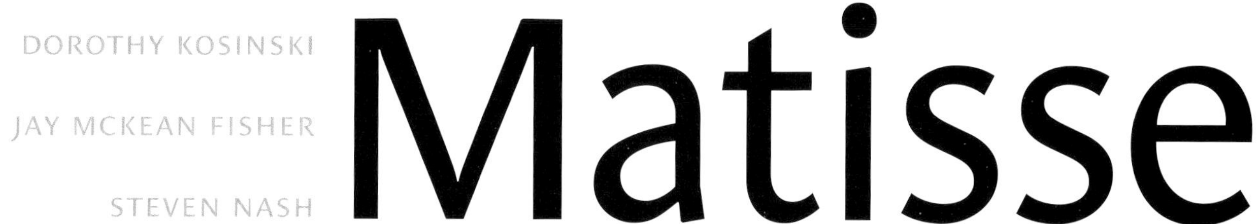

Matisse

painter as sculptor

ESSAYS BY

ANN BOULTON

OLIVER SHELL

CONTRIBUTIONS BY

HEATHER MACDONALD

JED MORSE

OLIVER SHELL

The Baltimore Museum of Art

Dallas Museum of Art

Nasher Sculpture Center

Yale University Press, New Haven and London

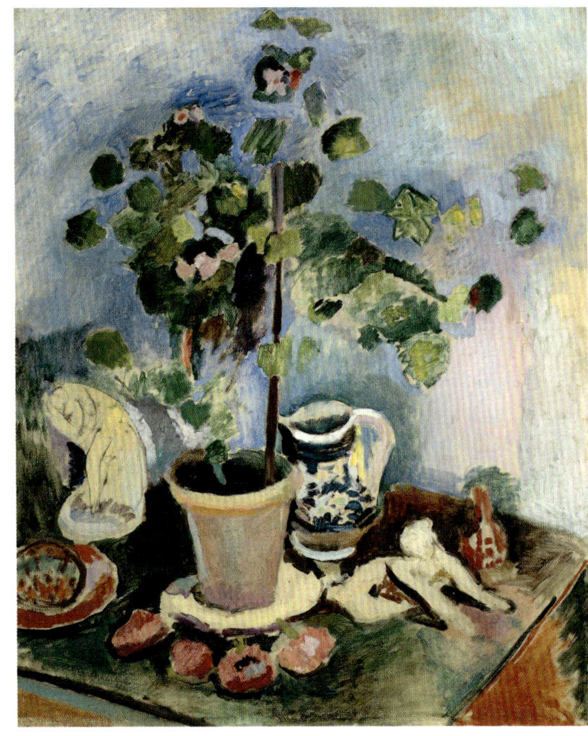

This catalogue has been published in conjunction with the exhibition *Matisse: Painter as Sculptor,* jointly organized by The Baltimore Museum of Art, the Dallas Museum of Art, and the Nasher Sculpture Center.

The national tour is presented by Bank of America, the exhibition's exclusive corporate partner.

This exhibition is supported by an indemnity from the Federal Council on the Arts and the Humanities.

Additional organizing support is provided by the National Endowment for the Arts and The Pierre and Maria-Gaetana Matisse Foundation.

Preparation of the exhibition catalogue was underwritten, in part, by The Richard C. von Hess Foundation. Additional support was provided through a Samuel H. Kress Paired Fellowship for Research in Conservation and the History of Art from the Center for Advanced Study in the Visual Arts, National Gallery of Art.

Exhibition Schedule

Dallas Museum of Art
1717 North Harwood Street, Dallas, Texas 75201
and
Nasher Sculpture Center
2001 Flora Street, Dallas, Texas 75201
January 21–April 29, 2007

The Dallas presentation is made possible by The Dallas Foundation.

San Francisco Museum of Modern Art
151 Third Street, San Francisco, California 94103
June 9–September 16, 2007

The San Francisco presentation is generously supported by the Koret Foundation Funds and the Evelyn D. Haas Exhibition Fund.

The Baltimore Museum of Art
10 Art Museum Drive, Baltimore, Maryland 21218
October 28, 2007–February 3, 2008

The Baltimore presentation is generously sponsored by The Rouse Company Foundation and Jeanette C. and Stanley H. Kimmel.

Contents

List of Lenders

Art Gallery of Ontario, Toronto
The Art Institute of Chicago
The Baltimore Museum of Art
Bridwell Library Special Collections, Perkins School of Theology, Southern Methodist University
Iris and B. Gerald Cantor Collection
Centre Pompidou, Paris; Musée national d'art moderne/Centre de création industrielle
Charles Janoray, LLC, New York
Dallas Museum of Art
The Detroit Institute of Arts
Mr. and Mrs. Claude Duthuit
Fine Arts Museums of San Francisco
Folkwang Museum, Essen
Fondation Beyeler, Riehen/Basel
Franklin D. Murphy Sculpture Garden, U.C.L.A., Courtesy of The Armand Hammer Museum, Los Angeles
Mr. and Mrs. Stanley R. Gumberg, Pittsburgh
Harry Ransom Center, University of Texas at Austin
Hirshhorn Museum and Sculpture Garden, Smithsonian Institution, Washington, D.C.
Los Angeles County Museum of Art
Stephen Mazoh
The Metropolitan Museum of Art, New York
The Minneapolis Institute of Arts
Dr. and Mrs. Morton Mower
Musée de Grenoble
Musée départemental Matisse, Le Cateau-Cambrésis
Musée Matisse, Nice
Museum Boijmans Van Beuningen, Rotterdam
The Museum of Modern Art, New York
Nancy A. Nasher and David J. Haemisegger
Raymond and Patsy Nasher Collection, Dallas
National Gallery of Canada, Ottawa
Noortman Master Paintings, Maastricht
The Perisset Trust, New York
Gerald and Kathleen Peters
Philadelphia Museum of Art
Pierre and Maria-Gaetana Matisse Foundation
San Francisco Museum of Modern Art
Solomon R. Guggenheim Museum, New York
Stedelijk Museum, Amsterdam
Tate
Yale University Art Gallery, New Haven, Connecticut
and several lenders who wish to remain anonymous

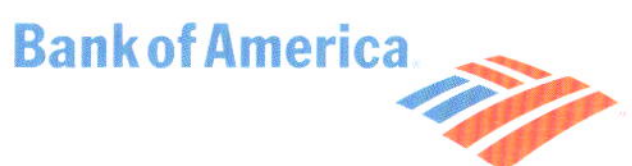

The publication of this volume was made possible by Bank of America.

Bank of America is proud to be the exclusive corporate partner of the national tour of *Matisse: Painter as Sculptor,* an exhibition organized jointly by The Baltimore Museum of Art, the Dallas Museum of Art, and the Nasher Sculpture Center.

At Bank of America we strive for higher standards in everything we do for our customers, shareholders, associates, and communities. It is therefore fitting that for this exhibition we are partnering with four of our country's—indeed the world's—greatest cultural institutions. We believe that our commitment to the arts translates into an enduring investment in the quality of life in communities served by Bank of America nationwide.

It is our hope that you will enjoy the opportunity to visit *Matisse: Painter as Sculptor* and encourage continued interest and support of the arts.

Foreword

Henri Matisse, long recognized as one of the twentieth century's leading artistic innovators, has been the subject of numerous exhibitions. Yet, his sculpture has not been fully explored—in its own right, in the context of his work across media, or in the history of modern sculpture. The first major exhibition of his sculpture in America to be held in over twenty years, *Matisse: Painter as Sculptor* presents this great French master, so widely appreciated for his elegant draftsmanship and brilliant paintings, as an equally accomplished artist in three dimensions. This landmark project, documented by this scholarly catalogue, has its origins in great American collections, a lively dialogue among scholars and curators, and an active partnership among its organizers, The Baltimore Museum of Art, the Dallas Museum of Art, and the Nasher Sculpture Center.

There has long been a fascination with Matisse and his sculpture among Americans, who became some of his earliest and most perceptive patrons. Several American collections form the artistic core of this exhibition. Works owned by pioneering patrons of modernism—Leo and Gertrude Stein, Michael and Sarah Stein, Harriet Lane Levy, and Claribel and Etta Cone—are highlighted in the exhibition and catalogue. These collectors were linked to one another by common interest and by friendship. Happily, examples of the works they acquired are today in the collections of The Baltimore Museum of Art and the San Francisco Museum of Modern Art, both venues for our exhibition. More recently, Raymond Nasher and his late wife Patsy developed an important collection of Matisse sculpture, now exhibited in the broader context of modern and contemporary sculpture at the Nasher Sculpture Center in Dallas.

Over Matisse's extended artistic career there was no more important single collector of his sculpture than Baltimore's Etta Cone. At first with her sister Claribel and then alone, Etta acquired twenty-six Matisse sculptures in all, those in The Cone Collection in Baltimore and a small group given to the Weatherspoon Art Museum at the University of North Carolina at Greensboro, the location of the Cone family textile mills. The richness of The Cone Collection in particular provided a body of Matisse's sculpture, purchased directly from him, that could serve as a touchstone for scholars studying his work in the medium and as a critical mass of loans for this ambitious exhibition.

Matisse's first sculpture exhibition was held in America, at Alfred Stieglitz's gallery 291 in 1908. The two major retrospectives held during the artist's lifetime also took place in the United States, the first at The Museum of Modern Art in New York in 1931, the second at the Philadelphia Museum of Art in 1948. Two more recent American exhibitions have concentrated on his sculpture, one in 1972 at The Museum of Modern Art, the other in 1984 at the Kimbell Art Museum in Fort Worth, Texas.

Matisse: Painter as Sculptor takes a broader view of Matisse's three-dimensional work than attempted before, demonstrating just how much the artist worked across media as he developed his sculpture. Prompted by the extensive American holdings of Matisse, this major retrospective examines the artist's sculptures within the totality of his work and includes important paintings, drawings, and prints that create a visual and conceptual dialogue with sculpture. We have considered Matisse's view of sculpture, as he did, in the round.

Also, Matisse's sculpture is examined within the continuum of a rich sculptural tradition, stretching from the late nineteenth-century French sculpture that served as Matisse's first inspiration to the international work of his contemporaries. This perspective, inspired in part by the Nasher Sculpture Center's mission and collection, provides the best view of the role Matisse's sculpture played within the history of twentieth-century art.

Three organizing institutions in Baltimore and Dallas have joined forces and worked closely together on every stage of the project, from the artistic conception of the exhibition to the complicated arrangements required for the care and shipment of such important works of art. This has been a collaborative and interactive process that has required both intellectual exchange and generosity of spirit. It is truly a case where the whole has become greater than the sum of its parts.

The Dallas Museum of Art first conceived the idea of this exhibition in 1999 and played the leadership role in shaping the exhibition and in initiating collaborations with both the BMA and the Nasher Sculpture Center. Dorothy Kosinski, Senior Curator of Painting and Sculpture and the Barbara Thomas Lemmon Curator of European Art at the Dallas Museum of Art, directed the organizational curatorial effort with Steven Nash, Director of the Nasher Sculpture Center, and Jay Fisher, Deputy Director for Curatorial Affairs and Senior Curator of Prints, Drawings, and Photographs at The Baltimore Museum of Art. These three then expanded the collaboration within their respective institutions with the addition of Heather MacDonald, the Lillian and James H. Clark Assistant Curator of Painting and Sculpture at the DMA, Jed Morse, Assistant Curator at the NSC, and Oliver Shell, Assistant Curator of European Painting and Sculpture, and Ann Boulton, Objects Conservator, both at the BMA. We are especially grateful to this remarkable group of professionals, who formulated and realized the mission of this exhibition and worked closely with other staff members in their respective museums.

At all three institutions we are fortunate to have dedicated educators, advocates for the needs and interests of our audience; we also benefit from the talents of our exhibition staffs, whose imaginative minds always find a new and completely effective way to present each exhibition. Added to these very visible results in the galleries are the unseen efforts of dozens of staff members at the three institutions—those who raise the funds that support museum programs, those who promote and market the exhibition, those who pack, ship, and preserve the art, and of course, those who protect the artworks every day.

It takes an equal commitment of financial support to realize the scholarship and exhibition planning required for such an ambitious project. We deeply appreciate the vision and leadership of Bank of America, the exhibition's national tour sponsor and exclusive corporate partner, which in each of our communities—Dallas, San Francisco, and Baltimore—plays a significant role in the support of cultural programs and institutions. We are grateful for the enthusiastic support of Walter B. Elcock, President of Bank of America Texas, who serves as President of the Board of Trustees of the Dallas Museum of Art, and for the engagement of his colleagues, John Berry, Senior Vice President of Sponsorship and Market Planning, Pam McQuitty, Central/Southwest Regional Manager Executive, and Andrew Pleplar, Senior Vice President, Corporate Philanthropy, in helping make the exhibition possible. A project of this magnitude would not have been achievable without such major support. Bank of America has been a remarkable partner in the collaboration that has brought this exhibition to the public.

In addition, we would like to acknowledge: an indemnity from the Federal Council on the Arts and the Humanities; the National Endowment for the Arts and The Pierre and Maria-Gaetana Matisse Foundation in New York for their support for research; and The Richard C. von Hess Foundation and the Center for Advanced Study in the Visual Arts for partial support of the publication.

The concentration of the artist's work at the BMA enabled us to undertake the first comprehensive technical examination of Matisse's practice of sculpture production. The study was supported in part by two Kress Curatorial Fellowships at the BMA, funded by the Samuel H. Kress Foundation, and by a remarkable Paired Fellowship for Research in Conservation and the History of Art at the Center for Advanced Study in the Visual Arts, National Gallery of Art, also funded by the Samuel H. Kress Foundation. This paired fellowship brought together conservator Ann Boulton and curator Oliver Shell. In Baltimore, organizational costs were supported by a grant from The Rouse Company Foundation and a generous donation from Jeanette Kimmel, a relative of Claribel and Etta Cone, and Stanley Kimmel. In Dallas we acknowledge the generous support of The Dallas Foundation. This grant is for the presentation of the exhibition in Dallas and is given in recognition of the inaugural partnership between the Dallas Museum of Art and the Nasher Sculpture Center.

We are pleased that *Matisse: Painter as Sculptor* will be presented at an additional venue, the San Francisco Museum of Modern Art. We sincerely appreciate the enthusiastic support that SFMOMA Director Neal Benezra and his colleagues have afforded the exhibition.

Finally, we wish to thank our numerous lenders, who were willing to relinquish these magnificent works for the exhibition tour. We are profoundly grateful for their generosity in making these loans, for each fulfills a specific charge in offering our audiences the best possible view of Matisse's sculpture and its crucial place in the history of modern art. In this regard we are particularly indebted to the family of Henri Matisse, and wish to express our gratitude for their loans and significant support of this exhibition.

Doreen Bolger, *Director,* The Baltimore Museum of Art
John R. Lane, *The Eugene McDermott Director,* Dallas Museum of Art
Steven Nash, *Director,* Nasher Sculpture Center

Acknowledgments

This exhibition and its publication are a testimony to the commitment of many individuals and the staff of three art museums. Dorothy Kosinski's proposal for a Matisse sculpture exhibition for the Dallas Museum of Art was soon embraced by Director Jack Lane and Deputy Director Bonnie Pitman, who were then joined by Director Doreen Bolger at The Baltimore Museum of Art and our curatorial colleague, Director Steven Nash at the Nasher Sculpture Center, with the strong support of that institution's founder, Raymond Nasher. Their solid support and encouragement prevailed through a long gestation period and has provided the foundation for the success of this project.

As should be well known to today's museum visitors, the curators who direct projects such as this may be the most visible figures in what must be a much larger effort. This collaboration among three museums is no exception, and we are first of all pleased to share any credit that may be derived from this exhibition with a large team of museum professionals, who committed their talents and diligence to making a project of this magnitude possible. Collaboration this extensive requires the knowledge and organization of an exhibition coordinator, and we are especially grateful to Tamara Wootton-Bonner, Director of Exhibitions and Publications at the DMA, who not only worked closely with her colleagues in Dallas but also was in constant communication with the staff in Baltimore. With her colleague Eric Zeidler, she also coordinated the publication, working with Michelle Boardman, Director of Creative Services at the BMA. Mitro Hood, Senior Photographer at the BMA, photographed innumerable works for the catalogue, and Chelsey Moore at the BMA was responsible for obtaining photographs and reproduction rights for the publication.

The complicated logistics of loans for this exhibition was overseen by DMA Director of Collections Management, Gabriela Truly, who worked closely with Senior Registrar Melanie Harwood at the BMA and Jennifer Ritchie, Head of Registration and Rights and Reproductions, at the NSC. The development staff at the Dallas Museum of Art took the lead in our fundraising efforts. We wish to thank Diana Duncan, Director of Development, Debra Phares, Director of Donor Relations, both at the DMA, and their colleagues Judy Gibbs, Deputy Director for Development at the BMA, and Jane Offenbach, Director of Marketing and Development at NSC. Bob Robertson, Chief Financial Officer at the DMA, oversaw the financial coordination with his colleagues Robin Churchill, former Deputy Director of Finance and Planning at the BMA, and Lista Hightower, Director of Finance at NSC. Public Relations for the exhibition has resulted from the collaboration of Judy Conner, Director of Marketing at the DMA, working with her colleagues Jane Offenbach, Director of Marketing and Development at NSC, and Becca Seitz, Deputy Director for Marketing and Communication, and Anne Mannix, Director of Communications, both at the BMA.

Recognizing the challenge that sometimes arises for museum visitors in the viewing of sculpture, we included in our exhibition planning a strong education and interpretive approach to

Matisse's sculpture. The overall education effort was supervised by former Deputy Director of Education and Interpretation at the BMA, Allison Perkins, and her staff, Kimberly Meisten, Linda Andre, and Marcia Gregory. The BMA's Education and Interpretation Division was in close contact with Gail Davitt, Director of Education at the DMA, and Rachel Schulze, Assistant Curator of Education at the NSC. We also wish to thank Dan Bailey and his staff from the Imaging Research Center at the University of Maryland, Baltimore County, for dynamic digital learning tools that enhance the appreciation of sculpture.

As senior curators directing this exhibition, we acknowledge the importance of our larger team of curatorial colleagues, each of whom made a major contribution to the creative and organizational work behind the project. Our overall project director, Dorothy Kosinski, was ably assisted by Heather MacDonald, the Lillian and James H. Clark Assistant Curator of Painting and Sculpture at the DMA, who, in addition to writing for the catalogue, supervised the development of the exhibition checklist. Over the course of the project Dorothy Kosinski was assisted by members of her staff, including Laura Bruck, Lisa Jones, Lora Sariaslan, Lauren Schell, and Leslie Ureña. At the NSC, Jed Morse, Assistant Curator, was an important author for this catalogue. Additional support at NSC was provided by Amy Henry, Executive Assistant, and Marin Sullivan, Curatorial Intern. Oliver Shell, Assistant Curator of European Painting and Sculpture at the BMA, wrote an essay for the catalogue and provided significant help coordinating with Jay Fisher. One of the hallmarks of this particular study of Matisse's sculpture has been the technical study, directed by Ann Boulton, Objects Conservator at the BMA, who, working closely with Oliver Shell and with cooperation from Jed Morse and Joanna Rowntree, Conservator at NSC, wrote an essay for this catalogue.

Our curatorial enterprise and technical research were greatly benefited by the generous advice and counsel of our colleagues, including Harry Abramson, Lee Aks, Anne Azano, Ida Balboul, Tony Bannon, Bernard Barryte, Jane Bassett, Arthur Beale, Theresa Beall, Larry Becker, Kevin Bellew, Roger Benjamin, Olivier Berggruen, Yve-Alain Bois, Peter Boris, Katherine Bourguignon, Ivor Braka, Emily Braun, John Buchanan, Cynthia Burlingham, Victor Carlson, Alessandra Carnielli, Harry Cooper, Elisabeth Cornu, Elizabeth Cropper, James Cuno, Sharon Dec, Lisa Dennison, Terry Drayman-Weisser, Douglas Druick, Jean Dubos, Laure Dussieux, Mr. and Mrs. Claude Duthuit, Bob Egan, John Elderfield, Carol Eliel, Sharon Elsen, Hartwig Fischer, Jack Flam, Laura Fleischmann, Valerie Fletcher, Barbara Freund, Matthew Gale, Lisha Glinsman, Carol Grissom, Jennifer Gross, Wanda de Guébriant, Anne d'Harnoncourt, Phyllis Hattis, Charles Janoray, Caitlin Jenkins, Yale Kneeland, Elizabeth Kujarski, Hubert Lacroix, Susan Lake, Julie Lauffenburger, Jacques Laurent, Elisabeth Lebon, Franziska Lentzsch, Astrid Lorenzen-Branger, Peter Lukehart, Georges Matisse, Paul Matisse, Jacqueline Matisse-Monnier, Steven Mazoh, Jeff Mechlinski, Melissa Meighan, Ellen McBreen, Thomas McGill, Charles Millard, Robert Mnuchin, Isabelle Monod-Fontaine, Yolanda Montañés Brunet, Kathryn Morales, Lynn Orr, Michael Parke-Taylor, Gerald Peters, Sarah Pinchin, Robert Pincus-Witten, Lionel Pissarro, Marie Thérèse Pulvénis de Séligny, Chantal Quirot, Rebecca Rabinow, Emily Rafferty, Michael Raphael, Eve Reid, Sabine Rewald, Jock Reynolds, René de la Rie, Joseph Rishel, D. Rosini, Deborah Schorsch, Martine Soria, William South, Shelley Sturman, Dominique Szymusiak, John L. Tancock, Helen Tangires, Michael Taylor, Gary Tinterow, Jia-sun Tsang, Charles Tumosa, Guy Tossato, Gijs van Tuyl, Olga Viso, Warren Weitman, Elizabeth and Paul Wilson, Kazuhito Yoshii, Joseph Young, and Lynda Zycherman.

For the production of the catalogue, we especially appreciate the patience and good humor of the editor, Frances Bowles, the attention to detail of the proofreader, Melissa Duffes, and the diligent efforts of the staff at Marquand Books, including Larissa Berry, Sara Billups, Ed Marquand, Linda McDougall, Marissa Meyer, Marie Weiler, Carrie Wicks, and Jeff Wincapaw. We are pleased to work with Yale University Press, and thank Patricia Fidler and Carmel Lyons for their efforts in this co-publication.

And we extend our sincerest appreciation to the many lenders, who have helped ensure the success of this exhibition and publication.

Dorothy Kosinski
Senior Curator of Painting and Sculpture and
The Barbara Thomas Lemmon Curator of European Art
Dallas Museum of Art

Jay McKean Fisher
Deputy Director for Curatorial Affairs and
Senior Curator of Prints, Drawings, and Photographs
The Baltimore Museum of Art

Steven Nash
Director
Nasher Sculpture Center

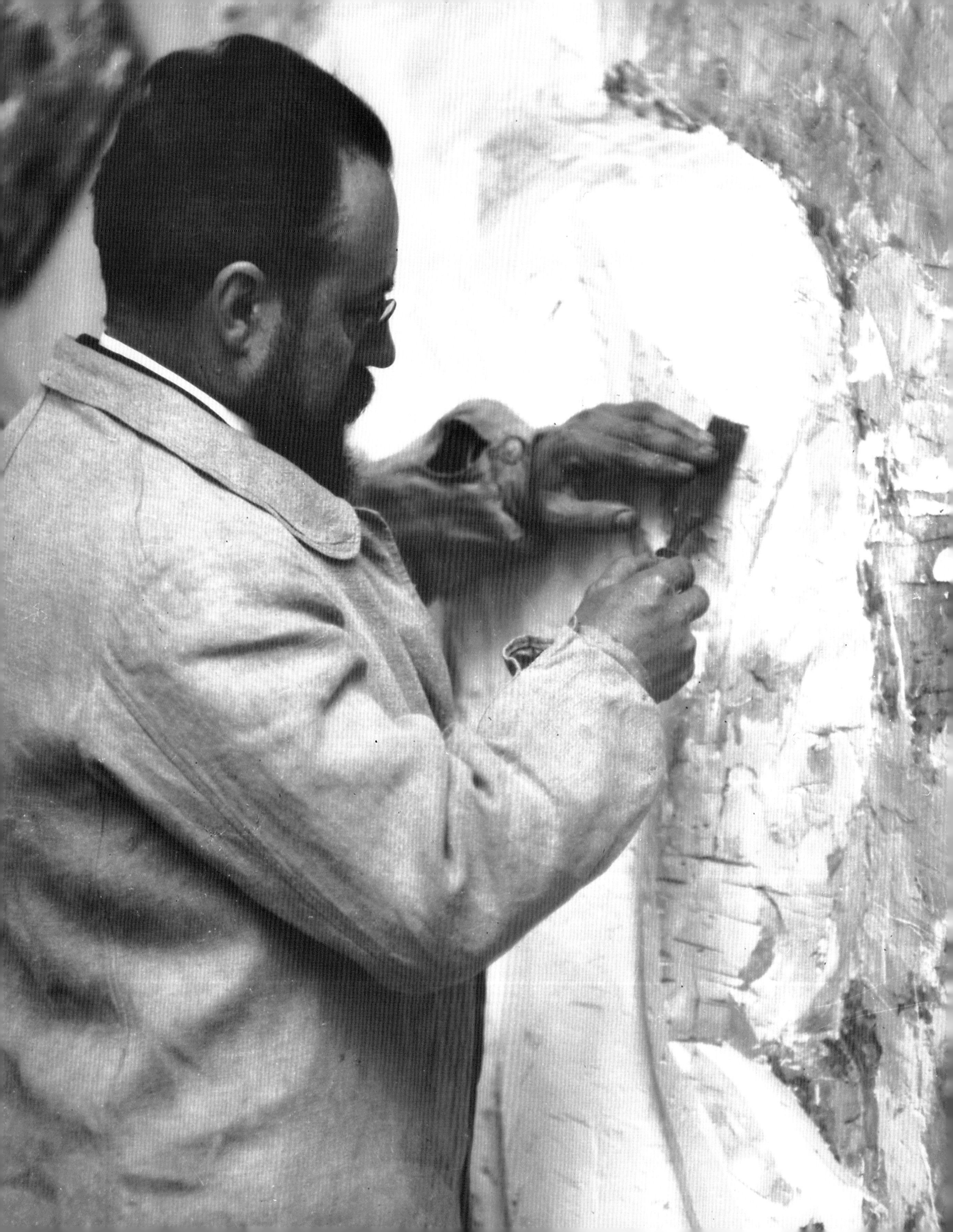

Steven Nash

The Other Matisse

. . . a sculpture must invite us to handle it as an object.

—Matisse to his students, 1908

In studies of Matisse's life and art, his sculpture is inevitably overshadowed. Painting, the main focus of his creative pursuits, dominates sculpture in both volume of production and expansiveness of achievement. His total output in sculpture was just over eighty works, and 75 percent of it dates from the first half of his career. This imbalance has, unfortunately, led too often to a bias that shortchanges the power and inventiveness of Matisse the sculptor, who, we read, "looked upon sculptures like paintings."[1] The literature on his sculpture is comparatively limited, and even fundamentally sympathetic writers have felt obliged to hedge their enthusiasm, observing, for example, that "all his conviction and inventiveness go into painting, with sculpture occasionally intervening to vary, confirm, complete or shed light upon discoveries which have usually already been made."[2]

Matisse himself helped stack the deck. "I sculpted as a painter. I did not sculpt like a sculptor."[3] Encouraging an assessment of his three-dimensional work vis-à-vis two-dimensional, pictorial issues, he added that he made sculpture "because what interested me in painting was the clarification of my ideas."[4] In the many instances when he absorbed images of his own sculptures into paintings to play symbolic or decorative roles or to explore spatial problems, such appropriations usually involved a surrendering of sculptural dimensionality to the painterly language of flattened drawing and thin skeins of color. All too readily the sculptures seem to sacrifice their fundamental identity. From all this, it might be assumed that sculpture for Matisse was marginal.

Not so. Matisse may have cultivated an image of himself as an amateur sculptor, a status that would give him considerable freedom in his exploration of the medium; several of his most inventive sculptures, for example, are essentially one-off efforts with no consequential development into other works, but there is no doubt that he valued the works and understood the overall import of sculpture in his artistic life. He exhibited sculptures early in his career and then fairly frequently and, although his commentaries on sculpture are not as highly developed as those on painting, they are articulate and revealing. Photographs taken at different points in his career show him posing proudly with sculptures. He worked on certain sculptures intently over lengthy periods of time, reporting in one case that he stood so long his feet became bloody.[5]

For Matisse, sculpture, like painting, was a matter of achieving a "condensation of sensations."[6] It was a means of resolving observation, feeling, and formal invention; formal issues in one medium were sometimes relevant and convertible to another. But sculpture also gave Matisse something that painting did not—a dialectic, in William Tucker's apt phrase, between "the grasped and the seen,"[7] between object and image, physicality and illusion. As Matisse put it: "Sculpture does not say what painting says. Painting does not say what music says. They are parallel ways, but you can't confuse them."[8] Sculpture for him was a resolutely haptic experience, not primarily visual or pictorial as often implied. It offered an art of volume, weight, density, and physical manipulation. He did not always come to sculptural solutions easily, but he had a distinct plastic sensibility and responded intuitively and emotionally to the process of working with physical form. Sculpture provided a means of thinking and feeling that painting did not and could not, in other words, a distinct epistemological system. In the consideration of Matisse's sculptural achievement that follows, we will

Fig. 1. Henri Matisse, *Madeline I,* 1901. Painted plaster, back view. Raymond and Patsy Nasher Collection, Dallas. Cat. 14.

attempt to understand better that sensibility, what it meant for the character of his work, and how it engaged key issues of perception, meaning, and representation.

Matisse's beginnings as a sculptor were not auspicious. His lack of formal training in sculpture shows both in the minor status of his few earliest works, produced before 1900,[9] and the laboriousness of his working methods throughout his career. He had little of the facile proficiency shown, for example, by Auguste Rodin and other leading nineteenth-century sculptors. His first major achievements came with the *Madeleine I* of 1901 (cat. 12–14, pp. 115, 120, 267) and *The Serf* of 1900–1903 (cat. 4–6, pp. 107, 109, 266), two works that seem inspired largely by problems he was dealing with at the time in his paintings. Albert Elsen characterized these two sculptures as indicative of opposing feminine and masculine modes.[10] Certainly, their formal and expressive natures are purposefully opposed.

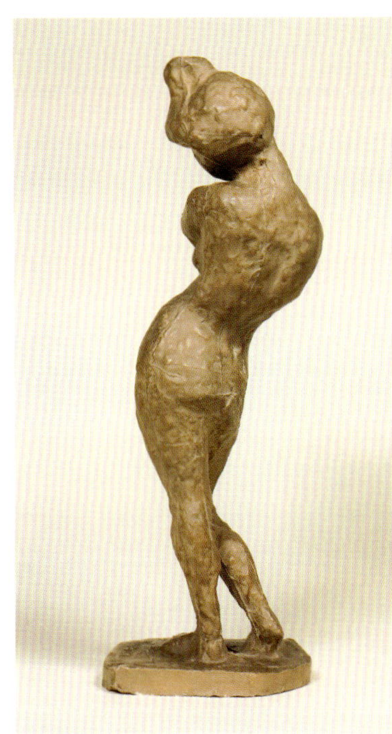

Madeleine I is an almost exact rendition in three dimensions of the pose and body type found in Matisse's painting *Standing Model (Nude Study in Blue)* (cat. 16, p. 117) from 1899–1900 and in the drawing *Study for Madeleine I* from 1901 (cat. 20, p. 120). Like these works, it provides an early example of his use of arabesque as a compositional device. But as sculpture, it required him to go beyond two dimensionality and to reconstruct his model—or *imagine* her, if working from paintings and drawings—from all perspectives. Thanks to its smooth, serpentine contours, the final sculpture when viewed from the front tends to look flat, implying a short depth of sculptural field. In reality, it carves out a dynamic, upward spiraling movement initiated by the lifting of the right foot off the base and terminated in the topknot of the coiffure. To be understood, this twisting of volume and space must be seen in the round (fig. 1); no one view is fully representative. By suppressing the arms of the figure, Matisse clarified even more its three-dimensional spin.

The painting and drawing of this figure must perforce strive to reconcile flatness and three dimensionality. Matisse's brushwork and coloration in the painting create a play of light and break up the figure's contours to allow space to intrude, thus helping to lock the body into its spatial ambience. His modeling is achieved with a variety of directional brushmarks, very much indebted to Paul Cézanne's structured brushwork, intended both to suggest plasticity and to underscore the independent patterning of the strokes. In the sculpture, a light texturing of surface hints at some of this same vibrancy.

In contrast to the lithe elegance of *Madeleine I, The Serf*, with its muscular anatomy, braced legs, protruding stomach, and craggy surfaces, is brusque and even brutal in effect. It, too, has close analogues in painting, especially the *Male Model* of c. 1900 (cat. 7, p. 110). In Matisse's effort to achieve some of the faceting of form and dynamic highlights of the painting, he carved up the surface of the sculpture much more aggressively than he had in *Madeleine I,* with robust sequences of cuts, furrows, knobby extrusions, and shadowed pockets that envelop the body and stray considerably from anatomical accuracy. Several large bumps, for example, protrude around the stomach, and deep hollows in the chest and right collarbone are answered by a giant lump on the right shoulder blade. Up and down the figure's back and legs, Matisse flattened or sliced wide, sharp-cornered planes with a modeling knife. Toned down from the even more excited surfaces documented in a photograph of the sculpture at an earlier stage of development (fig. 50, p. 52), these gestural inflections show not so much an analysis of light or structure as Matisse's intuitive reactions while working his soft and malleable material. His obvious points of reference in this work, as often noted, were Rodin's *Walking Man* and *John the Baptist.*[11] He even used the same model. But he declared his intent to distance himself from the powerful influence of his nineteenth-century predecessor. This is seen in the staunch immobility of his figure, which contrasts with Rodin's illusion of movement in order to focus on a stabile wholeness of form, and his exuberant display of expressive modeling, unusual in even the most freely worked of Rodin's exploratory studies. Stasis, a consistent

Fig. 2. Photograph of a model used by Matisse for *The Serpentine.* Archives Matisse, Paris.

sculptural principle in Matisse's work, is emphasized here by the figure's hefty center of gravity placed just above his sturdy hips, oriented further by the downward tilt of the head and the upward-pointing triangle of the spread legs.

The sculptural values shared by these various works, basic to Matisse's art at this time, gave way around 1903 to the pyrotechnics of color and brushwork in the paintings of his fauve period, developments that did not lend themselves to interpretation in sculpture, although Matisse isolated individual figures from his paintings in several small clay studies, including the *Seated Nude with Arms on Head, Woman Leaning on Her Hands, Reclining Figure with Chemise,* and *Standing Nude,* all from 1904–1906 (cat. 35, pp. 148–49; 24, pp. 127–28; 30, pp. 133–34; 32, pp. 137, 140), as if taking an inventory of his poses several of which he appropriated from Cézanne's bathing scenes.[12] By 1907, his interest rallied again, leading to the most fertile period of sculptural productivity in his entire career. Beginning with the *Reclining Nude I (Aurora),* finished in 1907 (cat. 44, p. 269; 45, pp. 153, 155–56), and continuing with such masterworks as *Two Negresses* (cat. 47, p. 159) and *Decorative Figure* from 1908 (cat. 66, p. 181), *The Serpentine* and *The Back I* from 1909 (cat. 58, pp. 170, 172; cat. 48, p. 162), and then the series of heads of *Jeannette* starting in 1909–1910, it was a record of remarkable achievement and ambition. This maturation as a sculptor corresponded closely with the time when Matisse ran his academy, teaching and clarifying his thoughts on art for his students. Key developments in his sculpture of this period remained lastingly important, including a heightened freedom of anatomical interpretation, new sexual candor, the use of photographs as sources and neutral points of interpretive departure, and the exploration of serial imagery as a means of developing and distilling motifs. Sculpture also began to strike out independently from his paintings.

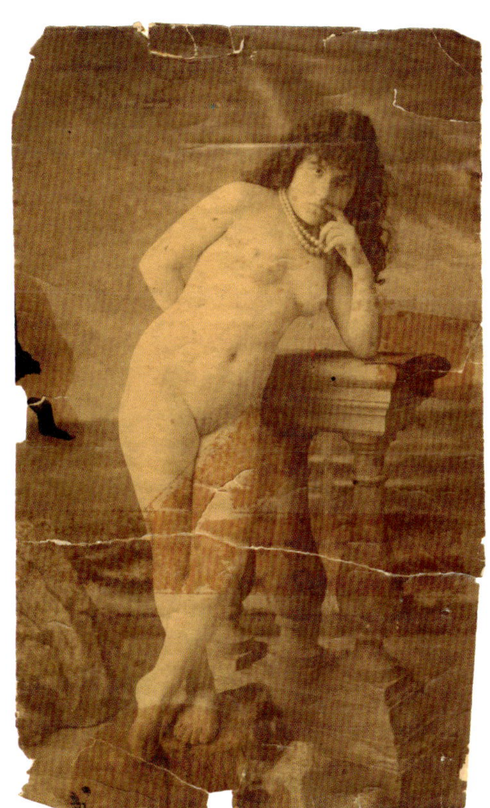

For an artist who had occasion to say, quite frequently, that he depended on the stimulation derived from direct encounters with models for inspiration in his work, it is odd that Matisse frequently based his sculptures on photographs of nude models rather than on actual models. He used a variety of photographic sources and sometimes worked quite literally from particular images. His reliance on photographs, for example, for *Two Negresses, The Serpentine* (fig. 2), and probably *Reclining Nude I (Aurora)* is well known.[13] We may well wonder about this practice, especially as it required the additional concern of translation from two-dimensional to three-dimensional form. On the most practical level, photographs provided a handy source of ideas for poses and may have been valued because they provided a set of conventional studio poses that distanced Matisse psychologically from the models, permitting a greater concentration on formal realization. Also, Matisse may have enjoyed their two dimensionality as a stimulus to sculptural imagination. As we have seen, he was known to adapt images from his paintings to develop and test in sculptures, and photographs provided another departure point for the dialogues between pictorial and plastic space, between image and object, that he cultivated in the different branches of his work.

In this period of exceptional productivity, we find a division between Matisse's small, handheld objects and his larger compositions. In smaller works such as *Seated Figure, Right Hand on Ground* from 1908 (fig. 3) and *Torso Without Arms or Head* from 1909 (cat. 57, p. 176), the reduced scale magnifies the impact of Matisse's touch. And the fact that the sculptures are so small may have induced greater freedom of manipulation. Both works are notable for the full-bodied, churning rhythms of their surfaces and the liberties Matisse took with representational form. In the first, the head and hair are three rough globules, and the right arm is like a long rope hanging limply to the ground. In the second, the fragmentation reduces the dancing or running figure to a basic silhouette that from the side or back seems more like an upright flint than a human body. Other small-scale sculptures from the period seem perfect embodiments of Matisse's own advice to his students about the essentials of form: "In addition to the sensations one derives from a drawing, a sculpture must invite us to handle it as an object; just so the sculptor must feel, in making it, the particular demands for volume

Fig. 3. Henri Matisse, *Seated Figure, Right Hand on Ground,* 1908. Bronze. The Museum of Modern Art, New York; the Abby Aldrich Rockefeller Fund.

Fig. 4. Henri Matisse, *Small Crouching Torso without Arms or Head,* 1908. Bronze. Direction des Musées de France, Gift of Jean Matisse, on deposit at the Musée Matisse, Nice, 1978.

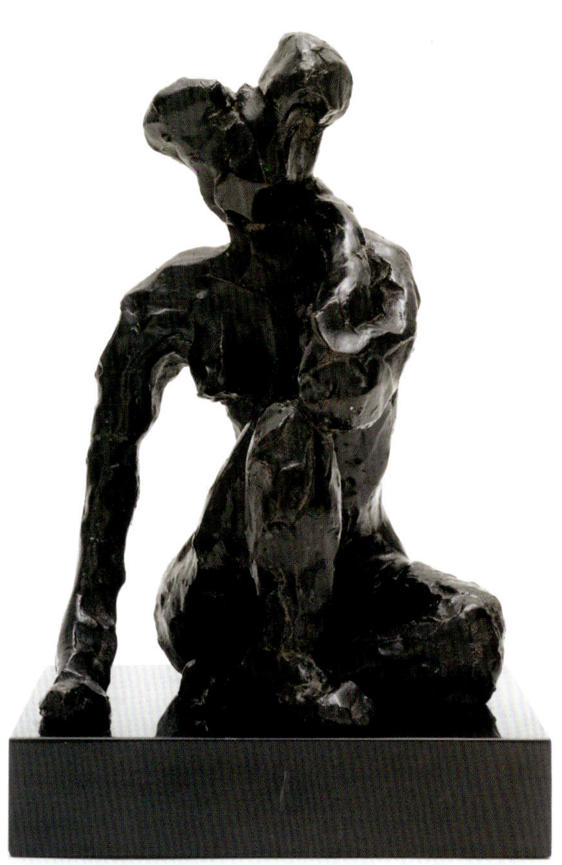

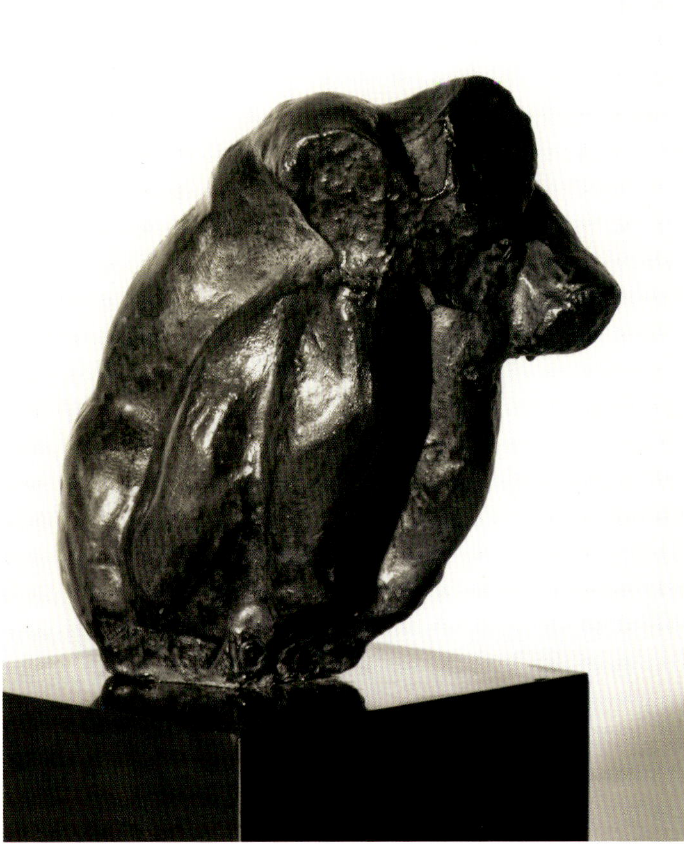

and mass. The smaller the bit of sculpture, the more the essentials of form must exist."[14] The *Small Crouching Torso without Arms or Head* from 1908 (fig. 4) is condensed into a rocklike ovoid in which indications of torso and legs hardly break through the solid mass. It is a wonder of concision. In the *Thorn Extractor* of 1906 (cat. 25, p. 129), with its pose from ancient art, the figure virtually merges with the rock on which it sits. The back of the left leg disappears into the rock, and the other leg, torso, and arms are pulled tightly together into a mass of undulating, rounded, barely articulated shapes, striking in their degree of abstraction.

Matisse may have been a direct inheritor of Rodin's figural language—this is how he is usually classified in studies of modern sculpture—but these objects broke new ground in the history of modeling. No parallels exist in early modern sculpture for the abstractions of form that Matisse achieved at this early date. In contrast, his dramatic manipulations of substance gave way, in larger sculptures of the period, to calmer, more measured surface treatments and an emphasis on what he called the architecture of full and complex volumes in space. This pattern is clear from a comparison of three complementary compositions, *Reclining Nude I (Aurora), Decorative Figure,* and *The Serpentine,* studies, respectively, of nudes reclining, seated, and standing. The story of the evolution of the first of these warrants recounting. Matisse began the sculpture in 1906. He apparently took the pose from a photograph but imbued the figure with a powerful sequence of twisting, thrusting, and compacted forms that have no trace in the bland photographs at his disposal. It was a pivotal sculpture for Matisse, involving a violent break from nature and a willful use of exaggeration and distortion for his own compositional needs. Indeed, the contrapuntal rhythms defining the contours are so strong they seem to break the work apart into separate, powerfully massed elements, centered around the chest and arms, left hip and thigh, and large feet. It is an innovative compositional device, with its horizontal episodic layout, and one that Pablo Picasso and Henry Moore, among

Fig. 5. Henri Matisse, *The Horse,* 1901. Bronze. Direction des Musées de France, Gift of Jean Matisse, on deposit at the Musée Matisse, Nice, 1978.

others, would make use of many years later. Every angle of view of the figure provides it own, sometimes rather startling, composition of interlocked and superimposed shapes.

After Matisse had developed the sculpture to a fairly advanced state, it fell from its stand and was badly damaged. At first he attempted to reconstruct the piece, but then decided instead to make a painting, the *Blue Nude: Memory of Biskra* (cat. 46, p. 157), noting later that he was "full of confidence in the trace that it [the sculpture] had left in my mind."[15] He adopted the same pose for the highly sculptural nude in his large painting, setting it in a lush, tropical landscape and emphasizing the curves of the body with modeled tones, a heavy application of blue shadows, and directional hatching of strokes. When the painting was complete, he returned to the sculpture. How much it may have changed from its earlier manifestation we do not know, but in its final version it has the torqued, powerful form of the much larger painted nude. For these two works the creative flow of formal ideas on pose, anatomical distortion, and spatial displacement ran from photography to sculpture to painting and back to sculpture. Images were re-presented three times, the artist learning lessons in one medium and applying them in another. These dialogues between formats in Matisse's work were always complex and not just the one-way street from painting to sculpture that is too often claimed with implications of prioritization.

With the *Decorative Figure,* Matisse adopted a pose related to that of the seated nude in his painting of *La coiffure* of 1907,[16] also a very sculptural figure, but seems to have set for himself the problem of resolving the tension between a pictorial schema—a frontal composition of intersecting arabesques—and a full, volumetric reading of the figure in space. The basic theme of the sculpture is the play of the coiled, serpentine movements in the body against the geometry of the base. In modeling the figure, Matisse made constant anatomical adjustments. The head is overly large, the thighs have an exaggerated swell, the left foot is bent downward to match the verticality of the front of the socle, the right arm is longer and thicker than the left as part of its bracing function, and so forth, all in concert with the carefully plotted flow of curves and surfaces. With its ungainly exaggerations and the hard symmetry of the breasts, the figure struck early critics as ugly, but it is undoubtedly a reflection of the growing influence on Matisse at this time of African art and the anatomical license it encouraged.

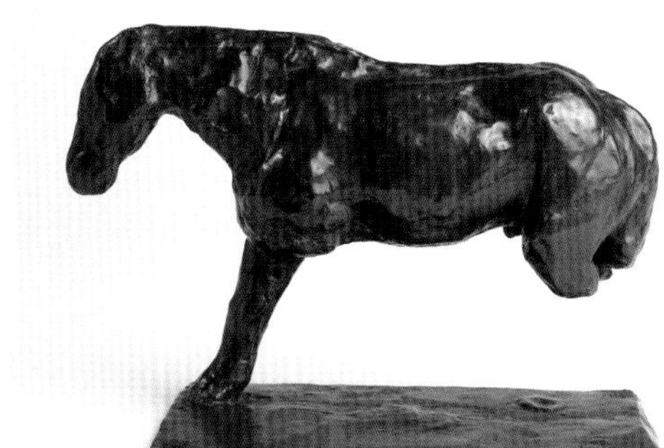

Despite the frontality of its presentation, the *Decorative Figure,* like *Reclining Nude I (Aurora),* pulls the viewer around it with an unfolding from every angle of different compositional solutions that are harmoniously integrated but still diverse and even surprising. From the front, no one could predict, for example, the powerful alignment of three circular masses with which Matisse defined the buttocks and pillow. And note his control of negative spaces, another lasting characteristic of his sculpture. In an early work such as *The Horse* from 1901 (fig. 5), the external spaces seem to press in upon the form, but by omitting the horse's back legs, Matisse has engaged negative space as a support. Space becomes corporeal. In *The Serpentine,* the sculpture is *largely* negative space, and the eye gravitates as quickly to the open and surrounding spaces, and the shapes they define, as to the actual solid masses. With the *Decorative Figure* and the holes that Matisse very consciously shaped in its forms, negative spaces take on their own compositional relationships; they seem to be graspable. They connect front and back and inner and outer volumes with a tactile certainty that helps counteract any initial impression of two dimensionality and anticipate the exploitation of negative space many years later by Henry Moore.

The relatively restrained surface treatment in *Decorative Figure* records the action of Matisse's hands as he pressed pellets of clay into his forms, smoothed and shaped them, built up highlights, and deepened areas of shadow. His modeling, he said, was for the purpose of formal structure rather than for pleasing effects: "We are already far from the palpitation of the flesh that was sought by traditional statuary arts, and even from Rodin's inflexions. . . . The surface registers all the marks

Fig. 6. Henri Matisse, *Dance (I),* 1909. Oil on canvas. The Museum of Modern Art, New York; Gift of Nelson A. Rockefeller in honor of Alfred H. Barr Jr.

of the act of modeling, rebuffing our eye's caress in order to stress the primacy of architecture."[17] A considerably sleeker handling of surface is found in *The Serpentine,* in keeping with the exaggerated elongation of its proportions and clarity of contours. Again, Matisse based this sculpture on a photograph (see fig. 2), and in its early stages he replicated more closely the stocky physique of the photographed model. He also gave his figure at this point distinctly Negroid facial features, another sign of the influence of African art. The extreme slimming of the figure that took place during the course of work, along with the smoothing of contours and broadening of spaces between the limbs, must have occurred as a sculptural response to problems with which Matisse was dealing at the time in his paintings. In March 1909 he painted his large oil sketch—*Dance (I)* (fig. 6)—depicting a subject he was proposing to his Russian patron Sergei Shchukin, and later in the year he was at work on the final canvas, *Dance (II).*[18] The stretching of the limbs of his figures in these paintings and the stress on their linear, sinuous contours are connected directly with the development of the composition of *The Serpentine,* worked on during the latter half of 1909. Simultaneously, he opened up the

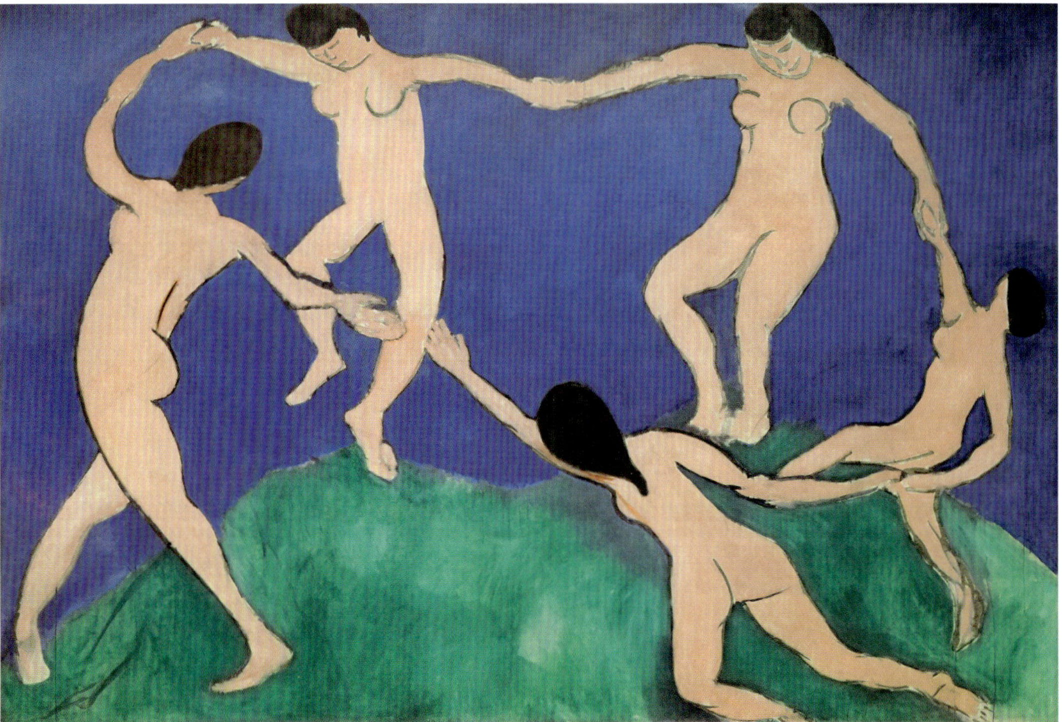

spaces between the parts of the sculpture to increase transparency and allow clear, unencumbered views of anatomical form from different angles, a projection into three dimensionality from the flat format of the paintings. That this sculpture, one of Matisse's most inventive, has no counterpart in the rest of his sculptural oeuvre helps affirm its interrelationship with contemporaneous pictorial investigations.

Another aspect of this figure that bears consideration and opens questions pertinent to several of Matisse's major sculptures is its sexuality. It has been said that Matisse's sculptures contain little metaphor, that their meanings are self-reflective, a matter of form for form's sake.[19] *The Serpentine* is, however, one of several sculptures that show the opposite to be true. Its figure has been interpreted in different ways: as a distant reference to the Farnese *Hercules at Rest,* as an evocation of plant growth, and most notably, as a symbolic and physical embodiment of sexuality, given the eroticism of her swelling hips and thighs and her conjunction with the phallic pedestal.[20] Such readings, particularly the latter, might seem strained at first but are more persuasive in the context of

Fig. 7. Matisse in his apartment at no. 1, place Charles-Félix, Nice, c. 1926, with an early version of the sculpture *Large Seated Nude.*

Fig. 8. Henri Matisse, *Large Seated Nude,* 1922–1929. Bronze, back view. Raymond and Patsy Nasher Collection, Dallas. Cat. 99.

other sculptures—*Two Negresses, Large Seated Nude,* and *Venus in a Shell II,* for example—with comparable sign languages.

Two Negresses is based fairly closely on a photograph of two Tuareg women standing side by side and facing in opposite directions, but Matisse developed the image into a three-dimensional investigation of paired opposites, influenced certainly by Picasso's famous essays on pairings of monumental figures seen front and back, but with added sexual nuance. This work of Matisse's has been linked to works commenting on lesbianism, a rare theme in early modern sculpture.[21] More to the point is its self-conscious confusion of sexual identities. When viewed from one side, the two figures, given their manliness of physique, seem to be an embracing pair of male and female lovers. One has to shift viewpoints to see that in fact both are women. The resulting *frisson* is part of Matisse's canny rhyming of opposites locked into the composition: back and front views, closed and open forms, movement upward and downward. And it fits into a pattern of sexual ambiguity or suggestiveness played out in other of his sculptures.

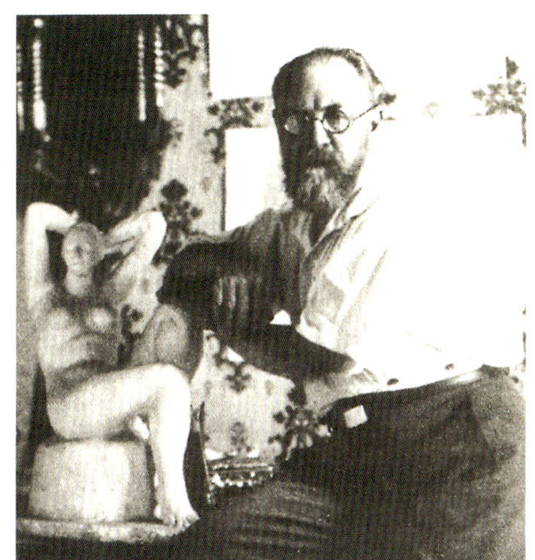

The *Large Seated Nude* of 1922–1929 (cat. 98, p. 217; 99, p. 275) and *Venus in a Shell II* of 1932 (cat. 124, p. 251), are particularly pertinent. Matisse labored on the first of these over a seven-year period, announcing numerous times that he was approaching a finished version, only to put it aside and return later for more work. A powerful statement, it is the largest of Matisse's sculptures excepting the *Back*s and the most important sculpture, along with *The Back IV* (cat. 51, p. 163), from the last thirty years of his life. Part of its strength comes from the daring asymmetrical composition, which immediately puts the viewer off balance. By lifting the model's arms up over her head and thrusting her upper body out into space at a most unlikely angle, Matisse created a physical impossibility but a powerful visual dynamic. The composition was worked and reworked into the image of a muscular amazon, with a rock-hard physique and a rounded, bulletlike head. It is known that Matisse drew heavily for this composition on Michelangelo's figure of *Night* in the Medici tomb, and Michelangelo's spirit is strongly felt both in the torsion of the body and its hermaphroditic anatomy.[22] The expressive twist that Matisse gave his pose, with its ancient connotations of proffered beauty, is more fully appreciated when one compares photographs of the early states of the composition, in which the body is smaller and more curvaceous and the pose more relaxed (fig. 7). Viewed head on, the final version embodies strong contrapuntal rhythms playing around the contours with positive and negative spaces beating back and forth to embolden the composition. A back view (fig. 8) reveals the same heavily faceted modeling of anatomy, with slices of the knife to harden form and enliven contour. The overall impression is strongly one of masculinization. The woman has the body of a weightlifter. The strength of her large thighs, flexed abdomen, and broad shoulders makes her a formidable physical specimen. The sense of maleness is heightened by the miniaturized breasts and hard simplifications of head and face, all contributing to the image of an androgynous hybrid.

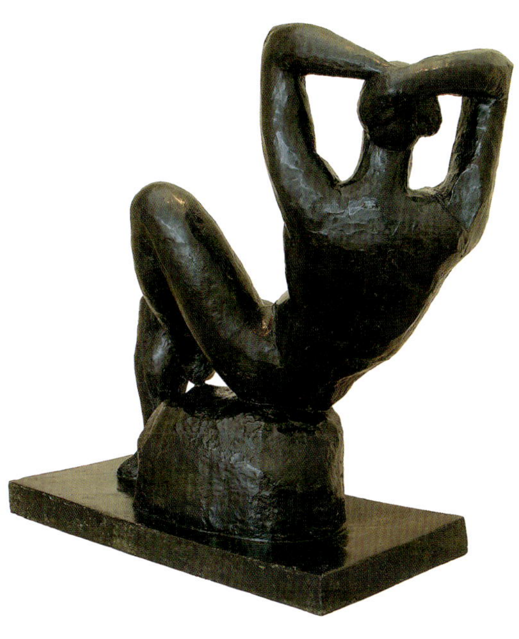

The *Venus in a Shell II* is a much smaller but still quite powerful work. Here, too, the pose has ancient precedents and overtones of classical decorum and beauty. Matisse, however, self-consciously rips asunder this inheritance. Anatomy is reshaped and reordered even more thoroughly than in the *Large Seated Nude.* The bent legs, for example, are separated from the torso and presented as two independent, upright motifs. The figure's back is excavated with a deep V-shaped furrow. Head, hair, and upraised arms are merged into one barely differentiated mass. Matisse's handling of form in this and related works is sometimes described as cubist, but the sliced planes that lead to this rubric are only one of several of his mark-making, volume-inducing gestures that actually are antithetical to cubism's real or implied shuffling of planes in space. Basic to the work is its sexual duality. Matisse very clearly transformed the body, with its longer upright torso and two shorter upright legs, into a phallus broadly faceted like a rocky outcrop. It is a strikingly masculinized reading of a theme traditionally presented as an apex of feminine sensuality.

Also relevant here is the *Tiari* of 1930 (cat. 77, p. 195; 78, pp. 196–97), where sensuous feminine folds enshrouding the flower/head are given a sleek smoothness attractive to the hand and unusual in Matisse's sculpture. The joining in this work of globular forehead and long narrow nose recalls a very similar formulation in the much earlier *Jeannette V* from 1913 (cat. 88, p. 206; 89, p. 274). Yve-Alain Bois refers to this motif as a "spoon-nose and forehead,"[23] but it can plausibly be interpreted as a distinctly phallic sign. This is the way Picasso saw the motif when he recycled it into his Boisgeloup *Heads* of 1931[24] to create some of the century's most vivid images of male and female coupling. Its rhyming language also brings to mind the sleek, tumescent stylizations and blatant eroticism of Brancusi's infamous *Princesse X.*[25]

Are such doublings of sexuality merely an inventive exercise, a calculated study of visual double entendres? Or do they say something more profound about Matisse's attitude toward women and models? This is complicated exegetical territory, especially considering the long and heated debates about the exploitiveness of Matisse's male gaze and possibly even misogynous feelings.[26] Even if we do discount such interpretations as flawed, we seem to have in certain of Matisse's sculptures, more than with his paintings, an expression closer to a rather fearful comment he once made that his sensations in front of a model were something akin to a rape.[27] This is exaggeration, to be sure. But we see in the works noted a vicarious possession of the models: a displacement of touching and handling from the model to the object, in some cases a tough-minded distortion of anatomy, and a transformation of bodies and body parts into maleness, androgyny, or sexual signs. We find a tactility of desire that belies any interpretation of Matisse's sculpture as lacking in metaphoric content. Matisse tells us as much: "She was a pretty girl, a perfect model. I touched her body, my hands enveloped her forms, and I transmitted into earth the equivalent of my sensation."[28]

Those with doubts about the healthiness of Matisse's attitude toward women might see in such transformations a reflection of repressed domination. Their mixture of attributes, however, speaks more of sexual potency, whether male or female, and desire. Consideration might also be given to a theme found in earlier works by Picasso, that is, the integration of male and female states in stages of human development. Leo Steinberg, in his examination of the ambiguity of gender in Picasso's *Three Women* of 1908, saw the figures as emblems of male and female bifurcation, as signs of "the sexes straining apart to position themselves as confronted halves" in the process of mental and physical growth.[29]

More convincing, however, is the erotic dimension recognized most revealingly by Picasso as basic to certain of Matisse's sculptures. As is often noted, a number of audaciously sexualized sculptures by Picasso from around 1929–1931, such as his *Seated Nude, Reclining Bather,* and the series of Boisgeloup *Heads,* took a strong cue from sculptures by Matisse as part of Picasso's general reassessment of his own work during the late twenties and early thirties.[30] This reevaluation was fueled in large part by Picasso's response to an exhibition in Paris of Matisse's sculptures and paintings in 1930 and a large retrospective of his work in 1931. Challenging him and attempting to stake out higher ground, Picasso pushed Matisse's subjects to his own extreme limits, but his initial indebtedness is clear, as is his interest in an eroticized Matisse. Such sexual candor is commonplace in Picasso's art in both paintings and sculpture but extremely rare in Matisse's paintings, where a tone of discrete decorum almost always prevails. Only infrequently, as, for example, in his *Nymph and Satyr* of 1908–1909, does sexual arousal become an explicit theme.[31] Sculpture gave him a voice for such instincts. As William Tucker recognized, "it is in the sculpture that the sexual content of [Matisse's] art is most directly realized."[32] Even when he was working from photographs rather than directly from a model, the manipulation of tangible matter opened different sensory experiences. In his reliance on bland studio poses, he eschewed any nineteenth-century rhetoric of posture or gesture. Distinctly modern as an agenda, sexuality came from sign and form rather than from narrative.

Fig. 9. Henri Matisse, *The Back 0,* 1909. Clay. Preliminary version, destroyed. Archives Matisse, Paris.

Fig. 10. Paul Cézanne, *Three Bathers,* c. 1879–1882. Oil on canvas. Musée du Petit Palais, Paris; formerly in the Collection of Henri Matisse.

Fig. 11. Gustave Courbet, *The Bathers,* 1853. Oil on canvas. Musée Fabre, Montpellier; Gift of Alfred Bruyas.

When claims for Matisse's contributions to modernism in sculpture are being asserted, special attention must be paid to two of his most important sculptural projects, *The Back I–IV* and *Jeannette I–V.* These works include some of his more daring inventions and illustrate his engagement with serial imagery, a key aspect of his working methods in sculpture and a strategy used by other early twentieth-century sculptors, including, for example, Alberto Giacometti with his *Women of Venice* and Constantin Brancusi with the *Bird in Space* series. Other well-known serial progressions in his work include the three busts of *Henriette* (1925–1929), and there are numerous works he repeated in a second version. In a sense, his *Large Seated Nude* also resulted from a series of individual states, although in this case he fixed only the final version in a bronze cast. Earlier states are recorded in photographs.[33]

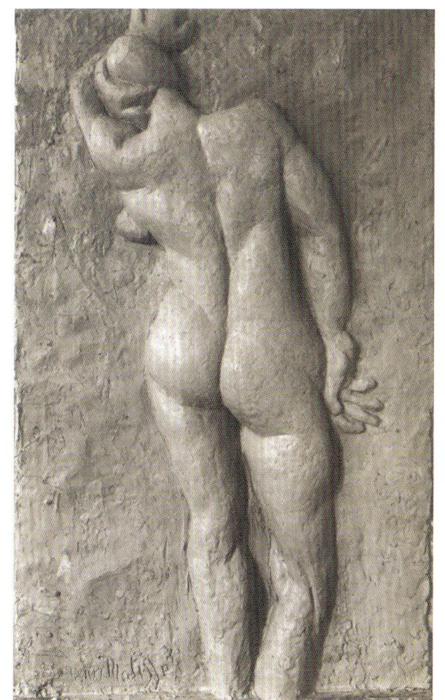

The Back, that powerful series of essays on mass and abstracted anatomy produced over a twenty-one-year period, stands as one of the great landmarks of modern sculpture. Albert Elsen's research revealed that, between 1909 and 1930, Matisse made five different versions of these relief compositions, four preserved in bronze (fig. 9). The relief format is sculpture at its most pictorial, and indeed, numerous painted and drawn precedents have been nominated as possible influences for the *Back*s, including works by Cézanne and Matisse himself. His 1909 *Bather* at the Museum of Modern Art is one such work, and his *Bathers by a River* of 1916, in the Art Institute of Chicago, is often cited as a key analogue for *The Back III* (cat. 50, p. 163) from the same year.[34] Cézanne's multifarious bathers—Matisse actually owned an important Cézanne bathing scene, purchased in 1899 (fig. 10)—provide numerous comparisons suggestively close in pose and even stylistic treatment of form. Courbet's *The Bathers* from 1853 (fig. 11) and *The Spring* from 1868,[35] those two celebrations of the ponderous backside anatomy of bathing nudes, offer other intriguing possibilities.

Beyond the issue of particular pictorial sources, different authors have analyzed instances in which the *Back*s seem to address representational or stylistic problems shared with contemporaneous paintings. Most important in this dialogue, however, is the way that Matisse, in the *Back*s, actually

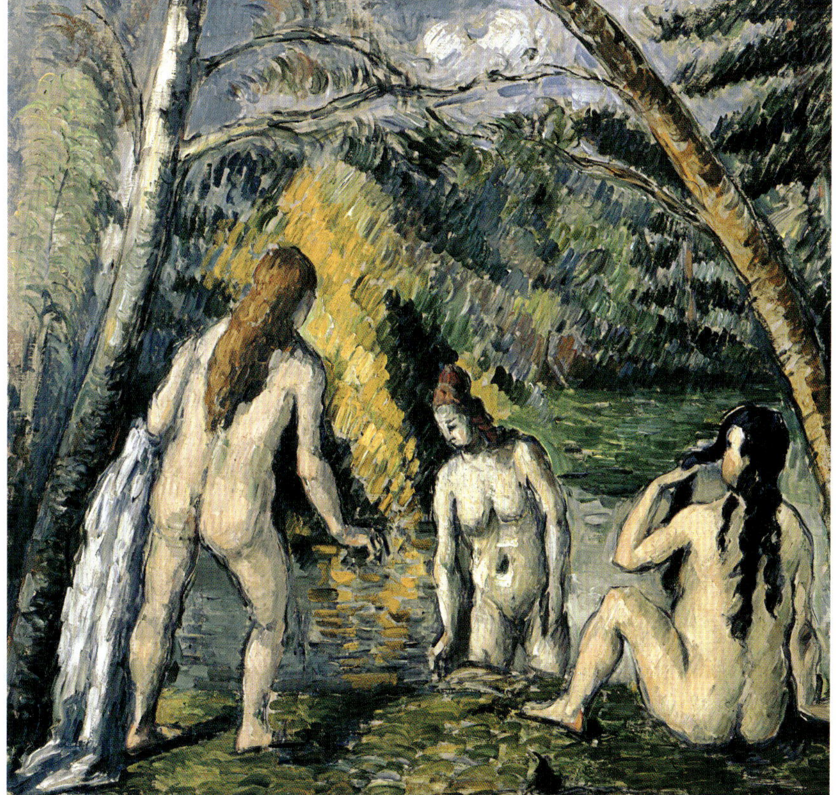

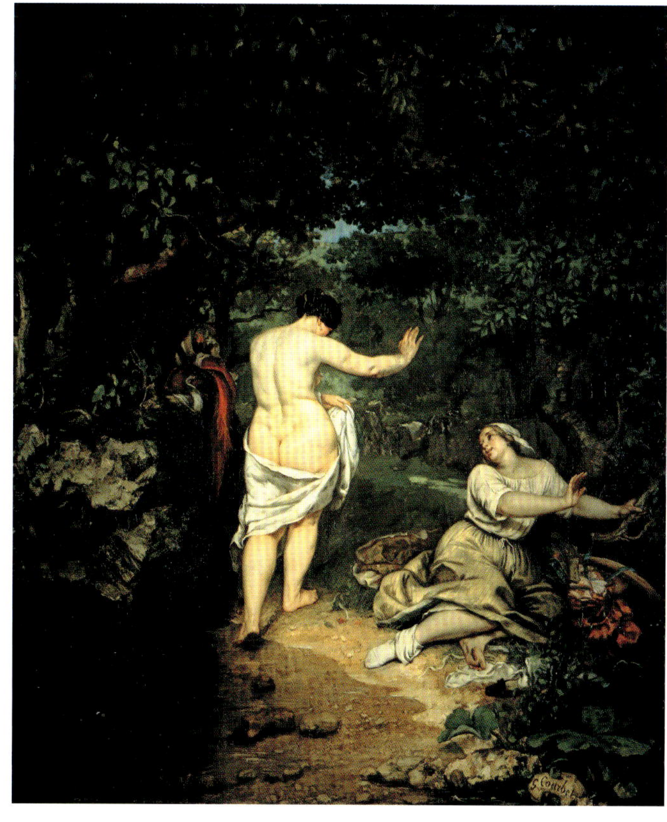

critiques or offers a strong counterpart to painting, turning fields of illusory form and space into extremes of dense substance. The depth of relief in all four bronzes is dramatic. The rectangular backgrounds are worked just as thoroughly as are the figures, the process diminishing distinctions between figure and ground and contributing to the sense of one massive, unified volume. All five figures are sunk ankle deep into a protruding ground plane (a device Matisse may have adopted from ancient kouroi that he knew, for example, from the Louvre)[36] and reach or extend up over the background wall, confounding any notion of confinement within the format and adding to the outward, expanding pressure created by each dense terrain of anatomy. Matisse stresses the sense of force with which each figure presses against the background planes by distending their right hands and left breasts to the side. His working methods are declared both by his modeling, and the extreme license it takes with the human body, and by the almost cinematic recording of the evolving states of the composition, as he distilled, condensed, and abstracted his figure step by step. There is about the *Back*s a sense of *terribilità* and aggressiveness rare in his paintings after the fauve period. The basic sensibility in their making is wonderfully, ambitiously sculptural.

For Matisse, the methodology of repeating a composition in different versions encouraged greater risk taking and increasingly subjective interpretation. Later states inevitably exhibit a more liberated reworking of the initial concept. It is fascinating, for example, to follow Matisse's progress from his first head of *Jeannette* (cat. 80, p. 200; 81, p. 273), made early in 1910, to his last, *Jeannette V* (cat. 88, p. 206; 89, p. 274), dated variously 1913 and 1916.[37] The first and second sculptures, which he made in rapid succession, give little promise of the explorations that would mark his later variations. In the shapes of the head and face and relatively naturalistic handling, they relate closely to a drawing and painting of the same model from the same years, both entitled *Girl with Tulips.*[38] But in fact, the sculptures are more timid in their recasting of visual reality than are their two-dimensional counterparts. Perhaps they represented for Matisse a relaxation, a safe step back from the extreme stylizations of *Dance (II)* and *Music,* both begun in 1909 and finished in the summer of 1910,[39] or the sleek abstractions of anatomy in *The Serpentine* of 1909.

Jeannette III and *IV* (cat. 84, p. 202; 85, p. 274; 86, p. 203; 87, p. 274) embody a leap away from naturalism, with manipulations of form more in tune with his paintings of the period. The coiffure in both is segmented into large, biomorphic globules that do not so much frame the face as protrude irregularly around it. No longer images of just the head, or head and neck, these are expanded into forcefully upright compositions, with head, neck, and chest set atop a freely modeled base that, in its visual instability, adds to the dynamism of upward movement in the lozenge or zigzag shape of the whole ensemble. Long cylindrical necks prop up the heads, another cue from African sculpture. The strong rhythms that he modeled and sliced into the woman's rather caricatured features provide a foil to the heavy, rolling contours of the hair.

Matisse's clear intent to create more of a mask than a face reaches fruition in his *Jeannette V,* where hair and skull, nose and forehead, eyes and bone structure fuse as part of a thorough reengineering of the head's anatomy. The strength and confidence of this move would seem to support a dating of the work to 1916, and an alignment with the powerful manipulations of form in *The Back III* from that year and the masklike faces in the *Piano Lesson* of 1916, *The Italian Woman* of 1916 (cat. 91, p. 204), and *Portrait of Auguste Pellerin (II)* from early 1917.[40] The sculpture does not, however, conceptually or visually recap such paintings. It goes beyond them in the achievement of a powerful simulacrum of a head, with a quality of *art brut* and incorporation of the jarring abstractions and emotional darkness that contemporary artists found so invigorating about African art. Its radical deconstruction of human form has no parallel in early modern sculpture before this time.

We see a progression of subjectivity, like that in the *Back*s from 1909–1930, in other of the sculptural series by Matisse: the *Henriette* series from 1925–1929 and the two versions of *Venus in a Shell*

Fig. 12. Henri Matisse, *Reclining Nude I (Aurora)*, 1907. Bronze, top view. Raymond and Patsy Nasher Collection, Dallas. Cat. 44.

from 1930–1932. What did seriality give Matisse? For one thing, it allowed him a running start on sculptural invention. With the *Back*s and certain of the *Jeannette*s, for example, he progressed from one stage to the next by making a plaster cast of one version and reworking that cast by cutting, reshaping, and adding and modeling new material. Thus he avoided a blank slate, saved labor, and undoubtedly drew inspiration from working a pre-existing form. Furthermore, because Matisse exhibited different, complete series of works at various times, we know he did not regard the later stages in a series as the more definitive or think of the early steps as works in progress. He obviously appreciated the exposure of different, evolutionary stages and thought of each as a work unto itself. A key theme of each series was process—the evidencing of a creative mind at work and actual physical transformation. Process becomes the implicit subject of each series. With certain of his paintings, Matisse revealed the prolonged evolution that led to their final states by publishing sequential photographs documenting the different stages of work like a cinematic scan.[41] His proclivity for serial imagery in prints and drawings is evidenced, among many other examples, by his extended series of ten charcoal, pen and ink, and black crayon drawings of a reclining woman in his *Themes and Variations* of 1941. Matisse referred to these successive studies as "a motion picture film of the feeling of

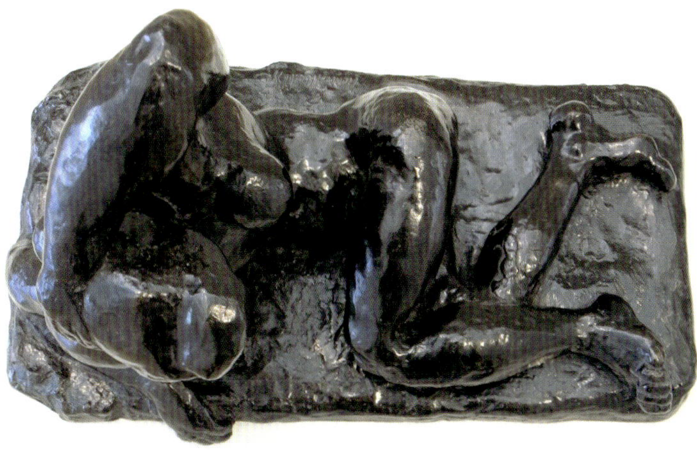

an artist."[42] This revelation of feeling, in finely tuned or more abrupt variations, with its accompanying documentation of process was to become a classic conceit in early modern and postwar art.

Matisse's sculpture also participated in modernism's drive toward the independent, literal object. He made certain works that verge on pure abstraction, and the meaning of the figures in his sculpture was not imitative as it always was with Rodin, no matter how extensive his fragmentations and distortions. For Matisse, the figure was a sculptural object on which to enact his sensations. Another move in this direction was his minimization or removal of bases, with their implication of an idealized sculptural space. The many small sculptures he made that are literally handy—meant to be picked up, hefted, examined, and set back down on a table or shelf without an intervening base—are a strong step in this direction. In *The Serf,* the figure stands at the very edges of the base, as if almost pushed off; in *Reclining Nude I (Aurora),* the right elbow engages the edge of the base and a foot and hand extend over it (fig. 12). It is as if the bases could no longer contain their assertive inhabitants. The figures in all of the *Back*s project beyond their solid backgrounds, and the cantilevered upper body of the *Large Seated Nude* bursts off its socle to encounter the viewer directly. All of these gestures help move the works into ambient space and stress their immediate formal objectness.

Fig. 13. Henri Matisse, *Maquette for Red Chasuble (back) Designed for the Chapel of the Rosary of the Dominican Nuns of Vence,* 1950–1952. Gouache on paper, cut and pasted. The Museum of Modern Art, New York; Acquired through the Lillie P. Bliss Bequest.

Fig. 14. Henri Matisse, Costume for a Mourner in *Le Chant du rossignol,* 1920. White felt robe with appliquéd dark blue velvet triangles. The Victoria and Albert Museum, London.

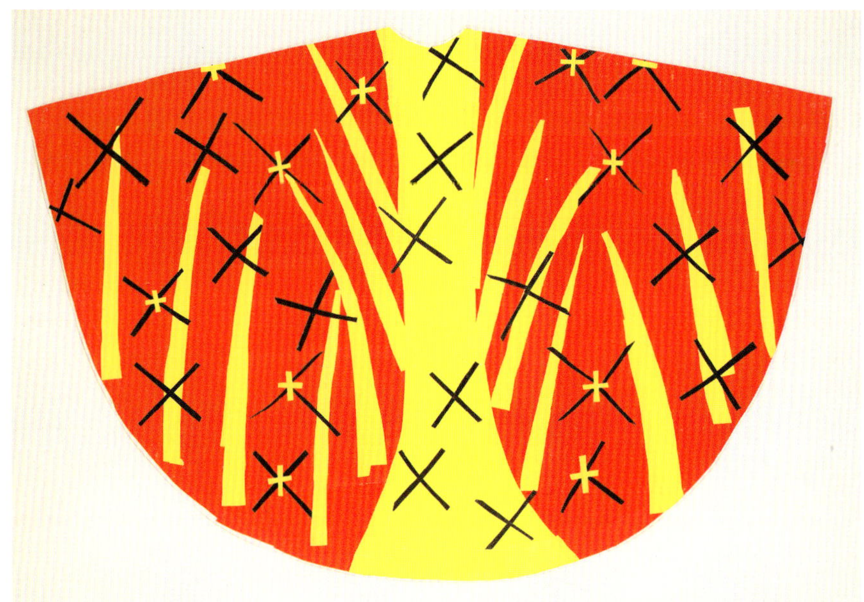

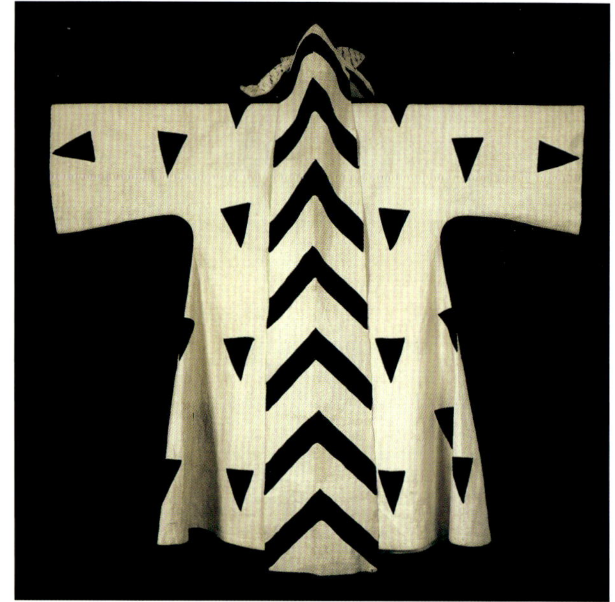

It is perhaps ironic, therefore, that one of Matisse's most dramatic contributions as a sculptor, his development of the cut-out, would free sculpture entirely from solidity and mass. As often recounted, Matisse had used paper cut-outs as maquettes or aids in the production of earlier paintings and decorative schemes but began in the 1940s to concentrate on the medium more intently, with stunning results.[43] Matisse equated the cut-outs with sculpture: "Cutting directly into vivid color reminds me of the direct carving of sculptors."[44] He sensed that the resilience of his colored papers painted with gouache gave them distinct materiality. The process of first pinning and then pasting the cut-outs onto backgrounds (performed by assistants) added other physical steps, and the layered cut-outs could, in effect, be considered very shallow reliefs. Undoubtedly thinking back to Michelangelo's comments about freeing figures from blocks of marble, Matisse felt that his slicing actions served to liberate images from paper. His special flair for the medium need hardly be stressed. It led to some of his most spectacular work and dominated the last years of his life. After about 1948, he made very few paintings and sculptures, concentrating instead on cut-outs and several decorative projects that involved them in the design process. Within his sculptural development, the cut-outs, another manifestation of Matisse's plastic sensibility, occupy their own category as a perfect synthesis between two-dimensional and three-dimensional work.

The sculptural analogy can be taken a step further. In various garments he designed, Matisse achieved with his cut-out technique not just the illusion of volume but actual volume. As part of his decorative program for the Dominican chapel at Vence, worked on from 1948 to 1952, he provided maquettes for a series of colorful chasubles (fig. 13); much earlier, in 1919–1920, he had designed costumes for Serge Diaghilev's production of *Le Chant du rossignol.*[45] In working on the chapel at Vence, he was mindful of the relevance of theatricality and theatrical tradition: "I'm not doing this to design a church. I'm doing it the way I'd design a stage set. For the Rossignol, which is set in a Chinese court, I did something derivative and many memories of churches went into it. The builders of the Gothic cathedrals were terrific stage designers."[46] The décor of *Le Chant du rossignol* has disappeared but some of the costumes survive (fig. 14). Matisse observed that he designed the décor "like a painting, only with colors that move," referring to the costumes.[47] Strongly patterned with a vocabulary of fairly simple shapes cut from different colors of textile and applied to backgrounds ranging from white to vibrant red, the costumes were devised to create their own luminous effects independent of the stage lighting. Once donned by the actors and dancers, the flat designs took shape. They became rounded, folded, hanging images that flowed in space and reacted to changing light. A kinesthetic element was introduced, animating the "sculptures" and producing a moving kaleidoscope of visual effects that struck witnesses as ingenious. They also mark the birth of the cut-out, revised by Matisse so vigorously more than twenty years later.

By the time of Matisse's triumphant work with cut-outs, the days of his main contributions in solid sculpture were past. Old age and infirmity made the physical labor required for modeling even a medium-sized form impossible and, at any rate, he had shifted his creative focus. Nevertheless, the cut-outs are another manifestation of Matisse's plastic intelligence and they continued to satisfy, at least partially, his innate will to shape with his hands the visions of his mind and eye. They advanced the dialogue in his work between the grasped and the seen and remind us, in their own way, of that basic truth, advocated to his students at the beginning of the century, that sculpture is a tactile experience.

The fundamental and most obvious attribute of his sculpture—its physicality—is also the *reductio ad essentia* of its meaning for his art. If painting represented illusion for Matisse, sculpture represented objectivity. It opened up for him a world of direct sensual involvement that painting could not, providing a way to "condense my sensations," as he put it, into solid matter and resolve perceptions and feelings in three-dimensional compositions that sometimes interacted with paintings but had their own strong character and life as felt form.

In this regard it is interesting to consider a revisionist view of Matisse now gaining currency that stresses his passionate side, not revealed so much by his general demeanor as by the fierce determination with which he pursued his art. This perspective rebuts the more traditional appraisal of Matisse as temperate, tasteful, and thoroughly bourgeois. His biographer Hilary Spurling notes the "brutal metaphors he used to describe his work in unguarded moments."[48] He spoke of painting as an act like "kicking down a door" or "slitting an abscess with a pen knife."[49] He could start a fresh canvas only "if he felt like throttling someone,"[50] and worked himself up into states of high anxiety and self-doubt if his art was not going well. Such sentiments are hard to square with the vast majority of Matisse's paintings and drawings but not with the distortions, eroticism, and harsh expressiveness found, for example, in the *Back*s, *Large Seated Nude, Venus in a Shell II,* or *Reclining Nude I (Aurora).* Such works are purposefully discomforting and put the lie to Matisse's trope about art providing the soothing effect of a well-used chair.[51] This expressiveness had few counterparts in paintings, especially after about 1909–1910. When it came to absorbing the discordant lessons of African art, allowing feelings of sexuality free reign, releasing other emotional states, and exploring the musicality and power of forms projected in space, sculpture gave Matisse an essential tool. If an example is needed of the power of Matisse's sculpture to influence his painting, we should consider the catalytic role that the *Large Seated Nude* played in the stylistic revolutions in his art of the mid-1920s, when he brought a sculptural paradigm to bear against the soft painterliness that had characterized his work from earlier in the Nice period.[52]

By choosing commonplace poses with which to work, devoid of rhetorical gesture, pose, or facial features, Matisse freed his subjects of associations in order to let his shaping of volumes and surfaces become the embodiment of meaning rather than its illustration. He understood sculpture as a visual but also a temporal and haptic experience that communicates through sight, tactility, and our bodily empathy for scale, weight, three dimensionality, and spatial location. His works invite touch and can best be understood when they *are* touched. None of Matisse's sculptures is larger than the human body; some are small enough to be handled and are meant to be picked up. Their inflections of surface always relate to the size and sensitivity of our own hands and fingers. And, in his fashioning of shape and surface, Matisse always captured a sense of spontaneity, even if the production was long and laborious, thus preserving immediacy and highlighting manual process. Surface has its expressiveness, but it also stresses the immediacy of volume and objectness.

Matisse's sculpture may strike us today as less adventuresome, less driven by polemical problems than that of some of his contemporaries such as Picasso and Giacometti. It has its conservative side, inherent in its acceptance of a Rodinesque figural tradition. Its creativity and accomplishment, however, lie not in a radicalization of that tradition but rather in its revision and extension with daring modeling and anatomical reinvention, deeply autobiographical metaphorical meanings, and a new concept of the object as object rather than as image that Rodin would not have been able to countenance. The works Matisse made contribute significantly to the development of modern sculpture on several levels. We must understand the achievement of this other Matisse if we are to appreciate more fully the complexity of his artistic personality.

Notes

1. Grohé 2005, 307. This is an attitude that permeates criticism of Matisse's sculpture. The same author asserts that "Henri Matisse's sculptures are staunchly painterly in the sense that Matisse lends them clear views. They may be executed in the round but above all demand to be viewed from a specific point of view" (310). To quote another related view: "For Matisse as for Picasso, sculpture was mainly a specular tool to confirm and conclude in three dimensions what their paintings had already accomplished" (Baldassari 2002, 265). Discussing this issue, John Elderfield notes that Matisse, in "choosing two-dimensional images as his sources and/or working from a restricted number of viewpoints when treating a sculpture suggest[s] that [his] sculptural ambitions were essentially pictorial," but concludes that the sculpture's "independence from painting—though motivated by painting and relevant to its issues—lends it endurance" (Elderfield 1972, 82–83). It is the present author's view that Matisse made sculpture not just to serve or reflect upon painting, and that the direction of motivating influence was sometimes reversed.

2. Monod-Fontaine 1984, 9. She adds, in discussing the dialogue in Matisse's art between painting and sculpture, that "painting always takes precedence."

3. Henri Matisse, interview by Georges Charbonnier; Charbonnier 1960, 2:7–16.

4. Henri Matisse, interview by Georges Charbonnier, 1941; (Charbonnier n.d., 66; reprinted in Flam 1995, 298 n.11). Matisse went on to say: "I changed my method, and worked in clay in order to have a rest from painting. . . . That is to say that it was done for the purpose of organization, to put order into my feelings and to find a style to suit me. When I found it in sculpture, it helped me in painting" (ibid.).

5. Spurling 2005a, 280.

6. This formulation was repeated by Matisse many times; see Flam 1995, 33, 38; and the quotation from Matisse by Gaston Diehl, in Fourcade 1972, 195.

7. Tucker 1975, 62.

8. See note 3.

9. See Duthuit 1997, cat. 1–5.

10. Elsen 1972, 56, 58. Elsen attributes the first use of this terminology in regard to modalities in Matisse's art to Meyer Schapiro.

11. See, for example, ibid., 28–35. The dates for these works are, respectively, 1875–1878 and 1878.

12. Duthuit 1997, cat. 22, 17, 19, 20.

13. Many authors have discussed Matisse's reliance on photographs for poses. For a summary of issues and sources involved, see Sykora 2005, esp. 333–36. Jack Flam proposes a different photographic source for *Reclining Nude I (Aurora)*; see Flam 1998, fig. 4.

14. From Matisse's comments on sculpture made to his students at the Matisse Academy, as recorded by Sarah Stein in 1908; published in, among other sources, Flam 1995, 50.

15. Guichard-Meili 1986, 59; trans. Duthuit 1997, 383.

16. Elderfield 1992, cat. 101.

17. See note 15.

18. For the chronology of Matisse's work on these paintings, see Elderfield 1992, 181–83 and cat. 112, 125.

19. For example, Elizabeth Cowling (in Cowling et al. 2002, 225), on the one hand, in an enlightening discussion of exchanges between the work of Matisse and Picasso in the late twenties and early thirties, suggests that Picasso, although "impressed by the revelation of Matisse's originality as a sculptor . . . consistently developed the metaphoric and symbolic dimension of his figurative imagery to a degree Matisse never attempted." Yve-Alain Bois (1999, 67), on the other hand, stresses the strong metaphorical nature of the sculpture, noting that Matisse, "eschewing metaphor in his painting, accepts it in his sculpture." See also his more general discussion in Duthuit 1997, 376–78.

20. Flam 1998, unpaged [10–11].

21. Flam 2003, 33.

22. See Elsen 1972, 144–46; and Cowling, in Cowling et al. 2002, 222–23.

23. Bois 1999, 67.

24. On the influence of Matisse's sculpture on Picasso's work from the early thirties, see ibid., 58, 64–72; and Baldassari 2002, 269.

25. See Monod-Fontaine 1985, 40 and fig. 58.

26. An informative survey of criticism dealing with purported antifeminist themes in Matisse's art is found in Elderfield 1996, esp. 9–18, 52–54 nn.5–10.

27. Spurling 2005b, 34; see also, Spurling 2005a, 24.

28. Quoted by Pierre Schneider (1972, 22); no source given.

29. Steinberg 1978, 120.

30. See note 24.

31. Elderfield 1972, cat. 117; discussed at length in Spurling 2005a, 5 ff.

32. Tucker 1975, 66.

33. Photographs taken at Matisse's apartment in Nice at 1, place Charles-Félix, over an uncertain period of years, record various stages of work on the *Large Seated Nude.* Different photographs have been published in numerous sources; see, in particular, Elderfield 1992, 294–95; Elsen 1972, fig. 194, 196–98, 225; and Monod-Fontaine 1984, fig. 54, 55.

34. Elderfield 1992, cat. 119. On the relationship between *Bathers by a River* and *The Back III,* see Elsen 1972, 188–92.

35. Fernier 1977–1978, cat. 140, 627. Interestingly, Matisse owned five paintings by Courbet, including two figure studies, one of them a highly sensual nude, *The Sleeping Blonde,* acquired in 1917; see Spurling 2005a, 197, 199, 479 n.62.

36. For a photograph of Matisse sketching one of these kouroi in the Louvre, see Elsen 1972, fig. 9; Elsen also reproduces (as fig. 10) the plaster cast of a kouros that Matisse eventually owned. Aristide Maillol, Matisse's friend, used the same device of sinking the feet into the ground plane; ibid., fig. 144, 145.

37. On the question of the dating of *Jeannette V,* see Baldassari 2002, 357 nn.21, 35.

38. Elderfield 1992, cat. 129, 130.

39. Ibid., cat. 125, 126.

40. Ibid., cat. 188, 200, 199.

41. Selections from the photographic sequences for *Large Reclining Nude* (1935), *Woman in Blue* (1937), and *Music* (1939) are published in ibid., 360–62.

42. Ibid., 357 and plates 355–44; all the drawings are in the Musée de Grenoble.

43. A useful summary of the history of Matisse's involvement with cut-outs, at first as a visual and mechanical aid and then as an independent art form, is found in Elderfield 1978, 7–39. Of Matisse's working process, Elderfield writes: "Taking a sheet of heavy paper—pre-painted with gouache by one of his studio assistants—from a stockpile in his studio, Matisse carved out the image he held in his mind in a few swift, fluid actions. It was the work of a moment, this liberation of the image from the paper: the scissors wide open, carving—never clipping—through the sheet of pure color. . . . It was a process with all the spontaneity of drawing. . . . Conceptually, however, it was more like a sculptor releasing an imagined form from inside a block of marble or stone" (ibid., 7).

44. From Matisse's notes for the publication *Jazz* (1947); reprinted in Flam 1995, 172.

45. On the history of Matisse's work on the chapel at Vence, see Schneider 2002, 669–94; on the production of designs for *Le Chant du rossignol,* see ibid., 624–26; and Spurling 2005a, 229–33.

46. Quoted by Schneider from conversations with Brother Rayssiguier, who was Matisse's confidante and the prime mover behind the commission for the chapel at Vence; Schneider 2002, 624–25.

47. Pierre Courthion n.d. (Getty Center), 80; quoted in Spurling 2005a, 231.

48. Spurling 2005b, 34.

49. Ibid., 34; and idem, 2005a, 429.

50. Ibid.

51. Matisse 1908, 731–45; reprinted by Flam 1995, 42.

52. Anne Baldassari (2002, 268) also notes that the *Large Seated Nude* "helped spark the renewal of [Matisse's] painting." Numerous authors have discussed the sculptural qualities of the nude in Matisse's painting *Decorative Figure on an Oriental Ground* from 1925–1926; see, for example, Elderfield 1996, 21–22.

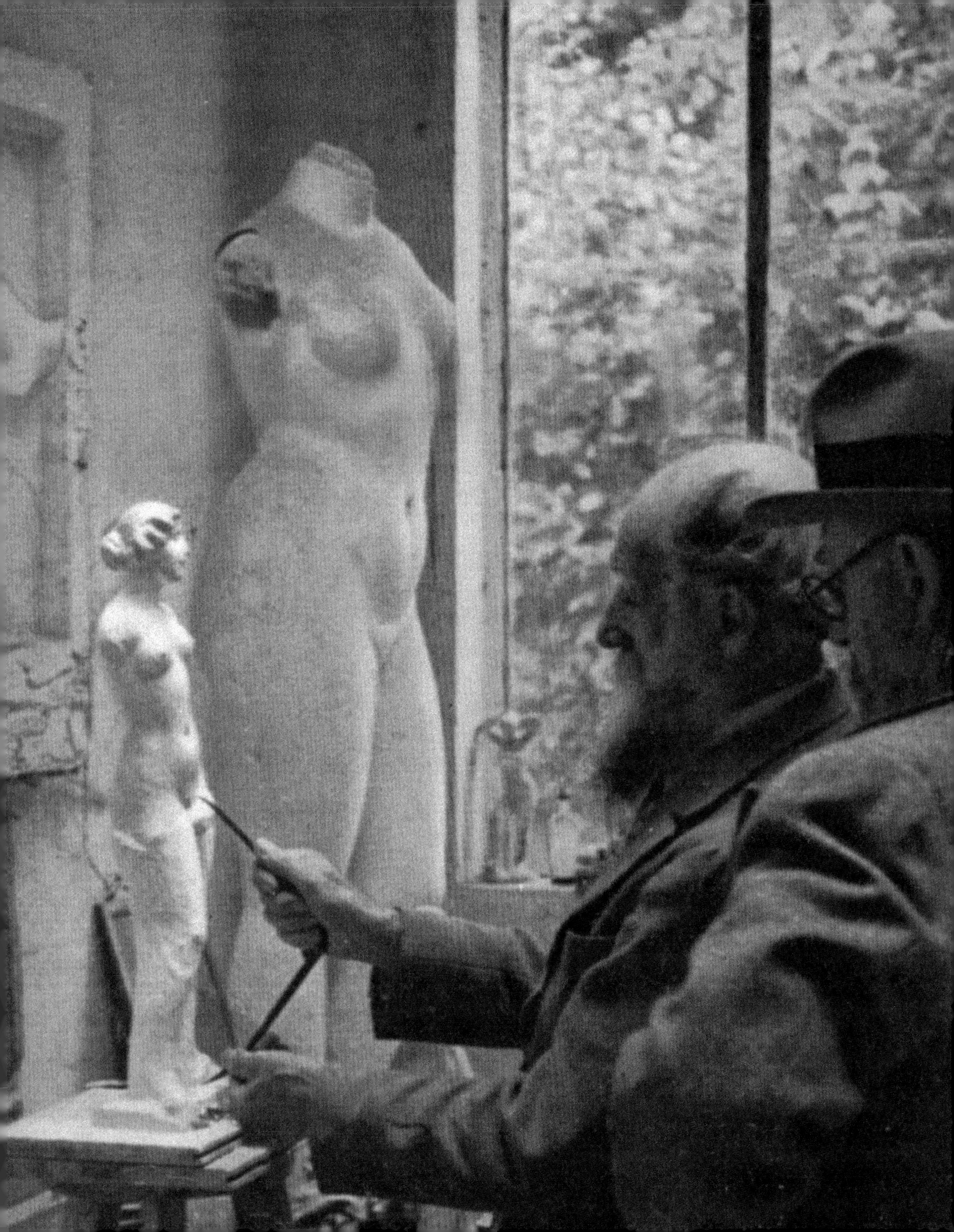

Dorothy Kosinski

Matisse

and His Contemporaries

I have never avoided the influence of others . . . I would have considered this a cowardice and a lack of sincerity toward myself. I believe that the personality of the artist develops and asserts itself through the struggles it has to go through when pitted against other personalities. If the fight is fatal and the personality succumbs, it means that this was bound to be its fate.

. . . I have worked to enrich my knowledge by satisfying the diverse curiosities of my mind, striving to ascertain the different thoughts of ancient and modern masters of plastic art. And this study was also material because I tried at the same time to understand their technique.[1]

—Henri Matisse, 1907

Our exhibition *Matisse: Painter as Sculptor* embraces works (and not all of them sculptures) by other artists: Archipenko, Barye, Bourdelle, Brancusi, Cézanne, Degas, Despiau, Giacometti, Laurens, Lipchitz, Maillol, Picasso, and Rodin. Some of the individual works (Laurens's terra-cotta, for instance; see cat. 155, p. 191)[2] were owned by Matisse, reflecting a deep and enduring friendship; others were the object of profound study, Barye's *Jaguar Devouring a Hare,* for example, or admiration (Cézanne's). Rodin was a starting point, a father figure, the object ultimately of Oedipal fury. If Matisse came away disappointed (if not disgusted) by the great master's commentaries on his drawings, he sought out at least briefly (and with apparent contentment) technical training from Emile-Antoine Bourdelle.[3] In this exhibition Gustave Moreau's absence is perhaps lamentable: Not only was he an important teacher of Matisse and the other "fauves" but also he is, like Degas, a painter-sculptor who experimented with modeling in wax, creating rather crude figurative assemblages.[4] Maillol was a longtime friend and acknowledged as an important proponent of modernism.[5] Matisse, however (and despite the friendship), emphasized the profound differences between their aesthetic foci. Others (Rodin or Giacometti) invite us to think more carefully about the importance and meaning of the expressionistic surface or, in an opposite extreme (Lipchitz or Archipenko), its eradication into a smooth anonymous skin. What is the significance of the antique tradition or its modern counterpart (Despiau) in terms of Matisse's repeated investigation of the human body; or how does the focus on the human torso, fragmented from the body as whole, reflect simultaneously the resonance of tradition and a modernist impulse toward the reductive? Degas's mastery of motion makes manifest Matisse's focus on stasis. Already in 1912, Roger Fry had anointed Matisse and Picasso—"at the present moment as leaders"—with a preeminence that does not dissipate and that results in a keen awareness, in each, of the other, moments of pointed contact, and episodes of creative dialogue.[6] The inclusion of these other artists is surely not an attempt to investigate the issue of influence; Matisse's appetite was voraciously catholic and any investigation would necessitate an unwieldy range of objects, from antique statuary to Iberian sculpture, African carvings, Michelangelo, and so on. The point is rather to provide a lens by which to clarify the meaning and importance of Matisse's sculpture in its time: How is it modern? What were the major issues that preoccupied him and his contemporaries? What did sculpture mean to him? The juxtaposition of Matisse's sculptures with a careful selection of works by other artists underlines issues of process and materials, the dominance of specific themes and concepts—the arabesque, the dance, and the treatment of surfaces.

Matisse claimed the female nude as his primary subject: "What interests me most is neither still life nor landscape but the human figure. It is through it that I best succeed in expressing the nearly religious feeling that I have toward life."[7] His passionate explanation reveals an importance for the sculptures that might not at first be apparent. The subject matter might be seen as conventional, perhaps repetitive, or even offensive to the feminist art historian.[8] The scale of the sculptures is relatively small. They inhabit a private realm, divorced from the rhetoric of the public monument. They might be understood as *mere* exercises, a notion that Matisse's statements would seem to encourage: "I took up sculpture because what interested me in painting was a clarification of my

Fig. 15. Windowsill with Matisse's sculptures. Archives Matisse, Paris.

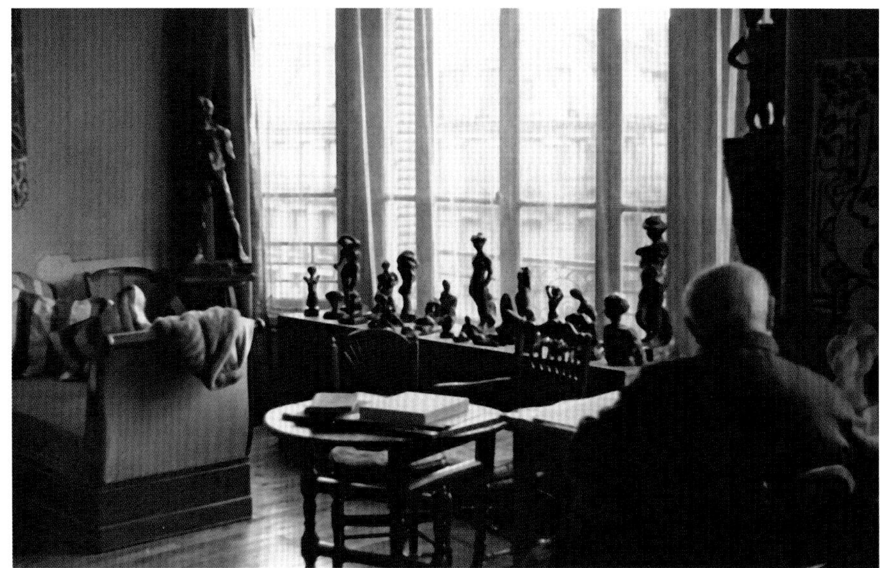

ideas. I changed my method and worked in clay in order to have a rest from painting. . . ."[9] "By changing the medium I do not change the goal. . . . I do not consider my sculpture anything but an exercise."[10] Matisse worked with the traditional sculptural process, carving and casting, while a teleological art history of the twentieth century would privilege the processes of collage and assemblage and the sculptures of the planar dimension.[11]

One must not, however, be misled by Matisse's comments about his fluid movement between the realms of painting and sculpture. His sculpture clearly meant a great deal to him. Some projects occupied his attention for years, and sculpture was an integral part of his creative process and problem solving. Beginning with the Salon d'automne in 1904, he included sculpture in almost every major exhibition.[12] His last exhibition at Alfred Stieglitz's 291 gallery in 1912 was devoted exclusively to sculpture.[13] Matisse seems to have embraced diminutive scale (fig. 15) as a challenge to succeed in achieving what he sought for synthesis: "The smaller the bit of sculpture, the more the essentials of form must exist."[14] He is not, of course, alone in his preoccupation with the female nude; this subject seems to be inscribed at the very heart of modern sculpture in the early years of the twentieth century, a time when, as Kenneth Clark suggests, "art was once more concerned with concepts rather than sensations [and] the nude was . . . the first concept that came to mind,"[15]—that the female nude was the ideal vehicle for an exploration of form emptied of narrative, emotion, and rhetoric.

This might imply that the form is a mere cipher and that the sculptures are somehow neutral in their effect, neither of which is the case with Matisse's sculptures, which all exude a subtle energy. Even the smallest work that we yearn to weigh in our palm has a compelling inner vitality. Larger works, such as *The Serpentine* (cat. 58, pp. 170, 172) or *Large Seated Nude* (cat. 98, p. 217; 99, p. 275), which demand that we circulate around them, confound our understanding by revealing an extraordinarily complex sequence of forms that resist easy adherence to the whole. Matisse speaks frequently about the necessity for the artist to internalize the bodily structure and pose of the model. Perhaps we might profitably borrow from Graham Dunstan Martin, a professor of French at the University of Edinburgh, who appropriated a neurological term, *proprioception,* coined by the Nobel prize–winning physiologist Sir Charles Sherrington in 1906 to mean "our imaging of our body's position and capacities of movement." Martin writes: "More concretely, it is like being inside your body and your limbs, knowing your way around them, as a hand is inside a glove."[16] Matisse demands that the artist literally feel or absorb the pose and internal structure of the subject, thereby infusing the work with authenticity. In 1908 he advised his students to "empathize with the model's postures."[17] Similarly he advised: "To one's work one must bring knowledge, much contemplation

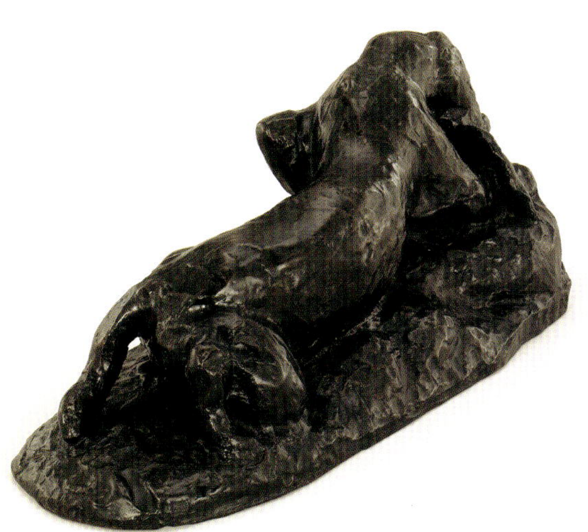

Fig. 16. Henri Matisse, *Jaguar Devouring a Hare,* 1899–1901. Bronze. The Baltimore Museum of Art; Purchase with exchange funds from the Nelson and Juanita Greif Gutman Collection. Cat. 1.

of the model . . . and the imagination to enrich what one sees. Close your eyes and hold the vision, and then do the work with your own sensibility. . . . If it is a model, try taking the same pose yourself. If you feel a strain, be glad, it is the key to movement."[18] Even more telling is the anecdote offered by his son-in-law, Georges Duthuit, about the work process that resulted in the painting *Dance:* "He crouched ready to leap as he had done one night some years before on the beach in Collioure in a round of Catalan fisherman. . . ."[19] This insistence on the internalized understanding of anatomy, balance, and pose is fundamental to Matisse's thinking about sculpture and is also key to an understanding of his attitudes about his predecessors and contemporaries.

An eloquent manifestation of Matisse's ability to give form to these internalized sensations is found in the arabesque, the powerful torsion of the figure in space.[20] This three-dimensional expression of balance and energy constitutes the essence, for example, of *Madeleine I* (cat. 12, p. 267; 13, p. 115; 14, p. 120) and *II* (cat. 15, p. 119) and *The Serpentine, Reclining Nude I (Aurora)* (cat. 44, p. 269; 45, pp. 153, 155–56), *Reclining Nude II* (cat. 112, p. 228), and *III* (cat. 113, p. 229). It is, however, in his years-long study of Antoine Barye's *Jaguar Devouring a Hare* (cat. 146, pp. 103–104) that Matisse comes to understand the force of the powerful S-curve, the sense of coiled energy in the tense musculature. He expressed his goal in a comment to Raymond Escholier: "[I] identified with the passion of the wild beast expressed in the rhythm of the masses."[21] Matisse's meticulous study of the Barye involved an intellectual process of identification with the ferocious beast's inner structure, rather than a preoccupation with expressive surface details or narrative elements (fig. 16). Moreover, Matisse's arabesque is not a line inscribed in space—that would suggest something far too linear and insubstantial. Rather, his arabesque is constructed of a set of lines that twist and spiral together and against one another to describe the curving contours of a powerful volume in space.[22] The pulling in of the arms, their eradication or absorption into the torso reinforces the torsion in the *Madeleine* figures. This radical editing effectively erases gesture and exemplifies Matisse's reaction against the histrionic poses of Rodin's *Eve,* who shields her face in shame, or his *Meditation* (cat. 162, p. 118), in which the arms coil around the head, revealing the tortured voluptuousness of the lower body. "Expression, to my way of thinking," he said, "does not consist of the passion mirrored upon a human face or betrayed by violent gesture."[23]

Matisse does not seek to capture the ephemeral nor to describe motion, but rather to find a "condensation of sensations," a "suggestive synthesis."[24] Rodin's work seems to have everything to do with flux and motion, essential characteristics that Leo Steinberg describes so eloquently: "We see firm flesh resolve itself into a symbol of perpetual flux . . . each human body but the fugitive configuration of a moment . . . the irresistible energy of liquefaction, in the molten pour of matter as every shape relinquishes its claim to permanence. . . . Rodin's intuition is of sculptural form in suspension. He finds bodies that coast and roll as if on air currents"; his art of "aerial detachment" and "restless fragments" is in stark contrast to Matisse's communication of an internal force and energy even when the figure is in stasis.[25] One might compare *Dance Movement Pas de Deux 'B'* (cat. 164, p. 175) by Rodin with *The Dance* (cat. 59, p. 174) by Matisse, whose approach can be characterized as the more intellectual or analytical: "Underneath this succession of moments which constitutes the superficial existence of things animate and inanimate and which is continually obscuring and transforming them, it is yet possible to search for a truer, more essential character which the artist will seize so that he may give to reality a more lasting interpretation."[26]

Extremely conscious of the limitations of depicting movement, Matisse mentioned the subject frequently: "Movement is itself unstable and does not correspond to something durable like a statue, unless the artist has an understanding of the entire movement of which he represents but a moment."[27] Quite naturally one identifies Edgar Degas with the theme of the dance (fig. 17), a subject that attracted him tremendously because of his interest in movement. Auguste Renoir

Fig. 17. Edgar Degas, *Arabesque over Right Leg, Left Arm in Front,* c. 1882–1895. Yellow brown wax, metal frame. National Gallery of Art, Washington, D.C.; Collection of Mr. and Mrs. Paul Mellon.

Fig. 18. Henri Matisse, *Woman Leaning on Her Hands,* 1905. Bronze. The Baltimore Museum of Art, The Cone Collection, formed by Dr. Claribel Cone and Miss Etta Cone of Baltimore, Maryland. Cat. 24.

Fig. 19. Edward Steichen, Matisse working on *La Serpentine,* from *Camera Work,* 1909. Photogravure. The Baltimore Museum of Art, E. Kirkbride Miller Library. Cat. 165.

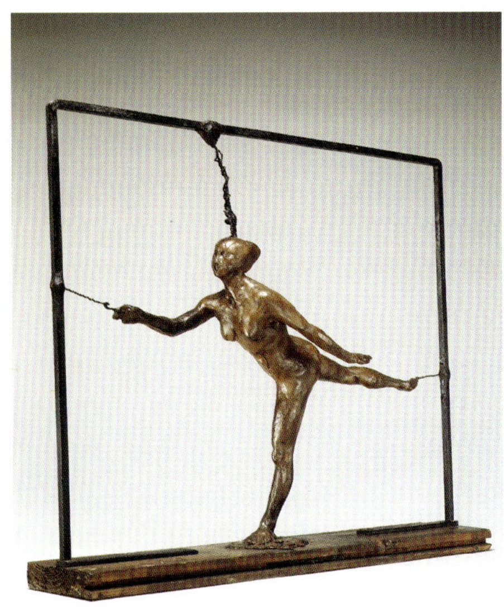

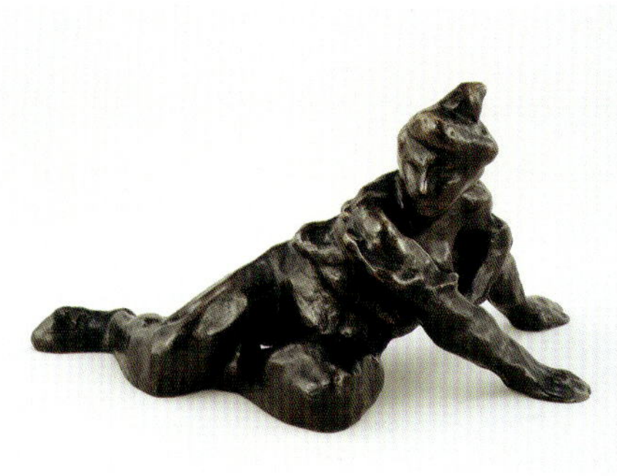

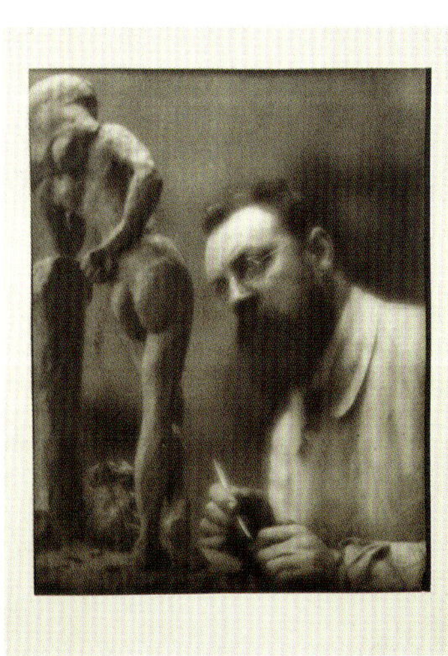

observed in admiration: "Degas found the means to express the malady of our contemporaries: I mean movement."[28] Degas's fascination with the chronophotographic studies of Eadweard Muybridge and his own experiments in projecting his sculptures against a cloth illuminated by candlelight and set on a rotating base are evidence of his obsession with the fleeting, with the fugitive, with the quintessentially symbolist, Bergsonian concepts of the interpenetrating and fluid realities of time, movement, and space.[29] Julius Meier-Graefe went so far so to describe Degas's subject as the "balance point between two movements."[30] It has been suggested that Matisse was inspired by the robust muscularity of Isadora Duncan's craft; in discussing *Woman Leaning on Her Hands* (fig. 18; cat. 24, pp. 127–28), Dominique Szymusiak makes an interesting point in this regard.[31] It is (very much unlike Degas's works) not about fleeting movements and fractions of seconds, but about the body in stasis but hardly at rest. The woman is in full contact with the floor, her torso twisted in a powerful arabesque as her limbs extend outward to engage the space around her.

Matisse's figures are never in flux; on the contrary, they are grounded, constructed with the thinking of an architect. He stressed "the mechanics of construction," the "essentials of form. . . . Never forget the constructive lines, axes of shoulders and pelvis; nor of legs, arms, neck, and head. This building up of the form gives its essential expression."[32] It is hardly surprising that Matisse held Courbet and Cézanne in such esteem. He owned a bather composition (now in the collection of the Petit Palais and unfortunately unavailable for this project; see fig. 10, p. 9).[33] He must have empathized with Cézanne's tormented and assiduous realization of these sensations, the building up of his figures. Matisse wrote about Courbet almost if he were a sculptor: "Courbet does not have atmosphere, he does without it. Even a beautiful Courbet is a little like marble: it's a solid thing . . . the sturdiness, the richness of the material is in Courbet."[34]

Matisse's *The Serpentine* is clearly related to his work on the *Dance* composition in 1919. There is a compelling similarity between the sculpture (fig. 19) and the *Study for Dance (II)* (cat. 62, p. 173), in which the limbs are treated like "rolls of clay" and there is equal focus on the figure and the surrounding space. The title may allude to Loie Fuller's dance of the veils, which was wildly popular at the turn of the century in France.[35] We know that *The Serpentine* is based on a photograph of a model resting on a studio prop (fig. 2, p. 3), and most probably relates as well to the Farnese *Hercules at Rest*, which he would have known.[36] It is ironic that this figure is at rest while it communicates a coiled intensity, the feet tense with alert energy, the body taut with the possibility of springing into action. We know that Matisse pared away at the initially plump body of the figure, reducing it dramatically to these tensile forms. When he wrote about allowing the movement to be "comprehensible from all points of view," perhaps he meant the revelation of internal energy in these thinned-down forms, or the energizing of the surrounding space that has been so thoroughly activated around the volumes, or perhaps it is his enabling us to intuitively grasp or "see" the entire body, thereby compelling us—first in our imagination, and then in reality—to circulate around the object in space.[37]

Emile-Antoine Bourdelle's *Large Bacchante* (cat. 147, p. 178) from just two years earlier offers an instructive point of comparison with *The Serpentine.* If Matisse's work addresses a tension between stasis and movement, Bourdelle's sculpture is explicitly about dance: the intoxicated follower of the wine god Bacchus writhes in orgiastic frenzy.[38] The dramatic movement of churning legs and outstretched arms creates a dynamic silhouette, the limbs framing, embracing, and energizing the surrounding space within the composition. The dynamism of surrounding space is clearly critical to both pieces. Significant differences become clear, however, as one circulates around each sculpture. Bourdelle's dancer seems to offer itself in discreet moments—front, back, and sides; the volumes and spaces of *The Serpentine* fold and unfold in a fluid and bafflingly complex three-dimensional envelope. Of course, Bourdelle overtly embraces a subject from antiquity, for instance, cleverly

Fig. 20. Emile-Antoine Bourdelle, *Fruit,* 1911. Bronze. The Baltimore Museum of Art; Alan and Janet Wurtzburger Collection.

Fig. 21. Aristide Maillol, *Flora,* 1911. Bronze. Dallas Museum of Art; Gift of Mr. and Mrs. Eugene McDermott.

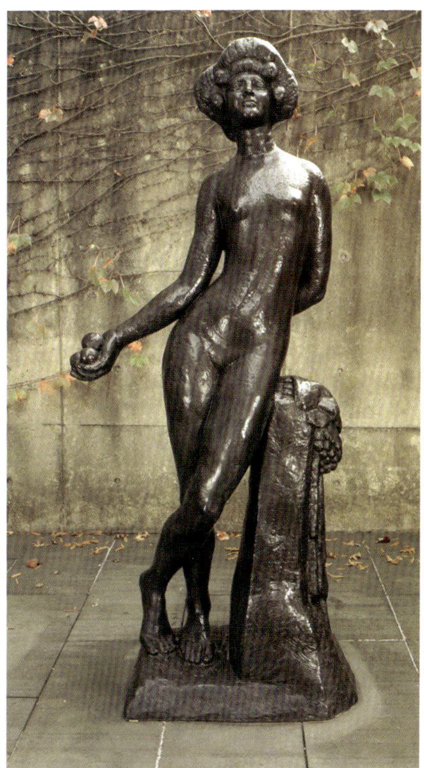

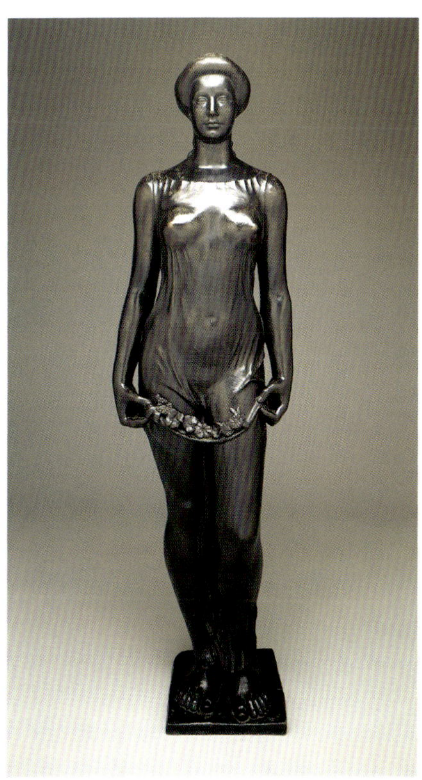

juxtaposing the twisting column of the polished wood base with the pose of the dancing figure (she seems to leaf or sprout out of the trunk) while using the gnarled trunk to reinforce the theme of revelry under the influence of the grape. For Matisse, it is never about narrative but rather, in this case, about a "marvelously taut and sure three-dimensional S," an inner inevitable vitality of a vegetal form.[39]

Bourdelle's *Fruit,* a noted sculpture that he worked on during an extended period from 1902–1911, may have influenced Matisse in terms of the pose of the leaning figure, legs crossed at knees (fig. 20). The differences are dramatic and prompt a clear distinction between Matisse's aesthetic and that of the artists of the contemporary "classical modernity," including Bourdelle, Maillol, Bernard, and Despiau, among others. Bourdelle's work is principally about elegant line and the contour of a columnar figure; Matisse's work is always about form as mass in space. He offered his students a clear maxim in this regard: "If an egg be conceived as a form, a nick will not hurt it; but if as a contour, it certainly will suffer,"[40] a phrase that sounds like William Tucker's notion of Matisse's "innocent experience of volume alone."[41]

The vocabulary that dominates the discourse of modern sculpture in the first decades of the twentieth century is remarkably consistent. Matisse talks about simplification, clarity, and condensation. The classical modernists seek "essential structures,"[42] "balance, harmony, and synthesis."[43] Bourdelle describes his lofty aesthetic mission: "I departed from the accidental plane in search of a permanent plane. I sought the essentials of structures, leaving in second place the transient waves, and moreover I sought universal rhythm."[44] Bourdelle aspired, too, to a monumentality, an architectural significance.[45] Classical modernity became especially prominent between the wars, but had already begun at the turn of the century as a reaction, especially among some artists who studied and worked in his studio, against the towering figure of Rodin.[46] These artists turned to the serene harmony they recognized in Greek sculpture as an antidote to the characteristics they identified in the work of Rodin: pathos, sentiment, heightened naturalism, and romantic literary content. The classic moderns sought to cleanse their work by returning to the sculptural values of elemental forms (volume) and mass. We know that Matisse was part of this reaction against Rodin, criticizing his obsession with the observation of details in nature, his fascination with motion, and his depiction of emotion. Rodin's working method—focusing on a detail, reworking it, replacing it, reacting to the implications of the alteration—was antithetical to Matisse's deliberate, deeply felt, and highly intellectual process and to his goal of constructing "a luminous ensemble."[47]

Matisse would never, however, embrace overt allusions to the classical past, nor could he ever compromise his highly personal intuitive and intellectual responses in order to adhere to an aesthetic philosophy. He was not reticent about articulating his differences with his sculptor contemporaries. About Maillol, whom he met first in 1904, and with whom he enjoyed a close friendship, Matisse said: "Maillol's sculpture and my work in that line have nothing in common."[48] Elaborating elsewhere, he said: "We never speak on the subject. For we couldn't understand one another. Maillol, like the ancient masters, proceeded by volume; I am concerned with arabesque like the renaissance artists. Maillol did not like risks and I was drawn to them. He did not like adventure."[49] Maillol, in turn, contrasting his own work to that of Rodin, said, "I search for beauty and not character."[50] Indeed, his work is about extreme simplification and transcendent qualities rather than about the depiction of reality or the expression of the artist's emotions. André Gide captures the cool elegance of Maillol's work in his description of *La Méditerranée* (cat. 157, p. 190), exhibited at the Salon d'automne in 1905: "She is beautiful, she does not signify anything, it is a silent work."[51] Despite figuration, his work tends toward the internalized meanings of abstraction.[52]

Matisse's sculpture—though retreating from Rodin's bombast, which he deeply distrusted—is never cool in the sense that Maillol's work is, the figure drained of meaning and tending toward

Fig. 22. Photograph of Matisse working on *Standing Nude (Katia).* Archives Matisse, Paris.

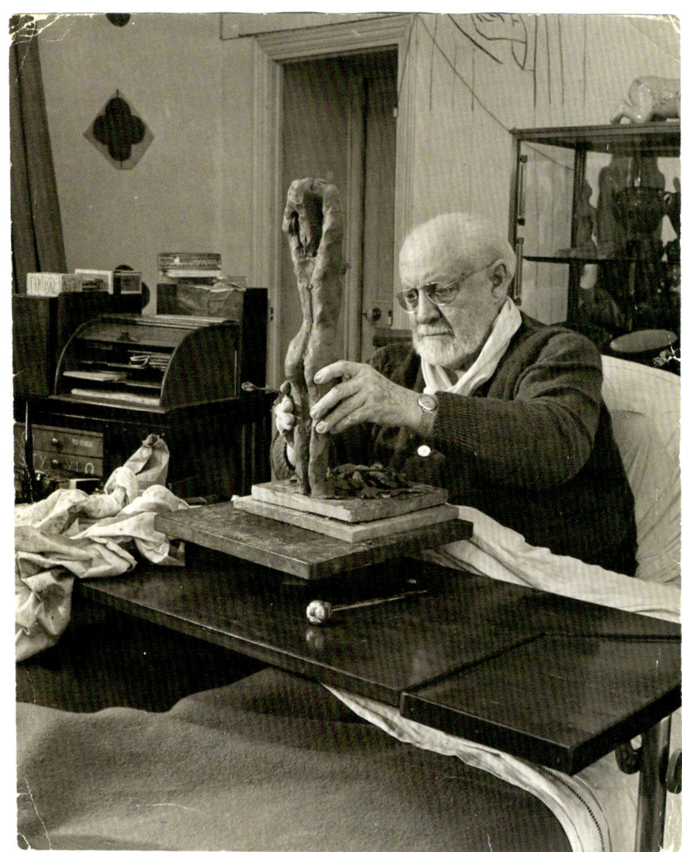

abstraction. *La Méditerranée* is contentedly inscribed within an imaginary cube; his standing figures—*Flora,* for example (fig. 21)—have the architectural clarity of a column or a caryatid. In Matisse's work (as we have explored already), meaning is invested in "the solid articulated core of the body."[53] The eloquence of *Large Seated Nude* is rooted in the violation of the cube, the way in which the figure leans improbably into space by means of an unimaginable equilibrium derived from an intuition of inner vitality deep within the abdominal musculature. Matisse returns again to his extraordinary understanding of the arabesque: the figure coils around a continuous central axis. *Standing Nude (Katia)* (cat. 132, p. 255) surely resonates with the tradition of the kourai or amphora, but it is less his response to tradition than his constant attention to the construction of the human body and the communication of physical energy that is remarkable. The tiny *Venus in a Shell I* (cat. 123, pp. 245–46, 248) has extraordinary explosive energy: the torso is taut, stretched upward, the breast unified within the contour of the body. Jack Flam has written about the

> underlying structures . . . firmly unified. . . . This unity was inherent in his working procedure. Throughout his career, Matisse began his sculptures by building them up, and he finished them by paring them down. Each of his sculptures attests to the central role that the stripping away of mass played in his work. He would first construct a solid and naturalistic image of a figure and then reduce it to essentials by a process that involved kneading, cutting, bending, gouging, scraping, and twisting the forms. In his sculpture, as in his painting, he worked from the objective to the subjective, from a concept of order based on the notion of a stable, naturalistic norm to a more difficult and subjective one based on the dynamic tensions that arose from different kinds of perceptual responses. This dialectic between opposing perceptions is one of the striking ways in which Matisse's early sculptures differ from Rodin's, even though both use a similarly based range of surface textures.[54]

Fig. 23. Medardo Rosso, *The Concierge,* 1883–1884 (detail). Wax over plaster. Raymond and Patsy Nasher Collection, Dallas.

Fig. 24. Henri Matisse, *Small Crouching Nude without an Arm,* 1908. Bronze. The Baltimore Museum of Art, The Cone Collection, formed by Dr. Claribel Cone and Miss Etta Cone of Baltimore, Maryland. Cat. 65.

Fig. 25. Henri Matisse, *Bathers with a Turtle,* 1908. Oil on canvas. The Saint Louis Art Museum; Gift of Mr. and Mrs. Joseph Pulitzer Jr.

The surfaces of his sculptures are very often maps of his process, traces of his work with the material.[55] The evidence of labor, of process embedded in the surface is, according to Yve-Alain Bois, "part of the meaning of his sculpture."[56] Matisse's surfaces (fig. 22) are totally dissimilar to Rodin's agitated pools of material, which initiate a play of light, and certainly different from Medardo Rosso's surfaces (fig. 23), where solid form seems to disintegrate in light. Matisse's surface is more a residue of his process and perhaps might be attributed to the influence of the untraditional working and reworking of malleable wax in the hands of his predecessors such as Gustave Moreau or Edgar Degas.[57]

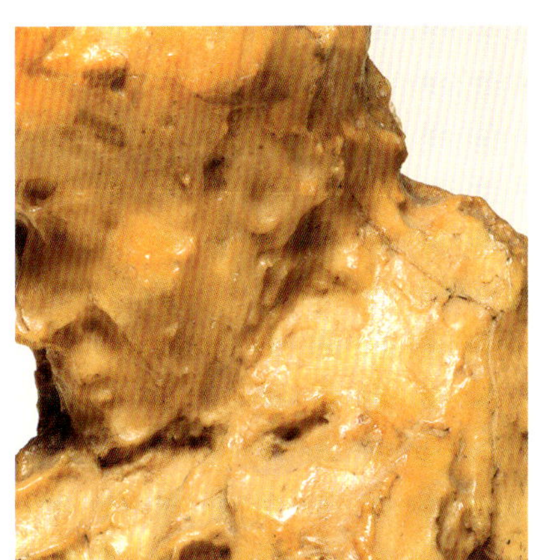

Throughout his career, Matisse experimented with very small and radically reduced sculptures of the human form. *Torso with Head (La Vie)* (cat. 37, p. 151) from 1906 depicts the female nude with dramatically truncated legs and arms, putting the emphasis on the curve of the belly, the arch of the back, the erect breasts, and full thigh and buttocks. *Small Crouching Nude without an Arm,* from 1908 (fig. 24; cat. 65, pp. 184–85), seems so modest as to resist our attention. The figure is without detail—no facial features, for example. The body is simply folded in on itself, a pose that is even more radical in *Small Crouching Torso without Arms or Head* (see fig. 4, p. 4) from the same year. This pose takes up again the position of figure explored already in his major painting, *Le bonheur de vivre,* from 1905–1906 (fig. 28, p. 29; see also cat. 31, p. 135). As the figure is not seated but rather crouches, there is tremendous physical tension in the vertebrae that are so radically stretched and taut. The dynamic tensile strength of the spine as it curls forward in space is the essence of this tiny sculpture and relates, of course, to contemporary explorations of this pose in his paintings, *Bathers with a Turtle* (fig. 25) and *Le Luxe I* and *II* (1907, 1908).

Small Torso (cat. 120, p. 235) and *Small Thin Torso* (fig. 26; cat. 118, p. 276; 119, pp. 236, 238), both from 1929, seem to follow this reductive impulse to an extreme. These tiny sculptures, between three and four inches in height, seem to embody in an almost perversely radical fashion the artist's statement about diminution of form demanding greater attention to "the essentials."[58] Each of these is like a projectile, a primitive weapon that we instinctively yearn to hold in our palms. Indeed, these small works most probably indicate Matisse's love of antique statuary, of the fragments of the human form that he copied as a student and continued to study in the collections he roamed.

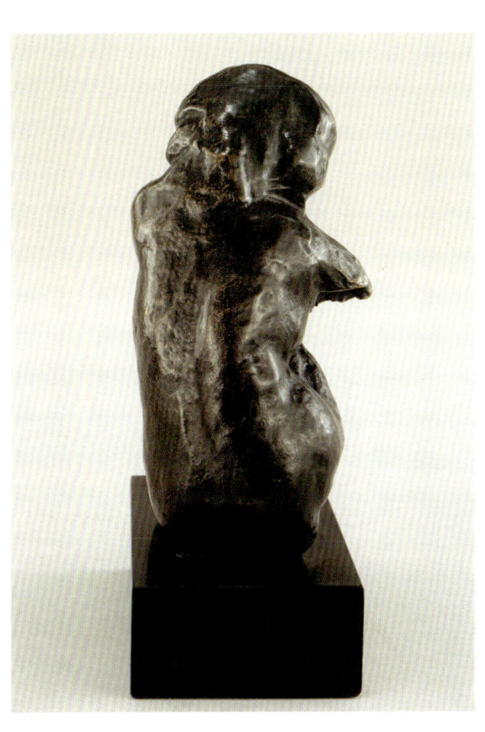

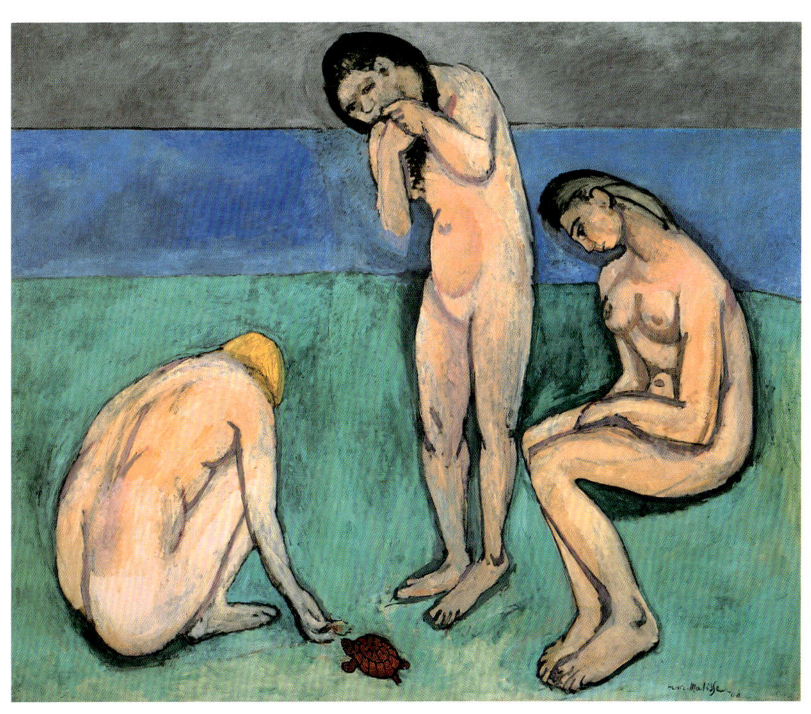

Fig. 26. *Small Thin Torso,* 1929. Bronze. Direction des Musées de France, Gift of Jean Matisse, on deposit at the Musée Matisse, Nice, 1978. Cat. 119.

Fig. 27. Charles Despiau, *Adolescent Girl (Torso),* 1929. Plaster. High Museum of Art, Atlanta; Purchase with funds from Irene and Howard Stein.

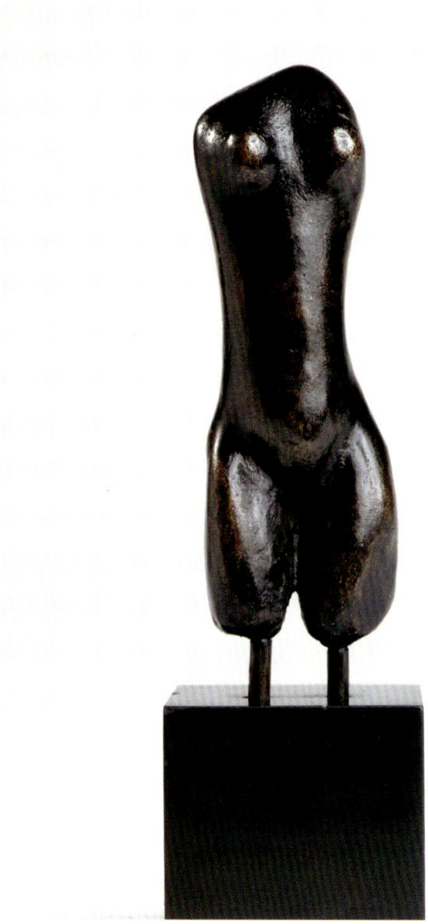

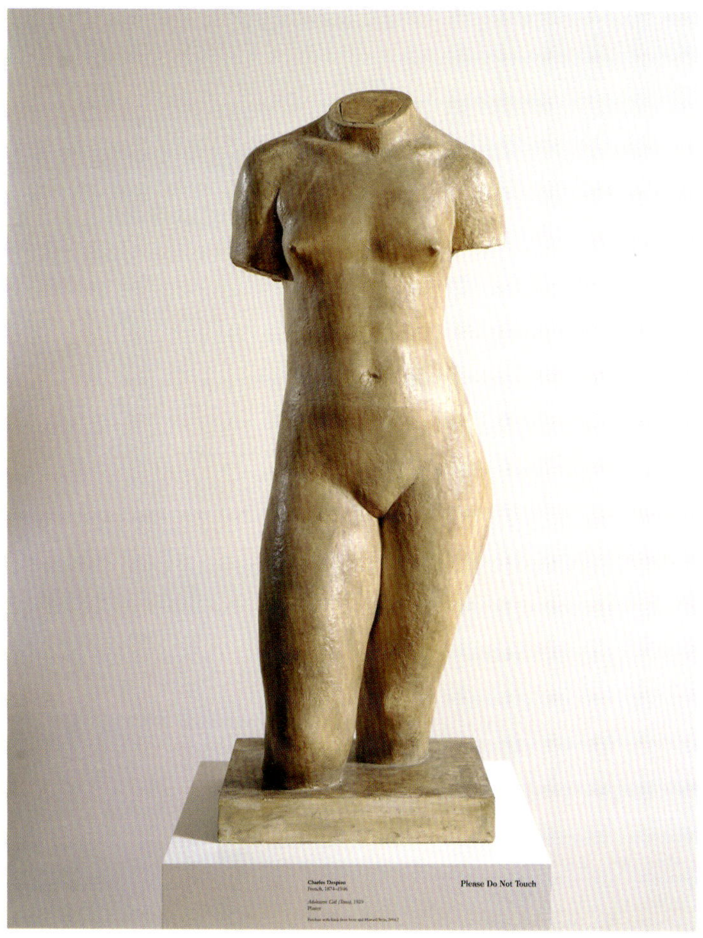

These small sculptures intersect with a broader issue of the importance of the fragments of the human torso to modernist sensibility.[59] One might even look to the possible influence of a modern classicist such as Charles Despiau, whose elegantly reductive plaster of *Adolescent Girl (Torso)* (fig. 27) was shown amidst contemporary sculpture at the Galerie Georges Bernheim in 1929. In looking at torsos from the twenties and thirties, one is struck by the rapport in reductive stylization that stretches from classicist to surrealist and cubist. Matisse's attraction to a highly polished surface—in these torsos from 1929, but also in *Henriette II* (cat. 93, p. 212) and *Tiari* (cat. 78, p. 195)—perhaps reveals an interest in the almost fetishization of surface found in contemporary works by Brancusi (cat. 148, p. 240), Archipenko (cat. 145, p. 242), or Lipchitz (cat. 156, p. 213).

Matisse—in doing away with head and limbs—has eradicated entirely any distraction from the expression of his own profound interiorized understanding of the structure of the body, its densest region, the source of its physical power and balance. In these tiny torsos, *mere* fragments, one confronts the two essential aspects of Matisse's achievement that we have tried to probe in this essay: the intellectual process whereby he knows and feels the essence of the human form, and his tactile work, the imprint of his thumbs creating the material vessel of that profound intuition. We perhaps come to understand Matisse's rather startling observation (made to André Verdet) about his work with the model: "She was a pretty girl, a perfect model. I felt her body, my hands enveloped the shapes, and then I transmitted in earth the equivalent of my sensation."[60]

> What matters is not so much to ask yourself where you are going, as to try to live with the materiality of things, to enter into all its possibilities.[61]

Notes

1. Matisse to Guillaume Apollinaire; Apollinaire 1907, in Barr 1951, 101.

2. Henri Matisse sent a photograph of his studio collection to Louis Aragon. The collection included Laurens's terra-cotta *Little Seated Nude.* The caption on the photograph reads: "Objects which have been of use to me nearly all my life."

3. Matisse recounted to Pierre Courthion the story of showing his drawings to Rodin, as suggested by his friend Lagare, who was working at Rodin's studio. When Rodin saw them, he responded, "You have an easy hand. You must be wary of it. It is necessary to make extremely worked drawings, even overworked, with the most details possible, and once you have done this show them to me!" Matisse mentioned that when he left he was more disappointed than flattered, and he commented that, "once I was able to make more detailed drawings I wouldn't need anyone to teach me, because my natural method consisted of working from the simple to the more complicated. . . ." (Courthion n.d. [Matisse Archives] fourth conversation).

4. Cooke 1986, 11–42.

5. Roger Fry included both Matisse and Maillol (and others) in his exhibition devoted to the postimpressionists, held at the Grafton Galleries in London, November 1910.

6. Fry 1912, 249–51.

7. Barr 1951, 122.

8. John Elderfield offers a retort to feminist readings of Matisse's works in his book *Pleasuring Painting: Matisse's Feminine Representations* (1995).

9. Elsen 1971, 45.

10. "En changeant de moyen je ne change pas de but . . . je ne considère ma sculpture que comme exercice" (Courthion n.d. [Matisse Archives], sixth conversation).

11. Up until World War II or some time thereafter, contemporary art exhibits were heterogeneous, embracing figurative and nonfigurative, avant-garde and modern classicists. See p. 21 and note 46, below, regarding this all-embracing view, which later became more rigidly canonical.

12. At the Salon d'automne of 1904 Matisse exhibited *The Serf* and *Madeleine;* see Cowling et al. 2002, 362.

13. It included six bronzes, five plasters, one terra-cotta, and twelve related drawings; see Cauman 2000b, 168.

14. Barr 1951, 551.

15. Clark 1956, 358.

16. Martin 2000, 199–214, esp. 205.

17. Elsen 1972, 20; see also Barr 1915, 550–52, for the entire text of Matisse's instructions to his student Sarah Stein in 1908.

18. Barr 1951, 550.

19. Ibid., 135.

20. Benjamin 1992, 15–22.

21. Escholier 1960, 46. The obvious source for this form is to be found in the Renaissance and baroque *figura serpentinata.* Matisse's admiration for Michelangelo, for example, is well documented.

22. Szymusiak (1993, 10–11) describes this arabesque as a double-helix construction.

23. Barr 1951, 119.

24. Ibid., 120; and Elsen 1972, 37.

25. Steinberg 1972, 325, 338.

26. Barr 1951, 120.

27. "Le mouvement est, par lui-même instable, et ne convient pas à quelque chose de durable comme un statue, à moins que l'artiste ait eu conscience de l'action entiere dont il ne représente qu'un moment" (Szymusiak 1993, 15; citing Fourcade 1972, 45–46).

28. Renoir 1962, 67.

29. The Nobel Prize–winning French philosopher, Henri Bergson (1859–1941) described human experience or consciousness as a continuously flowing process whereby time is experienced as duration.

30. Millard (1976, 104), referring to Julius Meier-Graefe's discussion in idem 1923.

31. Szymusiak 1993, 13; citing Girard 1993, 42.

32. Barr 1951, 551.

33. Matisse purchased Cézanne's *The Three Bathers* in 1899 and held it in high esteem throughout his career. In his conversations with Courthion he commented that this Cézanne painting "haunted" him; see Courthion n.d. (Matisse Archives), 56–67. See also Barr 1951, 38–40, for a discussion of how Matisse acquired the painting.

34. "Courbet n'a pas d'atmosphère, il s'en est passé. Même un beau Courbet, c'est un peu comme un marbre: c'est une chose dure . . . la solidité, la richesse de la matière est dans Courbet" (Courthion n.d. [Matisse Archives], second conversation).

35. Loie Fuller (1862–1928), the American dancer and theatrical innovator, was interested in experimenting with visual effects, using gels and slides to create special lighting that illuminated her voluminous serpentine dress, first introduced in 1892 in New York and a fantastic sensation later that year in Paris.

36. Mezzatesta 1984, 78.

37. Barr 1951, 139.

38. This work was apparently very special to the artist and he offered plasters of it as gifts to a few cultural figures who were important in his life, including the dancer Isadora Duncan.

39. Elsen 1972, 93; citing Tucker 1969.

40. Barr 1951, 551.

41. Tucker 1974, 87.

42. Elsen 1972, 43; citing Varenne 1937.

43. Jianou and Dufet 1965, 26.

44. Ibid.

45. André Saures in Le Marchant 1989, 14.

46. One of the best studies of this phenomenon is a modest exhibition catalogue (Champion and Janoray 2002) that accompanied an exhibition with works by Joseph Bernard, Bourdelle, Despiau, Léon Drivier, Marcel Gimond, Alfred-Auguste Janniot, and Robert Wlerick. It is especially interesting to be reminded of how integral the modern classics were to the world of modern art: Bernard was prominently exhibited at the 1919 Salon d'automne, both Bernard and Bourdelle exhibited at the Armory show, and the Museum of Modern Art in New York collected and exhibited works by Despiau in 1934, 1939, and 1949.

47. From Courthion (n.d. [Matisse Archives], sixth conversation) herewith the full quote: "And it resulted, in my opinion, in an assemblage of details that do not add up to a decorative ensemble, that do not reach the spectator's eye at the same instant, and this method seems to me to be distant from one that organizes sensations to construct a luminous ensemble for the spirit" (Il en résultait, à mon sens, un ensemble de détails qui ne compte pas dans l'ensemble décoratif, qui n'arrive pas à l'oeil des spectateurs dans un même instant. Cette méthode me paraît bien loin de celle qui consiste à organiser ses sensations pour construire un ensemble lumineux pour l'esprit).

48. Matisse speaks of Maillol with great warmth, noting their contact when Matisse lived in Collioure and Maillol in Banyuls and expressing a special admiration for Maillol's keen attention to materials, his work with clay, for instance (ibid., fourth conversation).

49. Escholier 1960, 140–41.

50. Elsen 1974, 14; citing Claudel 1937, 132.

51. "Elle est belle, elle ne signifie rien, c'est une oeuvre silencieuse" (Duval 2000, 28; citing Gide 1905, 475–85).

52. See, in this regard, an enlightening essay by Lorquin (2002, 54–59). "Maillol," he says, "brought figuration to the brink of formlessness" (ibid., 56).

53. Elsen 1972, 22.

54. Flam 1998, [5–6].

55. Interestingly, William Tucker (1974, 87) points to the worked surfaces as evidence of Matisse's lack of experience, virtuosity, or care when working the clay, evidence of his struggle against its inherent properties.

56. See the preface by Yve-Alain Bois in Duthuit 1997, 372. See also Tucker 1974, 87, 99: "That is to do with the innocent experience of volume alone. . . . The experience of volume was thus essentially abstract: it initially derived from his eye and mind, not from the handling of material."

57. Degas's wax sculptures have been thoroughly treated in the literature; less well known, however, are the small wax sculptures of Gustave Moreau, Matisse's teacher; see Lacambre 1999, 160; and Mathieu 1984, 128.

58. Barr 1951, 551.

59. See Leo Steinberg (1972, 272–76), an expansion on this subject originally published as "Torsos and Raoul Hague," *Art Magazine* (July 1956).

60. "C'était une jolie fille, un modèle parfait. Je palpais son corps, mes mains enveloppant les formes, et puis je transmettais en terre l'équivalent de ma sensation" (Szymusiak 1993, 13; citing Verdet 1952, 30).

61. Flam 1998, 3; citing Matisse as quoted in Diehl 1943.

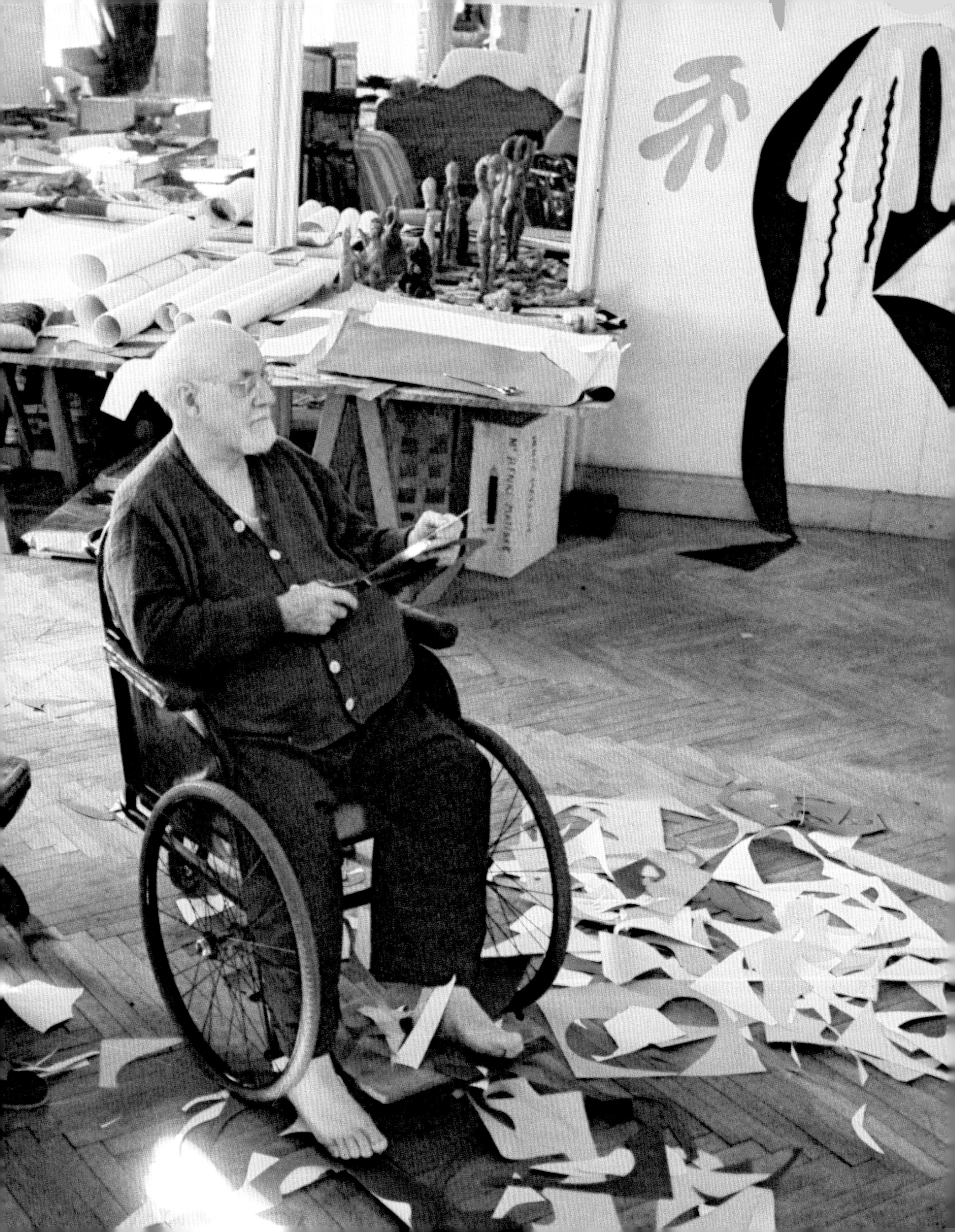

Jay McKean Fisher

Drawing Is

Sculpture Is Drawing

In an exhibition that focuses on Matisse's sculpture, the inclusion of drawings and related prints provides perspective on the artist's creative process. Matisse worked in the mediums of painting, sculpture, drawing, printmaking, and cut-paper collage, sometimes simultaneously, always with an interchange of ideas. In his own writings he emphasized a totality of artistic expression—an encompassing unity. To understand what was meant by the artist's equation of one medium to another, the different values brought to each of them must be identified. With this recognition it is possible to grasp how a specific drawing or sculpture may take up a particular artistic issue, and how, at times, one medium might lead the way while another lags behind. Through the comparative study of drawing and sculpture, it is possible to see how ideas might have evolved and, particularly, how an artist so focused on process chose different paths—drawing to sculpture, sculpture to drawing, and both to painting—in a search for transformation. For Matisse, the very legibility of his artistic process makes its apprehension by the viewer essential. The evidence of his working process is a deliberate visual statement, its subsequent revision and restatement assigning the viewer the role of witness to the artist's progress toward a new resolution. Each completed work of art answers a self-imposed challenge and, as such, provides a stopping place in an evolution that encompasses other works of art.

The formulation of any medium-centered exhibition, in this case sculpture contextualized through a broader view of Matisse's art, leads inevitably to a focus on the artist's creative choices. Specifically, the inclusion of a technical study of Matisse's sculptural practice can, in effect, transport us to the artist's studio, where we learn the limitations and possibilities of the alternatives explored as ideas take visual form. As for drawing, Matisse learned in a standard academic curriculum that had not changed much for decades, and his sculpture, too, grew from the traditions of the genre. There was nothing revolutionary in the technical aspects of his sculpture; it is the way in which he used traditional means to achieve unconventional results that asserts the immediacy of his art. His writings about making art embrace a commitment to explanation. Matisse was convincing, often eloquent, and in the expressed certainty of his convictions, personal. Not surprisingly then, his own perspective continues to control the conversation about his art, but not through any insistence on orthodoxy. Matisse never sought disciples among his students.

We can acknowledge the primacy of painting without valuing sculpture, drawing, or printmaking any less. Matisse's statement, "a drawing is a sculpture," can usefully be reversed to affirm that for him, sculpture is also drawing.[1] The study of his drawings, particularly those related to sculpture, engages attention to the formal aspects of Matisse's art. These drawings can provide us a revealing first-hand point of view from which to follow the artist's visual explorations. He wrote in 1939: "I have always considered drawing not as an exercise of particular dexterity, but above all as a means of expressing intimate feelings and descriptions of states of being, but a means deliberately simplified so as to give simplicity and spontaneity to the expression, which should speak without clumsiness, directly to the mind of the spectator."[2]

Can we challenge the notion that a drawing's function is almost always preparatory, so subservient, its value dependent on the outcome of a finished work of art—the final statement of a visual idea? Are drawings then intermediary, or can they be complete—fully resolved—a stopping place in the resolution of an idea still unfolding? For Matisse, the notion of equivalency is central to understanding his use of different mediums. In accepting that an idea can take form through different means, always inflected by the medium's unique characteristics, we allow the recognition of a drawing's individuality. "There are various kinds of drawing. . . . They have a particular meaning in my work. They precede, accompany, and follow my paintings—and by the dozen. Yet they have no clear-cut relation to the paintings themselves, because when I'm drawing I never think about the paintings, which is really the indirect motive."[3] Drawing did not mean the same thing to Matisse at all times, so his statements about drawing must be considered in the context of the art he was making at the time.

How can drawing be equivalent to sculpture or both drawing and sculpture to painting? In 1939, with his pen-and-ink drawings of the mid-1930s in mind, Matisse wrote: "My line drawing is the purest and most direct translation of my emotion. The simplification of the medium allows that."[4] But this cannot be said of all his drawings, such as his sketches of 1904, which are less a distillation and more a means of analysis. Scholars such as Isabelle Monod-Fontaine and John Elderfield sought to elucidate the interrelationship of Matisse's art as a give-and-take exchange, where an idea in drawing or sculpture might culminate in painting or might be further advanced in drawing, but not yet fully realized in painting or sculpture.[5] This acknowledgment of the different impacts that can be assigned to specific mediums at a given time sets the stage for the recognition of the cut-paper collage as the culmination of all his ideas—an ultimate synthesis, where the means of making is inseparable from the achieved form. This was the artist's goal—a totality, a wholeness at once apparent to the viewer. The works of art, not the artist's words, become the most eloquent explicators of Matisse's creative process.

Several of Matisse's sculptures were created in direct relation to paintings of the same subjects. *The Serf* (cat. 4–6, pp. 107, 109, 266), for instance, is accompanied by a painting of the same model; similarly there exists a painting closely related to the *Madeleine* sculptures. The sequence of sculpture and painting is not known and the approach to modeling the figures is different in each. In the paintings, the models are posed in the artist's studio and in that environment the creation of painting and sculpture are interlocked. In the period from 1904 to 1908, figural poses present in such seminal works as *Luxe, calme et volupté* and *Le bonheur de vivre* (fig. 28), are also given three-dimensional form in sculpture. Most direct, and a sequential pair, are the painting *Blue Nude: Memory of Biskra* (cat. 46, p. 157) and the sculpture *Reclining Nude I (Aurora)* (cat. 44, p. 269; 45, pp. 153, 155–56), each successively a study for the other. After Matisse's arrival in Nice, his work with the reclining-nude pose in painting, sculpture, and drawing was, in each medium, equivalent. In 1930–1932, a painting such as *The Yellow Dress* (cat. 128, p. 247) and a sculpture contemporary with it, *Venus in a Shell I* (cat. 123, pp. 245–46, 248), both seek, in different form and through different means, a formal transformation, a new visual synthesis. But what about drawing, a creative act understood principally in terms of its function? If a drawing is to be related to another work of art, what is the direct connection? Is it possible to determine in a drawing of a reclining nude, for instance, whether or not it was even made in some direct relationship to a sculpture of the same pose? Could it have been the exploration of an idea that was being explored simultaneously in painting? After all, Matisse used a relatively small repertoire of poses, amounting to a series of themes and variations extended across the chronology of his artistic production. He did not consistently date most of his drawings, and because so many exhibitions and studies of Matisse have concentrated repeatedly on a relatively small number of well-known works, most of the artist's drawing oeuvre remains unstudied. A comprehensive catalogue of the drawings has been underway for many years, but the documentation of such a prolific output, one that would consider chronology,

Fig 28. Henri Matisse, *Le Bonheur de vivre,* 1905–1906. Oil on canvas. The Barnes Foundation, Merion, Pennsylvania.

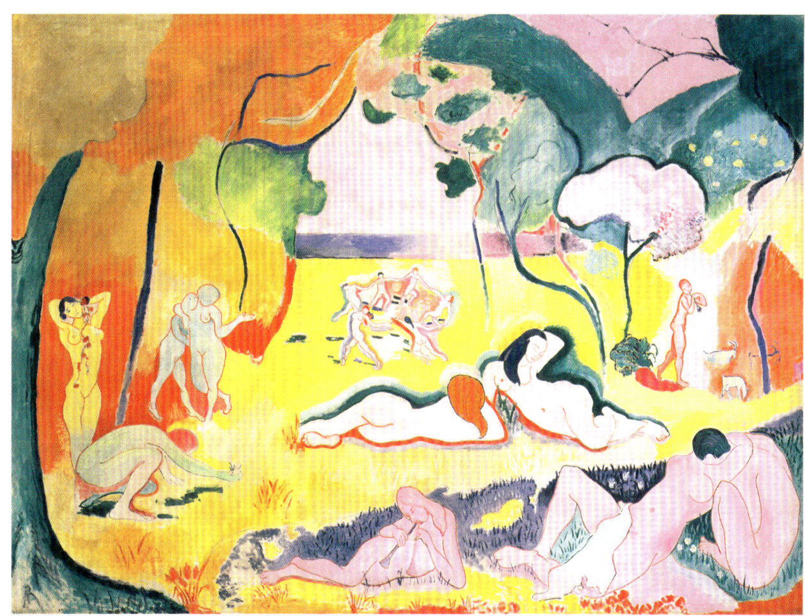

style, medium, and relationship to other works of art, is a Herculean task. Fortunately, through the generosity of the Pierre and Maria-Gaetana Matisse Foundation in New York, the organizing museums of this exhibition were able to include numerous drawings not previously exhibited.

The Academy: Cézanne

Between 1900 and 1903, the period in which Matisse's first sculptures were completed, is a time when the interrelationship between drawing and sculpture is best introduced. There are shared values and often a sequential order in the artist's process of works. This clarity in the relationship of sculpture and drawing at this time results in part from the nature of Matisse's own artistic training, a traditional orientation explained in his lectures to the students in his school.[6] In 1908, Sarah Stein, both student and patron of the artist, made notes to record the content of Matisse's lectures. Stein had assisted Matisse in organizing the school, which opened in 1908 and closed in 1911.[7] The artist's lessons reflected the traditional nature of his own artistic education, although his teachings, and his view of his role as a master, are often colored by a distaste for the rote academic practice he found so restrictive as a student. The standard methods of masters such as William Bouguereau and Jean-Léon Gérôme inspired him to redirect his teaching so that it offered, by his own example, a model of unity in artistic expression.[8] He valued the hard work of making art, using drawing as a means to develop vision, to learn about nature, to simplify form, and to recognize one's own creative impulses. The practice of drawing from memory could put a young artist in touch with nature as experienced first hand, not handed down as an example to be copied exactly. Matisse taught drawing from plaster casts and the model, painting of figures and still life, and sculpture. While his teachings provided clear insights about the inherent possibilities of each medium, his overall orientation emphasized the totality of artistic vision. Drawing with a pencil or charcoal could be analogous to sculpting in clay, something best illustrated by his own works. He told his students to perceive the form of a melon through a gesture of two opposing contours, much like the physical experience of making a sculpture:

> Give the round form of the parts, as in sculpture. Look for their volume and fullness. Their contours must do this. In speaking of a melon one uses both hands to express it by gesture, and so both lines defining a form must determine it. Drawing is like an expressive gesture, but it has the advantage of permanency. A drawing is a sculpture but it has the advantage

> that it can be viewed closely enough for one to detect suggestions of form that must be much more deliberately expressed in sculpture which must carry from a distance.[9]

Auguste Rodin had been shown a number of Matisse's earliest drawings and, while praising his facility as a draughtsman, advised the artist to concentrate on the drawing of details, making an example of his own work in sculpture, where he focused on parts to arrive at the conception of the whole. Matisse wrote about his meeting with Rodin many years after his visit and, in retrospect, probably made too much of their differences. Rodin's sculpture was clearly on his mind. There is no evidence of Matisse's reactions to Rodin's own drawings, particularly to the extraordinary late drawings that, while revealing different values in the representation of the figure, make a strong statement for Rodin's comprehension of the totality of figural form in movement. Rodin greatly admired the mid–nineteenth-century sculptor Antoine-Louis Barye, the legendary sculptor of animals in mortal combat, and may have encouraged Matisse to study his work. In 1900, Matisse made several drawings after a plaster cast of one of Barye's impressive combats, *Jaguar Devouring a Hare.*[10] The first of Barye's sculptures to enter the Louvre, this monumental work was among his best known and was duplicated in numerous plaster casts intended for the use of students. Significantly, in Matisse's time, the bronze that the government had commissioned after the plaster exhibited in the Salon of 1850 was eventually joined by a plaster model of a later version reworked by the artist, together with a bronze cast made from it, the first introduction of such demonstrations of sculptural process in the collection of the Louvre.[11] Matisse, working from a reproductive plaster of the 1850 work (a bronze version is included in this exhibition, cat. 146, p. 103–104), did not follow the typical academic practice valuing detailed copying above all. Two sketches after the plaster (cat. 2, p. 103; 3, p. 104) reveal that what interested the artist in Barye's sculpture was not his well-studied animal anatomy, the representation of animal flesh, or the narrative of mortal combat but, as Yve-Alain Bois noted, "the condensed energy of its sinuous arabesque which crushes everything in its path."[12] In looking at these studies of the outside contours of Barye's sculpture, each from a different point of view, we are alerted to Matisse's interest in the serpentine twist of the animal as it attacks the hare with such sudden force. It is his fascination with the tense muscular strength and the abrupt action that determines his description of the animal's contours. This is what he took from these drawings when he moved to the next step, the modeling of his copy in clay, a first-hand experience of the three-dimensional impact of the form. Just as he would for his first major sculpture, *The Serf,* which began while the continued revisions on the jaguar sculpture were being made, Matisse worked long and hard on this exercise in copying, probably making many more drawings (some we know are lost).[13] He is said to have studied the anatomy of a dissected cat to gather the information that Barye would have gleaned from similar study and repeated visits to the Jardin des Plantes in Paris. It is reported, Matisse closed his eyes and sculpted the clay from his well-rehearsed memory of the form, now internalized, allowing him to synthesize the muscular tension of the attacking jaguar to achieve a visual transformation far beyond the goals of academic copying (cat. 1, pp. 101–102, 105).[14]

In his study of Matisse's drawings, John Elderfield elucidates most clearly the parallels between sculpture and drawing.[15] First, in his view, both function as a study for the medium of painting, as Matisse stated: "I took up sculpture because what interested me in painting was a clarification of my ideas. . . . That is to say that it was done for the purpose of organization, to put order into my feelings, and find a style to suit me."[16] Drawing had a related role. Second, both provide a means for the study of form, specifically, how to shape volumes that meet surrounding space to contain the whole as an image. Third, the similarities in the physical making of both, drawing on paper being equivalent to tactile modeling in clay. Fourth, the most direct connection, the acknowledgment in both of the distance between the viewer and the image. "In addition to the sensations one derives from a

Fig. 29. Henri Matisse, *Nude Male Seated on a Stool,* 1895. Crayon. The Baltimore Museum of Art, The Cone Collection, formed by Dr. Claribel Cone and Miss Etta Cone of Baltimore, Maryland.

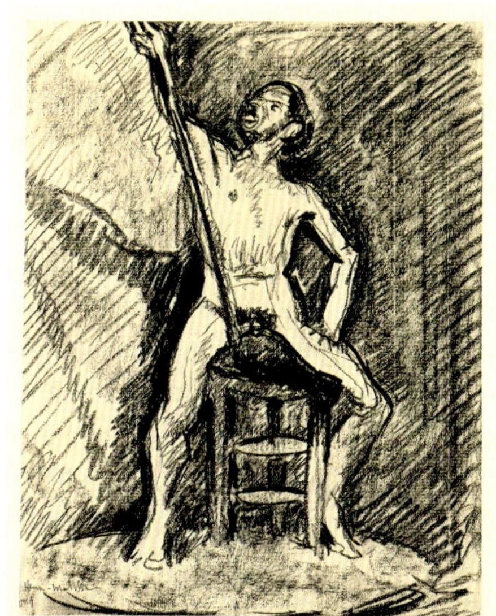

drawing," said Matisse, "a sculptor must invite us to handle it as an object; just so the sculptor must feel, in making it, the particular demands for volume and mass."[17] He needed the reality of experiencing volume and mass at first hand in order to understand how to realize the unity of the figure.[18]

Though Matisse never achieved formal admission to the École des Beaux-Arts in Paris, he was not ready to abandon his conviction that a traditional art education was important. The alternative he followed still brought him to the École, not formally enrolled, but studying there in the Cours Yvon, a grand courtyard where artists came to make copies from plaster casts, in hope of attracting the attention of one of the École's professors. One such master, the painter Gustave Moreau, was known to be particularly open minded and, after seeing examples of Matisse's work, invited him to work in his studio.[19] Matisse was impressed with Moreau's dedication to making art as well as by his interest in the history of art, which was much broader than the standard assignments for copies at the Louvre might indicate. Moreau was actively involved in the education of his students and would accompany them to the Louvre to offer advice. A good number of Matisse's early student drawings have survived but, like most such academic exercises, they are difficult to date. There are several in The Cone Collection at The Baltimore Museum of Art, including *Nude Male Seated on a Stool* (fig. 29), probably among the first purchases Etta Cone made after meeting Matisse in 1906. Moreau typically posed his models on a circular platform such as can be seen here, so that, possibly, the model could be turned for different points of view. This sketch has all the hallmarks of an academic drawing after the model, the figure set against a darkened background and the pole provided to hold steady the extension of the arm. It is tempting to recognize in his features the well-known studio model Bevilaqua, who posed for many artists including Rodin and whom Matisse used for several years of work on *The Serf.* What departs from academic practice here is Matisse's energetic drawing of the background with hardly any comparable interest in modeling the musculature of the figure. It is as if the figure, strongly silhouetted against the background, highlighted through the whiteness of the paper that remains in place of modeling, has become inseparable from the background. Much later in 1909, Matisse would make studies for *The Back I* (cat. 48, p. 162) using, as in this drawing, pen-and-ink strokes of equivalent character to join figure to ground.

Cézanne's drawings have been described as relying upon contrasts, the relationship between black and white, and it was the use of these contrasts that enabled him to structure his image and, at the same time, make forms tangible.[20] Cézanne insisted that "line and modeling do not exist," at least independently, as both were interchangeable.[21] In his *Sketch after Puget's Milo of Croton,* c. 1890 (fig. 30), one of twelve such studies of the famous sculpture from different points of view, Cézanne uses the white of the paper between areas of dense shading contained within curvilinear strokes of the graphite pencil. The rippling musculature of sculpture, now physically experienced, has become tangible. Matisse, too, studied Puget, making a sculptural copy of his *écorché* (flayed figure) in 1903 (fig. 31). The study of such figures, whether from models or after reproductive prints of classical prototypes, would have been a typical assignment for an art student. In his sculptural copy, Matisse used his fingers, prints visible on the surface, to apply the clay, building up this small figure gradually. Like the rubbing of charcoal in a drawing, the rough surface of the sculpture has been smoothed with his hand to accentuate the linear flow of tense muscles holding a timeless pose. Cézanne kept a cast of Puget's *écorché* in his studio and, significantly, chose to picture the sculpture in a painting, but his study of sculpture served his painting and his work in watercolor. Matisse needed to understand Puget in three dimensions and what was learned from that tangible experience of copying Puget's flayed nude took form in sculpture as well as drawing.

Among the studies related to *The Serf,* a drawing closest in character to Cézanne's draughtsmanship is a pen-and-ink study of the back of Bevilaqua (cat. 11, p. 113). In the drawing Matisse realizes the solidity and weight of the figure. Though the model's muscular bulk is evident, his attitude,

Fig. 30. Paul Cézanne, *Sketch after Puget's Milo of Croton,* c. 1890. Graphite. The Baltimore Museum of Art, Bequest of Frederic W. Cone.

Fig. 31. Henri Matisse, *Copy after Puget's Écorché,* 1903. Bronze. Direction des Musées de France, Gift of Jean Matisse, on deposit at the Musée Matisse, Nice, 1978.

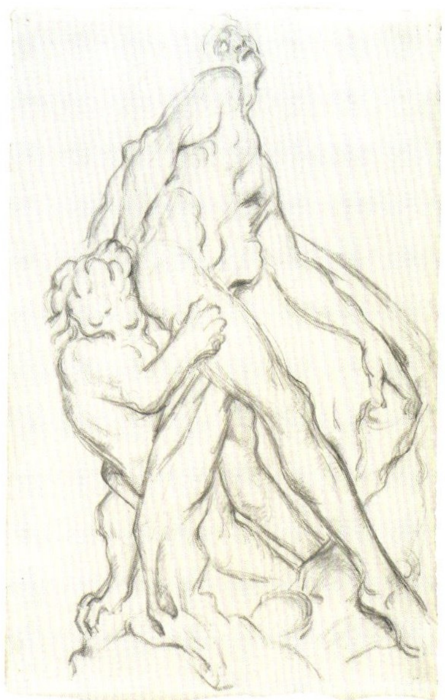

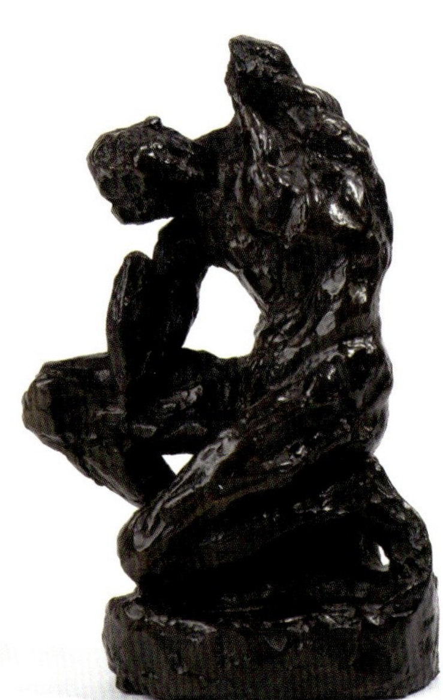

with hunched back, seems withdrawn. Two other studies for *The Serf* are also drawn from the model. The first, *Male Model* (cat. 9, p. 112), shows Bevilaqua in a wide, rearing stance, with arms extended out from his body as if in motion. Like Cézanne's bathers, the figure is immobilized, planted in the ground by the force of nature. Here the model's weight, and his complementary attitude of determination, is experienced. Using rapid, short strokes and squiggles to fill in shaded areas, Matisse sketches in the back wall to position the figure coming out from the corner. A second drawing (cat. 10, p. 112) shows Bevilaqua in a less assertive stance, closer to that of the painting of the model in the studio (cat. 7, p. 110). As before, Matisse concentrates on the outward contours of the figure in this position. The bright illumination on the chest, arms, and lower torso provides contrast to the shading on the back areas. This results in a relief-like projection enunciating the volume of the figure's mass without the use of modeling. Another drawing for *The Serf,* of entirely different character (cat. 8, p. 113), is a less common type of study in the artist's repertoire. The outside contour of the figure, drawn with sharp pencil lines like a quickly realized caricature, is an instantaneous record of an immediate impression. But more than the figure's pose, the sketch is recording an individualized quality, something personal implied in the attitude of the model's position. Such instantaneous drawing was something Matisse and other artists he associated with in the fauve years found engaging.[22] These sketches were made in front of the model, rather than from memory, perhaps with the object of making the sketch looking just at the model and not at the drawing itself, an exercise of direct hand-eye coordination—a distillation of visualized form experienced unmediated by a focus on drawing technique. "The model must not be made to agree with a preconceived theory or effect. It must impress you, awaken in you an emotion, which in turn you seek to express. . . . Put in no holes that hurt the ensemble, as between thumb and fingers lying at the side. Express by masses in relation to one another, and large sweeps of line in interrelation."[23] Drawings such as these are part of a process of study, practice in focusing on the particular model in various poses. Some exploration could be in pursuit of a specific issue with regard to the sculpture. What cannot be known with certainty is whether these sheets were specific studies for the painting of the model in the studio or for the sculpture of *The Serf.* In a study of artistic process, the recognition of sequence, a secure path in the evolution of an idea, would be ideal, but there is no conclusive method to determine this and such concerns are really beside the point because what Matisse's drawings do reveal is universal to all the mediums in which he worked.

Fig. 32. Auguste Rodin, Untitled (female nude with raised leg), c. 1905. Pen and ink, brush and wash. The Baltimore Museum of Art; Gift of Mrs. Richard Gimbel, Elkins Park, Pennsylvania.

In the case of another early sculpture, *Madeleine I* (cat. 12, p. 267; 13, p. 115; 14, p. 120) and its descendent, *Madeleine II* (cat. 15, p. 119), the related drawings are similar in character and purpose to those for *The Serf.* Again, there is a closely related painting, *Standing Model (Nude Study in Blue)* (cat. 16, p. 117). In the drawing *Standing Nude* (cat. 18, p. 123), Matisse takes a side view of the model, roughing in the shading on the front of her figure with broad areas of dense graphite strokes. Her back and side are brightly illuminated against the strong shadows on her front. At her left shoulder and to silhouette the line of her neck, Matisse has erased the graphite to modulate the shading. This achieves a spatial foreshortening across the chest. It appears the model has just turned toward us. The muscular tension of the back gives way as the torso rotates. Her crossed legs anchor the lower half of the figure against the turn.

Another mode of drawing similar to the "caricature" of Bevilaqua is a rapidly sketched study of figural contours. *Standing Figure* (cat. 17, p. 123) freezes the dancelike movement of a standing figure. The arms are raised and the head is turned to anticipate the coming rotation. This is a challenging point of view to capture as, with the torso turned to the right, the head and arms begin to turn in the other direction. It is instructive to compare such line drawings with Rodin's figure drawings of approximately the same date (fig. 32). Rodin's dancers, drawn with light pencil lines and an overlay of subtle color wash, do not function as Matisse's do to analyze figural form. Instead, something more fleeting is evoked—more like an impression or an abstracted reflection of experience.[24] A second contour drawing relating to *Madeleine I* depicts a different strained and unbalanced pose (cat. 21, p. 122). Seen from the back, this substantial model's right leg bends slightly forward, causing that side of the hip and buttocks to drop while, at the other side of the fulcrum, her massive hip juts outward. A crease at the waist indicates the muscles giving way, anticipating movement, and the turn of the head suggests that the torso has also turned. One can experience the effect of Matisse's instructions to his students: "Close your eyes and hold the vision, and then do the work with your own sensibility. If it be a model assume the pose of the model yourself; where the strain comes is the key of the movement."[25] In contrast, another drawing of the back of a standing figure (cat. 23, p. 122), dated by the artist October 1903, models the figure's volume with the use of shading.

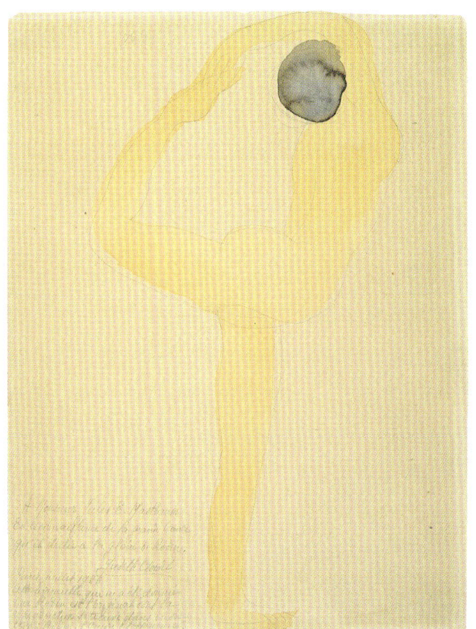

As confirmed by Ann Boulton's technical study in this catalogue, Matisse, rather than beginning again to make a second version, *Madeleine II,* stopped to make a plaster model, freezing his work at that point, while the clay was still wet. He could then return to the clay and proceed with revisions, setting the work up for the eventual casting of both versions.[26] As a proof is made to record a preliminary stage before work on a print is continued, these two intact versions, the second taking its point of departure from the completion of the first, manifest Matisse's characteristic process of revision and transformation. Though such revision is not unusual in sculptural practice, it is less common to make an intermediary model for casting or to create a series of progressive versions of an evolving clay model. In the more malleable mediums of graphite and charcoal, a succession of drawings will manifest the process of visual transformation. Whatever the medium, each version is a completed work of art, a stopping place, a variant resolution in the process of creation.

Two graphite drawings, one (cat. 20, p. 120), identified as preparatory for *Madeleine I,* and the other (cat. 22, p. 121), identified as a sketch for *Madeleine II,* both from a similar point of view, are quite close to the final composition. There are only a few cases where Matisse made drawings in series as a systematic study of the sculptural pose from different points of view, something one might expect of preparatory drawings for sculpture in the round. The sketch for *Madeleine I,* with evidence of erasure and repeated strokes to reinforce the delineation of contours, annunciates the rotation of the torso through the strong graphic diagonal of the clasped arms rising in the direction of the bent head. In the pose—one leg straight, the other slightly bent, and the right hip thrust upward—we perceive a counterbalancing twist constrained by the limits of muscular extension.

Fig. 33. Henri Matisse, *Study for Woman Leaning on Her Hands,* c. 1905. Reed pen and ink. Private collection, Baltimore.

In the drawing for *Madeleine II,* more in keeping with Cézanne (and thus the connection to *Madeleine II,* a stocky figure with rougher surface modeling), the concentration moves to the contours of muscular mass, the curvilinear volumes of the massive supporting legs achieved through short parallel strokes of the pencil. In this case, the mass and contour of the figure are more an issue than is the contortion and twist of its serpentine pose. In *Madeleine I,* the surface has been smoothed—refined to reflect the linearity of the curving pose; in *Madeleine II,* the comparatively rough surface, like a painted Cézanne bather, is completely different.

Le bonheur de vivre

The work surrounding a group of seminal Matisse's paintings, *Luxe, calme et volupté,* 1904–1905, *Le bonheur de vivre,* 1905–1906, and the two versions of *Le Luxe,* 1907–1908, encompass several sculptures including *Woman Leaning on Her Hands* (cat. 24, pp. 127–28) and *Reclining Figure with Chemise* (cat. 30, pp. 133–34). The latter emerges during the gestation period for *Le bonheur de vivre,* taking up, in the sculpture, a pose seen with slight modification, front and back, as the reclining figure at the center of the painting. As such it is the first sculpture to take up the reclining-nude theme, a transitionary work in advance of *Reclining Nude I (Aurora)* and therefore also related to the painting *Blue Nude.* This is a classical pose, static, with chiseled facial features, only the shift slipping off her shoulder to remind us of the leisurely arcadian world from which she came. In its rugged modeling and physicality, the sculpture shows little of the synthesized refinement in the figures in *Le bonheur de vivre.*

Woman Leaning on Her Hands connects to a figure in *Luxe, calme et volupté,* though in the painting, the seated figure leans back on her hands rather than forward. There is a number of drawings, several included in the exhibition and others published elsewhere, that relate to either the sculpture or the painting and particularly to modeling sessions, where Matisse explored this challenging pose. One of the published drawings related to *Woman Leaning on Her Hands* was annotated by the artist as a study for the sculpture *"La Chemise Relevée,"* the title given to this sculpture in one of Matisse's notebooks. This variant title recalls the close relation of this sculpture to *Reclining Figure with Chemise:* each would have derived from the same modeling session.[27] While not a traditional reclining pose, the relaxed attitude taken by the model seems appropriate for Arcadia, and it might also have been inspired by this model's individual style, her way of moving and posing, sometimes directed to hold strained and uncomfortable positions. Two graphite "life" drawings (cat. 27, 28, p. 131), show the model leaning either forward or back, and in both, Matisse focuses his attention on the torsion of the figure, a muscular tension that contrasts with a relaxed attitude of repose. The strain has to do with the leaning support of the figure. The arms act like strong buttresses while the padlike hands may anticipate the artist's decision, in the sculpture, to do away with any actual base, a convention that provides the illusion of support for a sculpture. These drawings reflect a more rapid study of the model: in cat. 28, the contour lines have been retraced several times as if to memorize and synthesize the pose; by contrast, cat. 27 is more a statement of distillation than of exploration. There is little interest here in modeling the volume of the figure; Matisse instead suggests volume through his drawing of the bodily contours.

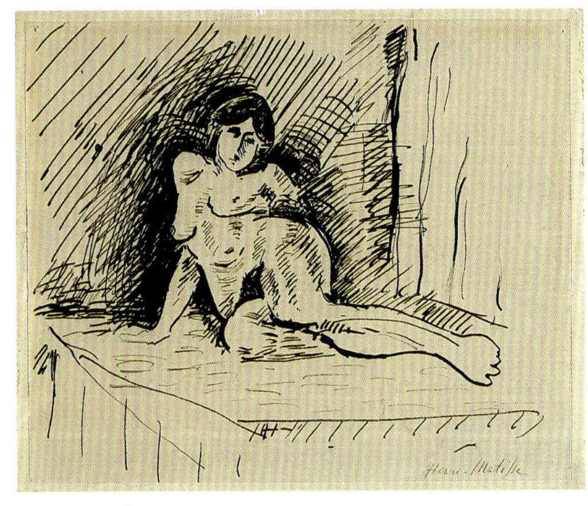

In his study of Matisse's sculpture, Albert Elsen writes of the different modalities that coexist in the artist's work, a reality exemplified clearly in drawings and prints of 1905–1906.[28] Two other drawings related to *Woman Leaning on Her Hands,* both probably from 1905, demonstrate one mode. They provide two views of the model. In the exhibited drawing (cat. 26, p. 130), we see the back side of the figure reclining parallel to the picture plane. She leans back on her hands. In a second sheet, previously unknown (fig. 33), the model is turned head on in a foreshortened perspective. No longer posed in a static, classical position, the figure now confronts the viewer directly in

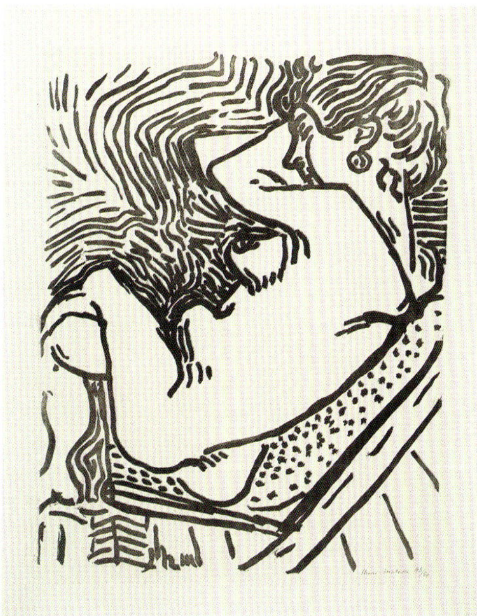

Fig. 34. Henri Matisse, *Large Woodcut (Seated Nude)*, 1906. Woodcut. The Baltimore Museum of Art, The Cone Collection, formed by Dr. Claribel and Miss Etta Cone of Baltimore, Maryland.

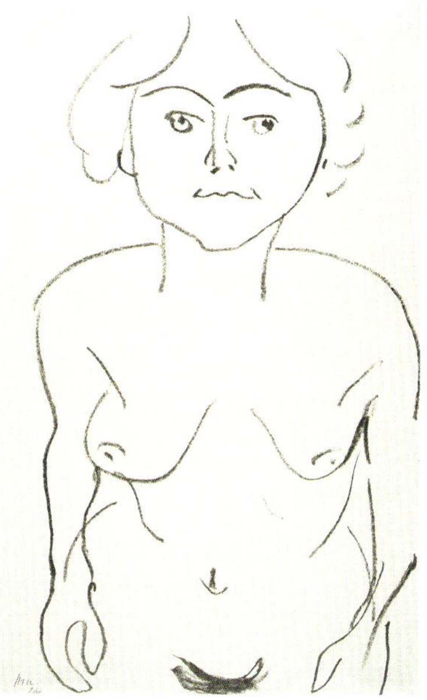

Fig 35. Henri Matisse, *Front of Nude, Looking Down*, 1906. Crayon transfer lithograph. The Baltimore Museum of Art, The Cone Collection, formed by Dr. Claribel and Miss Etta Cone of Baltimore, Maryland.

a dynamic formulation that exploits muscular tension held uncomfortably against anticipated relaxation. The strong directional thrust of the massive thigh gives way to the twist of the torso—a substantial weight supported by the model's strained left arm held back almost to the point of shoulder dislocation. Using black ink and a wide reed pen, Matisse reveals entirely different values in these drawings, compared with those of the previously discussed graphite life studies. These pen drawings are characterized by the strong contrast between dark ink lines and the gleaming white of the paper—a style characteristic of Matisse's fauve drawings. The heavily weighted contour lines contrast with the expressive short pen strokes. In these areas an especially vibrant relationship is established between figure and ground, represented by the white paper. The apprehension of figural form remains even though these strokes do not model volume through light. Instead, they signify its presence. The infusion of light we experience in these fauve drawings creates coloristic nuances from black-and-white contrasts. Just as in drawings by Vincent van Gogh, works that Matisse undoubtedly knew well, we become conscious of the artist's *fracktur*—the individuality of his own visual language. Though we perceive volume and space, the lines in these Matisse drawings are of equivalent tonal value across the surface of the sheet—equalized by our perception of strong illumination. Rather than perceiving an effect that we might describe as pictorial and two dimensional, we experience something physical, like a sculpture—a three-dimensional reading, where light now plays on a bronze surface, first modeled in clay.

The largest of Matisse's four woodcuts from 1906, where the cutting of the block closely follows a preliminary drawing, is a striking example of his fauve style. *Large Woodcut (Seated Nude)* (fig. 34) reveals an aggressive, two-dimensional approach to drawing. The reed pen seemingly gouges the surface of the paper, just as a cutter's tool would gouge the block.[29] For the striking lithograph *Large Nude* (cat. 101, p. 222), the artist drew directly on the stone instead of transferring the image from paper, his normal practice. Here the style of drawing is unusually angular, creating planar surfaces like a sculpture carved from stone. The pose, reclining and with arms above the head, looks forward to *Large Seated Nude* of 1922–1929 (cat. 98, p. 217; 99, p. 275), demonstrating how Matisse would return many years later to the exploration of a specific pose, in this case first inspired by his study of Michelangelo in the Medici chapel. The planar abstraction of *Large Nude* has suggested to some that it ought to be dated later, possibly to 1916 and associated with his cubist works, but this was not a pose that occupied Matisse at that time, and the print's exhibition in 1906 has been documented. In another lithograph of the same year, a transferred image, *Front of Nude, Looking Down* (fig. 35), Matisse adopts an alternative approach, using only contour lines without modeling to suggest volume. In a departure from Cézanne's practice, an alternate modality for Matisse, it is only these flowing curvilinear lines that lead us to the perception of mass assigned to the white areas of paper.

Rather than being based solely on the study of models in the studio, many of the poses in the sculptures and paintings in this period, such as *Seated Nude with Arms on Head* and *Standing Nude* (fig. 37), begin with photographs. Has the preparatory role of drawing from the model been supplanted by an alternative first step, the use of an anonymous photograph from a compendium of posed nudes? "Photography," wrote Matisse,

> has greatly disturbed the imagination, because one has seen things devoid of feeling. When I wanted to get rid of all influences that prevented me from seeing nature in a personal way, I copied photographs. . . . We are encumbered by the sensibilities of the artists who have preceded us. Photography can rid us of previous imaginations. Photography has very clearly determined the distinction between painting as a translation of feelings and descriptive painting. The latter has become useless.[30]

These words, written in 1933, reflect an attitude that long prevailed among many artists. Matisse's first published comments on photography, based on an interview, appeared in Alfred Stieglitz's periodical *Camera Work* in 1908. In this same issue, photographs by Edward Steichen showed the artist at work on *The Serpentine* (cat. 165, p. 172). Matisse understood and clearly endorsed the more subjective pictorialist values that Steichen brought to this portrait of romanticized creative genius. The precedent was obviously Steichen's earlier photographs of Rodin at work on his Balzac sculpture. But, in the interview, instead of discussing the portrait of himself at work, Matisse preferred to focus on the role of the photograph as a means of studying nature, noting that "photographs will also be impressive because they show us nature, and all artists will find in them a world of sensations. The photographer must therefore intervene as little as possible, so as not to cause photography to lose the objective charm which it naturally possesses."[31] Under Stieglitz's editorial control, *Camera Work* advocated for photography the status of fine art, as the equivalent of painting. This orientation may have suggested that Matisse temper his views, sidestepping the interviewer's question about the aesthetics of the medium. Most significant, he did not acknowledge his own use of photographs, beginning in 1904, and particularly as a source for *The Serpentine* (cat. 58, pp. 170, 172), the very sculpture shown in Steichen's portrait.[32]

Continuing until around 1909, Matisse used these photographs (see fig. 36 and 38 for examples) as direct sources for both paintings and sculptures and as a point of departure for drawing studies as well. Isabelle Monod-Fontaine was the first to seriously consider the influence of these images on Matisse's sculptures and paintings.[33] The photographs themselves were published in magazines that featured posed images of nude women. Such magazines were popular with artists, taking the place of life-drawing sessions at the academy, but their appeal to collectors of erotica is also demonstrable, a topic recently pursued by Katharina Sykora.[34] *L'Humanité feminin,* a magazine with an ethnographic orientation, published the image of two Tuareg girls from Africa that is a direct source for *Two Negresses* (cat. 47, p. 159). Others, among them *Mes modèles* and *L'Étude académique,* featured nude women in a range of unconventional but contrived poses, and several of those were used for sculptures such as *Standing Nude* (cat. 32, pp. 137, 140), *Seated Nude with Arms on Head, Small Crouching Nude without an Arm* (cat. 65, pp. 184–85), *Reclining Nude I (Aurora),* and *The Serpentine.* As we have seen in numerous drawings, Matisse had previously found ample opportunity to explore

Fig 36. Photograph, *Standing Nude,* from *Mes modèles,* 1906. Archives Matisse, Paris.

Fig 37. Henri Matisse, *Standing Nude,* 1906–1907. Oil on canvas. Tate.

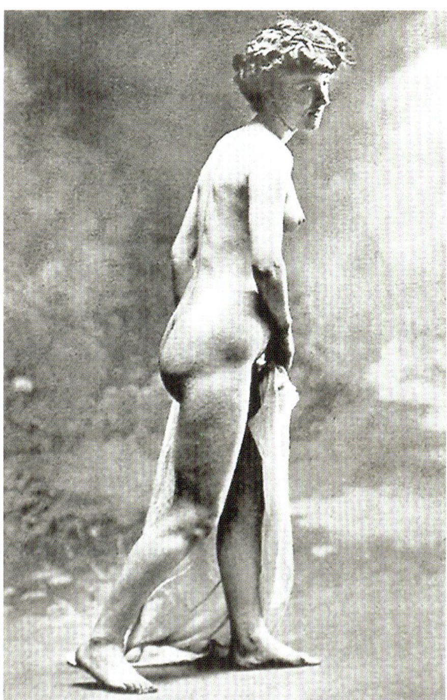

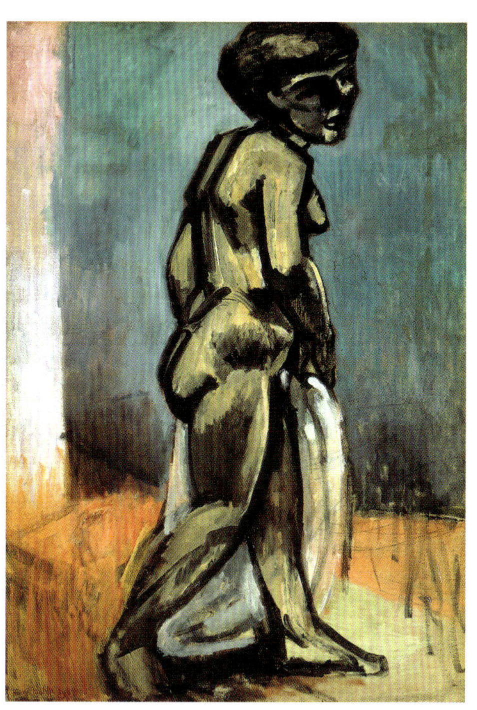

figural poses in studies directly from the model, so why now turn to these particular photographs? Monod-Fontaine asserts that the number of fresh poses and the occasional inclusion of multiple points of view introduced a new repertoire of possibilities. They stimulated a departure from a reliance on more traditional academic poses, those taken from classical sculpture, for instance. The photographs also provided a range of physical types, "factory girls and seamstresses," as Monod-Fontaine put it.[35] In his studio Matisse surrounded himself with images of the figure from other works of art as well as photographs like these. Sykora writes that these photographs had a "purgative function," allowing Matisse to address the pose with a desensitized neutrality, enabling a focus on structure and surface, a veritable clean state on which to apply his own sensations.[36]

A photograph (fig. 36) cited as the source for the pose for *Standing Nude* (cat. 32, pp. 137, 140), is directly linked to a 1907 painting of the same figure in the collection of the Tate in London (fig. 37). Though this photograph was published in 1906, a drawing currently dated c. 1904, *Nude, Seen from the Back, on a Hatched Ground* (cat. 19, p. 122) may have been derived from a related photographic source. Here the focus is on the back rather than on the striding pose seen from the side. The shift to the back view would require only a quarter turn of the side pose in the photograph. The models are of the same body type, and in the drawing, as in the photograph, there is a contrived, artificial quality to the pose unlike life studies of the model. Shading is achieved with rapid, scribble-line strokes. The drawing might very well be counted among those for *The Back I* or *II* (cat. 49, p. 162) as the verticality of the figure, inclined to the left, announces a pending serpentine twist that begins with the parted and turned legs, progresses in the backward turn of the left buttock, and is resolved in the opposing torsion of the upper torso with the neck and head. The articulation of the figure's musculature in the process of movement—the strained extension in a pose that would otherwise seem relaxed and static—is unexpected. If the viewer attempts to emulate the pose, the tension of anticipated movement is readily experienced. Another contour drawing, dated 1914–1915 (cat. 56, p. 167), shows a woman, again from the back, whose figure rotates to the right, the turn beginning with her neck and head. The large scale of this work is unusual among Matisse's figure drawings and, although the suggested date of the work is perplexingly late, it is worth considering the possibility that the drawing is based on a sculpture rather than on a model and may be preparatory for the appearance of the sculpture in a painting.

Fig 38. Photographs, *Nudes,* from *Mes modèles,* 1906. Archives Matisse, Paris.

Fig. 39. Eugène Delacroix, *Perseus and Andromeda,* 1847. Oil on canvas. The Baltimore Museum of Art, The Cone Collection, formed by Dr. Claribel Cone and Miss Etta Cone of Baltimore, Maryland.

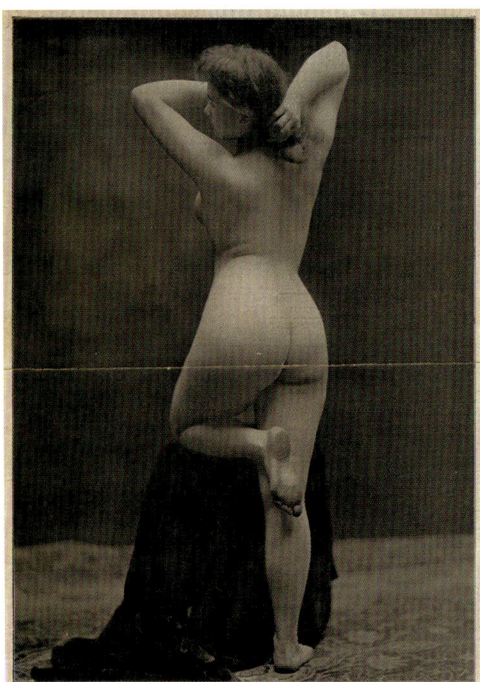

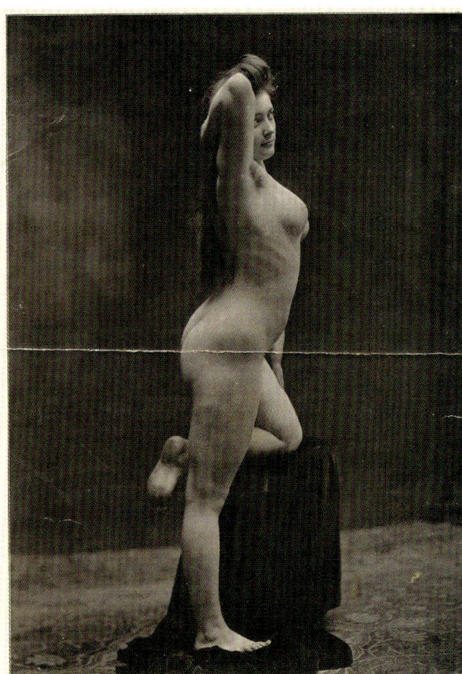

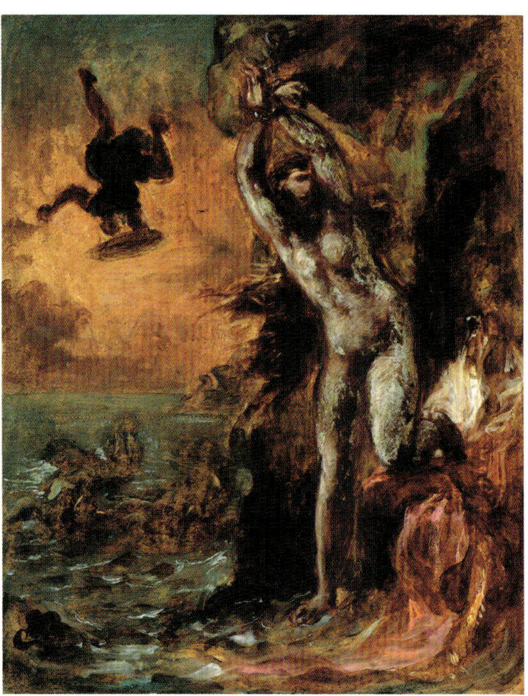

The pose for Matisse's two 1904 sculptures, *Upright Nude with Arched Back (Andromeda)* and *Seated Nude with Arms on Head,* is also derived from photographs, such as two published as alternative views (fig. 38). A second source has been cited for the pose of the *Arched Back* sculpture—a painted sketch, *Perseus and Andromeda* by Eugène Delacroix, that at one time hung in the apartment of Leo and Gertrude Stein and today is in The Cone Collection in Baltimore (fig. 39).

In 1906, Matisse continued his interest in the standing nude pose with two further sculptures, *Standing Nude, Arms on Head* (cat. 36, p. 144) and *Standing Nude.* Three drawings (cat. 41–43, p. 145) are described as different versions of the *Standing Nude, Arms on Head* sculpture and are numbered by the artist in sequence: 1, 2, 3. Together they read almost cinematically as stills of stages in a preparatory sequence. The figure's pose, seen from the side, is reminiscent of a bather in Cézanne's lithograph *Small Bathers* of 1896–1897 (fig. 40). In the drawings, the model, halted in mid-stride, is drawn four times (the third sheet has two drawings), the figure progressively taking on mass, particularly at mid-torso. In the third sheet, the model's right leg—the thigh, calf, and large, weight-bearing foot—acquires a volume equivalent to that of the back and buttocks. The sculpture by contrast, while rough and massive at the base, becomes more refined and contoured, like the drawings, in the upper torso. Two other slightly earlier drawings show the model in a frontal pose. These, one graphite and dated 1904, *Nude* (cat. 38, p. 147), the other charcoal, *Standing Nude* (cat. 39, p. 150), are distinguished by Matisse's use of more malleable materials such as graphite and charcoal to model the figure's volume. This is essentially different from the values brought forth in his reed-pen and ink drawings, which assertively express the figure's contours. In both sheets, the features of the frontal pose are brightly illuminated, creating areas of strong contrast between the shading and the whiteness of the paper. In the graphite drawing, tightly contained areas of shading are achieved with short parallel strokes, similar to those made with charcoal in the later drawing. The charcoal study is less restrained and reveals the model's more personal and relaxed attitude. The figure comes forward in sharp relief, strong contour lines silhouetting her form against the shaded wall behind her. This emphasizes the frontal plane from which the body moves forward and back in a tight serpentine twist at mid-torso.

In the process of creating the two major paintings of 1904–1906, *Luxe, calme et volupté* and *Le bonheur de vivre,* Matisse turned his attention to works by Edgar Degas (cat. 151, p. 252) and Henri

Fig. 40. Paul Cézanne, *Small Bathers,* 1896–1897. Color lithograph. The Baltimore Museum of Art, The Cone Collection, formed by Dr. Claribel Cone and Miss Etta Cone of Baltimore, Maryland.

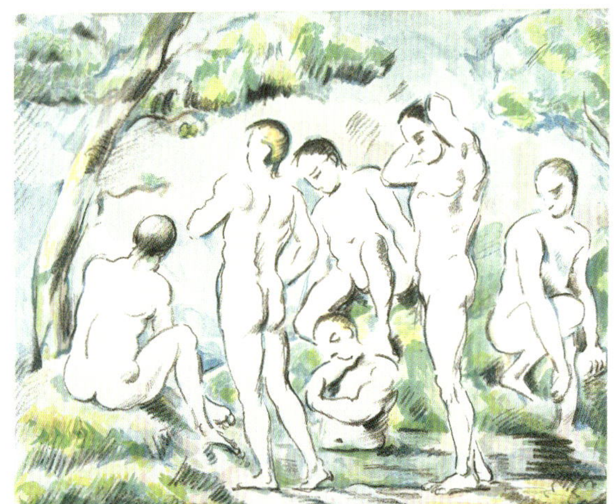

de Toulouse-Lautrec depicting women posed in domestic situations—intimate, private moments such as bathing. Two drawings in the exhibition take up the theme of *la toilette.* In one, *The Bath* (cat. 126, p. 253), a woman, just finished with her bath, begins to step out of the circular tub as her maid dries her foot.[37] In the second sheet, *Woman Standing in Tub* (cat. 125, p. 253), the woman is alone, facing us, her arms raised as she towels her shoulder and neck. These intimate, self-contained poses, where the viewer is cast as a voyeur, relate closely to the figures that inhabit the arcadian world of the paintings. *Girl with Ivy in Hair* (cat. 40, p. 143), a whimsical, spontaneous pen-and-ink sketch of a figure found in *Le bonheur de vivre*, can be related to this group.The sculptures of standing figures in 1906, with arms down or raised and, ultimately, the figure in the *Back*s, take on the same relaxed pose of these drawings—an attitude of refreshed rebirth after the bath—private in a domestic setting. Matisse would return to this theme in 1930 with his *Venus in a Shell.*

Matisse made numerous drawings for *The Back I* but few for the other versions. Perhaps the direct work of shaping the plaster originals took the place of extended drawing from the model. Two of the drawings (cat. 53, 54, p. 164) selected for this exhibition date from 1909 and relate to *The Back I,* and one sheet, *Back Study* (cat. 52, p. 166), also drawn that year, indicates the progressive refinement of the pose at the stage of *The Back II.* A final work in this group, *Study for The Back II* (cat. 55, p. 167), dated 1913, is a small sketch on a larger sheet. Recalling the drawing of a standing nude, *Nude, Seen from the Back, on a Hatched Ground* (c. 1903), *Standing Woman Seen from Behind (Study for The Back I),* drawn in pen and ink, places the figure against a wall (Matisse's studio at Issy-les-Moulineaux), with a prominent shadow cast by strong illumination from the right. The figure stands out as in relief and the study of the pose concentrates on the curving line of the spine as the back bends from the hip to the shoulder. In a second pen-and-ink drawing of a model against the same back wall, *Study of a Model's Back,* we are closer to the figure which, flat against the wall, appears more massive. Musculature is modeled with strongly contrasted shading of parallel strokes. Her head is turned as it is in the sculpture but the pose remains more vertical, the figure composed in the center of the sheet. Though dated 1909, the third drawing, *Back Study,* looks forward to the sculpted distillation of the pose that is manifested in *The Back II* (1913). Heavy, reinforced graphite lines emphasize the contour lines that silhouette the figure against a now unshaded background. The pose has been simplified, made more precise with a structured, geometric character such as can be seen in the rounded shaping of the buttocks. The purpose of the 1913 sketch, *Study for The Back II* was the consideration of the compositional placement of the figure within the rectangle of the entire sculptural relief. This focus on the figure in relation to surrounding space is not unlike that of the lithographs Matisse produced in 1906, in which figures drawn in contour are carefully positioned within the parameters of the sheet (or lithographic plate). In the relief sculptures of the *Back*s, the composition of the figure within the rectangular relief plaque adds emphasis to the figure's serpentine curve.

> When I see that my work has become more and more obviously detached from reliance upon the model, I do think that I have made some progress. . . . One day I would like to be able to do without models altogether. . . . I do not think I will be able to do so because I have not developed my memory for forms sufficiently. . . . I know perfectly well what a human body looks like—for me, a model is a springboard, a door I have to break down so as to get into the garden in which I am so alone and so happy."[38]

Written thirty years later, these words are equally valid to characterize Matisse's process in 1909, and through his drawings we see most clearly his investigations into the use of the model. For *The Serpentine,* Matisse again takes a pose from a photograph, this of a rounded and stocky nude leaning against a balustrade, finger to her lips (fig. 2, p. 3). But this borrowing coexists with drawings made from the model, including a pen-and-ink sketch, *Bather Leaning against a Tree* (cat. 61, p. 171), and *Nude,* a pencil drawing of a model seated, resting her arms on a pedestal (cat. 60, p. 171). Between the focus on the body's linear arabesque and the modeling of the figure's mass, the composition of the sculpture emerged: "Matisse succeeds in transposing volume into *lines* which are so subtly modulated that they themselves can evoke a third dimension."[39] The transformation of the sculpture's form directly parallels the process of refinement in his drawings relating to the paintings *Dance I* and *II.* In the great charcoal drawing of the dance composition, from Grenoble (cat. 62, p. 173), or in a drawing of a single figure to the left of this composition (cat. 63, p. 175), we experience a process of synthesis as he distills a choreographed circular movement to create an arabesque of figural contours. Both of these drawings relate most closely to the more refined composition of *Dance II.* The single figure of the one sheet has a compositional role crucial to capturing the circular dynamic, holding it within the composition and slinging the energy back around to the top. It is the Grenoble drawing that is most relevant to Matisse's related work in sculpture for it most likely postdates the painting *Dance I* and quite possibly *Dance II* as well. It represents a continuing process of refinement in the search for a more inclusive synthesis of form.[40] The original owner of the Grenoble drawing, Marcel Sembat, Matisse's friend and a commentator on his art, expressed disappointment in the lack of repose and calm in *Dance I.* The drawing may have been Matisse's answer, for the composition is simplified even further as the limbs and bodies are straightened. A drawing (cat. 64, p. 179) for the 1931–1933 murals of *The Dance* leads us to Matisse's later reprise of the dance theme, extending the process of transformation inspired by the movement of these mythic dancing figures.[41]

There are few known drawings related to sculpture after those for *The Back I* and *II* and *The Serpentine,* and between 1918 and 1923, Matisse made no sculpture at all. This results in an accompanying gap in the chronology of drawings featured in this exhibition. In the period before his move to Nice in December 1917, in both sculpture and painting, Matisse concentrated on the portrait, most significantly the progressive sculpture series of the *Jeannette* heads. In Nice, Matisse returned to the odalisque in both painting and sculpture, first taking up the pose of the seated figure clasping her knee, a theme explored first in 1909–1910 with *Seated Nude (Olga)* (cat. 67, p. 183). There are several powerful drawings from 1909, among them *Study, Heads and a Figure* (cat. 69, p. 187), characterized by their heavy pen-and-ink lines dryly applied to textured paper using the now-familiar wide reed pen. The 1918 sculpture of *Seated Nude Clasping Her Right Leg,* made in Nice (cat. 68, pp. 186–87), returns to a pose close to that of the figure in this drawing and unlike the sculpture *Seated Nude (Olga),* which is actually contemporary with this sheet. *Olga,* by contrast, is more angular in conception, with rough modeling that constrains the rhythmic contours present in the drawing. It is as if Matisse put aside the thoughts behind his 1909 drawing, taking them up again only in 1918. Another instance of a figure study looking forward to a much later work is *Face and Two Nudes with Gourds* (cat. 134, p. 256), dated 1912–1913, contemporary with the *Jeanette* series. Though the figural studies foreshadow the sculpture *Standing Nude (Katia),* the striking face study, a cubist masklike abstraction of facial features, has been related stylistically to the painting *Bathers by a River* and also the progressive *Back I–IV* reliefs.[42]

Study, Heads and a Figure has the added interest of several head studies drawn separately from a figure whose head is only partially shown. Such head studies are contemporary with the beginning of the *Jeannette* series. In each case the rounded heads appear fixed on stiff supporting shafts. Matisse once said to his students, emphasizing the importance of recognizing structure: "In the antique, the head is a ball upon which the features are delineated."[43] One final drawing, *Head of a Woman* (cat. 79, p. 194), is part of a group of drawings made during visits to cafés-concerts, where Matisse and his friend and fellow artist Albert Marquet would go to sketch the audience and performers.[44] This notation of a disembodied head looking down emphasizes its form, a study of its

Fig. 41. Henri Matisse, *Untitled, Head Study,* 1906–1907. Graphite. Centre Pompidou, Paris; Musée national d'art moderne/Centre de création industrielle.

Fig. 42. Photograph of Matisse in Nice studio with plaster cast of early version, *Large Seated Nude,* 1925–1926. The Museum of Modern Art, New York.

Fig. 43. Henri Matisse, *Seated Nude, Left Arm on Head,* 1926. Crayon transfer lithograph. The Baltimore Museum of Art, The Cone Collection, formed by Dr. Claribel and Miss Etta Cone of Baltimore, Maryland.

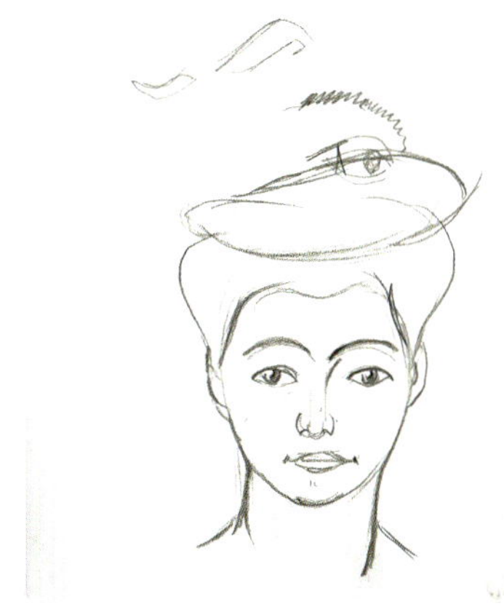

mass inclusive of the prominent arrangement of hair on top of the head, not unlike what is seen in sculptures such as *Small Head with Comb* (cat. 73, p. 194). *Untitled, Head Study* (fig. 41) reveals the process of distillation in the mass of head and hair—a transformation that began with the drawing of contours.[45] Matisse's later *Study for Henriette II* (cat. 95, p. 211) takes that process to a greater degree of synthesis.

Nice: Analysis Precedes Synthesis

Matisse's exploration of the reclining nude pose, so prevalent in his painting and sculpture of 1904–1908, was significantly advanced by the study of Michelangelo's figures from the Medici tomb, which he first saw in person in 1907. Even before he visited Florence, two prints from 1906, the woodcut *Seated Nude* (fig. 34) and the lithograph *Large Nude,* suggest the study of Michelangelo as a point of departure, leading not long after to the sculpture *Reclining Nude I (Aurora)* and the painting *Blue Nude: Memory of Biskra.* In 1910–1911, Matisse made several drawings of the Michelangesque pose, among them *Study of a Reclining Nude* (cat. 103, p. 224). Ann Baldassari has related this particular sketch to a painting of 1911, *La Nuit (Grand Nu à la colle),* now lost.[46] Shortly after his move to Nice, Matisse returned to studies of the Medici figures, copying plaster casts at the art school there. He wrote to his friend Charles Camoin at that time: "I am also working at the École des Arts décoratifs . . . I am drawing Night and modeling it. . . . I hope to understand the clear and complex construction of Michelangelo."[47] Two lithographs of 1922, both figures drawn in contour, *Day* and *Night* (cat. 104, 106, p. 223), attest to this close study and could be said to mark the beginning of his work on the sculpture *Large Seated Nude.* Another sculpture based on sketches made at the École des Arts décoratifs, *Crouching Venus* (cat. 97, p. 220), is based on studies from a plaster cast of a Hellenistic sculpture (the Rhodian Venus). The number of paintings, drawings, and prints of variant compositions produced in these years demonstrates the artist's intense concentration on the pose of the reclining nude or seated nude with arms raised. In a photograph of his studio taken in about 1927 (fig. 42), where a variant plaster of the *Large Seated Nude* may be seen, the artist is surrounded by similar images including recent lithographs, among them *Seated Nude, Left Arm on Head* (fig. 43). On the door is a reproduction of Michelangelo's figure of *Night* and, nearby, Matisse's lithograph of the same subject.

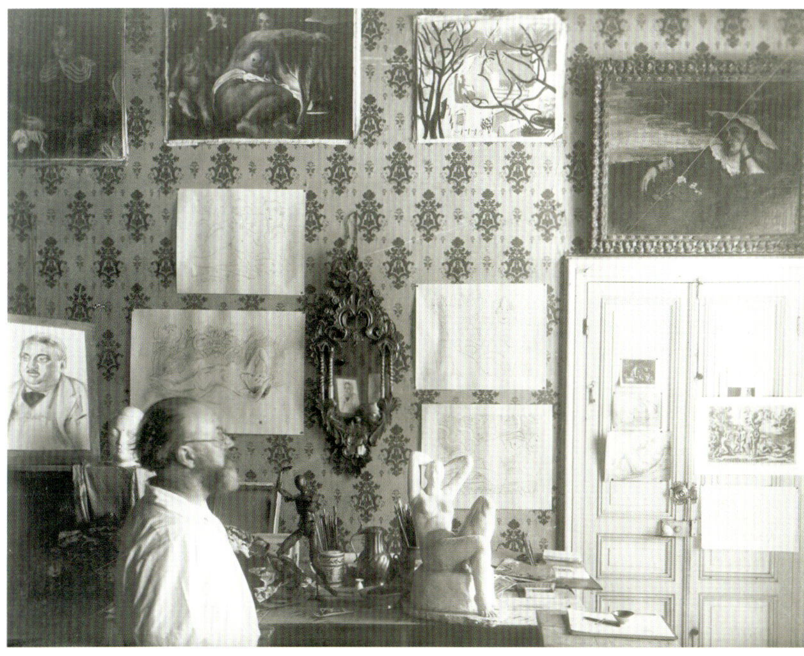

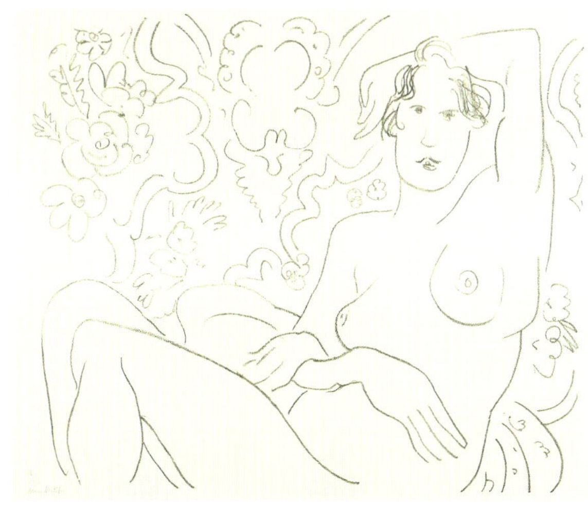

Fig. 44
a. Henri Matisse, *Turkish Blouse, Study of Legs,* 1925. Crayon transfer lithograph.
b. Henri Matisse, *Study of Legs,* 1925. Crayon transfer lithograph.
c. Henri Matisse, *Study of Legs,* 1925. Crayon transfer lithograph.
d. Henri Matisse, *Nude, Leg Bent—Study of Legs,* 1925. Crayon transfer lithograph.
All four works: The Baltimore Museum of Art, The Cone Collection, formed by Dr. Claribel and Miss Etta Cone, Baltimore, Maryland.

For almost all of this work including most of his painted odalisques, Matisse used the same model, Henriette Darricarrère. Looking at the assemblage of drawings and prints of her reclining poses, observed "at liberty," one can sense her relaxed attitude—a studied consistency informed by her memory of past sessions in their collaborative exploration of the figural pose. In 1922, after an eight-year hiatus, Matisse returned to lithography making nearly one hundred prints that freely explore a vast array of images of Henriette in portraits, as a ballet dancer, variously costumed in interiors decorated with intricately patterned Islamic textiles, or reclining as an exotic odalisque.

> My models, human figures, are never just "extras" in an interior. They are the principal theme of my work. I depend absolutely on my model, whom I observe at liberty, and then I decide on the pose which best suits "her nature." When I take a new model, it is from the unselfconscious attitudes she takes when she rests that I intuit the pose that will best suit her, and then I become the slave of that pose.[48]

Reflective of the openness that must have characterized the modeling sessions with Henriette is a group of four lithographs from 1925 (fig. 44 a–d). Here Matisse drew in his contour mode without modeling. The character of his line is both sure and spontaneous or even playful—one line was crossed through with diagonal lines and replaced by a new one. Each image offers a variation on the reclining pose with leg raised. In one, the head and one breast are cut off by the edge of the image, in another, both the foot and the top of the head are invisible, as if the figure had grown beyond

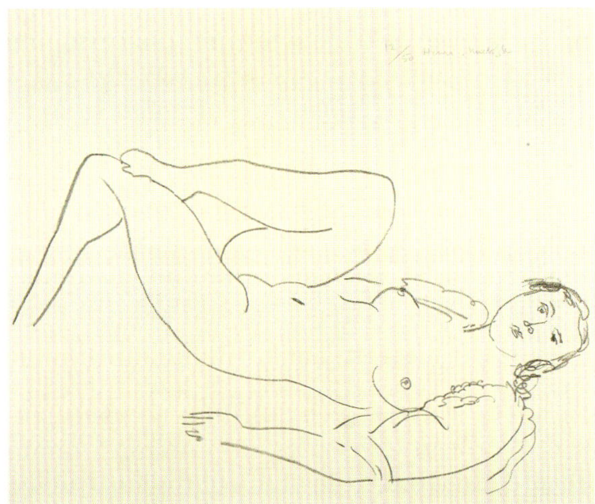
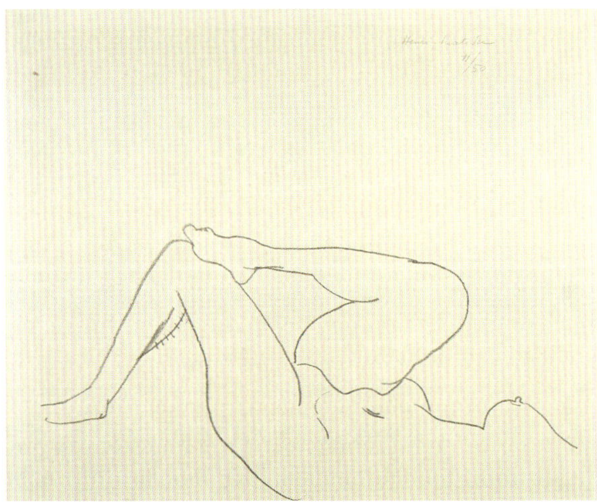
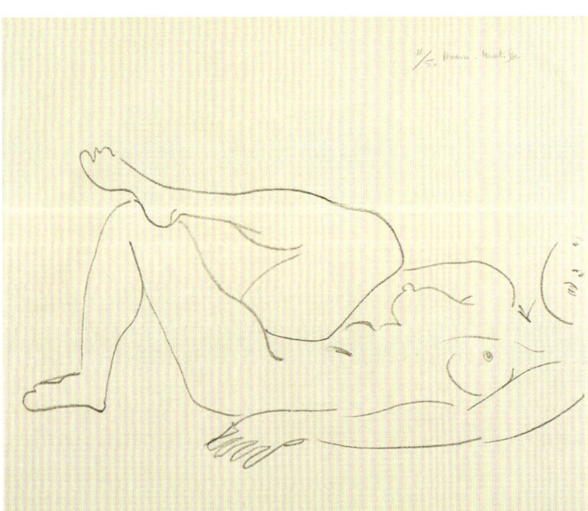
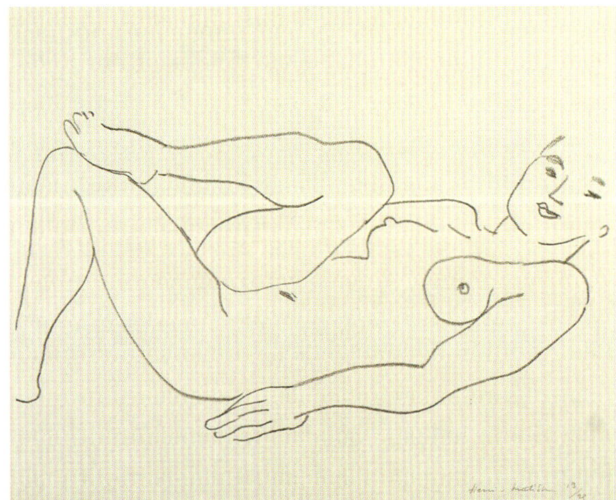

the space allowed. A drawing of contour lines from c. 1925, *Nude, Legs Crossed* (cat. 108, p. 225), is further evidence of the theme of the crossed-leg pose with its many variations. Matisse also produced his largest and most ambitious lithographs, three images of Henriette, with legs crossed and arms raised, reclining in a chair. The first, *Nude with Blue Cushion* (cat. 107, p. 219), shows the model sitting sideways in an enfolding upholstered armchair, an image elaborated in a second print, where interior furnishings are added and the chair is ornamented with a decorative textile. In a third, related image, *Large Odalisque with Bayadère Culottes* (1925), Henriette wears brilliant striped pants, her arms now relaxed on the arms of the chair. These lithographs are made through transfer from a drawing on paper to a lithographic stone or plate for printing. Here, in an alternative mode to the contour lithographs, the crayon is used more like a stick of charcoal and the images share with his charcoal and stump drawings a volumetric luminosity.

The charcoal and stump drawings from 1922–1924, most brilliantly represented by *Reclining Model with a Flowered Robe* (cat. 105, p. 219), best illustrate Matisse's intention "to consider simultaneously the character of the model, her human expression, the quality of surrounding light, the atmosphere and all that can only be expressed by drawing."[49] In these years, charcoal drawings joined painting to sculpture in a new synthesis of light and form. The manipulation (rubbing and erasure) of the charcoal with the stumping tool produces an array of modulated tones from dark to light. The tool, known in French as an *estompe,* is sometimes referred to in English as a "stump," thus the common term *stumping,* referring to the manipulation of the already applied charcoal with this tool, which is made from tightly rolled paper. By means of erasure, revealing the white of the paper, strong highlights are achieved. This manner of drawing, which could be characterized as pictorial, thus most closely related to painting, has parallels with the actual physical working of clay in the modeling of sculptures. With the infusion of light, Matisse could model the figure in terms of volume while also contrasting the strong perception of three-dimensionality against areas of decorative detail that are two dimensional.

In the last stages of work on *Large Seated Nude,* Matisse returned to the consideration of the reclining pose of *Blue Nude* and *Reclining Nude I (Aurora)* of 1907. The series of sculptures continued with two new works, *Reclining Nude II* (cat. 112, p. 228), and *Reclining Nude III* (cat. 113, p. 229). After two decades, the evolution of this pose moved further toward simplification—a refinement of the arabesque achieving a continuous linear unity. In a lithograph of 1927, *Sleeping Figure* (cat. 114, p. 232), the *Large Seated Nude* is instead reclining languidly on a cushioned bed, her chiseled musculature now relaxed, the tension in her back released. Three strong drawings of reclining figures, the first, in crayon, dated 1907–1908, the second, a charcoal drawing dated 1929, and a third drawing in graphite dated 1927–1928, demonstrate Matisse's tireless absorption with the reclining-nude pose, as he sought to simplify even further his articulation of the figure. The c. 1907–1908 drawing, *Reclining Nude* (cat. 102, p. 224), is contemporary with the first nude in the sculpture series, *Reclining Nude I (Aurora).* This extraordinary sheet announces the transformation that would occur two decades later in the subsequent sculptures. With an almost violent expressiveness, the drawing emphasizes the fractured angularity of the reclining pose. Slashing strokes gather along the figure's contours, some repeatedly reinforced to emphasize the abrupt changes of direction in the articulation of the figural pose. The point of view from above is unusual, but in a series of photographs now published in the Duthuit catalogue raisonné, Matisse indicates various preferred views of sculptures including this perspective on *Reclining Nude (Aurora).*[50] The figure stretches out before us, foreshortened and spatially distorted. A 1929 drawing (cat. 116, p. 232) appears more decisively analytical. Strong charcoal strokes, so definite they might have been applied with a straight edge, structure the pose of the figure. Like the limbs of the wooden puppets found in an art school classroom, one leg rotates forward while the other holds to the picture plane. The lower torso flattens to the base with

Fig. 45. Photograph of Matisse working on a preliminary version of *Venus in a Shell,* c. 1930. Archives Matisse, Paris.

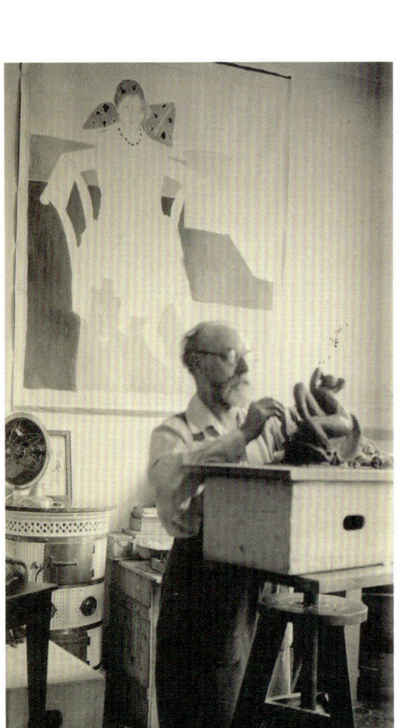

a hingelike bend as the upper torso rises to the raised arm. This drawing would relate most closely to the 1929 sculpture *Reclining Nude III.* By comparison, the angular delineation in these sheets coexists with a different drawing style in a slightly earlier sheet, *Reclining Nude,* c. 1927–1928 (cat. 110, p. 225), with more subtle modeling achieved in part through stumping and erasure of the malleable graphite strokes.

In 1929, Matisse also returned to the study of the torso in two sculptures, *Small Thin Torso* (cat. 118, p. 276; 119, pp. 236, 238) and *Small Torso* (cat. 120, p. 235), partial figures such as that of his 1906 sculpture *Torso with Head (La Vie)* (cat. 37, p. 151). In a scale suitable for holding in the hand, the two sculptures also express the physical act of clay modeling, the surface rubbed to achieve a distillation of form. The result becomes so purified beyond the realistic representation of the body to become an abstract form, though one clearly derived from nature. A sketch from this year reveals the progress toward abstraction (cat. 121, p. 237). There are two figures, the first, in the foreground to the right is more fully worked. Matisse focuses on the figure's torso, dispensing with the head and arms just as he had for *Torso with Head.* The body is posed in profile, turning just slightly toward the viewer. Heavier lines reinforce the outer contours of the body's profile and the minimal use of shading subtly models the figure's volume. To the left is another drawing, more simplified, of the torso without head, arms, or feet. This sketch is a frontal view such as one would have of the sculpture *Small Torso.* The figure is abstracted to a vaselike form that prefigures the positive/negative cut-out of *Forms* (cat. 122, p. 239), a plate from *Jazz.*

This transformation of the figural form represents a new synthesis of organic refinement also manifested in a number of sculptures of 1927–1930, including *Tiari* (cat. 77, 78, pp. 195–97) and *The Back IV* (cat. 51, p. 163), but nowhere more tangibly than in the sculpture *Venus in a Shell I.* These pieces would mark the conclusion of a productive and transformative phase of sculptural production. Monod-Fontaine has pointed out that these works are the equivalent of line drawings made in the period, such as those made as part of the artist's book commission to illustrate the *Poésies de Stéphane Mallarmé* or drawings related to the *Dance* murals.[51] Two graphite drawings, *Seated Nude* (cat. 127, p. 248) and *Standing Nude* (cat. 129, p. 249), one from the front and one from the back, capture the cylindrical compactness of the simplified torso. For these Matisse used the graphite pencil both for linear control and the opportunity for revision and refinement through erasure. In *Seated Nude,* a drawing for *Venus in the Shell I,* there is no self-consciousness or contrivance in the natural pose of the figure, which, seen from the back, is seated but will soon stand. She has already straightened up from a crouched position recalling earlier sketches of figures rising from the bath. This unfolding is like the gradual emergence of a tulip flower—stem straightening and blossom taking form as it rises from the ground. This particular study, as well as the next drawing to be discussed, relates most closely to a destroyed version of the *Venus* sculpture pictured in a studio photograph (fig. 45). In his drawing of *Nude with Raised Arms* (cat. 130, p. 249) Matisse seems to revisit his earlier studies from 1905–1906, where the model rises from the bath with an attitude of liberation and the exhilaration of rebirth.[52] This marvelous contour drawing of a woman about to stand has the unabashed exuberance of a flower's first brilliant bloom. It is closely related to preparatory drawings for the Mallarmé book, specifically the drawing and subsequent etching for the poem *Hommage III* (cat. 131, p. 250) but also to figures taking form in the *Dance* murals. In the sculpture *Venus in a Shell I,* a more emotional response is tempered by a new discipline of formal restraint, but the point of departure remains the same observation of the model.

Again, the creative process surrounding the *Venus* sculptures is inseparable from the character of work for the Mallarmé illustrations. Monod-Fontaine writes of "his creation of purified plastic signs which provide an equivalent to the poet's images without imitating them."[53] As in *Le bonheur de vivre,* we return to the world of classical mythology, revisiting Arcadia. Matisse's

Fig. 46. Henri Matisse, *The Frigate,* 1938. Linoleum cut. The Baltimore Museum of Art; Purchased as the Gift of Jeanette Kimmel and Edward T. Cone, in memory of Mrs. Edward Loewenstein.

figures are again isolated from any setting or directed action, and their idealization removes any sense of contemporaneity. The extended preparation for the Mallarmé illustrations is elucidated in the maquette of drawings and proofs for the etchings compiled by Matisse and sold to Etta Cone in 1932. With a successive progression of revisions made through tracing, erasure, and restatement Matisse continues his distillation of figural form. In the preliminary drawing for *Hommage III*, we experience at once both the final synthesis and the manifestation of Matisse's process of refinement —ever reductive. This progress is finally realized in the most essential linear expression of the pure etched line in the final Mallarmé illustrations. In this and other drawings, or in a painting such as *The Yellow Dress* (cat. 128, p. 247), we apprehend a figure that takes form as a growing plant, at the same time acquiring monumentality. A transformation of temporal nature occurs in an artistic vision, where the real and the ideal are tangibly joined in a Matissian synthesis.

One of Matisse's last sculptures is the *Standing Nude (Katia).* In its totemlike verticality, its other-worldliness, it is essentially different from the earlier sculpture of 1906, *Standing Nude, Arms on Head.* There, we sense the presence of the model in the studio as there is an immediacy to the more casual attitude of the pose, legs apart, weight shifted, one foot in front of the other. A strongly modeled charcoal drawing of 1908–1909, *Standing Nude, Seen from the Side* (cat. 133, p. 257) further illuminates the contrast with *Katia.* The early, standing pose is developed further as the forceful rendering of the nude's massive form silhouetted against the white ground of the paper achieves forceful monumentality. No space exists to separate the viewer from this assertive figure. In a sheet discussed earlier, *Face and Two Nudes with Gourds*, the exotic, Gauguin-like figures carrying vessels on their heads, to the left of the drawn face, reflect the same primitivism apparent in the *Katia* sculpture.

Drawing with Scissors / Cutting into Stone

In his illustrated book *Pasiphaë,* published in 1943, Matisse used the technique of linoleum cut, gouging the matrix to achieve in the print sinuous white lines that gleam from the surrounding printed black. Matisse wrote of these linoleum cuts: "The gouge, like the violin bow, is in direct rapport with the feelings of the engraver."[54] Recalling earlier images such as *Blue Nude,* his linoleum print *The Frigate* of 1938 (fig. 46) depicts again the pose of the reclining nude with raised arm, but here distilled in a pure linear expression, just a few white lines against the surrounding black ground. The incisiveness of this printmaking technique becomes physically tangible through the evidence of its making. The artist must draw (gouge) against the physical resistance of the actual substance of the linoleum material. But linoleum is more supple than wood and so gives way to the pressure of the tool, just as an etching needle easily finds its way through the plate's protective ground. What results is the purity of line as the articulation of form—a synthesis of method (making) and the final expression of an idea directly comparable to what Matisse would achieve with the cut-out technique. There his scissors cut (drew) through a paper he described as "almost like cardboard, a paper that resists the striking of the scissors."[55]

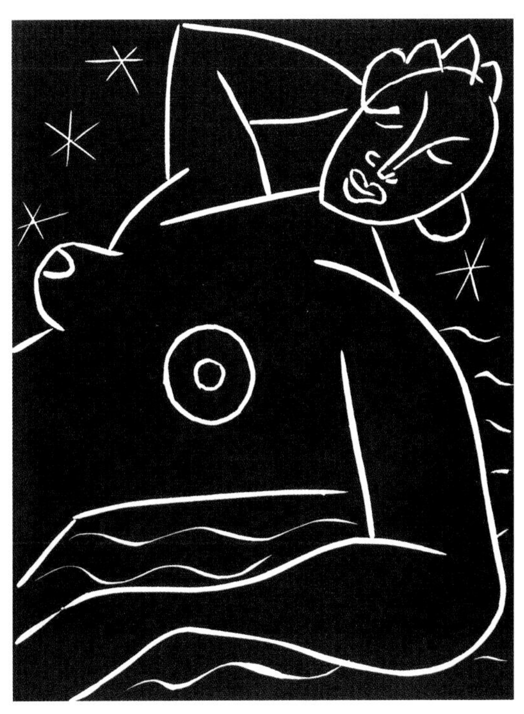

His four cut-paper *Blue Nude*s of 1952, including *Blue Nude I* (cat. 141, p. 265), revisit his masterwork of 1907, *Blue Nude: Memory of Biskra.* In the cut-out, the figure is composed through cut-out shapes joined as continuous fields of flat color, each piece adhered to a white ground. The limbs of the nude, intertwined in a self-contained crouching pose, are beginning to unfold. The progress toward a new monumentality evident in the sculpture *Venus in a Shell I* or the painting *The Yellow Dress* is here eloquently simplified to an expression of wholeness, a synthesis of serpentine form. The white ground of the support paper silhouettes the contoured shapes of the figure, but the flatness of the collaged cut-out pieces, the perception of volume is accentuated, an aspect achieved and also signified in the contours of the blue cut-out forms. The space that surrounds the figure is contained

Fig. 47. Henri Matisse, *Model in Studio,* 1948. Pen and ink. Collection of Steve Mazoh.

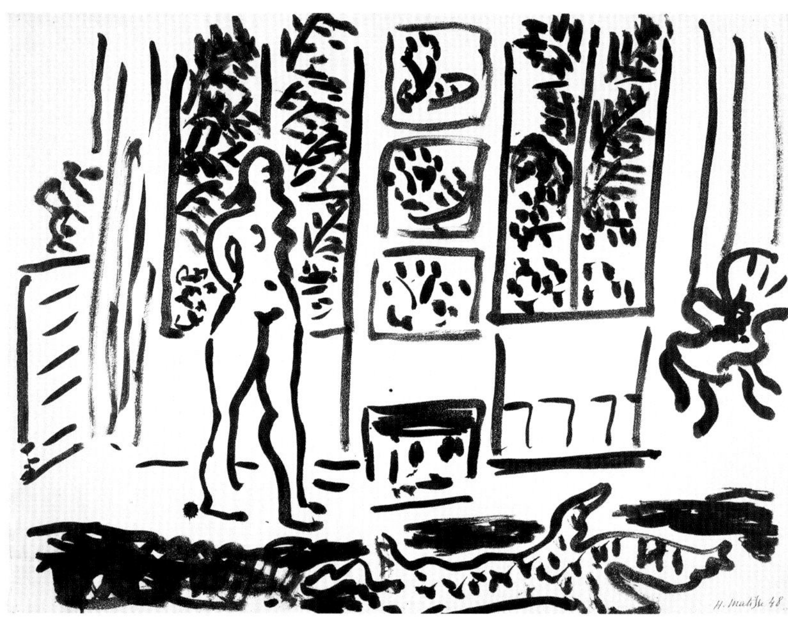

by a rectangular box that both compresses and enunciates our reading of the nude's mass. Just as *Forms,* from *Jazz,* the cut-out pieces become both positive and negative shapes.

Among Matisse's last drawings are striking brush works made in Vence in 1947–1948. They are the equivalent in drawing of the visual distillation expressed in the cut-out collages. Such drawings were sometimes actually joined to cut-out compositions such as a decorative scheme, *Large Decoration with Masks* (1953). In brush drawings such as *Model in Studio* (fig. 47), a rich black ink is applied with a broad brush to achieve lines that flow across often large sheets of white paper. Such broadly expressive drawings correlate directly to his contemporary paintings of interiors painted in Vence, such as *Interior in Yellow and Blue* (1946). In the drawing, Matisse recalls his earlier sculptures, such as *Madeleine I.* This standing nude, drawn only with expressively contoured lines, arms held back to reveal, unabashedly, her breasts, sustains the same linear rhythm as his depictions of other elements in this lively interior. Two pen-and-ink drawings from 1950, *Acrobat, Study* and *Four Studies of an Acrobat* (cat. 143, 144, p. 264), capture what could be a rehearsal exercise for a series of large brush-and-ink drawings of acrobats from 1952. The elasticity of these figures, recoiling like a spring, foretells a dynamic circuit from the ground to the air and back again. In the sheet of four studies, the acrobats, drawn only in contour, flip through space as if lighter than air. Contemporary with the brush drawings is one of the artist's last cut-outs showing two acrobats cut from blue paper. In a liberation from any constraint, they are reminiscent of figures in *The Swimming Pool* (1953), now at the Museum of Modern Art in New York, a frieze of swimmers that once moved along the upper walls of a room in Matisse's Nice apartment—blue forms, flowing in and out of a ribbon of space like a school of dolphins or a procession of naiads from an idyllic world.

> The work is the emanation, the projection of self. My drawing and my canvases are pieces of myself. Their totality constitutes Henri Matisse. The work represents, expresses, perpetuates. . . . An artist must therefore force himself to express himself totally from the beginning. Thus, he will not grow old: if he is sincere, human and constructive, he will always find an echo in following generations.[56]

Notes

1. Flam 1995, 48.

2. Ibid., 131.

3. Ibid., 102.

4. Ibid., 130.

5. Monod-Fontaine 1984; and Elderfield 1984.

6. Flam 1995, 46–52.

7. The best summaries of the activities of the Matisse school can be found in Flam 1986, 221–23, and Flam 1995, 44–46.

8. Elderfield 1984, 24.

9. Flam 1995, 48.

10. Elsen 1972, 16–22.

11. Anne Pingeot of the Musée d'Orsay, lecture at the Jane Voorhees Zimmerli Art Museum, October 22, 2005.

12. Bois 1997, 375.

13. Two drawings that had been in the collection of the Musée départemental Matisse, Le Cateau-Cambrésis, were, according to the current staff, destroyed in the process of a conservation treatment. They are illustrated in Szymusiak 1993, 26.

14. Elsen 1972, 16, 18–21; Aragon 1972, 81.

15. Elderfield 1984, 35; and Elderfield 1972, 77–85.

16. Flam 1995, 298 n.11.

17. Ibid., 50.

18. In Elderfield's words (1984, 50), "in order to achieve that union of the physical and the pictorial he desired." The question of "distance" in the perception of sculpture is dealt with more thoroughly in Oliver Shell's essay in this volume.

19. Flam 1986, 32–33.

20. Elderfield 1995, 31.

21. Chappuis 1973, 12–13.

22. Grammont 2002, 33–47.

23. Flam 1995, 49–50.

24. In spite of Matisse's disappointment over Rodin's comments on his drawings and his criticism, particularly, of Rodin's concentration on parts of the figure instead of the whole, Rodin's late drawings have many parallels with Matisse's own contour drawings and practice of keeping the eye on the model instead of on the act of drawing on the paper; see Varnedoe 1981, 153–89; and Elsen and Varnedoe 1971, 69–102.

25. Flam 1995, 47.

26. Ann Boulton's essay in this volume, pp. 75–76.

27. Szymusiak 1993, 44–47. One of the drawings illustrated in Szymusiak, fig. 28 on page 44, is annotated by the artist: "Dessin pour la sculpture 'La chemise relevée'"—the title given as well to fig. 27 on page 45. Those two drawings were sequenced by the artist with the annotation "3" and "4," respectively. A similar sequencing is found on drawings for the sculpture *Standing Nude, Arms on Head* (cat. 36, p. 144; and see also cat. 41–43, p. 145). The Matisse notebook is illustrated in Duthuit 1997, 311.

28. Elsen 1972, 56–58.

29. Elderfield 1984, 40.

30. Flam 1995, 106.

31. Flam 1984, 43–44.

32. Sykora 2005, 331.

33. Monod-Fontaine 1984, 12–17.

34. Sykora 2005, 331–35.

35. Monod-Fontaine 1984, 13.

36. Sykora 2005, 332.

37. Baldassari 1989 147–49.

38. Monod-Fontaine 1984, 17. A different translation, though with the same meaning, appears in Aragon 1972, 235.

39. Monod-Fontaine 1984, 17.

40. Neff 1975, 44; Elderfield 1984, 58–59.

41. A closely related drawing, *Untitled (Dancer),* is in the collection of the Musée nationale d'art moderne, Centre Georges Pompidou, Paris (Monod-Fontaine, Baldassari, and Laugier 1989, 221, no. 78).

42. Ibid., 168–70.

43. Flam 1995, 46.

44. This drawing was identified by Wanda de Guébriant; written communication with the author.

45. Monod-Fontaine, Baldassari, and Laugier 1989, 152–53.

46. Ibid., 162–63.

47. Elsen 1972, 146.

48. Flam 1995, 131.

49. Ibid., 131. For the flowered robe drawing, see Elderfield 1984, 88; and Carlson 1971, 106.

50. Flam 2001, 42–43.

51. Monod-Fontaine 1984, 41.

52. Monod-Fontaine, Baldassari, and Laugier 1989, 226–28.

53. Monod-Fontaine 1984, 41.

54. Flam 1995, 168.

55. Ibid., 302 n.6.

56. Matisse, interview with André Verdet, April–May, 1952; in ibid., 212.

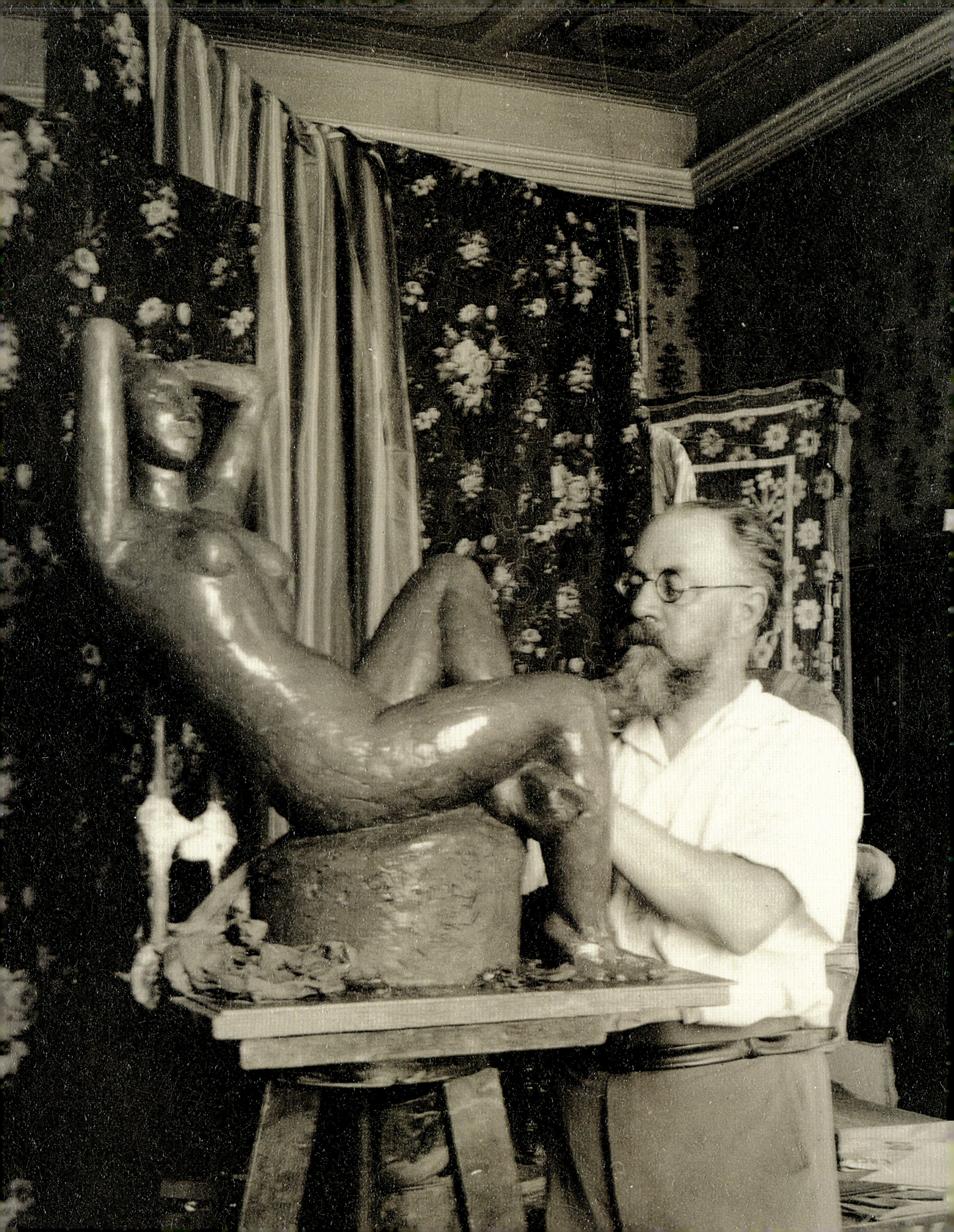

Oliver Shell

Seeing Figures

Exhibition and Vision in Matisse's Sculpture

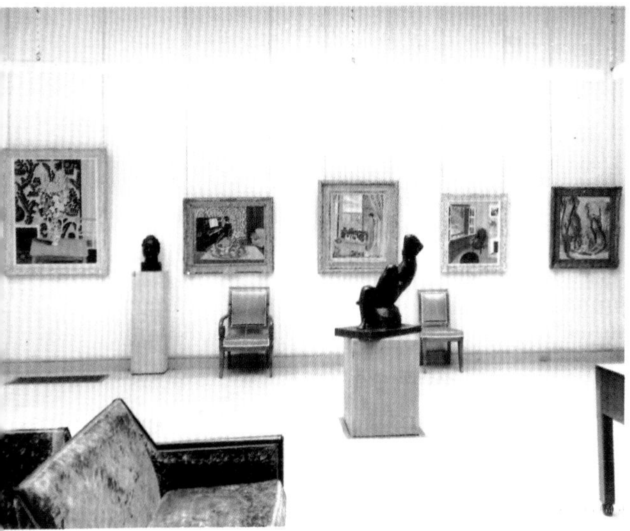

Fig. 48. Installation of exhibition of work by Henri Matisse, Galerie Bernheim-Jeune, Paris, 1958.

Four years after Matisse's death, the Galerie Bernheim-Jeune in Paris held a retrospective exhibition of his works. An installation shot from that 1958 exhibition depicts three of the artist's better-known sculptures—*The Serpentine* (cat. 58, pp. 170, 172), a head of *Henriette,* and the *Large Seated Nude* (cat. 98, p. 217; 99, p. 275)—and five paintings (fig. 48). The paintings, among them still lifes, interiors, views of windows, and a landscape, are all set in ornate frames suspended from the ceiling on conspicuous wires, which add to the modernist sense of an installation that imposes a grid throughout the gallery with rigorous efficiency. This is also reinforced by the cubic pedestals, suspended lighting, and placement of furniture. Two of the chairs set against the wall have cords stretched across their seats to prevent the public from using them. Apparently, their function is purely aesthetic, evoking a faux domesticity but intended, in their alignment with the verticals of the frames and support wires, to extend the grid to the floor plane. No visually disruptive labels are evident. At left, *The Serpentine* set against the wall assumes an attendant role, as does the portrait bust of *Henriette* flanking the other side of a heating grate. *Large Seated Nude,* placed out and away from the wall on a large stone pedestal, plays the leading role. Innovatively, the curator has twisted *Large Seated Nude* almost forty-five degrees off from the alignment of the pedestal, as if the sculpted figure had grown tired of seeing the paintings before her and turned to look at her sisters, *The Serpentine* and *Henriette*—who in turn refract her gaze throughout the exhibition space. This whimsical privileging of the representational figure over the sculpture as a whole—base and all—is the single violation of an otherwise strict ninety-degree coordination of elements in the gallery. Of course, sculpture that comes alive and moves is as old as the Pygmalion myth, which is why we do not expect it from a canonic modern artist such as Matisse. Formalist modernism taught its public to prefer abstract relationships to the representational elements of a work of art. Treating the sculpted figure as though it were an actor within the gallery space hardly conforms to such expectations. The peculiarities of the exhibition raise several questions. Was there any precedent within Matisse's lifetime for this sort of sculpturally centered installation? And did the curator violate Matisse's intent or simply respond to latent features in his sculpture that encourage interactive visual play?

It is hard to make generalizations about Matisse's sculpture because, in the words of William Tucker—one of his most thoughtful interpreters—none of his sculptures "has a solution whose authority exceeds the particular work."[1] Efforts to define their shared qualities do not easily progress beyond affirming that they all posses what can loosely be termed a sense of "made-to-be-looked-at-ness." This aspect of visual self-consciousness, which constitutes the essence of all visual arts, is felt more acutely with regard to Matisse's sculptures precisely because of his lack of a definitive solution. Each work activates this quality through a variety of means; it requires (using Tucker's word) a new "solution" for each piece. Several factors, singly or in conjunction, contribute to this sense: Matisse's manipulation of the monumental aspects of the plinth; his frequent copying either of known sculptures or of standard academic poses—poses that already carry a certain visual charge; his reliance on sexually coded gestures of figural self display; and his creation of figures that embody sightedness, appearing to return the viewer's gaze or to survey their environment. We recognize that our own act of looking is highlighted by the sense of that gaze being reflected back at us.

To understand this somewhat unwieldy notion of visual self-consciousness and to assess Matisse's sculpture within his larger oeuvre, we might begin by addressing some basic questions. When and how did Matisse become known as a sculptor? How did he want his sculpture to be seen by the public? How did he want to be seen as a sculptor? Among these questions the subject shifts from historical context to author, artwork, and audience, and one is reminded of an observation made by Roger Benjamin in comparing Matisse's teacher Gustave Moreau with the poet Stéphane Mallarmé—a point made to suggest a source for Matisse's understanding: "Mallarmé had a highly sophisticated understanding of how the poem mediates between its author and its reader; so too Moreau sought to describe the functioning of communication by means of a painting."[2] A similarly complex mediation occurs with Matisse's sculpture where, as we shall see, the artist occupied and conceptualized vision from multiple vantage points. Matisse conceived the entire spatial, visual, and even historical field in which his sculpture intervenes, and he sought to shape the spectatorial experience through a fluid exchange of the positions of object and subject. Such an understanding not only determined the forms and figures he created but also affected the ways in which sculpture was displayed and photographed or represented in paintings.[3]

Exhibitions

In June of 1904, Matisse had his first one-man show at Ambroise Vollard's gallery in the rue Lafitte.[4] It included forty-five paintings, one drawing, and not a single sculpture. This is surprising because the exhibition was an important opportunity for Matisse to present himself comprehensively to the public and he had been actively sculpting for five years. We know that Vollard dealt in sculpture at least as early as 1899, when he purchased nine terra-cotta figurines from Aristide Maillol, which he then cast repeatedly in bronze and sold in his gallery. Later he bought important early sculptures from Pablo Picasso, including celebrated portraits of Fernande Olivier. He never showed Matisse's sculpture, possibly because he would buy not only the sculptures, but also the rights of their reproduction.[5] This was the case with Picasso's cubist *Head of a Woman (Fernande).* Once he owned the rights to a sculpture, Vollard would produce any number of casts, depending on demand. This practice conflicted with an emerging ethos among a number of early modernists that sought to limit sculptural reproduction to a set number of casts. Maillol, who was close to Matisse by 1904, claimed with some exaggeration that the limited editions of ten casts produced for Vollard frequently ended up being nearer to ten thousand. Matisse certainly knew of Maillol's complaints, and his well-documented distrust of dealers would have disinclined him to let Vollard gain control of his sculpture.[6] Such concerns would have been consistent with Matisse's lifelong attempt to limit the editions of his sculptures to ten examples.[7]

The earliest evidence that Matisse publicly exhibited his sculpture comes from the catalogue for the Salon d'automne in 1904, in which two sculptures are listed, an "*Étude* (buste, plâtre), [and] *Femme* (buste, plâtre)."[8] The first critical mention appears in a review by Louis Vauxcelles, who devotes most of his article to the fourteen paintings Matisse submitted, but concludes by describing two sculptures, "a nude man, vigorously accentuated" and a "young girl, quite amusingly curved."[9] Clearly these are not the plaster busts Matisse had planned to submit; in fact, the descriptions most closely fit Matisse's *The Serf* (cat. 4–6, pp. 107, 109, 266) and *Madeleine I* (cat. 12–14, pp. 115, 120, 267).

The Serf, begun in 1900, was his earliest large-scale, conceptually original sculpture.[10] He worked on it for more than three years, but did not remove the arms until 1908, when the figure was first cast in bronze.[11] *The Serf* stands alone among Matisse's prewar sculptures both in its ambition and as a summary of the artist's early aesthetic ideas. With its literary subject, the work looks backward to nineteenth-century allegorical representations of labor.[12] The pedestal, with its prominent inscription, contributes to a sense of the monumental, making *The Serf* appear a timeless embodiment of stoic endurance.

In 1899, in spite of his poverty, Matisse purchased two artworks from Vollard: a plaster bust by Auguste Rodin and a painting by Paul Cézanne.[13] *The Serf* has been convincingly interpreted as a sophisticated artistic response to both of these sources. In hiring the same Italian model (Bevilaqua), who many years earlier posed for Rodin's *John the Baptist* and *Walking Man,* Matisse deliberately confronted the aesthetic challenge of the older sculptor.[14] *The Serf*'s most radical innovation, however, rests in its divergence from Rodinian prototypes. When Matisse began *The Serf,* he was painting studio works, from the model, that are recognized as heavily indebted to Cézanne. Among these, *Male Model* (cat. 7, p. 110) depicts the same model (Bevilaqua), whose pose closely resembles *The Serf.* The near-abstract application of discrete constructive blocks of paint has an analogue in the modeled and cut surfaces of *The Serf,* composed as they are of discrete, light-modulating masses and accents that construct the figure without direct reference to anatomy.[15] His translation of a kind of expressive facture taken from two-dimensional painting into a three-dimensional sculptural equivalent is unprecedented.[16]

Shortly after he began *The Serf,* Matisse also started work on *Madeleine I,* the first of two closely related sculptures based on a studio model of that name.[17] The sculpture is sometimes considered to be the female counterpart to *The Serf.* Both works arise from Matisse's renewed interest in figure studies around the turn of the century, but they differ fundamentally in scale and in style. Where *The Serf* is stable, immobile in pose, and constructed in terms of lumpy, architectural units, *Madeleine I* sways with a dynamic, unified spiral rhythm. Her surfaces are smooth, and there is little sign of the sort of editing with a sculptor's knife that is so evident in *The Serf. Madeleine I,* with its exaggerated *contrapposto* stance, recalling Michelangelo's *Dying Slave,* constitutes one of the earliest expressions of Matisse's lifelong interest in the unifying form of the arabesque or serpentine.[18] *Madeleine I* also reveals Matisse's debt to Rodin in the tightly wrapped arms reminiscent of the older sculptor's *Eve* (fig. 60) and in the dramatic, active contour lines that lead the viewer around the constantly shifting figure. Matisse shared Rodin's belief that sculpture should be seen from all sides and conceived fully in the round, a belief that contradicted the influential contemporary theories of Adolf von Hildebrand, who advocated a frontal sculpture.[19]

In 1904, the Salon d'automne was in only its second year of existence. Matisse exhibited his works together with paintings by Charles Camoin, Henri Manguin, and Albert Marquet, other former students of Gustave Moreau.[20] *The Serf* and *Madeleine I* would have stood out not only as the lone sculptures in the room but also because they were monochrome white plaster casts—neither had been executed in bronze at this point. No installation photographs exist of Matisse's contribution that year, but we do get a sense of the opulence of the Grand Palais exhibition spaces and the novel display strategies in three rare photographs depicting one of the highlights of the 1904 exhibition, the "salle Cézanne" (fig. 49).[21] Arranged by Vollard, this was Cézanne's first official exhibition in Paris. Matisse, perhaps prompted by Vollard, lent his own Cézanne, *Three Bathers* (fig. 10, p. 9), to the show, where it can be seen in one of the installation photos, oddly juxtaposed with an angled glass case containing a sculpture by Medardo Rosso, who, like Cézanne, was also recognized at the 1904 Salon d'automne with his own section. Why his work is included in the Cézanne room remains somewhat unclear. It may have acted as a segue to the area dedicated to Rosso; it is more likely, however, that Vollard was suggesting some affinity between the painter and the sculptor, perhaps emphasizing the impressionist roots of both. One wonders how Matisse, who had created arguably the most Cézannian sculpture to date in *The Serf,* felt about this. Perhaps this is what prompted

Fig. 49. Installation of the "salle Cézanne" at the Salon d'automne, Petit Palais, Paris, 1904.

Fig. 50. Photograph of Matisse and *The Serf* with arms, c. 1904. Dr. Claribel and Miss Etta Cone Papers, Manuscripts Collections, The Baltimore Museum of Art.

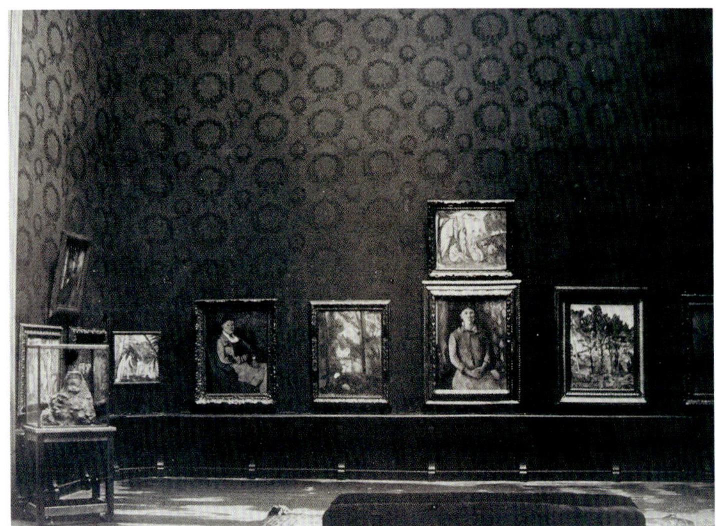

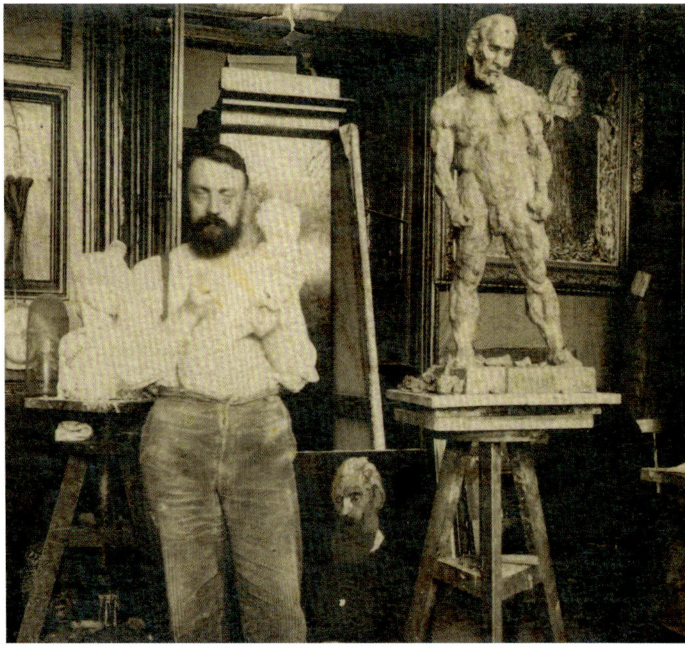

him to substitute *The Serf* for the "plaster bust" previously announced in the catalogue. If Matisse wished his connection to the Master from Aix to be underscored, he apparently succeeded; one reviewer, Raymond Bouer, commented: "Henri Matisse is more *cézannien* than Cézanne."[22]

The Serf, at the time still with arms, was depicted in a revealing photograph (fig. 50), most probably from 1904, of Matisse in his quai St-Michel studio.[23] The artist stands next to the uncompleted clay model.[24] Never commented on, because it is so difficult to see against the white of his shirt, is that Matisse holds a plaster cast of *Madeleine I* in his hands, cradling it against his chest. Madeleine's head is just to the right of Matisse's cheek and silhouetted against the upright rectangular shape of the tall armoire behind him. The edge of the sculpture's base is aligned with the waistline of his dark pants. Standing behind Matisse, on his proper right side—to his left in the photograph—is his plaster *Bust of a Woman* (1900)—undoubtedly one of the two "plaster busts" he intended to submit to the 1904 Salon.[25] On the ground is a veiled self-portrait of Matisse in the guise of a monk entitled *Monk in Meditation.* The 1904 dating of the photograph is strongly suggested once we recognize that most of the works in the photograph were exhibited for the first time in that year, including *Monk in Meditation,* shown both at Vollard's and at the Independents, *The Serf* and *Madeleine I,* shown at the Salon d'automne, and even the *Bust of a Woman,* which Matisse changed his mind about showing.

What are we to make of this photograph? John Elderfield sees in it an act of "unmistakable self-projection" on the part of Matisse—but just what is he self-projecting? Elderfield observes that "he is sending a mixed message: mostly masculine assertion, but also self-sacrifice and servitude."[26] These last two attributes, appropriate to monk and serf respectively, are certainly present in the image. Given the presentational gesture with which Matisse holds the plaster and the way in which, surrounded by the accumulation of his sculptural and painterly labors, he addresses the viewer, Matisse projects an image of himself as the complete artist. He is most probably posing for friends and there may be a hint of irony in the posture; yet he assumes the ambitious role of Renaissance artist in the vein of Michelangelo, both a sculptor and painter and a figure he repeatedly turned to for inspiration. Sculpture in this photograph confers a palpable sense of the physical, material effort of Matisse's labor.

Matisse submitted no sculpture to the notorious 1905 Salon d'automne. This exhibition, which cemented the artist's reputation as leader of the Parisian avant-garde and chief amongst the colorist painters henceforth known as the *fauves* (wild beasts), was not, however, without sculpture. In fact, the way in which the relationship between sculpture and painting in public exhibition spaces was conceptualized and discussed in the criticism of the 1905 Salon d'automne reveals ways in which early twentieth-century audiences perceived an animated exchange between three- and two-dimensional works. This clearly had a lasting impact and informed Matisse's own attitudes so it is worth recapitulating the events. As is well known, it was Louis Vauxcelles who coined the term *fauvism,* using it twice in quite different ways in his reviews. He saluted Matisse for his courage, speculating that his entry would "fare about as well as a Christian virgin fed to wild beasts [*fauves*] in the arena." At another point, referring to the paintings of Matisse and his colleagues while discussing a traditional sculptural head by Albert Marque shown in the center of the same exhibition room, Vauxcelles describes the head as "a Donatello among the fauves!"[27] There is a kind of mirroring between the public, on the one hand, which is compared to ravenous beasts threatening the virginal art, and the paintings, on the other hand, also likened to beasts, who surround and threaten the sculpture of a child's head—and by implication the Renaissance tradition of Donatello.[28] That the relationship between sculpture and paintings in an exhibition space could be regarded as a dynamic dialogue was not just Vauxcelle's fantasy. The idea was picked up and given a more bizarre, sexualized interpretation in a review by Jules de Saint-Hilaire, who commented:

> One really has to pity the delicate and candid head of a little girl, Mlle Marthe Lebasque! [Marque's sculpture] The poor child, obliged to contemplate all day the strange pictorial lubrications that surround her, must sense her lily-pure soul absolutely galled by these effluvia, so contrary to her moral being. One is even astonished that this marble, lost in the midst of the shameless profligacy of accents of all these palettes in breach of all good sense, maintains intact her whiteness.[29]

This will not be the last time that criticism of modern art—and specifically Matisse's art—is tinged with evocations of sexual immorality and even brimstone. More interesting is that here we have the image of a seeing sculpture. The writer assumes that a French public, educated by centuries spent in attending art exhibitions, will easily recognize an imaginary flow of psychological forces (be they violent or corrupting) visually transmitted between paintings and sculptures and running between art and the public in the metaphorical coliseum of the art gallery. The 1905 Salon d'automne and its criticism left Matisse with a deepened awareness of the psychologized space of the gallery and of sculpture's potential to shape such experiences. The full exploration of such relationships emerged only gradually, as Matisse's sculptural oeuvre grew and took on a greater presence in his exhibitions.

In 1906, Matisse again showed a small group of sculptures, three in all, including *The Serf* for the second time, along with fifty-five paintings in an exhibition held at the Galerie E. Druet.[30] This exhibition was ignored by the critics, overwhelmed by the attention given to Matisse's *Le bonheur de vivre,* his single contribution to the Salon des Independents of that year, which opened the same week. *Le bonheur de vivre* (fig. 28, p. 29), as Yve-Alain Bois points out, "is programmatic and encapsulates in many respects Matisse's entire enterprise."[31] In his arcadian landscape we find not only the early expression of figural poses he would explore in major sculptures—such as the *Reclining Nudes* (cat. 44, p. 269; 45, pp. 153, 155–56; 112, p. 228; 113, p. 229), *Standing Nude, Arms on Head* (cat. 36, p. 144), *Torso with Head (La Vie)* (cat. 37, p. 151), the *Small Crouching Torso without Arms or Head,* and *Two Negresses* (cat. 47, p. 159)—but also an expression of Matisse's lifelong fascination with luxuriant gestures of self-display and two-sided viewing relationships. *Le bonheur de vivre* presents a broad thematic of vision, directed both inward and outward, and the implicit negation of vision, through closure or distancing, which prefigures the major preoccupation of much of Matisse's

Fig. 51. Photograph of Matisse's sculpture class in the Couvent du Sacré-Coeur, boulevard des Invalides, Paris, c. 1909. Left to right: Jean Heiberg, unknown woman, Sarah Stein, Hans Purrmann, Henri Matisse, Patrick Henry Bruce. Archives Matisse, Paris.

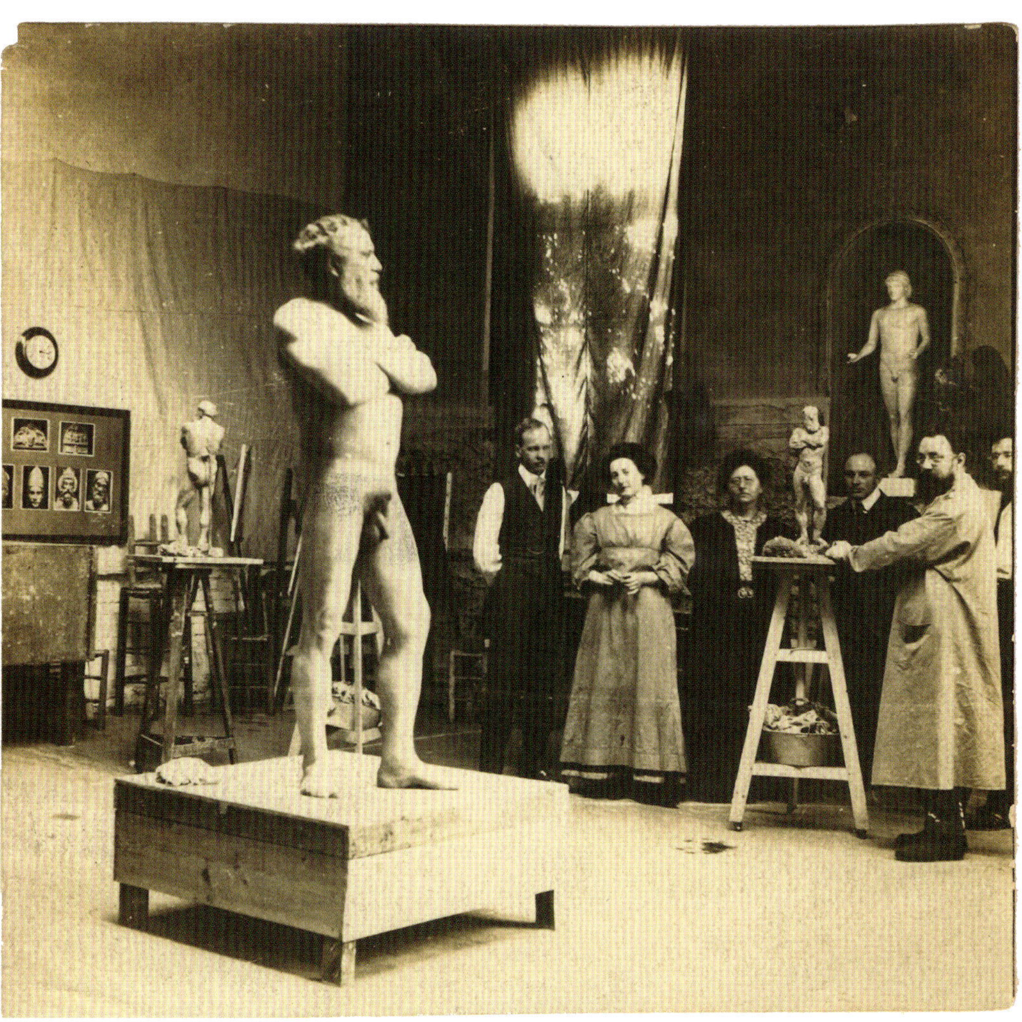

subsequent sculpture and art. The exhibition of *Le bonheur de vivre* reinforced Matisse's position, first recognized by the public at large in 1905, as the leader of the avant-garde. This status was based predominantly on his activity as a painter; however, his search for significant figures to inhabit his Arcadia was deeply connected to a sculptural understanding of expressive types and gestures.

His leadership would prove to be short lived. Only two years later, in 1908, Matisse received his first retrospective at the Salon d'automne, an honor hitherto reserved for artists such as Renoir, Gauguin, and Cézanne. Although he had not yet won over the public or the conservative critics, he was now presented as a "modern master" and as such he no longer led the avant-garde—a role increasingly assumed by Picasso.[32] It is at precisely this juncture that Matisse decides for the first time to present a sizable group of thirteen sculptures. What better way to challenge the public's limited perception of him as a purely sensational, wild hedonistic colorist? The painter who sculpts lays claim to a more universal outlook than does the specialist in a single medium—an outlook associated with humanism and Renaissance paradigms of genius. Matisse's efforts to broaden his appeal coincided fairly closely with the first publication of his artistic credo "Notes of a Painter," in which he dreamt of "an art of balance, of purity, and serenity."[33] These rhetorical goals hardly promote values associated with a radical, and do not conform easily to the genuine difficulty of his art, but they do record his desire to present his artistic goals as traditional. The same can perhaps be said about another venture of this period, Matisse's teaching, which began in late 1907 and occupied a considerable amount of his energies in 1908. In accordance with standard academic practice, Matisse included sculpture prominently in his curriculum, as is reflected in Sarah Stein's "Notes," a detailed record of his pedagogical dicta on painting, drawing, and sculpture.[34] Photographs also survive (fig. 51) that depict Matisse's students modeling in clay from the figure—Elsen speculates that this is the considerably aged Bevilaqua, the same model who had previously served both Rodin and Matisse. We see Matisse apparently going through the motions of being an academic master, even before he had won any critical acclaim as a sculptor.

With the Salon d'automne of 1908, the public had an opportunity to assess a broad selection of Matisse's sculpture.[35] Selection of the pieces would have been easy as Matisse's friend Maillol, together with Albert Marque, were on the sculpture jury that year.[36] *The Serf* was shown for a third time, but now in bronze and missing its arms. The cast in the exhibition was one of the two early bronzes belonging either to Leo Stein or to Michael and Sarah Stein.[37] Indeed, somewhat unusually, eleven of the thirteen sculptures exhibited were bronzes. These must have come, fairly directly, from the Bingen and Costenoble foundry, with which Matisse had only recently begun working.[38] From the titles of the works listed in the catalogue, we can identify most, but not all, of the sculptures. Is "*Femme couchée se soulevant sur bras*" the same as *Reclining Nude I (Aurora)?* It is generally assumed to be so. The list includes the earliest reference to the work commonly named *Two Negresses,* calling it *Groupe de deux jeunes filles* (Group of two girls)—a title that is in some ways more accurate.[39] The list also includes enigmatic works such as a mysterious bronze so-called study for *Seated Woman,* a title that could refer to several sculptures.

The thirteen sculptures clearly engaged Parisian critics and gave them a new aspect of Matisse's art to consider.[40] Excluding conservative critics who either ignored or dismissed Matisse, reaction to the painter's sculpture was largely favorable. Roger Marx, a critic who had championed Matisse in 1904 but had later become less enthusiastic, was once again laudatory: "M. Henri Matisse shows that he possesses the most enviable gifts: I refer here to certain of his sculptures, to his figure studies after the model, and to that still life whose sumptuousness captivates and conquers one irrevocably [*Blue Still Life,* 1907, now in the Barnes Collection]."[41] Louis Vauxcelles, who had long supported Matisse but was not always without criticism, discussed the glass cabinet of Matisse sculptures as containing works "in which the forms sometimes twist and writhe strangely, but where the character is spirited and very much alive."[42] The most extensive commentary came from Pierre Hepp, a reviewer for the *Gazette des Beaux-Arts.* Hepp was critical of Matisse's art and noted its underlying inconsistency: "The most serious reproach, which M. Matisse incurs, is that the relationship between his works is a haphazard one. Each represents an experiment that seems to be sufficient unto itself, made without concern for the one that precedes or follows it."[43]

Hepp's take on Matisse, as Roger Benjamin has demonstrated, derived from a broader criticism, launched by Maurice Denis, accusing Matisse of being overly theoretical and programmatic.[44] Thus Hepp finds favor with what he identifies as Matisse's "intuitive side," which "produces unexpected refinements as well as novel visual graces. It models clay with expressive movement of the thumb—it is the sure guarantee of M. Matisse's authority." At times Hepp almost appears enthusiastic: "M. Matisse has achieved something; the wall filled by his paintings and the glass cabinet furnished with his bronzes prove that the fruit which grows in Utopia is tangible, even if unusual."[45] In aggregate, the criticism of the Salon d'automne of 1908 demonstrates that Matisse's sculpture was not only assimilated into the larger appreciation of his art but also was repeatedly singled out for special mention.

In the years following the 1908 Salon d'automne, from 1908 to 1915, a broad international audience had the opportunity to see Matisse's early sculptural works. Ten sculptures were shown at Paul Cassirer's gallery in Berlin in 1908–1909. Eight each were included in the *Post-Impressionism* exhibitions organized by Roger Fry at the Grafton Gallery in London in 1910 and 1912.[46] Twelve were featured in the earliest exhibition focused primarily on Matisse's sculpture held at Alfred Stieglitz's Little Galleries of the Photo-Secession in New York in 1912. Thirteen works were shown

Fig. 52. Edward Steichen, Rodin with *Hand of God,* c. 1902(?). Gum bichromate print. Musée Rodin, Paris.

Fig. 53. Edward Steichen, Matisse with plaster cast of *The Serpentine,* Issy-les-Moulineaux, 1909. Archives Matisse, Paris.

in an exhibition, *Henri Matisse: Tableaux du Maroc et sculpture,* organized in 1913 by Félix Fénéon at the gallery of Bernheim-Jeune, Matisse's main dealer. And in 1915, during the early part of World War I, Walter Pach at the Montross Gallery in New York was able to arrange a comprehensive exhibition that included drawing, etching, lithography, painting, and eleven sculptures—seventy-four works in all. The catalogues that survive confirm that the same sculptures were resubmitted repeatedly—usually consisting of *The Serf, Reclining Nude I (Aurora), The Serpentine, Woman Leaning On Her Hands* (cat. 24, pp. 127–28), and sometimes *Two Negresses* and the heads of *Jeannette* (cat. 80–89, pp. 200–203, 206, 273, 274).

Much of the critical commentary about those exhibitions is brief and journalistic. Unusual for its detail is Roger Fry's discussion of Matisse's sculpture published in defense of his second postimpressionist exhibition, in 1912.[47] Of course, Fry had organized the show. Unlike Pierre Hepp who, in 1908, had reproached Matisse for the "haphazard" relationship between his works, Fry believed that the artist's sculpture evolved coherently. Citing the *Jeannette* series as proof, he writes of Matisse:

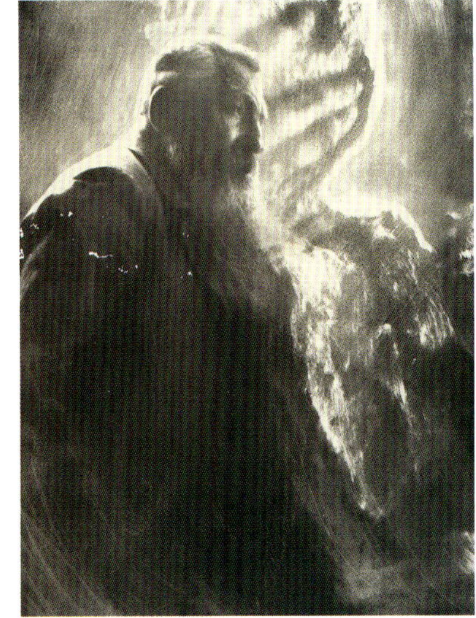

> He indeed is a singularly precise and methodical artist—one whose intelligence keeps pace with his sensibility, making clear to him at each point the next position to be gained. There is absolutely nothing fantastical or whimsical about Matisse, nothing, when one has seized his method of expression, that is bewildering or disconcerting. All proceeds by singularly clear and deliberate steps towards a definite end. As an illustration of his method the four busts of a woman [the *Jeannettes*] are particularly instructive. In the first state he has rendered the head more or less naturalistically. In each successive state he has amplified the forms, working always towards a more complete and inevitable plastic unity.[48]

The difference between Fry's and Hepp's assessments of the cohesiveness of Matisse's production may lie in the fact that, in 1908, Matisse had not yet produced the serial *Jeannettes*. These challenging pieces, together with the *Serpentine,* were by far the most radical in their deformation of anatomy; they caused considerable resistance and even outrage when they were exhibited in America.

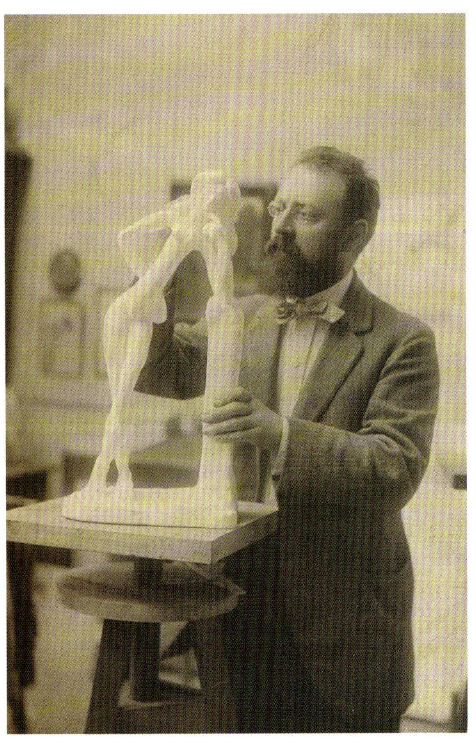

In the spring of 1908, Alfred Stieglitz launched the first of three remarkable exhibitions (the others in 1910 and 1912) that introduced Matisse's art to American audiences. The earliest efforts to import cutting-edge European modernism to New York, they were a result of the collaboration of the photographers Edward Steichen and Alfred Stieglitz, co-editors of the publication *Camera Work* and curators of the Little Galleries of the Photo-Secession—known more concisely as 291 (the address on Fifth Avenue). John Cauman has described Steichen's "scouting expedition" to Paris, where he befriended the Steins, Leo and his sister Gertrude and their older brother Michael and his wife Sarah.[49] Through them, Steichen learned of the latest developments in French art and saw some of the greatest fauve canvases hanging on the walls of their apartments. He met Matisse through Sarah Stein in 1907 and would photograph him in his studio at Issy-les-Moulineaux in 1909.

Steichen's photographs survive, two depicting Matisse wearing a smock, wielding a modeling tool, and working on the unfinished clay of *The Serpentine.* The anatomy of the figure is fully fleshed out and, in one of the photographs, we appear to witness the moment where the legs are pared down. In the second photograph (cat. 165, p. 172), later published in *Camera Work,* Matisse gazes intently at the female figure, his head cocked at an angle that collides at right angles with the cant of the spine of the figure and the poised sculpting tool. The sculptural figure, shot up close with its back to the viewer, hovers in an indeterminate space between the artist and the spectator. Steichen had perfected this sort of pictorialist rhetoric—rhetoric specific to the depiction of artistic genius—in dramatic photographs he had taken of Rodin a number of years previously (fig. 52).

Fig. 54. Photograph of *The Serf* and *Reclining Nude (Aurora)* in Michael and Sarah Stein's apartment, rue Madame, Paris, 1908.

A third photograph was taken at a later date and depicts Matisse, wearing a jacket and bowtie, inspecting the finished plaster of *The Serpentine.* Several months must have passed between the two photographic sessions, time for Matisse to finish the clay, to produce a mold, and to cast the sculpture in plaster. Matisse must have been aware of the photographer's intentions and cooperated with Steichen to produce what amounts to a brief essay on the process involved in the creation of one of his most radical sculptures.

In 1912, Steichen and Matisse collaborated again in the selection of works for the first exhibition held anywhere devoted primarily to Matisse's sculpture. Six bronzes, five plaster casts, one terracotta, and twelve drawings were exhibited in the third Matisse exhibition held at Stieglitz's gallery, 291. It ran from March 14 to April 6, 1912.[50] The choices were supposed to reflect Matisse's evolution as a sculptor. Once again *The Serf* was exhibited but so were some of his far more difficult pieces: *The Serpentine* and plasters of the first three states of the head of *Jeannette.* While *The Serf* at least received occasional praise from the press, one critic calling it a "work of genius" and comparing it to Jean-François Millet's *Man with the Hoe,* there was little sympathy for Matisse's more daring works. Charles DeKay, writing in *American Art News,* describes Matisse's modeling of *The Serpentine:* "He takes, let us say, a female figure and models it as well as he can. But it's too commonplace; too human. So he cuts away the flesh and some of the ribs from the torso, slaps enormous calves on the legs, draws out the neck, slams down the forehead, pulls out the ears, gives a twist to the whole figure and calls it 'Serpentine.'" Arthur Hoeber, writing for the *New York Globe,* could not fathom why Matisse should "ignore the human figure as the good Lord has made it and as men know it." He was particularly troubled by the three heads of *Jeannette,* whose meaning he confessed was beyond him but which he nonetheless found to be: "decadent, unhealthy, certainly unreal, like some dreadful nightmare." David Lloyd, writing for the *New York Evening Post,* was a touch wittier, observing: "The sculptor goes after the gargoyle in human nature, but then apparently realities begin to cramp him, and as in the parable, the last state is worse than the first." James Huneker of the *New York Sun* at least understood Matisse's historical context when he wrote: "After Rodin—what? Surely not Henri Matisse. We can see the power and individuality of Matisse as a painter, particularly as a draughtsman, but in modeling he produces gooseflesh." Interestingly, all these disparaging reviews and numerous others were collected and reprinted in *Camera Work,*[51] but Stieglitz did not see fit to include a laudatory assessment by Felix Grendon, of the radical monthly *The International,* who had asserted that "Matisse's work is the most valuable contemporary contribution to sculpture after the masterpieces of Rodin."[52] Clearly, Stieglitz had a keen sense of the value of scandal in the promotion of modern art in America. The exhibition was exceedingly well attended, drawing more than four thousand visitors over a three-week period.[53]

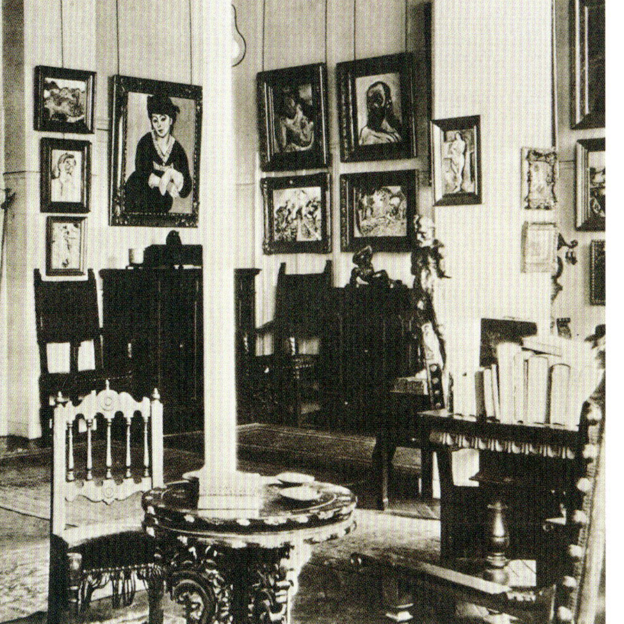

Visual Documentation

No installation photographs exist for the earliest exhibitions of Matisse's sculpture, including the 1904 and 1908 Salons d'automne and the 1906 Druet exhibition. The only photographs from this period that give a sense of his sculptures in situ date from early 1908 and show his work in Sarah and Michael Stein's apartment on the rue Madame, Paris. The Steins amassed a considerable collection of Matisse's paintings so the effect bears some analogy to a gallery setting. We know that Gertrude Stein enjoyed rearranging her collections on the rue des Fleurus in accordance with a kind of gamesmanship: visiting artists such as Matisse or Picasso were seated so as to be able take in their own work.[54] Sarah Stein, who was considerably closer to Matisse than was her sister-in-law, would have arranged the artist's works with great consideration and might even have consulted Matisse, who was a frequent visitor. In one of the surviving photographs we see both *The Serf* and *Reclining Nude I (Aurora)* carefully placed in the corner of a lush, carpeted room (fig. 54). They are

Fig. 55. Roger Fry, *A Room in the Second Post-Impressionist Exhibition (The Matisse Room),* 1912. Oil on canvas, Musée d'Orsay, Paris; Gift of Mrs. Pamela Diamand.

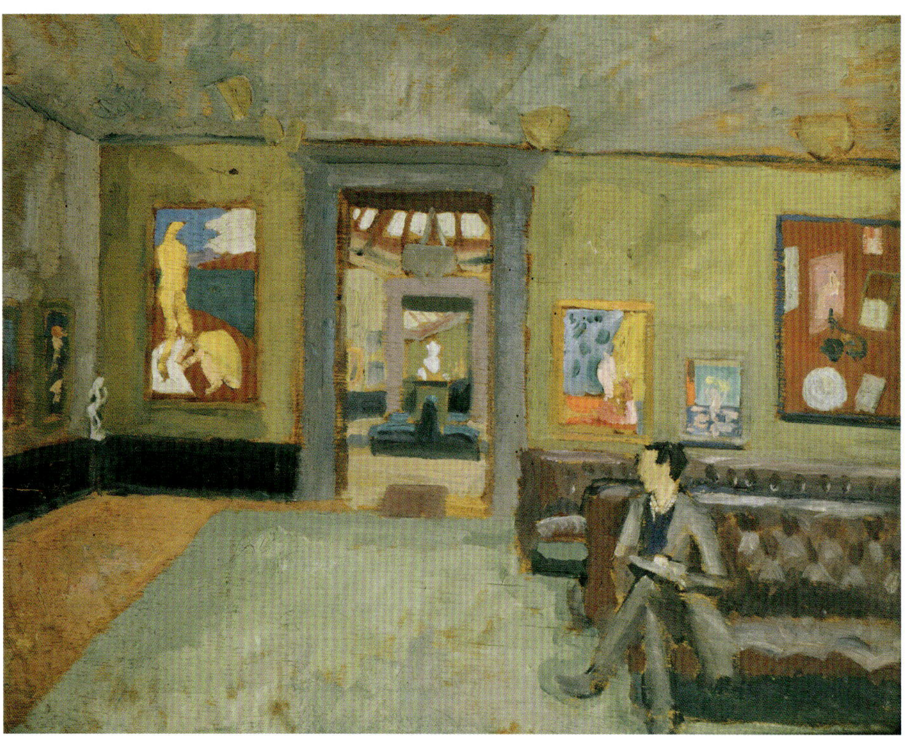

surrounded by paintings of Matisse's family and landscapes. A large portrait of Marguerite hangs slightly above and to the left of Madame Matisse in *The Red Madras Hat* (1907). On the adjacent wall, Matisse's celebrated *Self-Portrait* (1906) is mirrored in the highly self-referential figure of *The Serf.* The placement of *Reclining Nude I (Aurora)* directly in front of Matisse's *Oil Sketch for The Joy of Life (Le bonheur de vivre)* (cat. 31, p. 135) underscores the close conceptual relationship of the nymph to her arcadian home. This is far from casual and establishes the kind of dialogue between sculpture and painting that we will see repeated in the installation of Matisse's works.[55]

Looking for other visual documentation of early Matisse sculpture exhibition, we find a painting by Roger Fry depicting the "Matisse Room" (fig. 55) at the *Second Post-Impressionism Exhibition* held at the Grafton Galleries, London, in 1912. A young man sits in the gallery drawing or taking notes. He cranes his neck to take in a plaster cast of *The Serpentine,* which is standing on some sort of pedestal, in front of the painting *Le Luxe (II).* Looking into the next room we see what appears to be a plaster of one of the states of the head of *Jeannette.* Directly behind the man we see *Still Life with Aubergines, Wild Daffodils,* and prominently, at right, *The Red Studio.*[56] Fry's painterly but realist depiction no doubt accurately records the arrangement of works. The cleverness of his installation lies in the placement of *The Serpentine* in front of *Le Luxe (II);* this mimics the relationship established by Matisse in *The Red Studio* in the same gallery.

Astonishingly, no photographs have surfaced of the Matisse sculpture exhibition held at Stieglitz's 291 gallery in 1912. Individual sculptures were documented and much of the critical commentary was republished in *Camera Work,* but the installation was not illustrated. It is hard to believe that with so many photographers on premise no one recorded this exhibition—especially as other exhibitions, of Brancusi's work in 1914, of African art the same year, and of Picasso and Braque in 1915, were all lavishly documented by Stieglitz.[57]

The earliest photographic images of a Matisse exhibition with a prominent sculptural component come from a show, entitled *Tableaux du Maroc et sculptures,* held at the gallery of his dealer Bernheim-Jeune in 1913 (figs. 56–59). Most of the paintings on display were already sold, which may explain why the show ran for only a week, from April 14 to April 19.[58] Nonetheless, it drew the favorable attention of two important writers, Marcel Sembat and Guillaume Apollinaire. The latter

Fig. 56. Installation photograph, *The Serf* and "The Moroccan Triptych," exhibited as *Tableaux du Maroc et sculptures,* Galerie Bernheim-Jeune, Paris, 1913.

Fig. 57. Installation photograph, *Decorative Figure, The Serpentine, The Serf,* and *Moroccan Café,* exhibited as *Tableaux du Maroc et sculptures,* Galerie Bernheim-Jeune, Paris, 1913.

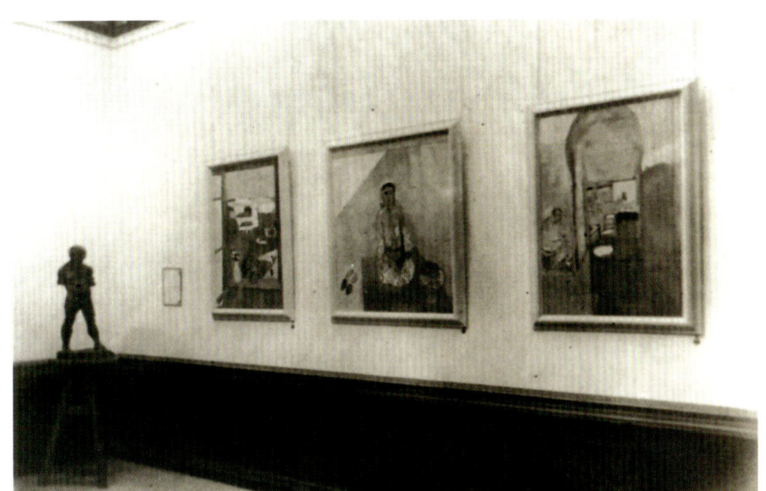

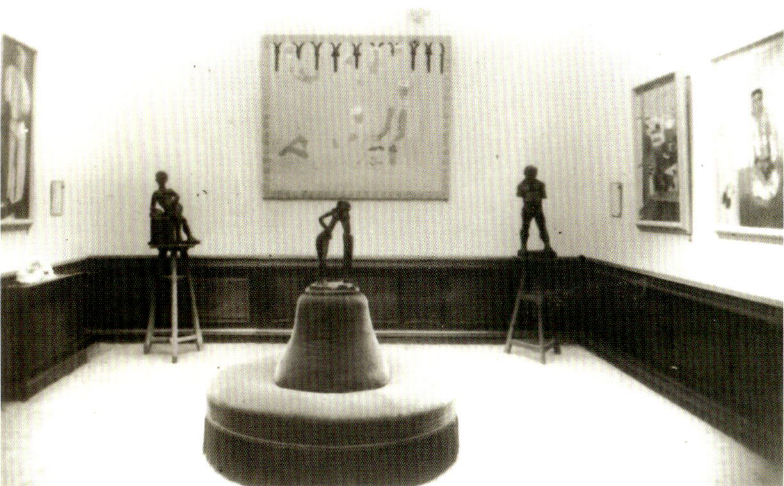

described Matisse's drawing as possessing "the most delicate and refined sensuality" and noted that "these were among the rare works inspired by contemporary North Africa that were not insufferable."[59] Apollinaire focused exclusively on the two-dimensional works. Félix Fénéon, who was in charge of the contemporary section of the otherwise somewhat stodgy Bernheim-Jeune establishment, arranged the exhibition. Correspondence makes it clear, however, that Matisse was consulted on most aspects of the show.[60] Scholars believe that Matisse either hung or approved the hanging of the exhibition.[61]

Sculpture, it would seem, was not the primary subject of *Tableaux du Maroc et sculptures,* which as the title implies was meant to highlight a remarkable group of paintings Matisse produced on two recent visits to Morocco, in early 1912 and the winter of 1912–1913. The sculpture, by contrast, included a survey of Matisse's earlier works, beginning with his first freestanding piece. The five installation photographs that survive illustrate a plaster cast of *Jaguar Devouring a Hare* (cat. 1, pp. 101–102, 105), *The Serf, Decorative Figure* (cat. 66, p. 181), *Seated Nude (Olga)* (cat. 67, p. 183), and *Jeannette II,* and plaster casts of *Jeannette I* and *Jeannette III.* Six additional works not visible in the photographs are listed in the exhibition catalogue. Most surprisingly, the photographs reveal one work that is not listed in the catalogue, *The Serpentine*. The figure is given pride of place, poised on top of a round settee in the middle of the room (fig. 57). Her absence from the catalogue is an important clue supporting the belief that Matisse was directly involved in the installation. It suggests that, once again, as he had in 1904 and at later Salon d'automne exhibitions, Matisse made last-minute changes to the checklist.[62] A letter survives, dated March 26, 1913, in which Fenéon seeks Matisse's approval regarding the drawings to be included in the catalogue—this is only nineteen days before the exhibition was to open. It hardly seems likely that Fenéon would have consulted Matisse on drawings but added a major sculpture without such approval. It is more probable that Matisse supervised at the hanging and added *The Serpentine* in its central position.

Evident in the photographs, most of the paintings in the *Tableaux du Maroc et sculptures* exhibition were deliberately displayed as triads.[63] Ivan Morosov purchased one of the most celebrated of these groupings, the so-called Moroccan triptych (fig. 56), which consisted of (from left to right): *Landscape Viewed from a Window, On the Terrace,* and *The Casbah Gate.* That the specific arrangement was determined by Matisse is known from a sketch he included in a letter to Morosov, dated April 19, 1913, the day the exhibition closed.[64] Matisse was so concerned with the hanging of the paintings that he made his own frames for them, painted a neutral gray.[65] The installation photographs show the way in which Matisse employed sculptures to distinguish and separate different triadic groups (fig. 57). *The Serf* we see used to mark the transition between the Moroccan triptych and the end wall. Like the outer attendant figures of a multipaneled altarpiece, *The Serf* and *Decorative*

Fig. 58. Installation photograph, *Jaguar Devouring a Hare* and *Decorative Figure,* exhibited as *Tableaux du Maroc et sculptures,* Galerie Bernheim-Jeune, Paris, 1913.

Fig. 59. Installation photograph, *Jeanette III, Seated Riffian,* and *Jeanette I,* exhibited as *Tableaux du Maroc et sculptures,* Galerie Bernheim-Jeune, Paris, 1913.

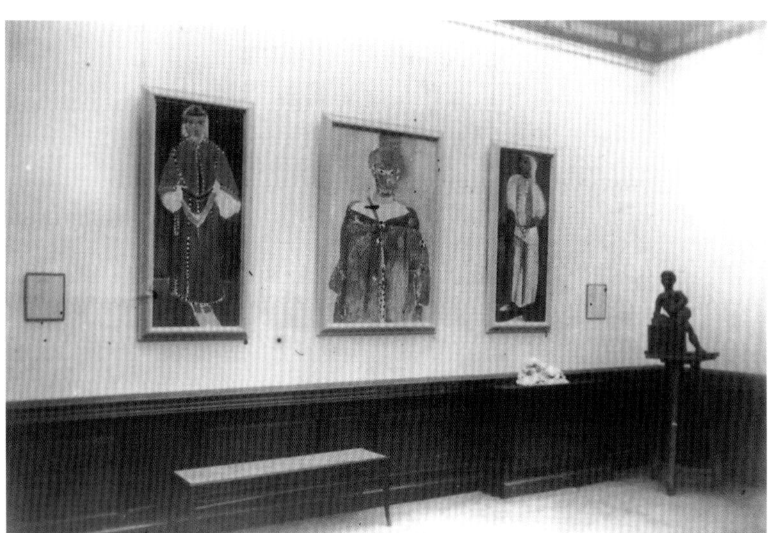

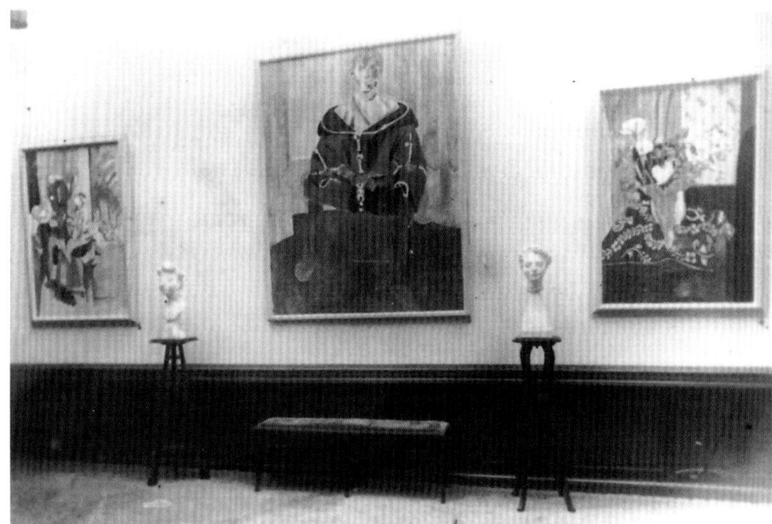

Figure flank the painting the *Moroccan Café*. Among the paintings, this large work dominated the exhibition both in terms of size and because it was not part of a triad. Its prominence was deliberate as it was one of the paintings available for sale—Shchukin would purchase it several months after the exhibition. *Decorative Figure* set up another triad (fig. 58) that included *Zora Standing, The Standing Riffian,* and *Fatma, the Mulatto Woman.* Unidentified drawings on either end of the triad also served to isolate this grouping. The plaster *Jaguar Devouring a Hare* resting beneath the image of Fatma, at right, created an element of asymmetry but, because of its light tone, it did not disrupt the ensemble. On the adjacent wall, one of the photographs (fig. 59) records a third triad of paintings dramatically interspersed with two plaster heads of *Jeannette.* From left to right, the ensemble included the painting *Calla Lilies,* the sculpture *Jeanette III, The Seated Riffian* (the largest iconic central painted work), *Jeannette I* (another sculpture), and the picture *Calla Lilies, Irises, and Mimosas.* Matisse used the two plaster *Jeannettes* like apotropaic guardians; they symmetrically reinforced the central *Riffian*'s direct stare to create an imposing triangular front of gazes.[66] *Jeannette I* and *III* were selected because they were both plasters. *Jeannette II,* normally part of the series, was exhibited separately, probably because the work was cast in bronze. Thus color and material consistency were more important to Matisse than maintaining the sculptural series intact.

So what does the installation of *Tableaux du Maroc et sculptures* teach us about the way Matisse viewed sculpture and wished the public to see it? Clearly he sought to create significant relationships between the paintings and sculptures. The latter can function as simple, rhythmic markers dividing the space, but they can also be placed so as to reinforce the various modalities of vision that Matisse had explored in the adjacent paintings. The *Riffian* and the *Jeannette*s work together, intensifying the spectator's sense of being aggressively scrutinized by a group. *The Serpentine* and the *Moroccan Café,* whose central figures gaze meditatively at two goldfish, seem calculated to reinforce a sense of contemplative viewing. Jack Flam addresses the interplay between two- and three-dimensional bodies somewhat differently when he discusses this flow of visual energies in more traditional formalist terms: Matisse's "inclusion of a representative selection of his sculptures with the Moroccan paintings at the Bernheim-Jeune exhibition is no coincidence. It reflects his concern at the time with Cézannian notions of balancing two- and three-dimensional forms of energetic, dematerialized pictorial space."[67]

The balanced energies are not, however, exclusively formal and they appear to be generated by the representational dynamics of figures whose intersecting visions unify and activate the entire gallery space. Nowhere do the trajectories of all these lines of sight converge with greater concentration than on the figure of *The Serpentine*—Matisse's late addition, which stands at the hub of the entire exhibition space. Matisse clearly must have recalled the potent relationships critics had perceived in the arrangement of the "salle des fauves" at the Salon d'automne in 1905. This time he would occupy the central sculptural position as well as the walls.

Matisse based *The Serpentine* on a photograph from a magazine, *Mes modèles,* which illustrated nude models in standard academic poses.[68] The photograph (fig. 2, p. 3) shows a dark-haired stocky woman leaning against a false balustrade before a studio screen depicting the sea. Her legs are crossed and a finger of her left hand is held to her mouth—features Matisse included in the sculpture. The artist revealed his source and artistic intentions to Alfred Barr: "I had to help me a photograph of a woman, a little fat but very harmonious in form and movement. I thinned and composed the forms so that the movement would be completely comprehensible from all points of view."[69] *The Serpentine*'s central placement in the gallery space on a round support invites the spectator to circle the work and observe its constantly shifting perspectives. Yet the invitation to comprehend movement through movement does not lead to any resolution or certainty. Yve-Alain Bois makes this point as he evokes the experience:

> To circle around a Matisse sculpture is to see an object constantly change identity, species, genus, and kingdom. The sculptural metaphor is no longer intended to assure your imaginary possession of the object and to rid it of its materiality, as it was in the Classical age; with Matisse it is even founded on this materiality in order to dispel all our certainties and sensitize us to the infinity of meanings.[70]

Matisse's installation invites us to examine *The Serpentine* from all perspectives, but in another sense, her placement makes her invisible. Seated on the settee that supports her, the audience can peruse the walls from her perspective and with her contemplative attitude, but they cannot see her. The multiple configurations of subject and object that this suggests enables us to regard the sculpture as a surrogate of sorts occupying our position. Within the larger gallery experience, Matisse's sculpture mimics its audience. Viewers who accept the invitation to sit with *The Serpentine* become part of the exhibit. The placement of the bronze figure on a comfortable-looking piece of furniture also brings to mind Matisse's most notorious and misconstrued metaphor about his art, his "dream" of "an art that could be for every mental worker, for the businessman as well as the man of letters, for example, a soothing, calming influence on the mind, something like a good armchair that provides relaxation from fatigue."[71] Matisse's dream of comfortable seatedness proves elusive and is rife with ironies when we consider the *Tableaux du Maroc et sculptures* installation. Seatedness implies positioning—the armchair suggests an ideal position from which all can be viewed in a passive, relaxed state. The circular settee, in spite of its promise of comfort, ensures the diffusion of the spectator's gaze and refutes the possibility of a singular commanding perspective.[72] The rest of the exhibition layout reinforces this sense: one Zora stares at another Zora while the seated *Riffian* confronts his standing counterpart on the next wall. Only through physical circulation can a multiplicity of satisfying relationships be apprehended, but none is definitive. Movement, of sorts, is structured into the installation just as it is into Matisse's best paintings.[73] It complements the marks of process encoded on the surfaces of his sculpture, the suggestion of mutability and future states—also witnessed in the serial heads of *Jeannette.* Such an emphasis on duration and flux, and on multiple reconfigurations of elements, may be informed by Matisse's growing awareness of cubist collage.

Photographs of Matisse's Sculpture

Matisse is known to have employed photographs from several magazines—*Mes modèles, Nu esthétique,* and *L'Humanité feminin*—as sources from which to model sculptures, including *The Serpentine, Small Crouching Nude with Arms, Two Negresses,* and perhaps also *Reclining Nude I.* His use of

Fig. 60. Eugène Druet, photograph of August Rodin's *Ève*, 1898. Gelatin silver print. Musée Rodin, Paris.

Fig. 61. Photograph of *Reclining Nude I (Aurora)*, copying the angle of the photograph by Eugène Druet and supposedly authorized by Matisse.

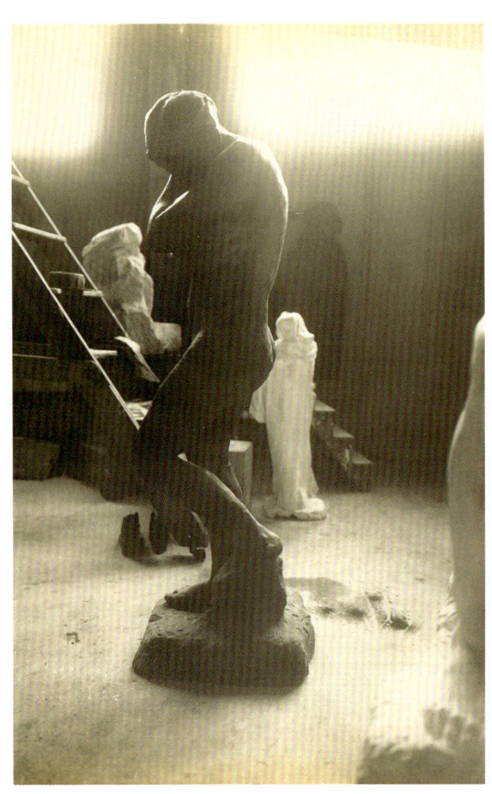

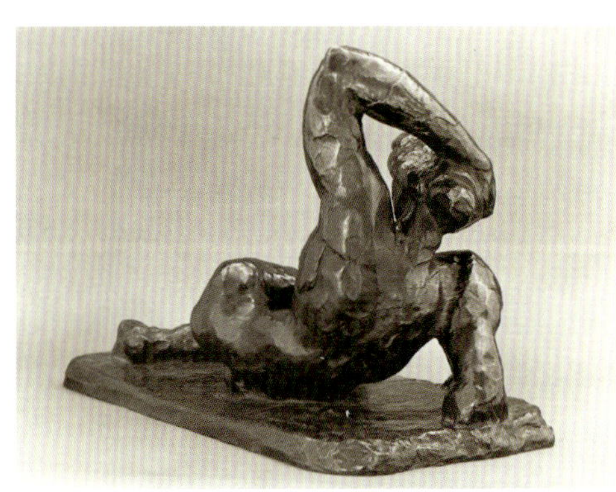

such photographic sources has received a fair amount of scholarly attention.[74] Less commented upon is his relationship with his primary early photographer Eugène Druet. Druet had a typical entrepreneurial career for his time, the late nineteenth and early twentieth century. He began as a café owner and amateur photographer and befriended Auguste Rodin in 1896.[75] For a period, until they had a partial falling out in 1900, the sculptor made Druet his official photographer and gave him unprecedented access to his studio and works. Druet also photographed the sculptures of Matisse's contemporaries, Emile-Antoine Bourdelle and Aristide Maillol. In 1903, Druet established his own art gallery and photographic reproduction business in the rue du faubourg Saint-Honoré. He was an innovator both in terms of his technique—which was rapid, versatile, and mobile—and because he provided accessible photographic services to artists and helped to create a truly modern, fluid economy of reproducible images.

A bill from the Galerie E. Druet addressed to Matisse and dated February 26, 1904, shows that the artist was quick to employ the photographer.[76] The document itemizes services including the reproduction of paintings, mounting of drawings, and purchase of twelve photographs of works by Rodin—calling into question the impression Matisse created in later interviews that he was no longer interested in Rodin after their brief meeting around 1900.[77] The Galerie d'estampes et photographie of the Bibliothèque national de France holds four boxes of folios containing Druet's photographs of Matisse's paintings and graphic works (not his sculpture), a collection that attests to a long professional relationship that continued with the Druet firm long after the photographer's death in 1916.[78] Although Druet's early photographs of Rodin's works were at times evocative studies executed in an atmospheric pictorialist style—see for instance the *Ève* (fig. 60)—the sixteen Druet photographs of Matisse's sculptures that this author has seen are straightforward and businesslike reproductions.[79] Photographs of Matisse's sculpture by Druet are not easily seen as none are preserved in the main French libraries.[80] Yve-Alain Bois, who was able to gain access to a number of these images, described them as "difficult to reproduce" owing to "too little or too much contrast."[81] Matisse apparently specified the angles from which his sculptures were shot, and, somewhat selectively, the same angles are reproduced in the photography of the *Catalogue raisonné de l'œuvre sculpté* published by Claude Duthuit in 1997.[82] We thus have a fairly good record of some of the angles Matisse preferred when viewing his sculptures. Seeking to characterize these views, Bois notes that "Matisse rarely chooses frontal perspective. . . . what matters most to him is to find the most eccentric, least expected point of view, which is often where the arabesques close the sculpture in on itself (and which therefore provides the least information on its contortions)."[83]

Three Druet photographs record the sculpture *Reclining Nude I (Aurora);* two are taken from its principal rectangular axes: straight on lengthwise and from the short side looking at the figure's feet. The third photograph (fig. 61) is taken at a diagonal angle looking at the figure's back from behind the raised arm. These multiple images of the same sculpture confirm Bois's larger observation that Matisse "seems to take pleasure in the sharp discordances from one to the next." Elsewhere, Bois notes more generally the difficulty of photographing Matisse's sculpture, mainly because "there is no good or bad way of going about it: each work requires as many points of view as can be obtained by physically moving around it."[84] Again we are left with an image of endless circulation and limitless perspectives.

At times Matisse did render definite views of his sculpture for functional purposes. Starting around 1936, he created a record book of sculptures with notations on the numbered casts (henceforth referred to as the *1936 Notebook*), which includes quick sketches of almost all of his sculptures produced up until then.[85] These are somewhat comical line-drawn caricatures of the sculptures, meant for quick recognition. As many of Matisse's titles were similar or kept shifting, this shorthand was actually more efficient. It allowed Matisse to send his family members Marguerite, Jean, and later on his assistant Lydia Delectorskaya, to visit his depositories of plasters in Paris and recognize the sculptures that were to be moved to the foundries for casting.[86] The drawings are not without wit and intelligence. Most of the views are simple and frontal (fig. 62); on occasion, however, Matisse employs the angle that most fascinated him. This is the case with the sketch for *Jaguar Devouring a Hare* (fig. 63), which replicates the high angle from the rear that best captures the arabesque—variants of which were also recorded in drawings he produced at the time he sculpted the work, currently in the collection of the Musée départemental Matisse, Le Cateau-Cambrésis.

Further evidence of the ways in which Matisse wished his sculpture to be seen and what role he assigned to it within the larger trajectory of his art can be ascertained from the sculptures themselves. The common element in a production at times viewed as experimental and "haphazard" seems to be that his sculptures possess a quality of visual self-consciousness or a shared sense of "made-to-be-looked-at-ness." Something about the sculptures themselves places them and us in a visual relationship constructed and desired by Matisse, a connection first observed by William Tucker in a thought-provoking essay, "Matisse's Sculpture: The Grasped and the Seen." Commenting on Matisse's figural sculpture, Tucker wrote:

> The figure is the motif which provides that particular tension between the physical and the visual, between concept and percept, which characterizes his sculpture. While the small size and the intense sensation of full volume push the work into the hand, the image subverts this physicality, distances the sculpture, withdraws it from our grasp. I say "image," not figure, advisedly, for Matisse consciously models the figure seen at a distance.[87]

Does a figure become an "image" when seen at a distance? Is the sensation of "made-to-be-looked-at-ness" comparable to Tucker's definition of "image"? To some degree yes, but there may be more to it. In a discussion of drawing and sculpture, Matisse commented on the issue of distance in both media. "A drawing," he explained, "is a sculpture, but it has the advantage that it can be viewed closely enough for one to detect suggestions of form that must be much more definitely expressed in sculpture, which must carry from a distance."[88] Matisse endorses an expressive

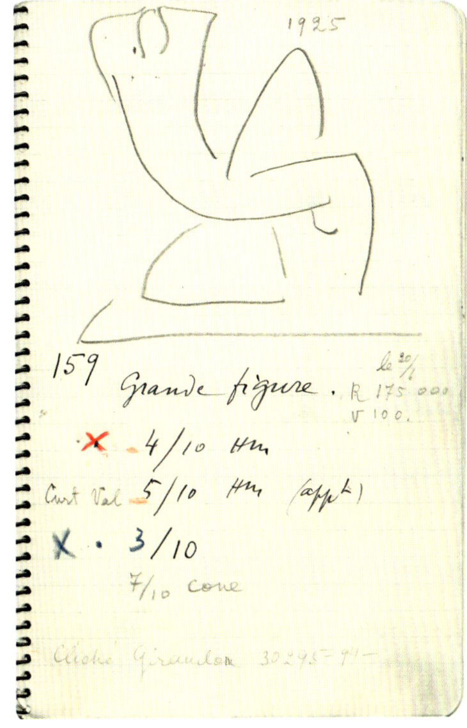

Fig. 62. Drawing of *Large Seated Nude* from Matisse's notebook of sculptures, dated 1936. Archives Matisse, Paris.

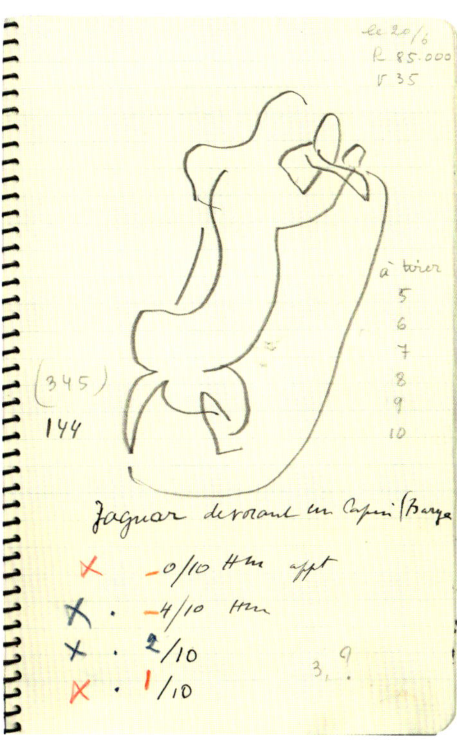

Fig. 63. Drawing of *Jaguar Devouring a Hare (copy after Barye)* from Matisse's notebook of sculptures, dated 1936. Archives Matisse, Paris.

exaggeration of form that anticipates the viewer's looking from a distance. Great sculpture tends to "carry" and this holds true of the distinctive profiles created by Matisse. The towering raised arm of *Reclining Nude I (Aurora)* or the curved S-shape of *Madeleine I* come to mind. Ironically, the drawing for *Large Seated Nude,* from Matisse's *1936 Notebook* (fig. 62), provides one of the clearest demonstrations of his notion of the "definite expression of form" required for sculpture to carry. In his caricature, Matisse distills the basics of the sculpture's form to illustrate it as if seen at a distance.

The quality of visual self-consciousness that Matisse's sculptures evoke includes and extends beyond both Tucker's notions of image and figures seen at a distance and Matisse's explanation. Distance alone eliminates optical detail and emphasizes gesture, but all manner of visual conventions and traditions also play a role. In particular, let us examine four areas of artistic manipulation that come under the headings plinths, copies, self-display, and seeing sculptures. Matisse made use of some of these elements in almost all of his sculpture. All four play a role in *Large Seated Nude,* making it the synthesis of most of his sculptural principles and discoveries.

The plinth in sculpture, like the frame in painting, establishes a mystical boundary between ordinary space occupied with things and artistic space filled by rarified visual material.[89] Rhetorically, the plinth proclaims that here is something monumental and worthy of being looked at. In *The Serf,* an early sculpture, Matisse sets the work on a large plinth cast in bronze and with the somewhat pompous literary title prominently inscribed on the front. This is in the grand tradition of the public works of the nineteenth century. Emmanuel Frémiet's *Age of Stone* comes to mind, or Constantin Meunier's various sculptures of labor; and, even without a cast inscription, Rodin's allegorical *Age of Bronze* carried on the tradition. Matisse launched *The Serf* with this sort of ambitious intention, but, in looking at the results, we see contradictions immediately. This muscular and highly masculine figure is armless and so rendered functionless; the monumental laborer is incapable of work. The underlying message, and *The Serf* by its very plinth still proclaims to have one, concerns impotence. The piece both employs and subverts the idea behind the monumental rhetorical sculpture still practiced by Rodin.[90] In the *1936 Notebook,* Matisse pokes fun at his sculpture, misspelling the title he himself had inscribed onto the base as "Le Cerf" (the stag).[91] Like a stag losing its antlers, *The Serf,* in losing his arms, has been emasculated. Much of the irony stems from the tension between plinth and sculpture, the plinth announcing the visual spectacle.

Although he never repeated the sort of inscribed plinth used for *The Serf,* Matisse experimented throughout his career with different rectangular bases, exploring the relationships between his figures and the hard-edged forms of the bases. The four-sidedness of bases holds the promise that sculpture might be easily integrated into its surrounding architecture. Matisse's figures almost always resist such comfortable accommodation; the twisting *Reclining Nude I (Aurora)* refuses to be satisfyingly revealed from any cardinal axis. When Matisse's figures do yield to the directional imperatives of the base, he makes fun of them, as he does in the small *Crouching Venus* (cat. 97, p. 220). For this figure, a copy after a well-known Greco-Roman prototype, Matisse has tilted her body up to flatten it for frontal viewing, as in the antique variants of the type. Although this is hard to see in photographs, the sculptor has pushed the figure all the way to the back edge of her plinth, effectively turning her into a bookend.[92] For *Large Seated Nude,* Matisse loosely borrowed the uncomfortable pose of Michelangelo's *Night,* in the Medici chapel, to develop his definitive base-resistant figure. Her upper body twists toward the frontal axis, carving out monumental negative spaces, but because the figure is not aligned with the plinth, the incomplete turn projects the internal tension of the anatomy into the surrounding architectural space. The work has confounded curators who sometimes resort to setting it at an angle—as it was for the installation at Galerie Bernheim-Jeune in 1958. Matisse did occasionally eliminate the plinth or bases altogether as in the cases of *Reclining Nude*s *II* and *III,* but he does not definitively banish it. The struggle he stages between the orientation of the figures and the architectural implications of the plinth does not, however, diminish the role such bases play as conventional monumental devices underscoring the visual spectacle.

Matisse's sculpture frequently doubles its visual, artistic appeal because he copies either well-known sculptures or standard academic poses derived from classical statuary. The modern copy, and especially the view of Matisse as a copyist, is still not prevalent in spite of considerable scholarship on the topic since the mid-1980s.[93] It is hard to overcome the weight of modernist interpretation for which authorship and originality are all-important; copying was, however, integral to Matisse's education and practice. With regard to Matisse's painting, this topic has been explored; his sculptural copying remains less studied. We know that his first free-standing sculpture was a copy after Barye's *Jaguar Devouring a Hare,* but he produced numerous direct and indirect copies throughout his career, including *Copy after Puget's Écorché* (fig. 31, p. 32), the *Thorn Extractor* (cat. 25, p. 129), *Vénus accroupie Michel-Ange* (in this exhibition as *Crouching Venus,* cat. 97), *The Serpentine* (based on a photograph of a model that was in turn based on a classical antecedent, most probably the Farnese *Hercules*), *Reclining Nudes I, II,* and *III,* derived from countless reclining nymphs of the Ariadne type, *Large Seated Nude,* based on Michelangelo's *Night* from the Medici chapel, and many more. With the exception of specific portrait heads and a few torsos, it is hard to think of any sculpture by Matisse that does not evoke a source in earlier statuary. Yve-Alain Bois broadens this claim when he observes that even the figures in Matisse's paintings derive their poses from these older sculptural antecedents.[94]

These sculptures of sculptures have much in common with his painted copies of paintings. Of the copy after Chardin's painting *The Ray,* Benjamin comments that "Matisse performs a modernist re-presentation of Chardin wherein the ambiguity of the brushwork forcibly asserts the presence of the copyist as originating author."[95] Similarly, it is the surface facture of Matisse's sculptures where the artist distinguishes his works from their sources. His surfaces are never representational in an illusionistic sense; rather they are marked with cuts and incident evoking the sculpting process. Indeed, in a comparison between Matisse's sculptures and their sources, it appears that the skin of those figures has somehow been removed and reformulated through additive modeling and subtractive cutting with sculpting tools. Matisse's choice to copy Puget's *Écorché* (a flayed man) thus evinces his process and was undoubtedly intended as ironic, self-referencing commentary on his treatment of surfaces. Whereas in his painterly copies Matisse tended to reproduce one master through another—for instance, Chardin's *Ray* executed with Cézanne's brushwork—in his sculptural copying, this sort of secondary stylistic appropriation is less clear.[96] One can argue that he employs surfaces inspired by Rodin or even translates Cézanne's brushwork into sculptural facture, but this argument creates a confusing series of (paternal) references. It is, however, the original sculptural source of his copy, lurking behind any secondary quotations in handling, that contributes the most to the sense of "made to-be-seen-ness." A sculpture of a sculpture carries an enhanced visual charge even where the recollection of the original source is unspecific or half-forgotten.

With the exception of *The Serf,* the *Copy after Puget's Écorché,* three portraits, and Christ from the chapel at Vence, the vast bulk of Matisse's sculpture depicts women. Among these works, a substantial number employ conventional, sexually coded gestures of luxuriating and self-display. These figural gestures already appeared in Matisse's early arcadian landscape *Le bonheur de vivre*—for example, the gestures of the standing garlanded woman with raised arms, at the far left of the painting, and of the central reclining nymph with the raised arm. Variants of these poses occur in *Seated Nude with Arms on Head* (cat. 35, pp. 148–49), *Standing Nude, Arms on Head, Upright Nude with Arched Back, Torso with Head (La Vie), Reclining Figure with Chemise* (cat. 30, pp. 133–34), *Reclining Nudes I (Aurora), II,* and *III, Small Nude in an Armchair* (cat. 100, p. 220), *Large Seated*

Nude, Standing Nude (Katia) (cat. 132, p. 255), and *Venus in a Shell I* and *II* (cat. 123, 124, pp. 245–46, 248, 251). The raised arm (or arms) motif with all its erotic suggestions extends backward through Ingres's *Vénus Anadyomène* and *Bain Turc* to Michelangelo's *Dying Slave* and Hellenistic sculptures such as the *Wounded Amazon,* the Barberini *Faun,* and various versions of the sleeping Ariadne.[97] By the nineteenth century the pose was usually reserved for female figures. Albert Elsen includes it among the "'platitudes' of salon postures" that Matisse renovates. He notes that the "model's gesture shows that thousands of similar interpretations have not deprived it of instinct and energy." He steps back, however, from the suggestion of innate, biological expressiveness, postulating a cultural basis for such a pose: "perhaps for the artist it was an emblem of femininity, no matter how unseductive."[98] Francis Frascina, presenting a postmodernist semiotic view, describes the "odalisque" pose, and its variant the "Vénus Anadyomène" pose, as a "gendered signifier of unblemished availability . . . a token of possession, a colonization of the 'other.'"[99] The notion that the meanings of these poses are fixed and stable and that such "othering" occurs every time they are invoked remains open to debate.[100] The sculptures employ the visual codes of gendered sexual self-display, and at times they seem to parody them—as with the *Venus in a Shell I,* whose raised elbows are so exaggerated that they become transformed into rabbit ears. The use of these conventional codes of display adds another layer to the imperative each sculpture produces for the viewer to look at it. Although voyeuristic expectations are perhaps aroused by the poses, Matisse denies us the pleasure of traditional anatomical surfaces; we are rewarded instead by free-floating marks of artistic deformation. This enhances the disjunction Tucker described between the tactile appeal of surfaces and the coded expectation created by the figure seen at a distance.

Occasionally, to activate vision and make it the proper subject of his sculpture, Matisse makes use of seeing figures. He rarely sculpted figures with eyes and even when he did so, mainly in portrait heads, these are not the figures evoking the most acute sense of sight. The impression that his figures can see results almost exclusively from the manipulation of posture and gestures of attentiveness. In such works, vision can be inwardly directed as it is in the *Two Negresses,* who are not only connected through their embrace but also by their locked eyes, or it can radiate outward. Matisse's early sculpture rarely confronts the viewer with a sense of returned sight. *The Serf* looks down at the soil before him, the locus of the labor that imprisons him and of the matter that in a biblical sense will reclaim him. *Reclining Nude I (Aurora)* appears to survey her own body, reinforcing the fantasy of her erotic self-absorption. It is only in the early sculptures from Nice that we begin to get apparently sighted sculptures, such as *Figure with Cushion* (cat. 111, p. 230), whose attentive posture suggests that she returns our gaze. One might, at the risk of overreaching, note that the figure's pose and attitude, in spite of its small scale, evoke Victorine Meurand confidently staring back at her spectators in Manet's modernist icon *Olympia.* It is difficult to understand how Matisse generates this sense from a few blobs of roughly modeled clay until one recalls Tucker's notion that Matisse sculpts the figure as if seen at a distance.[101] In public spaces, of course, we are aware that people are looking at us long before we can make out one another's eyes. Matisse appears to have studied the bodily clues that enable us to make such determinations. His other sculpture from 1918, *Seated Nude Clasping Her Right Leg* (cat. 68, pp. 186–87), lacks any facial features, yet clearly conveys the sense of looking intently to her proper left.

None of Matisse's sculptures possesses as commanding a sense of sight as *Large Seated Nude.* This impression is quite remarkable for, although Matisse modeled the rounded form of the eyes, there is no indication that they are open or closed.[102] The sculpture therefore employs multiple codes to suggest vision. Matisse's use of the conventional raised arm gesture would seem to be about self-display, making the figure the erotic subject of vision; but, curiously, it also contributes to the sense of her seeing. She leans back and gains an elevated position from where she surveys the world. *Large*

Fig. 64. Installation photograph of the Matisse retrospective exhibition held at the Thannhauser Gallery, Berlin, 1930.

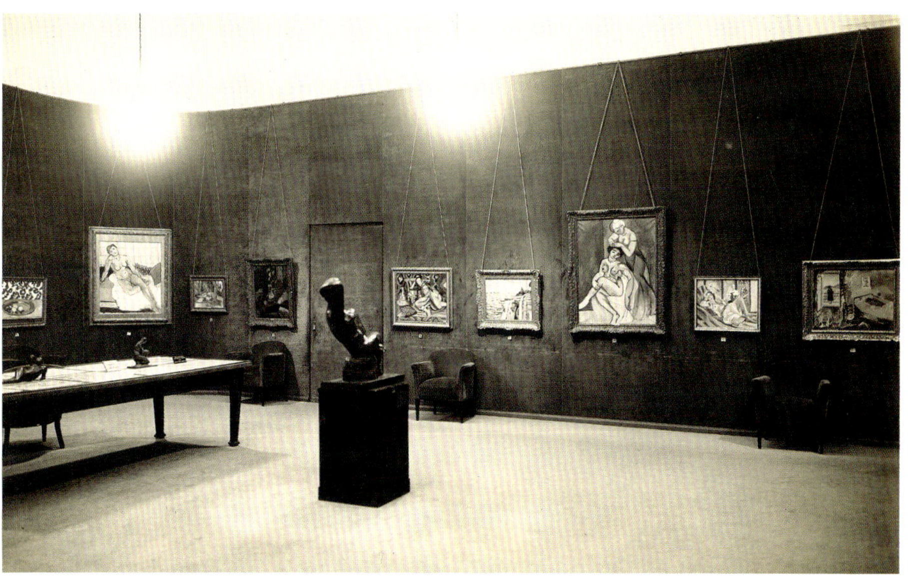

Seated Nude fuses self-display with sightedness in a sculptural reinterpretation of a theme Picasso had addressed in his notorious painting *Les Demoiselles d'Avignon*. Matisse's interest in the dual nature of vision, however, precedes Picasso's. Already in *Le bonheur de vivre,* the center of the painting was occupied by the two, paired nymphs who, it can be argued, appear as two sides of a single figure.[103] One of these aligns herself with the orientation of the viewer and thus turns her back to us; we assume that her vision, like ours, penetrates into the deeper space with its ring of dancers. The other figure faces the viewer and raises her arm in self-display. It is no coincidence that *Large Seated Nude* fuses these two possibilities of vision. Late in his life, Matisse confided in an interview: "from the *Joie de vivre* (*Le bonheur de vivre*)—I was thirty-five then—to this cut-out—I am now eighty-two—I have remained the same. . . . I have searched for the same things, which I have perhaps realized by different means."[104]

We know that Matisse worked on *Large Seated Nude* for at least seven years, from 1922 to 1929, dwarfing the former record of three years he spent completing *The Serf.* The initial inspiration for the sculpture can be traced to his interest in Michelangelo's figures in the Medici chapel—especially *Night* and *Day*—plasters of which he copied at the École des Arts décoratifs in Nice, in 1918.[105] The artist developed his own twisting Michelangelesque figures in numerous drawings, lithographs, and paintings produced during the 1920s.[106] Notable among these are his lithographs *Day* and *Night* (cat. 104, 106, p. 223), published in 1922 and 1924 respectively, and the painting *Nude with Blue Cushion* (cat. 107, p. 219), which most closely resembles *Large Seated Nude* in pose.[107] Matisse's model for almost all of these works was Henriette Darricarrère, a young dancer and painter, whom he employed for most of the Nice period.[108] Henriette is often depicted as an odalisque set in a decorative context and frequently seated comfortably on an armchair; in the sculpture, Matisse removed both the context and, most importantly, the support. This transforms what had been an "easy stance" or "indolent sprawl," into a surprisingly strained pose.[109] Mezzatesta describes her as "cantilevered into space, unsupported by anything but her own abdominal muscles."[110] What is most striking and deliberate in Matisse's final arrangement is the odd conjunction of ease and tension. The figure leans back and surveys her spectators with Olympian calm while her body, balanced on a small round support, holds a near impossible, uncomfortable pose.[111]

In its compression of a powerful sightedness with a traditional gesture of self-display, *Large Seated Nude* perfectly embodies the ambiguities in relationships between subject and object. The tense yet heroic balance achieved in this work takes on a nuanced significance if we consider the ways in which this sculpture was installed shortly after its completion in 1929. Of the five Matisse

Fig. 65. Installation of *Large Seated Nude* at the exhibition at Galerie George Petit, Paris, 1931.

exhibitions held in 1930 and 1931, the largest—if not the best received—was the massive Parisian retrospective sponsored by Bernheim-Jeune at the Galerie Georges Petit in 1931.[112] As the photographs reveal (figs. 64, 65), the installation returned to the idea of coordinating two-dimensional works around a dominant figural sculpture placed in the center of the room. This was almost certainly Matisse's idea; it was also used in the slightly earlier retrospective at Galerie Thannhauser in Berlin, most probably hung by Matisse's friend and former student Hans Purrmann, who also wrote the catalogue essay. The exhibition in 1931, organized by Étienne Bignou and hung by Matisse's son Pierre Matisse (whose own gallery in New York was beginning to achieve some success at this time),[113] turned out to be disappointing.[114] It included an unrepresentative sampling of a hundred and forty-three paintings (Bois calls them Bernheim "leftovers"—largely from the Nice period), roughly a hundred drawings, and, quite oddly, only one sculpture, *Large Seated Nude.*[115] In both exhibitions, Matisse did not simply recontextualize an older sculpture, as he had done with *The Serpentine* in *Tableaux du Maroc et sculptures,* but he employed a work that was the result of nearly a decade spent meditating on the topics of display, gesture, and vision.

Large Seated Nude was designed to play this role. Placed centrally within the gallery space, surrounded by Matisse's paintings, the figure enacts a pantomime of viewing; there is an oscillation between exhibition and exhibitionism. The figure becomes a surrogate viewer occupying the space of the museum-goers while conditioning and instructing them about the ideal mental attitude with which to confront art. Her seeing simulates our seeing, and where Matisse had once advocated an art "like a good armchair," the irony is that this work was born with his decision to remove the armchair from his odalisque models. Leaning tensely out into space, she is counterbalanced by all she surveys. Activity and passivity are fused into a precarious new ideal that replaces comfort as the goal of aesthetic contemplation.

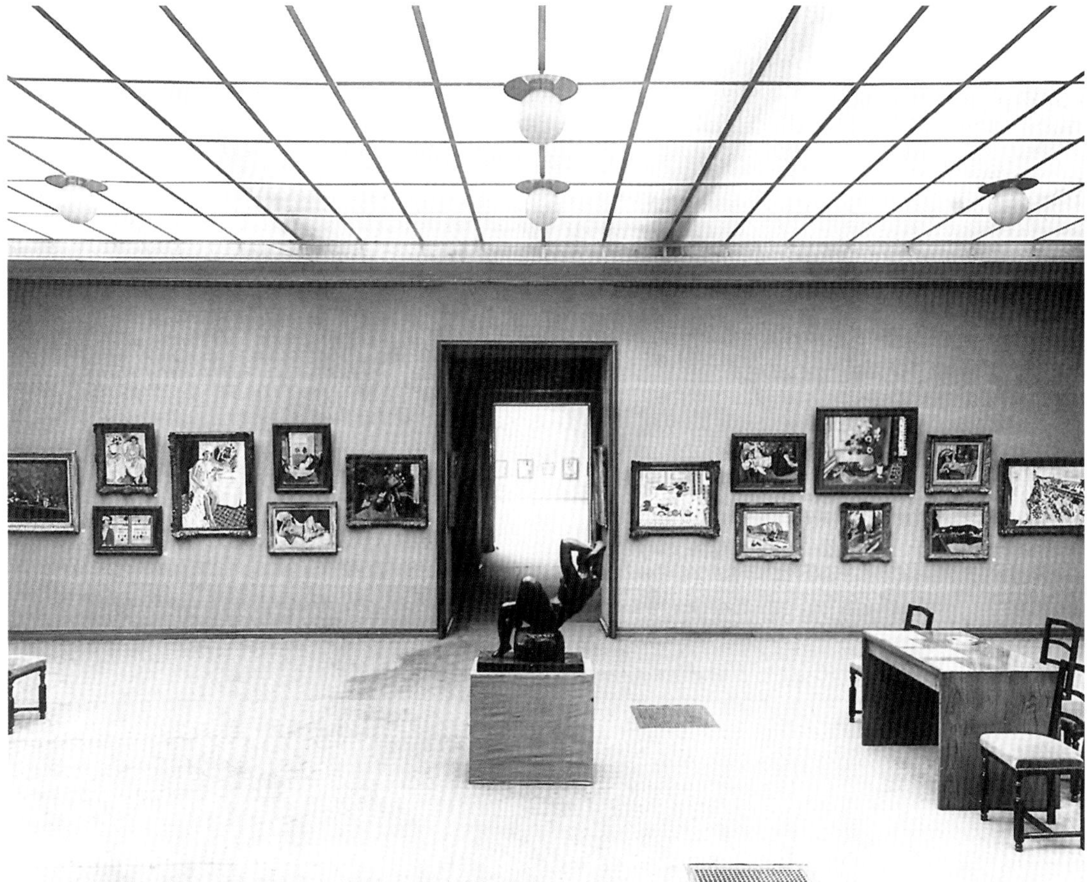

Notes

1. Tucker 1975, 63.

2. Benjamin 1987, 45.

3. The representation of Matisse's sculpture in his paintings is not a primary topic of this essay because it has received extensive attention from virtually all major Matisse scholars starting with Alfred Barr in his canonic *Matisse: His Art and His Public* (1951, 99–100) and Theodore Reff with his focused discussion "Matisse: Meditations on a Statuette and Goldfish" (1976, 109–15).

4. Flam 1986, 109.

5. Fletcher 2003, 171–72.

6. Flam 1986, 109, 487 n.5.

7. This is very different from nineteenth-century practice; Rodin, for example, rarely numbered his sculptures or limited their editions. In a letter to Roger Fry, from October 1912, Matisse responds to Fry's inquiry regarding the possible sale of plaster casts on exhibition at the Grafton Galleries, London: "These plaster proofs you should understand are numbered like the bronzes, which is to say they count toward the ten proofs (ces épreuves de plâtre serait bien entendu numerotises comme les bronzes c'est à dir compteraint dans les 10 épreuves)." Already in 1912, Matisse clearly understood that his editions would be limited to ten casts plus two possible artist proofs. Wanda de Guébriant of the Matisse Archives in Paris graciously provided access to this correspondence.

8. Catalogue information reprinted in Gordon 1974, 2:103.

9. Vauxcelles 1904, reprinted in Flam 1988, 45. The only other "nude man" Vauxcelles could be referring to is the *Copy after Puget's Écorché* (fig. 31, p. 32)—but it seems unlikely that a critic would neglect to mention that the work was a copy. The "amusingly curved" young girl could refer to *Madeleine II* but it is more likely to be *Madeleine I,* where the curvature of the figure is more fluidly pronounced.

10. Although it is indebted loosely to Rodin's *John the Baptist* and *Walking Man,* this is not a copy in the sense that Matisse copied Barye's *Jaguar Devouring a Hare* in the same years.

11. The work is still dated 1900–1903 in Duthuit 1997, 10. Arguments for a later date of completion appear in Mezzatesta 1984, 38–43; and Flam 1986, 85–88. Hans Purrmann (an artist who helped manage the Matisse Academy in 1908) contends that *The Serf* lost its arms accidentally, a view confirmed by Mme Duthuit (the artist's daughter), who adds that the mishap occurred during Matisse's move to his new studio at the Hôtel Biron, in 1908. Albert Elsen, followed by Flam and others, argues that the change more likely resulted from an aesthetic decision on Matisse's part; Elsen 1972, 30; Flam 1986, 487 n.18. Even if the arms were partially broken, close examination of the resulting bronze sculpture reveals that Matisse went much further and willfully amputated what remained.

12. Elsen 1972, 26; one thinks of the Belgian sculptor Constantin Meunier's large figures of workers—although these are usually clad in historically contemporary costume.

13. The Rodin bust depicts the journalist Henri Rochefort and comes from the collection of Édouard Manet; Elsen (1972, 17) dates this purchase 1898. Barr (1951, 38–40) suggests that the Rodin was acquired in 1899, together with Cézanne's *Three Bathers* (fig. 10, p. 9) and perhaps a Gauguin painting as well.

14. Elsen offers the most extensive discussion of the model "Bevilaqua" who formerly modeled for Rodin; Elsen 1972, 28–29. Who this individual was remains unclear; Raymond Escholier, whom Elsen cites as a source, calls him "Belivacque"; Escholier 1960, 73. Elsen notes that he was a peasant from Abruzzi and formerly named Pignatelli. This double name suggests some confusion. Hilary Spurling (1998, 213) suggests that "Bevilacqua" may have been a nickname for Pignatelli. Might two different models be involved? We know that Rodin employed other male Italian models; see Tancock 1976, 360–61.

15. Meyer Schapiro describes the surface as a "multiplication of small muscles [that] is the plastic equivalent in this work to subdivided flecking and pointillism in painting" (Schapiro, 1931, 35). Elsen (1972, 37) writes: "Matisse's facture involves a 'suggestive synthesis' of things known and observed about the body, subject to aesthetic intuition about when to stop in order to achieve an overall balance of accents." Flam (1986, 88) observes that the "modeling in *The Serf* alternates between description of anatomical detail and abstract modeling of mass that pools and disperses light and shadow in an almost painterly fashion."

16. With great subtlety John Elderfield discusses the "equivalence" between Matisse's painting and sculpture at this point; Elderfield 1978, 32. The one possible exception is Matisse's near-contemporary *Jaguar Devouring a Hare.*

17. *Madeleine I* was begun after *The Serf,* in 1901, but was the first major sculpture he completed. *Madeleine II* was begun in 1903.

18. Matisse later owned a copy of Michelangelo's *Dying Slave.* For an extensive discussion of the "arabesque" in Matisse's sculpture, see Benjamin 1992, 15–25; see also Yve-Alain Bois's discussion of the *figura serpentinata,* which he links back to Michelangelo and later mannerist sculpture; Bois 1997, 374.

19. For a discussion of the theories of Adolf von Hildebrand and their relevance to Matisse's sculpture, see Bois 1997, 372.

20. Benjamin 1990, 243.

21. See Boardingham 1995, 31–39.

22. Bouer 1904, 605; cited in Boardingham 1995, 38. The degree to which Bouer's comments were prompted by Matisse's sculpture rather than by his paintings is uncertain—the Cézannian impression of both would have been mutually reinforcing.

23. The photograph can be dated no earlier than 1904—as established by Michael Mezzatesta, who noted that the painting *Monk in Meditation,* visible between Matisse and *The Serf,* was not completed until late 1903 and 1904; Mezzatesta 1984, 40. Several copies of this photograph are known. One, located in the Special Collections library of the Museum of Modern Art in New York, was given to the museum by Erich S. Herrmann via Monroe Wheeler's office in 1954. The photograph was printed at the now-defunct Studio Madonnes in Paris. A second print, from the Cone Papers at The Baltimore Museum of Art, measures 7.2 × 7.8 cm. It was included in an envelope on stationery from the Lausanne Palace Hotel that bears Claribel Cone's inscription: "Photograph Le Serf & Matisse (with arms) from Mike." Emily Rafferty, Assistant Librarian at The Baltimore Museum of Art, advised me on this point and lent her expertise in all matters Cone. Claribel Cone died in 1929, so The Baltimore Museum of Art's photograph has a provenance going back at least to this date. More interestingly, the "Mike" in question is undoubtedly Michael Stein. Was he the photographer? Albert Elsen believed that the photograph came from Hans Purrmann, Matisse's friend and studio master when he ran his school, who first published the photograph in Purrmann 1960. Wanda de Guébriant of the Matisse Archives in Paris still maintains this belief. Since Purrmann did not meet Matisse until 1906, this would mean that the photograph would date from the period 1906 through 1908 (when the arms were removed from *The Serf*). With the rediscovery of the Cone photograph and its link to the Steins, who first introduced Purrmann to Matisse, it seems more likely, however, that one of the Steins took the picture. Michael and Sarah Stein would photograph Matisse many years later in a similar presentational mode standing in front of their portraits. The first two bronze casts ever made of *The Serf* were purchased in 1908 by Leo Stein and Michael and Sarah Stein, who are thus closely associated with the piece.

24. Although Elderfield suggests that the photograph represents a plaster, it is more likely that it represents the original clay model. The lumps of material around the base of the figure suggest pieces of removed clay. In the photograph the legs of the figure appear thicker and more knotted with muscles than they are in the more attenuated final bronze that survives today. This suggests that the clay was still soft enough to be carved off the sculpture—there is no evidence of chiseled dry plaster as occurred in some of the *Back*s. The photograph also shows several examples of plasters, which are far lighter in value than *The Serf* is—again suggesting a different material.

25. There is currently known no other bust, in the strict sense, that Matisse completed in time for the 1904 exhibition.

26. Elderfield 1992, 48–49.

27. Vauxcelles 1905b, reprinted in Flam 1988, 47.

28. Roger Benjamin interprets this use of language: "Vauxcelle's terminology connotes a sexualized release of uncontrolled instinct into the urbane milieu of the art exhibition. . . . The term *fauve* identified a twinned aggression in the ritual of the reception of new art: both exposing a captive public to the spectacle of 'unintelligible' works and exposing artists to the howls of public outrage" (Benjamin 1990, 253).

29. Saint-Hilaire 1905, translated and reprinted in Wright 2004, 62.

30. The other sculptures in the exhibition included "57 *Andromede* (plâtre)," thought by Flam (1986, 183) and others to be *Upright Nude with Arched Back* (Duthuit no. 14), and "58 *Buste d'enfant* (bronze)." It is unclear which sculpture this refers to but it would be the earliest known bronze cast, pushing the date of Matisse's bronze castings back by a year.

31. Bois 1994, 61.

32. Elderfield 1992, 18; see also Jack Flam's discussion of Matisse as "modern master" in Flam 1995, 31. Alfred Barr was perhaps the earliest scholar to observe that by 1908 Matisse's leadership of the Parisian avant-garde was in decline; Barr 1951, 87. Roger Benjamin describes Matisse's 1908 Salon d'automne and the publication of his "Notes of a Painter" later that year as "a kind of apotheosis" (Benjamin 1987, 112).

33. Matisse 1908, 731–45; reprinted in Flam 1995, 42.

34. Sarah Stein's "Notes" (1908) are reprinted in Flam 1995, 46–52.

35. According to the Société de Salon d'automne, *Catalogue 1908,* the following sculptures are listed: "Serf (bronze); Jeune fille debout [bronze]; Femme couchée se soulevant sur bras (bronze); Tête d'enfant [bronze]; Tête de fillette [bronze]; Femme s'appuyant sur les mains (bronze); Femme accroupie (bronze); Petit tête de femme [bronze]; Torse de fillette [bronze]; Femme assise [bronze]; Etude pour la précédente [bronze]; Tête de fillette (terre cuite, exemplaire unique); Groupe de deux jeunes filles (Tirages limités à 10 exemplaires numérotés)" (reprinted in Benjamin 1987, 290 n.196; Benjamin's interpolations in brackets).

36. Ibid., 112; Albert Marque was the sculptor whose rather conservative sculpture of a child's head prompted Vauxcelles's comment about "Donatello among the beasts" in 1905.

37. In his early career, Matisse would rarely cast sculptures in bronze until he had a client to pay the considerable expense. The Steins were probably instrumental in getting him to cast the piece. Michael and Sarah owned cast number 1/10 and Leo Stein owned 2/10. It would not be until 1910 that more *Serf*s were cast.

38. The earliest casts in bronze were produced starting in 1906 at the Bingen and Costenoble foundry; Maillol worked extensively at that foundry and may have recommended it to Matisse.

39. The work is based on a photograph of two Tuareg girls, not sub-Saharan Africans. See the discussion of this title in Herbert 1992, 157, 160.

40. My discussion of early critical responses to Matisse relies heavily on the research of Roger Benjamin, whom I wish to thank for the generosity of his time and for his responses to my questions.

41. Marx 1908; translated and reprinted in Benjamin 1987, 152.

42. "Aside from a plaster that one would think is half Gothic and half Hindu, there is a display cabinet of sculptures by the same artist in which the forms sometimes twist and writhe strangely, but where the character is spirited and very much alive" (Vauxcelles 1908, in Benjamin, 1987, 113).

43. Hepp 1908, 389; translated and reprinted in Benjamin 1987, 152–53; this is, of course, the same charge made far later by William Tucker.

44. Benjamin 1987, 87–98.

45. Hepp 1908, 389; in Benjamin 1987, 152–53.

46. *Manet and the Post-Impressionists,* November 8–January 15, 1910–1911; and *Second Post-Impressionist Exhibition,* October 5–December 31, 1912.

47. Roger Fry 1912, 249–51; reprinted in Reed 1996, 112–16.

48. Reed 1996, 114.

49. Cauman 2000, 83–96.

50. Ibid., 92–93.

51. These reviews were reprinted in *Camera Work* 38 (April 1912), 45–46.

52. Grendon 1912, 34–35; republished in Cauman 2000, 94.

53. Haviland 1912, 37. Cauman (2000, 94) speculates that the number may have been exaggerated but also concedes that the exhibition was well attended and drew a high-society crowd.

54. Stein 1933, 80.

55. *The Red Madras Hat,* The Barnes Foundation, Merion, Pennsylvania; *Self-Portrait,* Statens Museum for Kunst, Copenhagen.

56. The identification of the paintings appears in Elderfield 1972, 185; presently: *Le Luxe II,* Statens Museum for Kunst, Copenhagen; *Still Life with Aubergines* and *The Red Studio,* Museum of Modern Art, New York; *Wild Daffodils,* location unknown.

57. I believe that the exhibition was recorded photographically and that the photographs were either destroyed or await rediscovery.

58. Three of the paintings, the so-called Moroccan triptych, had already been sold to Ivan Morosov; many of the others are labeled, in the catalogue, as belonging to "M. S. S."—presumably Michael and Sarah Stein.

59. "Le dessin, qui est ici purement instinctif, s'esprime avec la sensualité la plus délicate et la plus raffiné qui soit aujourd'hui. Le Café turc, la Porte de la kasbah sont parmi les rares ouvrages supportables, inspirés par l'Afrique du Nord contemporaine" (Apollinaire 1960, 319).

60. See letters from Fenéon to Matisse, dated March 20 and 26, 1913; Archives Matisse, Paris.

61. Schneider, Cowart, and Coyle 1990, 270.

62. We saw that he had already done this in the 1904 Salon d'automne; the hanging of the salons was very contentious and political and Matisse was known, to the irritation of some, for his unpredictability and last-minute substitution of works. In 1907, Georges Lopisgich, a founder of the Salon d'automne and its general secretary since 1903, resigned in protest, mainly of the influence wielded by Matisse and his friends; he specifically complains about "irregularity having been committed in the reception of incoming works" (cited in Benjamin 1990, 261).

63. Other triads are discussed in Schneider, Cowart, and Coyle 1990, 270–74.

64. Ibid., 277.

65. Flam 1986, 360.

66. They also create a bridge between the painting and the viewer's space, furthering the sense of what one author has observed is already a "collapse in spectatorial distance" as occurs in the *Seated Riffian* painting; Wright 2004, 207, 267 n.39. These works are currently in the following collections: *Calla Lilies,* State Hermitage Museum, Saint Petersburg; *The Seated Riffian,* The Barnes Foundation, Merion, Pennsylvania; *Calla Lilies, Irises, and Mimosas,* State Pushkin Museum of Fine Arts, Moscow.

67. Flam 1986, 362.

68. Monod-Fontaine 1984, 17.

69. Barr 1951, 139.

70. Bois 1997, 378; elsewhere Bois gives an excellent description of the experience of looking at the sculpture *Seated Nude (Olga)* (cat. 67): "*Olga*—the Matisse sculpture that most forcefully demands circumnavigation, splendidly baffling the beholder's expectation. For this work epitomizes one of the most inventive features of Matisse's sculpture—the suppression of any geometric or muscular arris, of any demarcation between planes. Moving around Olga, you are always caught up short: you suddenly realize that you are looking at her back, though a split second earlier it was her belly that was in view—and no matter how many times you go around, you can never find the place where the shift occurs" (Bois 1998, 54).

71. Matisse 1908, in Flam 1995, 37. Yve-Alain Bois provides an important discussion of the meaning of Matisse's often misunderstood metaphor, relating it to an ideal state of receptiveness that Matisse wished his audience to achieve when looking at art that requires "a certain perceptual inattentiveness" (Bois 1994, 81).

72. Yve-Alain Bois describes the artist's strategy for evoking the "polysensoriality" of his memories and feelings in art: Matisse "renders the diffusion of his gaze, places the periphery in the center of his painting, and above all, he makes it impossible for our eye to come to rest, to settle on one spot. He teaches us not to look, that is, to really see; he sets out to blind us, to anagrammatize the visual, to work below the threshold of perception and move into the subliminal" (ibid., 79).

73. See ibid. The impetus for Bois's discussion comes from an observation made by Leo Steinberg about the circulatory mechanisms at play in *Le bonheur de vivre,* which he likens to "a city or . . . blood, where stoppage at any point implies a pathological condition, like a blood clot or traffic jam" (Steinberg 1972, 8). Bois (1994, 62) quotes this line with some minor alteration. The settee in Matisse's exhibition creates a circulatory flow among the spectators akin to that generated by a roundabout in an urban street system.

74. A sampling of sources on this topic includes Monod-Fontaine 1984, 12–17; idem 2003, 62–68; Flam 1998, unpaged; Herbert 1992, 156–57; Wright 2004, 168–69; and Sykora 2005, 331–42.

75. An excellent account of Druet's early career and relationship with Rodin is found in Pinet 2001, 275–95.

76. Archives Matisse, Paris.

77. The meeting of Matisse and Rodin is described in Escholier 1960, 138.

78. The photographer's wife continued to run the business until 1938. In 1939, the Druet archive of thirty thousand plates was purchased by the photographer, painter, and editor François Vizzavona, who carried on the business, expanding it greatly into a general photographic service; Schlesser 2005, unpaged.

79. Druet's photographs of Rodin's sculptures bear both Rodin's and Druet's signatures, but his photographs of Matisse's sculptures are embossed with a commercial stamp and inscribed with the anonymous designation: "Phot. Procédé druet." One wonders if Druet sent an employee or whether he shot the photographs himself?

80. The bulk of the surviving Druet photographs are currently stored in the Archives photographiques Fort de Saint-Cyr under the direction of the Médiathèque de l'architecture et du patrimoine; records were found of thirteen plates of Druet photographs of Matisse sculptures that are, "malheureusement," listed as missing. The only copies of Druet photographs of Matisse's sculpture that are known to this author are in the possession of Matisse's heirs.

81. Bois 1997, 375.

82. There is some confusion on this point; Duthuit 1997 indicates with a diamond symbol those photographs that reproduce Druet angles. At times, as in the critical case of

Reclining Nude I, Bois discusses three Druet views, but in the catalogue the triangular symbol is affixed only to a single view from the back. Although the Matisse-approved Druet photographs were available, the photographer of the catalogue raisonné chose not to reproduce them.

83. Bois 1997, 375–76.

84. Ibid., 376, 373.

85. Wanda de Guébriant provided me with the date of 1936 for this notebook, which is written in several different hands at different dates—some of the entries come from the late 1940s; the notebook is photographically reproduced in Duthuit 1997, 305–37.

86. Such errands are discussed in the correspondence of Matisse and Claude Valsuani (the owner of Matisse's preferred later foundry) and letters from Lydia Delectorskaya to Marguerite Matisse preserved in the Archives Matisse, Paris.

87. Tucker 1975, 65.

88. Stein 1908, in Flam 1995, 48.

89. It is for this reason that Vladimir Tatlin, seeking a utopian, radical destabilization of traditional nineteenth-century hierarchies, eliminates the plinth in his "counter-corner reliefs."

90. *The Serf*'s arms appear to have been willfully amputated. This almost crude sense of intention opens the sculpture up to potential rhetorical interpretation. If the purported message is about dysfunction, I would suggest that the target is self-referential and debunks the very possibility of still producing the sort of rhetorical public monument that, in part, *The Serf* set out to be. I am aware that using Rodin as a foil has its dangers. As Leo Steinberg lucidly outlines, Rodin is not easily condensed; there is both a public and a private Rodin, and Steinberg helped recoup the latter; see Steinberg 1972, 322–403 and esp. 393. My comments refer to the public, late nineteenth-century Rodin, whose rhetoric Steinberg describes as the will "to appeal, to afflict, to persuade—always to stir the heart up into fellow feeling" (ibid., 331).

91. Duthuit 1997, 306.

92. Curiously, Giorgio de Chirico employs a similar device in some of his depictions of Ariadne—with darker connotations of anxiety and the irrational.

93. Important essays about Matisse's copying include those by Roger Benjamin (1989, 176–201) and Richard Shiff (1995, 40–51); see also Shiff 1984, 55–69.

94. "It could even be said that the painting imparts nothing at all to the sculpture, apart from a repertoire of poses, and even then this repertoire is sculptural in origin, since it is largely derived from an old academic stock based on ancient statuary" (Bois 1997, 369).

95. Benjamin 1989, 182.

96. Ibid., 183.

97. The most famous sleeping Ariadne is the Roman copy of a second- to third-century BC Hellenistic original in the Museo Pio-Clementino, today the Vatican Museums.

98. Elsen 1972, 58.

99. Frascina 1993, 120.

100. Highly nuanced studies of Matisse's presentation of female subjects are found in Bourguignon 1998; and Elderfield 1995.

101. John Elderfield has discussed ways in which Matisse distances the figure's face in *Young Woman in White, Red Background* (1946, Musée national d'art moderne, Centre Georges Pompidou, Paris) and observes: "Whereas Giacometti, notably, seemed fascinated by the moment at which an advancing shape becomes recognizable to us as a figure, Matisse seemed to be fascinated by precisely the reverse. The face of this model appears more distant from us than the painted proximity of the whole figure suggests, certainly more distant than Matisse's proximity to the model allowed" (Elderfield 1992, 42). Matisse's sculptures fail, in my mind, to either advance or recede; in *Figure with Cushion* (cat. 111) there is simply a sense of an attentive figure looking across a spatial void.

102. Elderfield (ibid., 40) observes a similar ambivalence in Matisse's painting *Odalisque with Magnolias* (1923–1924, private collection, formerly in the collection of Leigh B. Block), produced in the same period, making the point that in some sense the viewer must determine whether to read the figure as asleep or open-eyed but unseeing. I would suggest that the model's reactive smile allows for an oscillation between reading her as asleep and oblivious or awake. With *Large Seated Nude,* Matisse quite deliberately leaves the open or closed state of the eyes ambiguous, permitting a similar oscillation of readings. It is interesting to compare also the eyeless seeing odalisque depicted in the painting *Nude with Tambourine* (1925–1926, Museum of Modern Art, New York). The dark shadows of paint obscuring the figure's eyes seem calculated to accentuate a sense of simultaneous blindness and vision.

103. The figures reciprocate but do not match each other and so are not truly mirrored; there is, however, a tradition of two-sided viewing as, for instance, in images such as Velázquez's *Rokeby Venus* (1647–1651, National Gallery, London), which Matisse's nymphs evoke.

104. Matisse speaking to Maria Luz, in 1951, quoted in Flam 1995, 207; also cited in Bois 1994, 62.

105. In 1918, Matisse writes to his friend the painter Charles Camoin: "I'm drawing *The Night* and modeling it. I'm also studying Michelangelo's *Laurent de Médicis.* I'm hoping to clearly and completely immerse myself in Michelangelo's construction" (reprinted in Duthuit 1997, 355 n.23). Albert Elsen published a photograph of Matisse's studio in which an early plaster of *Large Seated Nude* is seen next to a door on which there is a reproduction of the Michelangelo's figure of *Night* (Elsen 1972, 144). Mezzatesta observes that the lithographs *Day* and *Night* are "direct postural prototypes for the bronze" but also notes the differences from Michelangelo's sculptures; Mezzatesta 1984, 118.

106. Many related examples are discussed in Elderfield 1987, 215 n.2, 124–25, ill.

107. Elsen illustrates both Matisse's lithographs *Day* and *Night* and dates the former as 1924 rather than 1922 as given elsewhere; Elsen 1972, 145, 150. For the alternative dating, see Szymusiak 1993, 75.

108. Darricarrère would, in Jack Cowart's words, "incarnate the artistic and psychological atmosphere of the *niçoise* years, 1920 to 1927" (Cowart and Fourcade 1986, 26–27). For a discussion of Darricarrère with considerable bearing on Matisse's representation of women and relationship to his models, see Bourguignon 1998, 215–22.

109. Barr 1951, 213.

110. Mezzatesta 1984, 116.

111. Mezzatesta convincingly suggests that Matisse imbues the work with a "heroic quality" derived not only from Michelangelo's figures in the Medici chapel but also from the *Ignudi* of the ceiling of the Sistine chapel; ibid., 117–18.

112. Five major Matisse exhibitions were held in 1930 and 1931. An exhibition of around twenty sculptures was held at the Galerie Pierre and included the sizable personal collection of Pierre Loeb; the show opened on June 12, 1930; see Bois 1998, 57–58, 246 n.119. A major exhibition of Matisse's sculpture was held in New York at the Brummer Gallery in January and February 1931. No fewer than three Matisse retrospectives were also held in this period: one arranged by Hans Purrmann at the Galerie Thannhauser in Berlin; one put together by Alfred Barr at the Museum of Modern Art, New York; and the largest, sponsored by Bernheim-Jeune at the Galerie Georges Petit, in Paris in 1931; for an interesting discussion comparing the installations at the Galerie Thannhauser and the Museum of Modern Art, see O'Brian 1999, 106–108.

113. Hilary Spurling (2005a, 330) indicates that Matisse sent Pierre to "hang the Petit show."

114. Bois suggests that Matisse was too taken up with the Barnes commission to put much energy into the organization of the show; he just asked Étienne Bignou not to give him a "first class burial"—which, Bois concludes, is just what Matisse received; Bois 1998, 65; see also Barr 1915, 221–22. Jack Flam discusses the reception of the exhibition at the Petit gallery and, especially, Picasso's response; see Flam 2003, 151–57.

115. Bois 1998, 65.

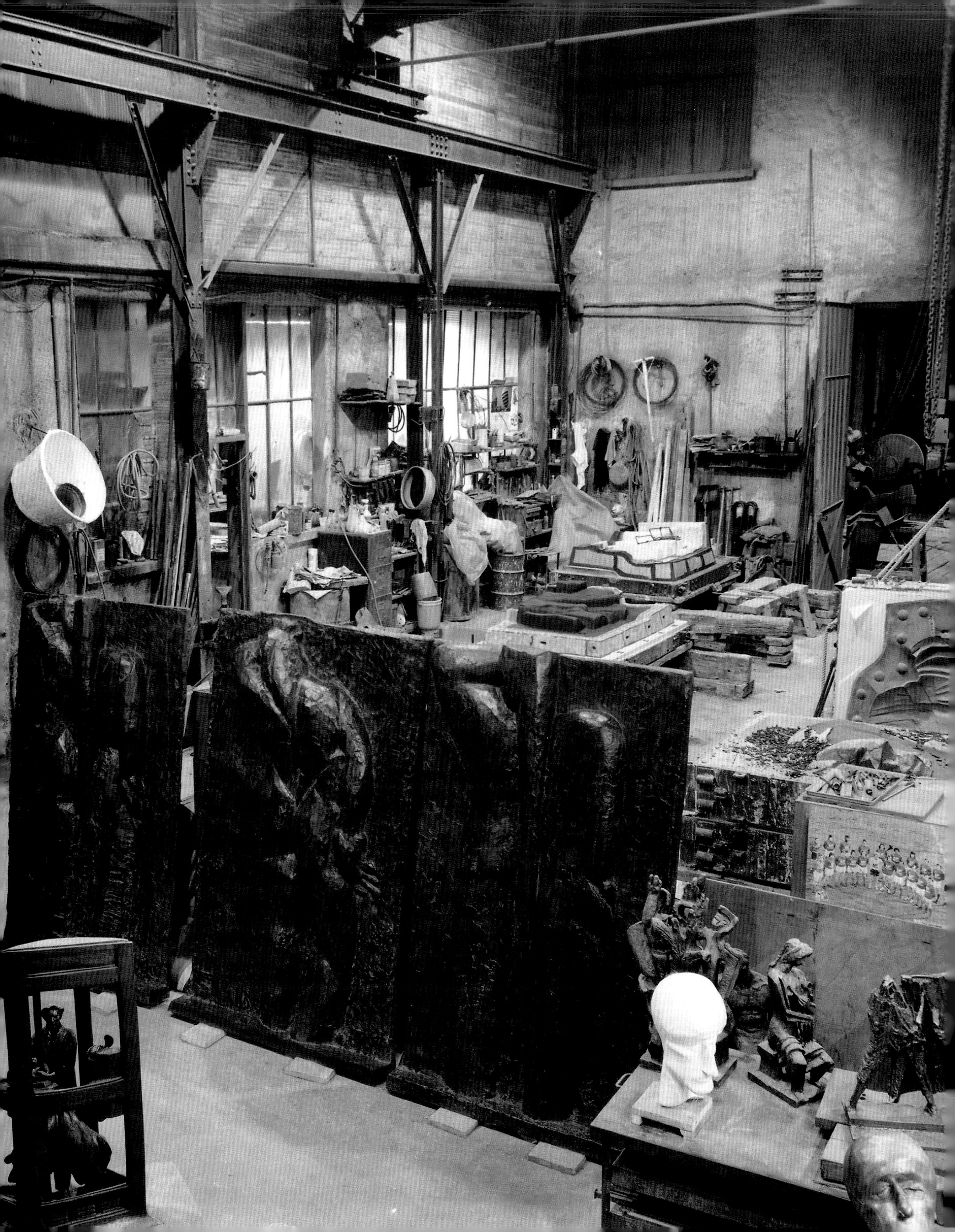

Ann Boulton

The Making of Matisse's Bronzes

The study of Matisse's painting has so overshadowed that of his sculpture that the lack of a published technical examination is not surprising. The complex fabrication process used to convert an artist's original work from clay to castings in bronze is often poorly understood, even by art historians, curators, and collectors. Object-based study is a crucial tool for connoisseurship, yet no technical examination of Matisse's sculptures has been published to date. This review of the examination of more than 120 bronze casts and most of the extant plaster, clay, and terra-cotta works from collections of Matisse's sculpture in the United States and France will, it is hoped, offer insights into how an artwork is made and the social and cultural context of its making.[1]

Matisse's struggle with modeling is well documented. Photographs of works in progress indicate that major changes would occur before sculptures were completed. Once that goal was met, however, and the sculpture ready for casting in bronze, Matisse never looked back. He was among the first sculptors to produce numbered limited editions in bronze and did so from his earliest casts. For seventeen years, he made use of the old-fashioned sand-casting technique for his work, even though serial lost-wax production was readily available. Even when he did switch, belatedly, to the lost-wax process, he did not exploit its creative potential. Comparisons of early sand casts and later lost-wax casts of the same work generally show little variation beyond that inherent in the technology, a reflection of the artist's grounding in nineteenth-century sculpture technique.[2]

Matisse's Working Method

Bronze sculptures are the end result of a multistep process that often begins with the artist sculpting his vision in a soft material, historically clay, plasticine, or wax. This soft model is then cast in a more durable material, commonly plaster and turned over to a foundry for casting in bronze. Only rarely do artists make their own bronzes; Matisse depended on others. He modeled his sculptures of clay or plasticine, a commercial modeling compound usually composed of clay, oil, pigment, and possibly sulfur. Small, compact works could be made without any internal support, but moderately sized works or those with only a small base required an armature. Matisse's only known extant original work in clay with its armature intact is *Standing Nude (Katia)* in the collection of the musée Matisse in Nice.[3] This work, his last sculpture, was modeled in 1950 when Matisse was bedridden, and it retains the wooden base and iron armature on which it was modeled. A lower section of the armature is replicated in the bronze casts (cat. 132, p. 255). Despite disliking plasticine,[4] Matisse still found a need for it. A core of plasticine was pressed onto the armature and then covered with a clay layer into which the surface details were modeled.[5] This exterior clay layer has dried and cracked at the waist revealing the inner, colored plasticine (fig. 66).[6] The crack occurred during Matisse's lifetime, and the earliest bronzes cast in 1958 retain the crack, clearly a design feature that appealed to him. A work from 1909, *Torso Without Arms or Head*, now extant only in bronze (cat. 57, p. 176), has a similar crack in the waist, perhaps also the result of the shrinkage differential between clay and plasticine.

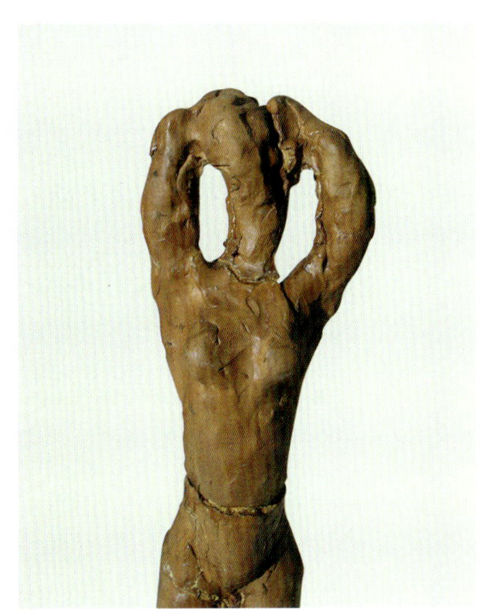

Fig. 66. Henri Matisse, *Standing Nude (Katia)*, 1950–1951 (detail). Clay and plasticine. Direction des Musées de France, Gift of Jean Matisse, on deposit at the Musée Matisse, Nice, 1978.

Mostly, Matisse modeled in clay alone. In the collection of the Musée départemental Matisse in Le Cateau-Cambrésis in northern France, are two small terra-cotta (fired-clay) heads that appear to be nearly solid clay and probably became the original models for the bronze editions of *Head of a*

Fig. 67. Henri Matisse, *Small Head with Upswept Hair*, 1906–1907. Terra-cotta. Musée départemental Matisse, Le Cateau-Cambrésis, Donated by Madame Marie Matisse in 1982.

Faun and *Small Head with Upswept Hair* (fig. 67).[7] The fact that they were fired indicates that they do not have internal armatures or plasticine cores. Rarely are clay sculptures preserved in this way; clay used for modeling has a smooth texture and does not contain the sand or grog required for successful firing,[8] and clay sculptures modeled on metal armatures cannot be fired at all because they would be destroyed by the shrinkage of the clay and the expansion of the metal during firing.

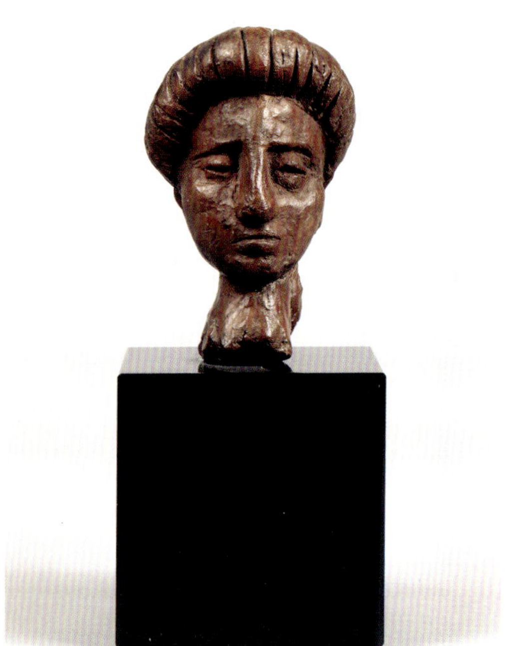

Most of Matisse's original clay sculptures no longer exist and were intended only as ephemeral creations. As long as a clay sculpture is in progress, it needs to be kept damp to prevent the surface from drying, shrinking, and cracking around the rigid armature. Before the advent of cheap plastic sheet, this was a recurring chore, requiring the constant rewetting of cloths applied to the surface. If a sculptor left town he would need someone to rewet the cloths on unfinished works. Matisse did this for Aristide Maillol when the two were neighbors in Collioure and Banyuls in about 1905–1907,[9] and the sculptor Etienne Terrus returned the favor in 1906 when Matisse left Collioure for Paris and the Salon d'automne.[10]

Waste Molds, Piece Molds, and Gelatin Molds

The quickest and best method to convert a clay sculpture to a plaster model is by employing a plaster waste mold, so-called because the original clay is destroyed in the making of the mold and the mold is subsequently destroyed to release the plaster cast. A waste mold is usually made in only two pieces. The soft complex clay form that is being molded is inevitably damaged as the two halves of the mold are pried apart when the plaster has set, and then it is thoroughly destroyed when the mold is cleaned out, as any soft clay caught in the undercuts must be dug or washed out. Once clean, the mold halves are rejoined and plaster is poured in. When that plaster has set, the rigid mold itself is chiseled off to release the plaster sculpture cast within. This plaster cast, the first plaster to be made directly from the clay, is then the only version of the original sculpture in existence and is usually referred to as the "original plaster." Because it expands very slightly when setting, plaster makes a high-quality, detailed reproduction of the original. The waste molding process is a necessary step in achieving a permanent version of their work, so sculptors were generally proficient in the process. Matisse helped Maillol mold *La Méditerranée* (cat. 157, p. 190), likely with a waste mold.[11]

By Matisse's day, a sculptor with resources could hire a professional mold maker to convert clay sculptures to plaster. To protect the precious original plaster, a sculptor who had the wherewithal to cast a work in bronze would have a plaster piece mold or a gelatin mold made of the original plaster and use that to make several more plaster casts to be used for the bronze casts. Unlike a waste mold, a piece mold requires greater skill, more time, and, for a complex sculpture, could involve as many as several hundred pieces, but the mold can be reused. Flexible gelatin molding, a time saver, began to replace piece molding during Matisse's working life.

Matisse and Mold Making

Even the most cursory glance at many of Matisse's bronze sculptures reveals multiple mold lines—impressions of the seams where two pieces of a mold abut—on the surface. Matisse's modern love of process, like Rodin's, led him to retain its traces, and even revel in then. The mold lines on Matisse's sculpture bear witness to the techniques used to create sculpture and their decoding offers a window into the creative process. Mold lines discussed in this section are those made by the artist or his mold maker when converting clay or plasticine to plaster or when press-molding clay.

Bills from the mold maker Léon Bertault in Paris, submitted between January 1928 and October 1929, show that four plaster waste molds, four gelatin molds, and thirteen plaster piece molds were produced for Matisse during that period.[12] Gelatin seems to have been the choice only for repairs of plasters or when molding from materials other than plaster, such as bronze or terra-cotta.[13] One of

Fig. 68. Henri Matisse, *Madeleine I,* 1901 (cast 1903). Painted plaster. Raymond and Patsy Nasher Collection, Dallas. Cat. 14. Detail showing piece-mold lines.

Bertault's piece molds, referred to as *"femme assise,"* is likely that for the *Large Seated Nude* (cat. 98, p. 217; 99, p. 275).[14]

Working in Nice, Matisse struggled with this sculpture from 1922 to 1929. In letters written to his wife and daughter, he describes his search in 1924 for a molder in Nice because the one he was planning to use "got away."[15] By 1926, he seems to have given up the search and explains that, although he made a mold of the bust he was working on and would like to do so for the statue, he hasn't because it "was too difficult" (probably due to the large size). In 1927, he appears to be on the verge of making a mold, needing only to wrap it up for travel back to Paris. Then, in May 1929, while he was in Nice, the sculpture was in Paris, where he wanted to have a piece mold made of it so that it could be cast in bronze. By July he understands that mold making is underway and wants to return to Paris before it is cast in bronze. The molder's bill for June lists a piece mold for *"femme assise"* and three (plaster) casts. The task of transporting a large, unfired, wet clay sculpture from Nice to Paris would have been inherently risky. It is likely that a waste mold was made in Nice, perhaps by Matisse himself, before the sculpture was moved to Paris. The plaster piece mold was likely taken from an original plaster so that more plasters—in this case three—could be cast as foundry models.[16]

But Matisse also had piece molds made directly on wet clay,[17] an unusual practice as the precision required for piece-mold production is difficult to attain with the soft clay. However, the molder's bill from February 1928 states unambiguously that a piece mold was made "directly on the clay" of a figure of a reclining woman, possibly *Reclining Nude II* (cat. 112, p. 228). The unusual description *"direct sur la terre"* indicates that the mold maker may have considered this to be out of the ordinary. A later bill, dated October 19, 1929, listing a gelatin mold made from a terra-cotta (*"terre cuite"*) head, probably *Small Head with Upswept Hair,* indicates that the molder was making a distinction between fired and unfired clay. Admittedly, the bill does not refer to *wet* clay, and it is possible that the clay might have been dry, therefore precluding waste molding for which clay must be soft and wet if it is to be removed thoroughly from the interior of the mold. Further evidence of Matisse's use of piece molds on wet clay exists, however.

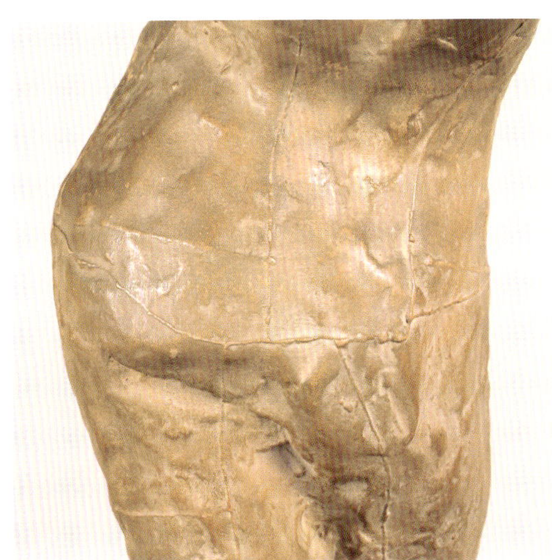

One of few extant plaster casts is that of *Madeleine I* (cat. 14, p. 120) in the Nasher Collection (fig. 68).[18] The original sculpture was modeled in 1903, when Matisse was probably too poor to hire a mold maker. The plaster exhibits many piece-mold lines with strange angles that, to a trained eye, appear poorly aligned, and the mold pieces seem to have slightly displaced the soft material they molded,[19] defects that perhaps Bertault feared when he carefully covered his bases with the description *"direct sur la terre"* in his bill. Matisse himself might have made this mold, which could account for the amateurish execution.[20]

Why would a sculptor want to make a bad piece mold on wet clay? Possibly, as Matisse did, because he wanted to record the state of a clay sculpture at a certain point and then continue to work on it. This idea may have come from Rodin via Emile-Antoine Bourdelle, Rodin's senior assistant, with whom Matisse studied for a few months in 1900.[21] Of the three methods for molding—waste mold, piece mold, and gelatin mold—it is only from the piece mold that the clay sculpture can be removed intact. (Gelatin is not generally used on unfired clay because the water in the gelatin can soften the surface.)[22] Writing to his daughter in June 1926, Matisse commented, "the bust has changed a lot from the state in which you last saw it, [from] which fortunately I made a mold."[23] The timing would be right for this to be *Henriette I* becoming transformed into *Henriette II* (cat. 92, p. 209; 93, p. 212).

Suggestions have been made that *Madeleine II* (cat. 15, p. 119) was made from a plaster cast of *Madeleine I,* and that each of the four large bas-relief *Back*s was made from a plaster cast of the preceding cast, except, of course, for the first. Examinations of the surfaces of these pieces and some

Fig. 69. Henri Matisse, *Madeleine II*, 1903. Bronze. Archives Matisse, Paris.

Fig. 70. Overlapped laser-scanned computer models of *Madeleine I* and *Madeleine II*. These models were made from thousands of precise measurements taken across the exterior surfaces of each sculpture. The two models were then superimposed on the computer screen and cut in cross-sections to create this image, which shows the close correspondence in shape and size between the upper torso and head of the two works, an indication that *Madeleine II* (purple lines) was made starting from *Madeleine I* (pink lines).

Fig. 71. Alvin Langdon Coburn. Matisse in his studio at Issy-les-Moulineaux, May 1913. Negative, gelatin on nitrocellulose roll film. George Eastman House; Gift of Alvin Langdon Coburn.

familiarity with the working of plaster and clay indicate otherwise. Although there is no longer an extant clay or plaster of the second *Madeleine,* the clay surface is faithfully recorded in the bronze (fig. 69). The modifications made to *Madeleine I* in order to arrive at *Madeleine II* show plastic deformation of the surface consistent only with the working of plastic media—clay or plasticine. One can add plaster to plaster in a wet state, but the removal of plaster from plaster must be done with files, chisels, and rasps, which would leave the surface abraded and cleaved, not deformed. *Madeleine I* was a temporary way station on the journey to *Madeleine II.* The comparison of three-dimensional computer models (fig. 70) indicates how closely the torsos and heads of these two works correspond in size and position.

The *Back*s are more complex. The extant plasters, although called "original plasters," are in fact foundry models, casts of the now-destroyed plaster originals.[24] There is no doubt that some rasping and chiseling was done directly on plaster surfaces, particularly on *The Back II* and *The Back III* (fig. 71). But once again, on all four pieces, there are plastic deformations consistent only with the working of clay or plasticine (fig. 72). Their large size and the thirteen years separating *III* and *IV* makes it unlikely, though not impossible, that one clay model served for all four; the clay would have to have been religiously covered with wet cloths, which seems unlikely for such a long period. Alternatively, they could have been made of plasticine, but this, too seems unlikely: that much plasticine would have been very expensive. More likely is that the piece mold used to record the state of *The Back III* was re-used.[25] Hypothetically, we can plot the developments: *The Back 0* (the title given by Elsen; it is known only by a photograph; fig. 9, p. 9)[26] is sculpted in clay but no mold is made of it. This clay is altered and piece molded. A plaster cast is made from the piece mold, to become *The Back I* (1909; cat. 48, p. 162). The clay is worked further and again piece molded. The plaster cast made from this mold is subjected to further work with rasps, files, and chisels, to become *The Back II* (1913; cat. 49, p. 162). The clay is worked further and yet again piece molded. The plaster cast made from this mold is subjected to alterations with rasps, files, and chisels, to become *The Back III* (1916–1917; cat. 50, p. 163). At this point, perhaps the clay dried out and was discarded or reused. Thirteen years later, when Matisse decides to continue on from *The Back III,* he presses sheets of clay into the piece mold and again alters the clay. A mold is made of this new state and becomes *The Back IV* (1930; cat. 51, p. 163).

It is well known that Matisse did not conceive the *Back*s as a series and they were never exhibited as such in his lifetime. Five bronze proofs were cast before he died, one of *The Back I* in 1948

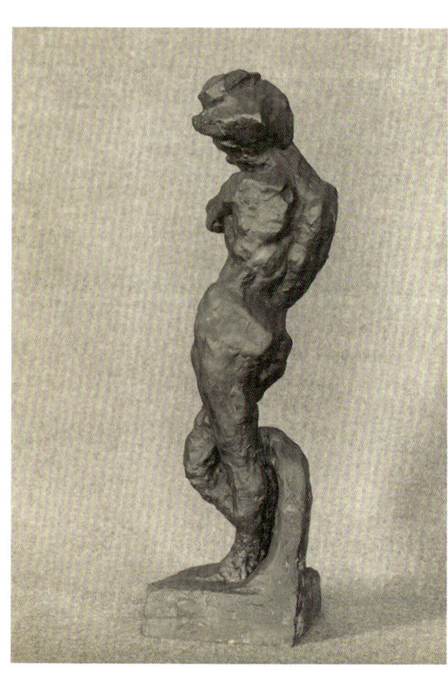

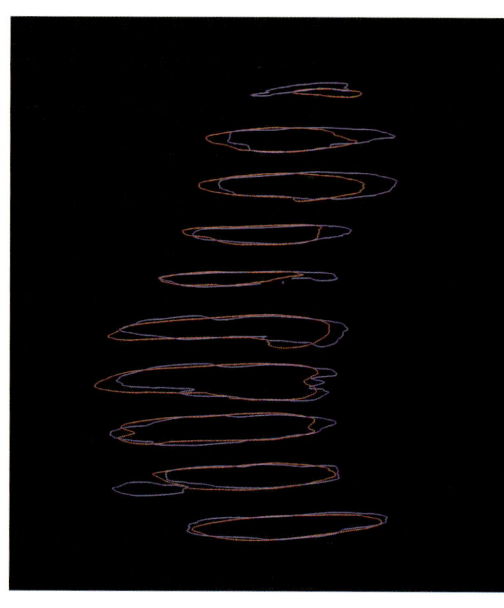

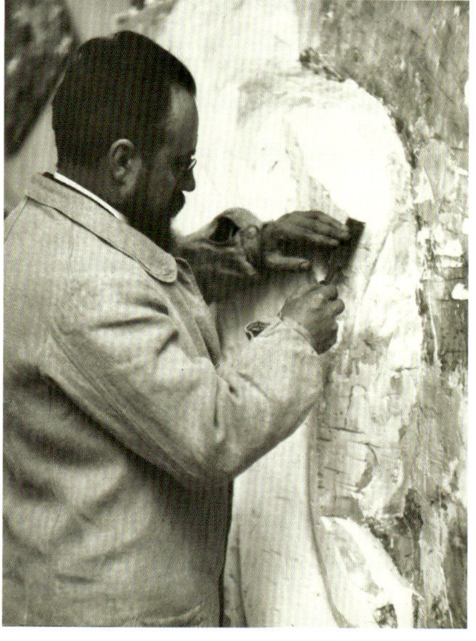

Fig. 72. Henri Matisse, *The Back III,* 1916–1917 (detail). Plaster. Musée départemental Matisse, Le Cateau-Cambrésis; Gift of the family of the artist, 1990.

Fig. 73. Overlapped laser-scanned computer models of two casts of Henri Matisse, *Head of a Child (Pierre Matisse).* The models of the two casts were superimposed on the computer screen and cut in cross-section to create this image, which shows that The Baltimore Museum of Art's cast (inner line) is smaller than that of the Weatherspoon Art Museum (outer line), demonstrating that the BMA's (smaller) cast was made, not from the plaster model, but rather from another bronze cast.

and, in 1950, two of *The Back I* and one each of *The Back III* and *The Back IV. The Back II* was unknown until after his death. It seems most likely that what have come to be called "the *Backs*" was one clay sculpture, always in progress but never completed. Luckily, Matisse recorded his hesitations along the way. Given the number of works by Matisse with piece-mold lines, it seems likely that the fits and starts evident in these sculptures reflect a similar course for numerous other works that have not survived.

Models

The term *model* here means a sculpture from which a mold is made in order that a copy, in either plaster or bronze, may be cast. The copy can be called a "proof." Once a bronze edition, usually comprising ten examples intended for sale and one or two to be kept by the artist, was completed, the plaster model was destroyed. Marguerite Duthuit, Matisse's daughter, commented that "the original plaster [of *Madeleine I*] was destroyed at the end of the casting of the bronze proofs."[27] In the 1990s, Matisse's heirs destroyed the remaining available plaster models after the outstanding editions were completed.[28] Ten plasters are known to survive. Of these, only *Profile of a Woman* and the unique work *Torso, Arms Raised,* are likely to be original plasters.[29] Others include the four foundry models of the *Backs*, three plaster proofs of *Madeleine I,* and one *Small Thin Torso.*[30] Two previously described terra-cotta works, *Head of a Faun* and *Small Head with Upswept Hair,* were used as models for their bronze editions.

Comparison of bronze casts for one edition, *Head of a Child (Pierre Matisse),* indicates that all the plaster models were lost at some time between 1912 and 1922, the chaos of World War I offering plenty of opportunity. Hilary Spurling, Matisse's biographer, relates that at one point the Matisse family, preparing hastily to evacuate Paris, buried sculpture in the yard of their home at Issy-les-Moulineaux, and that on another occasion two shells exploded on the roof of the studio there.[31] Measurements made by laser scanning of two bronze versions of this work bought from Matisse by the Cone sisters, one made in 1912, and the other cast in 1922 (fig. 73), show that the later version is about 1.5% smaller.[32] This size difference is the telltale marker of what is called a *surmoulage,* meaning, in its most literal sense, a cast made from another cast, the resulting bronze proof being necessarily smaller than the model as metal shrinks on cooling. The term is often used in the pejorative, implying a fake or unauthorized copy made by someone without access to the artist's plaster model. The airtight provenance for these two casts indicates that, once the plaster was accidentally

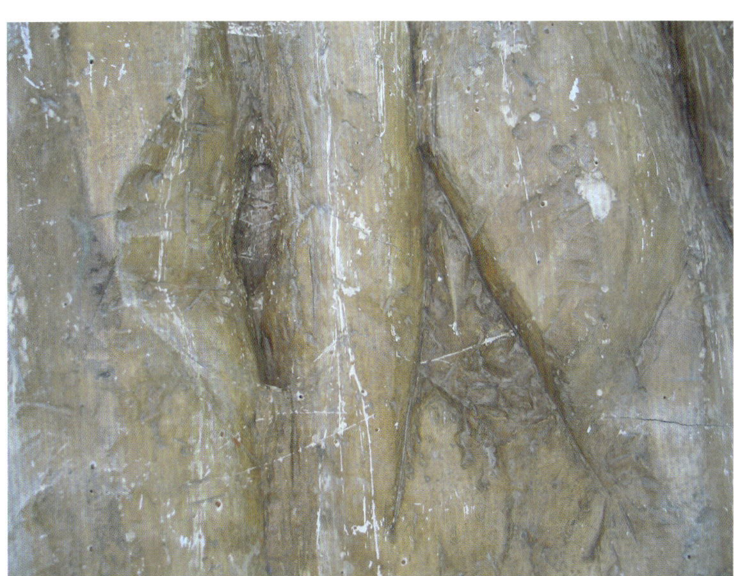

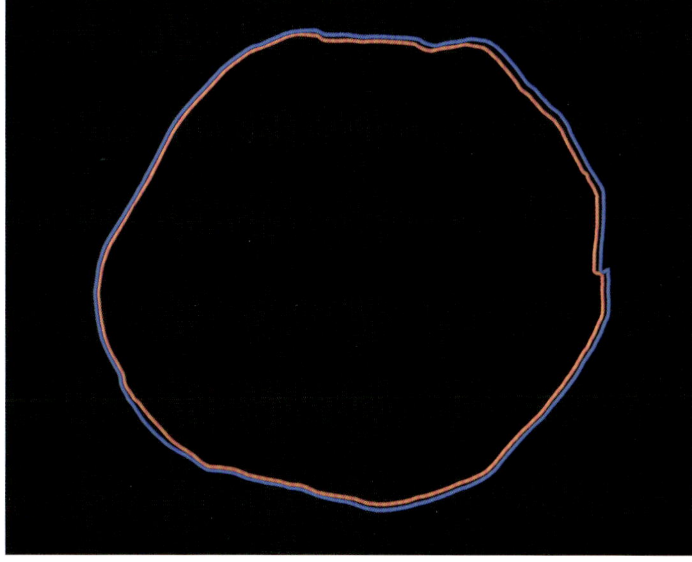

Fig. 74. Alexander Liberman, Matisse's studio: blue and white earthenware and *Reclining Nude I (Aurora)*, plaster, 1949–1951. Color slide. Alexander Liberman Photographic Collection and Archive, Research Library, The Getty Research Institute, Los Angeles.

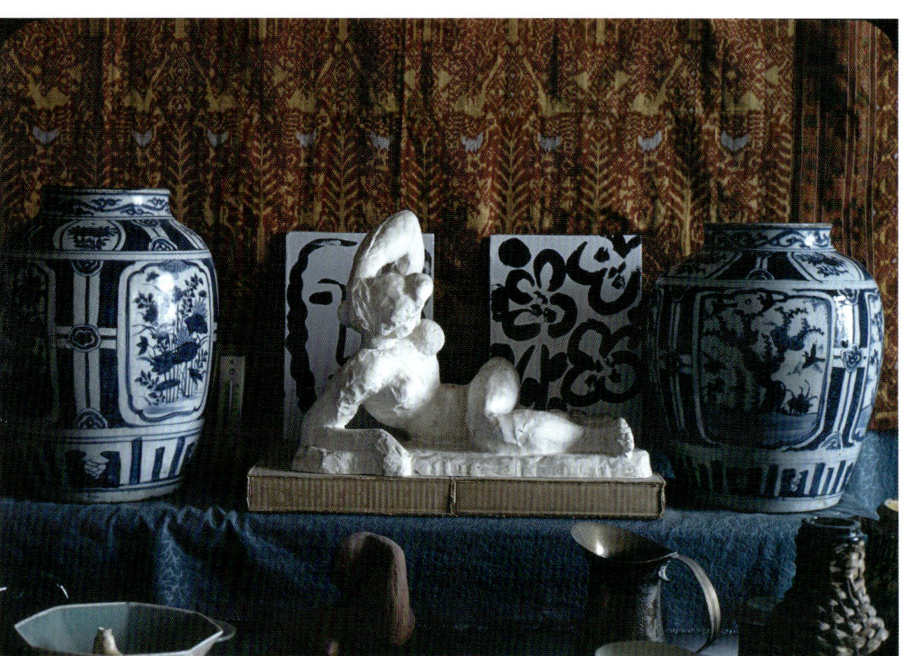

destroyed, Matisse himself selected a prewar bronze proof from which to produce the remainder of the edition. In this case, *surmoulage* takes on the more literal meaning used in nineteenth-century France, when large bronze editions were usually cast from bronze chief models.[33] The 1922 cast is indeed a *surmoulage,* but not a fake or unauthorized copy, and little, if any, of the surface detail has been lost on it.[34]

Two similar sand-cast versions of Matisse's *Reclining Nude I (Aurora)*, not accepted as genuine by the author of the catalogue raisonné, were examined as part of this study—one in a private collection and the other in an American museum collection.[35] These were found *not* to be *surmoulages* in the literal sense, in that they are the same size as other bronze versions known to have been made from the plaster model, but they may well be unauthorized copies made from the plaster model. It is likely that Matisse had not been consulted during the casting process, because all the mold lines, even those carefully preserved by the artist as design elements on the plaster model (which is now destroyed but known from photographs [fig. 74]), were thoroughly removed during the finishing process after casting, as is standard foundry practice, but not Matisse's. Two authorized bronze proofs, one a sand cast and the other a lost-wax cast (cat. 45, pp. 153, 155–56) made by two different foundries,[36] retain the mold lines from the plaster model after casting, undoubtedly at the artist's direction.

The Nasher Collection's *Reclining Nude I (Aurora)* (cat. 44, p. 269), a well-provenanced lost-wax cast made at the Valsuani foundry in 1951, is one of three bronzes cast after World War II to complete this edition. It is 4% smaller in size than a 1930 lost-wax cast and the 1912 sand-cast version,[37] an indication that perhaps another plaster model fell victim to war. Is this another case of a *surmoulage* that is an authorized copy? Photographs made between 1949 and 1951 of a plaster in Matisse's studio (fig. 74) would seem to prove that the model used for the prewar casts did survive the war. The plaster model shown is similar to the bronzes cast in 1912 and 1930 and includes certain detailed modeling on the front of the base that is not present on the Nasher work. Other slight differences (fig. 75) in the modeling of the Nasher work compared with the version in The Baltimore Museum of Art suggest that the former was not cast from an earlier bronze version. Were there in fact two different original versions of this work?

Two other works described as terra-cotta casts of the *Reclining Nude I (Aurora)* are included in the catalogue raisonné as part of a series of five produced by Matisse, who later destroyed three

Fig. 75. Overlapped laser-scanned computer models of two casts of Henri Matisse, *Reclining Nude I (Aurora),* one from The Baltimore Museum of Art (cat. 45), the other from the Raymond and Patsy Nasher Collection, Dallas (cat. 44). These superimposed computer models are colored to distinguish the Nasher's cast (red) from the BMA's cast (green). The Nasher cast is about 4% smaller; the size difference is most obvious here in the feet and indicates that these two bronze casts were not made from the same model.

Fig. 76. Overlapped laser-scanned computer models of two casts of Henri Matisse, *Reclining Nude I (Aurora),* a terra-cotta from the Hirshhorn Museum and Sculpture Garden, Washington, D.C., and a bronze from the Raymond and Patsy Nasher Collection, Dallas (cat. 44). These superimposed colored computer models show both casts to be the same size, an indication that the Hirshhorn plaster cast (blue) was made from a bronze model.

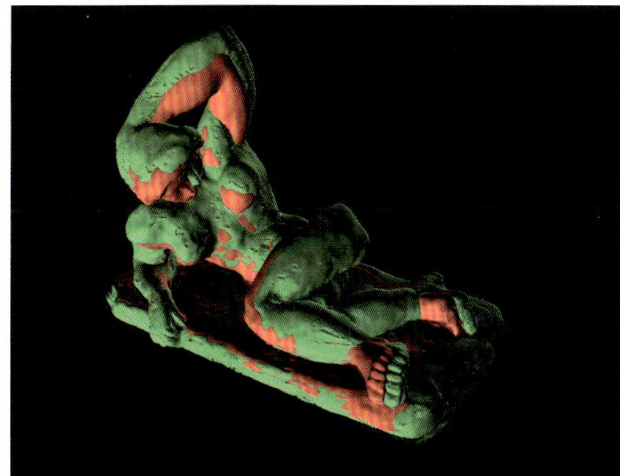

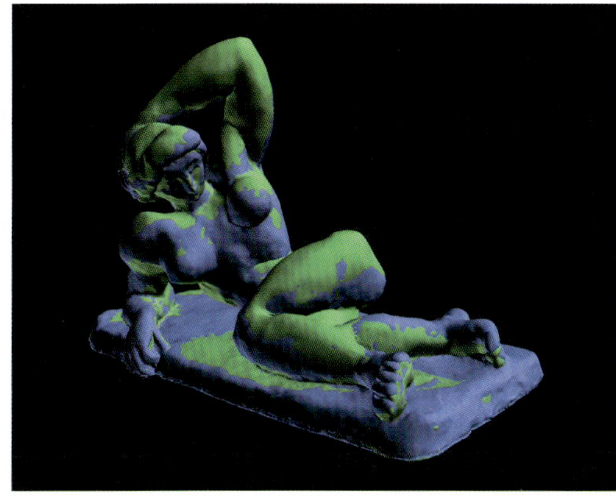

of them. The Hirshhorn example[38] resembles cast terra-cotta in color, texture, and hardness, and is probably hollow, but the bottom is closed up, with no apparent outlet to permit air to escape during firing, a necessary precaution to prevent explosion. In a comparison of three-dimensional computer models of this piece with similar computer models of two bronze casts of the sculpture, it and the bronze from the Nasher were found to be 4% smaller than that from The Baltimore Museum of Art (fig. 76). Terra-cotta would be expected to shrink substantially on drying and firing; but the fact that this one is exactly the same size as a bronze proof seems remarkably coincidental. This terra-cotta may actually be a plaster cast (plaster does not shrink) made from the Nasher bronze or another bronze of the same size, a possibility that can be confirmed through analysis.[39]

Matisse's Foundries

Matisse used four different foundries during his lifetime and, after his death, his family tapped three others in order to achieve his 744-piece bronze oeuvre. His lifetime production of bronzes, spanning nearly fifty years, occurred during a time of great upheaval in the French art bronze foundry industry. By 1958, wars and various financial crises had taken their toll, resulting in the loss of all but six of the sixty art foundries that had been operating in Paris at the beginning of the century.[40] Little art bronze was produced in France during the World War I; the workforce had been mobilized and the foundries converted for the war effort. During the German occupation in World War II, art bronze production was expressly prohibited.[41] Today, there is only a handful of foundries still in the business of art bronze production in the Paris region.

Matisse's first foray into bronze casting began at the Bingen and Costenoble foundry, 26, rue Bezout, Paris (the Petit-Montrouge quarter in the 14th arrondissement). It is likely that the sculptor Aristide Maillol, who trained there to finish and patinate his own sculpture and considered it the best sand-casting foundry at the time,[42] recommended the foundry to his friend Matisse.[43] Given that sand casting was cheaper and Matisse was struggling financially, he might have been influenced by Maillol's preference for the process. By 1914, Matisse was doing well enough to maintain two studios, one at his house in the suburbs, the other in the heart of Paris.[44] Still, he did not abandon sand casting for lost wax until his move to the Valsuani foundry in 1925. Between 1906 and 1910, Matisse had some thirty bronze casts completed at the Bingen and Costenoble foundry.[45] Sixteen more were made and marked by F. Costenoble alone between 1910 and 1915, after the pair split. Thirteen casts were examined as part of this study; all were sand casts, although the foundry also did work with the lost-wax process.[46]

After the war and the demise of the Bingen and Costenoble foundry (it was active from 1903 until 1920), Matisse turned to Florentin Godard, who made at least twenty-three bronze casts for him between about 1920 and 1925. None of this group of Matisse casts has a foundry mark and the catalogue raisonné erroneously attributes the casts to Émile Godard,[47] who did not become an art bronze founder until years later.[48] Nine casts attributed to Godard were examined for this study; all were sand casts.[49]

The catalogue raisonné attributes two casts to the founder Cullen (active between 1920 and 1925), a square bas-relief of *Profile of a Child (Marguerite)* dated 1905 and a bas-relief, *Standing Nude,* identified as a 1927 sand cast.[50] Neither of these casts was available for examination.

In about 1925, Matisse chose to have his bronzes cast by the firm of Claude Valsuani at 74, rue des Plantes (in the Plaisance quarter, also in the 14th arrondissement), and he switched from sand casting to lost-wax casting. Maillol had patronized Valsuani—who worked only in lost wax—in a small way since the foundry opened in 1908, but he always preferred sand casting.[51] It appears that after 1925, Matisse never had another sand cast made.[52] By the time Matisse came to Valsuani, Claude, the original founder, was dead and the firm was under the able direction of his son Marcel,

Fig. 77. Bronze versions of The *Backs* (center) at the Susse Foundry, 1980–1981. The Susse Fondeur Archive.

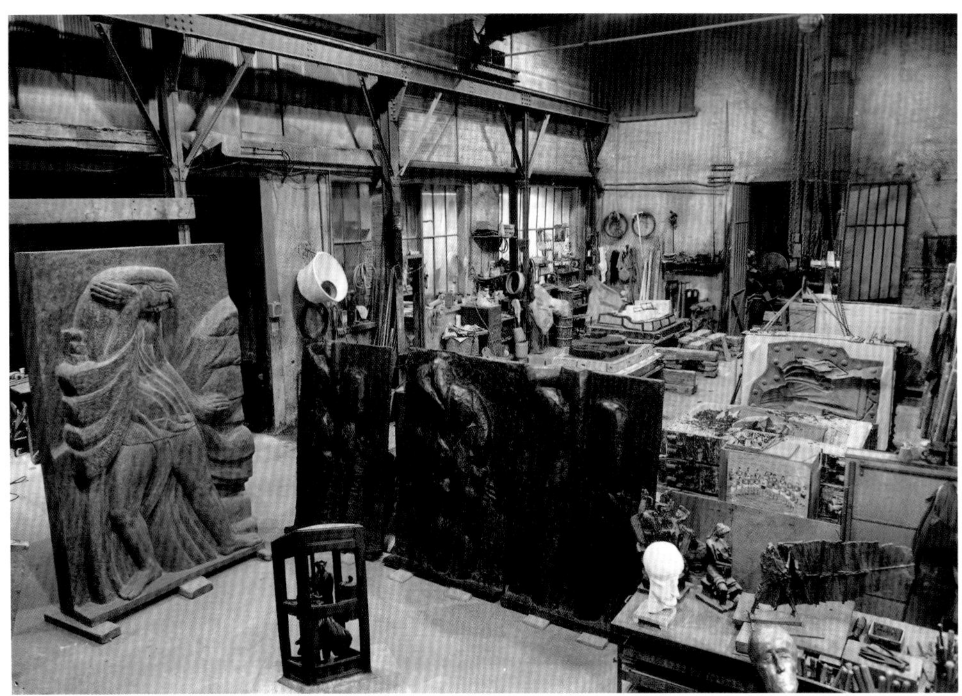

who continued to use his father's name and foundry mark until the 1970s; the firm itself was active until 1981.[53] Claude's father Marcello originally emigrated from Italy in 1902 to work for the founder Adrien-Aurélian Hébrard, who likely hired him for his skills in the lost-wax process and torch patination.[54] During his lifetime Matisse had more than four hundred lost-wax casts made at the Valsuani foundry. His family, particularly his daughter Marguerite, was often closely involved in assisting him throughout his life and continued posthumous production with Valsuani, completing about 150 casts in lost wax that, in appearance, closely resemble the casts made in Matisse's lifetime.[55]

Other founders involved in casting Matisse's work after his death include Georges Rudier, the estranged great-nephew of the company's founder, Alexis Rudier, who made thirty-five sand casts of the four *Backs* between 1955 and 1978; the Susse foundry, where twenty casts of various subjects including eight *Backs* were made between 1978 and 1984 (fig. 77); and the founder Thinot, who cast seven works in lost wax in 1996.

Numbering of Casts

From his earliest bronze production, Matisse numbered his casts and limited the number in each edition, a practice followed by few other sculptors at the time.[56] His most common edition size is ten, with one extra artist proof; there are fifty-seven editions of this size. Eight editions number ten casts with two artist proofs and there are two editions of four casts, one edition of five casts, and one edition of eight casts.[57] The number 10 is usually used as the denominator because casts beyond that number were considered artist proofs and not for sale, but a few numbered casts do not include the denominator.

Possibly his first work to be cast in bronze and his earliest numbered cast is *Small Head with Comb.* It was probably cast in 1906 by the Bingen and Costenoble foundry and is marked 3/10. Two other casts, likely completed in 1906, may be numbered 1/10 and 2/10, although this information was not collected for the catalogue raisonné.[58] Thus, Elisabeth Lebon must be in error in stating that, in 1908, Claude Valsuani was the first to include the total number of casts in a series as part of his numerical notation (e.g., 1/10).[59] Beginning in 1902, the founder Hébrard applied only one sequential number to each cast, although he would advise the buyer of the total number of casts in a given edition.

Matisse did not necessarily number the casts within an edition according to the sequence in which they were cast. Typically, he made only one or two casts of a given sculpture at any one time, as needed for a show or sale. Often the entire edition for one sculpture would be realized only incrementally over many decades. In the early years, poor record keeping resulted in several instances of duplicate numbers within editions. Between 1919 and 1940, and possibly later, casts marked 1 or 2 were exempt from U.S. import taxes, which could be as high as 60%, so some sculptors reserved these two numbers until they could be used specifically for an American client.[60] Matisse does not seem to have done this systematically.

Limited-Edition Serial Casting

The appearance of limited editions of sculpture in the early twentieth century was a response to massive, semi-industrial overproduction of small sand-cast sculpture.[61] Artistic quality had suffered and prices had plummeted. Artists were often virtually enslaved under contract to large commercial foundries that paid them little and offered even less in the determination of the final size or appearance of any given work.[62] The process became a byword for oppression and artistic degradation.

The first Frenchman to grasp and capitalize on the situation, A.-A. Hébrard, the son of a wealthy newspaper publisher and art collector, decided to restore the production of sculpture to the elite sphere that Houdon had occupied during the eighteenth century (and, in doing so, raise prices). He sought to attract artists as clients by offering the limited production of numbered casts and the irresistible opportunity for the artist to inspect and alter each individual wax just before it was cast in bronze, a step not possible in sand casting. The world of elite collectors was his natural social milieu and he had a flair for marketing. He failed, however, to grasp that artists were no longer willing to become ensnared in an oppressive contractual web. The door was open for small artisanal founders who were prepared to work cooperatively with artists. A handful of these founders, among them Bingen and Costenoble and Claude Valsuani, began working between 1903 and 1908.[63]

Sand Casting

Sand casting, known as *moulage à la française* in nineteenth-century Europe,[64] begins with a piece mold made of French casting sand that the founder builds up around a plaster model of a sculpture. The sand is actually a mixture that also includes clay and is very cohesive when tightly packed. When the piece mold has been made, the pieces are carefully taken apart and the model removed. The piece mold is then used to make a sand replica of the model to form a core to be placed inside the mold so that the bronze cast will be hollow. To make this core, the surface of the sand replica is very carefully scraped away to reduce its overall size by the desired thickness of the metal. Both core and piece mold are then baked hard, cooled, and assembled, with pins used to hold the core in position inside the piece mold. Molten bronze is poured into the void between the core and outer piece mold and, once it is cool, the piece mold and the core are destroyed to release the cast. During the nineteenth century the technique was extensively refined, and high-definition sand casting, as developed most notably in the work of the artist and founder Antoine-Louis Barye, was available at the Bingen and Costenoble foundry.

Carefully done, sand casting produces bronze sculpture that is remarkably faithful to the artist's original model. One of the earliest Matisse bronze casts made by Bingen and Costenoble, *Head with Necklace* (cat. 76, p. 272),[65] does not appear to have been altered, aside from patination, after casting. Once the circulation system required to distribute the metal evenly during casting—designed here so that it was attached only at the base and on the interior—was removed, little cold work, or finishing, was needed on the surface. Even some of the artist's fingerprints are reproduced in the

Fig. 78. Henri Matisse, *Head with Necklace,* 1907? (cast 1906?–1908); detail, hole in head. Bronze, sand cast. Direction des Musées de France, Gift of Jean Matisse, on deposit at the Musée Matisse, Nice, 1978. Cat. 76.

Fig. 79. Henri Matisse, *Head with Necklace,* 1907? (cast 1906?–1908); detail. Bronze, sand cast. Direction des Musées de France, Gift of Jean Matisse, on deposit at the Musée Matisse, Nice, 1978. Cat. 76.

Fig. 80. Henri Matisse, *Head with Necklace,* 1907 (cast 1930); detail. Bronze, lost-wax cast. The Baltimore Museum of Art, The Cone Collection, formed by Dr. Claribel Cone and Miss Etta Cone of Baltimore, Maryland. Cat. 74.

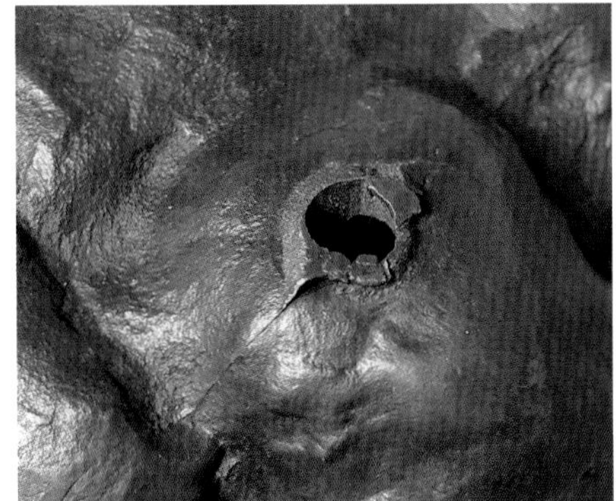

metal surface. Because the piece is small and has only a few undercuts, it could be molded in sand in just two pieces, the mold lines of which are intact on the sides of the work.

What is most striking about this particular cast is the large hole in the top of the head—the imprint of a combination core vent and core pin that allowed gases to escape the core and held the core in position to ensure an even gap between the mold wall and the core surface into which the metal would flow (fig. 78). In normal foundry practice this hole would have been filled with metal after the tube and core were removed, and the mold lines would have been erased. Possibly this work was a test piece, the artist challenging the founders to cast his sculpture in sand with the minimal cold work usually associated with lost-wax casting.[66] This piece is marked 00, indicating that it is an artist proof, and is the only documented Matisse cast by Bingen and Costenoble so marked, although two others are marked 0. Could this (fig. 79) be the artist's first bronze cast?[67]

This cast may be compared with a later lost-wax cast of the same sculpture produced by the Valsuani foundry in 1930 (fig. 80).[68] Of the two, the earlier sand cast more faithfully renders the original clay surface; the fingerprints are better preserved, and the slightly grainy texture of the clay more apparent. This is the opposite of what one might normally expect, the lost-wax process being considered superior in rendering fine detail, an assumption confirmed in the comparison of a lost-wax cast of the *Two Negresses* by Valsuani and a sand-cast version by Bingen and Costenoble.[69]

Lost-Wax Casting

Lost-wax casting is an ancient process. Direct lost-wax casting was practiced at least as early as 3000 BC in Mesopotamia.[70] Indirect lost-wax casting was known by the seventh century BC and was widely practiced by the ancient Greeks and Romans.[71] The critical distinction is that, in the direct process, the wax pattern (also called the wax positive) is shaped directly by the artist; in the indirect process, the wax pattern is made in a mold taken from a sculpture previously made by the artist and usually in another material. The disadvantage of the direct process is that a unique wax could be lost forever if the casting process failed. In the indirect method, a casting failure may be an inconvenience but will not be a catastrophe.

Lost-wax casting had been done in France before the Revolution, but by the early nineteenth century the process for the production of sculpture had been virtually lost,[72] replaced by sand casting. When the celebrated sand founder Honoré Gonon decided to take up lost-wax casting in about 1830, there was no one to learn from; he studied the fragments of lost-wax cast equestrian sculpture pulled down by revolutionary mobs and did his own experiments. In 1876, his son Eugène felt compelled to write a fifty-six-page description of the process and sell it to the government for fear the process would be lost when he died.[73] Gonon's was an indirect process using gelatin for molding wax positives.[74] But the founder Pierre Bingen apparently did not think much of that process and vowed

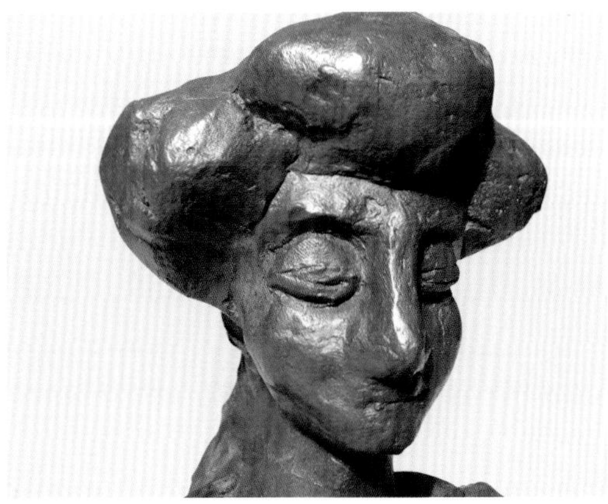

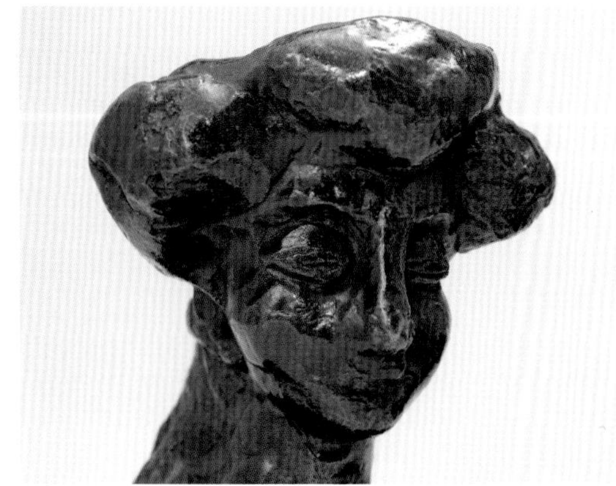

to discover "a method of lost-wax casting which in no way resembled that practiced by Mr. Gonon"[75] —perhaps because a direct lost-wax cast is likely to carry better detail than one made indirectly from a gelatin mold.[76] Bingen's process was a development of the more ancient, direct method similar to that described in the Renaissance by the sculptor Benvenuto Cellini for his *Nymph of Fontainebleau.*[77] This was the technique used during Matisse's time at the Bingen and Costenoble foundry,[78] as documented by Maillol's complaint, when pressed by a collector to produce for him a work in lost wax to be cast at that foundry: "I will make it for you because I promised, but it is the last time I will do it. It is a huge job, I must completely remake the figure."[79] During the last quarter of the century a few others, among them Victor Thiebault and E. Gruet Jeune, took up lost-wax casting, either direct or indirect, to produce unique works.[80]

In 1902, Adrien-Aurélien Hébrard brought several skilled Italian workmen to his foundry in Paris to provide serial lost-wax bronze casting. The early twentieth-century Italian method involved the use of a flexible mold made of gelatin to take impressions from an artist's plaster model.[81] Molten wax was brushed onto the interior of the mold and then more wax was poured into the gelatin impression to cast a wax positive of the sculpture. Up to about six wax positives of one sculpture could be cast in series using a single gelatin mold before it became too desiccated and had to be discarded.[82] Being flexible, the gelatin could be peeled away from the wax in large sections without damage to either the wax or the mold. More gelatin molds could be made as needed from the original plaster model to create a theoretically unlimited number of wax positives from one model.

At this stage, the artist could step in and rework the wax positives. He could merely sign his name in the soft wax, remove seams left by the gelatin mold, or radically modify the composition, even changing the wax positive so that each bronze cast would be different.[83] At the Valsuani foundry Matisse, for instance, typically put his initials into the wax; when he was absent, the mold maker used an oval stamp to apply the artist's initials. Matisse or the mold maker would carefully remove the mold lines created by the sections of the gelatin mold,[84] but the wax positives for the sculptures examined in this study had not been modified further.

Once the cast wax positive was prepared, it was covered with investment, a pasty molding material similar to plaster that set hard and was heat resistant. The Valsuani foundry was known for its use of investment with cow dung, *la potée à la bouse de vache,* and the so-called Italian core, *noyau à l'italienne.*[85] The core was made of investment poured inside the hollow wax positive to fill the interior so that the resulting bronze cast would be hollow. Next, the piece was heated to melt out the wax, leaving behind its impression entombed inside the investment, hence the term *lost* wax. Molten bronze was then poured into this mold to create the sculpture.

Surface Finishing

After a bronze sculpture has been cast, extensive surface finishing is required. This includes removing the residual mold material, whether sand or investment, cutting or sawing to remove the metal circulation system (sprues and vents) that begin as arterylike voids in the mold but become filled with metal during the casting process, filing off metal mold lines created by the sand piece mold or metal flash lines created by narrow cracks in the investment material, and plugging any holes in the cast caused either by the removal of core pins or core vents or from gas bubbles in the molten metal. Complex sand-cast sculptures with extensive undercuts are often cast in several pieces and then joined together mechanically. In large nineteenth-century foundries, skilled workmen, *monteurs,* assembled the parts; others, known as *ciseleurs,* disguised the joins by hammering, punching, and filing. This surface cold work can alter the artist's intention. Artists such as Barye and Maillol addressed this problem by doing their own finishing work. Matisse, a painter, was not so inclined

Fig. 81. X-ray: Henri Matisse, *Two Women,* 1908 (cast 1908). Bronze. Sand cast, Bingen and Costenoble. Hirshhorn Museum and Sculpture Garden. Arrow shows core vent.

Fig. 82. X-ray: Henri Matisse, *Two Negresses,* 1907–1908 (cast 1930). Bronze. Lost-wax cast, Valsuani foundry. The Baltimore Museum of Art.

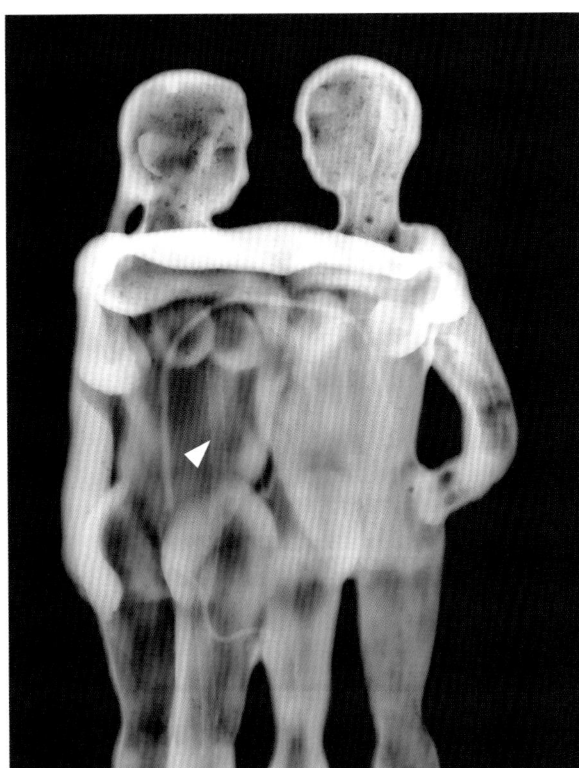

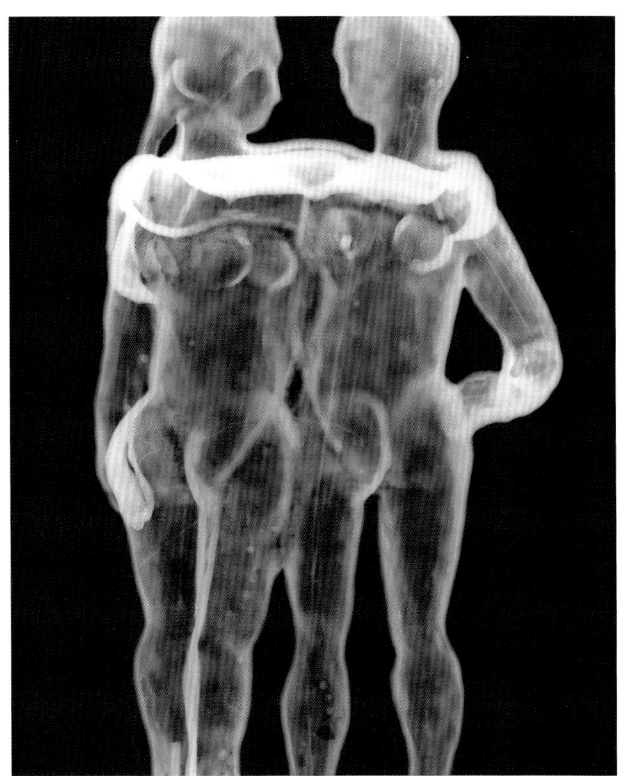

and relied on the founders to do it as sensitively as possible. His sand-cast sculptures made in more than one piece include the *Reclining Nude I (Aurora), The Serpentine,* and *The Serf.* Another sand-cast sculpture examined, the Hirshhorn's *Two Women,* is a complex form with many undercuts. It was nevertheless cast in one piece (fig. 81). This early work, cast in 1908, may reflect the superior workmanship in the foundry during the collaboration of Bingen and Costenoble; the *Reclining Nude I* and *The Serpentine* were cast later by Costenoble alone. *The Serf* (cat. 4, p. 266), although cast in the earlier period, is made in only two pieces with the figure intact and the base cast separately. One-piece casting seems to be easier in the lost-wax process; all Valsuani's casts that were radiographed for this study appear to have been done in that way (fig. 82).

Generally only the exterior surfaces of the sculptures were finished. The hollow interiors were not treated, except that bulk core material with its internal vents and armature was removed when accessible. Sand-cast interior surfaces tend to be clean and smooth with few flash lines (indications of cracks in the core) and only minor traces of loose gray sand trapped in deep recesses (fig. 83). (Later casts, from the 1950s, were generally found to be somewhat cleaner than those from the 1930s; fig. 84.) Mold lines do not occur on sand-cast interior surfaces because the core (of which the interior surface is an imprint) is usually made in one piece. A signature feature of sand casts from the Godard foundry is the silvery gray color of the interior surfaces. It looks like graphite and is the remnants of a surface treatment of the core that may have been used to facilitate removal of the sand after casting or to enhance the flow of the metal over the surface of the core. Lost-wax cast interior surfaces are irregular and sometimes X-rays will reveal obvious drip marks from the molten wax that is poured into the gelatin mold and because the mold is rolled so that the sides become coated with wax (fig. 85). Raised metal flash lines are common, and much residual white investment material is firmly attached to the bronze surface. Sprue stubs, remnants of the metal circulation system, are commonly found inside the bases of both sand and lost-wax casts, indicating that the molds were probably upside down during casting. Iron wires protruding from the interiors of inaccessible elements such as arms are remnants of core supports that became lodged within and could not be easily removed with the core.

Fig. 83. Henri Matisse, *Reclining Nude I (Aurora)*, 1907 (cast 1912); detail, underneath. Bronze, sand cast by Bingen and Costenoble foundry. Albright-Knox Art Gallery, Buffalo, Room of Contemporary Art Fund.

Fig. 84. Henri Matisse, *Reclining Nude I (Aurora)*, 1907 (cast c. 1930); detail, underneath. Bronze, lost-wax cast by the Valsuani Foundry. The Baltimore Museum of Art, The Cone Collection, formed by Dr. Claribel Cone and Miss Etta Cone of Baltimore, Maryland. Cat. 45.

X-radiography is useful for studying the interiors of bronze sculptures that have narrow or closed bases, providing information about the porosity of a bronze cast, and revealing hidden repairs or seams. Both lost-wax and sand casts were found to be quite porous but plugged repairs are rare.[86] In small heads cast in lost wax by Valsuani, such as the *Head of Marguerite,*[87] there were generally three core pins: a large-diameter (about ¼-inch) pin in the top of the head and smaller ones (about ⅛-inch diameter) on each side near the base. The pins themselves have been removed and the circular holes plugged with bronze. Existing core pins visible in the X-ray of the sand-cast version of the *Two Women*[88] were randomly spaced and are very small in diameter, the size of a straight pin (fig. 81). Similarly, the sand-cast *Serf* (fig. 86)[89] has dozens of 2-inch-long small-diameter pins still in place. These slender core pins did not need to be removed or plugged. Both sand casts were made by Bingen and Costenoble.

In some Bingen and Costenoble sand casts, including the *Two Women* and *Head of a Child (Pierre Matisse),*[90] where complete core removal was not possible, given the geometry of the work, a core vent (which probably also functioned as a core pin), slightly larger in diameter than a pencil and made from rolled sheet metal wrapped with fine-diameter wire, is visible in the X-radiographs (fig. 81).[91] These protruded from the tops of the heads during casting, and, rather than remove them, the founder pushed them back inside and plugged up the holes. Part of a similar core vent may be seen inside the Bingen and Costenoble cast of *Woman Leaning on Her Hands* (fig. 87).[92]

Patination

Once these repairs have been made and camouflaged by using small chisels, punches, and hammers to replicate the missing surface detail, the piece is patinated. Unpatinated raw bronze is a shiny bright copper color, similar to a new penny. Beginning in the 1820s, French founders began to devise myriad patination recipes and procedures using chemicals to produce various colors and surface effects. These effects were often enhanced, altered, or protected by the addition of tinted wax or varnish. Patination colors vary slightly on Matisse's works, but all are in the medium-brown to very dark brown or nearly black range, with warmer and cooler variations. Differences in patination seem to be the result of foundry techniques rather than of any particular aesthetic choice on Matisse's part,[93] except for a notable anomaly from the early 1930s. The Baltimore Museum of Art's version of *Tiari* (cat. 78, pp. 196–97), cast in 1930 by Valsuani, is quite different in finish from all the other casts examined as part of this study, including two casts of the same sculpture made that year.[94] The entire surface has been extensively cold worked with files, grinders, and abrasives to smooth the slightly undulating modeled surfaces that are apparent on the other two casts. The patination color

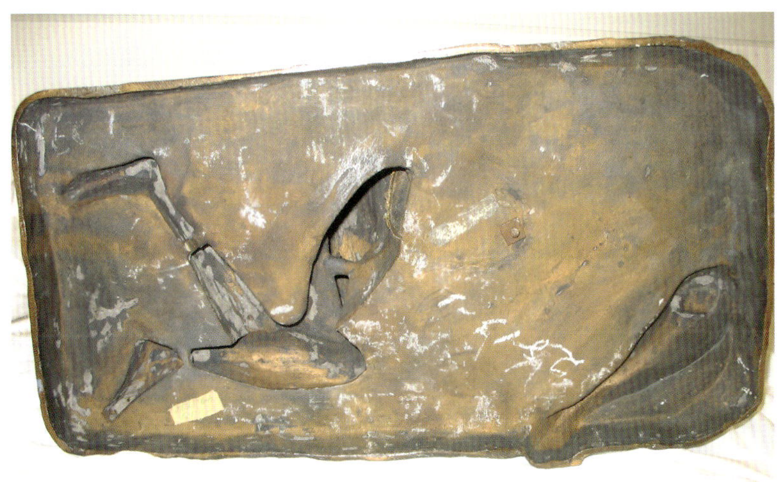

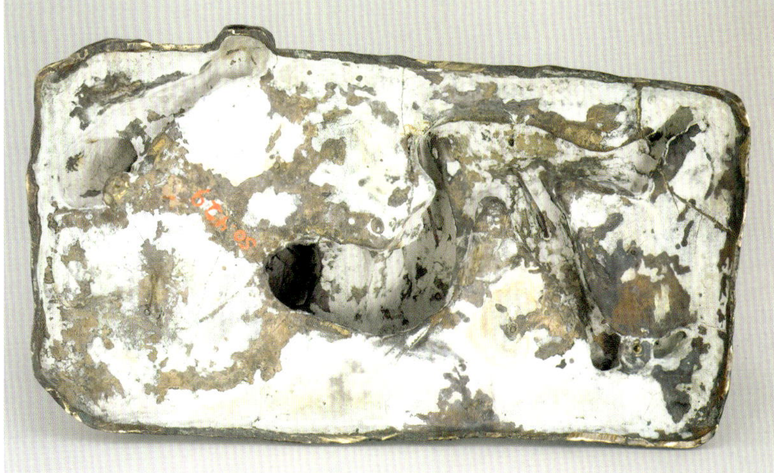

Fig. 85. X-ray: Henri Matisse, *Madeleine I*, 1901 (cast 1925). Bronze. The Baltimore Museum of Art. Cat. 12. Arrows show drip marks.

is a lighter golden brown and, most unusual, the necklace clasped around the neck is made of gold and silver. This unique work is numbered 1 in the edition and may well be the first proof cast in the series.[95] Perhaps it was intended as a special tribute to Etta Cone, the collector who purchased it.

Visual examination of the surfaces of the bronzes made by the three foundries revealed that the patination of the sand-cast works by Bingen and Costenoble and Godard were flatter, more opaque, and less lively than that of the lost-wax cast made at the Valsuani foundry. The Valsuani patina is deeper, richer, and more glossily nuanced than the others. The application of wax can heighten the gloss, but even on works from all three foundries, treated equally with wax for exhibition in a museum setting, Valsuani's casts come out the glossiest. Because many of Matisse's works have exuberantly modeled surfaces, the addition of the glossy Valsuani surface makes for a vibrant, impressionistic display. This distinctive patination can be recognized in Valsuani's work for other artists and does not seem to have been developed especially for Matisse. The rich, dense, and deep patina on the *Reclining Nude I (Aurora)* at The Baltimore Museum of Art (cat. 45, pp. 153, 155–56) is probably *noir Valsuani* (Valsuani black), one of the foundry's most famous patinas.[96]

How was the Valsuani patina achieved? The surface of the lost-wax cast metal was probably slightly less granular than that of a sand-cast surface, and the alloy composition may have been a factor. Analysis by X-ray fluorescence spectrometry (XRF) of the surfaces of sculptures at The Baltimore Museum of Art show that chromium is present in fourteen of the sixteen Valsuani patinas but not in those from the other two foundries.[97] Probably the biggest difference, however, has to do with the use of the blowtorch. Claude Valsuani in particular was celebrated for the beautiful patinas he created with a blowtorch "that did not leave a deposit of carbon."[98]

The blowtorch is such an integral part of the modern patination studio that it seems almost impossible to imagine its absence. Yet nineteenth-century French foundries patinated all manner of their immense bronze output without it. When torch patination came to Paris with the Italians and serial lost-wax casting in the early twentieth century,[99] French foundries were as slow to accept this finishing process as they were the serial lost-wax process itself. As late as 1920, in the Bingen and Costenoble foundry, multipiece sand casts were being joined mechanically in the traditional nineteenth-century manner by careful fitting and hand-tapped screws, an indication that even then the torch was not yet being used for brazing.[100]

Alloy Composition

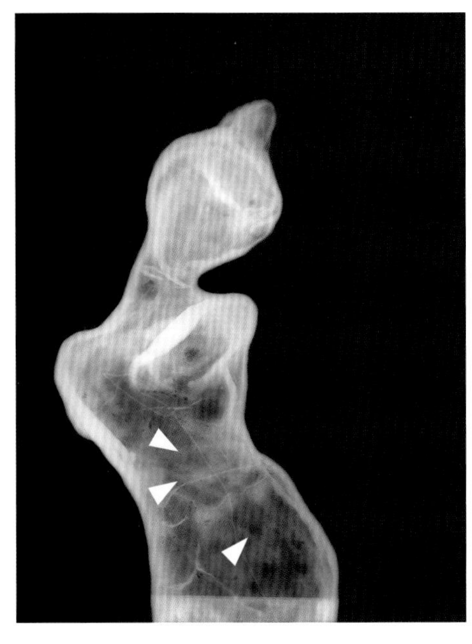

Bronze is a metal alloy—a mixture of several different metals. The composition of bronze varies widely; foundries often developed favorite recipes and were not always forthcoming about their compositions. Generally, bronze is a mixture of copper and tin, sometimes with a bit of lead. Zinc is a common additive and, in late nineteenth-century France, small quantities of silver and gold were added to emulate Japanese alloys.[101]

To distinguish the different alloys in use by different foundries and to see if differences existed between sand casts and lost-wax casts, the twenty-one Matisse bronzes at The Baltimore Museum of Art were analyzed by portable X-ray fluorescence spectrometry (XRF). One work from the Hirshhorn, *Two Women,* and four of The Baltimore Museum of Art's bronzes were analyzed by standard XRF for comparison (table 1).[102] The copper content of the six sand-cast works was found to be the highest, ranging from about 92% to 95%; that of the sixteen lost-wax works ranged from about 78% to 89%. Tin and zinc content varied (fig. 88). The two Bingen and Costenoble sand casts had nearly equal low levels of tin and zinc; the four Godard sand casts had slightly more than twice as much zinc as tin, although still at low levels.[103] Three early lost-wax works, made before 1929,[104] had about equal or higher percentages of tin than of zinc, whereas lost-wax works cast between 1929 and 1931 contained much more zinc, ranging from about 9% to 18%, with correspondingly much lower levels of tin,

Fig. 86. X-ray: Henri Matisse, *The Serf,* 1900–1903 (cast 1908). Bronze, sand cast by the Bingen and Costenoble foundry. The Baltimore Museum of Art. Cat. 4. Arrow shows core pin.

Fig. 87. Detail, Henri Matisse, *Woman Leaning on Her Hands,* 1906 (cast 1908). Bronze, sand cast by the Bingen and Costenoble foundry. The Metropolitan Museum of Art, New York. Arrow shows core vent.

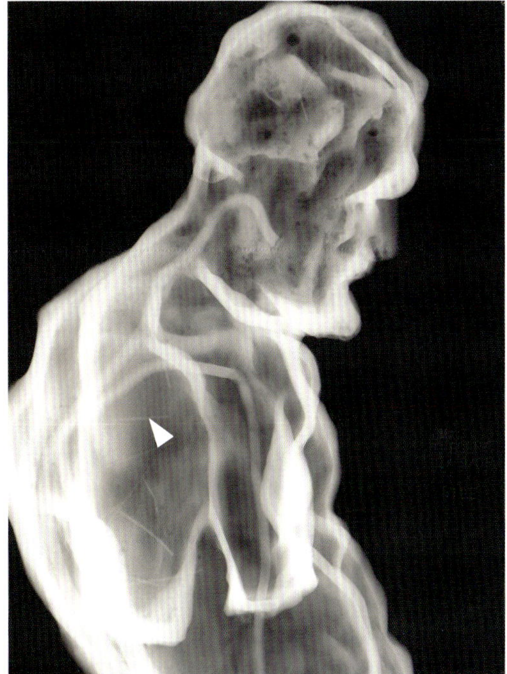

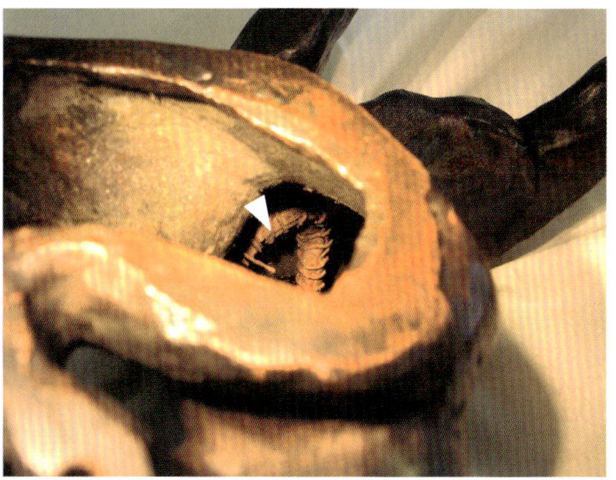

about 2% to 4%.[105] In all the sculptures, the lead content was generally below about 1%. Although the level of zinc in the later lost-wax casts is high enough that, technically, these alloys could be called brass, bronze is still an appropriate generic label for sculpture made of copper alloys.[106]

Henri Matisse's habit of making three-dimensional "snapshots" of a work in progress by piece molding on wet clay—an extrapolation of Rodin's method—has resulted in related works such as *Madeleine I* and *II* and *The Backs.* This window into his creative process helps explain his protracted struggle with some works for which he took the opportunity to return repeatedly to the earlier stages that he had recorded. His love of line, so evident in his painting, drawing, and cut-outs, is equally prominent in many of his most important sculptures, including *Madeleine I, The Serf, Reclining Nude I (Aurora),* and the *Large Seated Nude.* The transformation of a clay sculpture first to plaster, then often to wax, and finally to bronze offered as many as five separate opportunities to create mold lines on the surface of the finished work. Lines made at the foundry were carefully removed; only certain lines created by the artist himself or his mold maker were retained. These lines, the result of the artist's carefully considered and discriminating vision, were chosen to emphasize important contours or create surface decoration. Their importance to composition is especially highlighted in the strange case of the *Reclining Nude I (Aurora),* of which there are casts in bronze and terra-cotta—casts unlikely to have been produced under the artist's supervision—that lack these lines. The opportunity to compare the spurious with the genuine allows for an increased appreciation of the artist's preoccupation with line.

Although Matisse, unlike some sculptors, was not physically engaged in finishing his bronzes, the selection of his two most important foundries, Bingen and Costenoble and Valsuani, made on the basis of their reputations for collaborating with artists, indicates his concern that the finished product would replicate his artfully modeled and molded surfaces and his trust in the foundries chosen to do so. The many photographs taken of Marcel Valsuani visiting Matisse at his sickbed in Nice near the end of the artist's life is testament to their close friendship.

Matisse's bronze production came at a pivotal moment in the history of bronze casting in France, the understanding of which expands appreciation of his artistic vision. A nineteenth-century

Table 1. X-Ray Fluorescence Analysis of Selected Bronzes by Henri Matisse Cast 1908–1931, 1953

Title, by Casting Date and Foundry	Sample Location[a] by Instrument[b]	Composition of Alloy by Weight %				
		Cr	Cu	Zn	Sn	Pb
1. *The Serf*						
1908 sand cast, Bingen and Costenoble	Base: Innov-x	—	93.7	2.8	2.1	1.4
BMA 1950.422	Patina: Innov-x	—	94.9	2.1	2.2	0.6
	Patina: Innov-x	—	94.2	2.4	2.3	0.9
2. *Two Women*[c]						
1908 sand cast, Bingen and Costenoble	Base: Kevex	—	91.9	3.3	3.0	1.4
Hirshhorn 66.34.56	Patina: Kevex, site 1	—	92.1	2.9	3.2	1.5
	site 2	—	92.7	2.7	3.1	1.2
	site 3	—	92.0	2.7	3.1	1.8
3. *Head of Child (Pierre Matisse)*						
1922 sand cast, Godard	Patina: Innov-x	—	92.9	4.7	1.9	0.3
BMA 1950.425						
4. *Woman Leaning on Her Hands*						
1922 sand cast, Godard	Base: Innov-x	—	92.4	5.4	1.7	0.3
BMA 1950.424	Patina: Innov-x	—	92.7	4.9	1.7	0.5
5. *Small Head with Comb*						
1922 sand cast, Godard	Base: Innov-x	—	93.1	4.7	1.8	0.3
BMA 1950.427						
6. *Small Crouching Nude without an Arm*						
1922 sand cast, Godard	Base: Innov-x	—	93.3	4.3	2.1	—
BMA 1950.432	Patina: Innov-x	—	93.1	4.5	1.9	0.2
7. *Madeleine I*						
1925 lost-wax cast, Valsuani	Base: Innov-x	—	85.5	7.1	6.0	1.4
BMA 1950.423	Patina: Innov-x	0.6	84.7	5.5	6.5	0.3
	Base: Kevex	—	86.6	4.8	7.8	0.5
	Patina: Kevex, site 1	—	86.7	4.0	8.0	0.4
	site 2	—	87.1	4.2	7.6	0.2
	site 3	—	85.8	4.0	8.8	0.5
8. *Figure with Cushion*						
1925 lost -wax cast, Valsuani	Patina: Innov-x, site 1	—	87.3	4.8	6.7	0.7
BMA 1950.433	site 2	0.3	88.1	2.8	7.2	0.5
9. *Head of a Young Girl*						
1925 lost-wax cast, Valsuani	Base: Innov-x	—	86.5	5.3	7.5	0.5
BMA 1950.426	Patina: Innov-x	—	88.2	3.0	7.9	0.4
10. *Reclining Nude III*						
1929 lost-wax cast, Valsuani	Base: Innov-x	0.5	84.0	12.0	2.9	0.4
BMA 1950.437	Patina: Innov-x	1.6	83.7	11.2	2.4	0.3
	Base: Kevex	—	84.5	11.4	3.5	0.4
	Patina: Kevex, site 1	—	83.1	12.0	4.0	0.4
	site 2	—	87.1	8.3	3.5	0.6
	site 3	—	87.1	8.4	3.2	0.8
11. *Two Negresses*						
1930 lost-wax cast, Valsuani	Base: Innov-x	—	83.2	13.3	3.5	—
BMA 1950.430	Patina: Innov-x	0.8	86.3	9.9	2.5	—
	Base: Kevex	—	81.9	14.5	3.0	0.4
	Patina: Kevex, site 1	—	86.4	9.4	3.5	0.2
	site 2	—	87.0	5.9	5.7	1.0
	site 3	—	88.0	8.2	3.3	0.1
	site 4	—	85.6	10.0	3.5	0.4
12. *Seated Nude Clasping Her Right Leg*						
1930 lost-wax cast, Valsuani	Base: Innov-x	0.9	81.7	13.6	3.2	0.3
BMA 1950.434	Patina: Innov-x, site 1	2.7	83.0	11.0	2.7	—
	site 2	2.3	83.1	11.0	2.9	—

Title, by Casting Date and Foundry	Sample Location[a] by Instrument[b]	Composition of Alloy by Weight %				
		Cr	Cu	Zn	Sn	Pb
13. *Crouching Venus*						
1930 lost-wax cast, Valsuani	Base: Innov-x	0.6	79.9	13.9	2.6	2.7
BMA 1950.435	Patina: Innov-x	2.8	82.1	11.5	2.7	0.4
14. *Large Seated Nude*						
1930 lost-wax cast, Valsuani	Base: Innov-x	—	78.1	18.1	2.9	0.7
BMA 1950.436	Patina: Innov-x, site 1	1.2	80.9	14.9	2.7	0.2
	site 2	1.0	82.6	13.6	2.6	—
15. *Tiari (with Necklace)*						
1930 lost-wax cast, Valsuani	Base: Innov-x	—	84.5	12.3	3.1	—
BMA 1950.438	Patina: Innov-x	—	86.6	10.3	2.9	—
16. *Seated Nude with Arms on Head*						
1930 lost-wax cast, Valsuani	Base: Innov-x	0.5	82.7	13.9	2.7	0.2
BMA 1950.431	Patina: Innov-x	1.1	84.2	11.9	2.5	0.2
17. *Reclining Figure with Chemise*						
1930 lost-wax cast, Valsuani	Base: Innov-x	1.8	85.4	8.6	3.3	—
BMA 1955.164	Patina: Innov-x	1.1	86.1	10.0	2.2	—
	Base: Kevex	—	84.0	11.1	4.2	0.5
	Patina: Kevex site 1	—	82.2	14.1	3.1	0.2
	site 2	—	78.7	17.4	2.9	0.5
	site 3	—	87.2	8.1	3.8	0.4
18. *The Serpentine*						
1930 lost-wax cast, Valsuani	Base: Innov-x	0.3	82.6	15.2	1.7	—
BMA 1950.93	Patina: Innov-x	1.3	83.3	12.8	2.2	—
19. *Head with Necklace*						
1930 lost-wax cast, Valsuani	Base: Innov-x	—	85.2	12.2	2.1	0.3
BMA 1950.428	Patina: Innov-x	1.0	85.7	10.3	2.5	—
20. *Reclining Nude I (Aurora)*						
1930 lost-wax cast, Valsuani	Base: Innov-x	—	85.2	11.7	2.9	—
BMA 1950.429	Patina: Innov-x	2.1	81.4	13.0	2.9	—
21. *Venus in a Shell I*						
1931 lost-wax cast, Valsuani	Base: Innov-x	0.8	82.8	10.0	3.9	—
BMA 1950.439	Patina: Innov-x	1.1	82.5	11.1	3.0	1.8
22. *Jaguar Devouring a Hare*						
1953 lost-wax cast, Valsuani	Base: Innov-x	—	81.4	14.5	2.8	0.9
BMA 1999.3	Patina: Innov-x	1.1	84.5	11.0	2.9	0.2

Abbreviations

BMA = The Baltimore Museum of Art; Hirshhorn = Hirshhorn Museum and Sculpture Gardens, Smithsonian Institution, Washington, D.C.

Elements: Cr – chromium; Cu – copper; Pb = lead; Sn = tin; Zn = zinc

Notes

a. Sample sites:

Base: under the sculpture, taken in a flat area with little or no patination

Patina: on the exterior of the sculpture, taken in a flat area with patination; on some bronzes more than one site was analyzed

b. The instruments used were the handheld Innov-x Systems X-ray Fluorescence Spectrum Analyzer and the Kevex 0750A Spectrometer.

c. Matisse's original title for the sculpture also known as *Two Negresses*

Source

The Innov-x analyses were performed at The Baltimore Museum of Art by Jia-sun Tsang, Dr. Charles Tumosa, and Sarah Pinchin of the Smithsonian Center for Materials Research and Education, Washington, D.C., August 2004. The Kevex 0750A analyses were performed by Kathryn Morales at the National Gallery of Art, Washington, D.C., August 2004 and January 2005. The results of the Innov-x analyses are reported in Smithsonian Center for Materials Research and Education, Request No. 5914.

French founder who wanted to make more than one cast of a sculpture would have logically turned to sand casting, as lost wax was then viewed only as a way to make a unique work, an artistic work, not a mass-produced work. The idea of serial lost-wax casting thus had not developed in France, despite Gonon's innovative use of gelatin molding, because a perfectly acceptable method of serial casting already existed. The Italian method of serial lost-wax casting, then, represented, in France, not so much a technical innovation as a paradigm shift: bronzes made in series could be important, artistic works. Because the indirect nature afforded an artistic intervention not available in sand casting, the serial lost-wax process was lifted into the realm of fine art. Matisse's limited use of this opportunity to modify the wax surface—only removing foundry molding lines and signing his name—is proof that his artistic vision had come to fruition in plaster. His emphasis on recording the intellectual steps of the creative process stands in contrast to his indifference to the steps necessary for bronze casting. The loss of the original plasters is regrettable, but their skillful translation into limited edition bronzes by his trusted founders insures that his vision will endure.

Fig. 88. Composition of Tin and Zinc in 21 Bronze Sculptures by Henri Matisse
The Baltimore Museum of Art
Cast 1908–1931

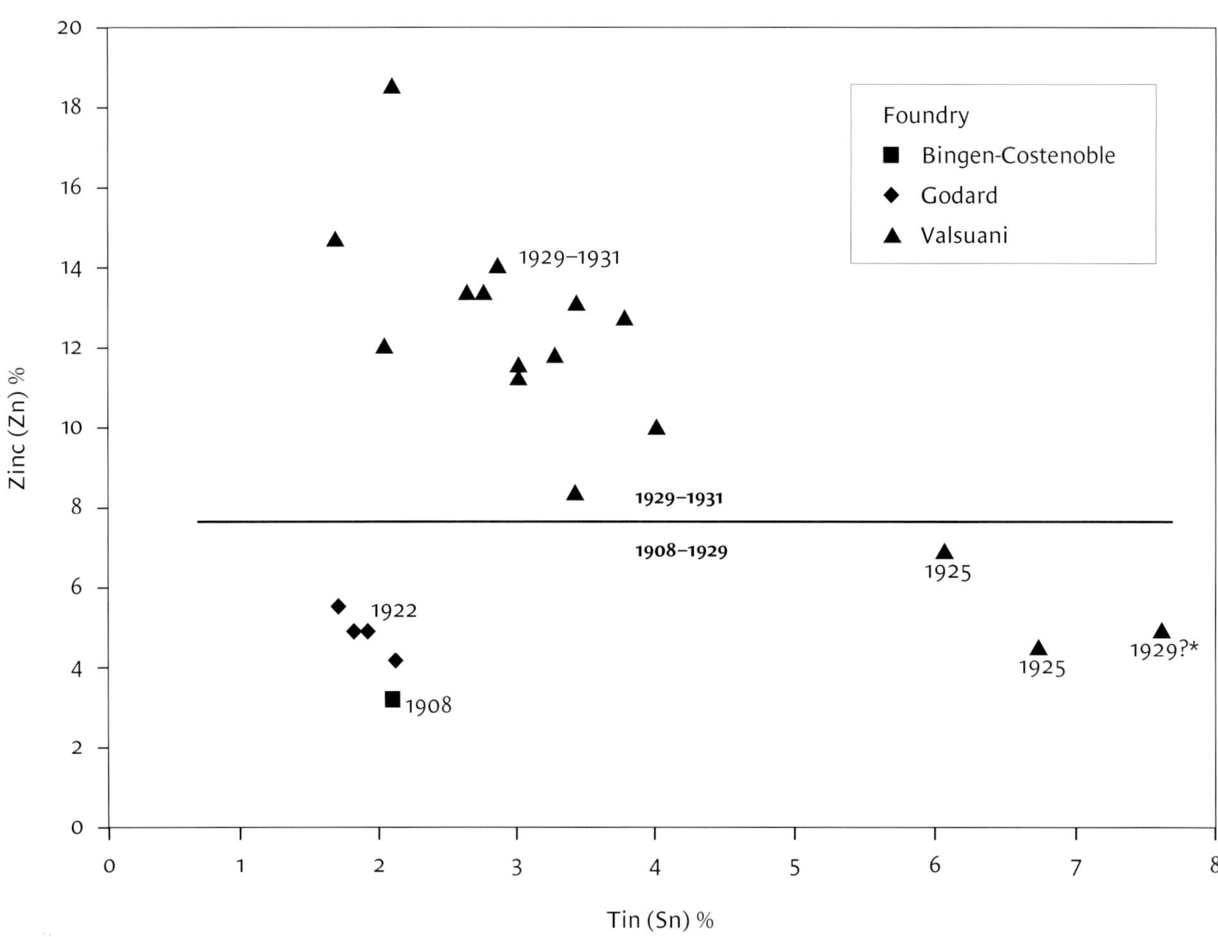

Each mark on this scatter plot represents one sculpture in the collection of The Baltimore Museum of Art.
The different shapes distinguish the casts made by the three primary foundries used by Matisse during his life: Bingen and Costenoble (square), Godard (diamond shape), and Valsuani (triangle). The three separate clusters are segregated by their differing tin-zinc ratios. The cluster of a square and diamond shapes in the bottom left quadrant represents sand-cast works made between 1908 and 1922 with low tin and zinc content; the small cluster of triangles in the bottom right quadrant below the dateline represents lost-wax casts made, before 1929, with more tin; the large cluster of triangles above the dateline represents lost-wax casts made, after 1929, with much higher quantities of zinc. This plot was prepared at the Smithsonian Center for Materials Research and Education.

* See note 104, p. 96.

Notes

1. The Baltimore Museum of Art; Hirshhorn Museum and Sculpture Garden, Washington, D.C.; Nasher Sculpture Center, Dallas, Texas; Museum of Modern Art, New York; San Francisco Museum of Modern Art; Philadelphia Museum of Art; The Rosenbach Library, Philadelphia; Weatherspoon Art Museum of the University of North Carolina at Greensboro; Albright-Knox Art Gallery, Buffalo, New York; The Metropolitan Museum of Art, New York; Musée Matisse, Nice; Musée national d'art moderne, centre Georges Pompidou, Paris; Musée départemental Matisse, Le Cateau-Cambrésis, France. The author gratefully acknowledges the important contribution of Oliver Shell to this work.

2. Albert Elsen states: "The credentials of Matisse as a sculptor are impressive," and reports that, in the late 1890s, he began an abbreviated yet concentrated effort to gain the skills he lacked by the study of human and animal anatomy, the making of copies of sculpture in his studio and at the Louvre, and through consultation with experienced sculptors such as Rodin and Bourdelle; Elsen 1972, 11.

3. Musée Matisse, Nice, 63.2.104.

4. Matisse's comments seem to imply that he had never before used plasticine: "I want to do a little more sculpture, smaller pieces, often working in bed. I had some wax ordered from Valsuani. He told me that I would have to use *plastilic* [*sic*]. I found it had an unpleasant feel to it, and I didn't like the surface either" (Duthuit 1997, 387). But a bill from Matisse's mold maker, Léon Bertault, dated February 17, 1928, lists a waste mold made on the plastiline (plasticine) of a study of the *écorché;* Archives Matisse, Paris. Perhaps the undated note to Laurens, believed to be from 1949, referred to a specific brand of commercial modeling clay. Oddly, the catalogue raisonné (Duthuit 1997) lists all bronzes of the *écorché* (fig. 31, p. 32) as cast in 1958, but a bronze version is depicted in a photograph of Matisse and Valsuani taken in 1953.

5. The term *plasticine* here is used in its most generic sense as a commercial modeling compound—no analysis was performed. The substance was identified by its yellowish color, the oil that appeared to be separating out, and its pliability. Plasticine, which began to be commercially available toward the end of the nineteenth century, initially contained sulfur, which was later found to corrode internal armatures. In later formulations sulfur was omitted; Arthur Beale, telephone interview by the author, February 2006.

6. The fifty-five-year-old plasticine has begun to deteriorate; oil has exuded onto the wooden base.

7. Musée départemental Matisse, Le Cateau-Cambrésis, 1982.33 and 1982.32. The supposition is based on their size—they are slightly larger than the bronze casts and bronze shrinks on cooling. In addition, a gelatin mold made from a terra-cotta head is documented in a bill from Matisse's mold maker, Léon Bertault, in 1929; Archives Matisse, Paris. *Small Head with Upswept Hair* was first cast in bronze in 1930. *Head of a Faun* was not cast in bronze until after Matisse's death. X-radiography, not possible in this study for these clay and terra-cotta objects, could show definitively the absence of armatures.

8. Clay formulated for modeling works that are not intended to be fired (*l'argile grasse à modeler* or *terre crue*) generally contains a lot of organic material and not much sand or grog. This results in greater shrinkage upon drying and sometimes cooked flour is added to counteract this. The best clay in France for modeling comes from Dreux, Houdan, Montereau, Gournay, and Gisors; Baudry et al. 1978, 95. Analysis of clay was not possible for this study.

9. Lorquin 1994, 56.

10. Spurling 1998, 369.

11. Ibid., 56.

12. Archives Matisse, Paris.

13. Although gelatin molding or at least flexible molding with glue dates to Roman times (Beale, telephone interview by author, fall 2004), it became newly appreciated in France beginning in the mid-nineteenth century. By the early twentieth century, the labor-saving advantages of flexible molding material increased its popularity over the labor-intensive and highly skilled rigid plaster piece-mold process; by mid-century flexible molding had virtually replaced it. Synthetic flexible molding materials such as silicone rubber then replaced gelatin. Matisse seems to have authorized the use of gelatin only rarely and clearly preferred the plaster piece-mold process.

14. Bertault's charge for making this mold, 700 francs, indicates that is was a large and time-consuming operation. By comparison, *Standing Woman (femme debout)*, a smaller, less complex work, cost 260 francs.

15. Duthuit 1997, 261–62, 385–86, where excerpts from letters are published in the original French and in English translation, which suffers from an imprecise use of technical terms.

16. That said, it is clear that Matisse did transport small, unfired clay sculptures from Nice to Paris; in another letter to his daughter, July 11, 1929, he says, "I'll bring back two clay pieces in two little portable boxes, and have them cast in Paris" (ibid., 387).

17. Wanda de Guébriant, interview by the author, December 2004, Matisse Archives, Paris.

18. Three-dimensional computer models of this work show that it is the same size as a bronze cast of the same work (The Baltimore Museum of Art, 1950.423), indicating that this plaster was cast from a mold made from a bronze. Had the plaster been cast from a mold made from the original clay or from a plaster model, it would be larger than the bronze because bronze shrinks on cooling and plaster does not. Identical piece-mold lines can be found on both casts, but are much easier to read on the plaster, which is light in color and has a matte surface.

19. M. Laurent, interview, December 2004, Atelier de moulage (formerly "du Louvre et des musées du France"; now separate), Paris.

20. According to the catalogue raisonné, the Nasher plaster and two others like it were cast in a piece mold made by Matisse himself, which accounts for the "imperfections and rusticity" of the plasters in comparison to the bronzes; Duthuit 1997, 20. In fact, this plaster is no more rustic or imperfect than are the bronzes; computer models show them to be virtually identical except for the bases. Matisse may well have made the plaster piece mold himself, but this plaster was not cast from that mold. Surface detail was transferred from the original clay to the original plaster to a bronze cast

and then to this plaster cast by way of several further molding operations. Imperfections are, in part, due to the fact that he made the first mold on a wet clay sculpture as well as to his limited molding skill. Had he been dissatisfied with the imperfections, he could easily have removed them from the original clay or plaster model.

21. Elsen 1972, 41. Matisse's daughter Mme Duthuit insisted that her father was not really a student of Bourdelle, but went to him only for technical assistance. Malvina Hoffman describes Rodin's method: "Frequently I knew him to start a portrait, and after a few sittings, to call in a plaster-caster and have a mould made as a record; then he would make a "squeeze" (*estampage*), that is, the fresh clay would be pressed into the negative of the piece-mould and with this stage of the portrait safely registered, he would feel more free to make bold changes or experiments, without fear of losing what had been achieved up to that point. The first plaster was a guide to which he could always refer if he felt himself in doubt during the subsequent sittings" (Hoffman 1966, 43; taken from Wasserman 1975, 146). This would seem to imply that the original clay was destroyed in a waste mold to produce an original plaster. From this a piece mold was made, and it was into this mold that Rodin put clay to make a copy of the first clay version, which had in the process been destroyed. (Arthur Beale disagrees with this interpretation and believes that Rodin was also making piece molds on wet clay; interview, February 2006.) Matisse skipped the waste mold step and went right to the piece mold onto the wet clay, perhaps to save time or money, as he probably could not afford a mold maker early in his career.

22. However, close examination of the unfired dry clay and plasticine sculpture *Katia* preserved at the Musée Matisse in Nice reveals intermittent shallow cut marks on the sides of the sculpture, clues that a gelatin mold was taken from this work, probably at the Valsuani foundry, where this work was cast in bronze after Matisse's death in 1958. This first mold was probably used to make a plaster cast from which further gelatin molds were made to produce wax positives for lost-wax casting. Unlike most of Matisse's sculptures, all ten bronze proofs were made in the same year, but more than one gelatin mold was probably needed for this. If more than one gelatin mold had been taken from *Katia,* there would have been more than one set of cut marks. (See Beale 1998, 97–108, for more on gelatin cut marks.) The catalogue raisonné calls this work "varnished clay" (Duthuit 1997, 236), and there is a darkened surface coating that may be varnish, perhaps applied to prevent the surface from being softened by water in the gelatin. Traces of gelatin are probably also present, remnants from the molding operation; analysis was not possible for this study.

23. Duthuit 1997, 386.

24. Musée départemental Matisse, Le Cateau-Cambrésis. They show clear evidence of foundry use both from gelatin molding for lost-wax casting (multiple shallow intermittent cuts in the surface of the plaster around the edges) and sand casting (sand caught in numerous small-diameter holes drilled into the surface). The purpose of these holes is not clear; they may have something to do with registration of the model. Although the examination of a cast plaster surface is instructive, an original worked plaster surface would have exhibited tool marks from chiseling and rasping and overlapping layers of plaster where plaster was added, evidence that is not present on these plasters except in a few small areas of restoration.

25. As was Rodin's practice; see note 21.

26. Elsen 1972, 183–84. Known only from a photograph taken in 1909 by Eugène Druet, the work depicted surely precedes *The Back I.* The facts that the clay is signed and that the artist allowed a photograph to be made signal another hesitation. If a plaster cast was made of it, as asserted in the catalogue raisonné (Duthuit 1997, 384), it has been lost, as was the mold used to make that cast. More likely, *The Back 0* was never molded and disappeared when the clay was further altered to make *The Back I.*

27. Letter, June 8, 1971. Archives Matisse, Paris.

28. De Guébriant, interview.

29. *Profile of a Woman* was not available as part of this study. This plaster relief was given by Matisse to Léon Vassaux, one of his first artist friends. Vassaux returned it more than fifty years later at the end of Matisse's life (Spurling 2005a, 435) and it is inscribed, "to friend Léon Vassaux, souvenir of good friendship." Spurling calls it "clay." All bronzes are posthumous and smaller than the plaster according to measurements in the catalogue raisonné; Duthuit 1997, 2. Perhaps this plaster was spared because of the inscription. *Torso, Arms Raised* is assumed to be the original plaster due to its status as a unique work.

30. This sculpture, which is at the Musée départemental Matisse, Le Cateau-Cambrésis, 1982.34, may be an original plaster. Shallow cut marks on one side indicate that a gelatin mold was made of this work, so it probably served as a model for the bronze edition, but it may be a foundry model.

31. Spurling 2005a, 160, 211.

32. Laser scanning of a bronze surface yields thousands of very precise measurements that are used to make a computer model of a sculpture. This model can be overlaid with a computer model of a similar sculpture to compare size and surface features. Nine sculptures for this project were scanned by Direct Dimensions of Owings Mills, Maryland, and two at the Nasher Sculpture Center were scanned by the Van Dusen Archives of Dallas, Texas. Computer models were made by Direct Dimensions using the eleven scans. The 1912 cast is at the Weatherspoon Art Museum at the University of North Carolina, 50.191; the 1922 cast is at The Baltimore Museum of Art, 1950.425.

33. The 1875 estate inventory for the sculptor Antoine-Louis Barye has an entire section entitled *Bronzes Surmoulés* to distinguish them from those in the *Modèles* section; Loffredo 1989, 144. Barye's practices were typical for his time in that he used bronze models rather than plaster to achieve his large unlimited editions. Plaster, although durable, could not hold up to constant use for sand molding because a new mold must be made for each cast. Some of Barye's more popular models were molded and cast more than eighty times during the artist's life.

34. According to the catalogue raisonné, Matisse elected to use bronze casts of two works, *Head of a Young Girl* and *Head of a Child (Pierre Manguin),* as models to complete the editions as the original plasters had been damaged; Duthuit 1997, 30, 257. In a letter dated 1978, Marguerite Duthuit lists "small head of a child" along with *Head of a Young Girl* as having been produced from bronze models; ibid., 257. It is possible that confusion in the catalogue raisonné exists between two works with similar titles: *Head of a Child (Pierre Matisse)* and *Head of a Child (Pierre Manguin).* No early examples of the latter were available for this study.

35. A third related cast in a Swiss museum collection was not examined but a base tracing provided by the museum staff indicates that it is the same size as the two described.

36. Albright-Knox Art Gallery, RCA45.3, cast by the Bingen and Costenoble foundry; and The Baltimore Museum of Art, 1950.429, cast by the Valsuani foundry.

37. Shrinkage of 4% suggests that this work is two casts away from the model. The first cast would have been about 2% smaller than the model; see also Beale 1975, 53, for more about the shrinkage of bronze. The 1930 cast is at The Baltimore Museum of Art, 1950.429, and the 1912 cast is at the Albright Knox Art Gallery, RCA45.3.

38. Hirshhorn Museum, 66.2460.

39. Analysis pending. Another troubling aspect of the piece is the absence of mold lines similar to the absence on the unauthorized sand casts discussed earlier. In contrast, the other extant terra-cotta, not examined as part of this study, but pictured in the catalogue raisonné (Duthuit 1997, 73), does retain mold lines like those on the original plaster model.

40. Michaelides 1958, 53.

41. Lebon 2003, 74, 221; the founder Eugène Rudier ignored this; others "made do" with scrap metal.

42. Ibid., 112.

43. Ibid.

44. Spurling 2005a, 145; she also notes the purchase of a costly violin the same year (154).

45. Although the catalogue raisonné gives 1907 as the earliest date for a bronze cast, the dealer Eugène Druet exhibited a bronze in 1906; Galerie Druet 1906, no. 58 ("buste d'enfant [bronze]").

46. Lebon (2003, 112) dates the split of the partners to 1914 or 1915 and believes that no Matisse cast marked "F. Costenoble" was made earlier than 1913; therefore, those marked "Bingen and Costenoble" could be as late as 1913.

47. Duthuit 1997, 249.

48. Lebon 2003, 165. She verified with the Matisse Archives that there is no documentation beyond "Godard fondeur." Two foundries named Godard were run by brothers, Désiré (Émile's father) and Florentin, during the 1920s. Florentin Godard was casting sculpture at 248, rue de Belleville, Paris (Saint-Fargeau quarter of the 20th arrondissement) (active 1909 to between 1933 and 1937). Aristide Maillol patronized Florentin Godard, who was known for his beautiful patinas, and because of this Lebon believes that Matisse was more likely to have used Florentin than Désiré; ibid., 167.

49. Duthuit (1997, 250) claims that Godard cast only in lost wax; Lebon (2003, 166) says that he cast only in sand.

50. *Profile of a Child (Marguerite) I* and *Standing Nude* (1920–1924); Duthuit 1997, 24, 108, 249. Wanda de Guébriant of the Matisse Archives, Paris, believes that the 1905 date may be wrong (interview by Oliver Shell, December 2005, Archives Matisse, Paris). Lebon (2003, 142) finds no trace of a founder by the name of Cullen working in Paris in the twentieth century (the reference to that name being found only in an inventory of work compiled by Mme Matisse in the 1920s), and speculates that the name could have been used by descendants of a better-documented founder active in the third quarter of the nineteenth century and variously spelled "Culan," "Culand," and "Culen."

51. Ibid., 261.

52. At least three of the five *Backs* (three of *The Back I* and one each of *The Back III* and *IV*) cast during Matisse's life were also made by Valsuani in lost wax. The three at the Museum of Modern Art, New York, were examined and found to be made by the lost-wax process, a determination made on their appearance: the edition numbers were inscribed in a soft material that caused a burr to be raised at the edges, the foundry mark (which is the usual one for Valsuani and includes the phrase "*cire perdue*") was impressed into a soft material, and photographs of the versos revealed an uneven surface, drip marks, and residual investment material. In addition, small, round, bronze "bubbles" were noted on the front surface, an indication that gelatin molds with some trapped air were used to cast the wax positives. The catalogue raisonné, citing letters in the Matisse Archives, erroneously assigns these casts marked Valsuani as being subcontracted to the Rudier foundry for sand casting; Duthuit 1997, 250. These letters must refer to later casts made by Rudier. Posthumous versions of the *Backs* are sand cast. These large bas-reliefs are of a size and shape probably more easily and practically made by sand casting. Matisse's decision to have the casts, at least during his lifetime, made in lost wax may indicate his loyalty to Valsuani.

53. The Valsuani mark was bought in 1981 by Leonardo Benatov. His foundry, Airaindor, still produces sculpture marked with the Valsuani cachet, sometimes slightly larger and squarer than that used by Marcel and Claude Valsuani; Lebon 2003, 259–60.

54. Ibid. Although Claude Valsuani was virtually alone among art bronze founders in managing to keep his foundry open during World War I, when he worked by himself, during World War II, the business was closed from 1940 to 1947. In 1952 the foundry had six workmen.

55. An exception is the Hirshhorn cast of *Bust of a Woman* (66.3458) cast in 1958, which has an unusual bright golden glow not seen on any other works examined in this study. All casts of this work are posthumous.

56. In a letter to Roger Fry written from Tangier in 1912, Matisse states that if he were to sell a plaster he would have to charge the same price as for a bronze because he makes only ten numbered examples of each sculpture and a plaster cast would have to count as one of the series; Archives Matisse.

57. Edition sizes were not limited by French law until 1968—a maximum of twelve, consisting of four artist proofs and eight for sale; further editions in different sizes are also allowed; Lebon 2003, 95.

58. De Guébriant, interview, December 2005.

59. Lebon 2003, 67. She believes that he was probably encouraged to do this by the artists who helped him start his business.

60. Ibid., 95.

61. Two sand foundries, Siot-Decauville and Blot and Drouard, made weak attempts at some limited editions in the last decade of the nineteenth century; ibid., 64.

62. Ibid., 87. Before April 9, 1910, a sculptor selling a work automatically transferred the rights of reproduction unless the rights were expressly reserved. After that date, the rights were reserved unless expressly transferred.

63. Ibid., 67. Lebon includes De Ferraris, Sutto, Gonot et Joret, Montagutelli, Bisceglia, and Carvillani on this list. The artists Rembrandt Bugatti and Joseph Bernard (whose son later

established the Coubertin foundry; see ibid., 140), burned by their contracts with Hébrard, helped Claude Valsuani establish his business, which found favor among painters making sculpture. The artists, conscious of the market and their rights, were very much in favor of limiting their editions; ibid., 77.

64. Simonds 1886, 8504.

65. Musée Matisse, Nice, inv. D 78.1.11, dépôt RF 3354.

66. Sand casting as performed in a semi-industrial setting had a reputation for requiring extensive cold work after casting, effacing the artist's touch. Because a sand cast is made in a piece mold similar in construction to a plaster piece mold but formed of sand, the resulting work has seam lines on the surface from the individual pieces of the mold. These seam lines are usually removed at the foundry as part of the finishing process. Lost-wax casts do not have these seam lines because the mold (investment) is applied wet over the entire surface of the wax positive and hardens into one piece without seams. However, because the investment material is less porous than the sand mold, lost-wax casts can have many more holes in the metal, caused by air bubbles, and metal flash lines, which are raised, seamlike lines caused when the molten metal runs into narrow cracks in the investment.

67. Matisse modeled twenty-eight sculptures in clay before this one. De Guébriant believes it is possible that this work could have been cast in bronze before *Small Head with Comb* (cat. 73), which is dated in the catalogue raisonné as the earliest bronze; interview, December 2005.

68. The Baltimore Museum of Art, 1950.428.

69. The Baltimore Museum of Art, 1950.430; Hirshhorn Museum and Sculpture Garden, 66.3456. The Hirshhorn work is titled *Two Women,* the title originally given to this work by Matisse.

70. Smith 1981, 134.

71. Mattusch 1996, 167.

72. Lebon 2003, 57.

73. Gonon 1876. Curiously, the process described in this document includes three important features—gelatin molding, the use of animal dung in investments, and the use of an alloy with a high zinc content—that were shared by the process imported to Paris by Hébrard's Italian workmen. Is it possible that, unbeknownst to his son, Honoré Gonon had received some training in Italy?

74. Eugène Gonon describes his father's use of gelatin molds for indirect wax positives. But the mold was destroyed in being removed from the sculpture, thus each was a unique work. Although there would have been nothing to stop Gonon from making more copies of the same model by making more gelatin molds, there is no evidence that this was done; ibid.

75. Shapiro 1985, 117.

76. Pierre Bingen described his process in great detail: The artist brings his sculpture to the foundry (presumably in plaster) and Bingen makes a clay cast. From this, he carefully removes a thin layer of clay to make the core—this preserves the general proportions of the work. The core is fired hard and then covered completely with modeling wax and given back to the sculptor who then completely remodels the surface of the sculpture in the wax. This is then invested, heated to drive off the wax, and so on, as done in serial indirect lost-wax casting; Lebon 2003, 114. Even though this process is direct, an original plaster model is saved.

The Gorham Manufacturing Company in Providence, Rhode Island, hired Pierre Bingen to establish a lost-wax casting foundry there in 1906; Shapiro 1985, 132. A bronze cast by the Belgian sculptor Paul Nocquet, *Man Crouched on a Rock* (The Baltimore Museum of Art, 1963.16.32), is inscribed "*cire-perdue* Gorham Mfg Co. 1906" and appears to have been made by Bingen's process. In contrast to Valsuani's casts, the interior is quite smooth and sculpted, much more like the interior of a sand-cast bronze. This is because Bingen's clay cores and cores formed in sand for sand casting are made in the same way—both begin as casts of the sculpture from which the surface is removed mechanically. In contrast, Valsuani's cores are poured in a semi-liquid state into an already prepared wax positive. In 1977, for the lost-wax cast figures of Rodin's *Gates of Hell,* the Coubertin foundry used cores similar to Bingen's; *Rodin* 1981.

77. The *Treatises of Benvenuto Cellini on Goldsmithing and Sculpture* were available in French at least as early as the 1847 translation by Leopold Laclanche. The *Nymph of Fontainebleau* was cast in France with the aid of French founders in 1543; Baudry et al. 1978, 293.

78. Lebon 2003, 67. Except for a very brief use of the name Bingen Jeune (Bingen junior) et Costenoble that implies a connection, Lebon could find no evidence that Jean-Augustin Bingen of Bingen and Costenoble was any relation to Pierre Bingen, nor that he was ever trained by him; ibid. 112.

79. Berger and Zutter 1996, 57.

80. Details of the lost-wax process used by Victor Thiebault and his successors are not known. A manuscript from the Thiebault archives (Thiebault n.d.), unsigned and undated but after 1927, when the foundry closed, describes the "Italian process," then in use by Italians in Paris, as employing gelatin molds. This would seem to indicate that the Thiebault foundry was not using gelatin, but it is certainly possible that it was doing indirect lost-wax casting using plaster piece molds.

E. Gruet Jeune shared workspace with Pierre Bingen for a year, 1897–1898, so he would certainly have known Bingen's process even if he did not use it; Lebon 2003, 178.

81. See Lie 2003 and Pullen 2003 for detailed descriptions of gelatin molding.

82. Lebon 2003, 67.

83. The American sculptor Frederick Remington used this to great advantage over the years at the Roman Bronze Works. His popular sculpture *Bronco Buster* evolved gradually and shows many changes made directly in the wax positives over the years, so that a number of these series casts are unique works; Shapiro 1985, 139–41. It was in 1900 that this foundry in Brooklyn, New York, began to work exclusively in the indirect serial lost-wax production of bronze sculpture, two years before Hébrard. The founder, Riccardo Bertelli, an Italian chemical engineer born in Genoa, had arrived in the United States in 1895; ibid., 136–37.

84. In a letter dated January 28, 1954, Matisse writes to Valsuani: "Jean Matisse who will bring the models to the foundry will surely speak to you about seams to remove. I think that as usual you should remove them from the wax" (Archives Matisse, Paris; also Lebon 2003, 78).

85. Ibid., 259. Lebon (ibid.) interviewed Pierre Thinot, the founder working in the most traditional manner today in Paris, about the meaning of these terms. The "Italian core," he said, is made up of a mixture of brick (presumably ground),

with plaster or crushed slate. Cow dung investment is made using, first, just the liquid pressed from the dung and mixed with fine sand. This mixture is applied to the wax positive in several layers and allowed to dry between applications. Horse dung mixed with sand is applied over this and then the same mixture as that used for the Italian core is applied. The vegetable matter in the dung burns out during the heating and leaves the investment porous, thus allowing gas to escape when the metal is cast. A slow process, the assembly can take days or weeks to achieve.

Eugène Gonon (1876, 56, 37) describes similar recipes for investment. His recipe number two, for *moule de terre au pinceau,* includes Montrouge sand, fire clay, and horse dung liquid for the first layers. A few of the many following steps include the application to the undercuts of small pieces of a dough made of four parts Montrouge sand and one part horse dung, and then bricks made of five parts Montrouge sand and one part horse dung are applied. His core recipe includes terra-cotta (presumably ground) mixed with sand and plaster.

La Fonte à Cire Perdue, a film made at the Valsuani foundry in 1980, the year it closed, shows the step-by-step method used to cast in bronze a large plaster model by the artist Andreas Beck. A large, four-piece gelatin mold is made of the simple form and the interior of the mold is brushed with a layer of high-quality, very refined beeswax and then a layer of a lesser quality beeswax. No additional wax was poured inside, perhaps because the mold was so large. The investment applied to the wax is a very homogeneous white plasterlike substance with nary a dollop of horse or cow dung in sight. The wax is burned out in an oven at 200°C and then the investment is dried and hardened at 600°C. The mold is lowered right side up into a large hole in the floor and completely surrounded by sand. The metal is poured into the top of the sculpture; Hocquard and Laupies 1980.

It appears that the Valsuani foundry abandoned the use of dung—*la potée de la bouse de vache*—sometime after 1951 as a photograph from that year shows a Valsuani worker applying investment material to a sculpture by Henri Laurens. The color of the investment is a dunglike brown, very different from that shown in the film of the process in 1980; Baudry et al. 1978, 236.

The use of cow and horse dung for lost-wax molds is also described in the Renaissance by Cellini (1967, 111), and in the twelfth century by Theophilus (1963, 132) in the earliest-known detailed description of lost-wax casting. He mixed his dung with clay, dried it, and then pulverized and sifted it, which would seem likely to have had the effect of eliminating the useful organic bits. Dung is still used in Normandy for bell founding today; Hubert Lacroix, interview by the author, December 2004, Susse Foundry, Arcueil.

86. Radiography was performed at the Walters Art Museum, Baltimore; the National Gallery of Art, Washington, D.C.; and The Metropolitan Museum of Art, New York. The author gratefully acknowledges the help of Julie Lauffenburger, Caitlin Jenkins, and Deborah Schorsch, respectively, and the approval of Terry Drayman-Weisser, Shelley Sturman, and Larry Becker for use of the respective facilities. Radiography of the two largest works, *The Serf* and the *Large Seated Nude,* was performed at The Baltimore Museum of Art by Maryland QC Laboratory.

87. The Baltimore Museum of Art, 1950.426.

88. Hirshhorn Museum and Sculpture Garden, 66.3456.

89. The Baltimore Museum of Art, 1950.422.

90. Hirshhorn Museum and Sculpture Garden, 66.3456; and Weatherspoon Art Museum, 50.191.

91. A similar sheet metal and wire-wrapped core vent was identified by radiography inside a sand-cast bronze, *Walking Tiger* (The Baltimore Museum of Art, 1998.116), probably cast in the mid-nineteenth century by the sculptor Antoine-Louis Barye. Dozens of very small diameter core pins like those inside the Hirshhorn sand cast, *Two Women,* are also present in the tiger. The wire-wrapped core vent and small-diameter core pins indicate a technical link between Barye and Bingen and Costenoble, both practitioners of high-definition sand casting.

92. The Metropolitan Museum of Art, 2002.456.141.

93. An unsigned letter at the Matisse Archives dated April 10, 1954 (also in Lebon 2003, 78), indicates that Matisse had some consideration for his client's preferences: "I am emphasizing that the current client of M. Matisse is very demanding about patinas. He has beautiful patinas [in his collection]."

94. The Baltimore Museum of Art, 1950.438; Nasher Sculpture Center 1986.A.06; and Museum of Modern Art, New York, 154.55.

95. This edition was not begun until 1930 and seems to have been achieved in a more orderly fashion than many. Numbers 0–3 are dated to 1930; the rest of the edition was completed in 1950 or later.

96. Lebon 2003, 260.

97. A few recipes from a patination handbook of 1887 contain chrome yellow; Lacombe, Debonliez, and Malepeyre 1979, 21, 24. A book from 1931 contains several; Michel 1931, 134, 137, 150, 154, 164. In both texts, the compound seems to be used more as a reagent than a pigment, but all of these recipes are for various shades of green. Michel (110) includes one recipe containing potassium bichromate for use on copper. Potassium bichromate and ammonium dichromate are used in France today for bronze patination; Patrick Labarre, patinator at the Coubertin foundry, Saint-Remy-les Chevreuse, interview by the author, December 2004.

Jean-Pierre Rama (1988, 340–41) gives several recipes for brown and black patinas for bronze that include chromium compounds.

Mahogany color: 100 g copper nitrate in 1 liter of water mixed with 100 g ammonium dichromate; 100 g copper nitrate in 1 liter of water mixed with potassium bichromate

Brown-red (applied hot): 100 g ammonium dichromate in 1 liter of water; or 60 g ammonium dichromate and 60 g potassium sulfate in 1 liter of water; 250 g ammonium bichromate and 250 g ammonium sulfate in 1 liter of water

Deep black with bluish reflections (applied hot): first green the piece with 100 g copper nitrate in 1 liter of water, then use several applications of 60 g to 80 g potassium ferrocyanide in 1 liter of water, followed by a water rinse, and finish with several applications of 100 g of potassium bichromate in 1 liter of water, rinsing with water between applications, until desired shade of black is obtained.

Foundries often follow chemical patination with a layer of tinted wax or lacquer. It is possible that chrome-based pigment is present on Matisse bronzes, although this does not seem likely to be chrome yellow or green as no green patination was observed except for that occurring naturally on some versions of the *Back*s that were exhibited outdoors. The so-called Italian method of patination described for making bronze medals look antique—feeding them to turkeys for a *voyage gastro-intestinal* (Michel 1931, 139) will surely have been impractical for Matisse bronzes.

98. Lebon 2003, 259.

99. Ibid.

100. Two types of commercially available torches were in use by the early twentieth century. The oxyacetylene torch, the first commercially feasible design of which is still in use today, was produced by Charles Picard, a French chemical engineer in 1910; http://chalumo29.free.fr/. The gasoline torch, for locations without piped-in gas, seems to have been invented in Sweden by Carl Nyberg in 1881 and was available in France in the early 1880s; http://www.sweden.se, http://lampes.a.souder.free.fr and http://perso.wanadoo.fr/laurent.bel.

Herbert Maryon describes in detail soldering lamps and torches in use in England (probably about 1912, the date of the first edition). The "blowpipe and bellows" pictured looks like an acetylene torch with its double hoses but used coal gas (piped-in gas, the forerunner of natural gas) and foot-operated bellows (now replaced by compressed air). For workshops without piped-in gas, he recommends soldering lamps burning alcohol or oil for small work and, for larger work, "Swedish blowlamps known as Aetnas . . . [and] Barthel brazing lamps. The most useful size . . . holds about a quart of [paraffin] oil and burn [*sic*] for an hour. The flame from an Aetna lamp, quart size, is about nine inches long, blue in colour and it roars considerably" (Maryon 1971, 27–34). These torches, which are described only in the section on soldering and are not included in the discussion of patination, were replaced in the 1950s by the propane torch common now.

Although Hébrard hired Italians, among them Marcello Valsuani and Albino Palazzolo, for their proficiency in the serial lost-wax process, he tapped a Frenchman, Adolf Gruet, in 1902, to be his patinator. Gruet was from a family of founders and had earlier worked for Rodin. In 1903, Hébrard fired Gruet, who told Rodin that he was going to sue Hébrard for stealing his process; Lebon 2003, 178. In 1905, the art critic Louis Vauxcelles described in detail his visit to the Hébrard foundry. Much is made of the complicated and lengthy process used to patinate Rodin's *The Thinker:* "Mr. A-A Hébrard treats his bronzes first with ammonium sulfide, then with nitric and muriatic acid. Then the sculpture is buried one month in a mixture of compost and beach sand. It is washed. It is dried. Ten days in the oven. New washing. New burial. Drying. It is wiped with a soft chamois impregnated with barium sulfate and gold chloride, etc., etc., [a] series of operations quite delicate and complex." The total time spent on this patina was six months for a result called "wet crow" (*corbeau mouillé*); Vauxcelles 1905a, 195. The mention of a torch is conspicuously absent here, but curiously turns up in a footnote about the patination of plaster and terra-cotta by way of iron and copper oxides; ibid., 194. The application of a torch flame to the surface of either plaster or terra-cotta seems very likely to have disastrous consequences. Could it be that Hébrard was also doing torch patination for some bronzes and Vauxcelles misunderstood the context? Or, that Hébrard deliberately misled him to keep it a secret? Certainly the description of the patination technique for *The Thinker,* whether stolen from Gruet or not, is a rather extreme (or exaggerated) example of techniques in common use by French patinators of the nineteenth century. Lacking a torch, they used other methods such as the oven baking for hot patinas, but also made patinas without heat. Burial in various substances was common and two months was sometimes needed to create certain patinas; see Lacombe, Debonliez, and Malepeyre 1979 and Adil and DePhillips 1991 for many patination recipes made without the use of a torch—some as late as 1895. Michel (1931, 109, 73) lists only two patination processes that call for torches, a *chalumeau à gaz* (probably an oxyacetylene torch) dated 1924 and the *lampe à souder* (probably a gasoline torch) from 1915. Torch patination had the advantage of being much quicker, certainly an asset in the production of serial bronzes, and probably offered more control. However, overly complex, lengthy, arcane processes were the hallmark of art bronze patination, as distinguished from the process for industrially produced, quickly patinated knickknacks, so use of the torch may well have been considered Hébrard's dirty little secret.

101. By law in France, the terms *bronze, Bronzium, bronze d'art,* and *bronze composition* could not be used after 1910 for products not made of bronze. In 1935 a law was passed that anything called "bronze" must be at least 35% copper and must be marked "bronze," but only the Susse and Barbedienne foundries followed the rule for marking; Lebon 2003, 90.

102. Two different XRF units were used. The Innov-x Systems X-ray Fluorescence Spectrum Analyzer, a hand-held portable unit, was used by Jia-sun Tsang, Dr. Charles Tumosa, and Sarah Pinchin of the Smithsonian Center for Research and Education, and that analysis was performed at The Baltimore Museum of Art. Five XRF analyses were performed at the National Gallery of Art by Kathryn Morales using the Kevex 0750A spectrometer. These two analyses are recorded in Report no. 5914. LA-ICP-MS was performed by Laure Dussieux at the Smithsonian Center for Research and Education with the Cetac LSX-200 Laser Ablation and Perkin Elmer Elan 6000 Inductively Coupled Plasma Mass Spectrometer. Results of the LA-ICP-MS are still to be reported. The author gratefully acknowledges the researchers' hard work and the approval of René de la Rie and Lisha Glinsman for the work at the National Gallery.

XRF determines elemental surface composition by weight percent within 5% for major elements and within 30%–40% for minor elements comprising less than 1%. Results are qualitative and can be used only to determine relative amounts. The Innov-x unit can measure twenty-five elements from potassium to bismuth. The stationary Kevex unit has better resolution (meaning the accuracy with which the detector can differentiate peaks of various elements) than the Innov-x. Sample sites were selected for flatness. At least one patinated spot and one unpatinated spot were analyzed for each work.

103. The Godard group showed remarkably little variation in composition, perhaps indicating these were all cast from the same metal pour.

104. One of this group, *Head of a Young Girl* (The Baltimore Museum of Art, 1950.426), is dated as cast in 1929 because that is the year it was acquired by Etta Cone. The sculpture was modeled by Matisse in 1906 and first cast in bronze in 1908. This example, cast by Valsuani, has a metal composition that is similar to that of two other works cast in 1925 and dissimilar to that of thirteen other casts made in 1929 or later. Therefore it seems possible that this work was cast before 1929. The only other work in this study that was cast by Valsuani and dated to 1929, *Reclining Nude III,* was not sculpted by Matisse until that year and its metal composition resembles that of works cast in 1930–1931.

105. The addition of zinc could have been an economic decision. The cost of bronze jumped from 2,650 francs per ton to 64,000 francs per ton in one year, between May 1936 and May 1937; Lebon 2003, 82. The cheaper zinc would have lowered the cost of bronze, and more zinc would have lowered the melting point of the alloy, resulting in a savings of fuel.

106. Eugène Gonon (1876, 56) gives several alloy compositions used for lost-wax casting, each containing very high concentrations of zinc (as much as 33%) with either very little tin or none at all. He calls these alloys both "bronze" and "brass." He prevented the volatilization of the zinc during heating by adding powdered charcoal to the crucible. In a manuscript from the Thiebault archives (Thiebault n.d.) an alloy in use by Italian founders in Paris is said to consist of 30% zinc and 70% copper. Vauxcelles's description of the lost-wax process at the Hébrard foundry in 1905 includes this nugget: "The serious defect of this process is that it will permit only the casting of bad bronze, poor alloys with antimony and lead: the refractory material made of brick and plaster is not able to support the high temperatures necessary to obtain the beautiful bronze" (Vauxcelles 1905a, 190; also in Lebon 2003, 58). Alloys with higher tin content were considered "modern alloys" in the later nineteenth century. Tin affects pourability and helps the metal flow better into small spaces, giving better surface detail. It also makes the surface harder, more brittle and more difficult to chase. Thus, a higher tin alloy allows for a high-quality cast surface in preference to extensive surface chasing; Elisabeth Lebon, e-mail communication, February 2006.

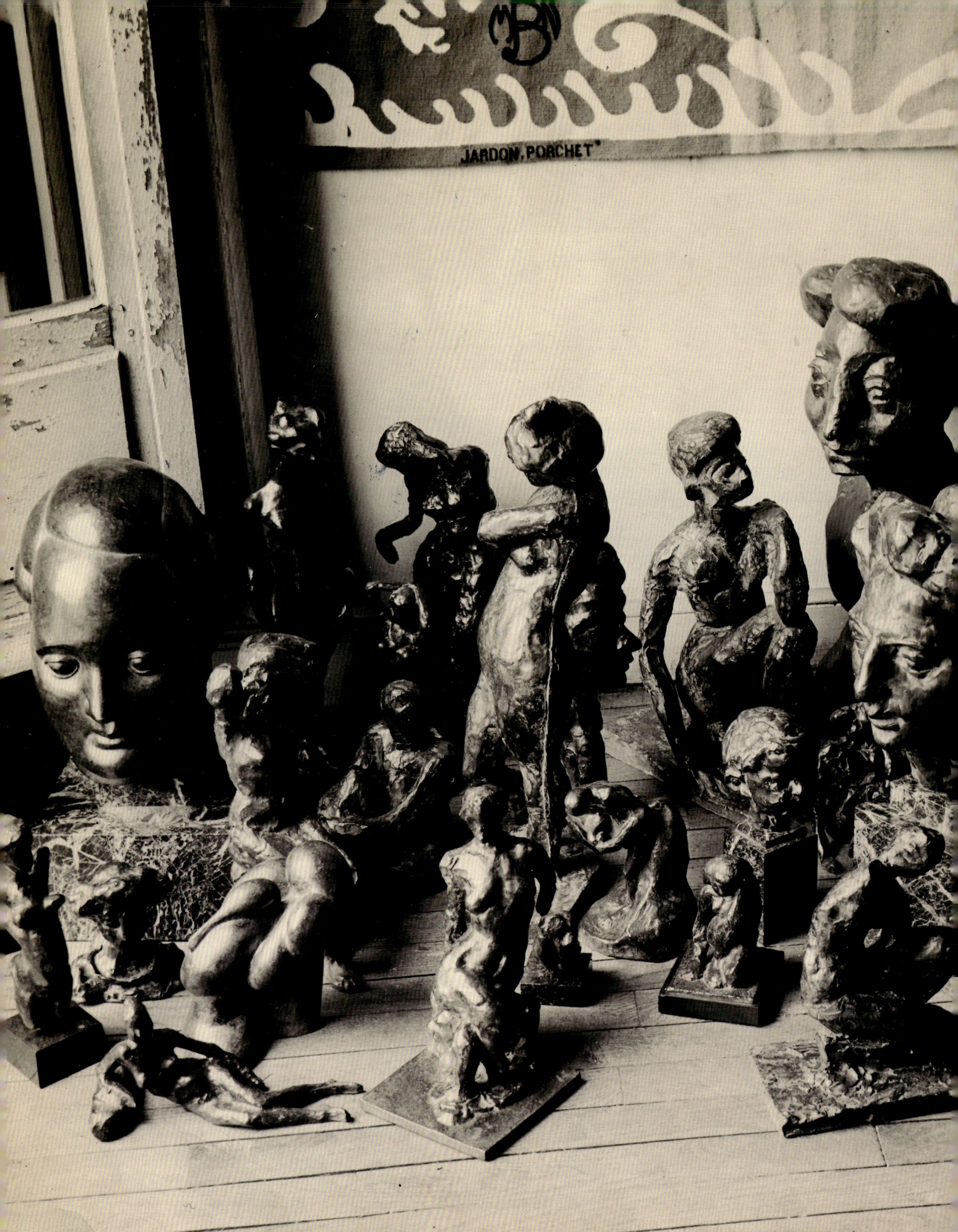
JARDON, PORCHET

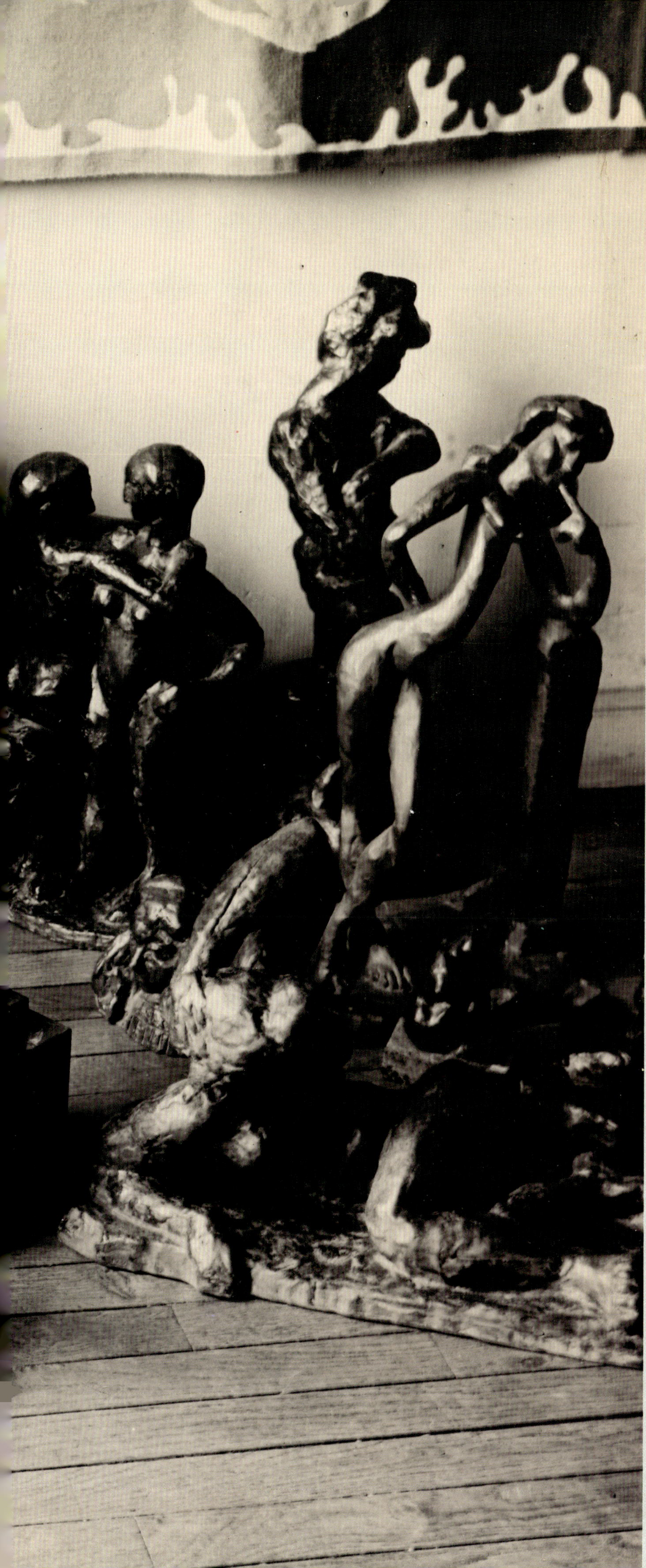

Catalogue

The catalogue of works is organized by sculptural subject. Each section of the catalogue consists of a core group of Henri Matisse's sculptural masterworks, together with related paintings and works on paper and works by sculptors and painters who influenced or were influenced by Matisse's sculpture. In this exhibition and catalogue, the dates and titles are those established in the catalogue raisonné of Matisse's sculptures by Claude Duthuit (Duthuit 1997).

The checklist follows the arrangement of the catalogue sections. Works for each entry are listed in two groups, the sculpture first, followed by other works by Matisse. Within each group, works are listed chronologically. Works by other artists are listed alphabetically by name of artist at the end of the checklist.

The entry for each of Matisse's sculptures includes dates of creation followed by cast dates and name of foundry. Medium is accompanied by method of casting, number of edition, and a reference to the catalogue raisonné entry number (Duthuit no.). English titles have been used throughout, except in those rare instances where the English translation does not fully convey the meaning of the original French title. In such cases, the French title is included in parentheses.

Dimensions, which have been supplied by the lenders, are listed as height by width by depth.

Page references in the checklist refer to illustrations.

Jaguar Devouring a Hare

Brutal conflict is hardly a subject we associate with the harmonious art of Henri Matisse, yet, between 1899 and 1901, he became obsessed with the theme. With the exception of a small horse produced in 1901, *Jaguar Devouring a Hare* is Matisse's only sculpture representing an animal and his only depiction of a violent action scene. Already an accomplished painter, Matisse attended evening courses at the École communale de la ville de Paris in order to learn sculpting. As part of nineteenth-century academic training, each student produced a copy after a cast of a masterpiece from the Louvre. Matisse selected Antoine-Louis Barye's *Jaguar Devouring a Hare*. For the next two years he devoted himself to the investigation of Barye's example. To gain a tactile understanding of its twisting masses, he worked on his sculpture while blindfolded, and he even studied a dissected cat, as Barye was known to have done.[1] Jack Flam describes Matisse's prolonged engagement with this violent theme as "obsessive" and an "act of sublimation" at a difficult point in the artist's life.[2] Matisse told Raymond Escholier that he "identified with the passion of the wild beast expressed by the rhythm of the masses."[3] This was a breakthrough piece, establishing sculpture as an important part of his art. His earliest freestanding work, *Jaguar Devouring a Hare* defines Matisse's assimilation of lessons learned from Auguste Rodin and his own painterly approach to the medium. In 1899, Matisse had purchased a plaster bust by Rodin and a painting by Cézanne (fig. 10) from the art dealer Ambroise Vollard. He learned from both of these important sources and synthesizes aspects of their approaches in his early sculpture, translating Barye's dynamic realism into a highly personal idiom, a combination of additive modeling and subtractive editing with the knife. The abstract marks of this process remain visible on the surface, while the structural principles underlying Barye's jaguar are retained as a unified gesture that concentrates all the power of the animal into a sinuous arabesque. As Matisse analyzes Barye's sculpture, we can trace his thought process in related drawings. One of these shows the jaguar, viewed from slightly above and behind, and reveals Matisse's fascination with the line that begins with the tail and spirals through the rib cage and shoulders almost like a helix to animate the beast. This serpentine form recurs throughout Matisse's career, dynamically coordinating mass in sculptures such as *Madeleine I, Reclining Nude I (Aurora)*, and *The Serpentine* and becoming the point of departure for his celebrated series of backs.

The first stage in translating a sculpture from clay into bronze is to cast it in plaster. Later on in his career, Matisse was able to afford a professional *mouleur* (plaster caster), but it is likely that he cast this early piece himself. Matisse's plasters inhabited the artist's studio and living quarters and at times became subjects in their own right as part of the staffage recorded in the artist's paintings. One of these, *Studio Interior,* 1903–1904, depicts three plasters stored on top of a tall armoire in Matisse's studio on the quai Saint-Michel. From left to right these are recognizable as the *Jaguar Devouring a Hare, Bust of a Woman,* and *The Serf*. In his early years as a sculptor, Matisse rarely had bronzes made from his plasters until he found a client willing to pay the considerable expense.

Henri Matisse, *Jaguar Devouring a Hare,* copy after Barye, 1899–1901. Bronze

The Baltimore Museum of Art, Purchase with exchange funds from the Nelson and Juanita Greif Gutman Collection. Cat. 1

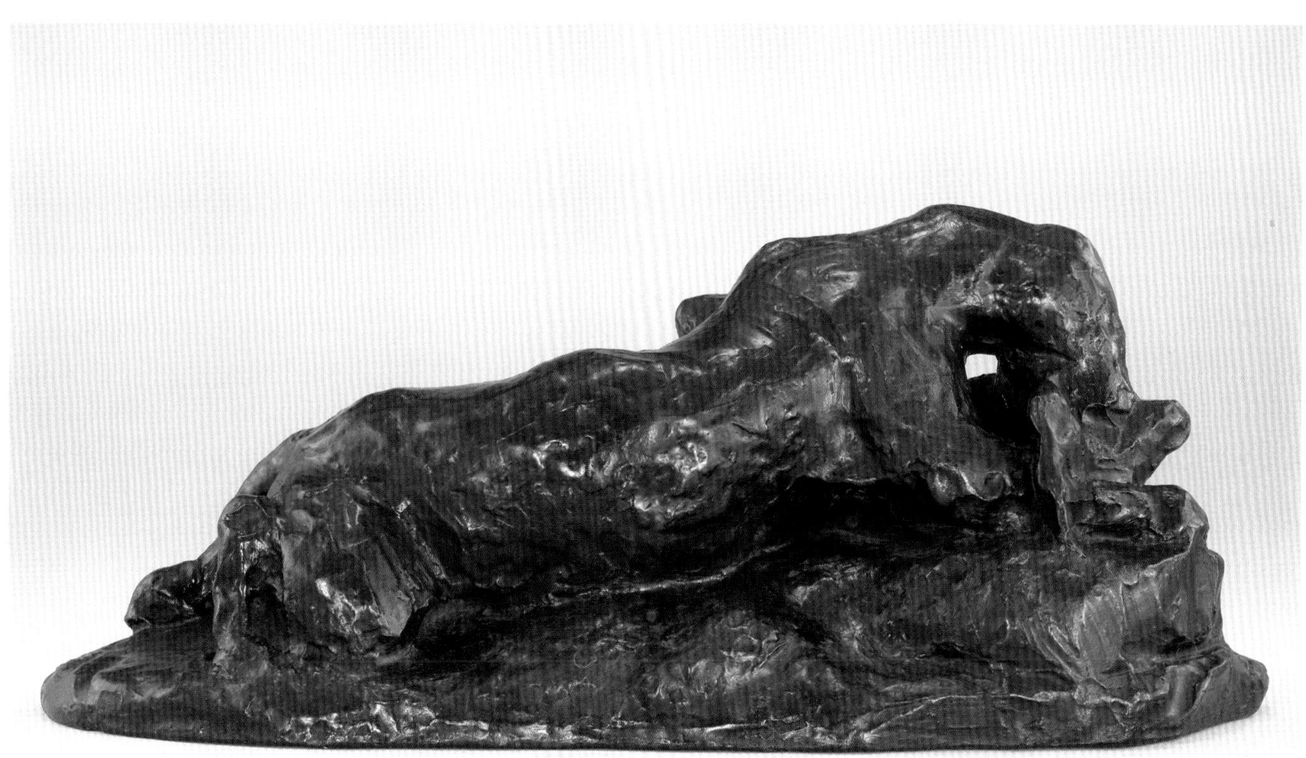

Jaguar Devouring a Hare was not cast in bronze until 1930, but this did not prevent Matisse from exhibiting it as a plaster in various influential early exhibitions, including one organized by Roger Fry at the Grafton Galleries in London in 1912 and another at the Galerie Bernheim-Jeune in Paris in 1913.[4]

OS

Notes

1. Escholier 1960, 141; Barr 1951, 52; Elsen 1972, 20; Flam 1986, 75–77.
2. Flam 1986, 76.
3. Cited in Elsen 1972, 18–19.
4. Duthuit 1997, 305.

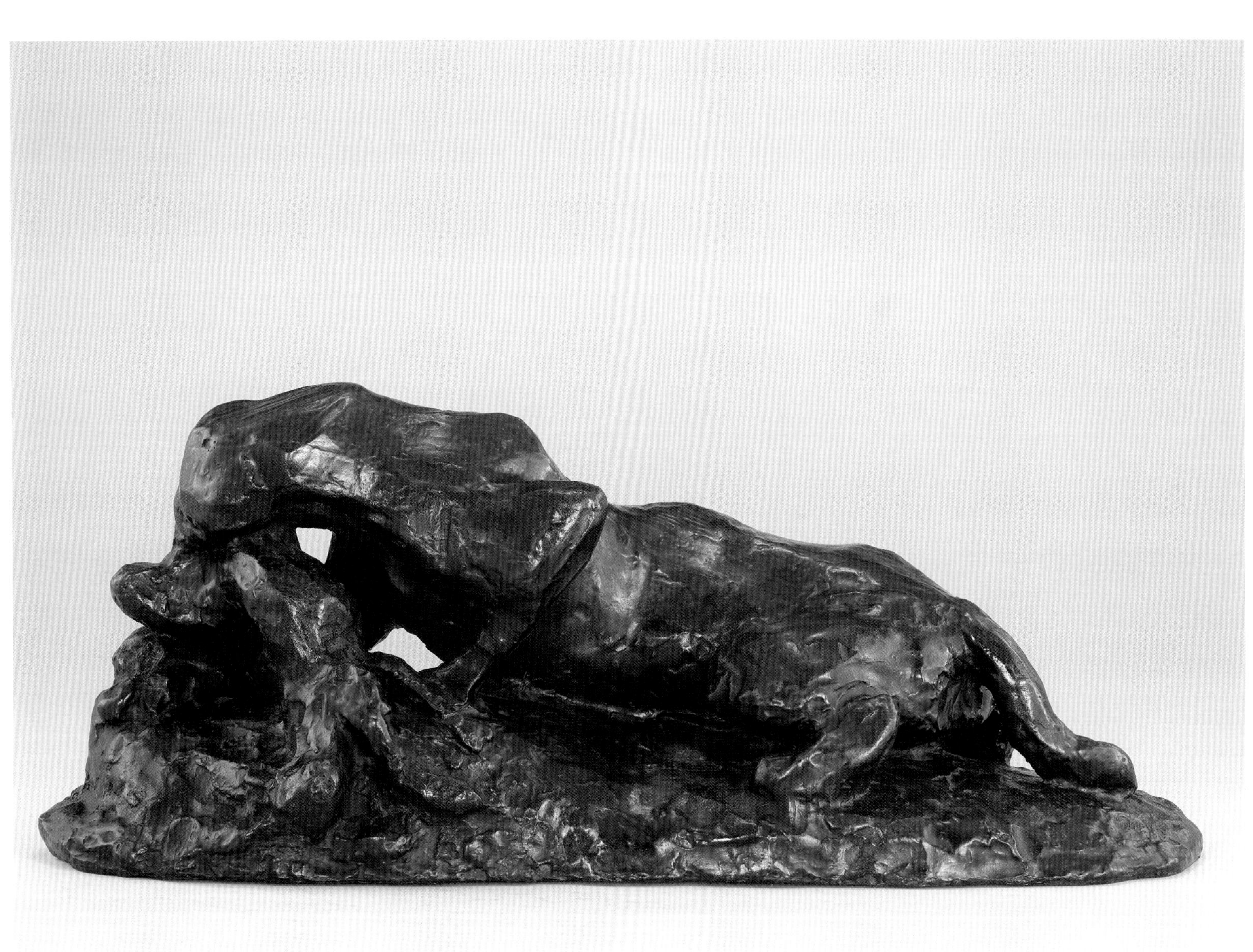

Henri Matisse, *Jaguar Devouring a Hare,*
copy after Barye, 1899–1901. Bronze
The Baltimore Museum of Art, Purchase with exchange funds from the Nelson and Juanita Greif Gutman Collection.
Cat. 1

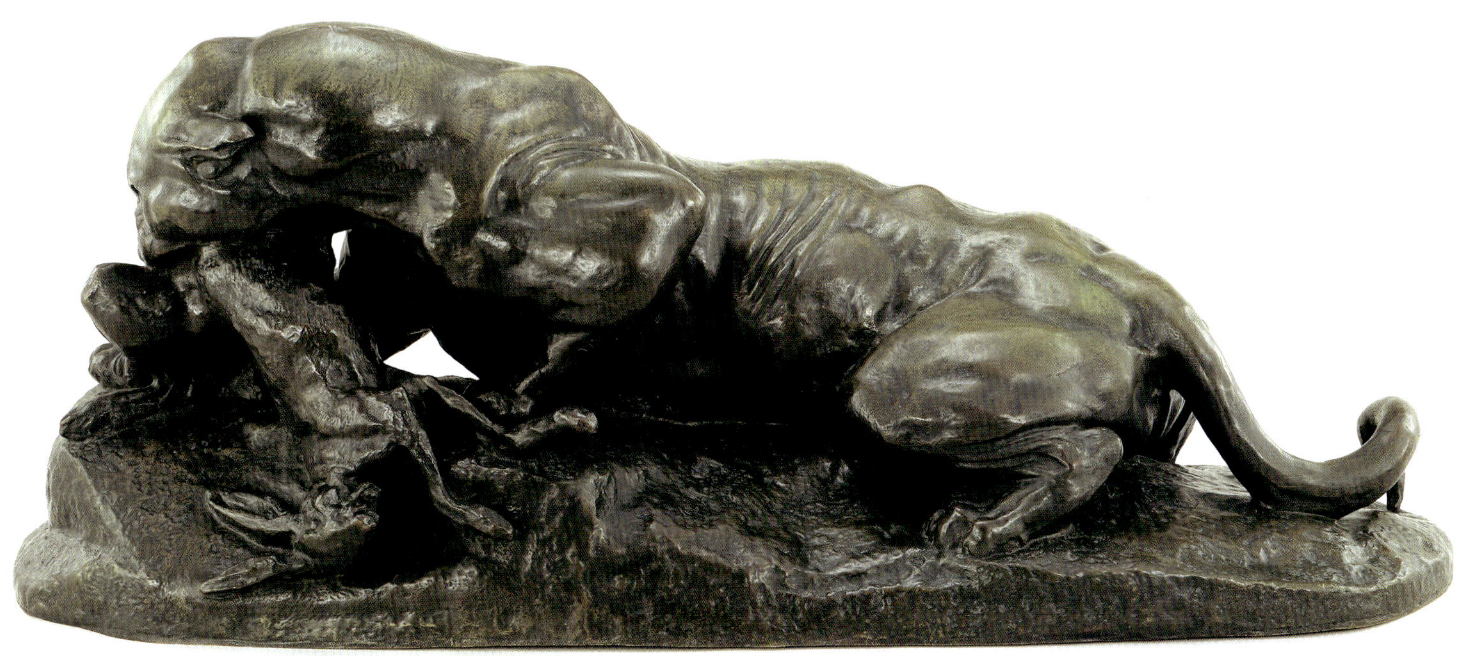

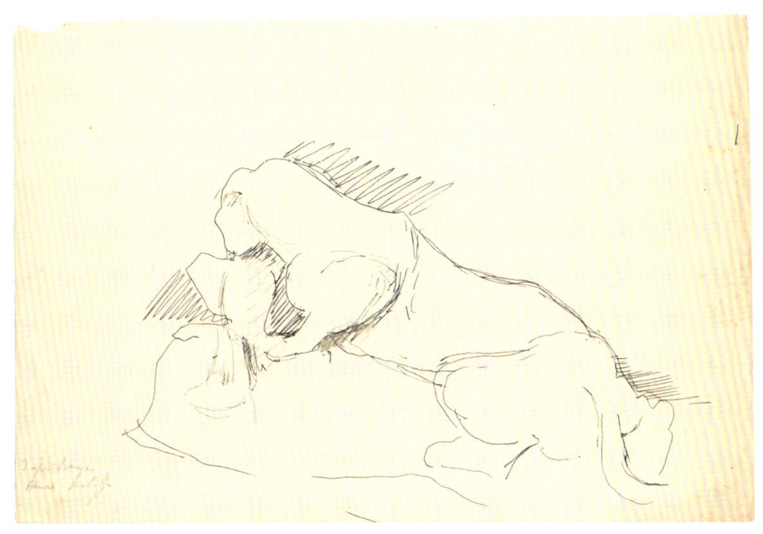

Antoine Barye, *Jaguar Devouring a Hare,* 1850
Bronze

The Baltimore Museum of Art, Purchased in Honor of Stiles Tuttle Colwill on his 50th Birthday with funds contributed by his Friends and Colleagues. Cat. 146

Henri Matisse, *Study for Jaguar Devouring a Hare,* c. 1900. Pen and india ink

Musée départemental Matisse, Le Cateau-Cambrésis, Gift of Marie Matisse, 1982. Cat. 2

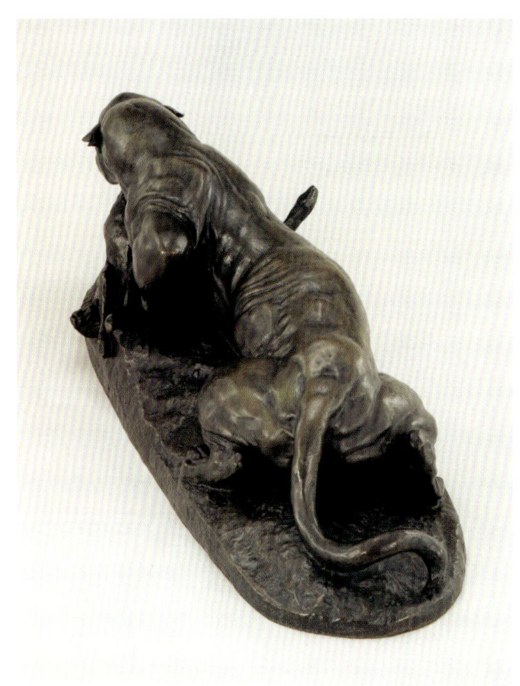

Antoine Barye, *Jaguar Devouring a Hare,* 1850
Bronze

The Baltimore Museum of Art, Purchased in Honor of Stiles Tuttle Colwill on his 50th Birthday with funds contributed by his Friends and Colleagues. Cat. 146

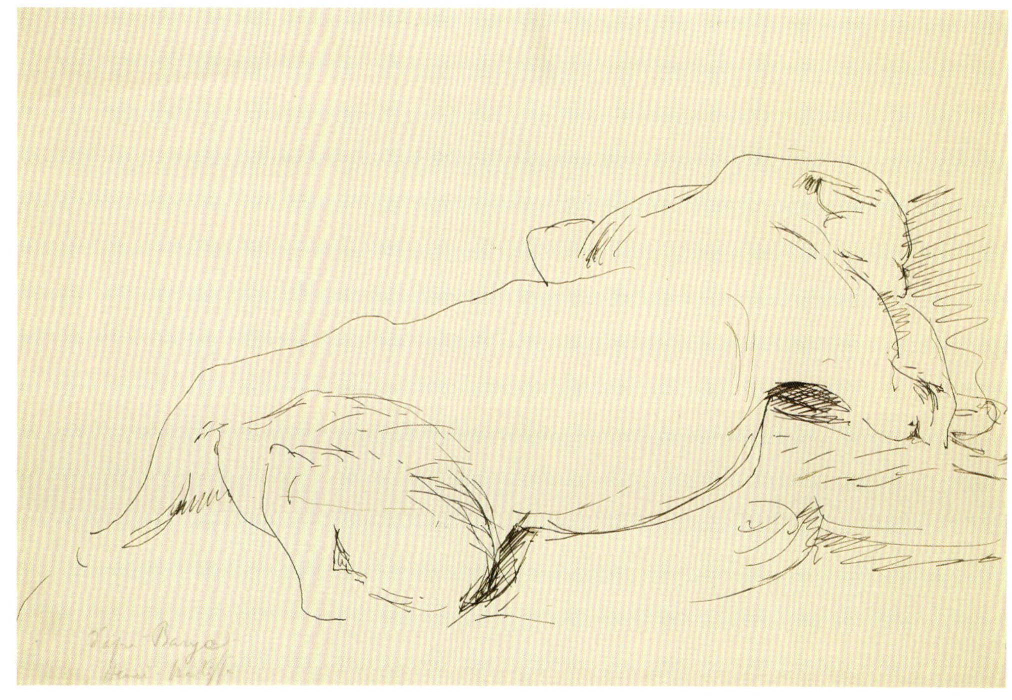

Henri Matisse, *Study for Jaguar Devouring a Hare,* c. 1900. Pen and india ink

Private collection. Cat. 3

Henri Matisse, *Jaguar Devouring a Hare,* copy after Barye, 1899–1901. Bronze

The Baltimore Museum of Art, Purchase with exchange funds from the Nelson and Juanita Greif Gutman Collection. Cat. 1

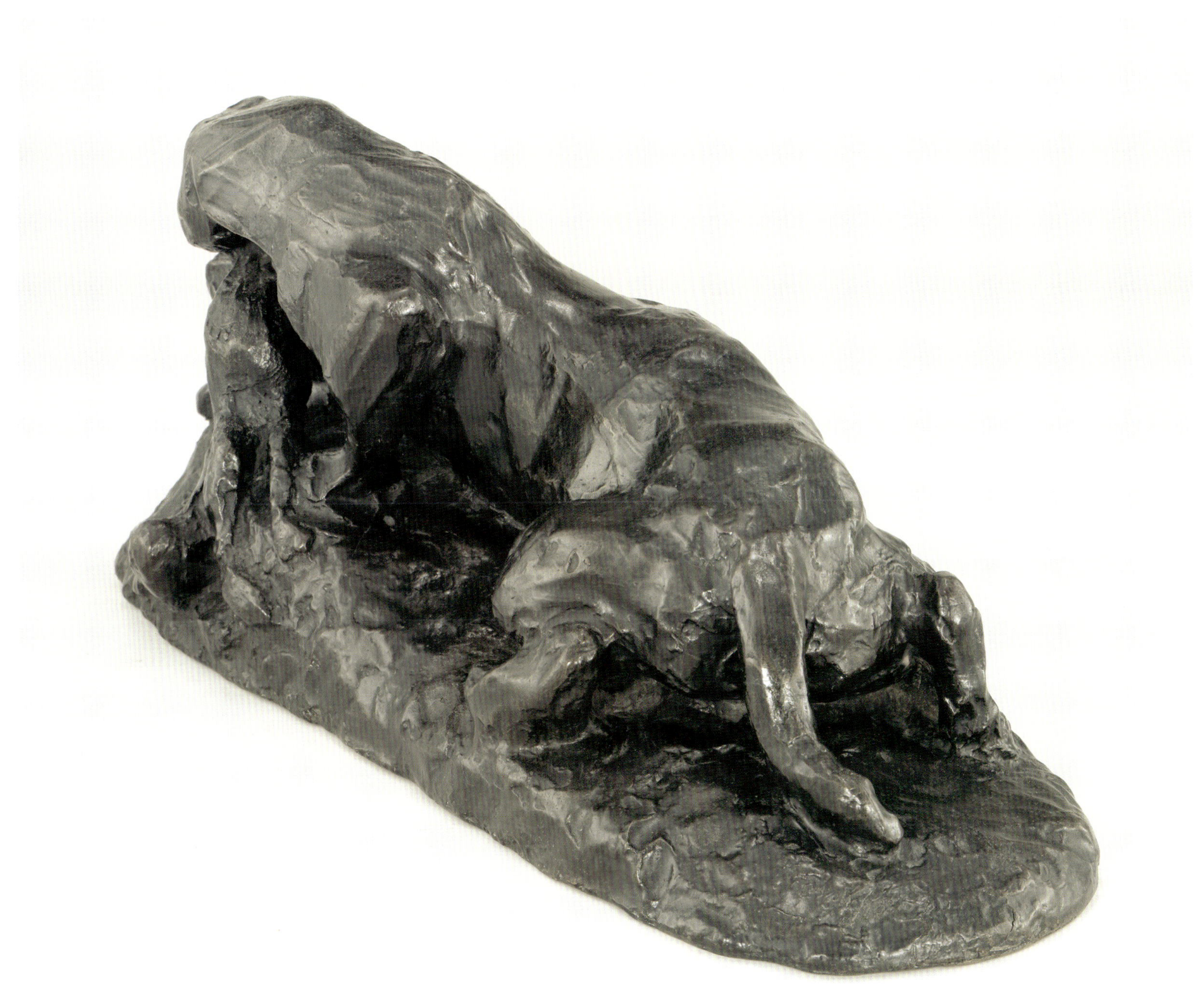

The Serf

Among his earliest and most ambitious sculptures, *The Serf* consumed Matisse's attention for at least three years, from 1900 to 1903, but did not acquire its present form until 1908, when Matisse removed the arms and had the figure cast in bronze.[1] According to some reports, the work involved up to five hundred modeling sessions.[2] Matisse—quite daringly for an inexperienced sculptor—hired a well-known Italian model named Bevilaqua, who had worked previously for Auguste Rodin, posing for some of the master's most celebrated sculptures, including his *John the Baptist* and *Walking Man.* Jean Puy, a fellow artist who shared models with Matisse in this early period, could not understand Matisse's interest in the aged Bevilaqua, whom he referred to a as "a sort of anthropoid."[3] It was precisely the connection to Rodin that attracted Matisse—who, in spite of his dire poverty, had purchased a plaster bust by Rodin in 1899. The influence is apparent, not only in the frequently observed relationship of *The Serf* to *Walking Man,* but also in the figure's wide-spaced stance and protruding paunch, reminiscent of versions of Rodin's *Balzac.* An early photograph of Matisse's original model of *The Serf* before he removed the arms reveals that it originally had balled fists held in a pose that is strikingly similar to that of Rodin's *Jean d'Aire.*[4]

Matisse would have seen some of these works when he met Rodin at his studio in the rue de l'Université, a visit that has been variously interpreted.[5] Linking the beginning of *The Serf* to Matisse's encounter with Rodin, Alfred Barr suggests that the younger artist hoped "that he might be permitted to work in the great man's studio," but was "rebuffed."[6] Matisse would later recount a different story. Rather than seeking out the great Rodin of his own accord, Matisse suggests that he went only as a favor for one of the master's acolytes: "I was taken to Rodin's studio in the rue de l'Université by one of his pupils, who wanted to show my drawings to his master. Rodin, who received me kindly, was only moderately interested. He told me I had a 'facility of hand,' which wasn't true. He advised me to do detailed drawings and show them to him. I never went back."[7] The exchange, it seems, was courteous but the advice that he received was what he would have been given by any beaux-arts academician. As Matisse developed his own sculptural ideas, he increasingly rejected the example of Rodin, and by 1908 was publicly criticizing Rodin's method of assembling "fragments" and the resulting "confusion in the expression."[8] Given his subsequent disparagement, it is clear that many of Matisse's later statements must be read cautiously as they tend to deny the early influence of Rodin in his sculptural development.

The Serf, with its deliberate fragmentation, un-effaced traces of process, and rhetorical theme is unabashedly a meditation on Rodin, yet differs from Rodin in terms of its surface. The pitted, broken surfaces of Rodin's figures evoke perfect anatomies that have suffered the ravages of accident and time; Matisse's *Serf,* in contrast, is modeled with a lumpy agitation that points to a new expressive freedom. Meyer Schapiro, one of the early commentators to observe this change, noted that "the multiplication of small muscles is the plastic equivalent in this work to subdivided flecking

Henri Matisse, *The Serf,* 1900–1903. Bronze

San Francisco Museum of Modern Art, Bequest of Harriet Lane Levy. Cat. 6

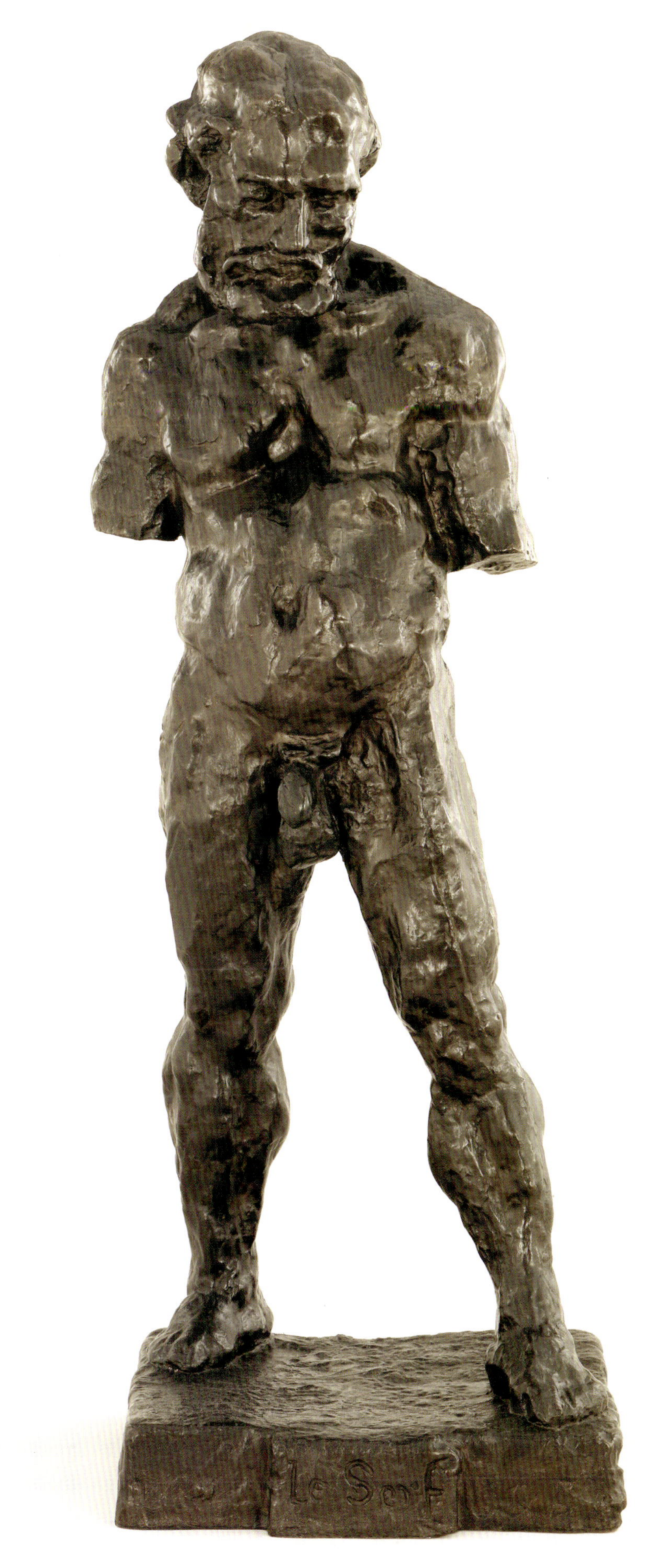
le Serf

and pointillism in painting . . . it is a development within Rodin's sense beyond Rodin."[9] Albert Elsen and Jack Flam, two influential interpreters of Matisse's sculpture, agree that the artist brings a painterly quality to his sculpting of *The Serf,* and that the subjective mark of the artist is applied through accents or discrete light-reflecting masses that construct the figure without representing anatomical surfaces.[10]

In 1899, Matisse acquired Cézanne's *Three Bathers* (fig. 10, p. 9). At this time, the older painter's work was barely known and still poorly understood.[11] The extent and speed with which Matisse absorbed the lessons of that work are apparent a year later in a group of drawings and paintings he executed of the model Bevilaqua. The most significant of these works is his oil painting, *Male Model,* a work that is the painted equivalent of *The Serf.* Not only is the same model used but also the figure's stance is almost identical, especially to the early version of *The Serf* with arms intact. *Male Model* marks a high point of Matisse's early engagement with Cézanne in part because of his use of a similar blue palette and the near-abstract construction of the surface out of distinct blocks of paint.[12] Much of the originality of *The Serf* lies in Matisse's appropriation of a surface taken from paintings by Cézanne, and the adaptation of the underlying principles of his method to create a sculptural equivalent. With the possible exception of Matisse's *Jaguar Devouring a Hare,* no such an attempt had been made before this. In Elsen's words: "The conceit of Matisse, shared with Cézanne, was that he could make a body which appeared more solidly put together than in actual life. By not truing his knife-made accents, Matisse called attention to his hand and the feeling behind each decision."[13]

Flam, noting the "physical similarity" of the sculpture and the bearded, stocky artist, suggests that Matisse seems "psychologically to have identified" with *The Serf.*[14] Given his hard work and poverty in these years, Matisse might well have felt a kinship with the stoic laboring serf. He certainly appears to have been satisfied with the sculpture, exhibiting it four times in Paris alone before World War I. By 1912, Matisse had commissioned five bronzes from the Bingen and Costenoble foundry, an unusually high number suggesting considerable demand for the work early on. *The Serf* was also greatly admired by students in the Académie Matisse (1907–1911), who studied sculpture using the same model.[15]

OS

Notes

1. The work is still dated 1900–1903 in Duthuit 1997, 10. Arguments for a later date of completion appear in Mezzatesta 1984, 38–43, and Flam 1986, 85–88. Hans Purrmann (an artist who helped manage the Matisse academy in 1908) contends that *The Serf* lost its arms accidentally, a view confirmed by Mme Duthuit (the artist's daughter), who adds that the mishap occurred during Matisse's move to his new studio at the Hôtel Biron, in 1908. Elsen, followed by Flam and others, argue that the change more likely resulted from an aesthetic decision on Matisse's part; Elsen 1972, 30; Flam 1986, 487 n.18.

2. Elsen 1972, 26.

3. Jean Puy, cited in Spurling 1998, 215.

4. The connection with *Walking Man* is discussed in Elsen 1972, 28. Pierre Schneider (1984, 123) suggests the possible influence of the *Jean d'Aire* figure, the model for which may also have been Bevilaqua.

5. Schneider (ibid., 546) suggests that there was more than one meeting between the two artists. After his move in 1908, Matisse must have run into Rodin frequently when they became neighbors in the former convent of the Sacré-Coeur at the Hôtel Biron.

6. Barr 1951, 52.

7. Escholier 1960, 138.

8. Ibid.

9. Schapiro 1932, 35.

10. Elsen 1972, 37; Flam 1986, 88.

11. Schneider 1984, 138.

12. Ibid., 140–41.

13. Elsen 1972, 39.

14. Flam 1986, 88.

15. Franzke 1983, 29–34.

Henri Matisse, *The Serf,* 1900–1903. Bronze

San Francisco Museum of Modern Art, Bequest of Harriet Lane Levy. Cat. 6

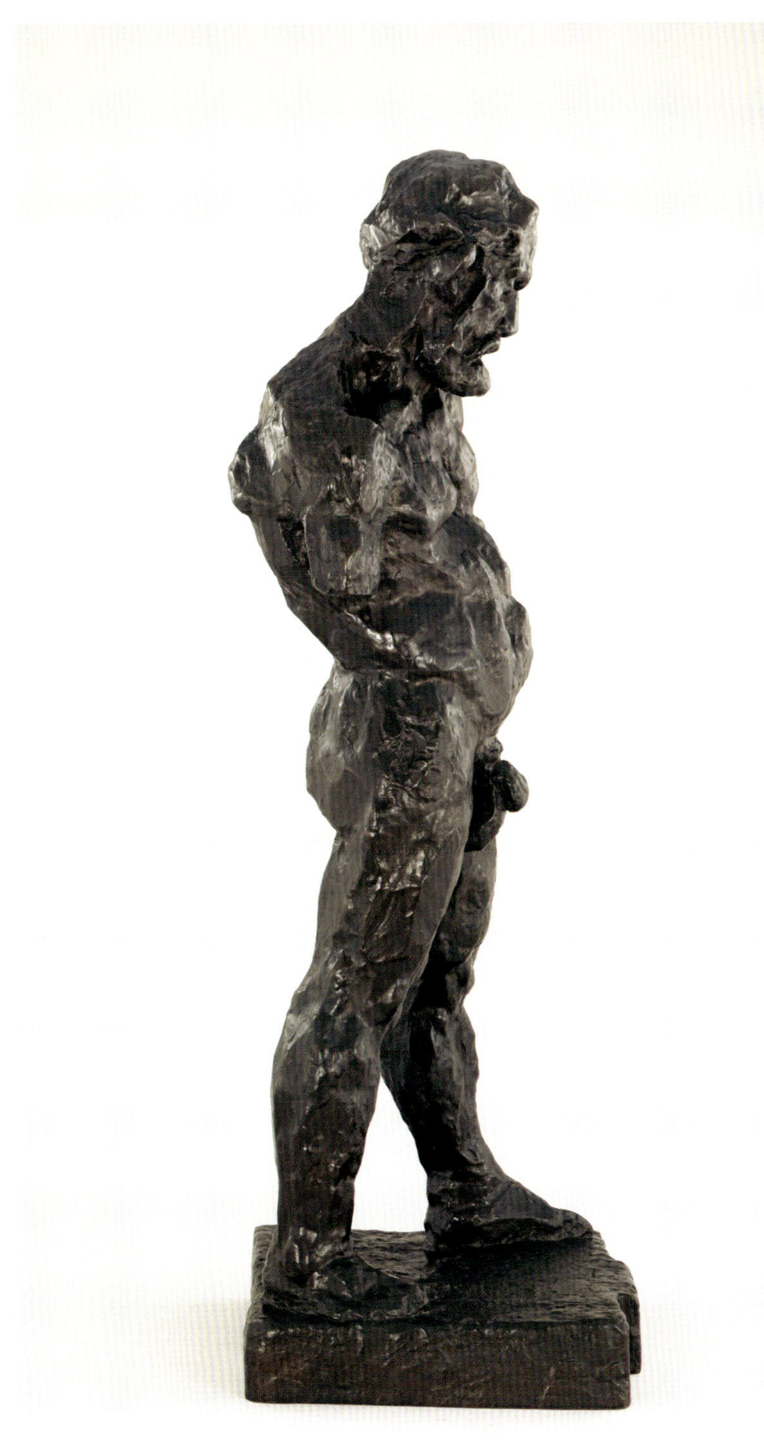

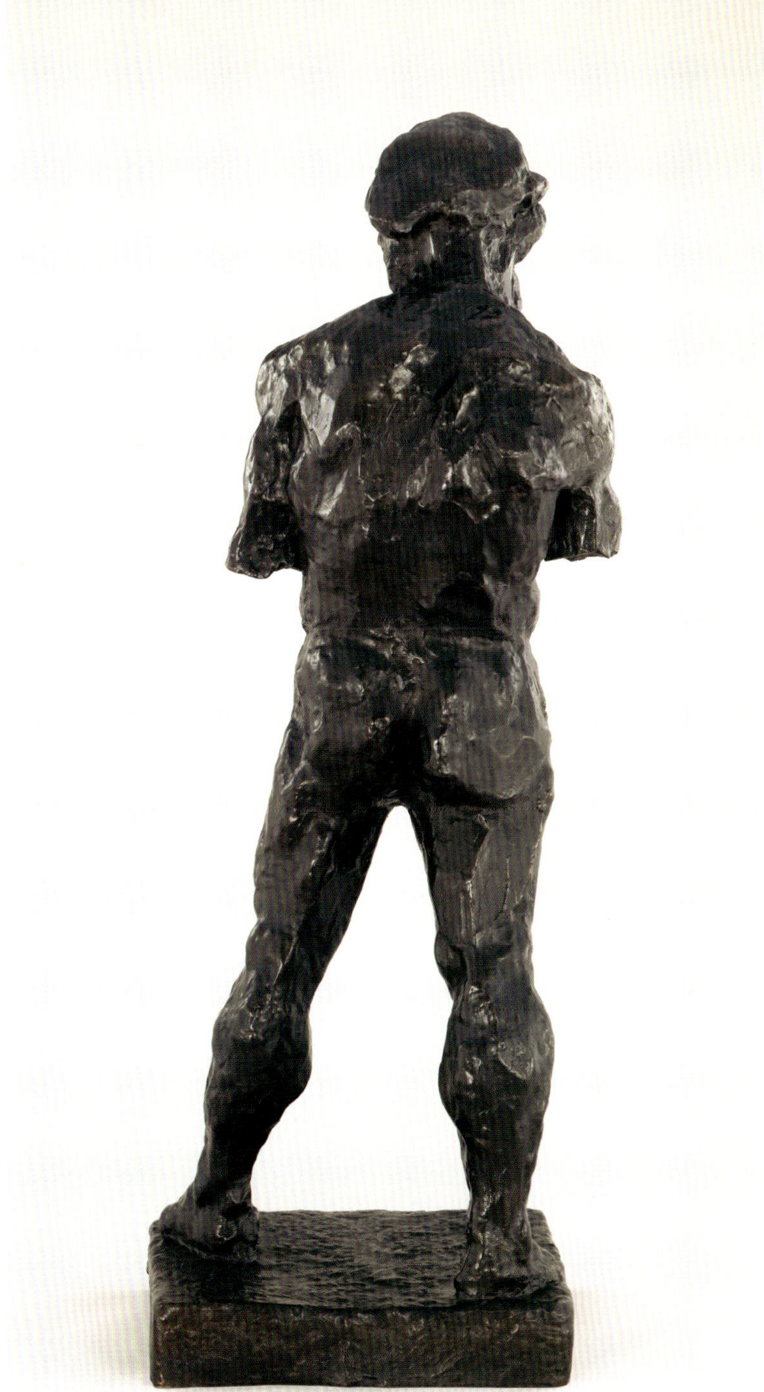

Henri Matisse, *Male Model,* c. 1900. Oil on canvas

The Museum of Modern Art, New York; Kay Sage Tanguy and Abby Aldrich Rockefeller Funds, 1975. Cat. 7

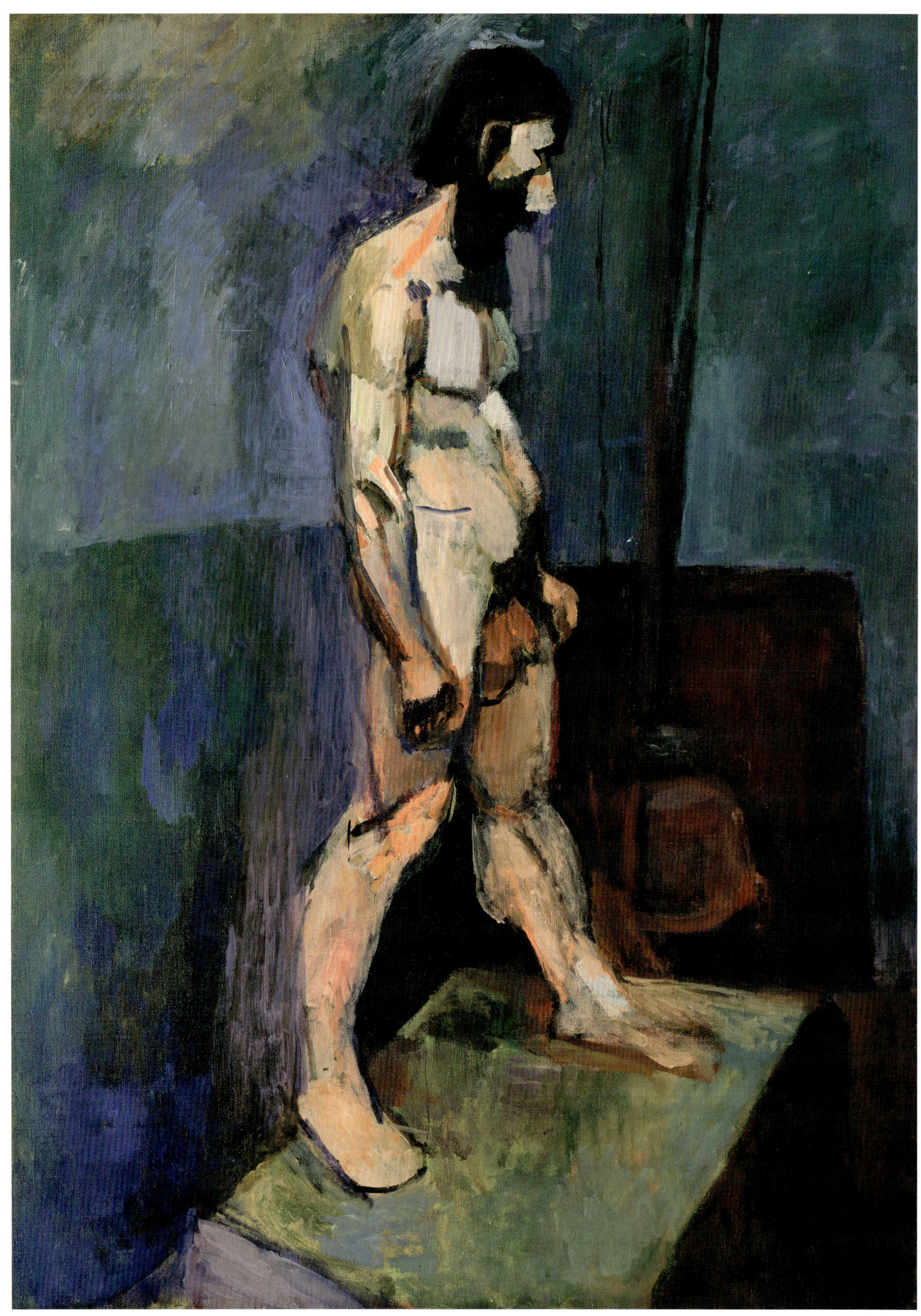

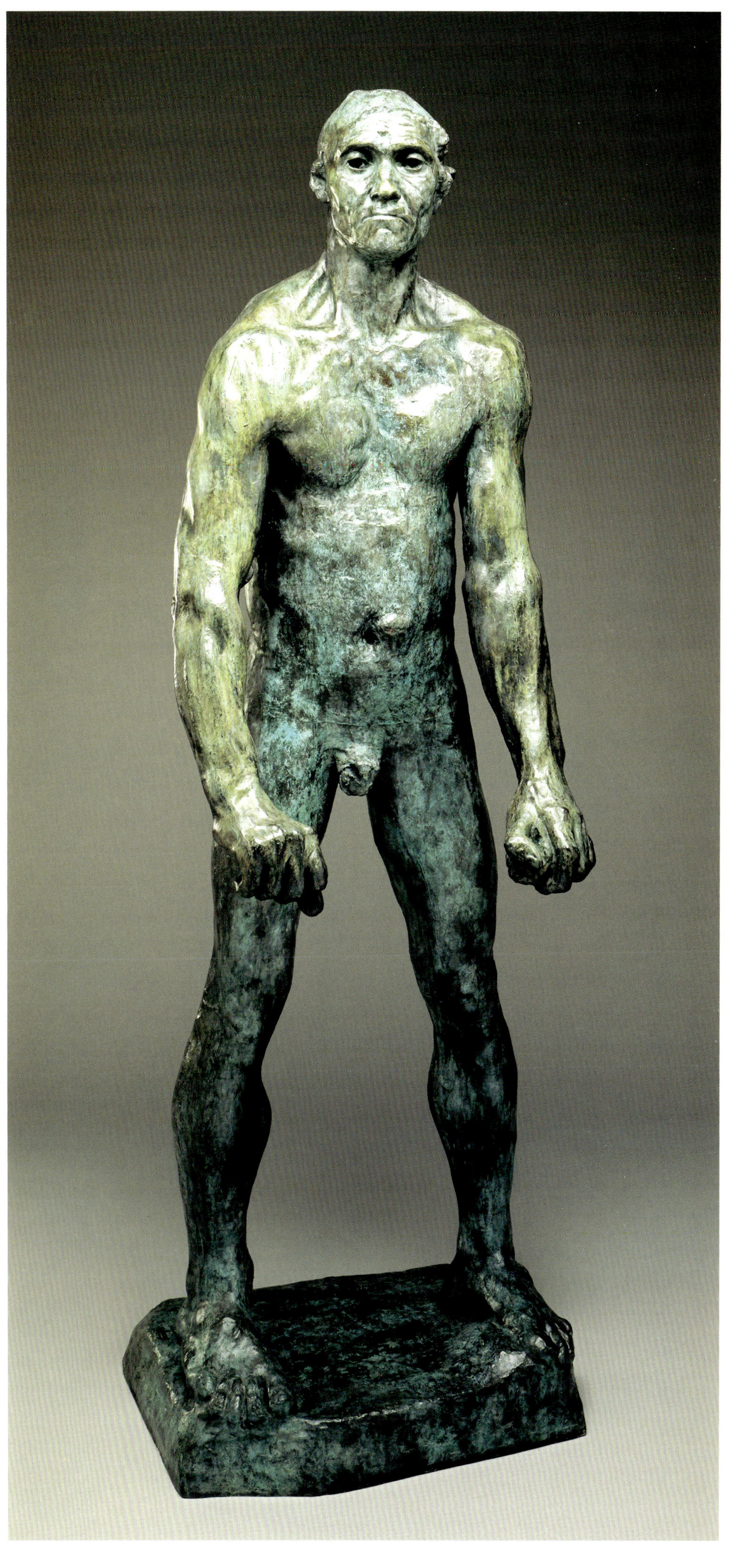

Auguste Rodin, *Jean d'Aire,* from the *Burghers of Calais,* 1895. Bronze

Dallas Museum of Art, Given in memory of Louie N. Bromberg and Mina Bromberg by their sister Essie Bromberg Joseph. Cat. 163

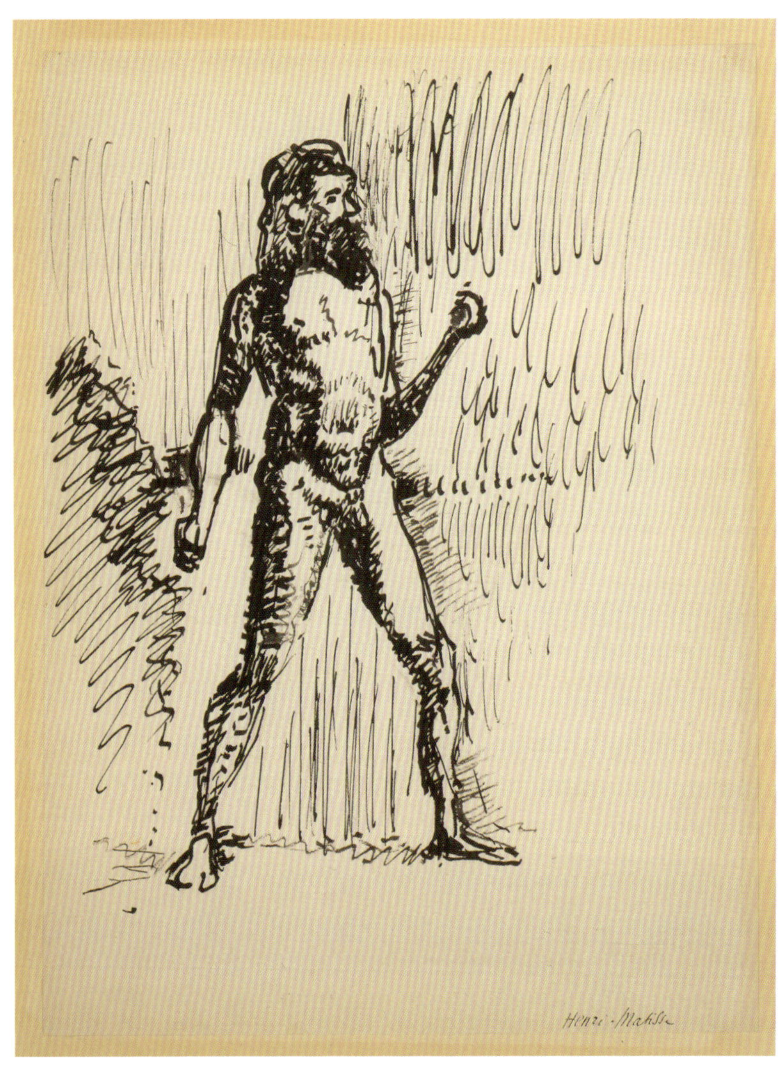

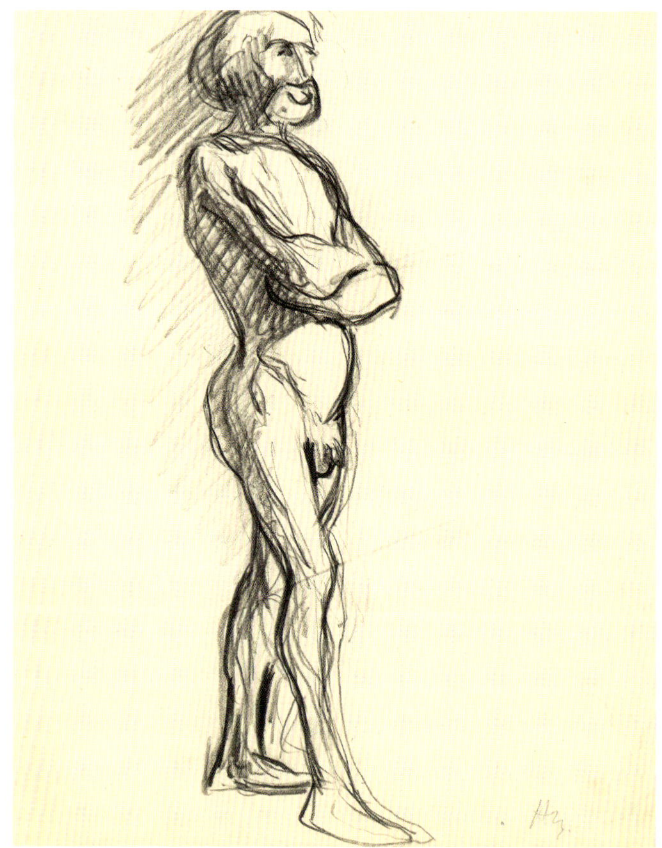

Henri Matisse, *Male Model,* c. 1900. Pen and ink

Solomon R. Guggenheim Museum, New York; Thannhauser Collection, Gift, Justin K. Thannhauser, 1978. Cat. 9

Henri Matisse, *Study for The Serf,* 1900–1902 Graphite

Private collection. Cat. 10

Henri Matisse, *Study for The Serf,* 1900. Graphite

Musée départemental Matisse, Le Cateau-Cambrésis, Purchase 1991. Cat. 8

Henri Matisse, *Standing Man, Seen from the Back,* 1900–1903. Pen and ink

Pierre and Maria-Gaetana Matisse Foundation Collection. Cat. 11

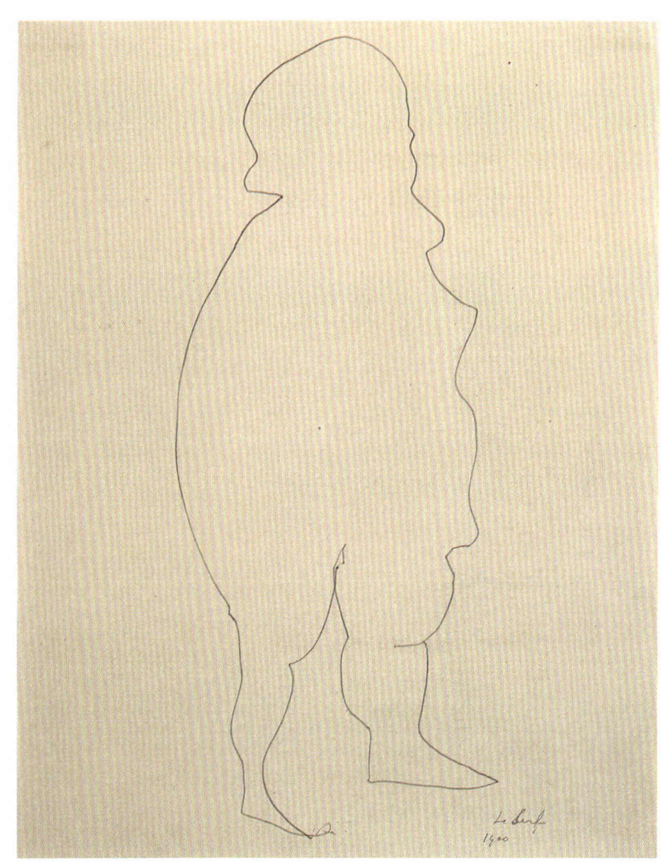

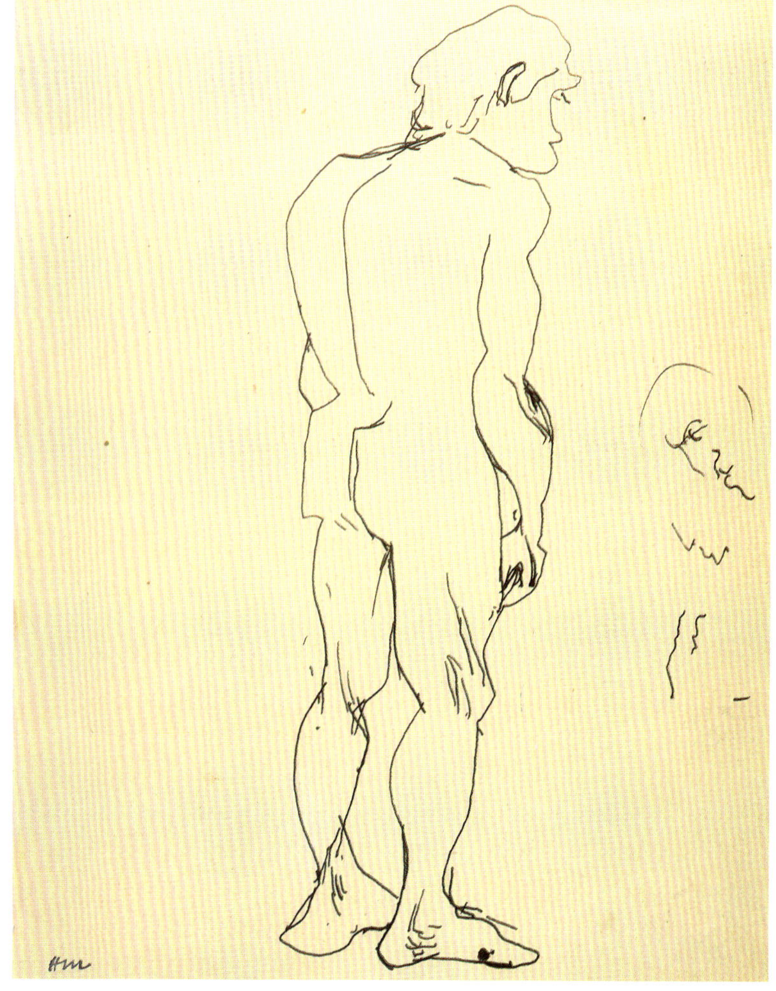

Madeleine

Although approximating the scale of work by Edgar Degas, Matisse's sculpted figures generally avoid strenuous movement. Nonetheless, even the static poses engage the mechanics of the body in a struggle with gravity. With *Madeleine I* and *Madeleine II,* sculpted in 1901 and 1903 respectively, Matisse concentrated on the model's *contrapposto* stance. He accentuates all of the consequences of the weight-bearing leg, which tilts the figure's pelvis and produces a series of pronounced and subtle counterbalanced bodily shifts. Although the figure does not technically move, it is animated by an internal spiraling rhythm that Matisse referred to as the *arabesque.*[1] Comparing himself to his friend the sculptor Aristide Maillol, Matisse would write, "Maillol, like the Antique masters, proceeds by volume, I am concerned with arabesque like the Renaissance artists."[2] In linking his own sculptural sources to the Renaissance, Matisse may well have been thinking of Michelangelo's *Bound Slave* and *Dying Slave,* works he knew intimately from his daily visits to the Louvre as a student of Gustave Moreau. Matisse would later acquire a plaster copy of the *Dying Slave,* and a number of commentators have compared its serpentine curvature to the arabesque of the *Madeleine* sculptures.[3] It is perhaps no coincidence that Matisse was also modeling *The Serf* in these years, a work that is conceptually if not formally linked to the *Slave.* Matisse's preoccupation with chiastic, shifted anatomies endured and would later receive monumental treatment in the bas-relief series *The Back I–IV,* which he produced over a period of twenty years, beginning in 1909.[4]

Moreau encouraged his students to balance what they learned at the Louvre against the direct study of nature. The series of studies related to *Madeleine I* and *II* reveal the sophistication with which Matisse combined visual observation and an awareness of numerous historical sources—not only Michelangelo's *Slave*s but also sculptures such as Rodin's guilt-ridden, self-hugging *Eve* (fig. 60, p. 62) and his *Meditation.*[5] Unlike these figures by Rodin, however, where the inward twisting poses are meant to express such notions as guilt or thought, *Madeleine* makes no attempt to cloak the nude with literary meanings—she is simply a model and in this she is more modern than *The Serf.*

In *Madeleine I* and several related studies, Matisse addresses the artistic problem of dealing with a figure's arms so that they do not interfere with the silhouette of the torso—an issue he struggled with in *The Serf.* The painting *Standing Model (Nude Study in Blue)* depicts the same model in a similar serpentine stance but with arms down in the familiar self-covering gesture of the classical *Venus pudica.* Perhaps unsatisfied, in the drawing *Study for Madeleine I* Matisse raises and crosses the figure's arms almost as in the sculpture—except that a portion of the figure's proper right arm in the sculpture is actually missing. This use of fragmentation again recalls Rodin and can be related to the suggestive erasure evident in Matisse drawings. As in the related studies, the figure's facial features are omitted, so attention becomes focused on the overall structure. Far from looking generic, however, the sculpture conveys a sense of vision at a distance, the surface activated with abstract incident and a complex modulation of light.

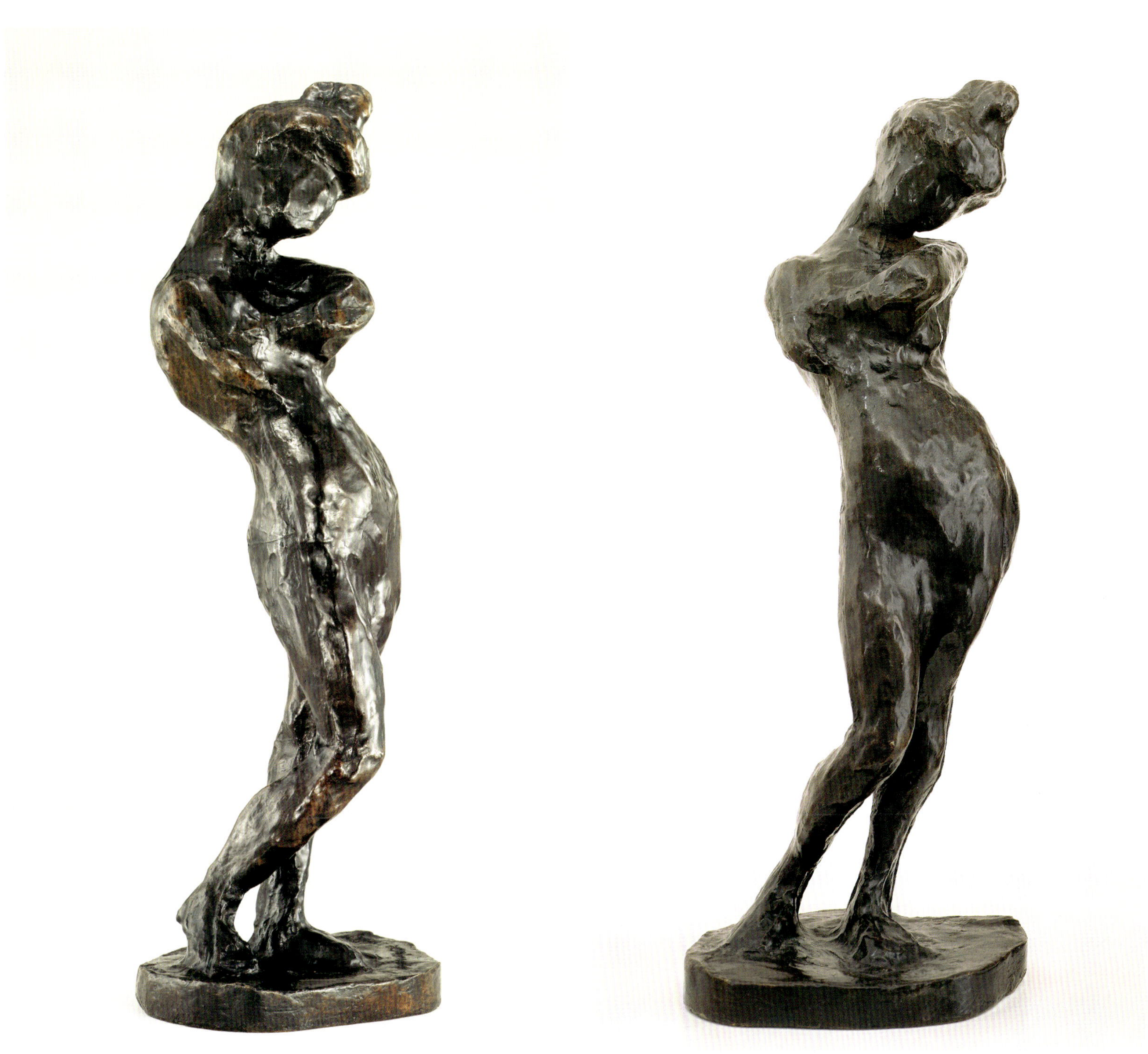

Henri Matisse, *Madeleine I,* 1901. Bronze

San Francisco Museum of Modern Art, Bequest of Harriet Lane Levy. Cat. 13

Madeleine I is one of the few sculptures by Matisse of which plaster versions survive. One of the most notable examples is the painted plaster in the Nasher Collection, its distinct mold lines bearing the traces of Matisse's process. The artist is said to have taken the piece molds himself and produced three plaster casts.[6] There is evidence that a mold was made from the wet clay original,[7] an unusual procedure that would have enabled Matisse to continue to elaborate the original clay, transforming it eventually into the second version of the piece, *Madeleine II.* This helps explain passages that, in laser scans taken from each sculpture (fig. 70, p. 76), are nearly identical.[8] Artistically it demonstrates Matisse's early use of a process that allowed him to work in series, a practice that he would take up again in series such as the *Jeannette*s, the *Henriette*s, and the *Back*s.

Compared with its predecessor, *Madeleine II* appears less smooth yet also more stable—broken down into blocklike architectural units. In this, and in its rough, less sinuous surface, the figure is closer to *The Serf.* Ironically, Matisse did not choose to exhibit this version together with *The Serf,* preferring to pair the male figure with the earlier, smoother *Madeleine I.* The art critic Louis Vauxcelles described the pair, which he'd seen together at the 1904 Salon d'automne, as "a nude man, vigorously accentuated" and a "young girl, quite amusingly curved."[9]

OS

Notes

1. For a discussion of Matisse's use of the arabesque, see Benjamin 1992, 15–25. Using the Renaissance term *figura serpentinata,* Yve-Alain Bois (1997, 374) discusses the same concept, which he links to Michelangelo and later mannerist sculpture.

2. Matisse in Escholier 1960, 140–41.

3. Elsen 1972, 50; and Bois 1997, 374.

4. *The Back I* and the now-lost *The Back 0,* recorded in a photograph by Eugène Druet (see fig. 9, p. 9), are the most powerful examples of this connection; see Elsen 1972, 184.

5. Ibid., 50.

6. Duthuit 1997, 20; one, given by Matisse to Albert Marquet, is currently in the Musée des Beaux-Arts, Bordeaux; another is in the Nasher Sculpture Center (cat. 14); the third is reported to be in a private collection in San Francisco.

7. Digital photographs of the mold lines of the Nasher piece were shown to M. Laurent, one of the most experienced plaster molders at the Atelier de moulage (formerly "du Louvre et des musées du France"; now separate) in Paris. He concluded that the irregularities in these lines resulted from piece-molding a wet clay original.

8. This research was conducted by Oliver Shell, Assistant Curator of European Painting and Sculpture, and Ann Boulton, Objects Conservator, both of The Baltimore Museum of Art, and employed the technical services of Direct Dimensions, Owings Mills, Maryland.

9. Vauxcelles 1904; reprinted in Flam 1988.

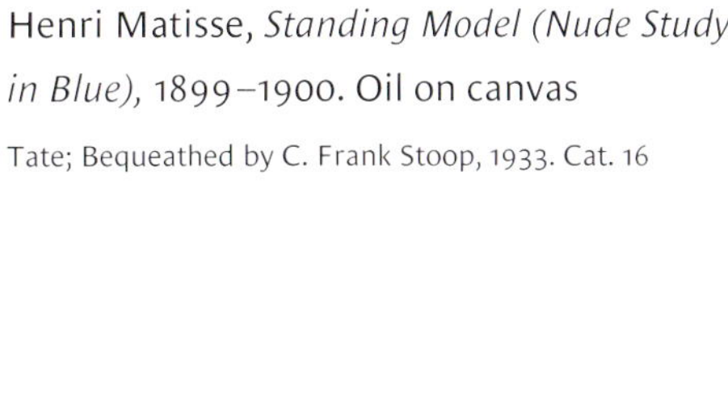

Henri Matisse, *Standing Model (Nude Study in Blue),* 1899–1900. Oil on canvas

Tate; Bequeathed by C. Frank Stoop, 1933. Cat. 16

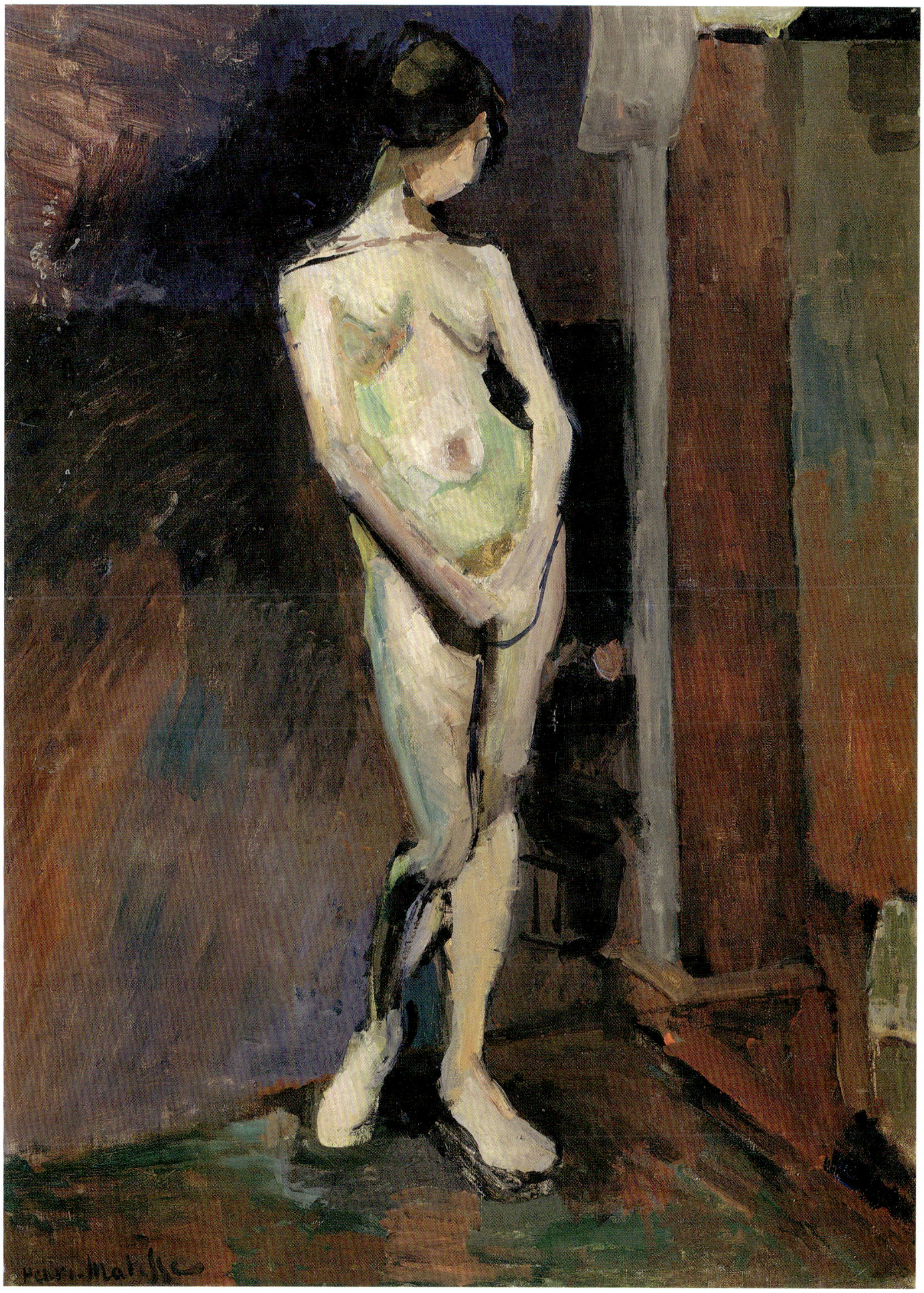

Auguste Rodin, *Meditation,* 1885. Bronze

Philadelphia Museum of Art, Bequest of Jules E. Mastbaum, 1929. Cat. 162

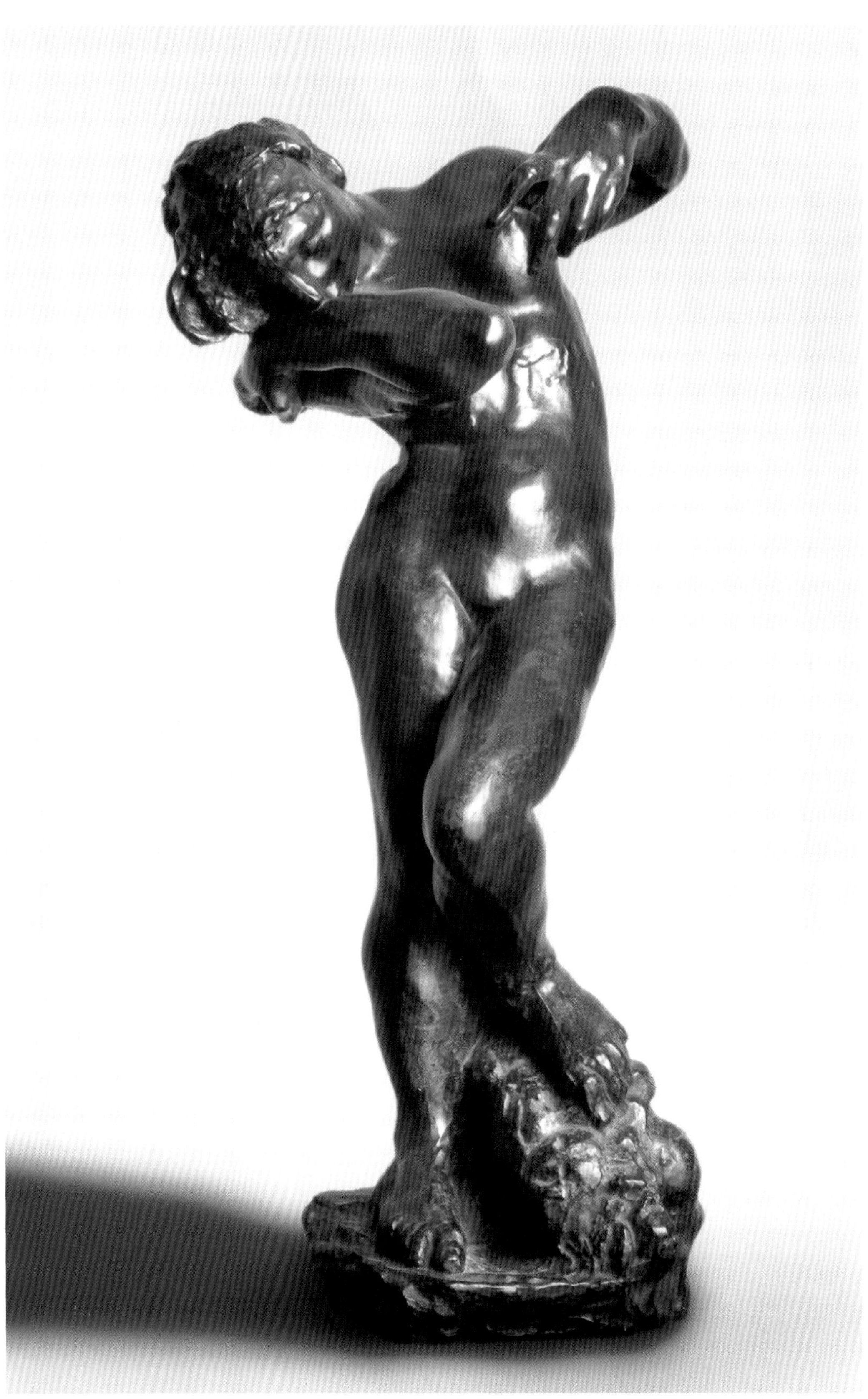

Henri Matisse, *Madeleine II,* 1903. Bronze

Centre Pompidou, Paris; Musée national d'art moderne/ Centre de création industrielle; Remittance in lieu of inheritance taxes to the government of France, 1991. Cat. 15

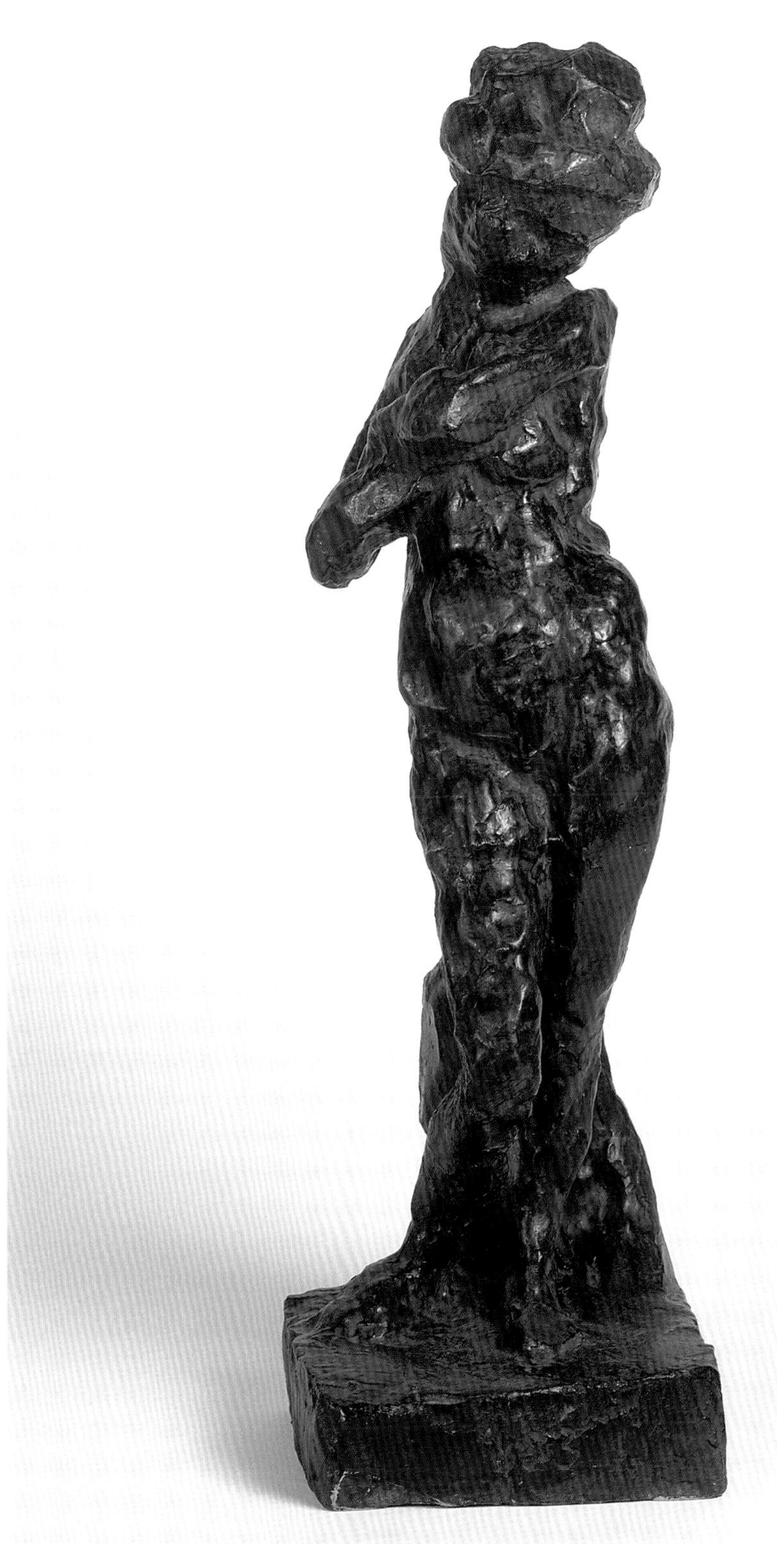

Henri Matisse, *Madeleine I,* 1901. Painted plaster

Raymond and Patsy Nasher Collection, Dallas. Cat. 14

Henri Matisse, *Study for Madeleine I,* 1901

Graphite

The Museum of Modern Art, New York; Gift of Mr. and Mrs. Pierre Matisse in honor and memory of Victor Leventritt. Cat. 20

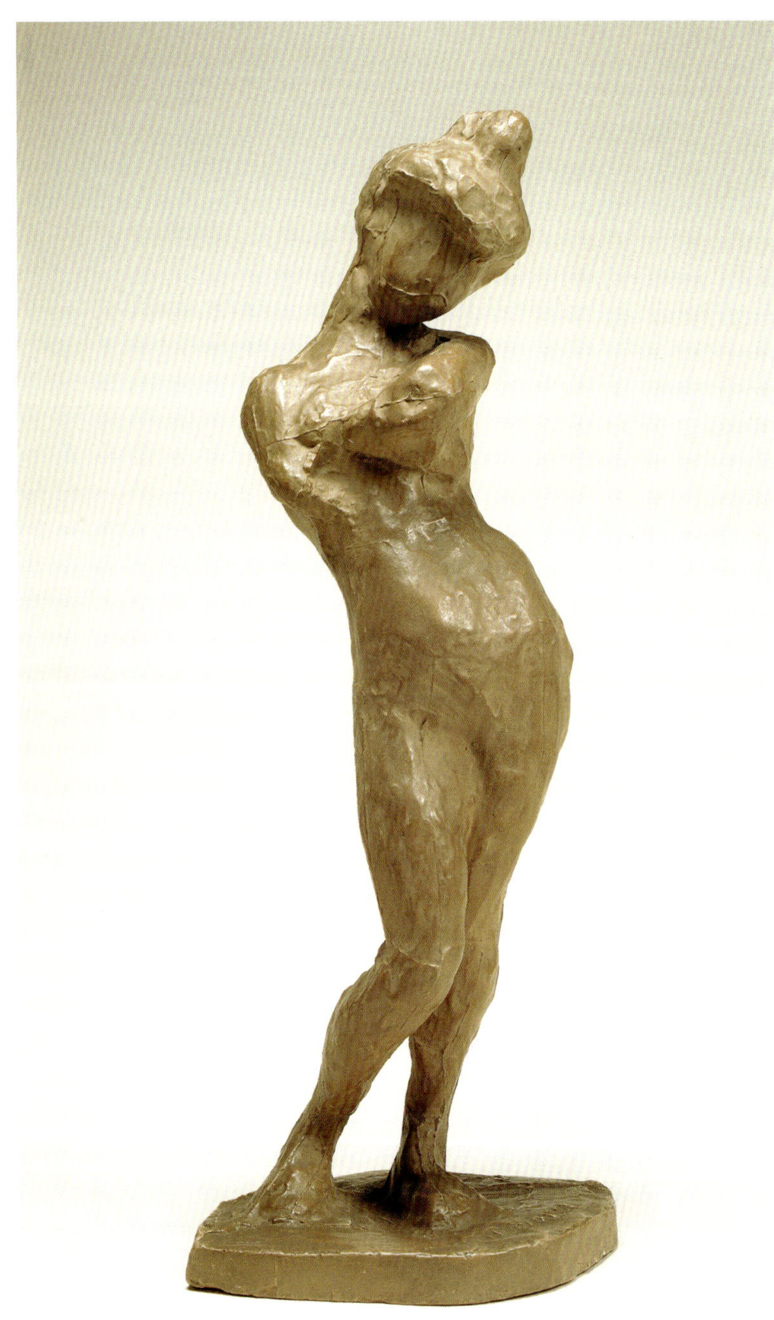

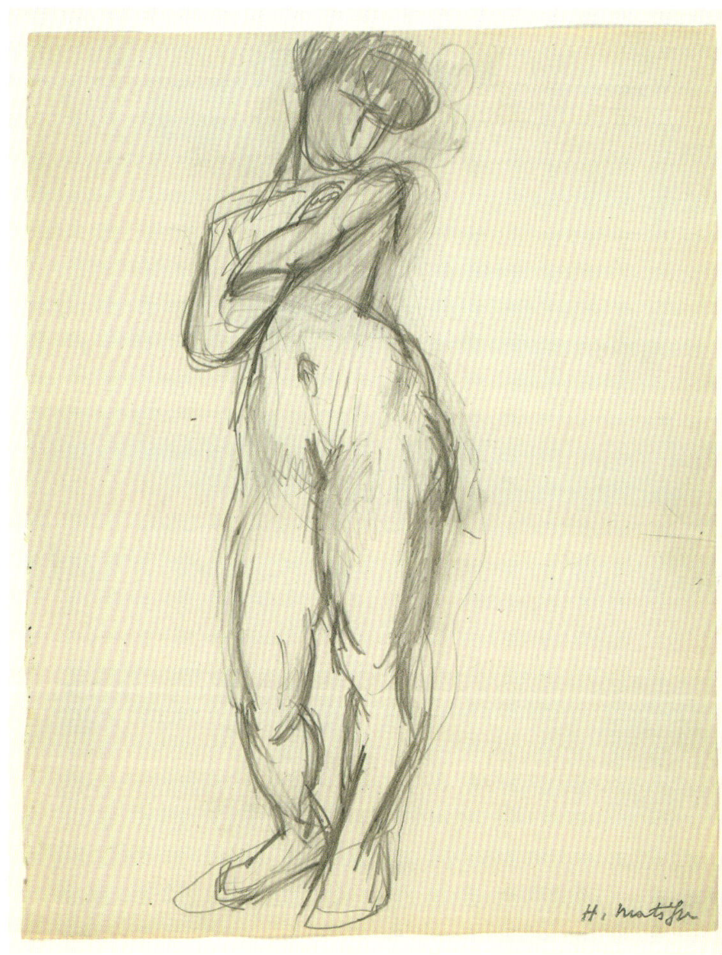

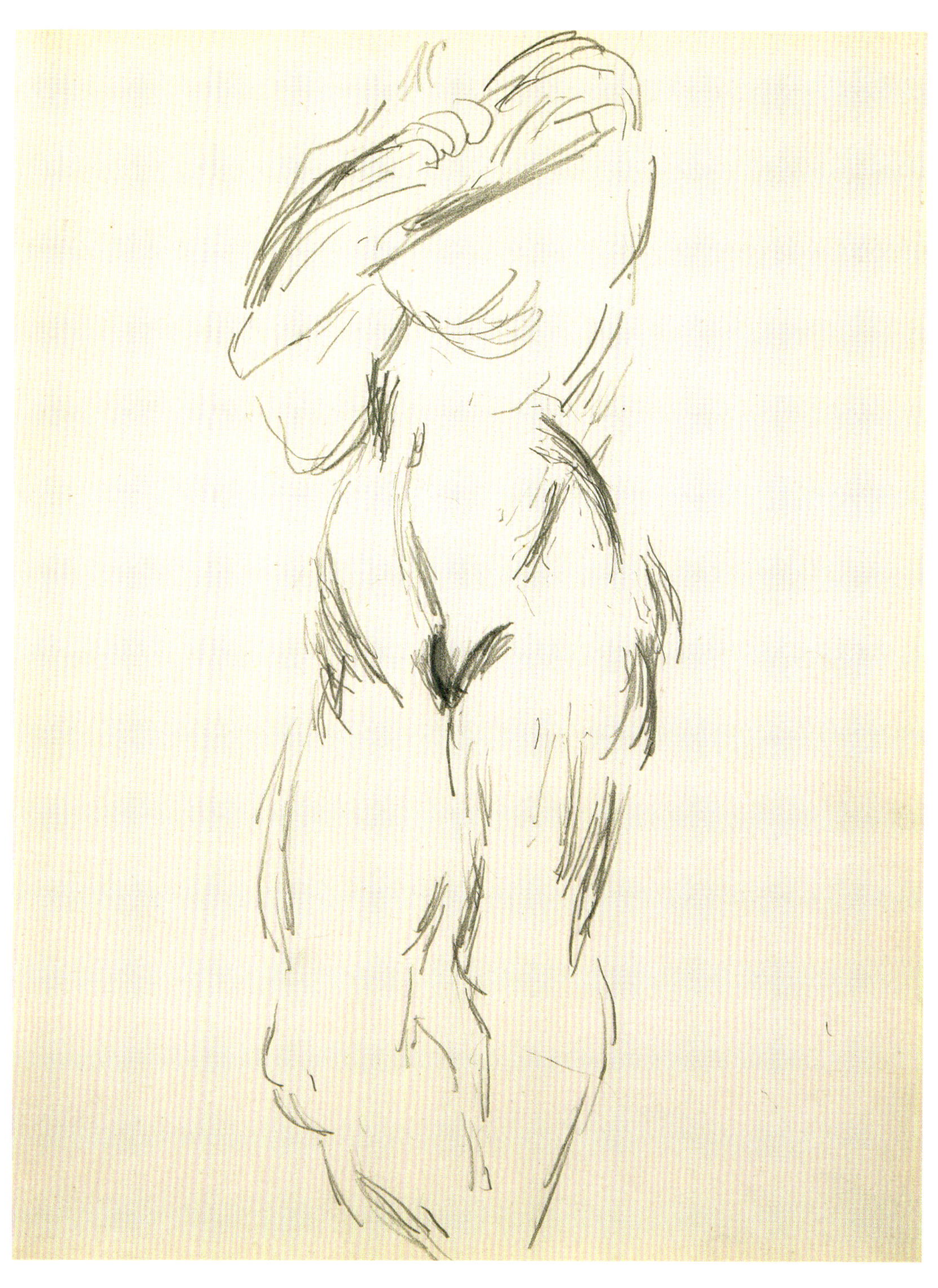

Henri Matisse, *Study for Madeleine II,* 1903

Graphite

Musée départemental Matisse, Le Cateau-Cambrésis,

Gift of Marie Matisse, 1993. Cat. 22

Henri Matisse, *Nude, Seen from the Back, on a Hatched Ground,* 1900–1903. Graphite

Pierre and Maria-Gaetana Matisse Foundation Collection. Cat. 19

Henri Matisse, *Standing Nude, Seen from the Back,* 1903. Graphite with stumping and scraping

Dr. and Mrs. Morton Mower. Cat. 23

Henri Matisse, *Nude, Seen from the Back,* 1901–1903. Graphite

Pierre and Maria-Gaetana Matisse Foundation Collection. Cat. 21

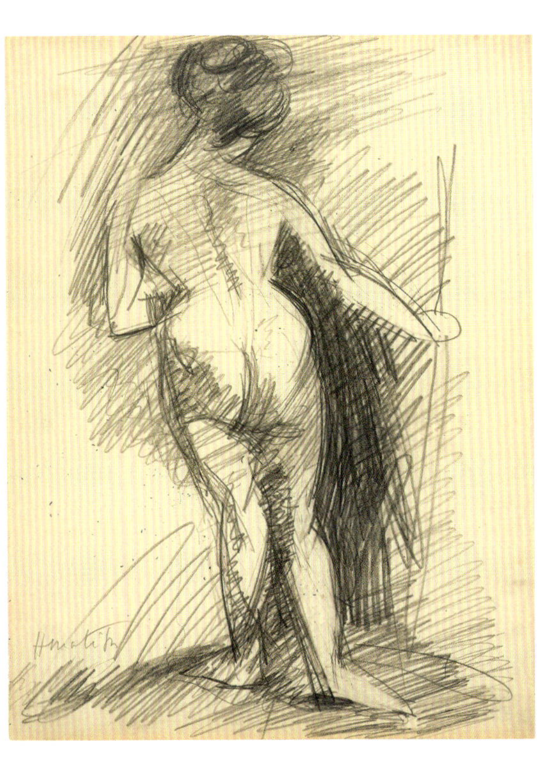

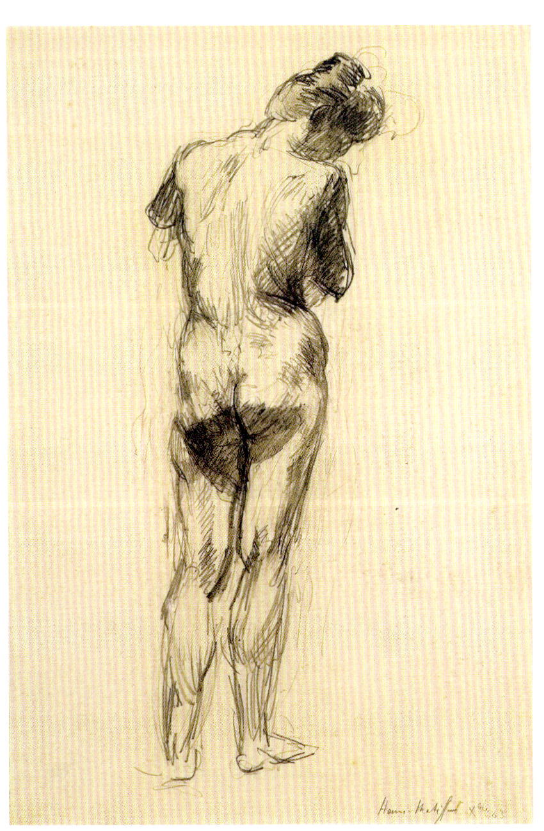

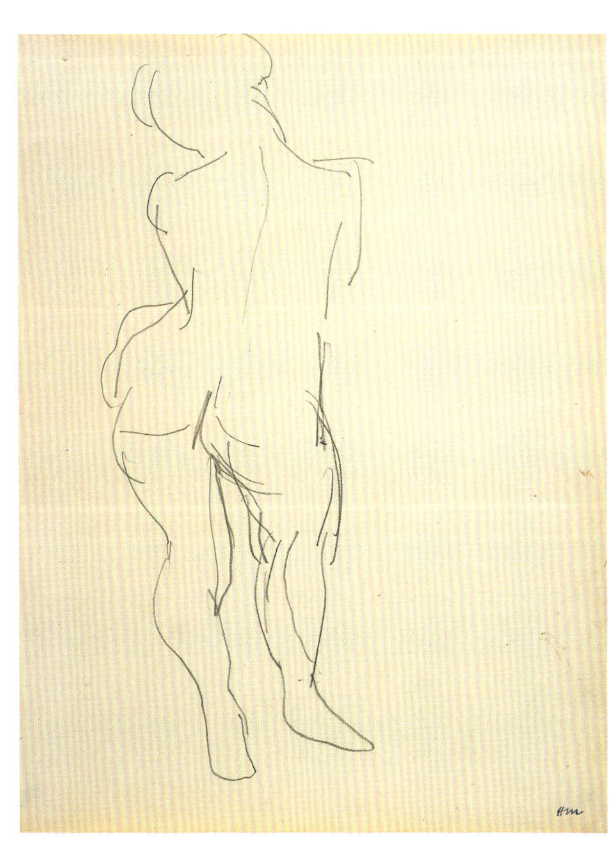

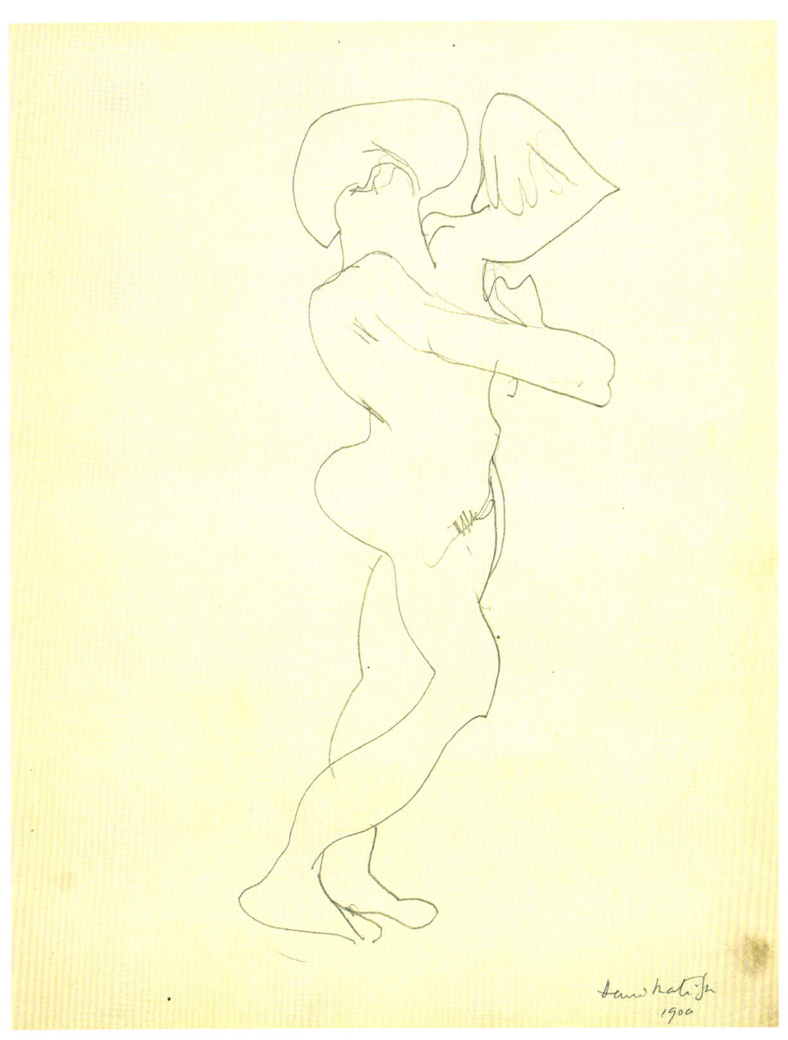

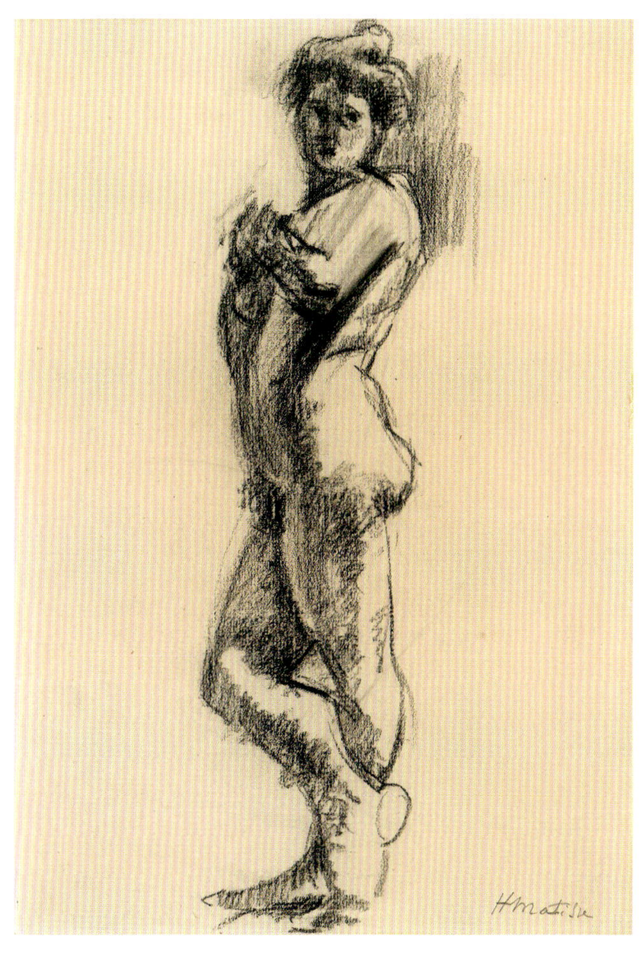

Henri Matisse, *Standing Figure,* 1900. Graphite

Pierre and Maria-Gaetana Matisse Foundation Collection.

Cat. 17

Henri Matisse, *Standing Nude,* c. 1900

Black crayon with stumping

Stedelijk Museum, Amsterdam. Cat. 18

Woman Leaning on Her Hands and *Thorn Extractor*

Woman Leaning on Her Hands is one of only two sculptures Matisse produced of clothed figures; the other is the more classically inspired *Reclining Figure with Chemise.* In the ledger of sculptures Matisse began in 1936, he underscores their close relationship, titling the former *Chemise relevée* and the latter *La Chemise.*[1] Alfred Barr describes *Woman Leaning on Her Hands* as "smooth in surface but complex in pose with radiating limbs and rhythmic counterpoise of head and torso."[2] Isabelle Monod-Fontaine notes the emphasis upon "the continuous arabesque, on the smooth transitions and the polished roundness of the shoulders, which echoes that of the chignon and the knees."[3] The sculpture has no base and the figure, rooted to the ground by gravity, is supported on oversized hands that have been variously described as "paws" or "suction pads."[4]

Woman Leaning on Her Hands has been compared to the figure in the right foreground of *Luxe, calme et volupté,* a critical painting in Matisse's development, coming from a period when he worked in close proximity with Paul Signac and Henri-Edmond Cross.[5] Although the painted and sculpted figures share complex twisting motions, the poses are not identical. It is, however, in the context of *Luxe, calme et volupté,* and the subsequent *Le bonheur de vivre* (fig. 28, p. 29) that this work is potentially revealing. Following Cross and perhaps Puvis de Chavannes (more than the indifferent figure painter Signac), Matisse was seeking ways to integrate figures into classically inspired idyllic landscapes.[6] Cross had worked toward this goal in *The Shaded Beach* (1902)—a painting, populated by several twisting nudes, that Matisse knew—and in other works inspired by symbolist poetry. These paintings include female figures whose costume varies from the contemporary to the mythological.[7] *Woman Leaning on Her Hands* shares the temporal ambiguity of these works and of *Luxe, calme et volupté,* which has been interpreted as a vision of the modern picnic with classical nymphs.[8]

From certain angles the sculpted figure appears to be wearing a loose-fitting toga or shift; in fact she wears only a shirt, as Matisse makes clear when he refers to the piece as the *Chemise relevée.* This incomplete contemporary costume is unusual, for as Matisse emphasizes in a related drawing, it is the figure's breasts that are "revealed" (*relevée*) by the loose-fitting shirt; she is nude below the waist. This sartorial arrangement is the exact opposite of that employed by Puvis de Chavannes in his paintings of overtly classical beachgoers, such as the *Pleasant Land*, where female figures expose their breasts and wear vaguely Greek-looking wraps below.

The sculpture was produced in Paris, beginning in late 1904, after Matisse had spent the summer in Saint-Tropez, making the initial sketch for *Luxe, calme et volupté,* and completed in 1905, perhaps overlapping with the beginning of *Le bonheur de vivre.* It is a sculptural exploration of the sorts of figures that would serve him in the landscapes. Although no figure in the latter painting echoes exactly the pose of *Woman Leaning on Her Hands,* the sculpture has a smooth, molten quality analogous to the fluid rhythms of the contours of the figures in *Le bonheur de vivre*—whose lines are cloaked beneath soft, colored auras. This quality is achieved through the omission of angular marks of cutting tools and may also result from an original model sculpted in wax.[9]

Where *Woman Leaning on Her Hands* teeters uncertainly on the brink between the observed world and classical fantasy, Matisse achieves a comparable balance in his *Thorn Extractor* indulging his fascination with classical models without hiding the fact that his is a modern copy of the well-known Roman prototype. Albert Elsen notes that Matisse reworked the theme, that he "reversed the ancient posture of the legs and made a standing rather than a seated figure, giving more energy and a more precarious balance to the motif."[10]

Both sculptures are brought together in the ground-breaking painting *Still Life with a Geranium,* where the internal gyrating energy of each of the two sculptures is mirrored by the larger centripetal composition revolving around the geranium pot. With the exception of the earlier *Studio Interior*, this is among the earliest examples of Matisse's using his sculptures to populate his paintings—a practice he would pursue most extensively in nine paintings he created depicting *Reclining Nude I (Aurora).*[11] I use the term *populate* advisedly because in *Still Life with a Geranium* the sculptures serve to animate the scene while retaining both the status of sculpted objects and of pure medium: crudely applied paint, drawn lines, and color. Arcadian references are brought emphatically down to earth as the figures must contend with everyday things: four onions, a rustic pitcher, and a flowerpot. Like the nymphs at the center of *Le bonheur de vivre,* however, the two main protagonists of *Still Life with a Geranium* face opposite directions and enact their own wheeling motion around the hub of the flowerpot as surely as does the circle of dancers in the pastoral scene.

OS

Notes

1. The ledger entry includes small illustrations and is published in Duthuit 1997, 311. Wanda de Guébriant of the Matisse Archives in Paris has stated that this notebook dates to 1936; some entries were clearly added later.

2. Barr 1951, 100.

3. Monod-Fontaine 1984, 10.

4. Ibid.; Schneider (1984, 548) writes: "The *Woman Leaning on Her Hands* clings to the earth, as if her outspread hands were suction pads."

5. Mezzatesta 1984, 52; Monod-Fontaine 1984, 10. Matisse spent part of the summer of 1904 staying with Signac, and he developed a close friendship with Cross; Spurling, 1998, 283–89.

6. The 1904 Salon d'automne, to which Matisse was a major contributor, included retrospective exhibitions of Cézanne and Puvis de Chavannes.

7. See also *Bord méditerranéens* (1895, Walter F. Brown Collection) and *Le bois* (1906, Musée de l'Annonciade, Saint-Tropez) in Baligand et al. 1998, 40, 58, 75.

8. Flam 1986, 118–20.

9. The BMA cast of this piece comes from the Godard foundry and appears to have been sand cast; I suspect that the smoothness has more to do with the initial model than with the casting technique.

10. Elsen 1972, 63.

11. See Duthuit 1997, 265–66, for the complete list of Matisse's paintings representing his sculptures.

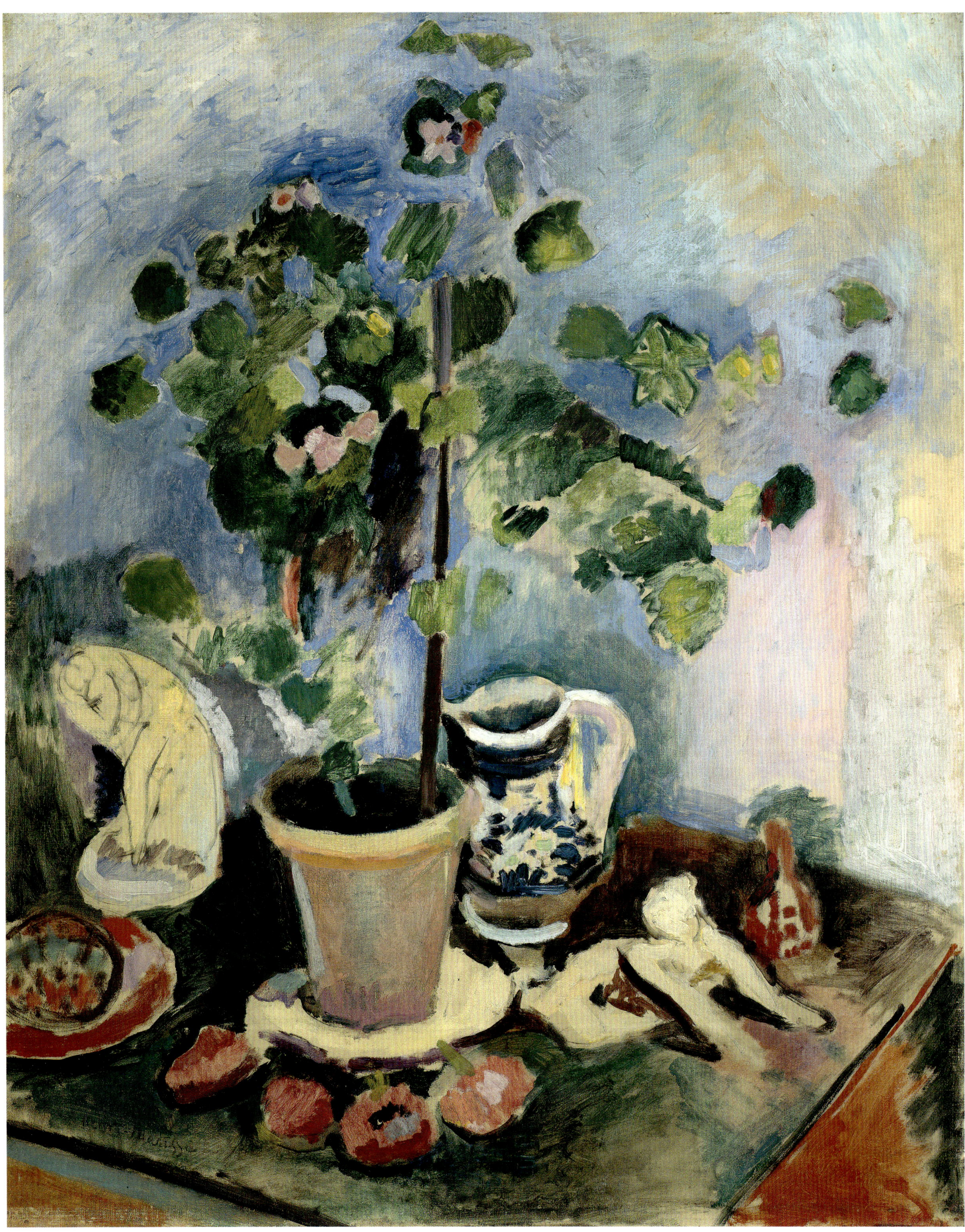

Henri Matisse, *Still Life with a Geranium,* 1906

Oil on canvas

The Art Institute of Chicago, Joseph Winterbotham Collection. Cat. 29

Below and following:

Henri Matisse, *Woman Leaning on Her Hands,* 1905. Bronze

The Baltimore Museum of Art, The Cone Collection, formed by Dr. Claribel Cone and Miss Etta Cone of Baltimore, Maryland. Cat. 24

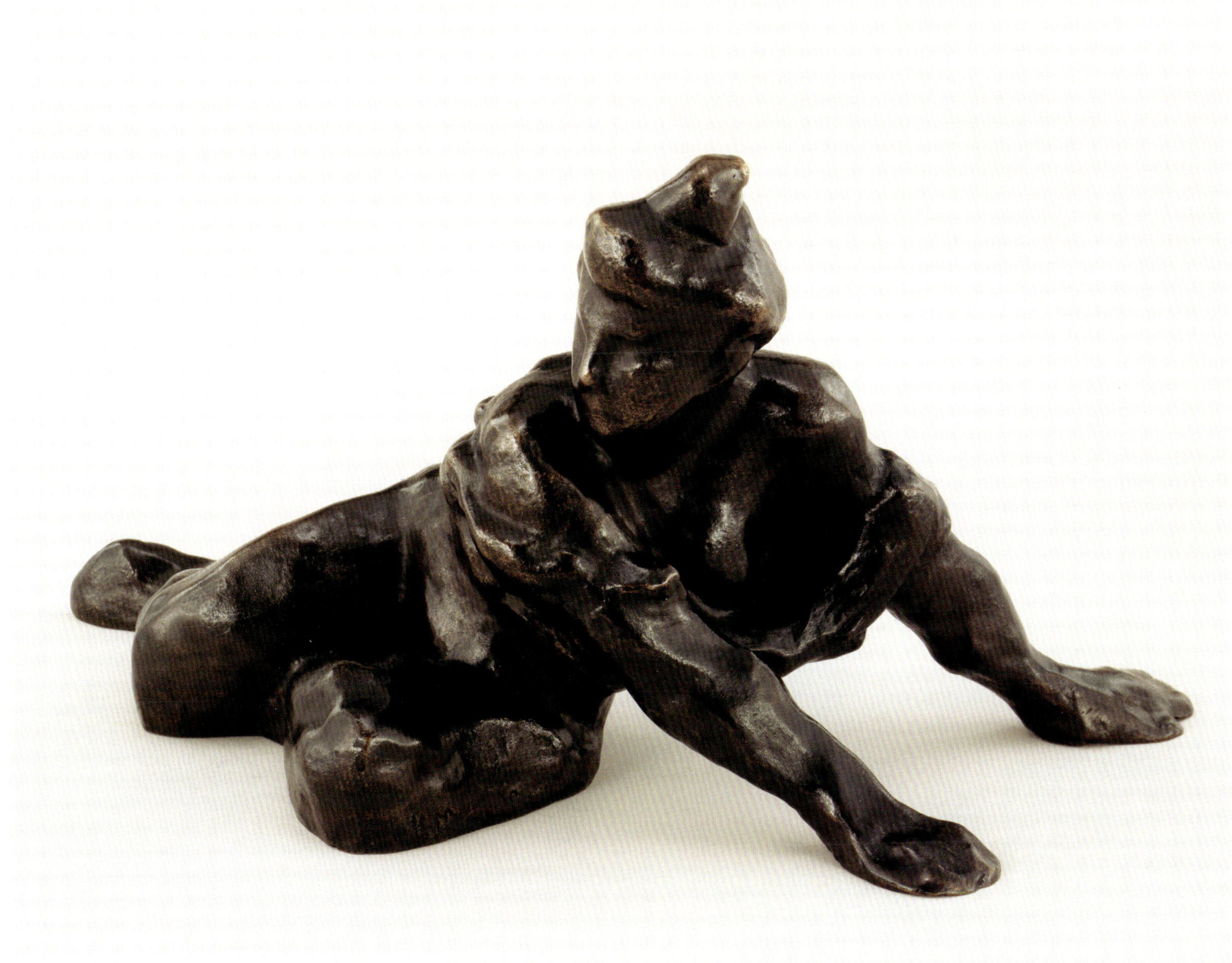

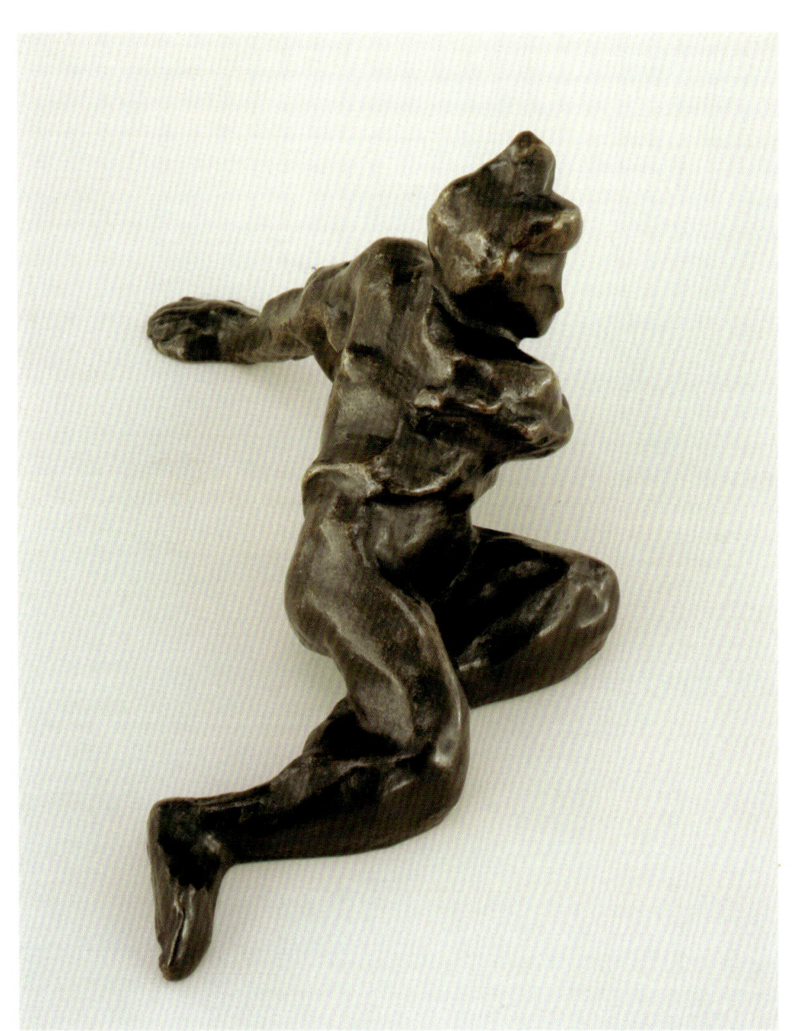

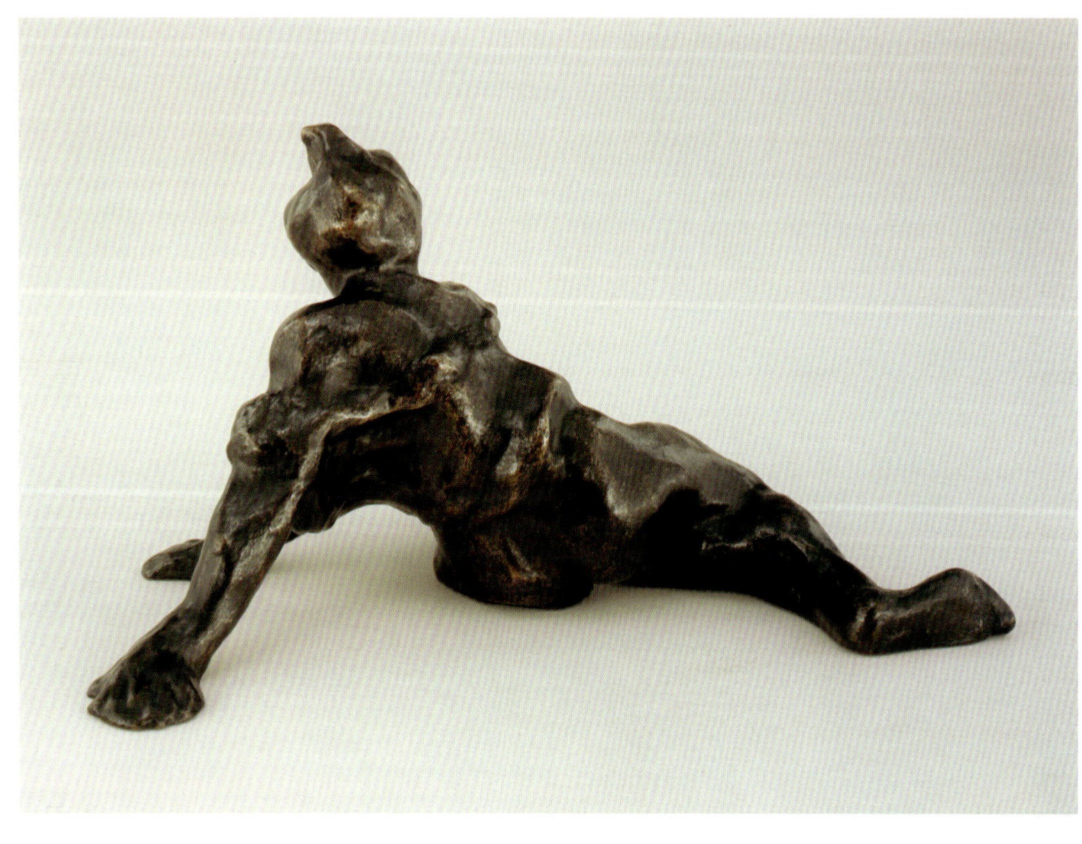

Henri Matisse, *Thorn Extractor,* 1906. Bronze

Collection, Art Gallery of Ontario, Toronto; Gift of Sam and Ayala Zacks, 1970. Cat. 25

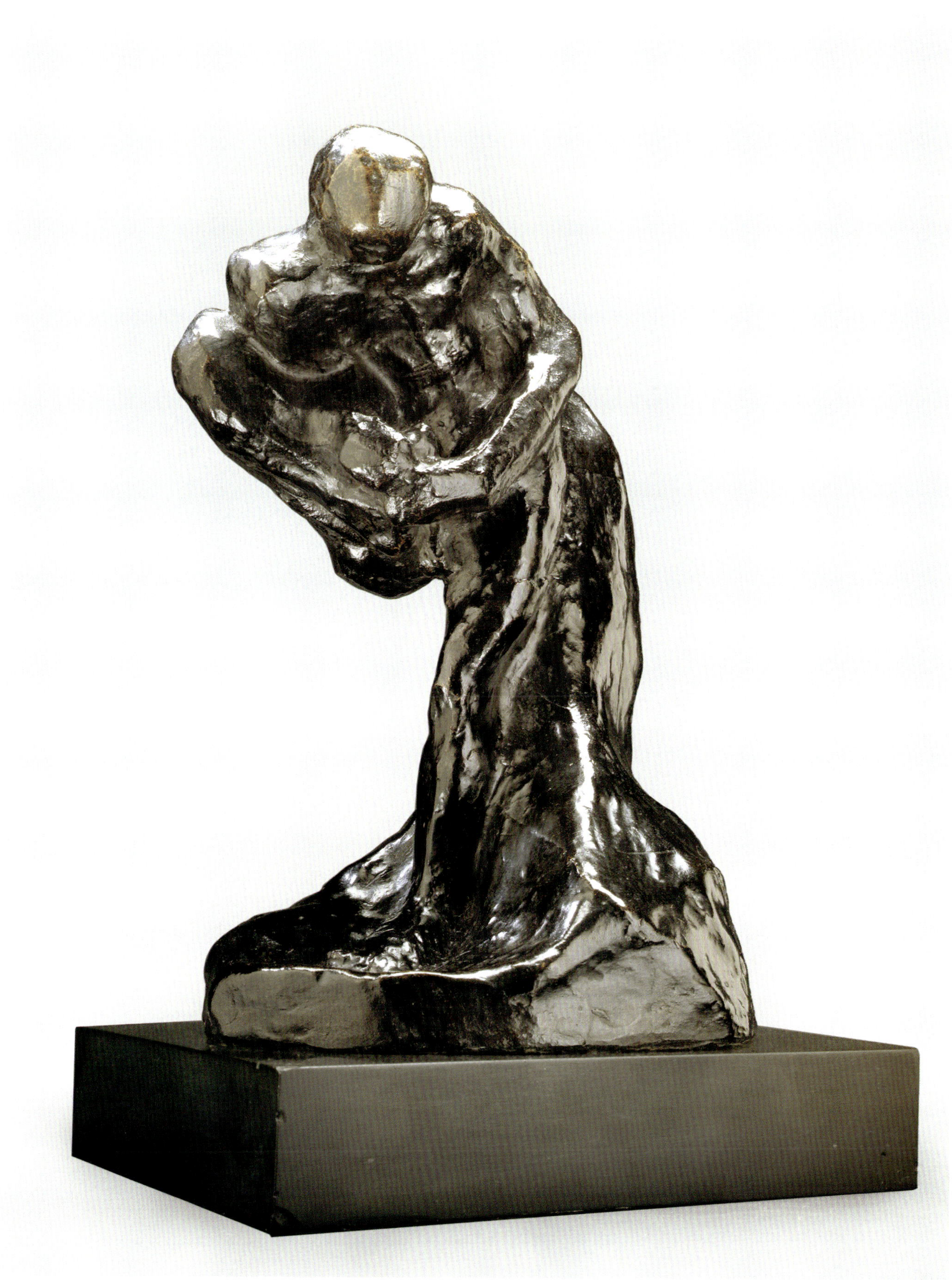

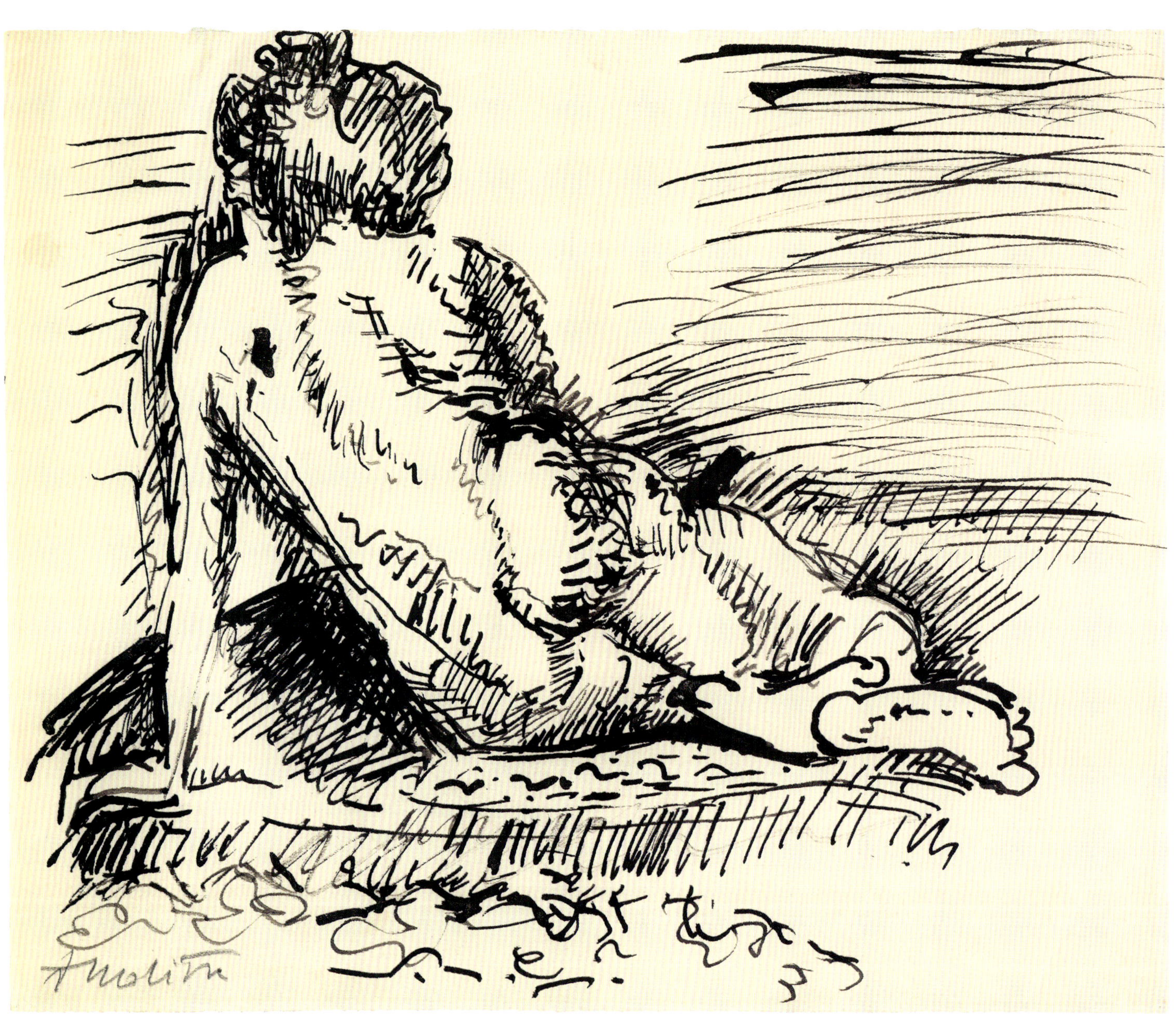

Henri Matisse, *Reclining Nude, Back View,* 1905
Pen and ink
Private collection. Cat. 26

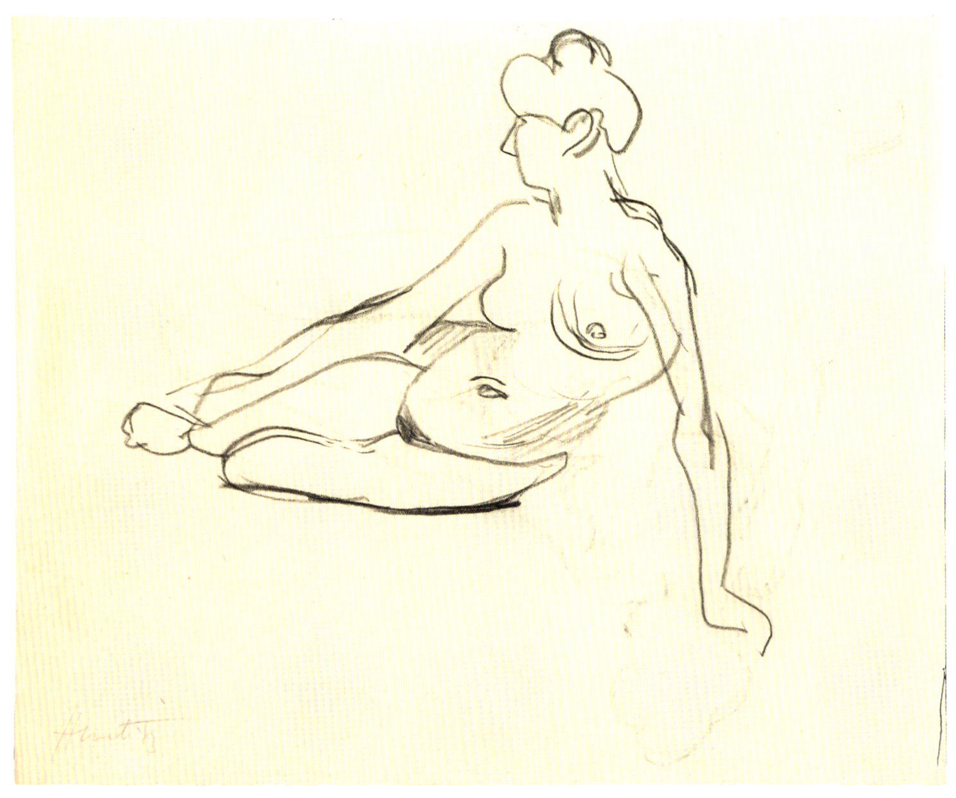

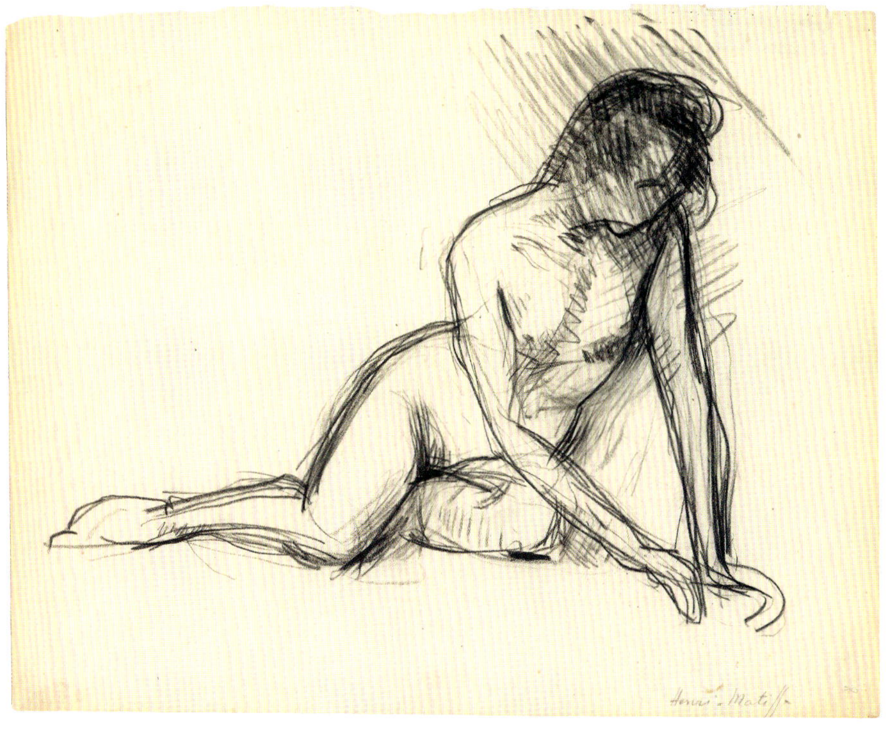

Henri Matisse, *Reclining Woman Leaning on Hands,* c. 1905. Graphite

Private collection. Cat. 27

Henri Matisse, *Reclining Woman Leaning on Hands,* c. 1905. Graphite

Private collection. Cat. 28

Reclining Figure with Chemise

As one of only two sculptures of clothed female figures, *Reclining Figure with Chemise* is conceptually related to *Woman Leaning on Her Hands,* modeled a year earlier. Both are associated with Matisse's interest in the arcadian, golden-age imagery explored in *Luxe, calme et volupté* and more explicitly in *Le bonheur de vivre* (fig. 28, p. 29). Summering in Collioure in 1906, Matisse developed a close friendship with the sculptor Aristide Maillol, although they saw sculpture very differently. Maillol would recite Virgil's *Eclogues* and encourage Matisse's interest in classical themes.[1] Scholars have related *Reclining Figure with Chemise* directly to the right central figure of *Le bonheur de vivre*—although one is nude, the other clothed.[2] Yve-Alain Bois describes their connection as "a game of Ping-Pong."[3] The rippling folds of the sculpture's chemise make the connection with antique statuary and with the classical world even more explicit than it is in the painting. *Reclining Figure with Chemise* is derived loosely from Hellenistic prototypes such as the *Sleeping Ariadne* existing in many copies and variants, most famously in the Museo Pio-Clementino at the Vatican in Rome, but also in versions at the Louvre and in the gardens at Versailles, as well as in prints.[4] Curiously, when compared with typical representations of Ariadne, Matisse's figure is laterally reversed. Over the course of twenty-three years Matisse would produce three more sculptural versions of reclining nudes with raised arms. The first two are oriented toward the right, the third assumes the more traditional arrangement; this underscores the close connection between the early versions and the similarly oriented reclining figure in *Bonheur de vivre.*

Historians frequently discuss *Reclining Figure with Chemise* in the context of the larger and slightly later *Reclining Nude I (Aurora).* Isabelle Monod-Fontaine suggests that the "floating folds [of *Reclining Figure*] . . . get in the way of a clear view of the counterpoints and torsions."[5] It may be a mistake to see this languorous Grecian figure in terms of her bodybuilding sister, but Albert Elsen follows this line as well, insisting against visual evidence that she reflects Matisse's "taste for strenuous postures in passive situations."[6] Comparing the two works, Jack Flam takes a different approach. He suggests that for *Reclining Figure with Chemise* Matisse relied on a model, leading to a balance of "visual and tactile elements," whereas in *Reclining Nude I (Aurora),* he "worked from memory and imagination," increasing the "tactile" quality of the latter work.[7] Some evidence suggests that Flam may be wrong about Matisse's reliance on memory alone. Monod-Fontaine argues that for *Reclining Nude I (Aurora),* Matisse relied on a photograph published in the periodical *L'Humanité feminin.*[8]

It is however this painterly quality of *Reclining Figure with Chemise,* which Flam attributes to a "sensation-by-sensation procedure" of recording the optical experience before the live model, that helps to explain the work in its own terms. Both Elsen and Elderfield describe the modeling of the sculpture as "coarse," yet it is precisely this activation of the surfaced that contributes to the sense of painterly visual notation.[9] Matisse had employed similar means since his first work, the copy of Barye's *Jaguar Devouring a Hare.*

OS

Henri Matisse, *Reclining Figure with Chemise,* 1906. Bronze

The Baltimore Museum of Art, Gift of Mr. and Mrs. Albert Lion Jr. Cat. 30

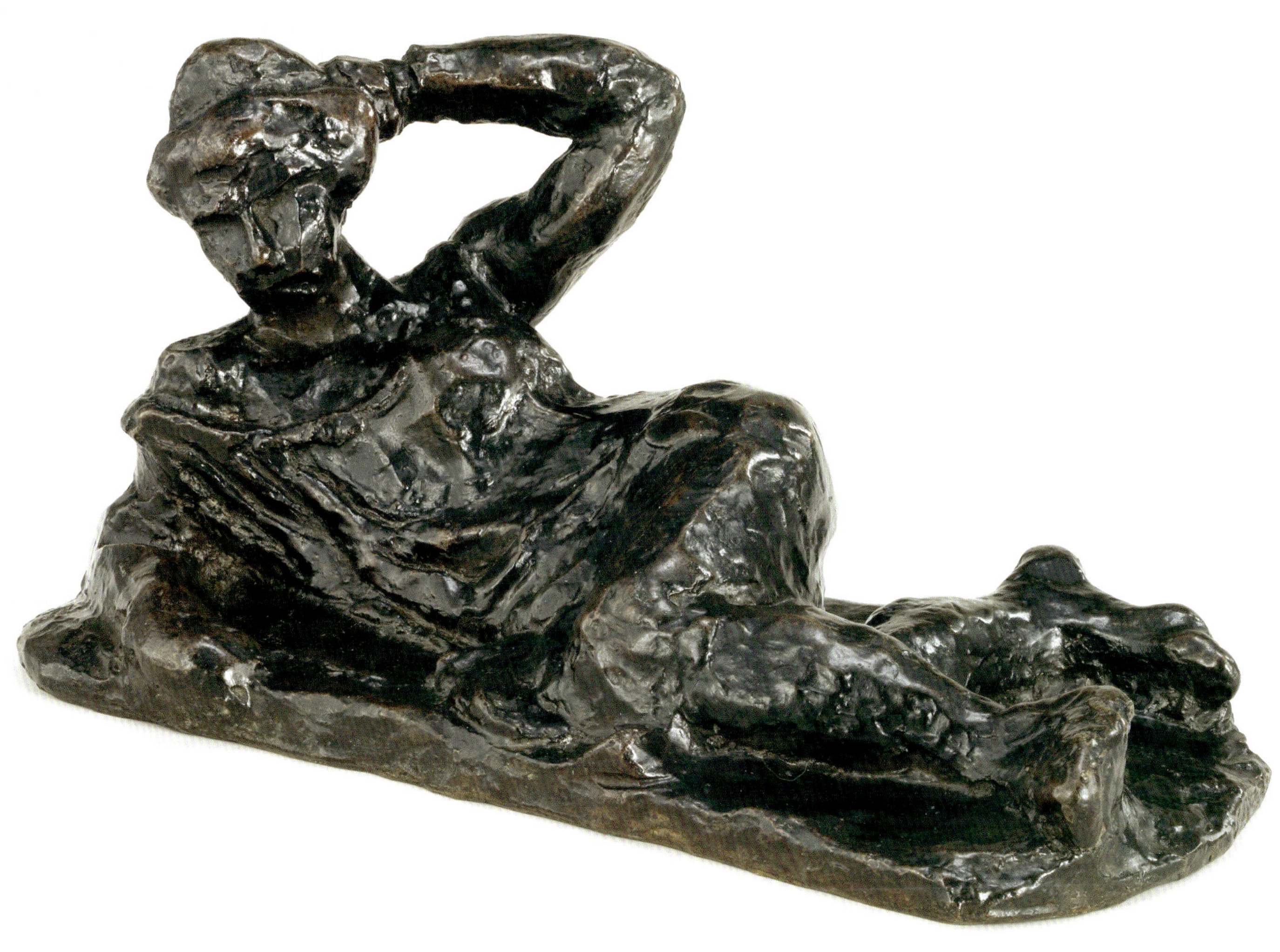

Notes

1. Schneider 1984, 558–59.

2. Flam 1986, 191.

3. Bois 1997, 369, 379 n.1.

4. Flam 1986, 191; Monod-Fontaine 2003, 64; Rosenthal 1956, 10. Rosenthal notes that Matisse had produced a copy of another Hellenistic sculpture, the *Thorn Extractor,* in the same year. If one adds the copy he produced of Puget's *Écorché* (fig. 31, p. 32) in 1903 and his *Vénus accroupie Michel-Ange* (1918–1919, in this exhibition as *Crouching Venus*), it becomes clear that Matisse copied sculptures regularly throughout his career.

5. Monod-Fontaine 2003, 64.

6. Elsen 1972, 71; Michael Mezzatesta (1984, 61) correctly observes that Matisse's intentions here are quite different from his intentions in *Reclining Nude I:* "Matisse was most concerned with establishing a subdued, ideal quality"; he [Mezzatesta] describes the pose as "relaxed."

7. Flam 1986, 191.

8. Monod-Fontaine (2003, 66–67) views a photograph of a nude woman that she claims was published in the December 22, 1906, edition of *L'Humanité feminin* as a source for Matisse's *Blue Nude: Memory of Biskra* and *Reclining Nude I;* her case is somewhat convincing in spite of the differences of the pose. There is some confusion, however, in the dating of the photograph, which, according to Alastair Wright (2004, 169, 259 n.25) was not published until March 23, 1907—too late to have inspired *Blue Nude,* which was exhibited that same year at the Salon des Indépendents, beginning March 20. Wright speculates that the photograph may have been published previously.

9. Elderfield 1995, 51.

Henri Matisse, *Reclining Figure with Chemise,* 1906. Bronze

The Baltimore Museum of Art, Gift of Mr. and Mrs. Albert Lion Jr. Cat. 30

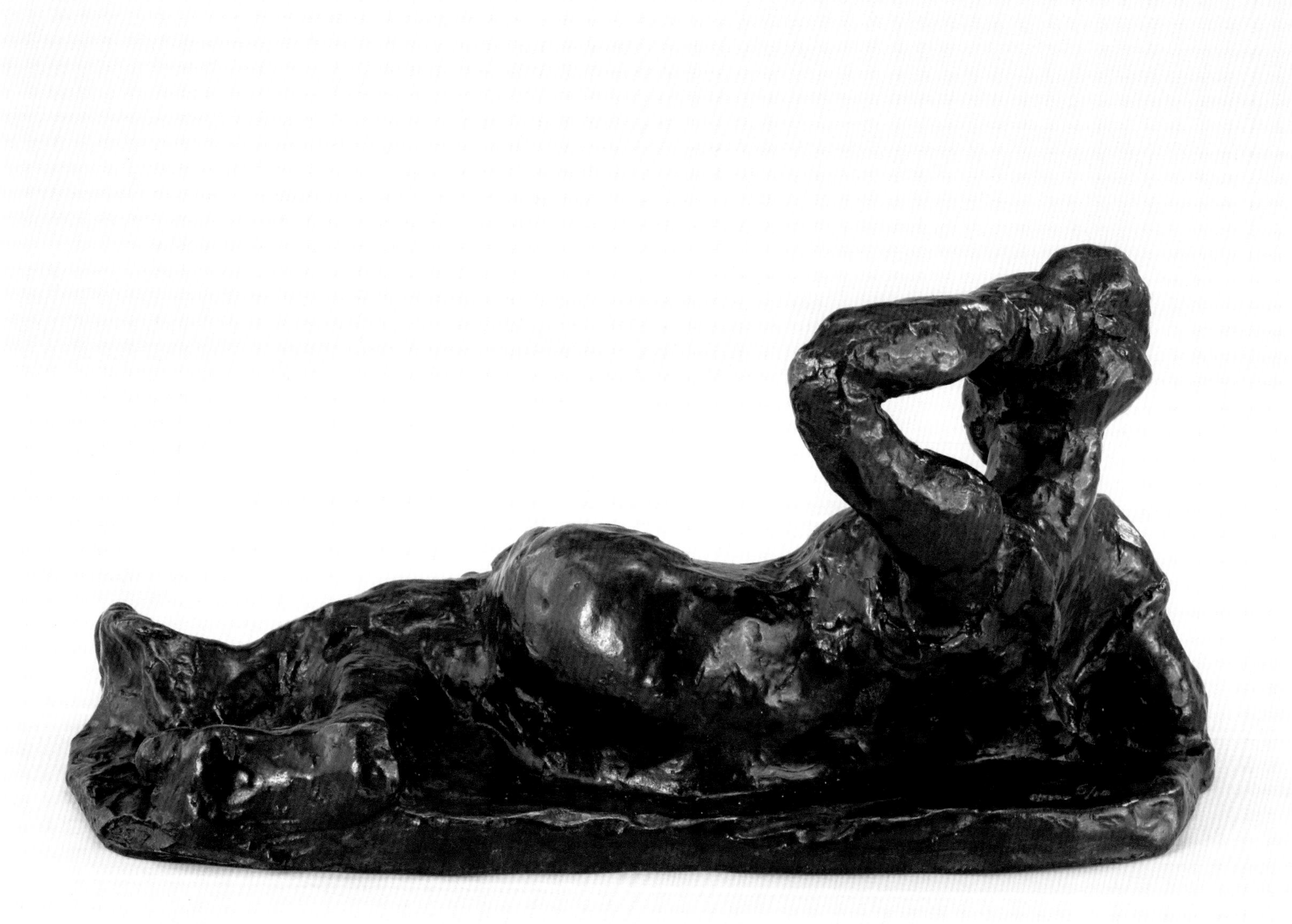

Henri Matisse, *Oil Sketch for The Joy of Life* (*Le bonheur de vivre*), 1905–1906. Oil on canvas

San Francisco Museum of Modern Art, Bequest of Elise S. Haas. Cat. 31

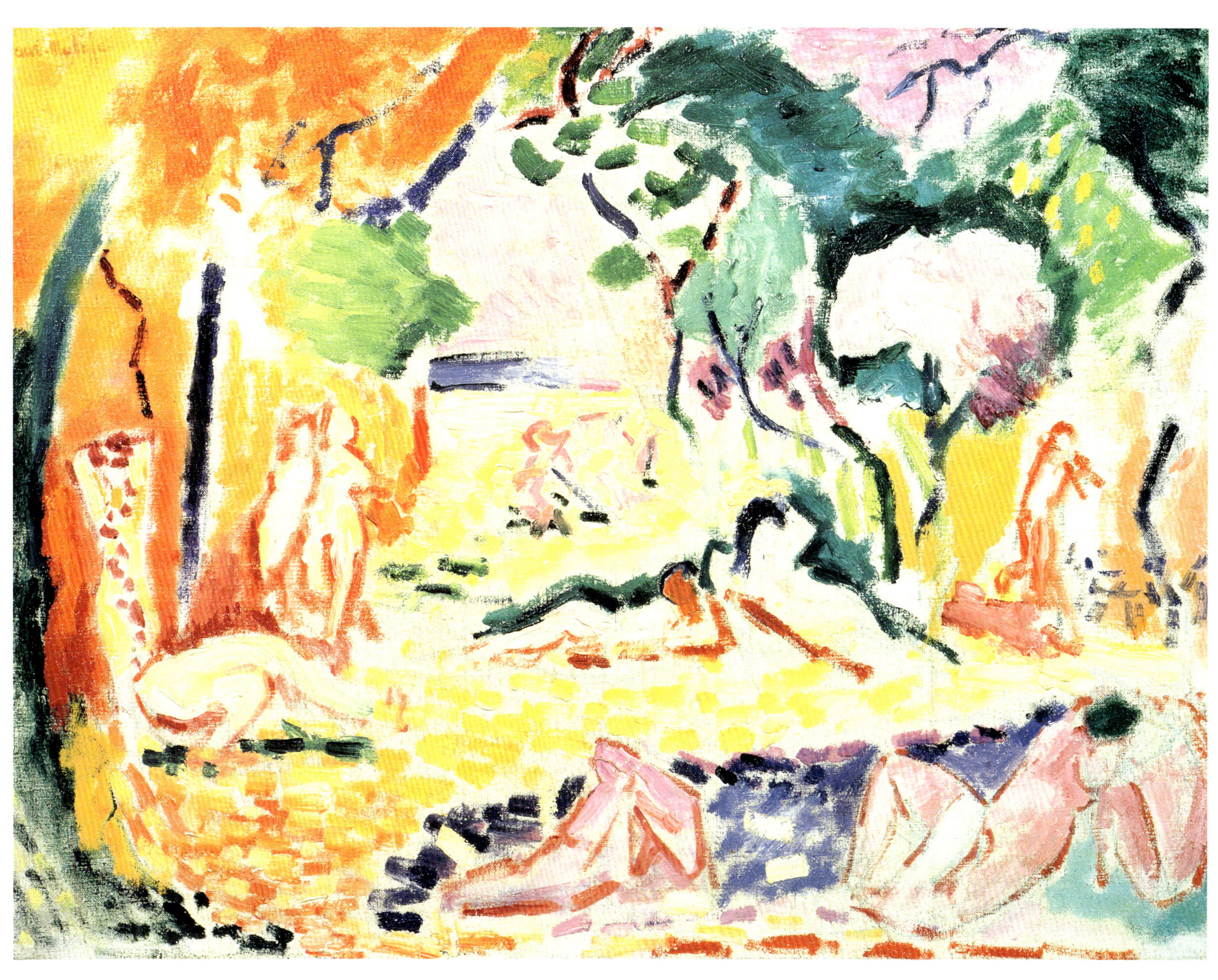

Standing Nude

Standing Nude was sculpted in the summer of 1906, while Matisse was staying with his family in Collioure. Earlier in the year he had traveled to North Africa, and the sculpture is often described as a synthesis between his classicism and a new expressionism, learned from looking at the exaggeration and figural distortions of African sculpture.[1] The summer after his trip was one of fertile creativity: in addition to *Standing Nude,* he worked on *Reclining Figure with Chemise, Thorn Extractor, Head of a Young Girl (Marguerite), Small Head with Comb, Standing Nude, Arms on Head,* and *Torso with Head (La Vie)* during that time.

The French title of this sculpture, *Nu de fillette* (young girl nude), reminds us that it represents his daughter, Marguerite, who was just twelve years old in 1906. She was an important model for her father that summer, sitting for the painting *Marguerite Reading* during the day, with her hair loose about her shoulders and wearing a childish dress with a pleated yoke collar, and then spending the evening hours posing nude for the sculpture, with her hair piled on her head in a loose bun. The anatomical exaggerations that Matisse may have borrowed from African sculpture at this moment distort the figure of Marguerite so that she is no longer recognizable as an adolescent girl, still less as an individual sitter. These exaggerations—the long, elegant neck, swelling breasts, and projecting buttocks—tend to give the figure the anatomy of a mature woman. Her remarkably still pose was a departure from the emphatic and athletic postures of other female nudes that Matisse was sculpting at the time, such as *Torso with Head (La Vie)* and *Woman Leaning on her Hands.* Many commentators have seen in this figure a reference to the figural sculpture of the archaic Greeks and Etruscans.[2] Only the slight turn of the head to the left disrupts her calm symmetry.

The painting of *Marguerite Reading* is unquestionably intended as a portrait of his daughter, as is *Head of a Young Girl (Marguerite),* a closely related bronze. *Standing Nude* explores instead a specific bodily attitude. In *Standing Nude,* painted in Paris around 1901, Matisse represents a professional model in a very similar pose: feet together, arms held at her sides, shoulders back, and head erect. Matisse may well have returned to the idea several years later, posing Marguerite to explore the motif further in sculptural form. Some of the apparent anatomical deformations that Matisse introduces into the sculpture, such as the pronounced roundedness of the belly and breasts and the long neck, may refer to the body of his earlier model, as remembered by Matisse, rather than to the twelve-year-old Marguerite. These changes both disguise the sculpture as a representation of a specific individual and create a tension between the "demure and chaste" pose and the pronounced womanliness of the figure.[3]

In *Still Life with Plaster Figure,* Matisse incorporates a plaster cast of *Standing Nude* into a group of other familiar studio props from the period in Collioure, including fruit and souvenirs of Matisse's recent trip to North Africa: a red carpet spread over the tabletop and two painted ceramic bowls. His sculpture is shown surrounded by other works of art within his studio, which is presented as a space of self-reflexive creativity. The painting pays homage to Cézanne's *Still Life with a Plaster Cupid*,

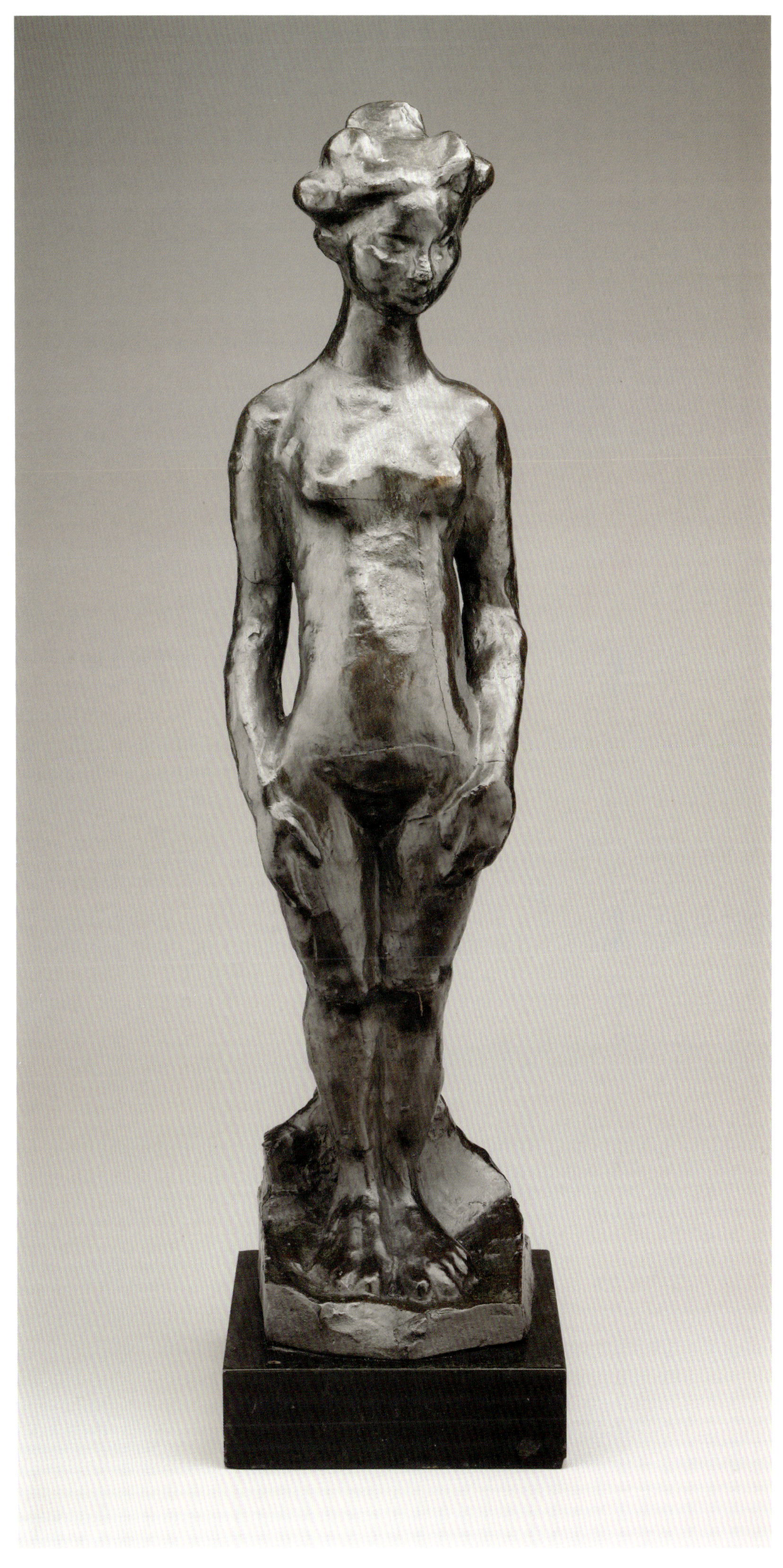

Henri Matisse, *Standing Nude,* 1906. Bronze

The Metropolitan Museum of Art, New York; The Pierre and Maria-Gaetana Matisse Collection, 2002. Cat. 32

which similarly uses a slim, vertical plaster figure as an indicator of the complex play between the two-dimensionality of the painted surface and the three-dimensionality of the objects represented. In Matisse's other paintings featuring his sculptures, such as *Still Life with a Geranium* and *The Branch of Lilac,* he paints the sculpted figures schematically, with strongly drawn outlines and relatively flat applications of color, allowing the three-dimensional sculptures to be integrated into the abstracting terms of the paintings. In *Still Life with Plaster Figure,* however, a chalky impasto of white paint gives the cast of *Standing Nude* a kind of tactility and bulk that comes forward from the decorative pattern of color surrounding it. One of Matisse's paintings of that year, *Flowers,* serves as a backdrop within the still life, almost closing off our access to the space beyond, except for a narrow strip of blue along the right edge of the canvas. This reiteration or doubling of the picture plane, with the resolutely material plaster sculpture sandwiched between the actual and represented canvases, offers an examination of the tension between surface and depth, color and space, artifice and illusion that is typical of Matisse's work of the period.

HMacD

Notes

1. Matisse purchased his first piece of African sculpture, a Villi figure of a seated man, later that year in Paris.

2. See, for instance, Szymusiak 1993, 14.

3. Mezzatesta 1984, 57.

Henri Matisse, *Still Life with Plaster Figure,* 1906

Oil on canvas

Yale University Art Gallery, New Haven; Bequest of

Mrs. Kate L. Brewster. Cat. 34

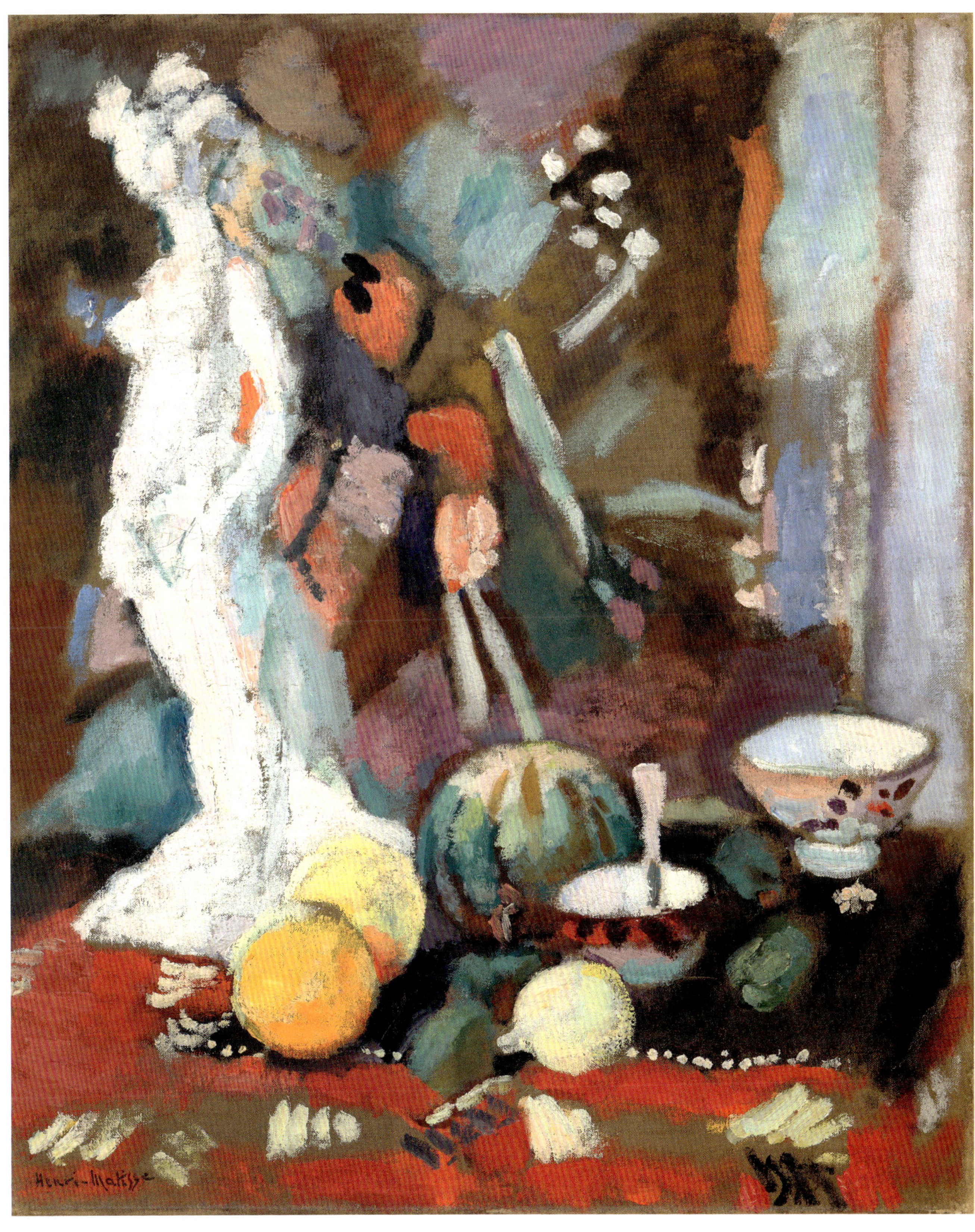

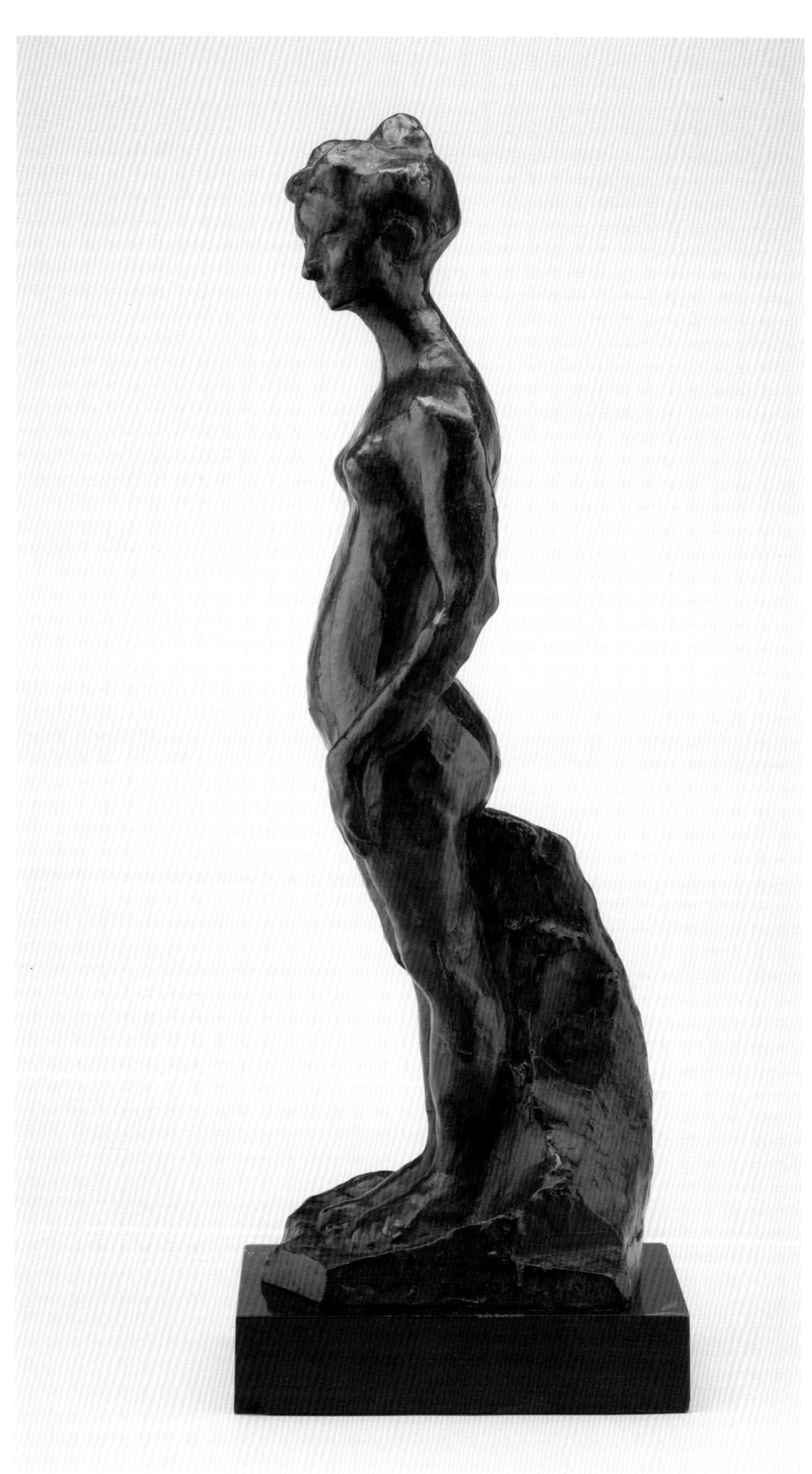

Henri Matisse, *Standing Nude,* 1906. Bronze

The Metropolitan Museum of Art, New York; The Pierre and Maria-Gaetana Matisse Collection, 2002. Cat. 32

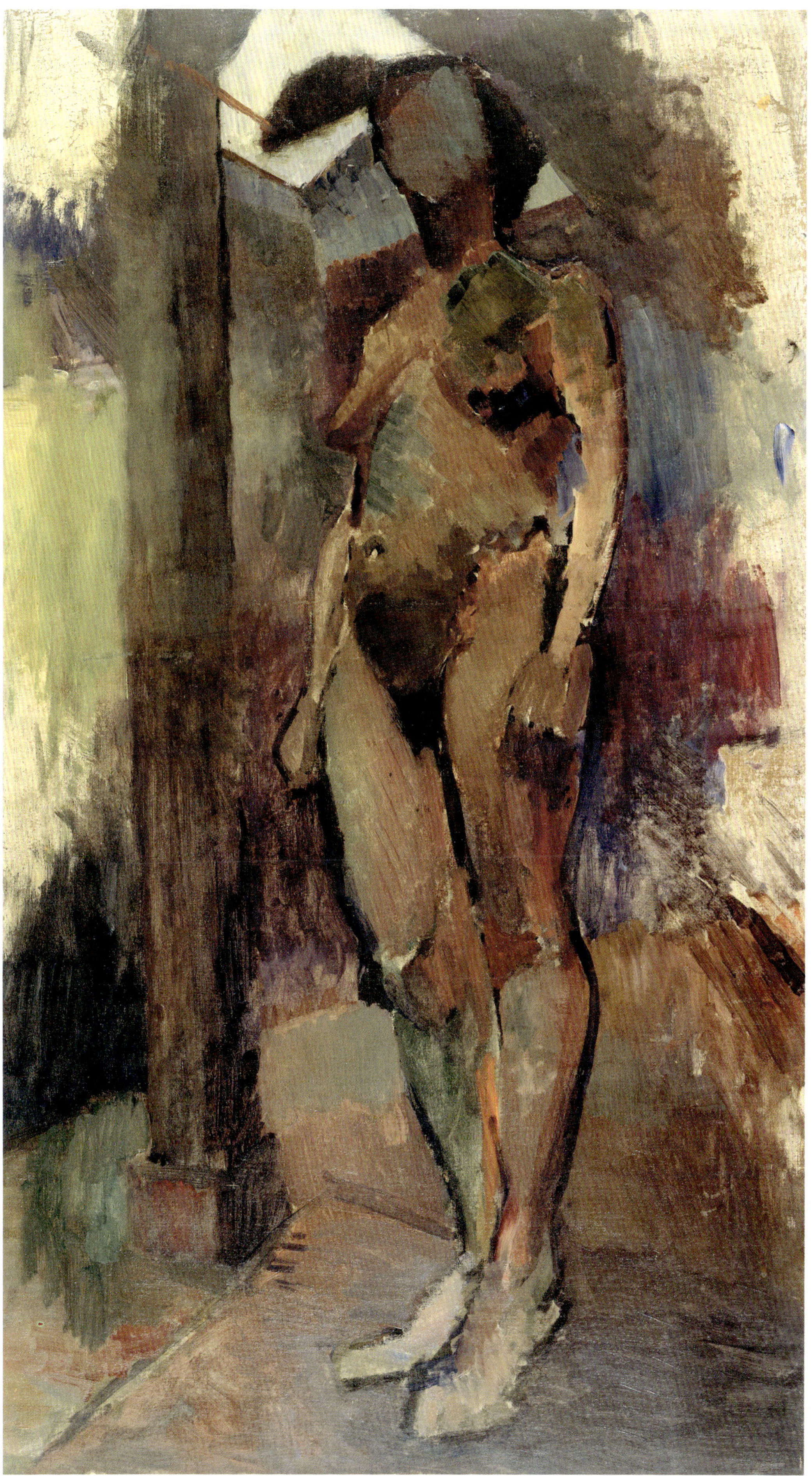

Henri Matisse, *Standing Nude,* c. 1901
Oil on canvas

Fine Arts Museums of San Francisco, Bequest of Aurelie Henwood to the de Young Museum in memory of Lucille and Gardner Dailey. Cat. 33

Standing Nude, Arms on Head

Standing Nude, Arms on Head belongs to a long line of works by Matisse in a variety of media that explore the formal and metaphorical qualities of the female nude posed with arms raised and hands clasped behind her head. Showing her variously seated or standing, relaxed or tense, frontally aligned or contorted, Matisse imbued the figure with expressive qualities ranging from the sensuous to the brutish. Fully exposing the naked figure, accentuating or exaggerating its forms, and stressing the sequence of complementary or opposing volumes, the pose lends itself to sculptural treatment even in two-dimensional media and elicits a tension that serves as a hallmark of some of Matisse's most radical inventions.

Standing Nude, Arms on Head descends from such cursory sculptural studies of classical and academic poses as *Upright Nude with Arched Back (Andromeda)* and *Seated Nude with Arms on Head,* both from 1904, and from the stretching nymph on the far left side of the painting *Le bonheur de vivre* (fig. 28, p. 29). Charcoal, ink, and pencil studies of a model in a similar pose from the same period substantiate the critical influence of Cézanne on Matisse's conception of this figure. Cézanne's many paintings of bathers and nudes provided Matisse with an encyclopedia of poses, which he drew upon often in both paintings and sculptures, attracted by their architectonic quality and by Cézanne's varied solutions of the relationship between figure and ground and figure and composition. His especially sculptural rendering of the model in *Standing Female Nude* provides a prototypical example of different works that Matisse may have had in mind in his production of *Standing Nude, Arms on Head* and related drawings. The monumentality of this large figure study recalls Cézanne's famous *Bather* from c. 1885. Ambroise Vollard, the well-known dealer and supporter of modernism, owned *Standing Female Nude* during the first decade of the century, and Matisse possibly saw it at his gallery or knew the reincarnation of the figure in Cézanne's *Large Bathers.* Matisse's charcoal *Standing Nude* from 1905 is particularly close in its depiction of the model's pose and proportions.

With a sense of strong, three-dimensional form that reflects his interest in ancient sculpture and the work of Michelangelo (he made numerous drawings from both sources), Cézanne plotted the physicality of his model in objective, dispassionate terms. The upward reach of the arms, spread stance, and arched back stretch open the body, silhouetted to dramatic effect against the blank background wall. John Rewald noted about this nude "an abstract quality" and a "desire for synthesis" that separates it from a more naturalistic preparatory study. "The facture is lively, with the marks of pentimenti in the leg and impasto the length of the body, where it detaches itself from the background. Similarly, to better set off the nude, its silhouette is outlined in dark lines."[1] Matisse's sculpture, although small in scale and sketchy in modeling, carries a similar air of poised monumentality. As did Cézanne, he stresses the tension of a body that is simultaneously pulled upward and firmly anchored to the ground, with spread feet and one leg extended forward. To both artists, the clean arabesque of outer contours is critical.

Henri Matisse, *Girl with Ivy in Hair,* 1905–1906

Pen and india ink

Private collection. Cat. 40

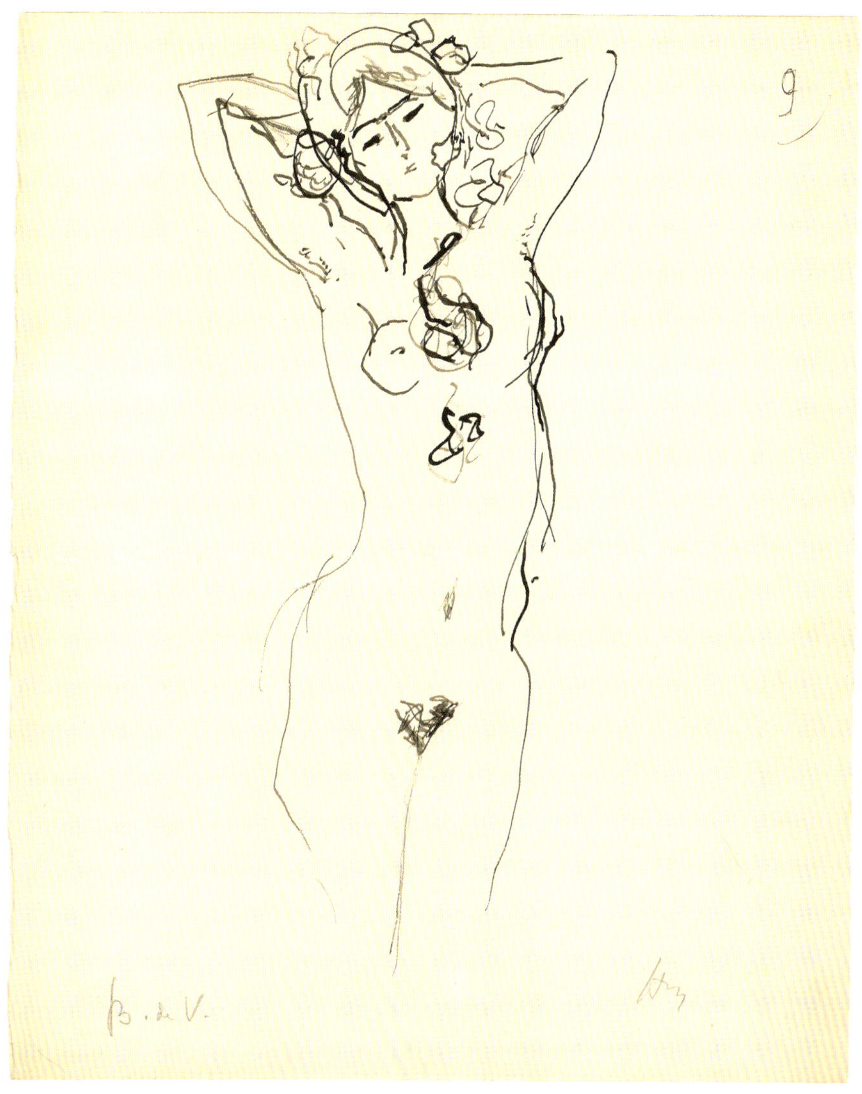

Modeled in 1906, shortly after Matisse's return from his first trip to North Africa, *Standing Nude, Arms on Head* exhibits some of the distortions of anatomy that signal his exposure to African sculpture. This tendency is carried even further in *Torso with Head (La Vie)* from the same year. Isolating the arched torso, Matisse emphasized the figure's bulging stomach, rounded posterior, and jutting breasts. In its fragmented state, this diminutive, palm-sized figurine suggests ancient fertility idols. Both sculptures anticipate, in quiet ways, the more brutal exaggerations and physical tension Matisse examined in later studies of figures with raised arms, such as *Reclining Nude I (Aurora)* and *Large Seated Nude.*

JM

Note

1. Rewald 1996, 1:527–28.

Henri Matisse, *Standing Nude, Arms on Head,*

1906. Bronze

Raymond and Patsy Nasher Collection, Dallas. Cat. 36

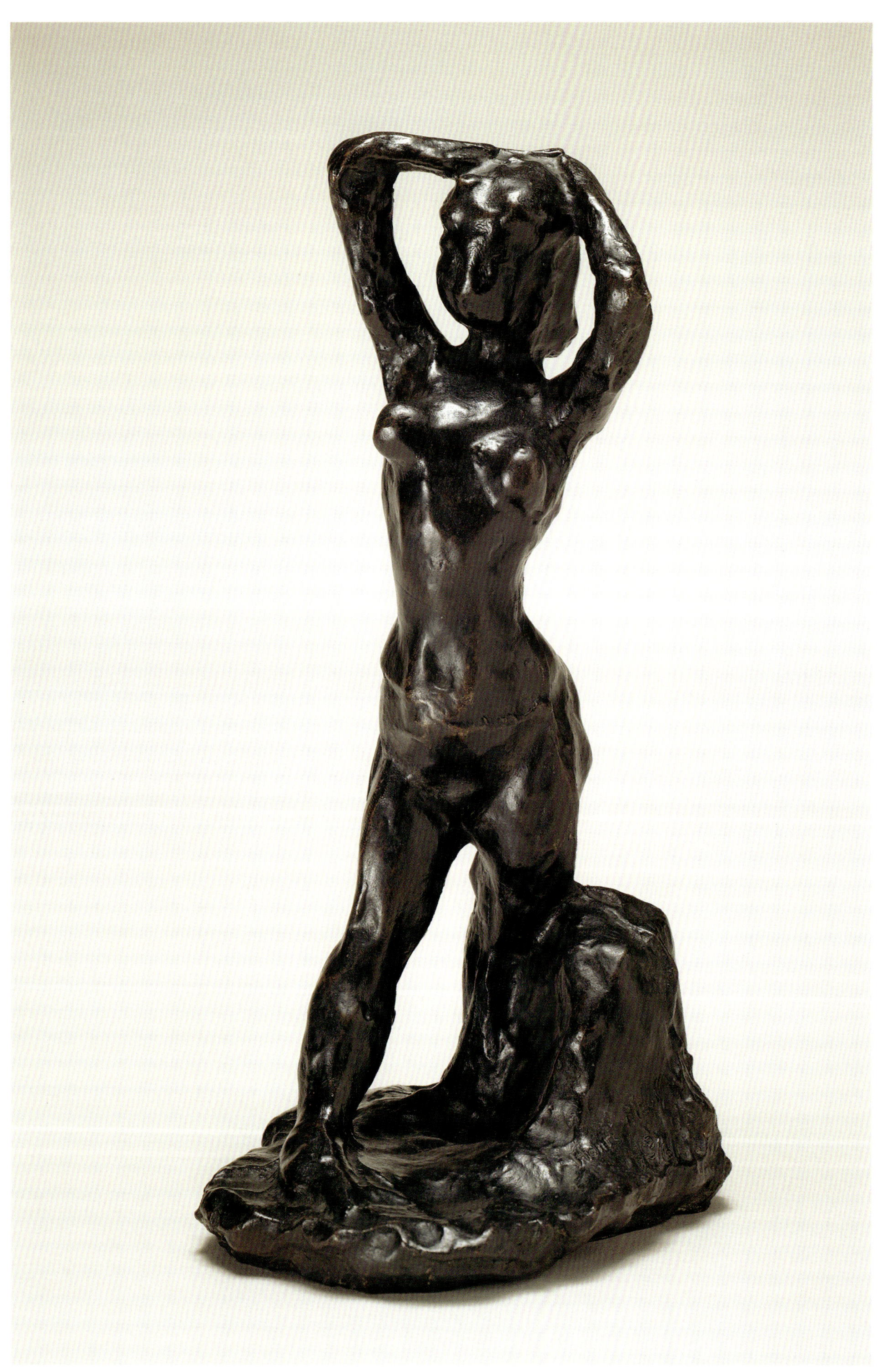

Henri Matisse, *Standing Nude, Version 1,* 1905–1908. Reed pen and india ink
Folkwang Museum, Essen. Cat. 41

Henri Matisse, *Standing Nude, Version 2,* 1905–1908. Reed pen and india ink
Folkwang Museum, Essen. Cat. 42

Henri Matisse, *Standing Nude, Version 3,* 1905–1908. Reed pen and india ink
Folkwang Museum, Essen. Cat. 43

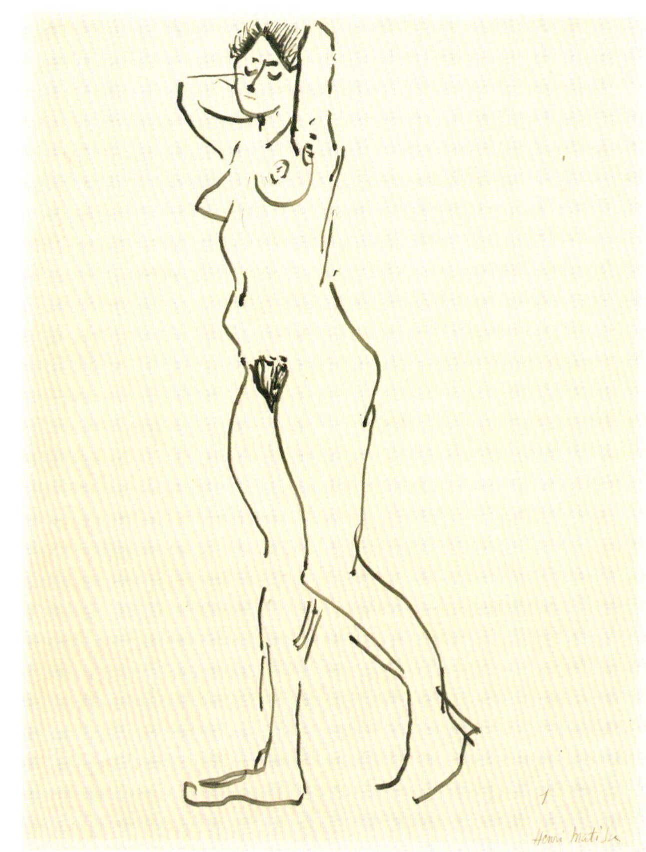

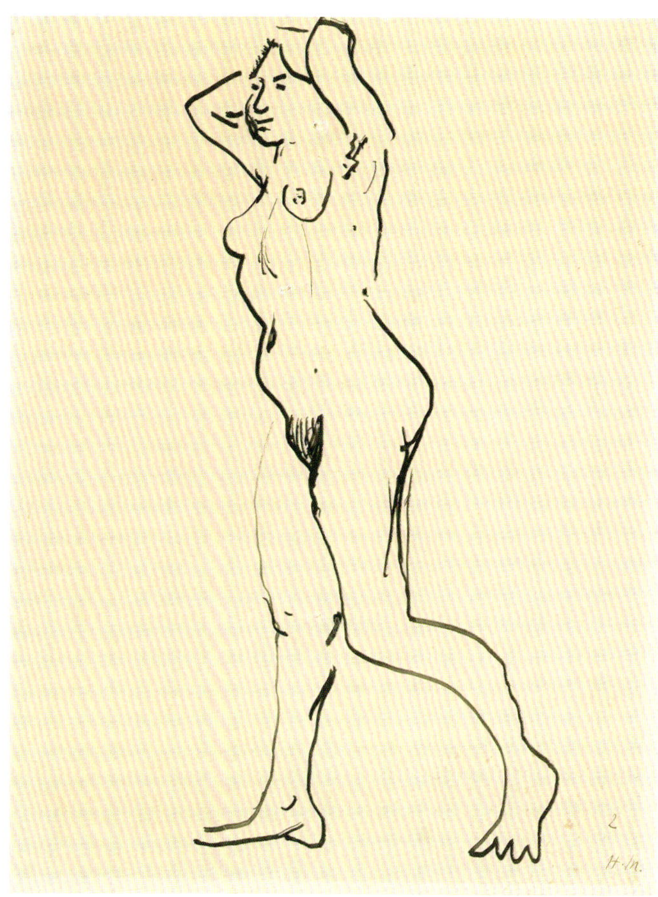

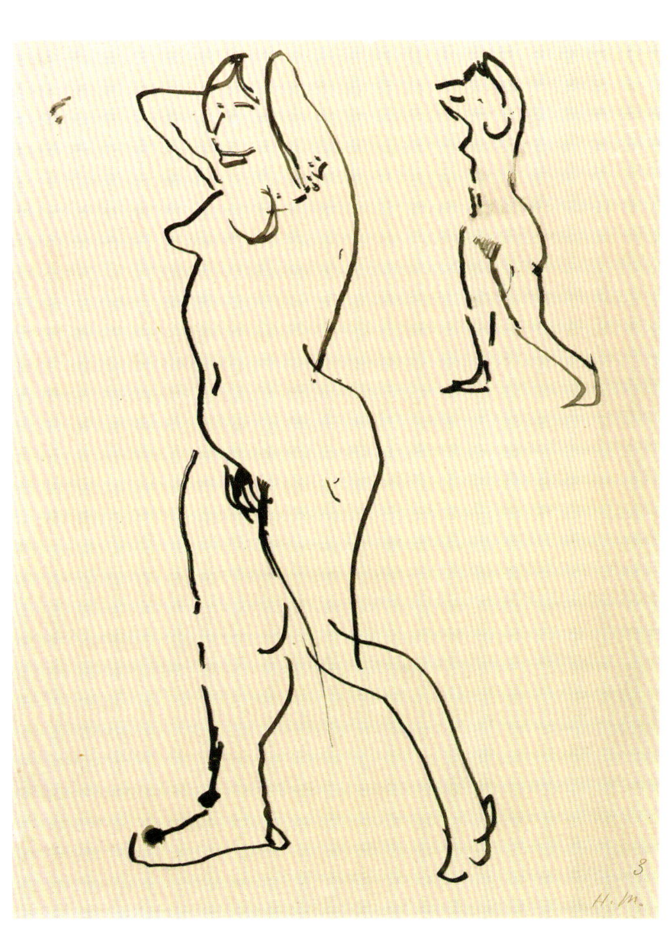

Paul Cézanne, *Standing Female Nude,*
1898–1899. Oil on canvas
Property of a Trust. Cat. 150

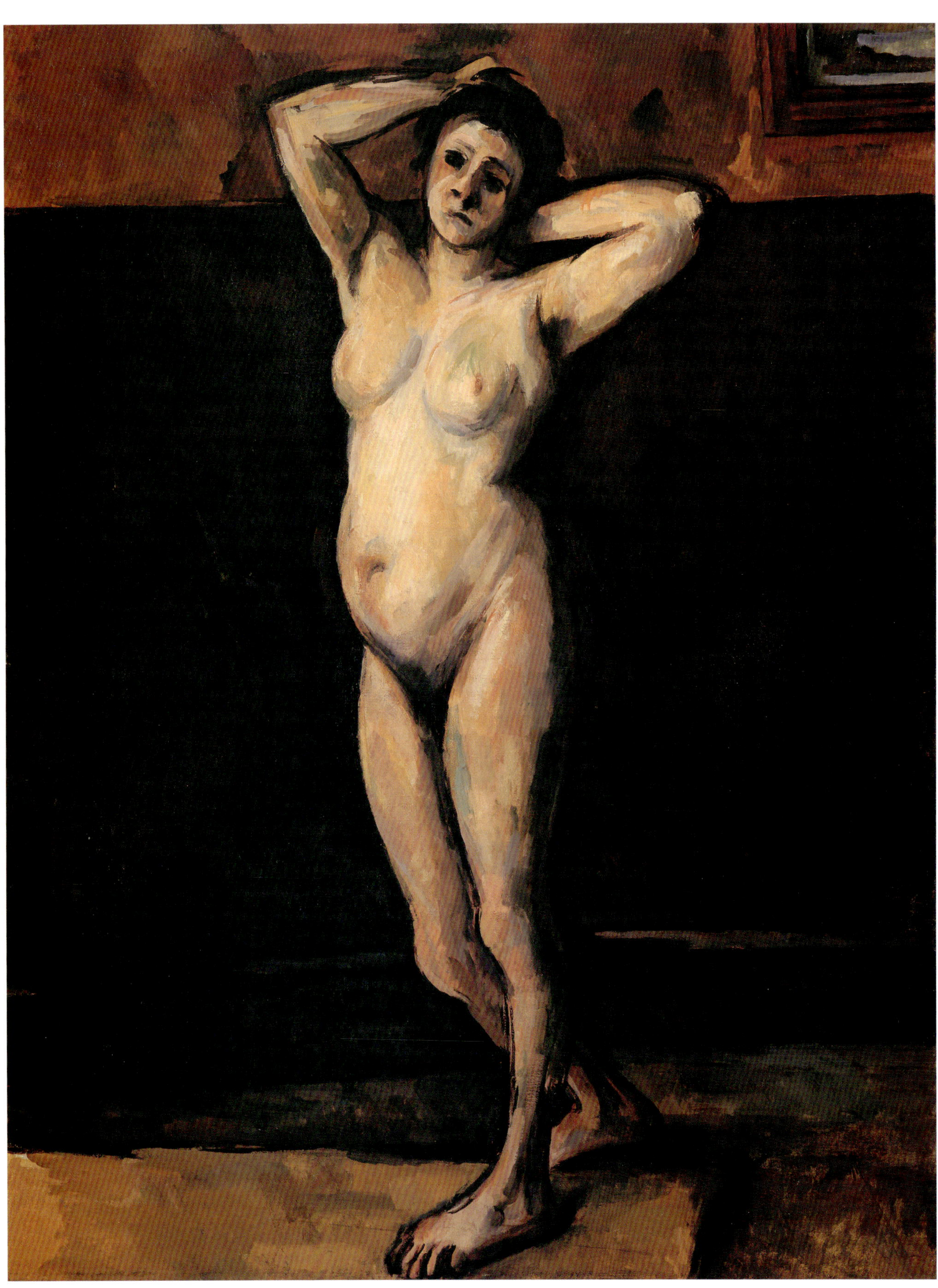

Henri Matisse, *Nude,* 1904. Graphite

Pierre and Maria-Gaetana Matisse Foundation Collection.

Cat. 38

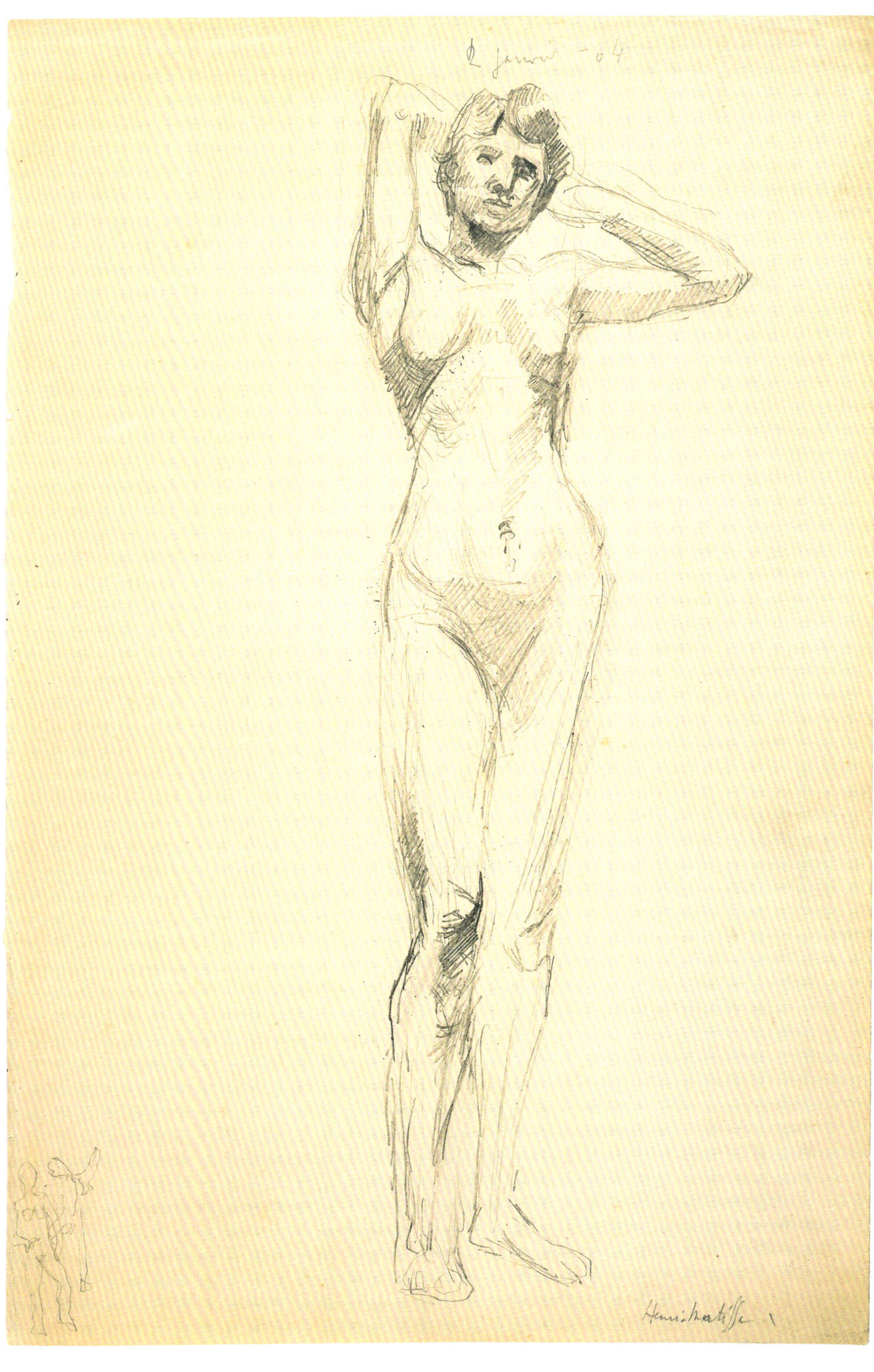

Henri Matisse, *Seated Nude with Arms on Head,* 1904. Bronze

The Baltimore Museum of Art, The Cone Collection, formed by Dr. Claribel Cone and Miss Etta Cone of Baltimore, Maryland. Cat. 35

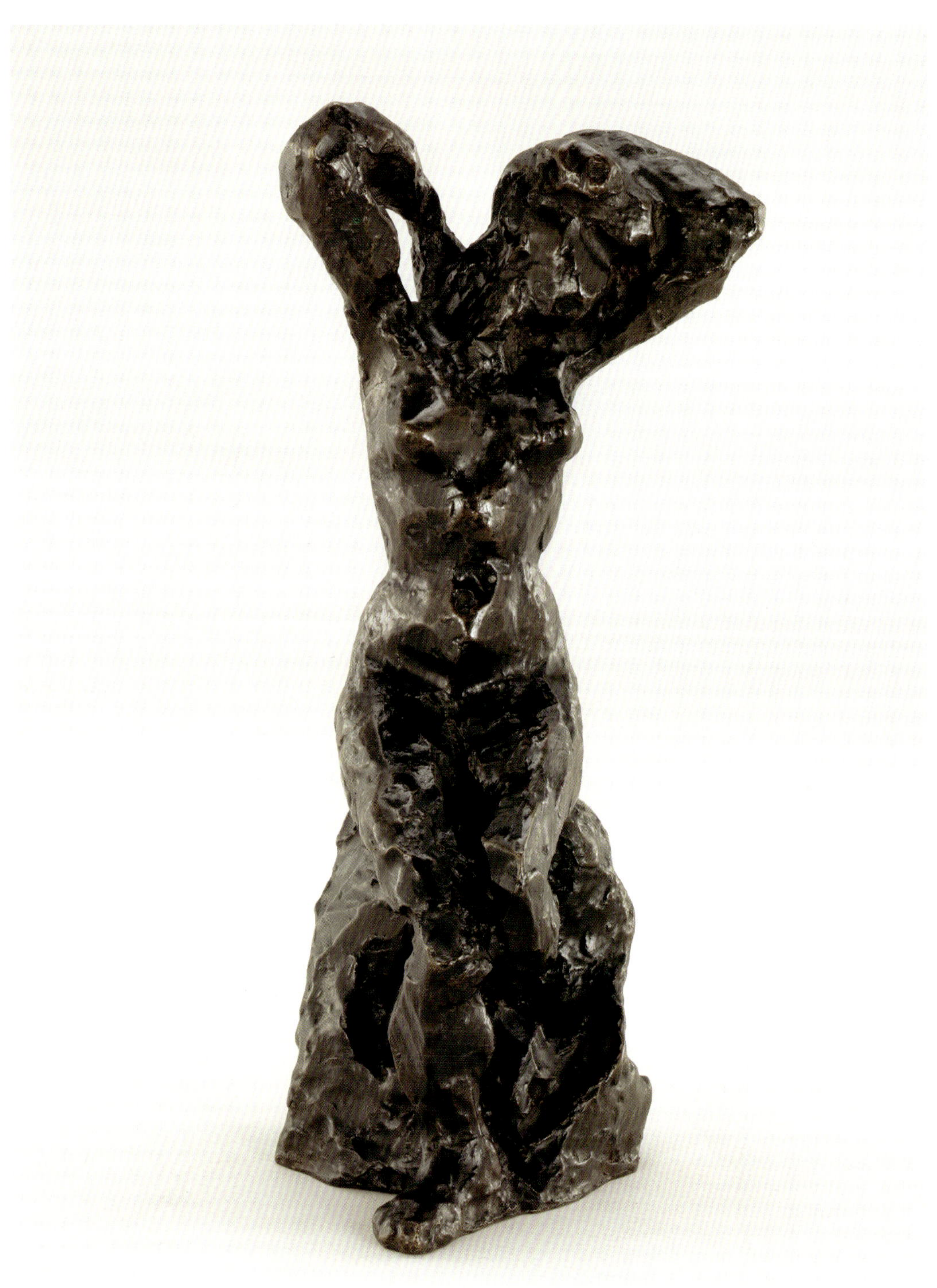

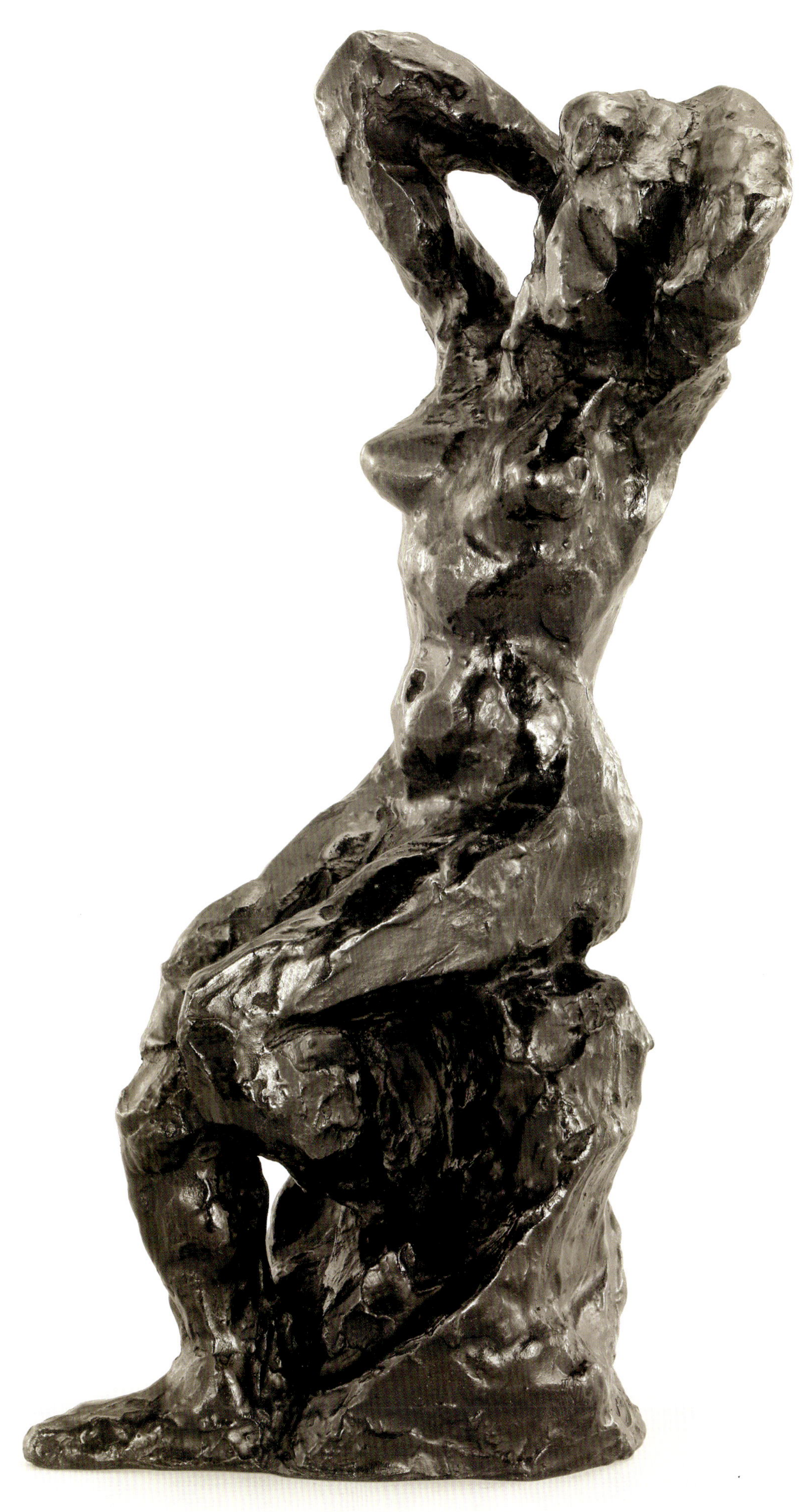

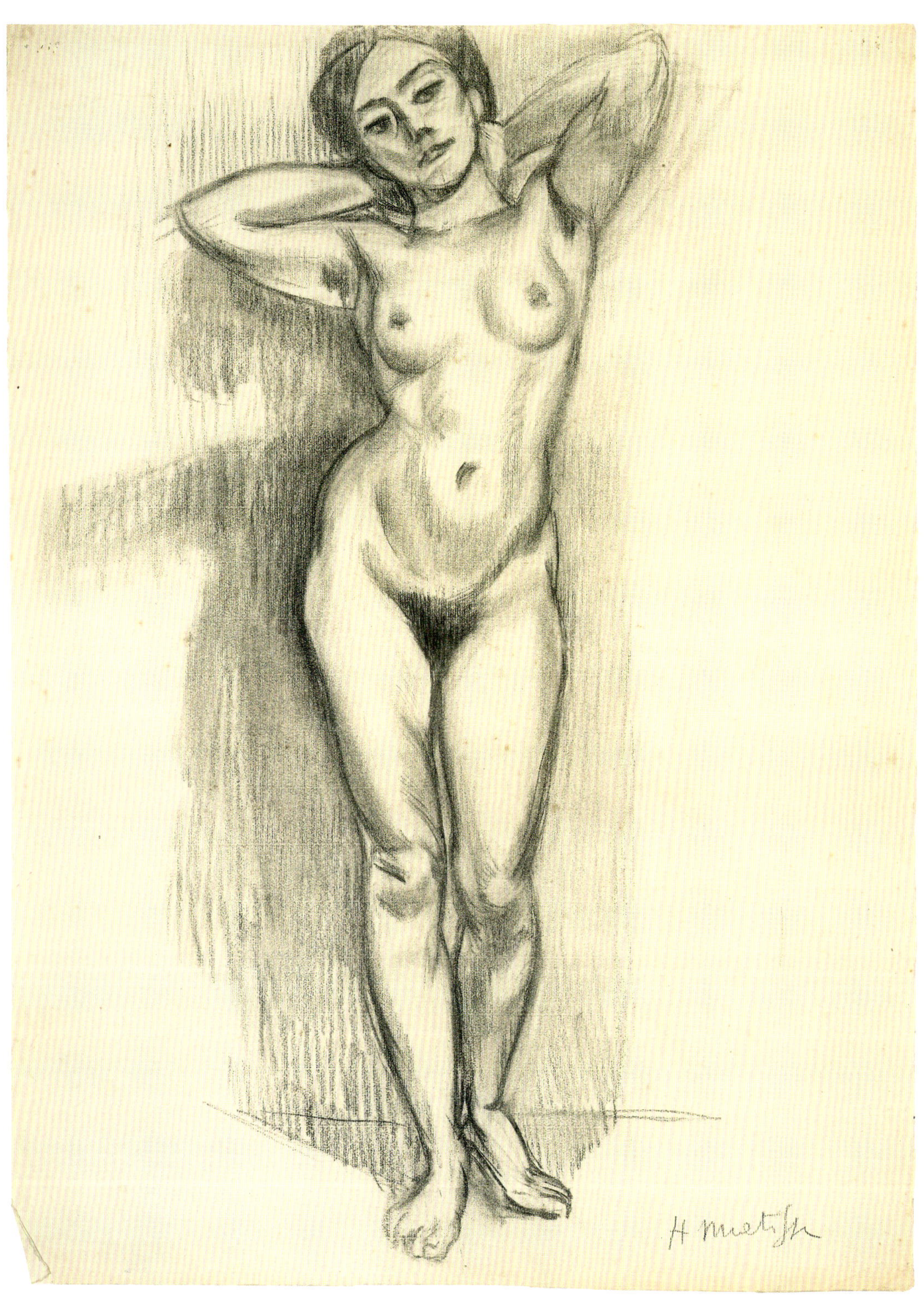

Henri Matisse, *Standing Nude,* 1905. Charcoal with erasing

Pierre and Maria-Gaetana Matisse Foundation Collection. Cat. 39

Henri Matisse, *Torso with Head (La Vie),* 1906 Bronze

The Metropolitan Museum of Art, New York; Alfred Stieglitz Collection, 1949. Cat. 37

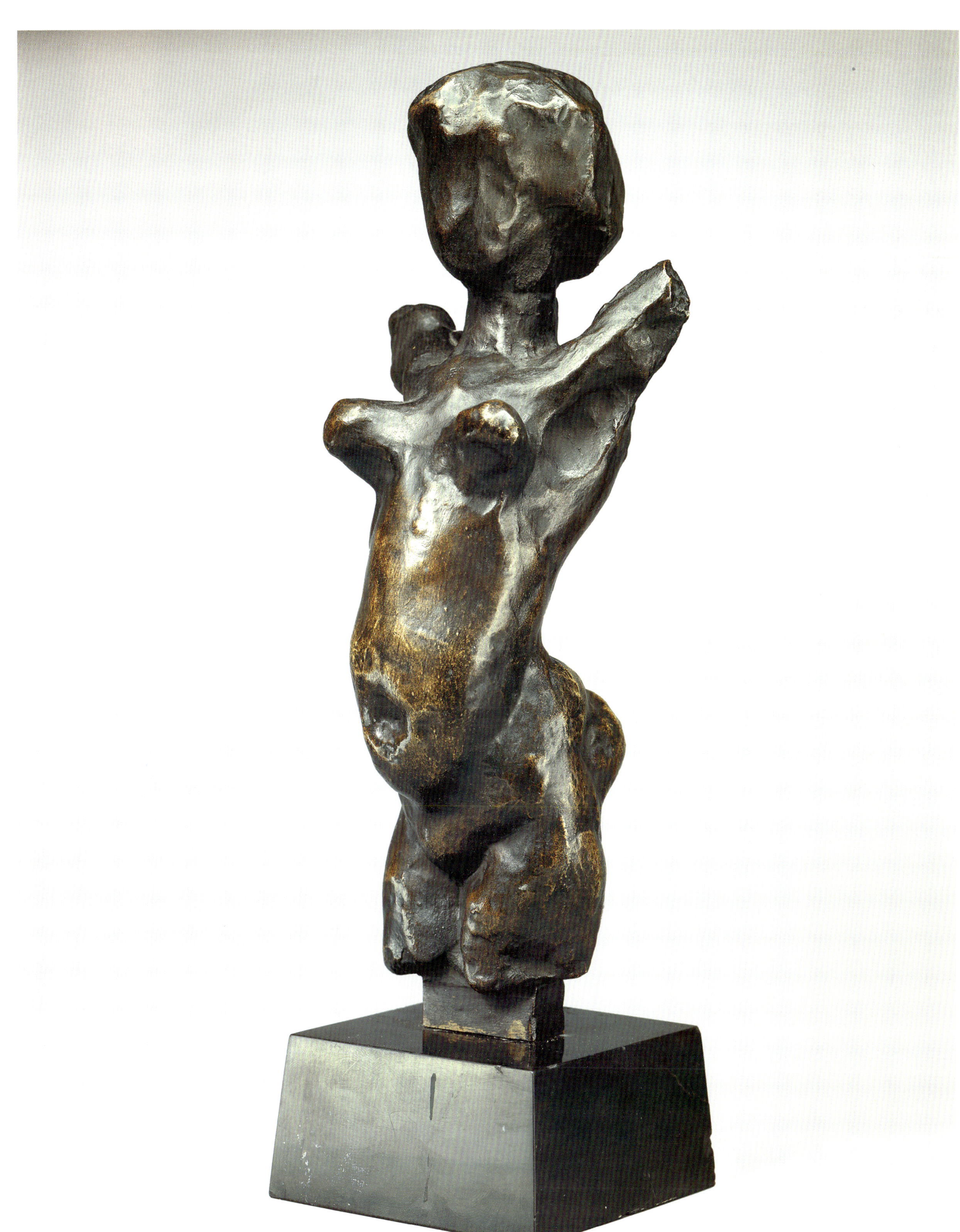

Reclining Nude I (Aurora)

In *Reclining Nude I (Aurora),* Matisse extends a meditation on the classical figure of the reclining nymph first begun in 1905–1906 with *Reclining Figure with Chemise* and the central figures in the painting *Le bonheur de vivre.* The secondary title *Aurora* may reflect Matisse's awareness that his nymph is derived from Hellenistic images of the *Sleeping Ariadne.* In versions of that myth, Ariadne, abandoned by Theseus on the island of Naxos, falls asleep in despair only to be awakened and rescued by her immortal lover Bacchus and his band of exotic revelers. Matisse's title *Aurora,* or "dawn," suggests the moment of joyous awakening into a world transformed by bacchanalian festivities—the same theme he addressed in *Le bonheur de vivre.*

Reclining Nude I (Aurora), when compared with the restrained *Reclining Figure with Chemise,* embodies a dramatic enhancement of scale and expressive power, much like the work of Michelangelo. Not only is the figure nude but also her physique is oversized and muscular. A colossal left arm is thrust up in the odalisque posture, rhymed by the exaggerated hip and complemented by the arabesque formed with her supporting right arm.

The origin of *Reclining Nude I (Aurora)* is closely tied to that of Matisse's painting *Blue Nude: Memory of Biskra.* According to Alfred Barr, Matisse, while modeling the sculpture, "wet the clay too freely so that when he turned the stand the figure fell off on its head and was ruined. Exasperated, he began to paint the figure instead, putting in some palm leaves which he remembered from his fortnight in Biskra [North Africa] the year before."[1] Pierre Schneider offers a more vivid account in which Madame Matisse rushes into the studio to calm her distraught husband. The following day, Matisse "picked up the clay sculpture and managed to restore it to its original shape. . . . Meanwhile," he takes a large canvas and begins painting *Blue Nude.*[2] Schneider's "meanwhile" leaves open the sequence of production. James Herbert is more categorical: "*Reclining Nude I* . . . served as a model for Matisse's *Blue Nude,* which he painted from the clay sculptural original rather than from a living woman."[3] Barr suggests the exact opposite sequence: "in a sense, the big painting actually served as a study for the sculpture."[4]

What light do these stories shed on the surviving sculpture? For Barr there is a lost original and the current "salvaged version," which may be somewhat different.[5] Close examination of the bronze is revealing. Numerous seams and sutures can be detected and are probably the result of both plaster piece molding and gelatin molding. In one passage, on the side of the ribcage adjacent to the figure's left breast, there is evidence of a layer of clay, perhaps added to reconnect and reinforce the protruding left arm—which would have been the first thing to break in a fall.[6]

Debate has centered on the role and degree to which Matisse's interest in African sculpture (he acquired his first piece in 1906) and his trip to Algeria influenced the bold, expressive handling of form in *Reclining Nude I (Aurora)* and *Blue Nude.* Jack Flam argues that in these works Matisse desired to "create not only a modern equivalent of the ancient Venus but even more significantly . . . a kind of 'African' Venus . . . [the] large head, spherical breasts, and bulbous buttocks recall common

Henri Matisse, *Reclining Nude I (Aurora),* 1907
Bronze
The Baltimore Museum of Art, The Cone Collection, formed by Dr. Claribel Cone and Miss Etta Cone of Baltimore, Maryland. Cat. 45

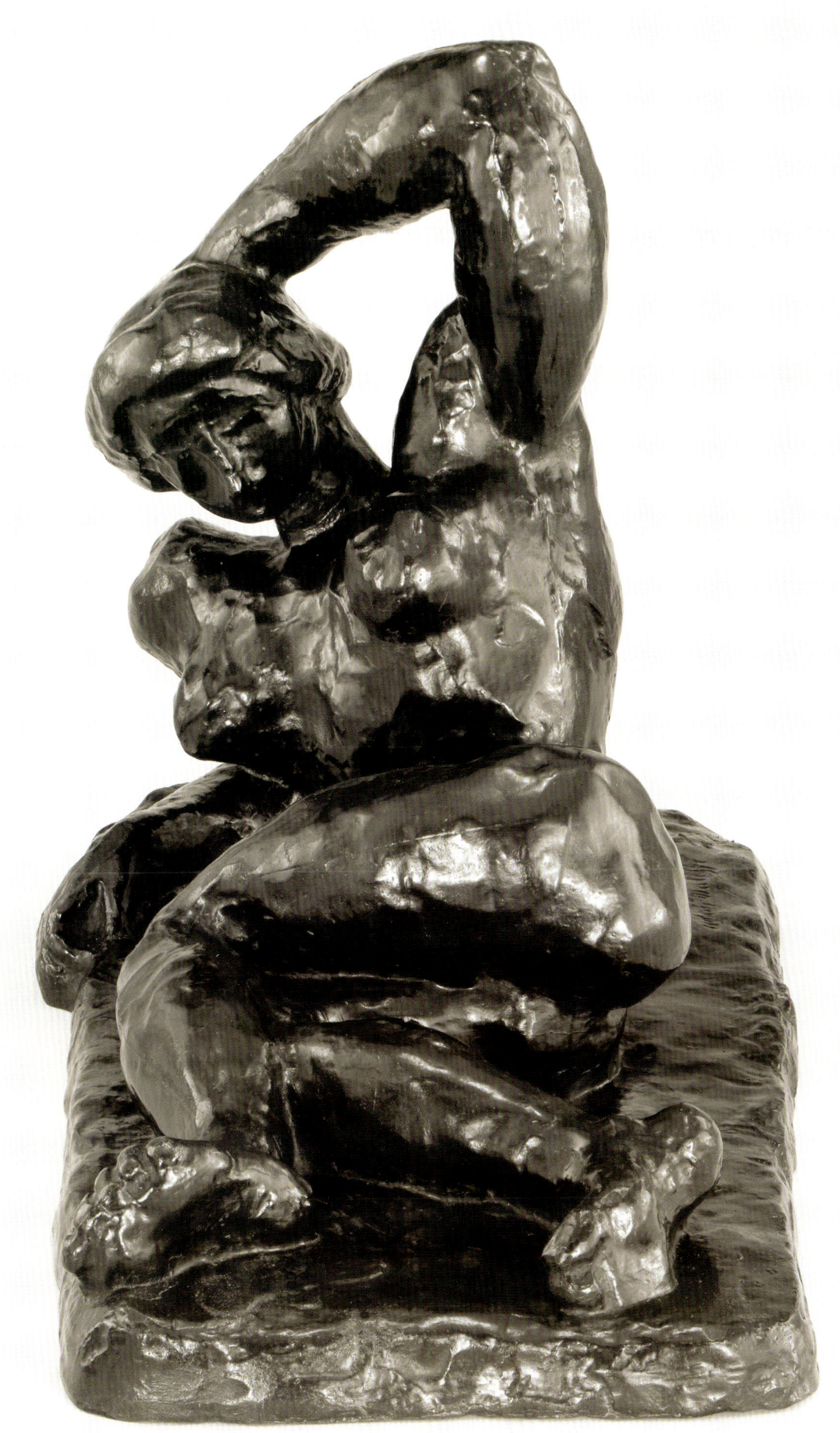

features of African sculpture."[7] Herbert, noting a resemblance between the buttocks in Matisse's sculpture and anthropological descriptions of the steatopygia of Hottentot women, goes to the extreme of suggesting that "undoubtedly Matisse and most of his contemporaries would have associated his bronzes—themselves dark in color—less with the 'white world' of Europe than with the 'black world' of Africa."[8] This argument is overstated and the deformation of anatomy could also be explained in terms of the influence of Cézanne. What is clear is that Matisse wished to evoke the primitive through a bold, sexualized pose that challenges the yielding passivity of salon favorites such as the depictions of Venus by Alexandre Cabanel or Henri Gervex.

The fact that *Reclining Nude I (Aurora)* was an unusually important sculpture for Matisse is attested to by its numerous depictions in his paintings, among them, *Sculpture and Persian Vase* (1908), *Still Life with Pewter Pitcher* (1910), *Goldfish* (1910), *Goldfish and Sculpture* (1911), and perhaps, most grandly, *Music Lesson* (1917). Many of these instances are thoughtfully discussed by Theodore Reff in his essay "Matisse: Meditations on a Statuette and Goldfish."[9]

OS

Notes

1. Barr 1951, 94.

2. Schneider 1984, 349; Schneider cites Pierre Courthion as his source, yet this is unpublished material; Hilary Spurling (1998, 461 n.131) includes the same anecdote and locates the source in Courthion n.d. (Getty Center).

3. Herbert 1992, 158.

4. He continues, "The sculpture is more powerfully composed, the distortions bolder, particularly in the bent but towering left arm" (Barr 1951, 100).

5. Ibid., 94.

6. In other instances, Matisse makes no effort to hide breakages that occurred in his sculptures. See for example the left wrist (where it is attached to the head) of *Reclining Figure with Chemise* and the elbow on *Upright Nude with Arched Back (Andromeda)* (Duthuit no. 14).

7. Flam 1984, 1:225. It is no reflection on Flam's participation, but the universalizing notion of affinity that guided this notorious exhibition (as well as the ethnocentric notion of justifying the aesthetic display of non-Western art in terms of modernist art) has been broadly ridiculed by anthropologists and art historians. Michael Mezzatesta (1984, 62), while agreeing with Flam on the role of African art in this piece, cautions—correctly in my view—that "the influence of African art is often subtle and at times so fully assimilated by Matisse that it is difficult to identify."

8. Herbert 1992, 158; his generalizing to all of Matisse's bronzes undermines what is otherwise a sophisticated discussion of the receptive context in which these works would have been seen.

9. Reff 1976, 108–15.

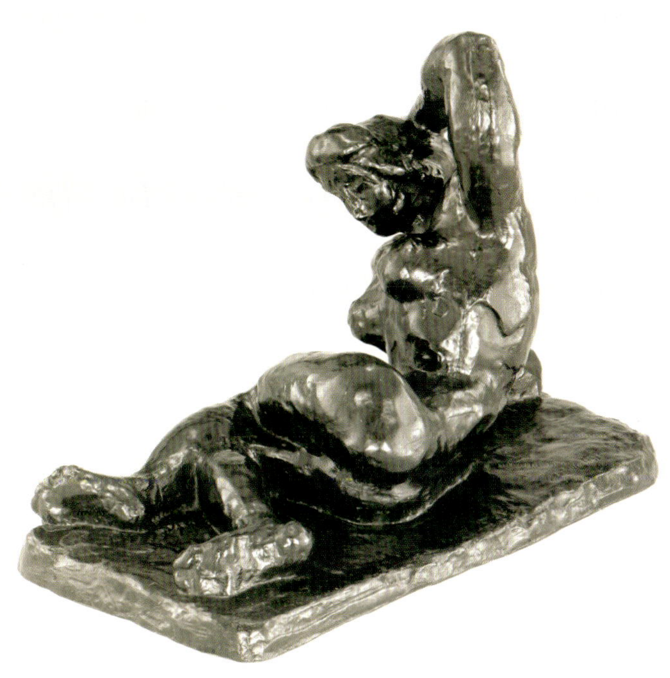

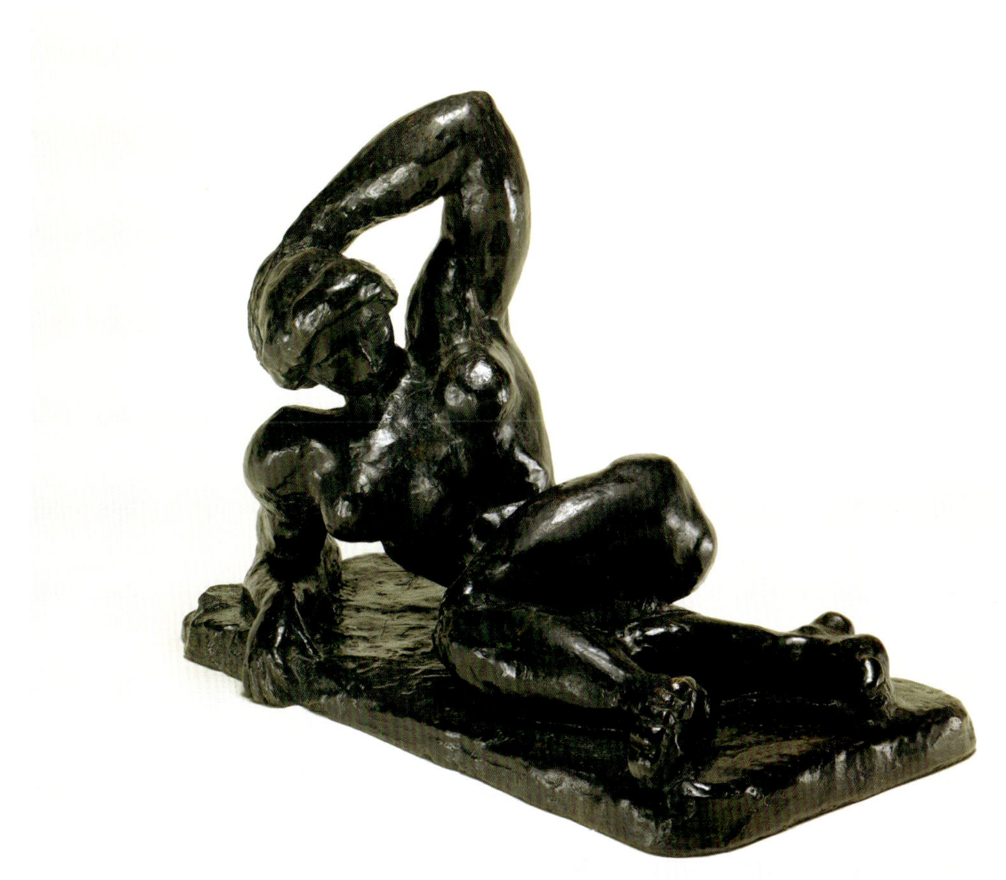

Henri Matisse, *Reclining Nude I (Aurora),* 1907

Bronze

The Baltimore Museum of Art, The Cone Collection, formed by Dr. Claribel Cone and Miss Etta Cone of Baltimore, Maryland. Cat. 45

Henri Matisse, *Reclining Nude I (Aurora)*, 1907

Bronze

The Baltimore Museum of Art, The Cone Collection, formed by Dr. Claribel Cone and Miss Etta Cone of Baltimore, Maryland. Cat. 45

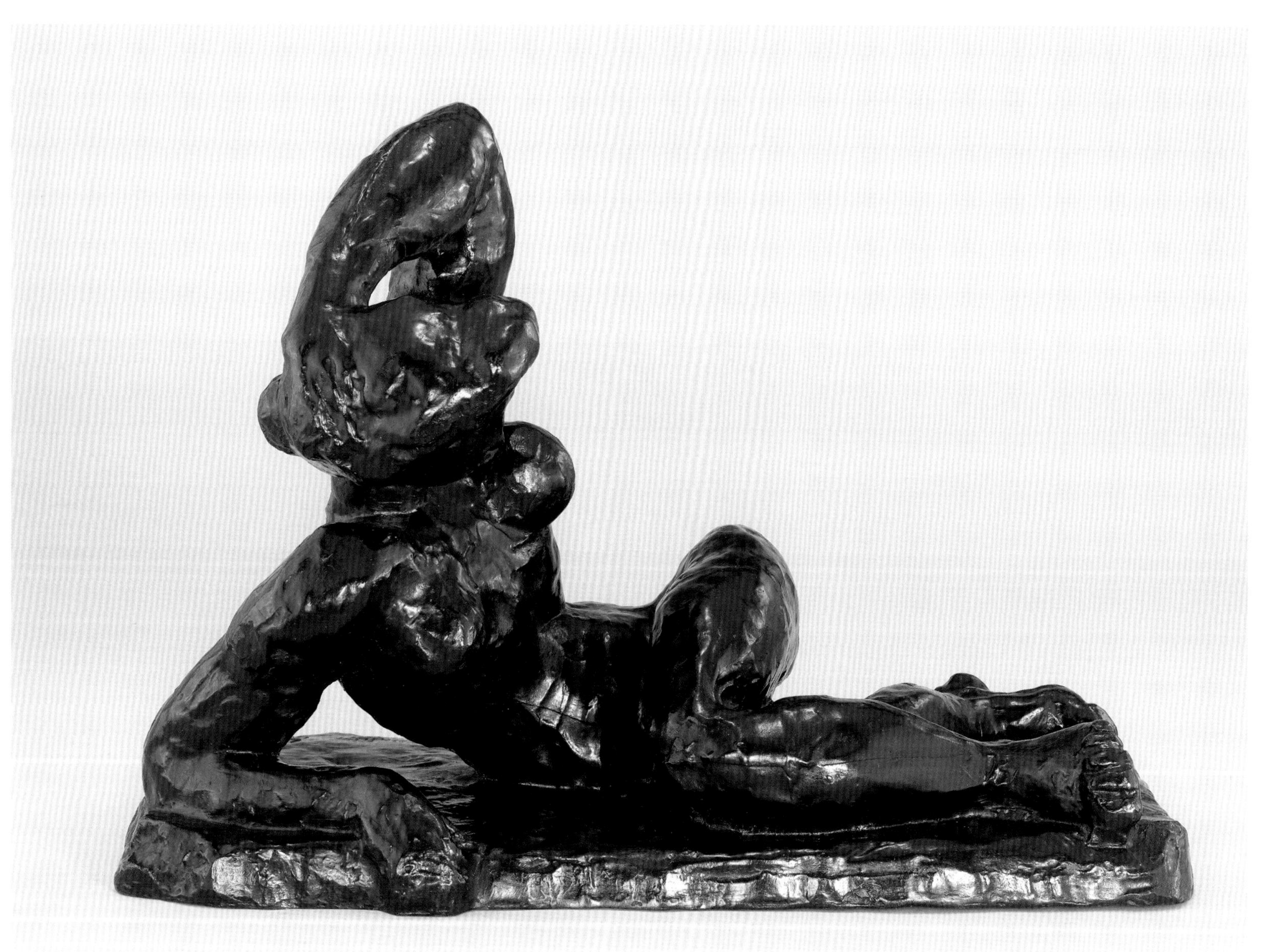

Henri Matisse, *Blue Nude: Memory of Biskra (Nu bleu: Souvenir de Biskra)*, 1907. Oil on canvas

The Baltimore Museum of Art, The Cone Collection, formed by Dr. Claribel Cone and Miss Etta Cone of Baltimore, Maryland. Cat. 46

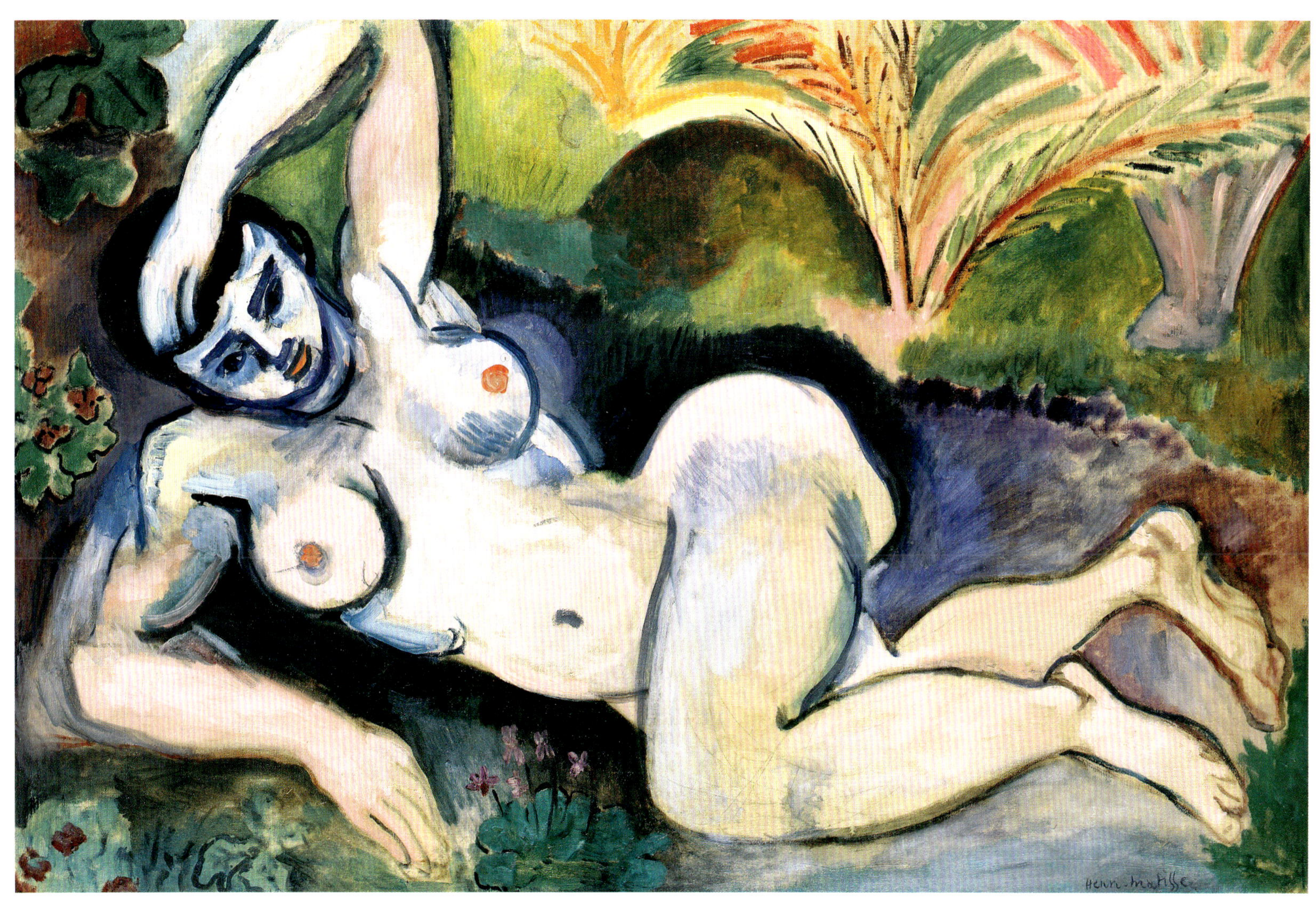

Two Negresses

Two Negresses is the only sculpture in Matisse's oeuvre that includes more than one figure and, perhaps more than any other sculpture, highlights the variety of sources on which Matisse drew at the end of the first decade of the century in his efforts to surpass outmoded, nineteenth-century sculptural conventions. Although he had previously treated the subject of two women embracing in the paintings *Le bonheur de vivre* (fig. 28, p. 29) and *Music (Sketch)* (1907), the sculpture is based on a now well-known photograph of two Tuareg girls from a French ethnographic magazine. Matisse recreated the pose in the photograph, but with significant differences. In the sculpture, the anatomy is exaggerated and the figures are pared down to their essential forms, eliciting the exoticism and brutal formalism that Matisse found in African and ancient art. Matisse also shortened the girls' legs and increased their mass, giving the figures a solidity and structural strength that they lacked in the photograph and recalling the suggestion made to his students at the time to "consider this Negro model as a cathedral, built up of parts which form a solid, noble, towering structure."[1] The position of the figures, standing side by side but facing opposite directions, gives the sculpture two fronts, aligned and planar, that emphasize its three-dimensionality by requiring the viewer to walk around the sculpture to view it entirely. This formal opposition subtly heightens a metaphorical duality: the figures stand as mirror reflections of each other, but their locked glance and the smooth, masculine head of one of them suggest a certain sexual ambiguity. A primitivizing formalism and exploration of duality can also be seen in works by Picasso, such as *Two Nudes* from 1906, the year Matisse was reported to have introduced the young Spaniard to African art.

JM

NOTE

1. Flam 1995, 47.

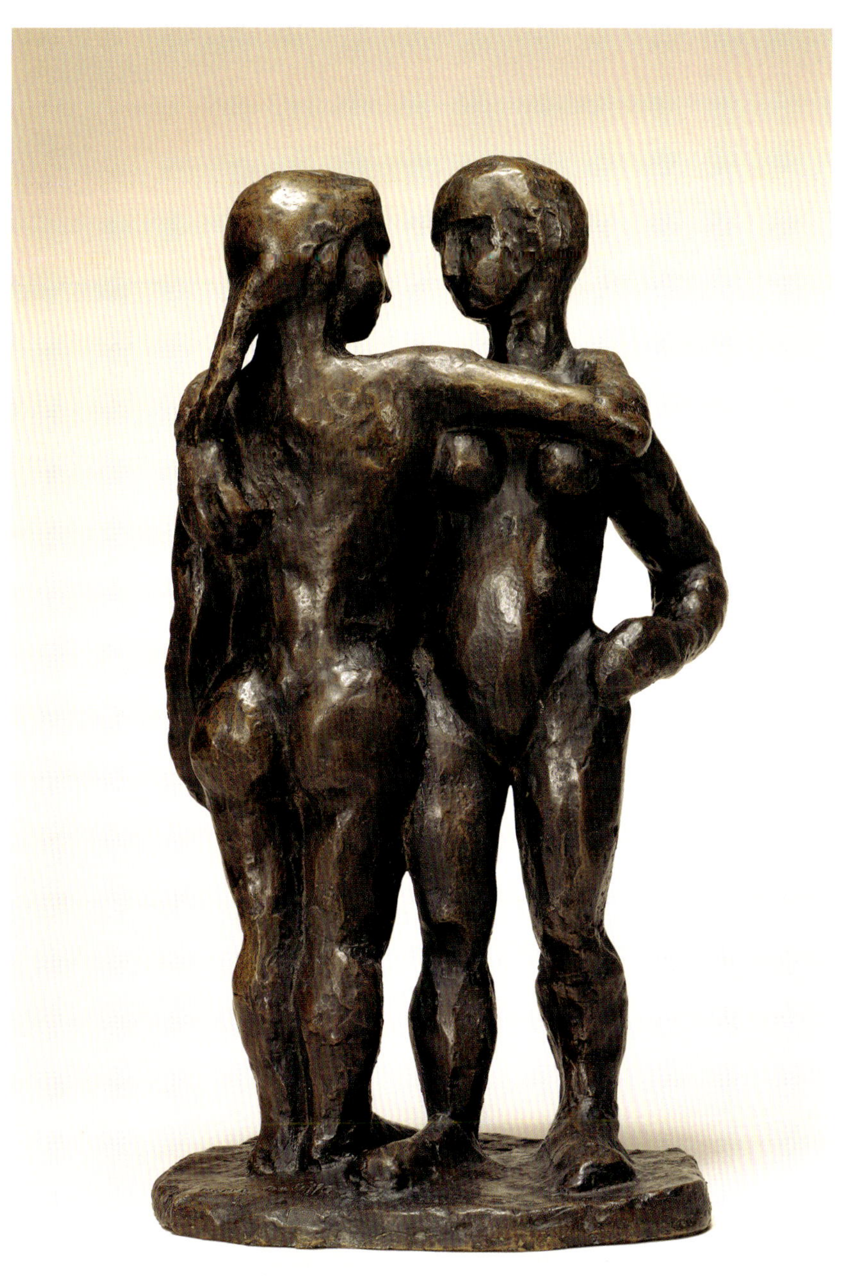

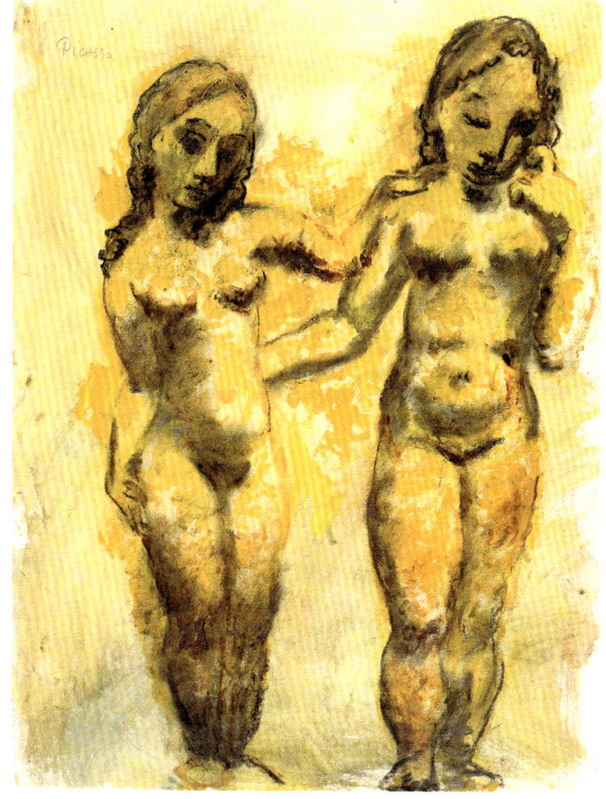

Henri Matisse, *Two Negresses,* 1907–1908. Bronze

Raymond and Patsy Nasher Collection, Dallas. Cat. 47

Pablo Picasso, *Two Nudes,* 1906. Brush and gouache, charcoal, watercolor, and black crayon

The Baltimore Museum of Art, The Cone Collection, formed by Dr. Claribel Cone and Miss Etta Cone of Baltimore, Maryland. Cat. 161

The Back

The four bronze iterations of *The Back* are among the most significant sculptural achievements of Matisse's career, not only for their size (they are the largest works in his sculptural oeuvre) but also for their chronological scope and their effect on the artist's development at crucial points throughout his career. Although they were not initially conceived as a coherent series, they represent a concerted focus on and elaboration of a single motif, the female nude leaning against a wall and seen from behind. Each figure is formed in high relief against a solid, sculpted background and stands ankle-deep in a projecting ground plane. The compositions move from a relatively naturalistic rendering of the figure in *The Back I* through progressively simplified, increasingly geometric anatomies to the startlingly stripped down, columnar figure in the last *Back.* As many scholars have noted, the tension between pictorial two-dimensionality and sculptural three-dimensionality inherent in the relief format of the *Back*s reflects Matisse's exploration of the relationship between figure and ground in paintings and drawings.

Matisse worked on *The Back I* in concert with a major commission for his Russian patron Sergei Shchukin, which included the large-scale paintings *Dance (II)* and *Music* (both 1910). In addition to the striking color combinations and idyllic themes, these paintings are largely concerned with the relationship of the figures to the background. Working on a life-sized relief allowed Matisse "to analyze the relationship of the figure's mass to the flat ground" on the same scale as that of the paintings.[1] In *The Back I,* Matisse modeled the figure naturalistically, composing the form in a gentle S-curve that traces the body from the right leg, up the spine, and around the left arm cradling the head. The woman seems to press her weight against the background, with her left breast and right hand pressed out to the side in complementary forms. The rounded anatomy, pleasantly defined musculature, and smooth surface give the figure a sense of fleshiness and mass that stands in contrast to the flat, roughly textured ground.

Throughout his career Matisse explored this subject in drawings and at this time executed numerous studies, in pen and ink or pencil on paper, of the nude seen from the back, with only slight variations in the position of arms, legs, and head. Each drawing accentuates the sculptural form of the figure: the outer contours are carved with dark, hard-edged lines, the three-dimensional volume of the forms modeled through shading. These techniques lend the figures a sense of mass and solidity. The treatment of the ground ranges widely, from completely absent, as in the pencil study from Kunsthaus Zürich (cat. 52, p. 166), to heavily articulated with dark hatchings around the figure, as in *Standing Woman Seen from Behind.* All of these figure studies show the entire model, including her feet. In *Study for The Back II,* Matisse is clearly working from the sculpture. The figure is shown in the same manner as in the relief, from ankles to head against a rectangular ground, but her anatomy has been simplified and her *contrapposto* stance exaggerated.

Matisse worked in a similar fashion on the series of reliefs, each time revisiting and refining the previous version. In *The Back II* and *The Back III,* he progressively softened the prominent

S-curve of the figure's stance in *The Back I,* straightening it a bit more in each version to the point of completely unifying the head, neck, and spine. This simplification and greater rectilinearity reflects a corresponding trend in painting. Matisse worked on *The Back II* and *The Back III* while he was creating the great painting *Bathers by a River* (1909–1916), initially proposed to Shchukin as the third large-scale panel in the commission that included *Dance (II)* and *Music,* but subsequently rejected. *The Back II* and *The Back III*—particularly the latter—bear a striking resemblance, in their pared-down, geometric anatomy, columnar verticality, and integration with their surrounds, to the figure on the far left side of *Bathers by a River.* Although Matisse maintained the volume and three-dimensionality of the figures in the *Back*s, always modeled in high relief, he integrated the surfaces of the figure and ground more and more in each version. These trends reach their culmination in *The Back IV*. Here Matisse reduced the figure to three massive vertical columns, recalling his advice to his students to "build your figure as a carpenter does a house. Everything must be constructed—built up of parts that make a unit: a tree like a human body, a human body like a cathedral."[2] Any previous articulation of musculature or anatomy has been smoothed out, subordinated to compositional unity.

Like much of Matisse's work, the *Back*s owe a debt to the example of Cézanne, whom he held in the highest esteem, calling him "a sort of god of painting," and turning to the example of his work for encouragement and moral fortitude throughout his career.[3] Cézanne's paintings of bathers, one of which Matisse owned (fig. 10, p. 9), provided him with a seemingly endless array of figure studies and poses. Several examples of bathers seen from behind, such as those depicted in *Three Bathers,* seem to have informed the *Back*s. Their anatomy is subtly articulated and yet they maintain a palpable weight and well-defined, almost sculptural presence. More importantly, Cézanne's paintings provided a crucial example of how to integrate the figure with the ground while not denying it its independence or sense of solidity. This is most evident in *The Back IV,* where the uniformly textured surface is the sculptural equivalent to Cézanne's painterly *passage,* subtly knitting together figure and ground.

JM

Notes

1. Mezzatesta 1984, 80.
2. Flam 1995, 47.
3. Ibid., 80.

Henri Matisse, *The Back I,* 1909. Bronze

Franklin D. Murphy Sculpture Garden, University of California, Los Angeles; Gift of Michael J. Connell Memorial Fund; Courtesy of the Hammer Museum. Cat. 48

Henri Matisse, *The Back II,* 1913. Bronze

Franklin D. Murphy Sculpture Garden, University of California, Los Angeles; Gift of the UCLA Art Council Fund; Courtesy of the Hammer Museum. Cat. 49

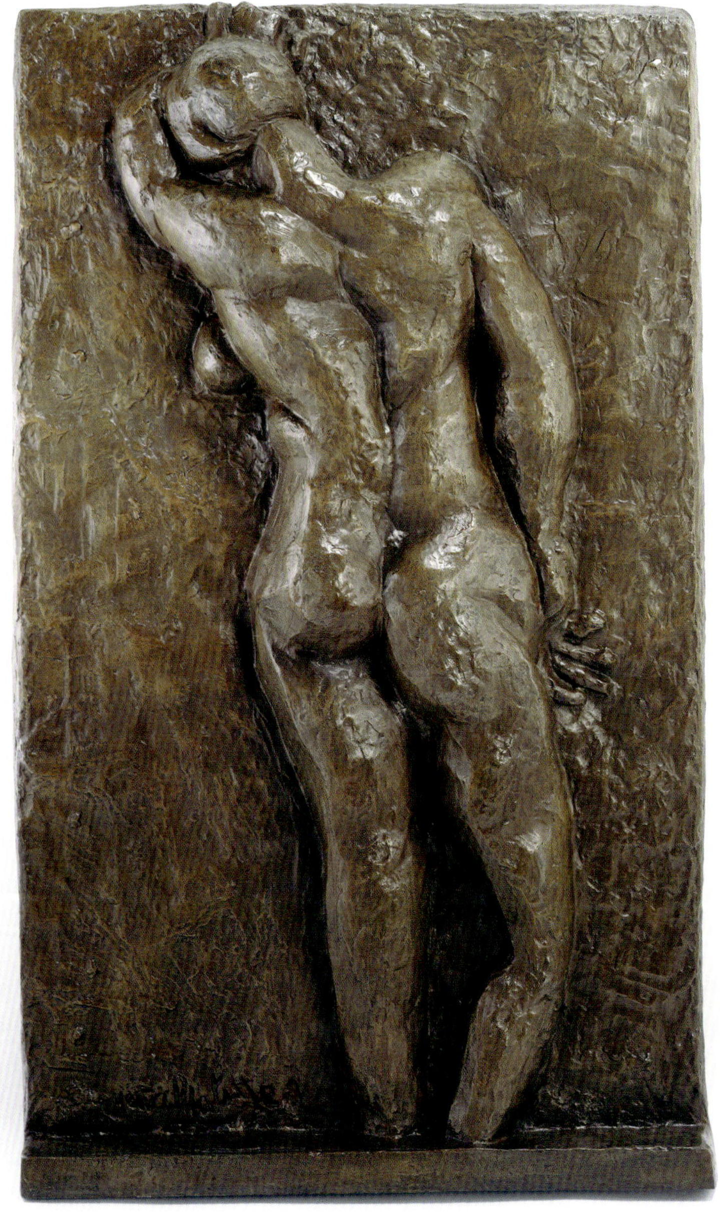

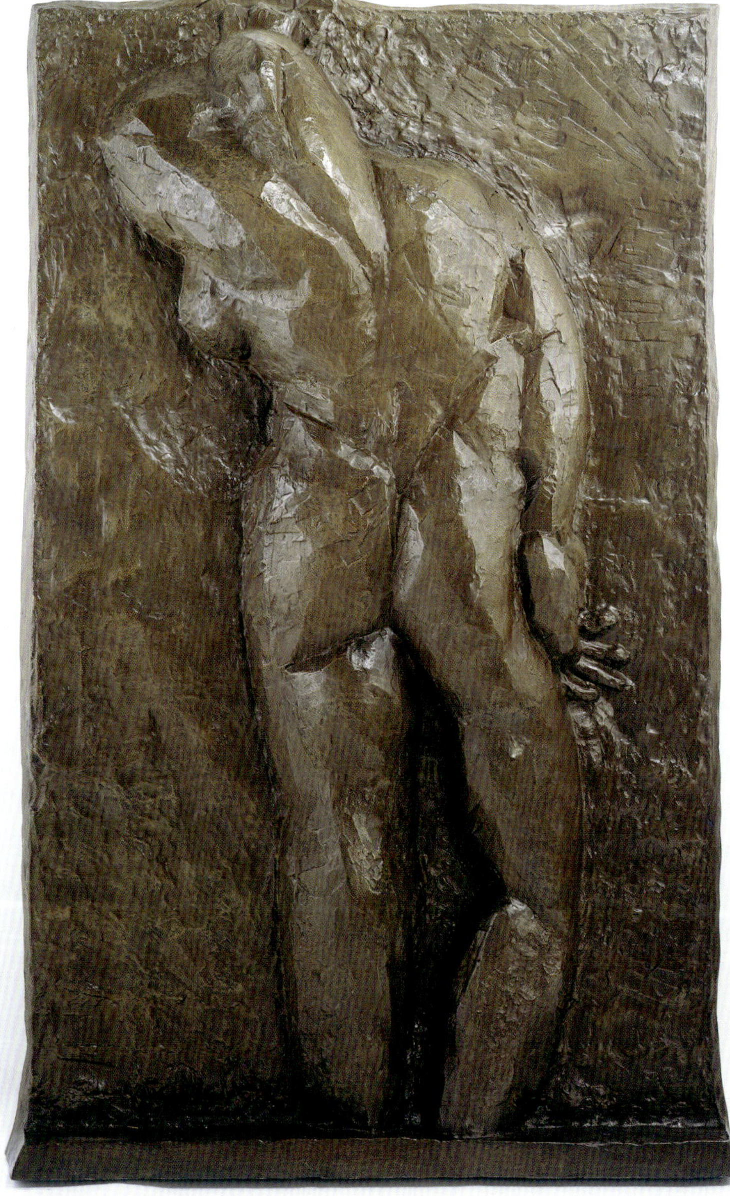

Henri Matisse, *The Back III,* 1916–1917. Bronze

Franklin D. Murphy Sculpture Garden, University of California, Los Angeles; Gift of the UCLA Art Council through the generosity of Mrs. Robert E. Gross and Mrs. Charles E. Ducommun; Courtesy of the Hammer Museum. Cat. 50

Henri Matisse, *The Back IV,* 1930. Bronze

Franklin D. Murphy Sculpture Garden, University of California, Los Angeles; Gift of Mr. and Mrs. Sidney F. Brody in honor of the UCLA Art Council; Courtesy of the Hammer Museum. Cat. 51

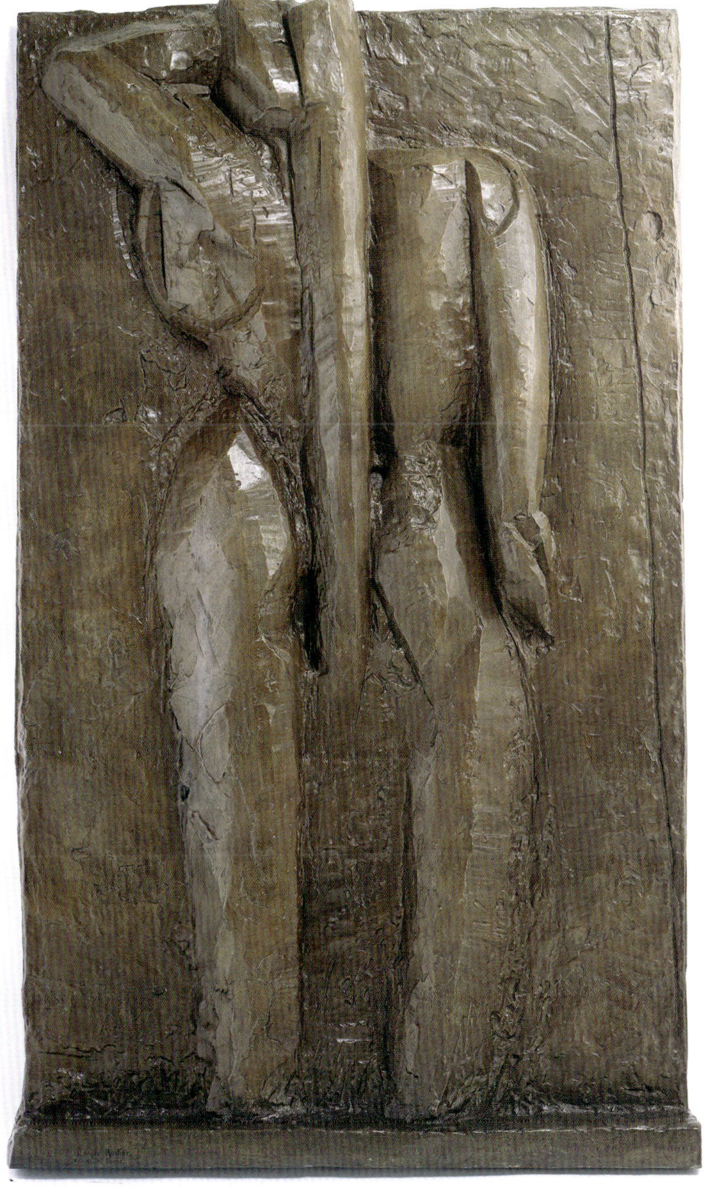

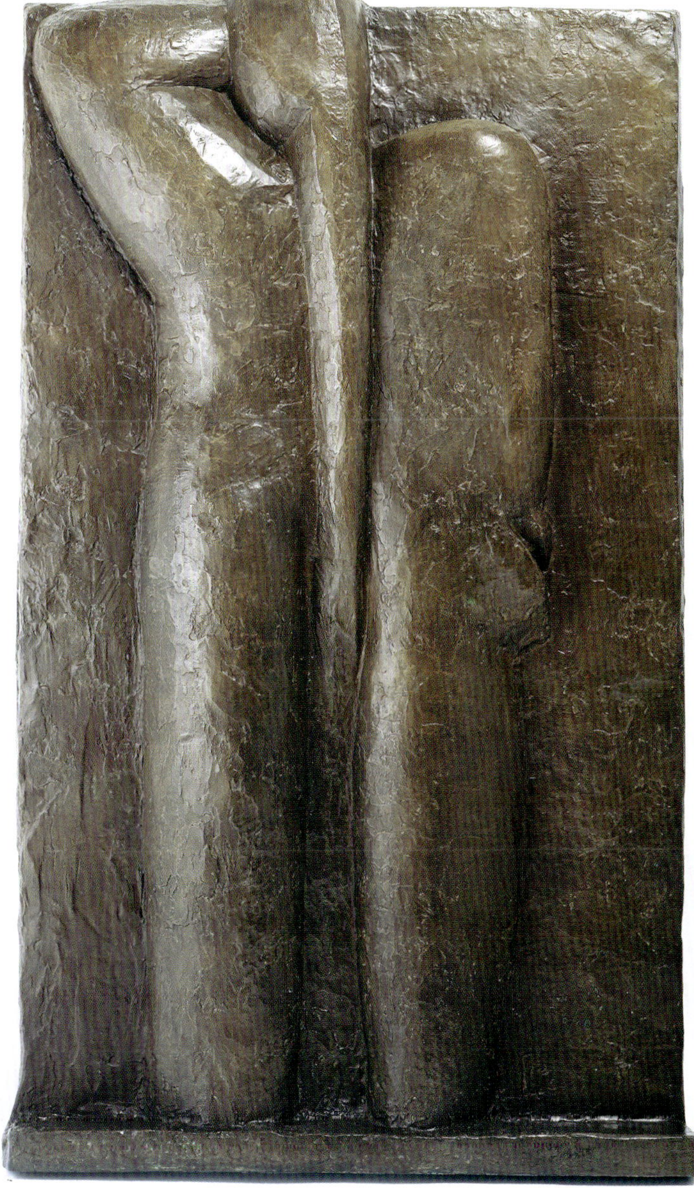

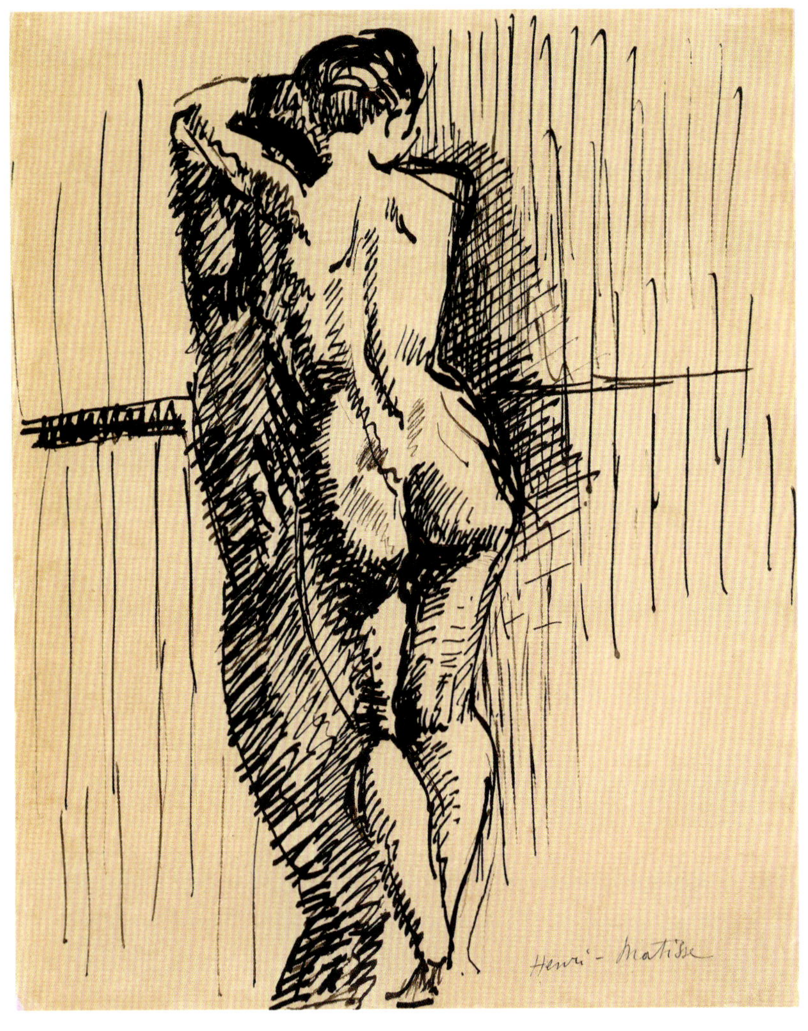

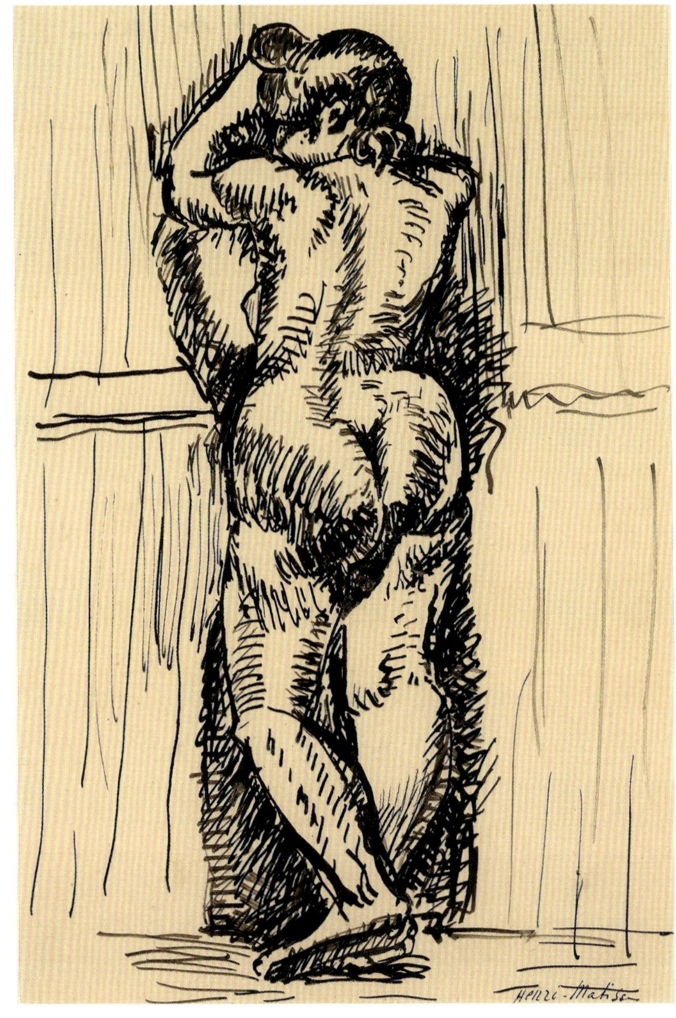

Henri Matisse, *Standing Woman Seen from Behind* (*Study for The Back I*), 1909. Pen and ink

The Museum of Modern Art, New York; Carol Buttenweiser Loeb Memorial Fund. Cat. 53

Henri Matisse, *Study of a Model's Back,* 1909

Pen and dark brown ink

National Gallery of Canada, Ottawa; Purchase 1974. Cat. 54

Paul Cézanne, *Three Bathers,* c. 1875

Oil on canvas

Private collection. Cat. 149

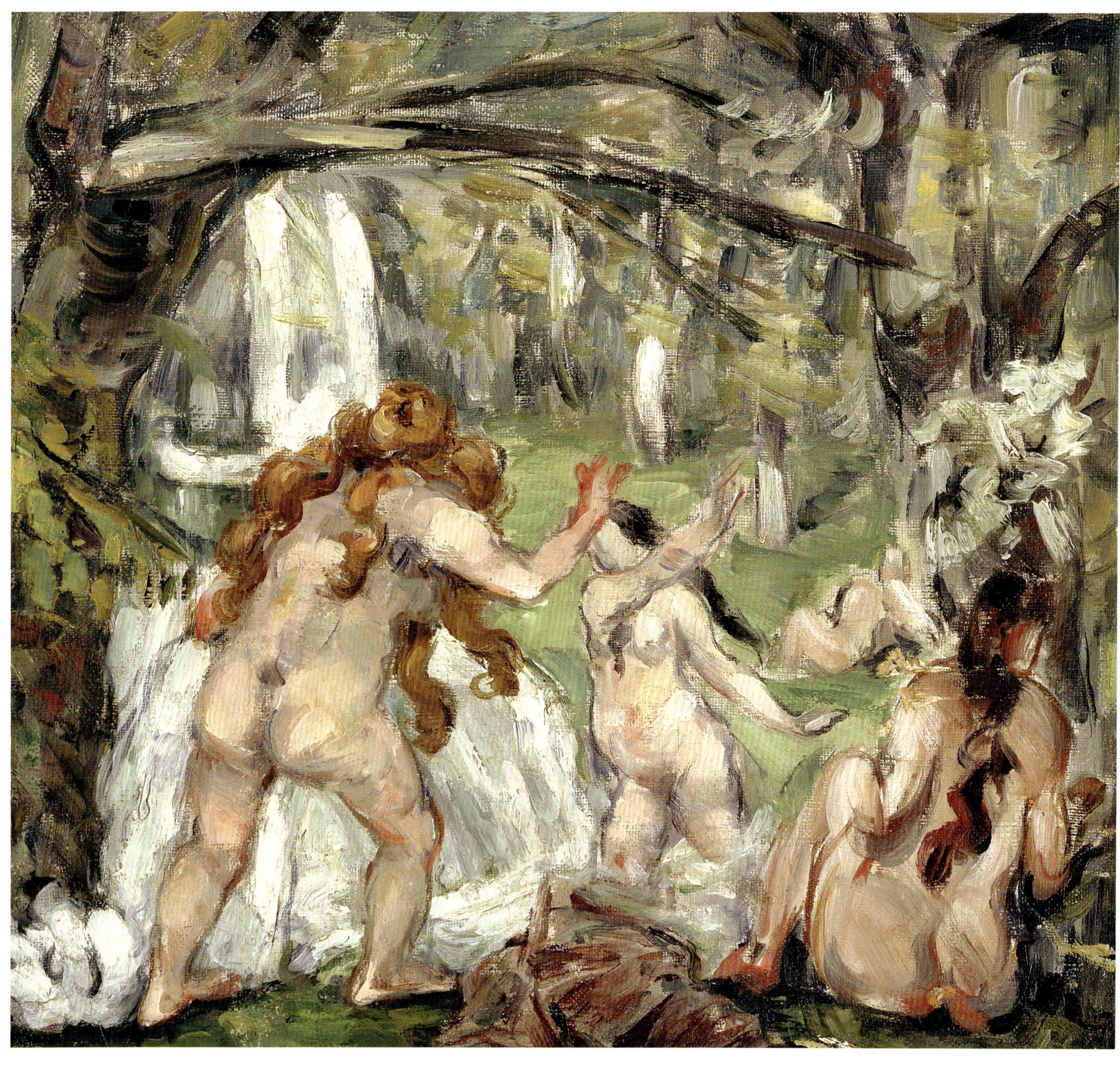

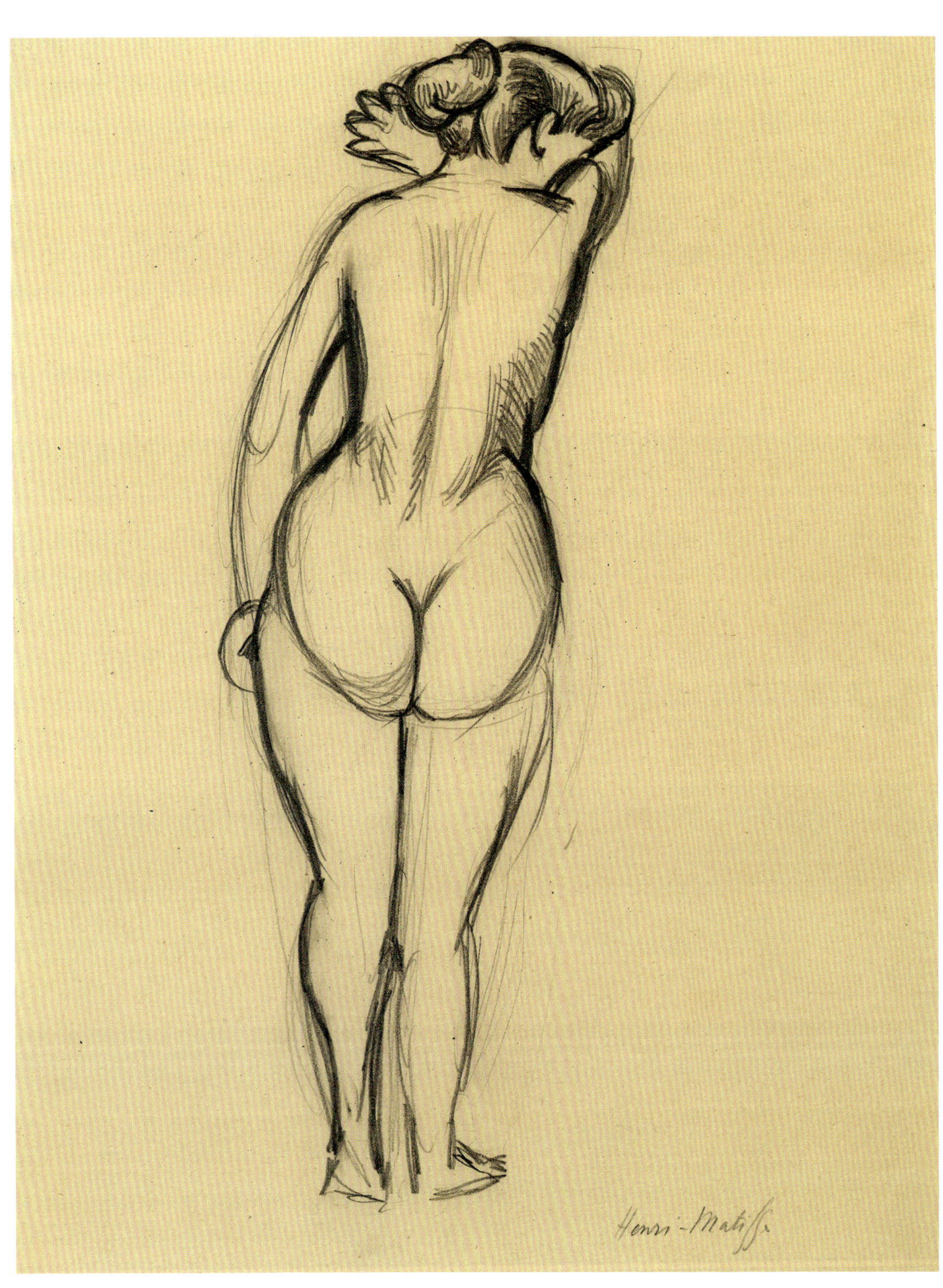

Henri Matisse, *Back Study,* c. 1907–1909

Graphite with stumping

Kunsthaus Zürich, Grafische Sammlung. Cat. 52

• Not in the exhibition

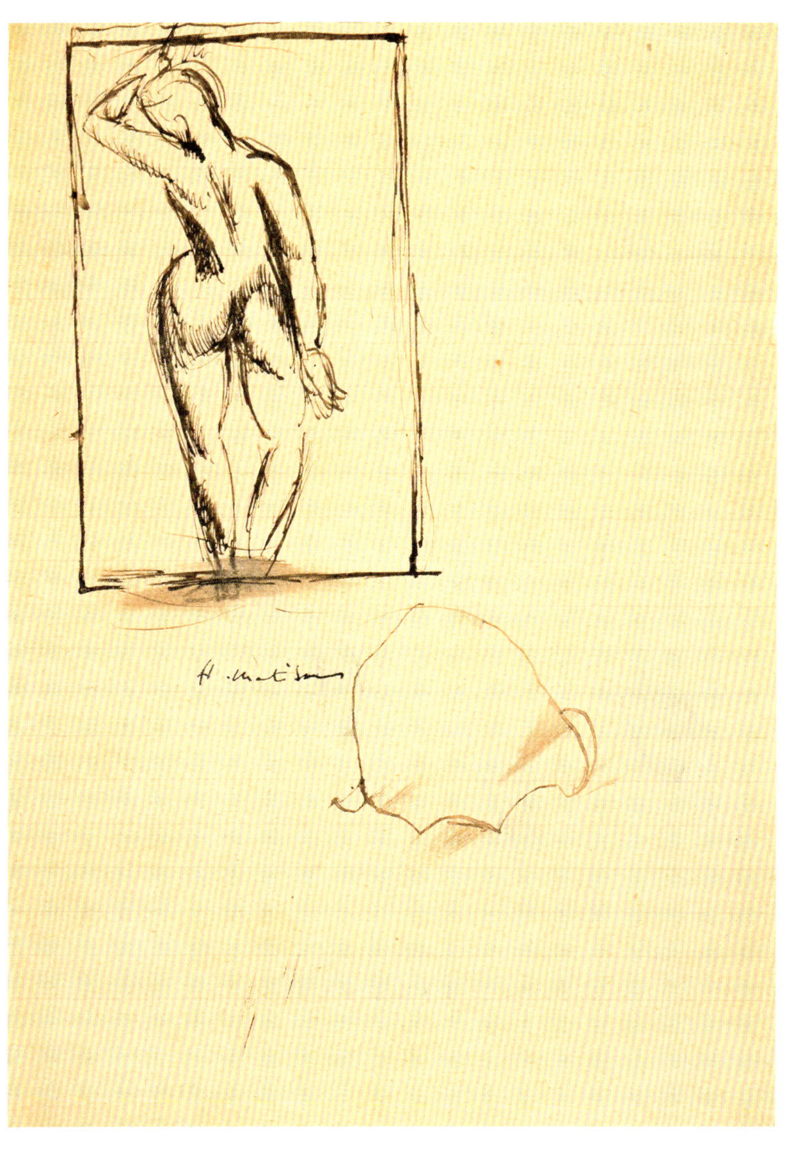

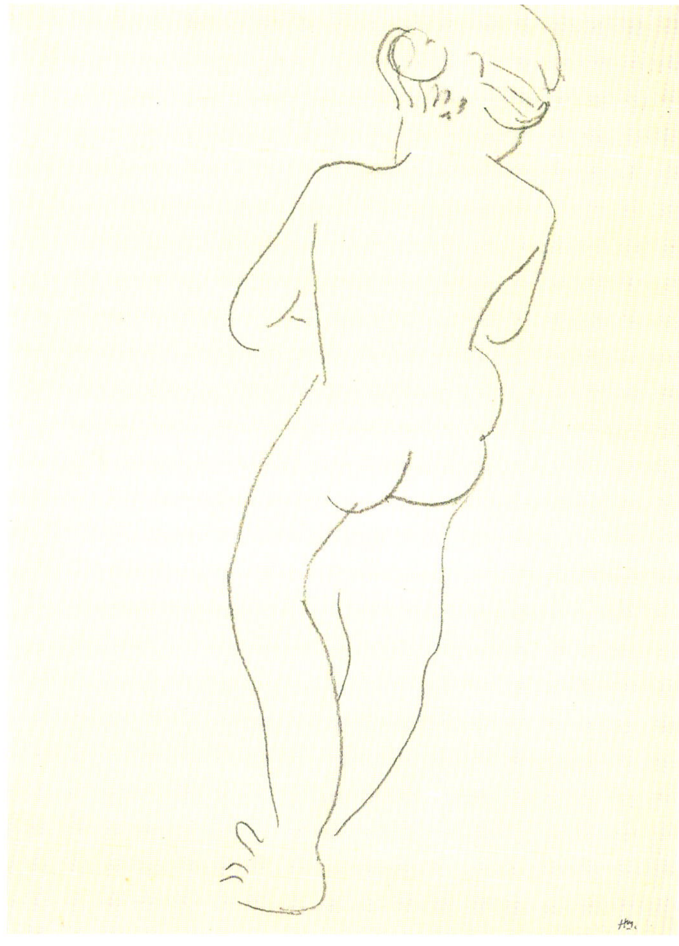

Henri Matisse, *Study for The Back II,* 1913
Pen and ink
The Museum of Modern Art, New York; Gift of Pierre Matisse.
Cat. 55

Henri Matisse, *Nude, Seen from the Back,*
1914–1915. Crayon
Pierre and Maria-Gaetana Matisse Foundation Collection.
Cat. 56

The Serpentine and *The Dance*

The theme of the dance provided a central motif for Matisse throughout his career, from the circle of revelers in his groundbreaking fauvist composition, *Le bonheur de vivre* (fig. 28, p. 29) to the over-life-sized figures in *Dance* (1932–1933), the trio of panels he painted for the home of Dr. Albert Barnes. Exploration of this theme in a variety of media was key to the artist's understanding of bodies in motion and yielded some of his most surprising and accomplished sculptural compositions. While working on the painting *Dance (II)* for the Shchukin commission, Matisse sculpted several studies of dancers or figures in motion. Foremost among these is *The Serpentine.* Although the sculpture depicts a figure at rest, the composition of looping, intertwined limbs suggests the smooth, rhythmical movements of dance and is a primary embodiment of the fluid, arabesque lines that characterized Matisse's painting for most of his life.

As many scholars have noted, the pose of *The Serpentine* has its origins in ancient and Renaissance sculptures and was part of the current academic stock-in-trade. A female nude stands with legs crossed at the ankles, leaning an elbow on a low post or stump to support her chin on her hand, the other hand resting behind her back. Matisse had experimented with variations of this pose in drawings of the same year. In *Bather Leaning against a Tree,* the figure leans against a vertical prop, resting her head on her arms. The pose is not unlike that of the figure in *The Back I,* a work of this same year, seen from the side. A pencil study, *Nude* (1908), also depicts a figure leaning on a prop or architectural element. The figure here is seated and could possibly be an intermediate composition between the seated nude in *Decorative Figure* and the standing woman in *The Serpentine.* Rather than ancient Greece or Rome, Matisse's immediate source was a contemporary photograph of a model, "a little fat but very harmonious in form and movement," leaning against a studio prop (fig. 2, p. 3).[1] Photographs by Edward Steichen of Matisse at work on an early state of *The Serpentine* show the figure as a shapely woman, not quite as plump as the model in the magazine, but not yet as thin as in the final sculpture.

As Matisse's comment suggests, it was the harmony and sense of movement in the pose that interested him. To accentuate these aspects, he "thinned and composed forms so that the movement would be completely comprehensible from all points of view."[2] Although the artist claimed to sculpt as a painter, not as a sculptor, *The Serpentine* demonstrates a careful consideration and profound understanding of working in three dimensions. The limbs wrap around the body, encircling her, reaching out into the surrounding space and returning again to the figure. The composition leads the eye on a similar path and entices the viewer to move around it to see it completely. Aside from the crucifix Matisse produced for the altar in the Chapel of the Rosary at Vence, the insistent linearity of the figure is unique in his sculptural oeuvre. *The Serpentine* emphasizes line and movement over mass and volume and in this way, although more sedate and restrained, anticipates Rodin's loose, experimental studies of dancers in the midst of acrobatic kicks, known as the *Dance*

Movements (see, for example, cat. 164, p. 175). Indeed, the sweeping lines and lyrical arabesques that animate the three-dimensionality of *The Serpentine* were among the hallmarks of Matisse's paintings.

Many scholars have noted that his work on *The Serpentine* helped Matisse determine the appropriate form for the figures in *Dance (II).* One recognizes in the painted figures, even in an early charcoal study for the painting (cat. 62, p. 173), the thin, ropey limbs and rhythmical composition of the sculpture, so crucial to expressing the dynamic movement of the dance or what Matisse called "that whirling round on top of the hill."[3] *The Serpentine* is still quite calm compared with the bacchic revelry depicted in the painting. Perhaps to clarify his understanding of the physical expression of this exuberant display, Matisse modeled *Torso Without Arms or Head.* Here, he focused on the torso in motion, much as Rodin and Degas would sculpt fragments to isolate an expression of bodies in motion (cat. 152, p. 177). Matisse had attempted to render a circle of ecstatic dancers in sculpture once before, in a carved wood stele of 1907, which matches in expressiveness and exuberance, if not in scale and virtuosity, the *Large Bacchante* that Emile-Antoine Bourdelle produced that same year.

When Matisse returned to the theme later, he intentionally slowed down the frenzy. In *The Dance,* he again modeled only a portion of the figure, concentrating on the position of the knees, hips, bust, arms, and head, leaving out the distracting details of hands and feet. Here, the suspended motion of the figure expresses a calm repose in the midst of slower, fluid movements. This shift from high to low gear is also visible in the paintings of his studio from this period, such as *Nasturtiums with Dance (I)* (1912), that include portions of *Dance (I),* deliberately revised to express the calm motion and stability he now desired in the composition.[4]

JM

Notes

1. Barr 1951, 139.
2. Ibid.
3. Flam 1995, 55.
4. Mezzatesta 1984, 94–95.

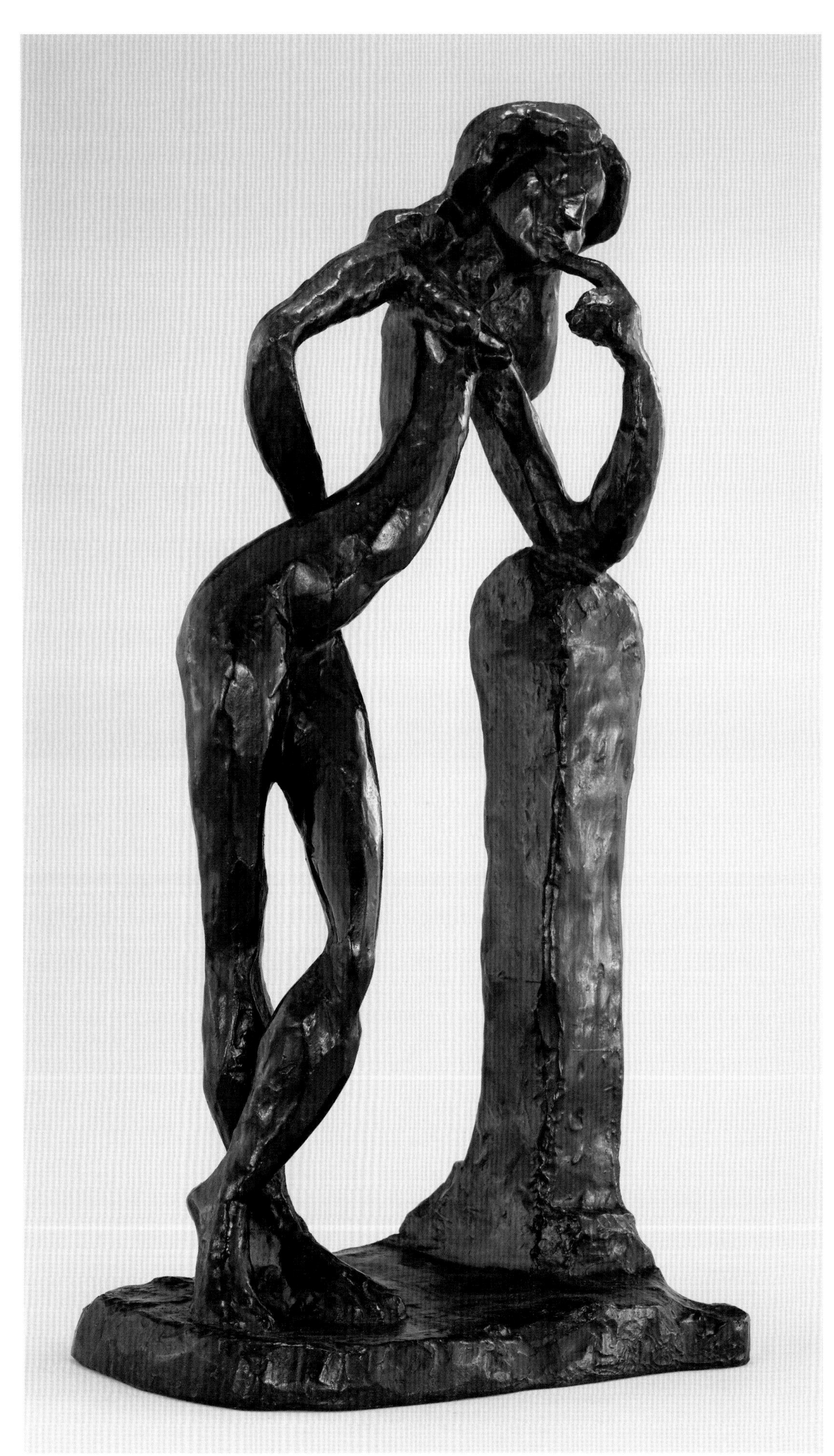

Henri Matisse, *The Serpentine,* 1909. Bronze

The Baltimore Museum of Art, Gift of a Group of Friends. Cat. 58

Henri Matisse, *Nude,* 1908. Pencil

The Metropolitan Museum of Art, New York; The Alfred Stieglitz Collection. Cat. 60

Henri Matisse, *Bather Leaning against a Tree,* c. 1909. Pen and ink

Private collection. Cat. 61

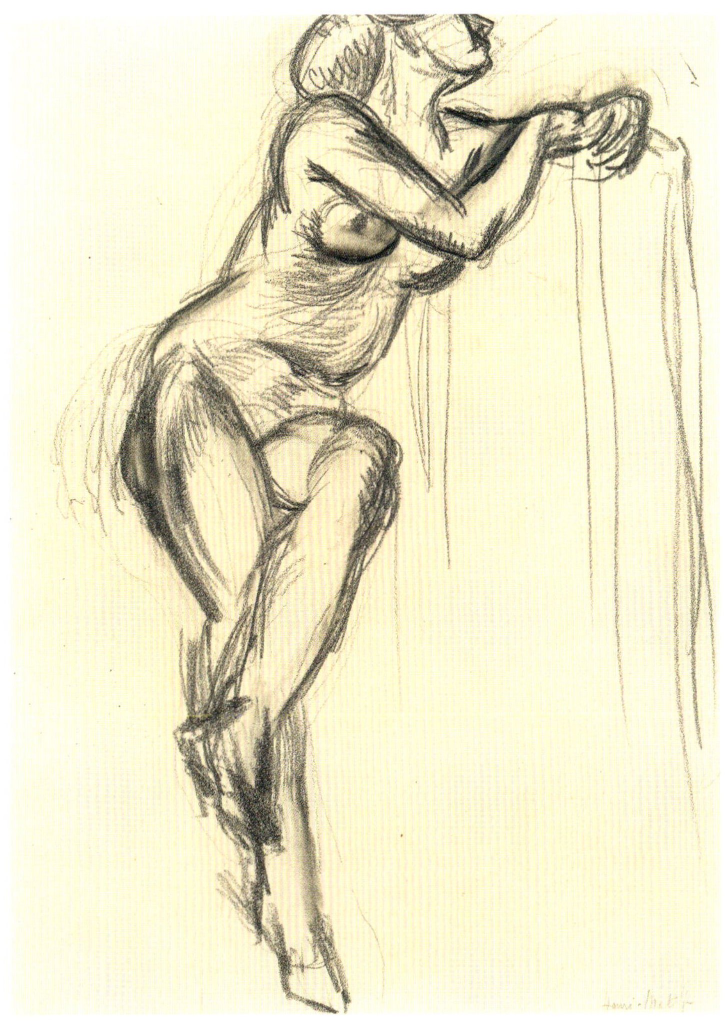

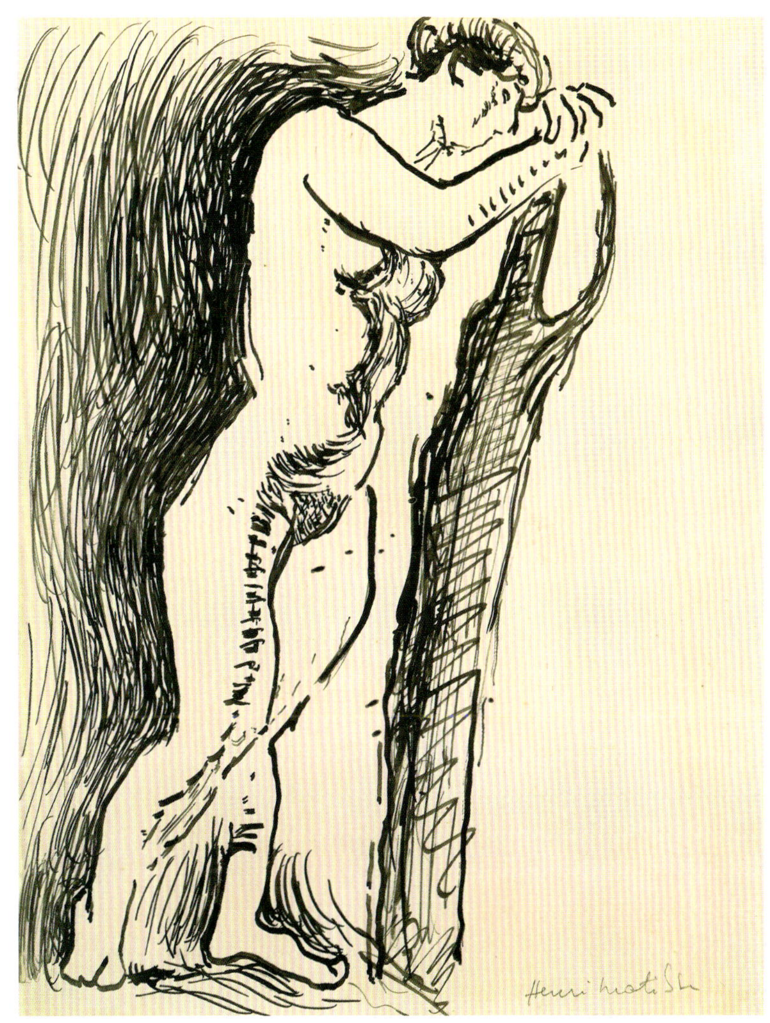

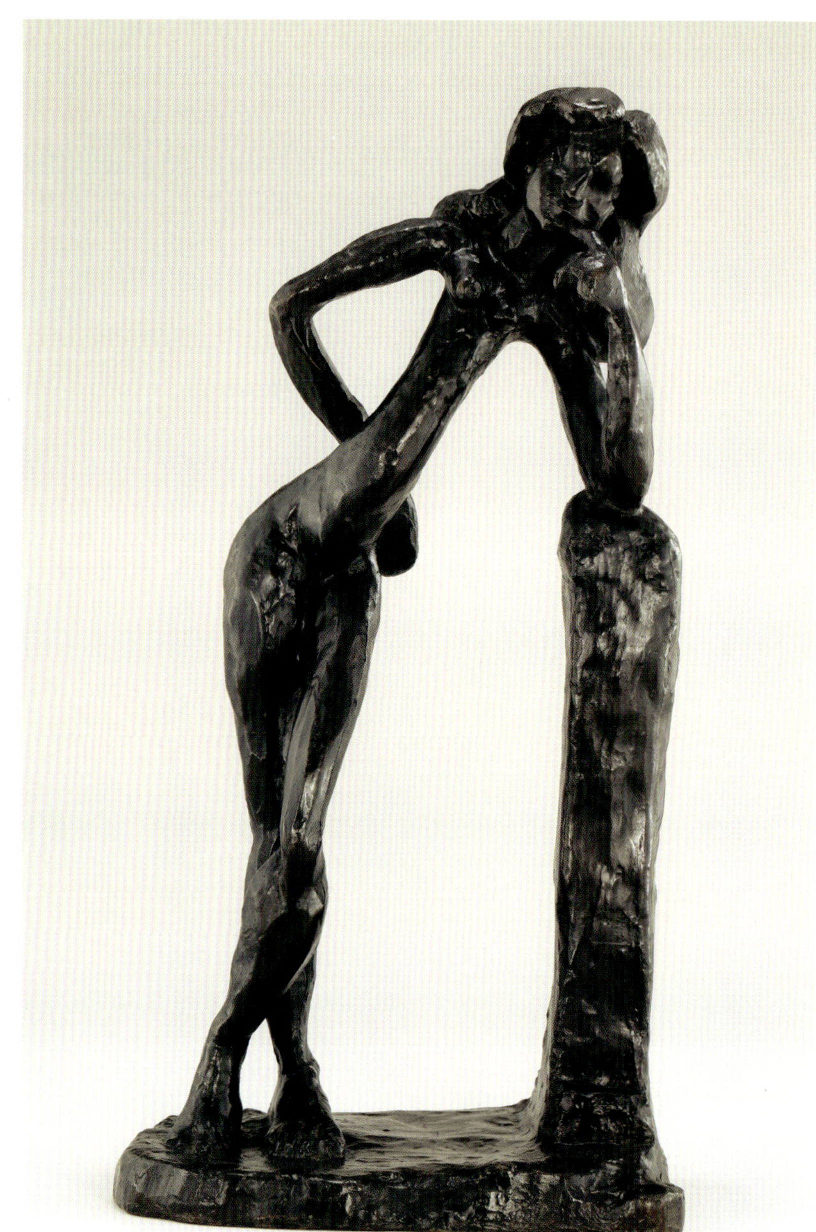

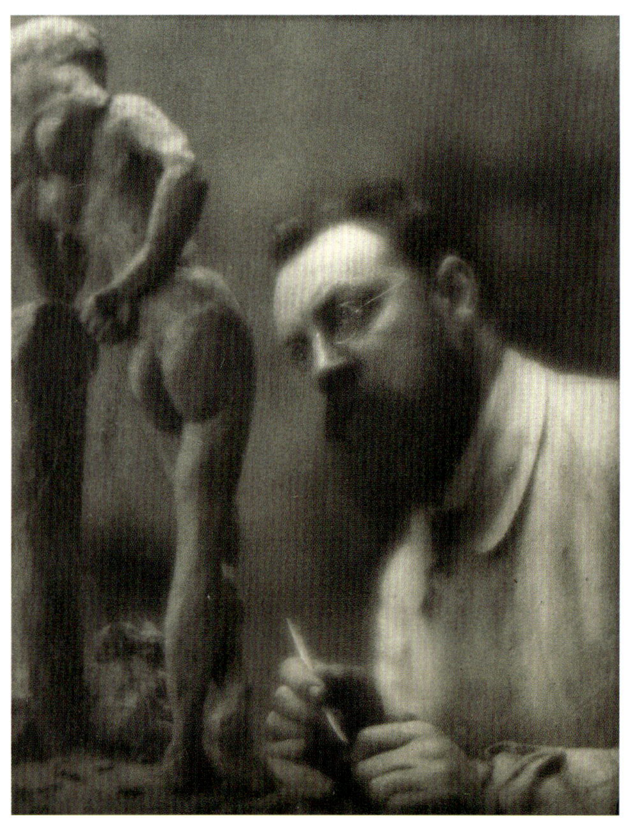

Edward Steichen. Matisse working on *La Serpentine,* from *Camera Work,* 1909
Photogravure

The Baltimore Museum of Art, E. Kirkbride Miller Library.
Cat. 165

Henri Matisse, *The Serpentine,* 1909. Bronze

The Baltimore Museum of Art, Gift of a Group of Friends.
Cat. 58

Henri Matisse, *Study for Dance (II)*, 1909–1910

Charcoal with stumping

Musée de Grenoble. Cat. 62

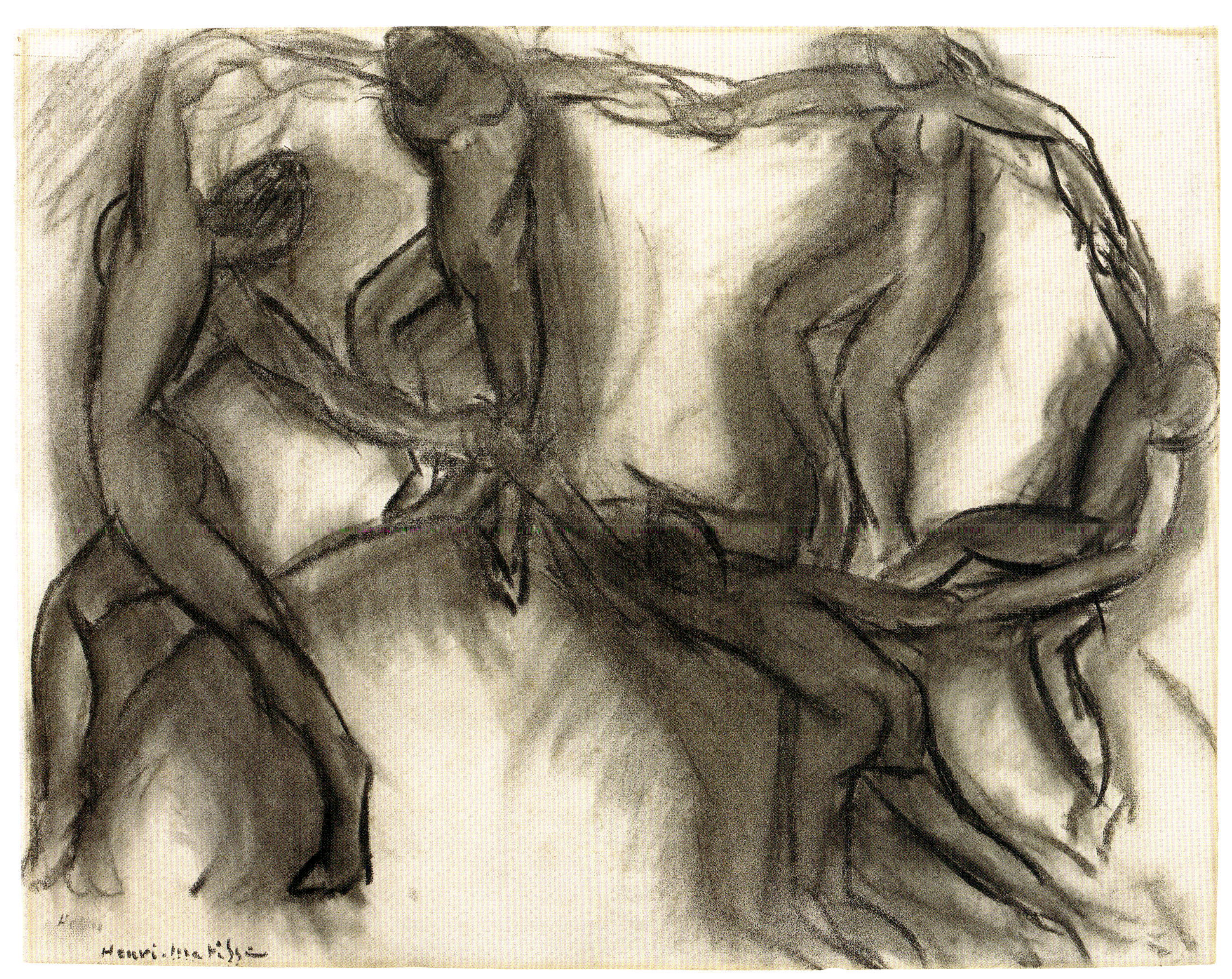

Henri Matisse, *The Dance,* 1911. Bronze

Hirshhorn Museum and Sculpture Garden, Smithsonian Institution, Washington D.C.; Gift of Joseph H. Hirshhorn, 1966. Cat. 59

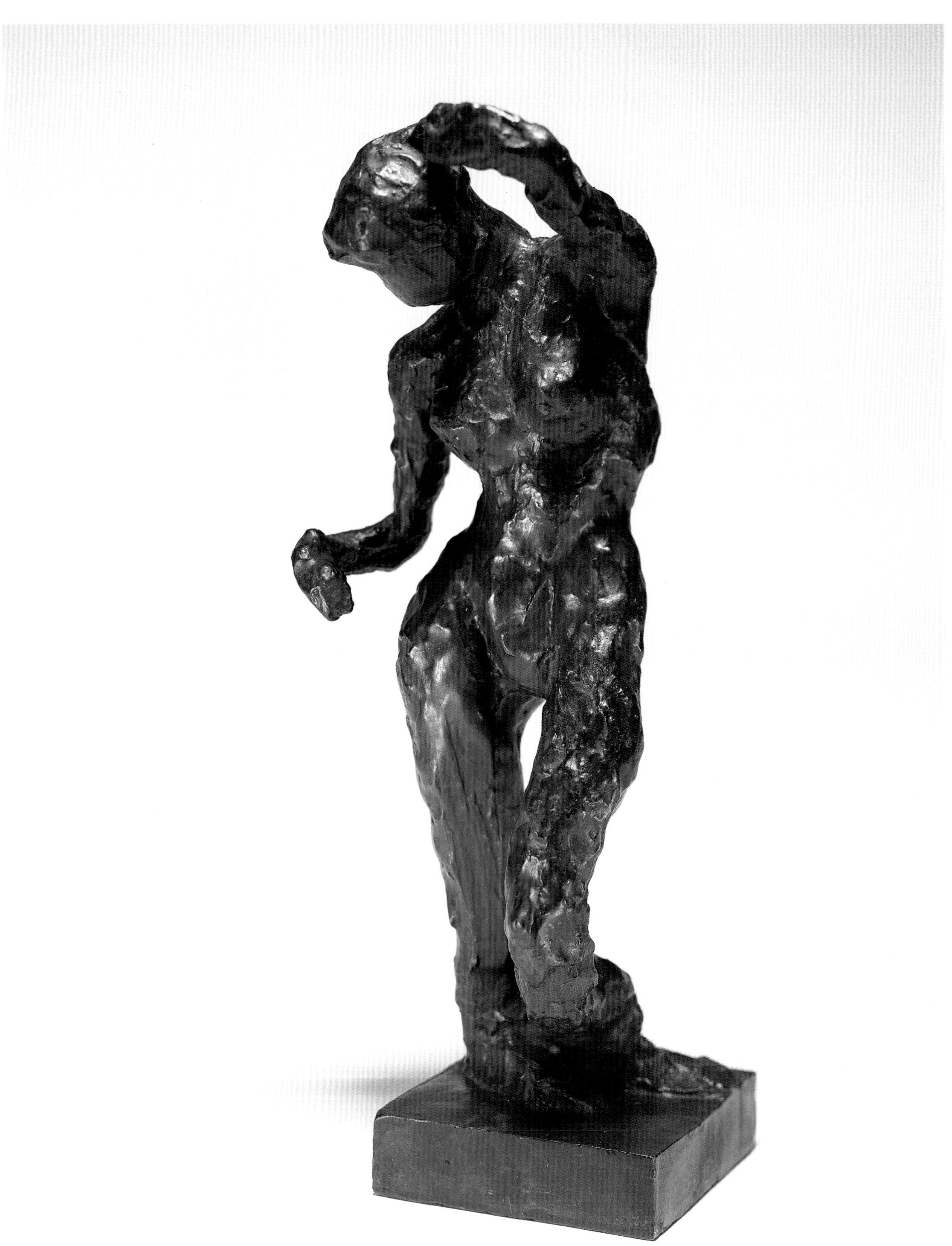

Henri Matisse, *Study for The Dance,* 1909–1910
Graphite
Pierre and Maria-Gaetana Matisse Foundation Collection.
Cat. 63

Auguste Rodin, *Dance Movement Pas de Deux 'B,'* c. 1910–1911. Bronze
Iris & B. Gerald Cantor Collection. Cat. 164

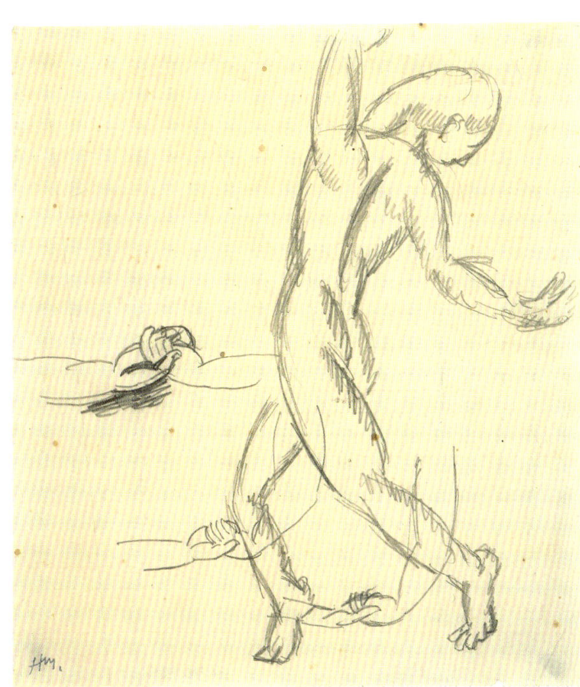

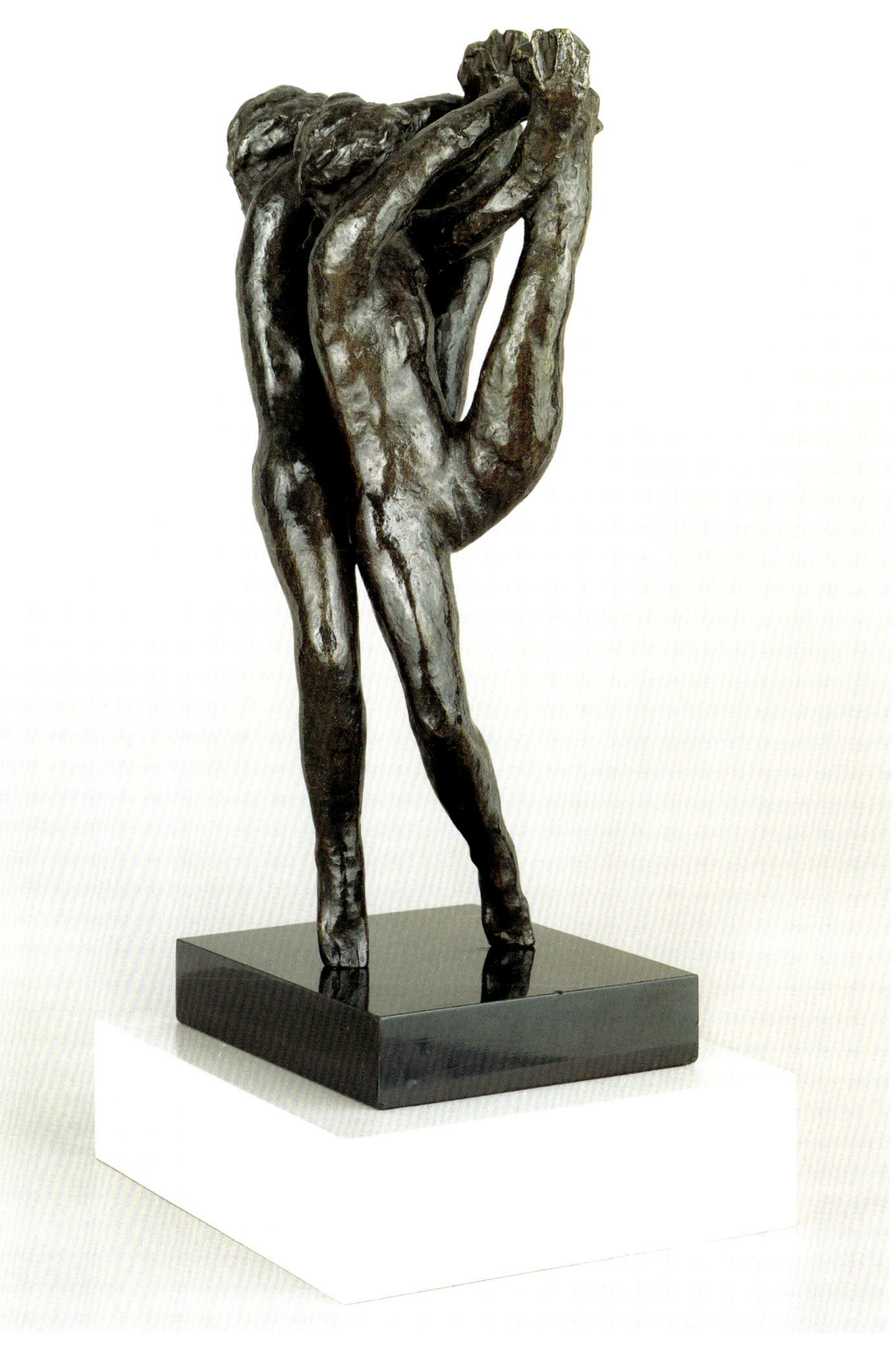

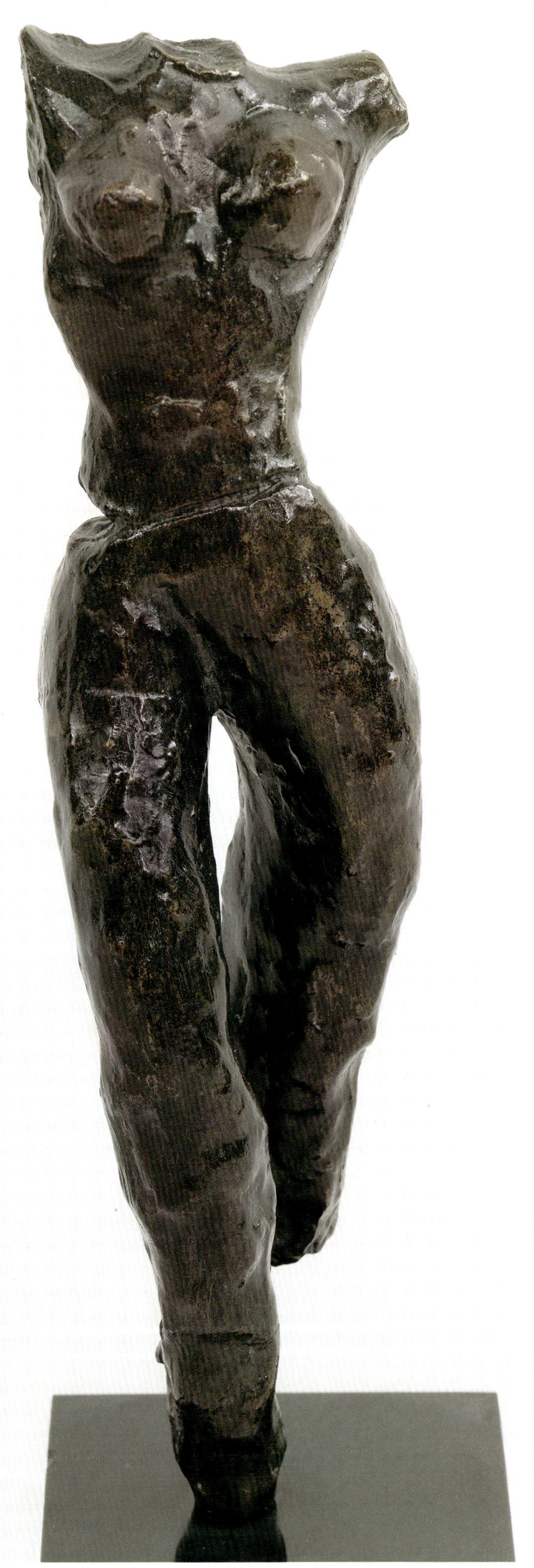

Henri Matisse, *Torso Without Arms or Head,* 1909. Bronze

Private collection. Cat. 57

Edgar Degas, *Woman Getting out of the Bath, fragment,* 1896–1911. Bronze

Noortman Master Paintings, Maastricht. Cat. 152

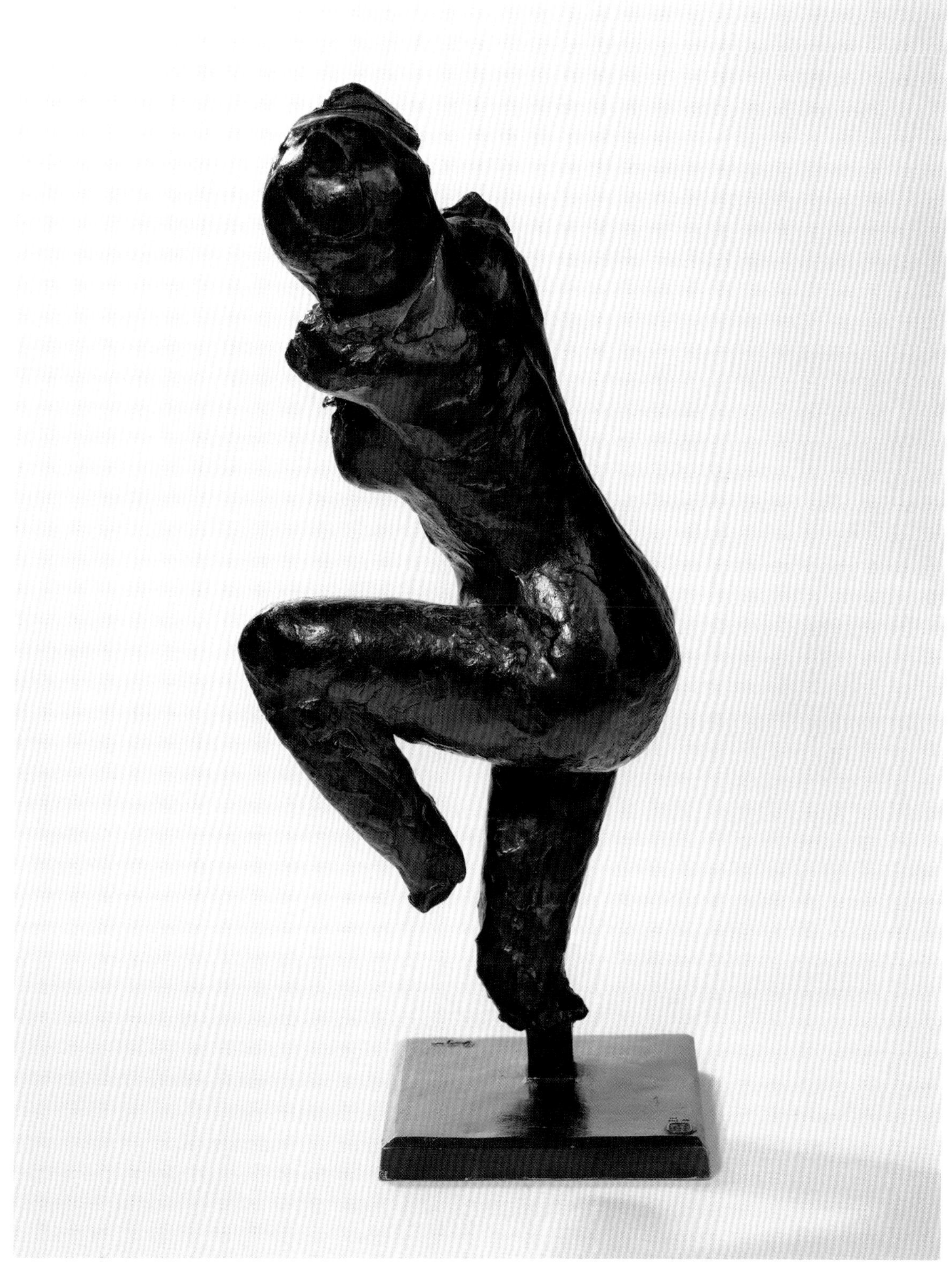

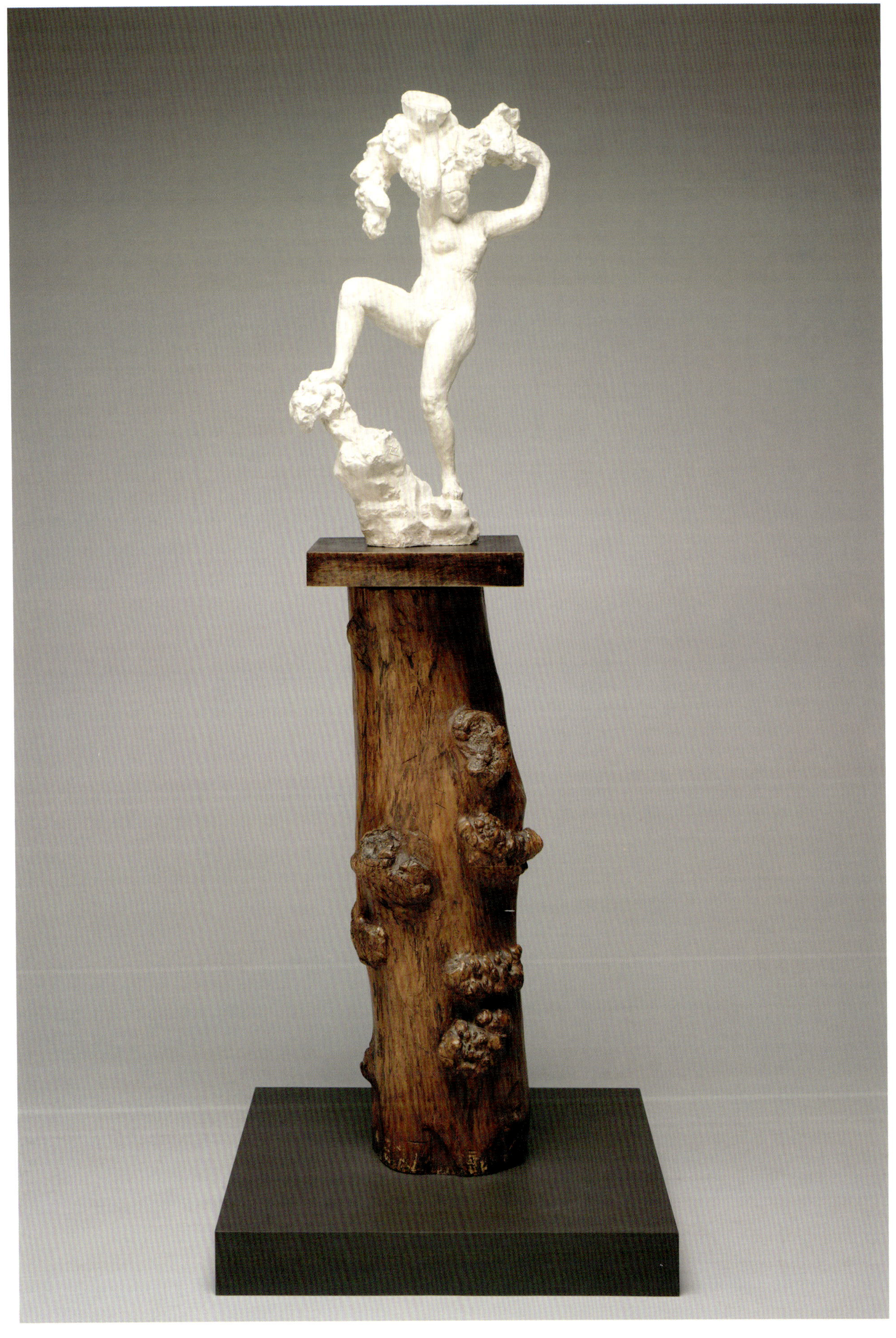

Emile-Antoine Bourdelle, *Large Bacchante,* 1907
Plaster on a pedestal of sculpted wood
Dallas Museum of Art, General Acquisitions Fund. Cat. 147

Henri Matisse, *Study for The Dance,*
c. 1930–1931. Graphite and pen and ink
Private collection. Cat. 64

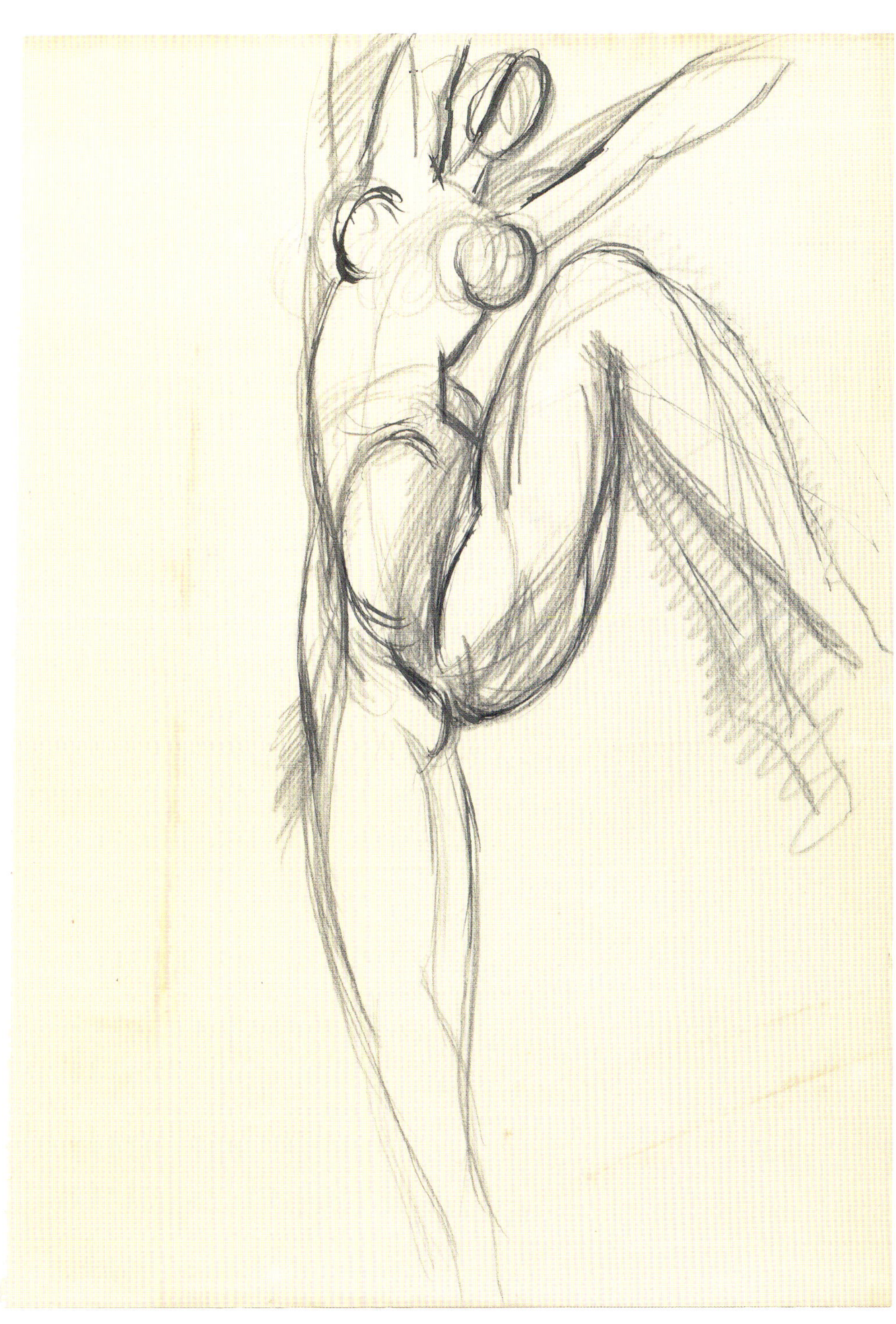

Seated Nudes and Crouching Nudes

Before 1908 Matisse had almost exclusively represented the human form either standing or reclining. He returned to these two postures again and again, modulating and reimagining the figure, usually the female nude. She was sometimes depicted as an upright structure, either rigidly symmetrical or twisting about a vertical axis, and sometimes as a sprawling odalisque, supporting herself on splayed hands or elbows. In 1908 Matisse began to work on a sequence of sculptures that instead captured the female nude seated or crouching, with knees bent to her chest and arms pulled in toward her body.

The initial sculpture in this group was *Small Crouching Nude with Arms*, which, like so much of Matisse's work from this period, was based on a photograph. A plaster cast of the sculpture is included in a still-life painting, *The Branch of Lilac,* painted in 1914. The small scale of the sculpture, which is just five-and-a-half inches high, is exaggerated by its juxtaposition with the enormous vase of lilacs. When the right arm of this figure was accidentally broken, the accident gave rise to the next work in the series, *Small Crouching Nude without an Arm.* For this second version, the flat base supporting the sculpture was also subtracted, and the figure rests directly on her right foot, left shin, and buttocks. In the last sculpture in the 1908 series, *Small Crouching Torso without Arms or Head* (fig. 4, p. 4), the head and vestigial remnants of the arms and legs are removed, the figure's hunched back becoming the most expressive component of her truncated anatomy. Pierre Schneider has described this series of sculptures in terms of an imagined interaction between the pliable clay model and the hand of the sculptor, a hand into which each of the sculptures would comfortably fit: "With each version, he increased the pressure of the invisible hand."[1]

Although *Decorative Figure* is not often discussed in relationship to the series of crouching nude figures, it represents a key moment in Matisse's exploration of this complex, involuted figural motif. In comparison with the earlier works, this, at nearly twenty-nine inches high, is monumentally scaled. Here the momentum that had characterized the earlier series is reversed. The imagined hand that had closed around the clay model uncloses, and the seated figure opens—at least in the frontal view—in a flat pattern of limbs, like the palm of an outstretched hand. The blank front of the large cube on which the figure perches reinforces our awareness of a flat rectilinear structure organizing this frontal view, over and around which Matisse carves a sinuous line with the muscular forms of the limbs. Matisse once said of the solid, monumental works of Aristide Maillol (cat. 157, p. 190), a sculptor he greatly admired, "Maillol worked with mass, like the Ancients, and I worked with the arabesque, like the sculptors of the Renaissance."[2] In *Decorative Figure,* Matisse's arabesque winds around and through the figure in intersecting lines that cohere as a complex, three-dimensional form. These flowing contours create a series of negative spaces that are effectively incorporated into the sculpture, an approach the Matisse would develop further the next year in *The Serpentine.*

Matisse once again took up the motif of the seated or crouching nude in 1910 or 1911, when he sculpted his student, the Russian painter Olga Meerson. *Seated Nude (Olga)* echoes both the

Henri Matisse, *Decorative Figure,* 1908. Bronze

Raymond and Patsy Nasher Collection, Dallas. Cat. 66

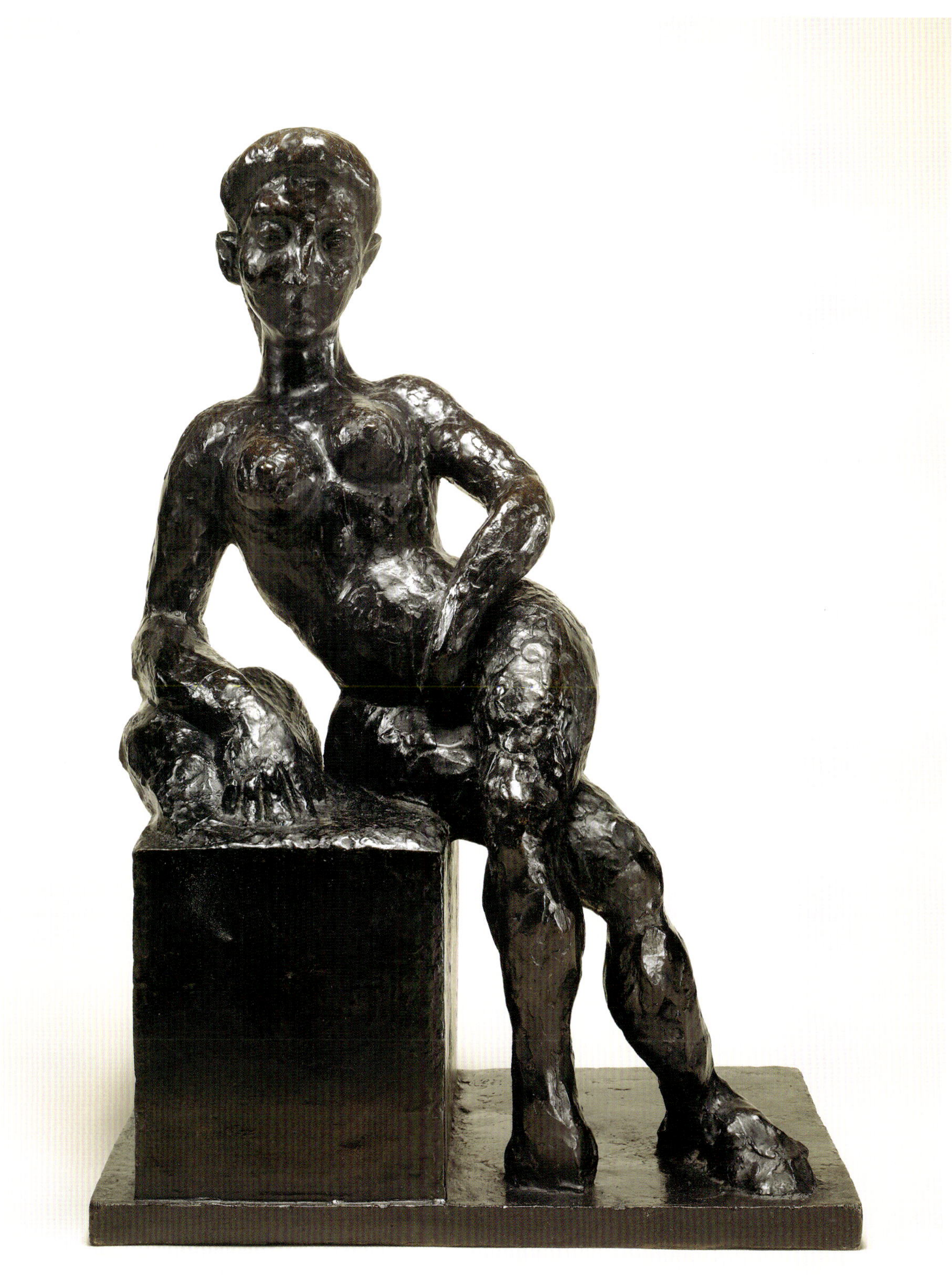

Crouching Nude series and a closely related work from 1908, *Seated Figure, Right Hand on Ground* (fig. 3, p. 4). Matisse also painted Meerson's portrait in the summer of 1911, but the sculpture is not intended as a portrait. It evokes a sense not of Meerson as an individual but rather of Matisse's new understanding of how to apply the lessons learned from his work with *Decorative Figure* and *The Serpentine* to the motif that had preoccupied him in 1908. In *Seated Nude (Olga),* Matisse pulls back gently from the development that caused the first series of crouching torsos to fold progressively in on themselves. This work, at more than three times the height of *Small Crouching Nude without an Arm,* is not one that might be held in the hand. Freed from the pressure of that imaginary hand, the figure is allowed to open in a new set of complex torsions. Ten years later, at the outset of his work in Nice, Matisse returned to this pose once more, with *Seated Nude Clasping Her Right Leg.* In this sculpture, the figure is more open still, and the limbs, freed from their fusion to the mass of the body, are given an elastic strength. This figure calls to mind Matisse's advice to his students, recorded by Sarah Stein: "Arms are like rolls of clay, but forearms are also like ropes because torsion can be placed on them."[3] This last seated nude, made before Matisse launched his work on the *Large Seated Nude* in 1922, is imbued with a muscular energy that relates it as closely to that late masterpiece as to its sculptural heritage in Matisse's earlier explorations of the crouching nude.

HMacD

Notes

1. Schneider 1984, 557.
2. Quoted in Escholier 1956, 163–64.
3. Quoted in Fourcade 1972, 67.

Henri Matisse, *Seated Nude (Olga),* 1909–1910

Bronze

Private collection, Courtesy of Ivor Braka, Ltd., London. Cat. 67

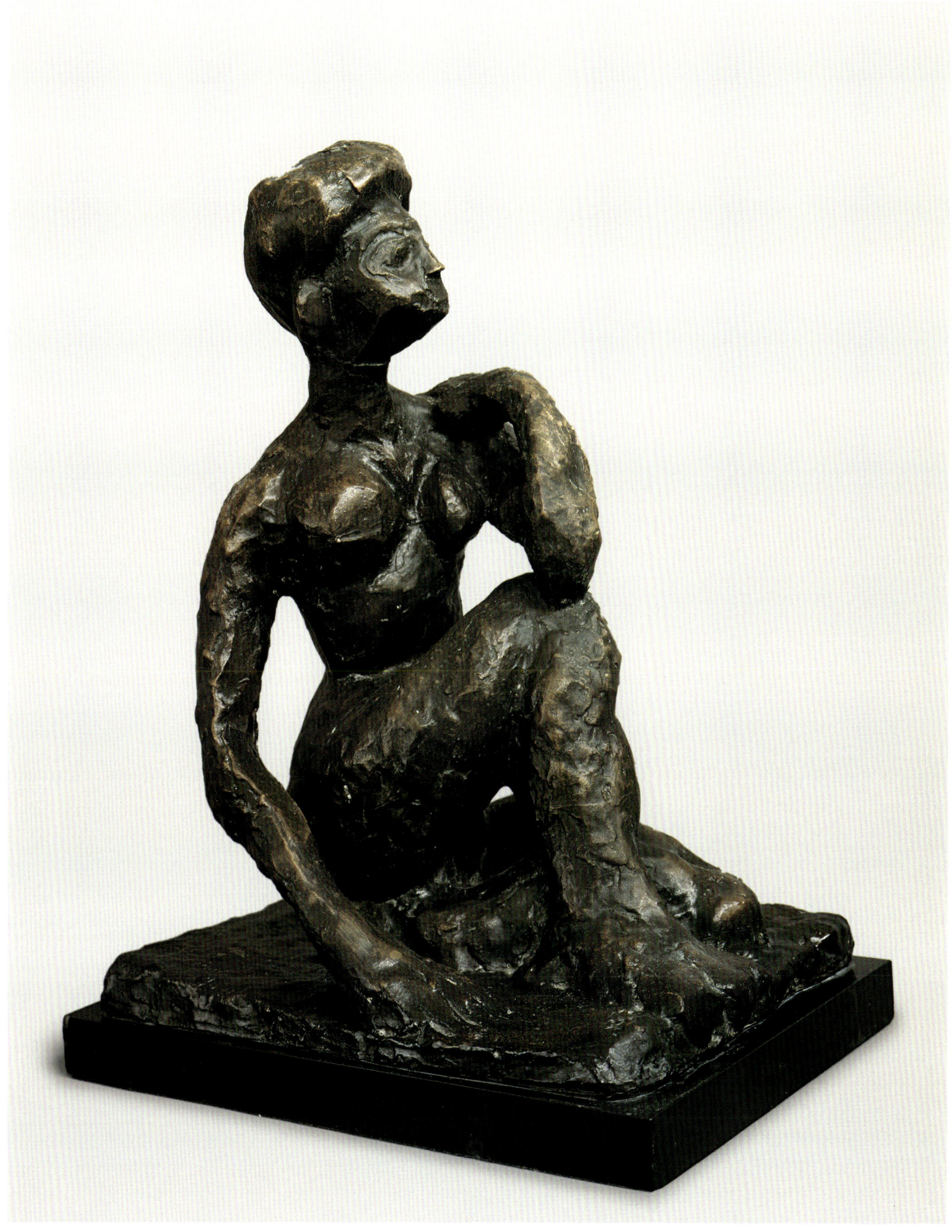

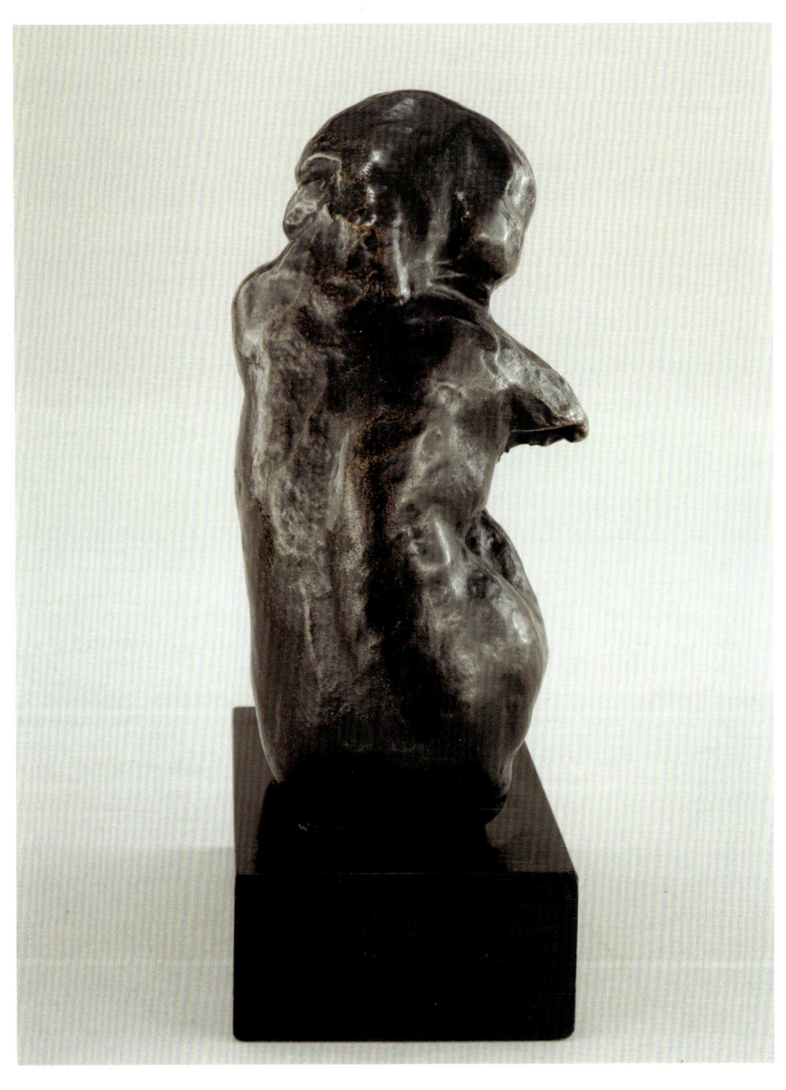

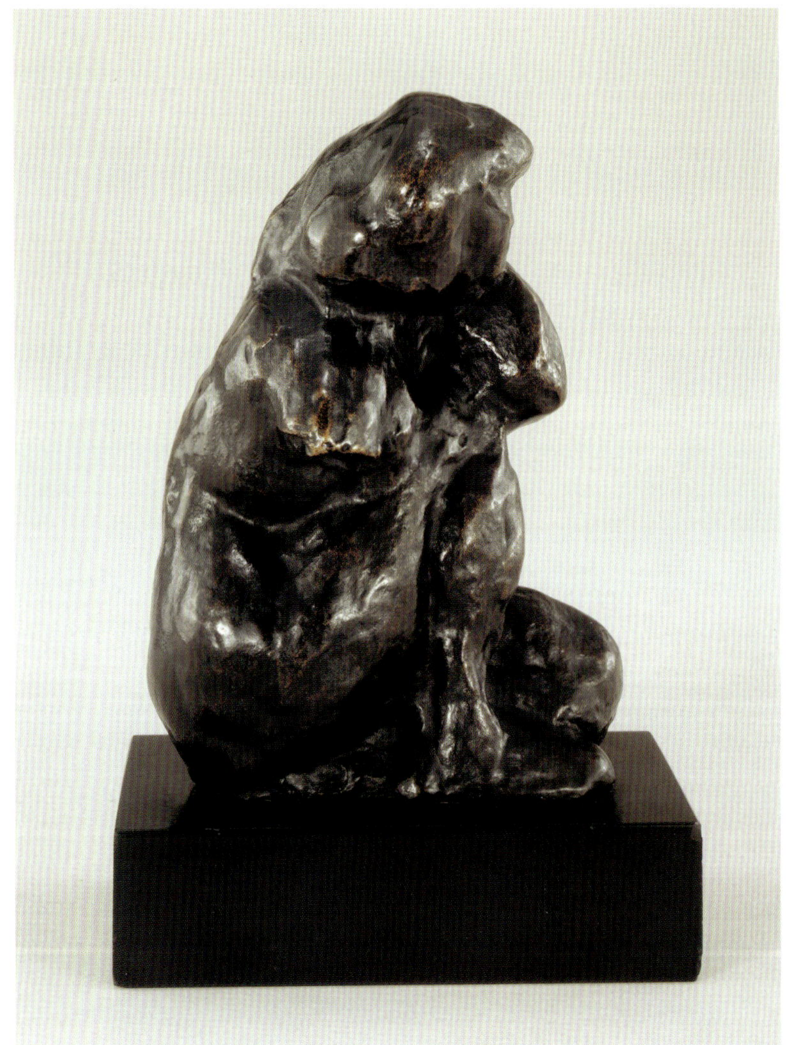

Henri Matisse, *Small Crouching Nude without an Arm,* 1908

Bronze

The Baltimore Museum of Art, The Cone Collection, formed by Dr. Claribel Cone and Miss Etta Cone of Baltimore, Maryland. Cat. 65

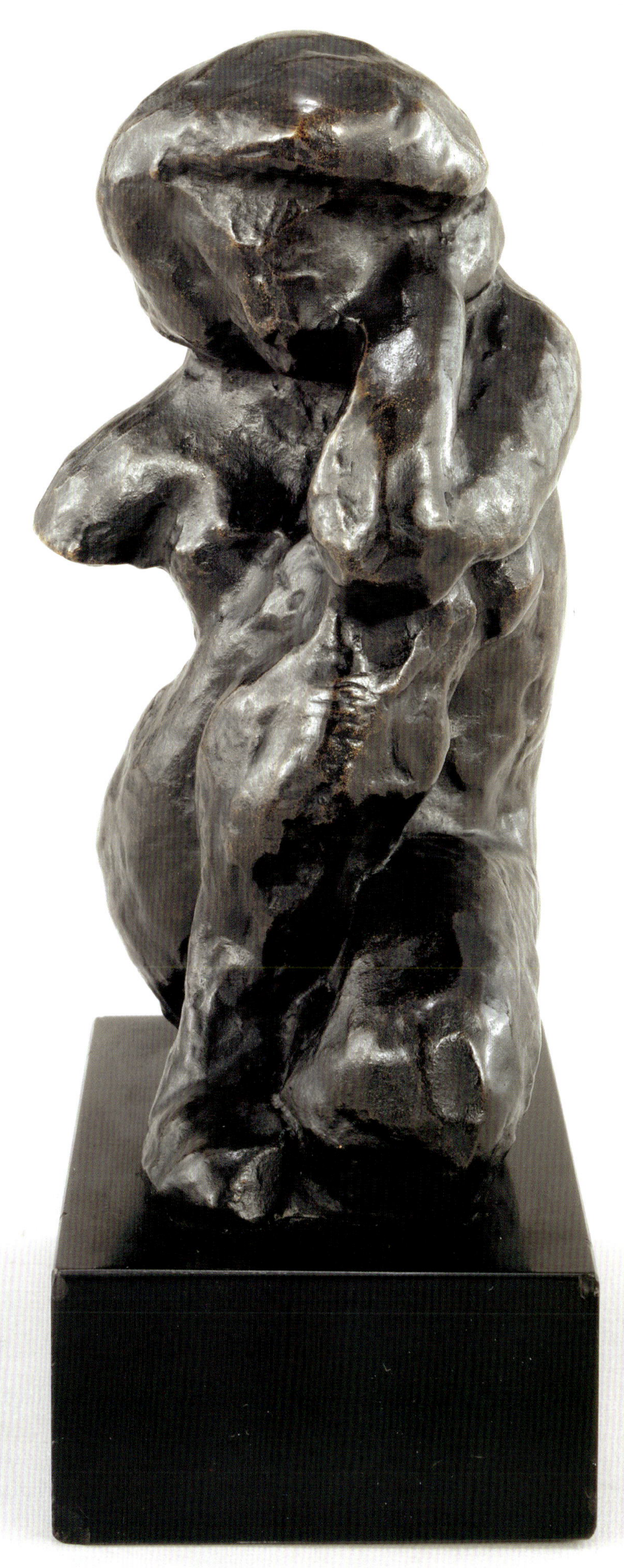

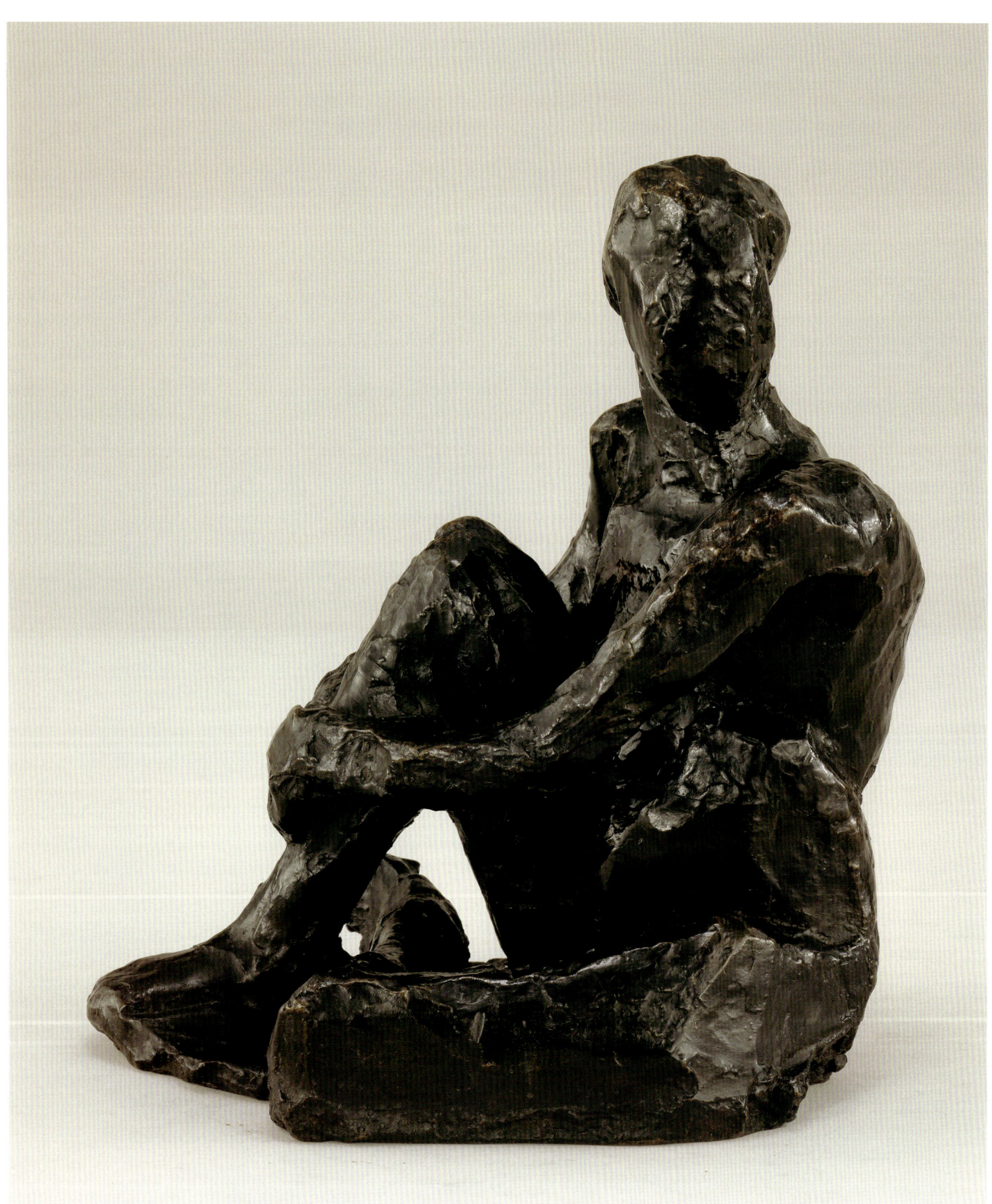

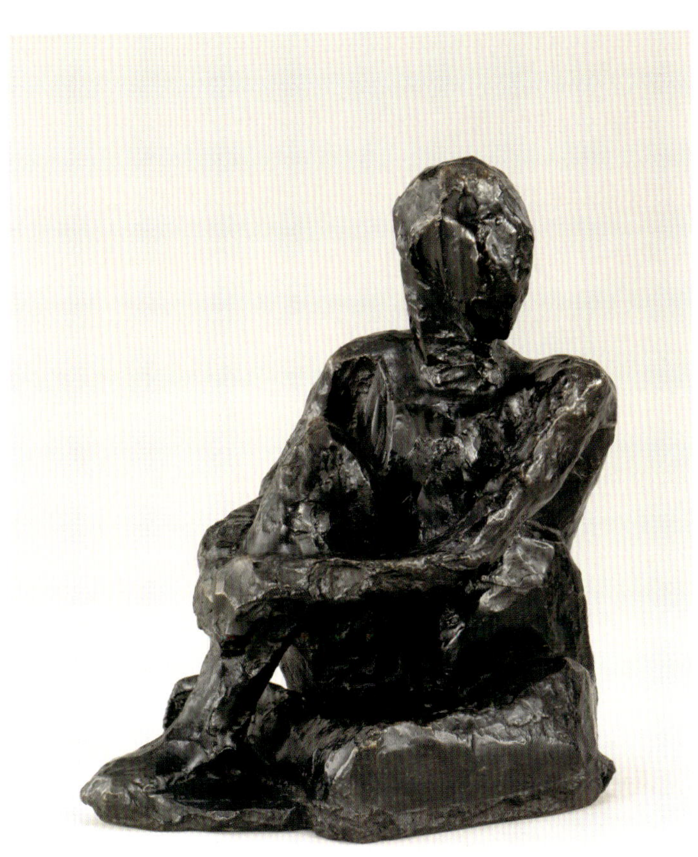

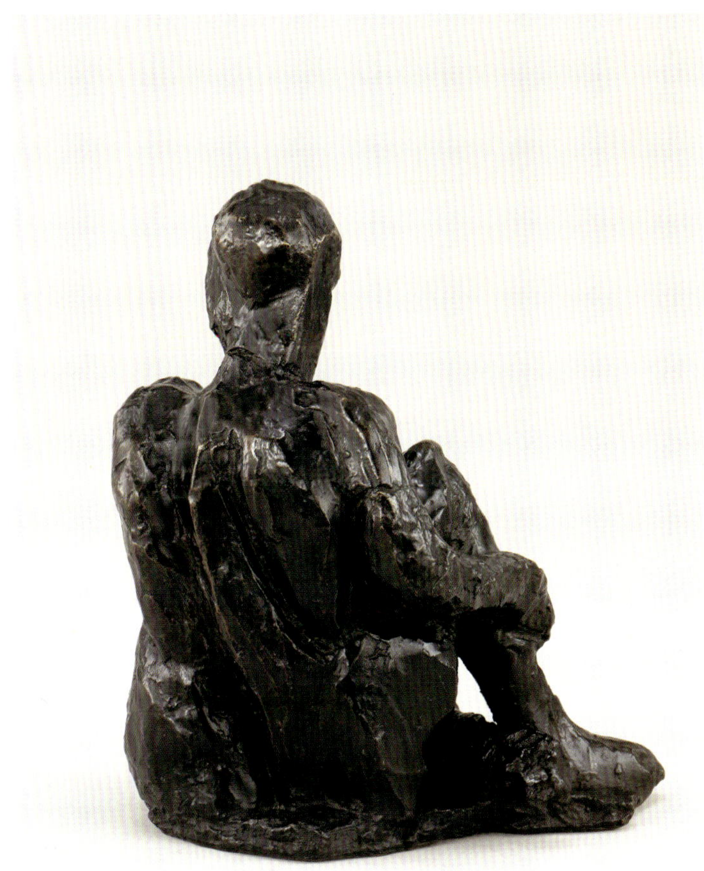

Henri Matisse, *Seated Nude Clasping Her Right Leg,* 1918. Bronze

The Baltimore Museum of Art, The Cone Collection, formed by Dr. Claribel Cone and Miss Etta Cone of Baltimore, Maryland. Cat. 68

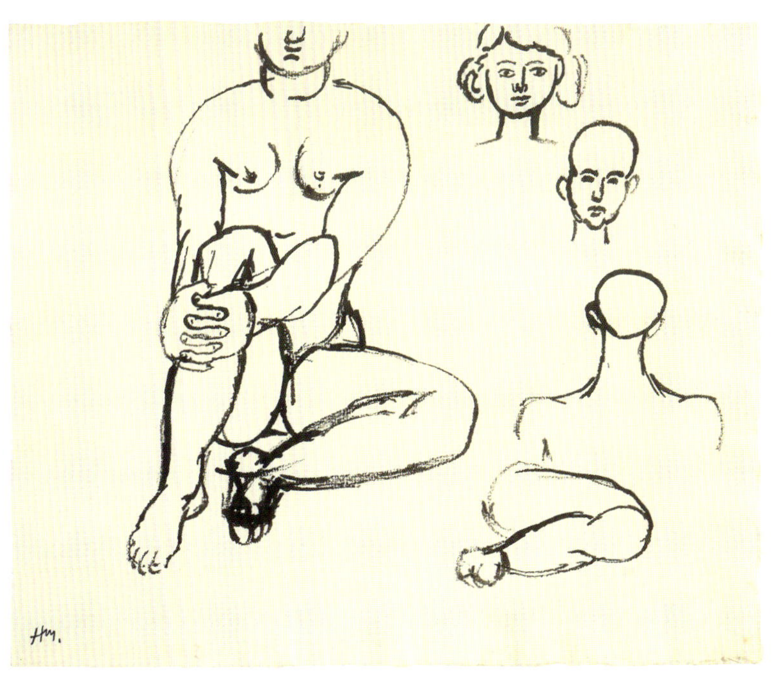

Henri Matisse, *Study, Heads and a Figure,* 1909 Reed pen and ink

Pierre and Maria-Gaetana Matisse Foundation Collection. Cat. 69

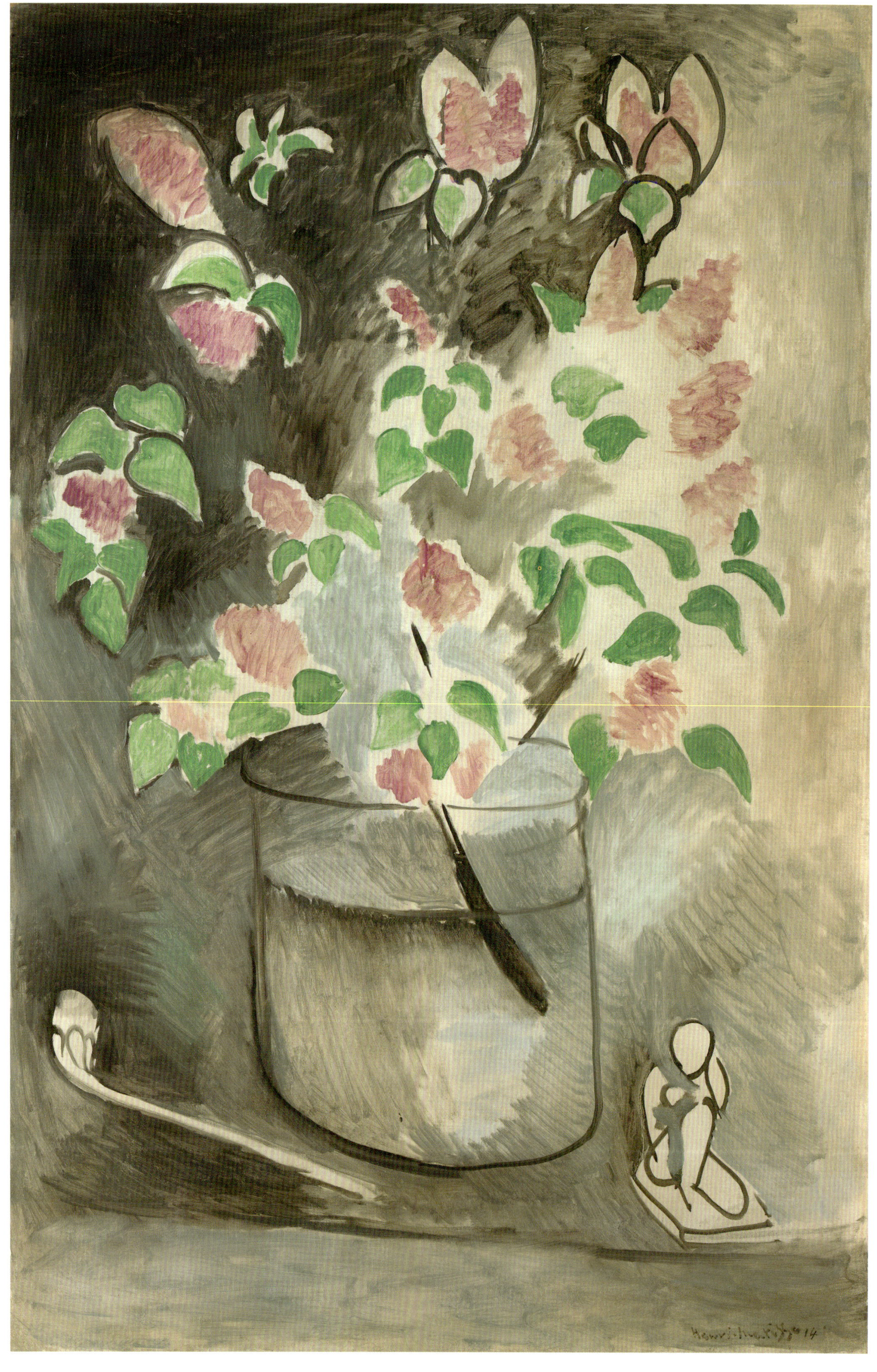

Henri Matisse, *The Branch of Lilac,* 1914
Oil on canvas
The Metropolitan Museum of Art, New York; The Pierre and Maria-Gaetana Matisse Collection, 2002. Cat. 70

Henri Matisse, *Seated Figure on a Decorative Background,* 1925–1926. Charcoal with stumping and erasing
Private collection, New York. Cat. 71

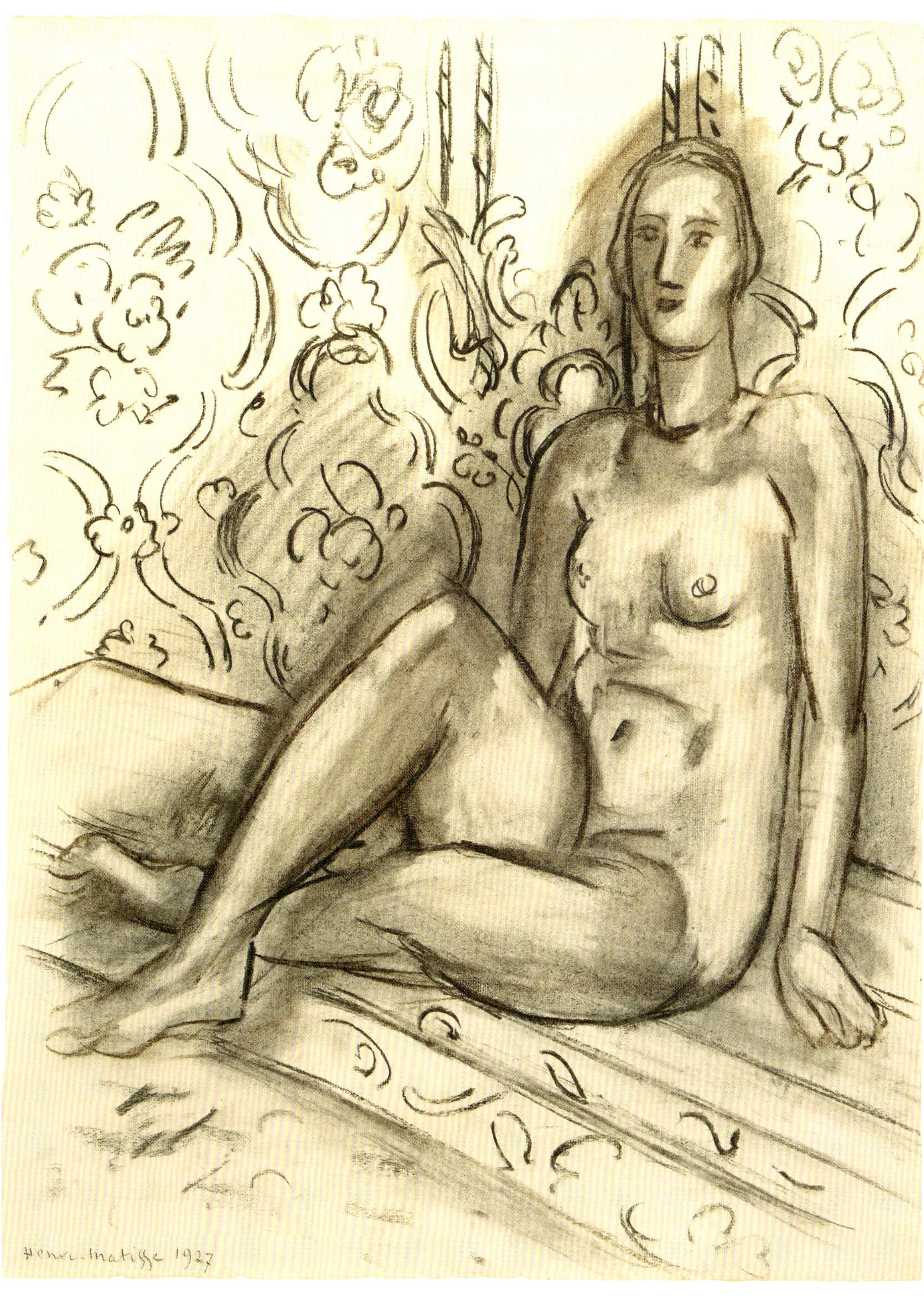

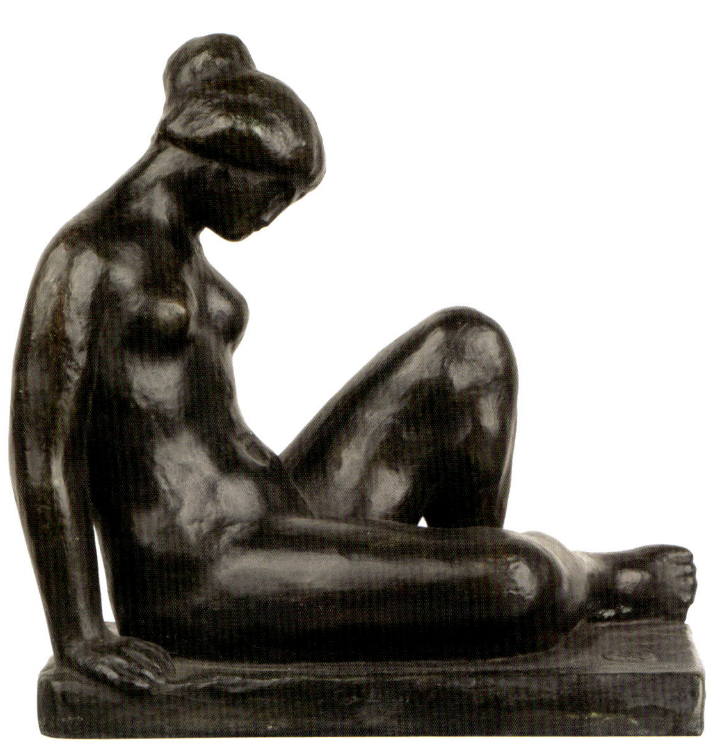

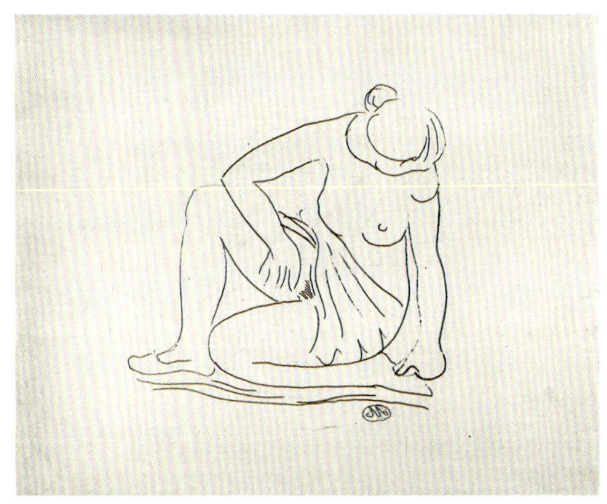

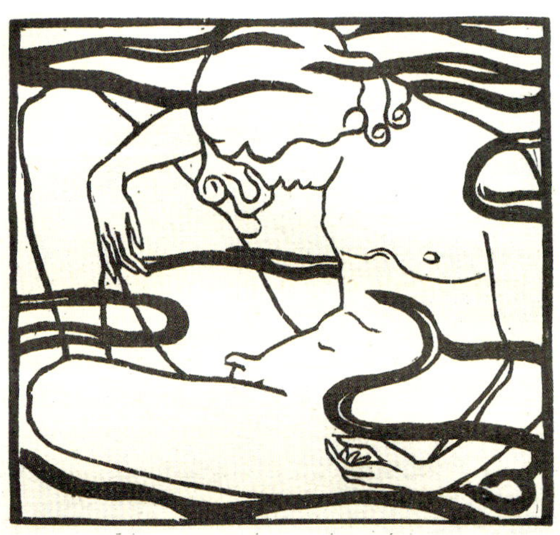

Aristide Maillol, *Study for La Méditerranée,* 1902
Bronze
Museum Boijmans Van Beuningen, Rotterdam. Cat. 157

Aristide Maillol, *Woman Kneeling Down with One Knee Raised,* c. 1926. Etching
Dallas Museum of Art, Foundation for the Arts Collection, Gift of Mrs. Alfred L. Bromberg. Cat. 158

Aristide Maillol, *Hylas disparu dans une fontaine,* from *The Eclogues of Virgil,* 1927. Woodcut
Harry Ransom Center, University of Texas, Austin. Cat. 159

Henri Matisse, *Still Life with Statuette by Henri Laurens,* 1942. Pen and ink

Musée Matisse, Nice; Bequest of Madame Henri Matisse, 1960. Cat. 72

Henri Laurens, *Little Seated Nude,* 1932
Terra-cotta

Musée Matisse, Nice; formerly Collection of Henri Matisse; Bequest of Madame Henri Matisse, 1960. Cat. 155

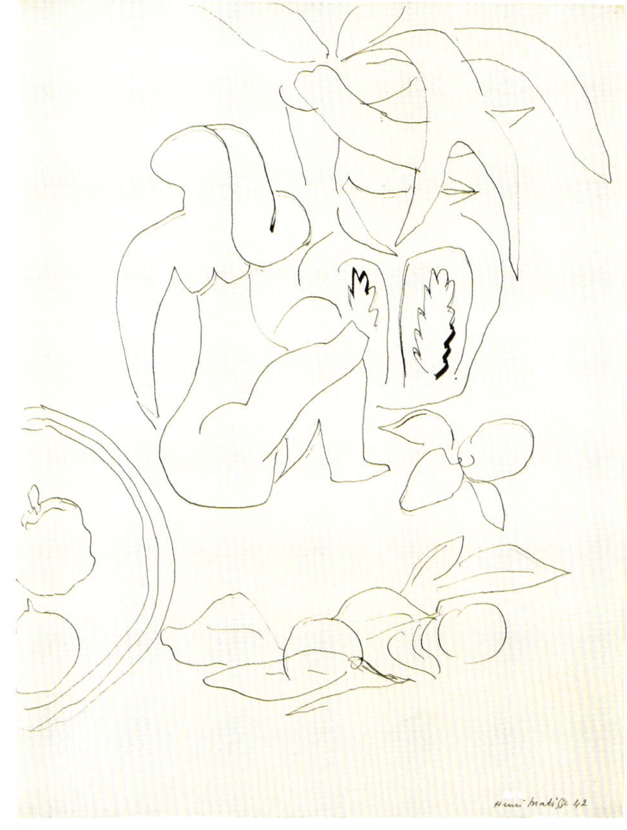

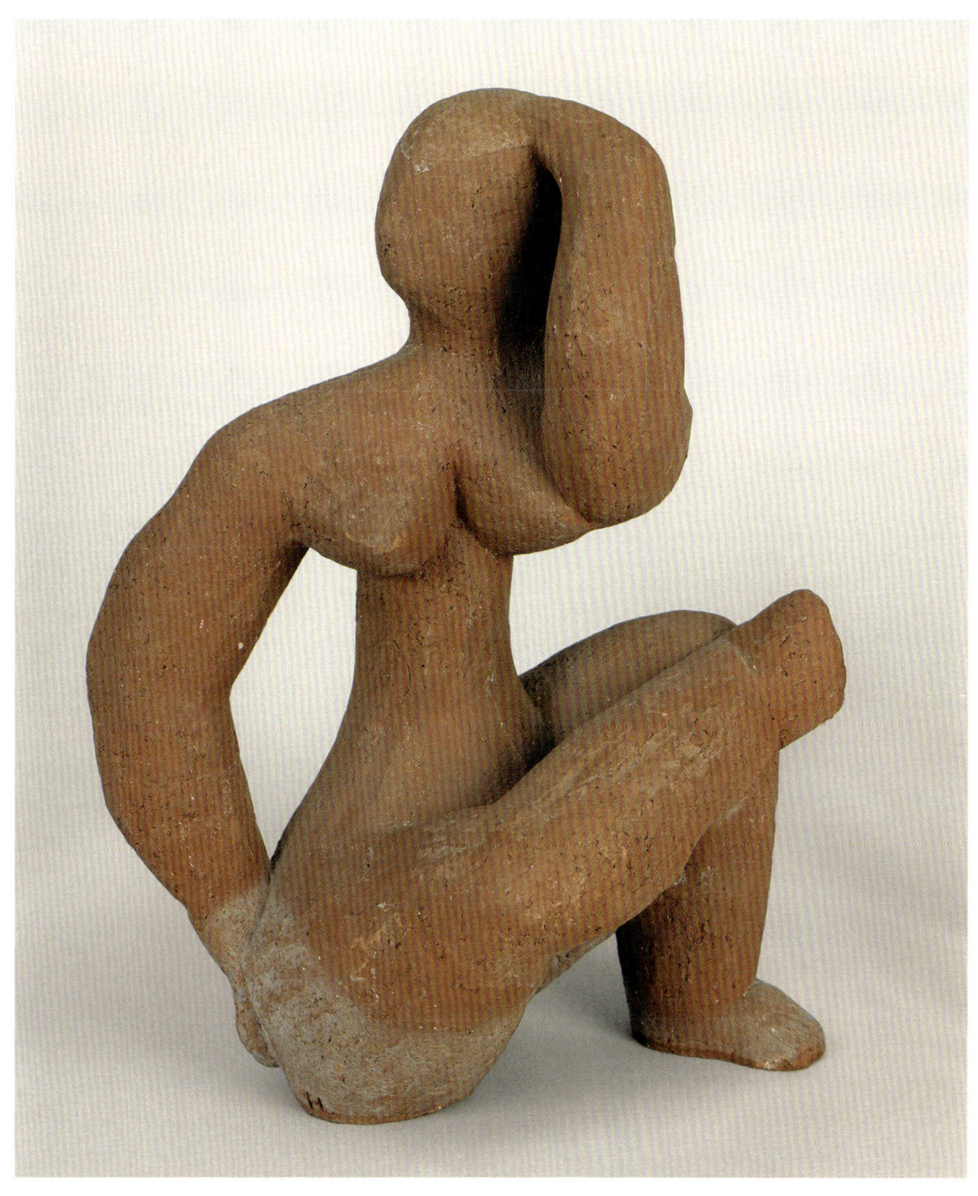

Tiari and Small Heads

Along with larger busts and sculptural portraits, such as the heads of *Jeannette* and *Henriette,* Matisse, throughout his career, made small, intimate studies of heads. These works range from tiny portraits of his children to summary examinations of various models and more abstract distillations of cranial forms. All of them reflect the artist's sensitivity to the unique characters of the models and attest to his careful consideration of the head or bust as a composition of volumes and masses.

The early sculptural heads, such as *Small Head with Comb* and *Head with Necklace,* are spontaneous and playful. Matisse lovingly modeled the tiny facial features and earnest expression of *Small Head with Comb,* yet seems more interested in harmonizing the relationship between the two most prominent elements, the voluminous cap of hair and the solid, round head that peers from beneath it. These two masses fit together like a ball and socket, the ears accentuated to help carry and balance the seemingly weighty coiffure. In *Head with Necklace,* Matisse composes the bust into a sequence of complementary forms and masses: the width of the hair matching the spread of the shoulders; the curve of the necklace reflecting the incised orbitals of the eye sockets; the softly modeled facial features leading fluidly up to the rolls of hair. As Michael Mezzatesta has remarked: "The small scale of the head favored experimentation as well as the quick and economical exploration of his ideas. The simplicity of the overall form and the informality of the modeling give it the freshness of a child's work. This quality is especially evident in the necklace draped over the shoulders, just as one of Matisse's children might have done."[1]

In *Tiari,* Matisse returned to the intimate scale and playfulness of the earlier heads, but now raised to a pinnacle of formal purity. Modeled shortly after his return from a trip to the South Seas, the sculpture presents a clever elision of the human and the floral. The shapes of the nose, head, and hair are reduced to suggest the petals, stems, and leaves of the *tiari* or Tahitian gardenia. In a slightly surrealist touch, Matisse added a real necklace to the first cast of the sculpture, "as if to stress even more the play between floral and human and between abstraction and reality."[2] The bulbous forms of the head in *Tiari* recall the artist's earlier busts, particularly *Jeannette III–V,* and the stylization and surface refinement reflect later developments to be seen in *Henriette I–III.* The surface of *Tiari* is unusually smooth for Matisse, perhaps reflecting the fleeting influence of Brancusi, an influence also to be detected, possibly, in the heads' rounded, abstracted shapes.

JM

Notes

1. Mezzatesta 1984, 67.
2. Nash 1987, 173.

Henri Matisse, *Head with Necklace,* 1907. Bronze

Raymond and Patsy Nasher Collection, Dallas. Cat. 75

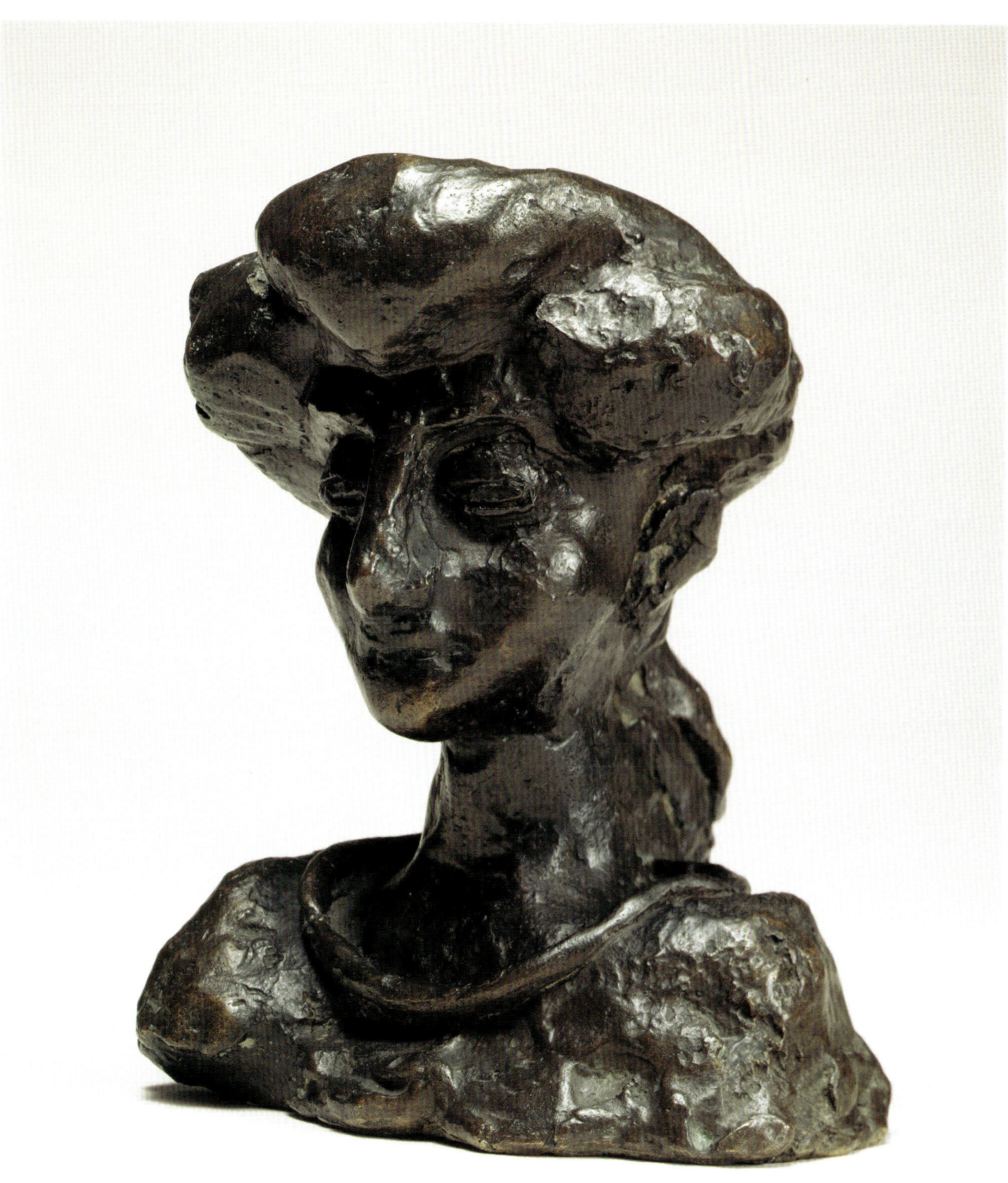

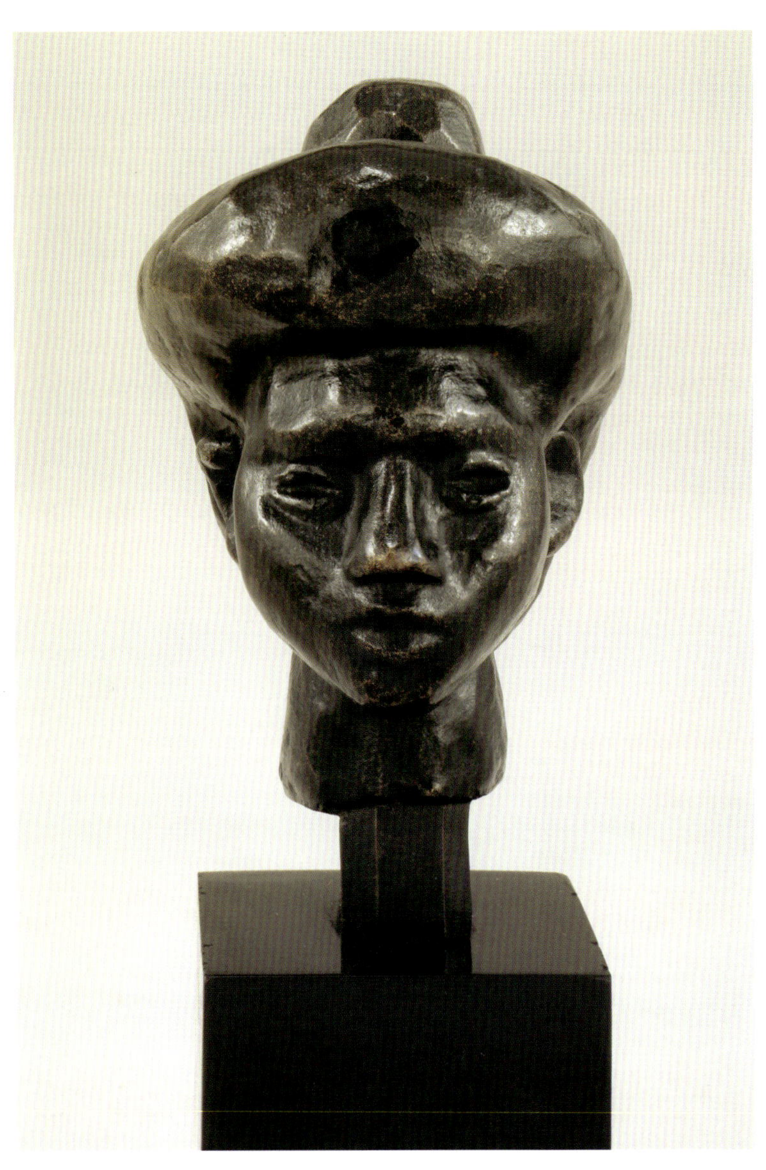

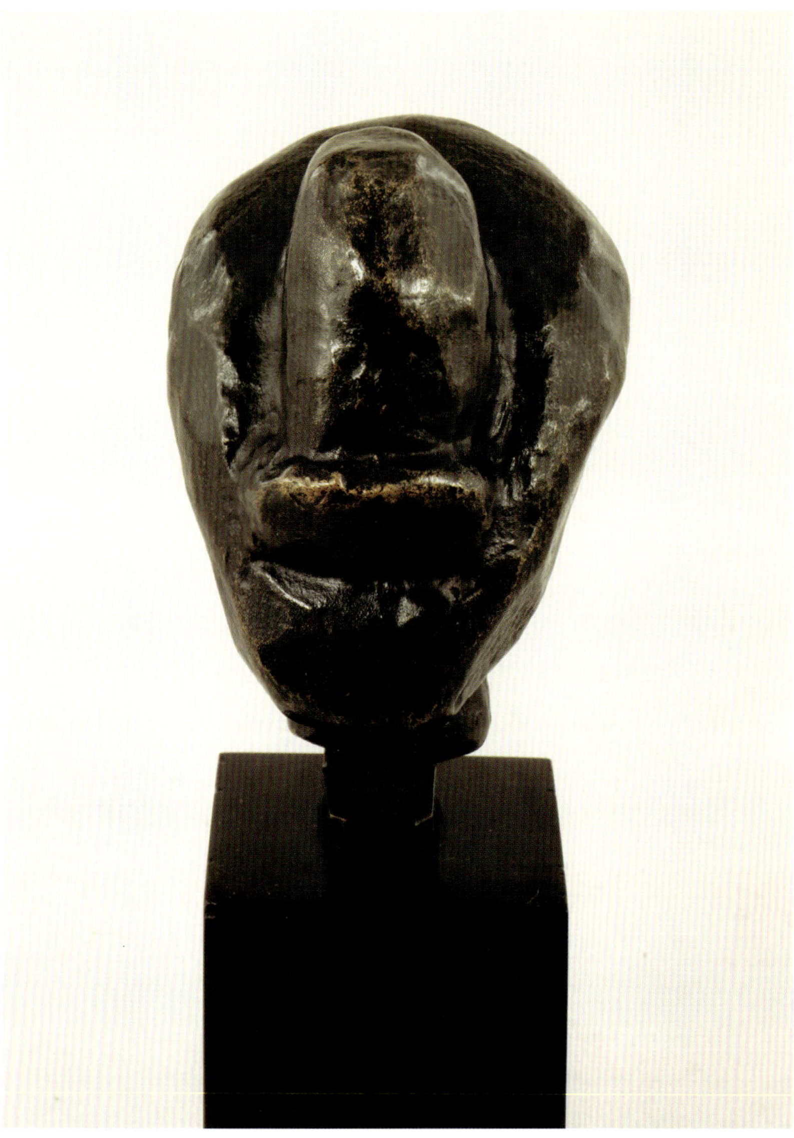

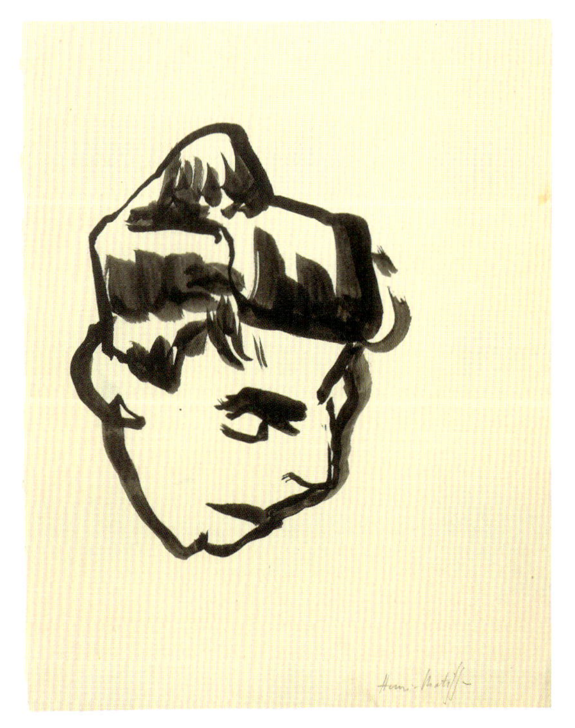

Henri Matisse, *Small Head with Comb,* 1907

Bronze

The Baltimore Museum of Art, The Cone Collection, formed by Dr. Claribel Cone and Miss Etta Cone of Baltimore, Maryland. Cat. 73

Henri Matisse, *Head of a Woman,* c. 1900

Brush and ink

Pierre and Maria-Gaetana Matisse Foundation Collection. Cat. 79

Henri Matisse, *Tiari,* 1930. Bronze

Raymond and Patsy Nasher Collection, Dallas. Cat. 77

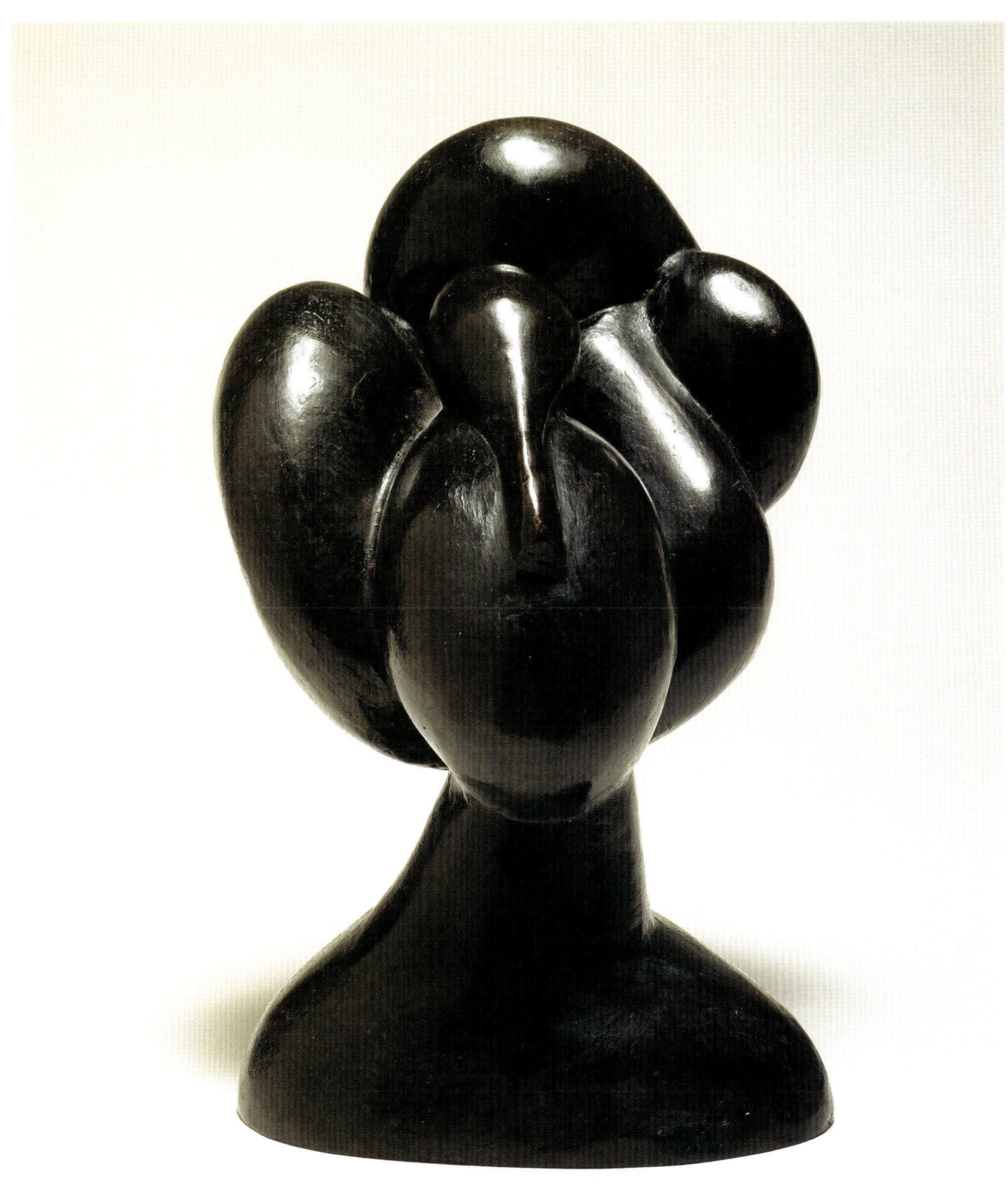

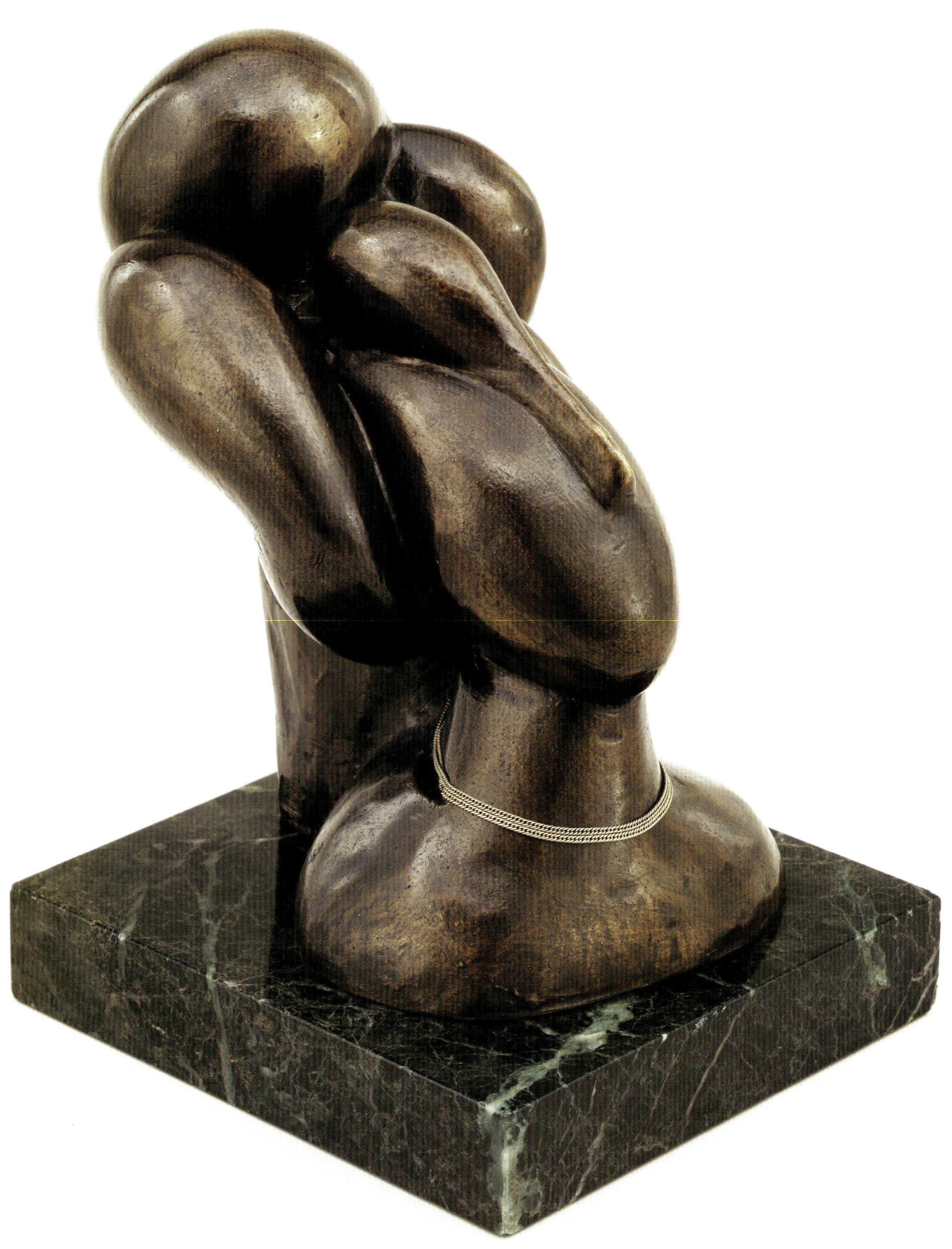

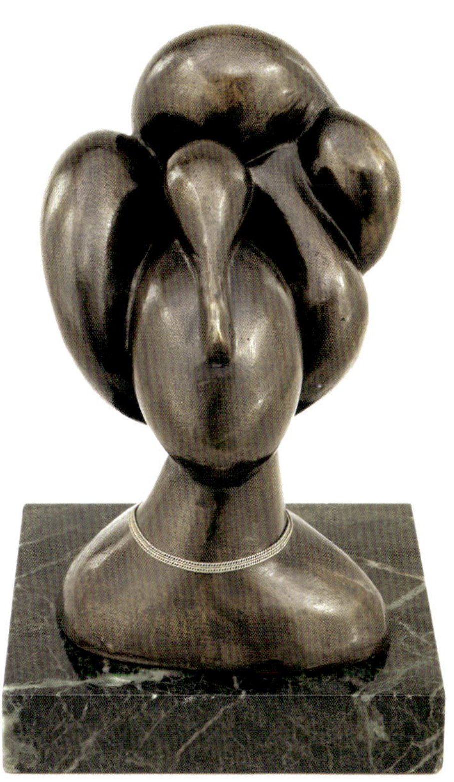
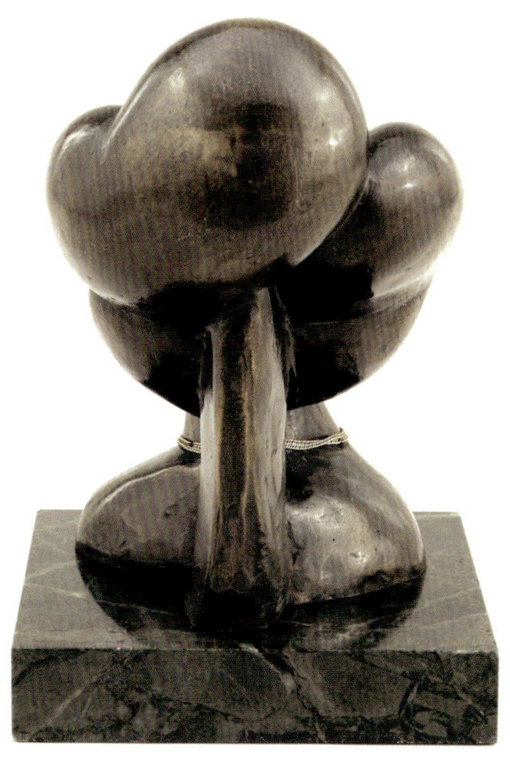

Henri Matisse, *Tiari (with Necklace),* 1930

Bronze with gold and silver necklace

The Baltimore Museum of Art, The Cone Collection, formed by Dr. Claribel Cone and Miss Etta Cone of Baltimore, Maryland. Cat. 78

Jeannette

The five heads of *Jeannette* are often cited as one of the greatest achievements of Matisse's work as a sculptor. Their stylistic range and creative bravado are unparalleled in his previous three-dimensional work. They are also illustrative of the artist's working process in sculpture as a whole. Matisse produced the *Jeannette*s independently over a period of three years, returning to the subject numerous times and refining or completely re-conceiving it, sometimes using a plaster cast of the previous head as the starting point for the next. Like the *Back*s, the *Jeannette* heads represent a serial examination of a single subject, each one becoming progressively more abstract. Also like the *Back*s, these heads were not planned as a series but developed as a natural outgrowth of the artist's investigation of increasingly abstract modes of representation.

The group begins with *Jeannette I,* a naturalistic portrait of Jeanne Vaderin, who also served as the model for the painting *Girl with Tulips* (1910). The bust faithfully renders features—pointy chin, prominent nose, heavy-lidded eyes, strongly defined brow, and voluminous cap of hair—that will help to identify the model through the series even as her visage becomes ever more abstract and distorted. Matisse's investigation here of the head as a sculptural form is similar to earlier, smaller heads such as *Head with Necklace* and *Small Head with Comb.* Over the previous decade Matisse had worked to move away from late nineteenth-century sculptural traditions, but here the modeling recalls his earliest sculptural experiments and their debt to Rodin. With each successive reconsideration of Jeannette's head, Matisse would move farther away from those conventions.

Although Matisse modeled *Jeannette II* from a cast of its predecessor, he drastically altered the presentation, smoothing and simplifying the features and reworking the composition with a knife. He cut away the neck from the base of the chin to the underside of the crown of hair, sliced off the topknot of her *chignon,* and excised a portion of the head at the back on the left side. He also removed the ear on the left side of the head and refashioned the right ear into a small circular appendage—all changes that isolate the face and give the work the fragmented quality of an ancient bust.[1]

Jeannette III represents a wholly new conception of the head. Matisse modeled the sculpture anew with clay, working from memory and with a liberated creativity. With the addition of the breastplate and classical socle, or stand, Matisse reconstructs the composition as a vertical arrangement of related masses. The features have been simplified and exaggerated: the eyes are enlarged and bulge behind their thick lids; the nose is forceful and aquiline; the chin juts forward to culminate in a sharp point. The hair, which appeared as a uniform ring in the first two *Jeannette*s has been re-imagined as a series of bulbous, hand-sized clumps. Many observers, Alfred Barr the first among them, note the tactile or haptic qualities of *Jeannette III,* so unlike the primarily optic or visual rendering of the model in *Jeannette I;* the difference, as William Tucker described it, between the grasped and the seen.[2] Matisse created the first *Jeannette* head by looking at his model, studying her features, and attempting to create a faithful likeness that also expressed something of how he saw and felt about her. *Jeannette III* appears to be based on a more tactile engagement with form, the parts modeled in graspable, hand-sized masses.

Jeannette IV is a refinement of *Jeannette III,* the face narrowed, the cheeks carved out, the nose and front prow of hair accentuated, the eyes reduced to their massive lids. But *Jeannette V* is a severe and radical reconstruction of the sculpture. Starting from a cast of *Jeannette III,* Matisse drastically cut away at the composition, hacking off the voluminous bulbs of hair, carving the orbital of the eyes deeply and far back on the sides of the head to accentuate the jutting nose and forehead, and planing flat the left eye. The brutal immediacy of the sculpture evokes the African figures that Matisse held in such high esteem, but, as many scholars have noted, also signifies the experimental and liberating influence of cubism. The radical geometric style developed by Picasso and Braque freed Western art from the obligation of natural representation and opened the possibility of composition solely according to the dictates of formal construction and the artist's creativity. Although decidedly not a cubist sculpture, *Jeannette V* exhibits the influence of cubism in the dissection of its volume into a series of separate but related parts. Many have noted that an exhibition of Matisse's sculpture at Galerie Pierre in 1930 intrigued Picasso, perhaps encouraging him to return to sculpture. In 1931 at his farmhouse in Boisgeloup, Picasso would produce a series of his own, distinctly erotic portraits, such as *Head of a Woman,* of his young lover, Marie-Thérèse Walter; the bulbous, appended forms bearing a striking formal connection to three-dimensional works by Matisse.

The simplicity and austerity achieved in *Jeannette V* extended into his paintings. In works such as *Portrait of Sarah Stein* and *The Italian Woman,* Matisse rendered the features of the models as a series of simple lines and planes. In both portraits, the side of the nose, orbital of the eye, and brow are again joined into a single line; the eyes and mouth are expressed as simple lozenge shapes, and the face and hair are defined as broad planes of contrasting tones.

JM

NOTES

1. Mezzatesta 1984, 90.

2. Tucker 1975, 62–66.

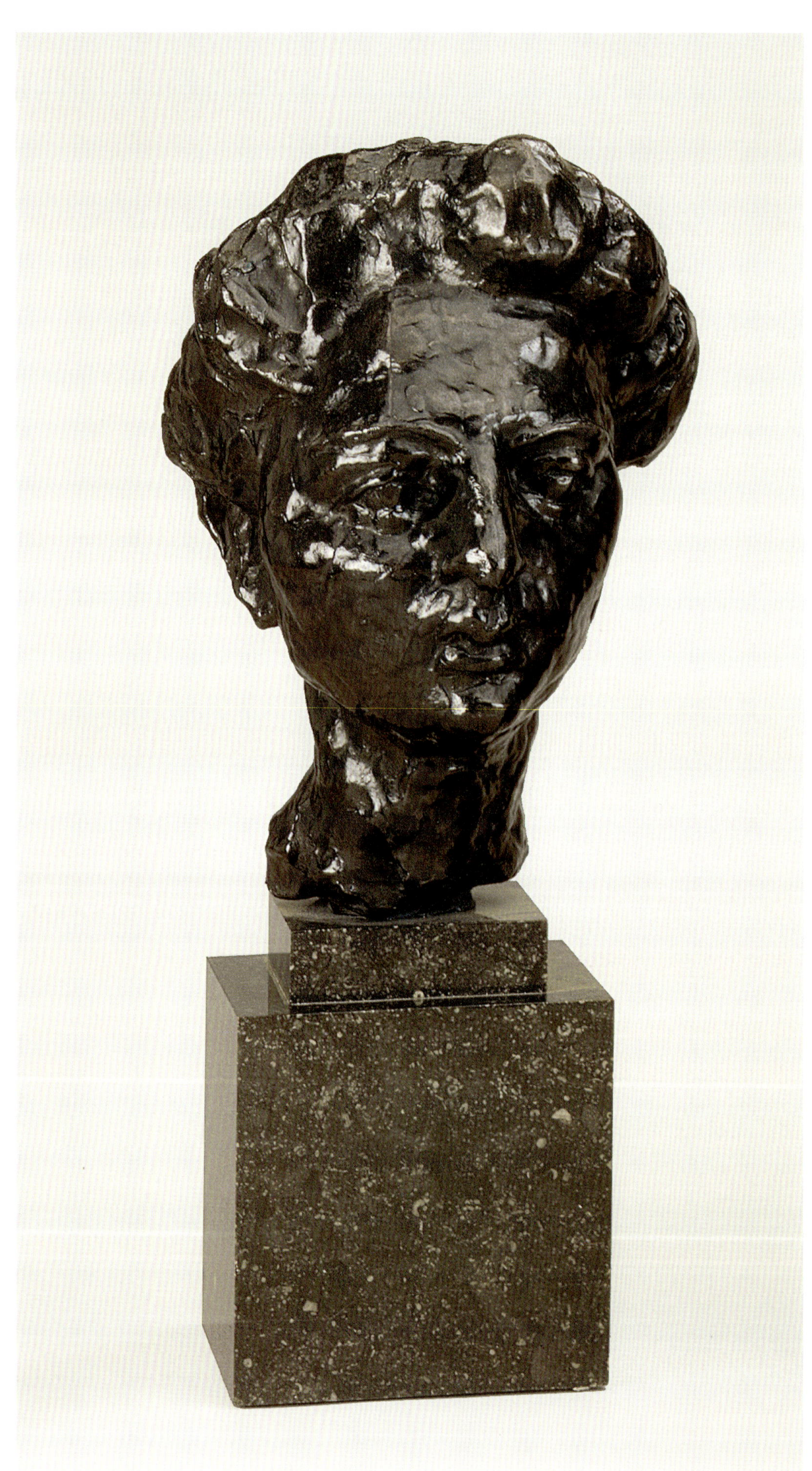

Henri Matisse, *Jeannette I,* 1910. Bronze

Los Angeles County Museum of Art, Gift of the Art Museum Council in memory of Penelope Rigby. Cat. 80

Henri Matisse, *Jeannette II,* 1910. Bronze

Los Angeles County Museum of Art, Gift of the Art Museum Council in memory of Penelope Rigby. Cat. 82

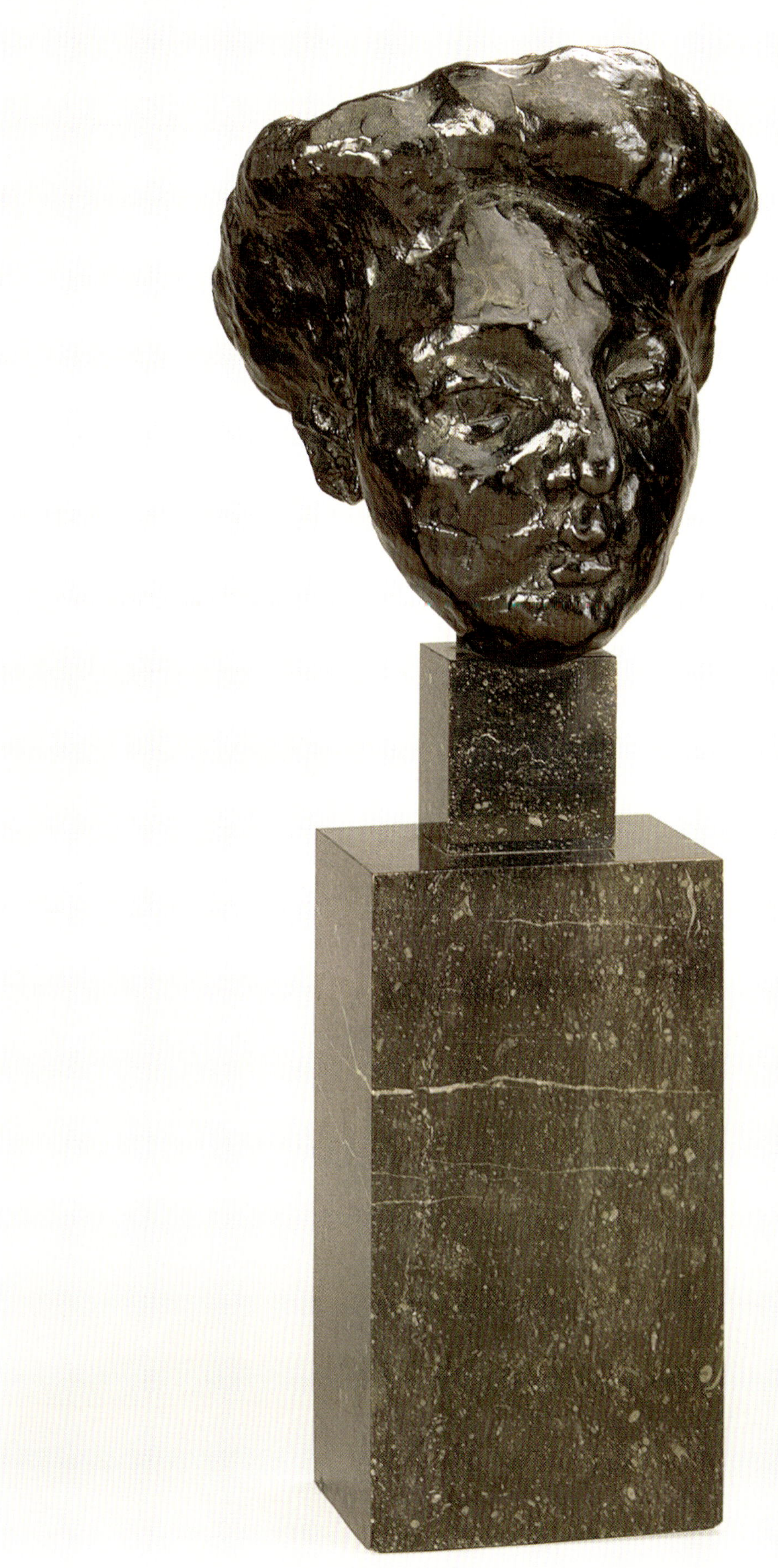

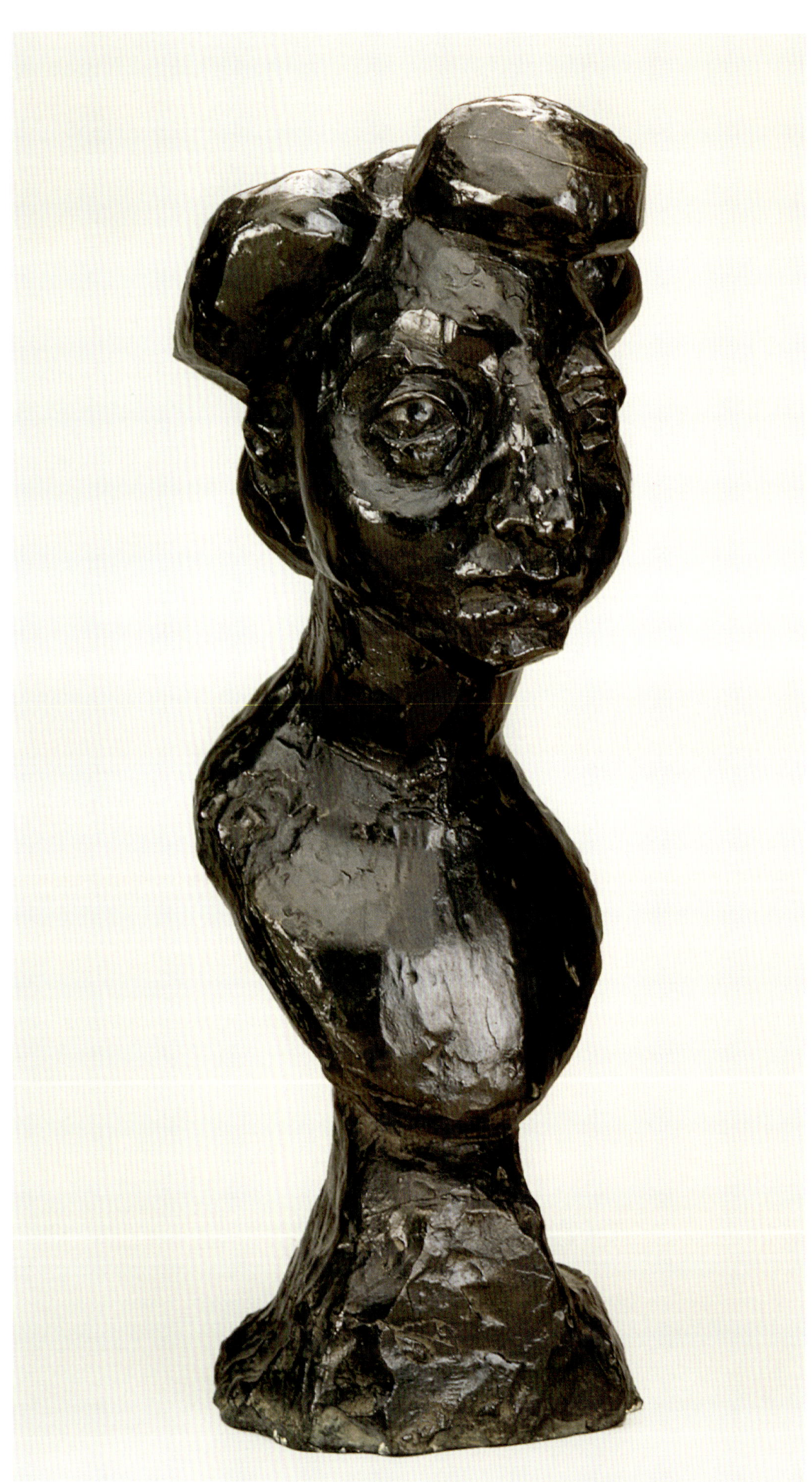

Henri Matisse, *Jeannette III,* 1911. Bronze

Los Angeles County Museum of Art, Gift of the Art Museum Council in memory of Penelope Rigby. Cat. 84

Henri Matisse, *Jeannette IV,* 1912. Bronze

Los Angeles County Museum of Art, Gift of the Art Museum Council in memory of Penelope Rigby. Cat. 86

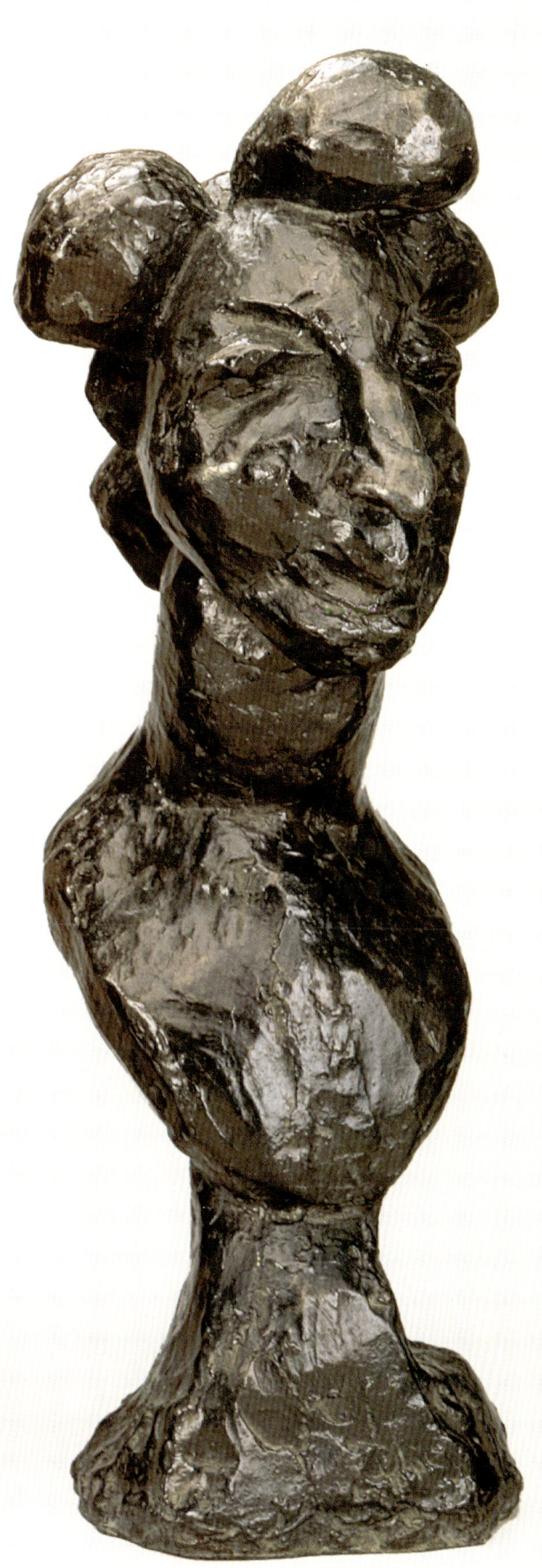

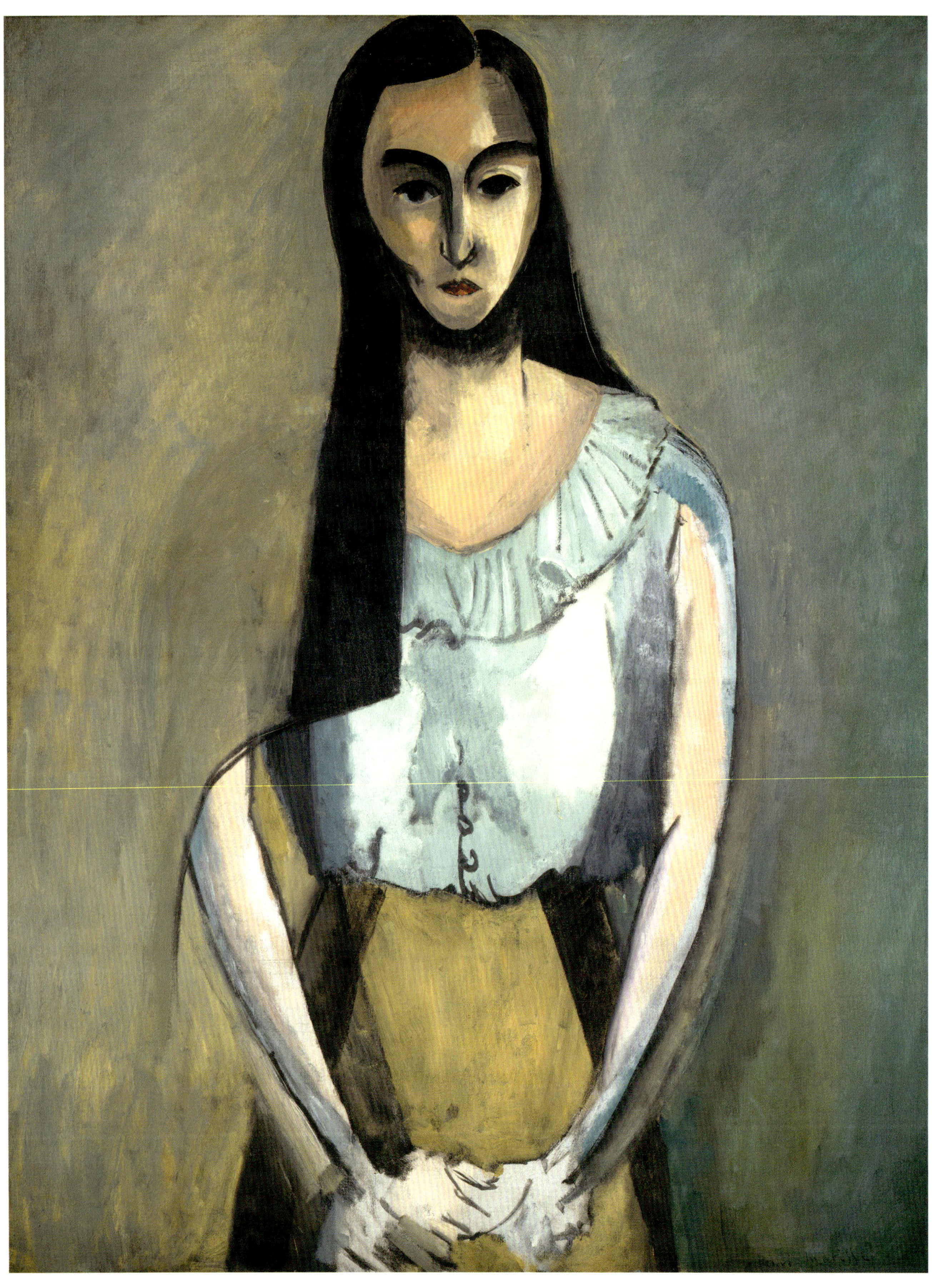

Henri Matisse, *The Italian Woman,* 1916

Oil on canvas

Solomon R. Guggenheim Museum, New York; by exchange, 1982. Cat. 91

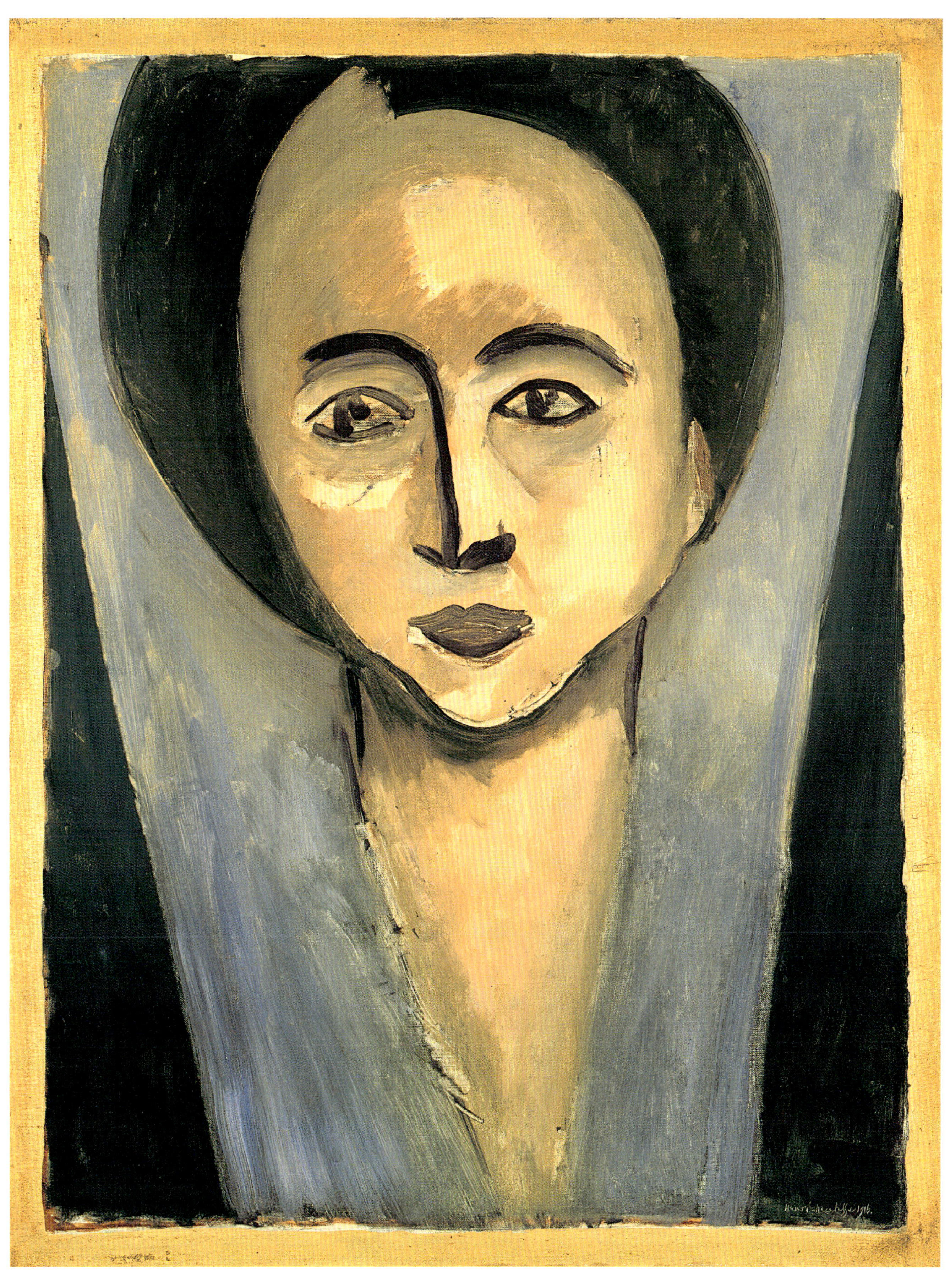

Henri Matisse, *Portrait of Sarah Stein,* 1916

Oil on canvas

San Francisco Museum of Modern Art, Sarah and Michael Stein Memorial Collection, Gift of Elise S. Haas. Cat. 90

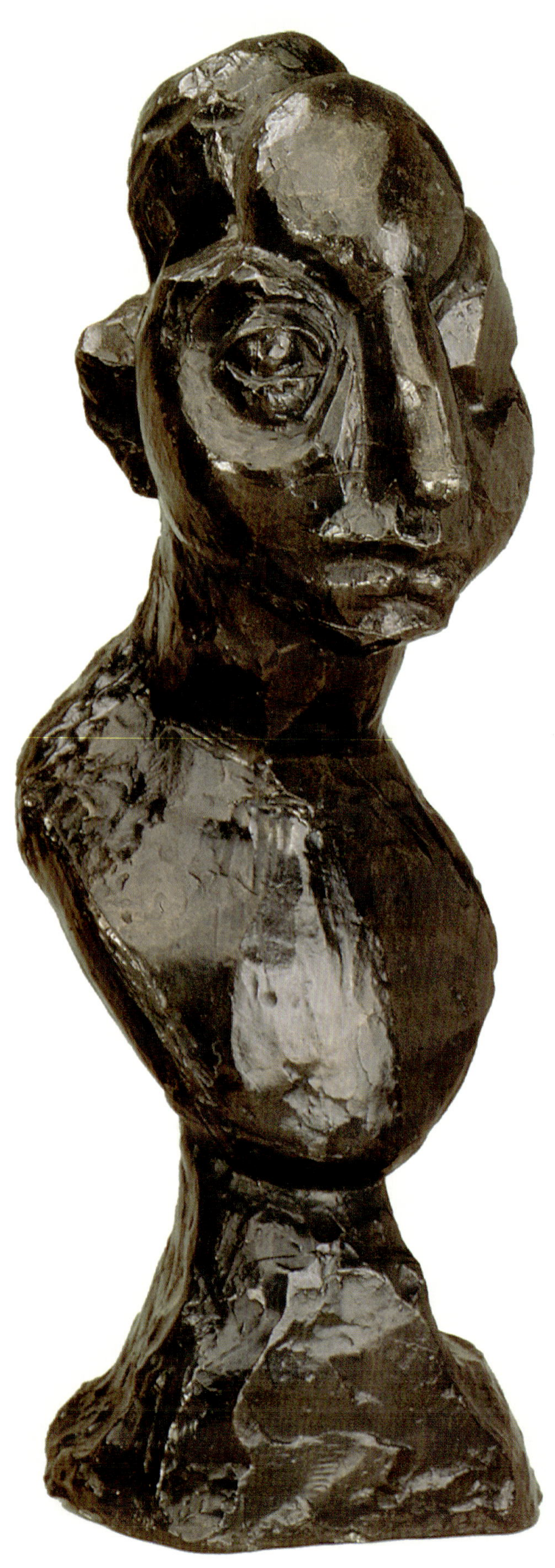

Henri Matisse, *Jeannette V,* 1913. Bronze

Los Angeles County Museum of Art, Gift of the Art Museum Council in memory of Penelope Rigby. Cat. 88

Pablo Picasso, *Head of a Woman,* 1931. Bronze

Raymond and Patsy Nasher Collection, Dallas. Cat. 160

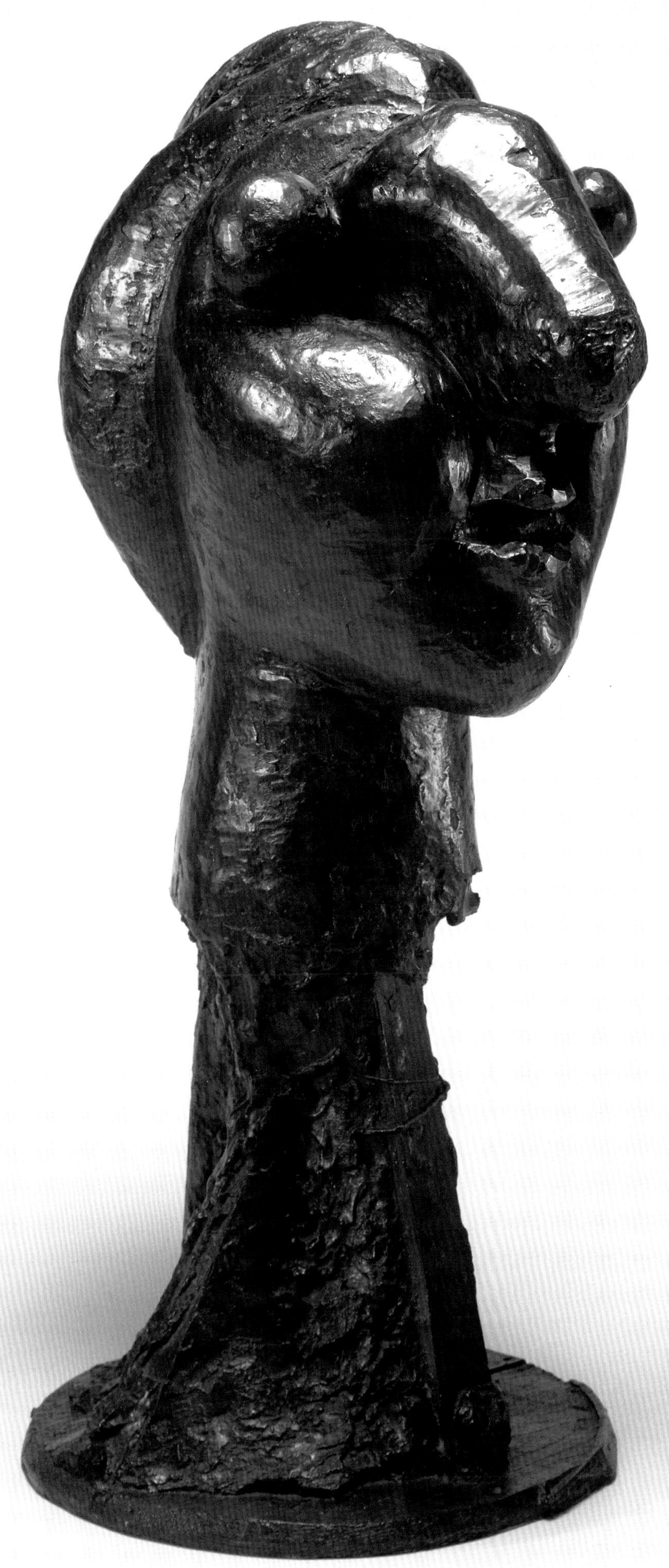

Henriette

During the seven-year period in which Matisse worked on his *Large Seated Nude,* he also made three sculpted heads of Henriette Darricarrère, the model for that important work. Each is remarkably different in character. The first, *Henriette I,* made in 1925, comes closest to being a true portrait of Darricarrère. Her strong, rounded features and the Olympian calm of her expression are familiar from the *Large Seated Nude* and from the many paintings and drawings Matisse made of her during the 1920s. For Isabelle Monod-Fontaine, "it is almost as though, having drawn and painted innumerable images of her body and having sculpted a synthesis of them all in the *Large Seated Nude,* he wanted to attempt a true portrait that has an intensity which, to my knowledge, he never achieved in a painting."[1] Her features, particularly the nose and lips, are modeled with a sensitive touch, but there is a degree of generalization in the treatment of the head as a whole. The hair is reduced to a kind of helmet, with the barest suggestion of a part, and the neck is cut off just below the jaw line, a truncation that abruptly disassociates the head from any notion of a body. One of the most arresting elements of this sculpture is the lump on the forehead, just above her right brow. According to the reminiscences of Matisse's family, this was what he called a "*pastille,*" or lozenge. The lump of clay, something like a flaw, applied to the clay model at the end of each session served Matisse at the outset of a new modeling session to reengage with the sculpture.[2] His reasons for leaving the *pastille* in place and casting it into the final bronze are unknown, but Ann Boulton describes Matisse's love of the traces of process and mold making, which he often elected to leave visible in the clay and cast into the bronze.[3]

When Matisse returned to the head of Henriette Darricarrère two years later, he seems to have decided to eliminate those qualities of his sitter's physiognomy that marked her as an individual. Instead he accentuated the generalization that was latent in the first version. Darricarrère's high forehead, prominent brow, and deep cleft above the lips remain, but Matisse has radically changed the profile and the shape of the nose, so distinctive in *Henriette I.* The hair is far more articulated than it is in the first sculpture, rendered as a series of smooth ovoid masses that have the effect of distancing the sculpture yet further from a portrait of a flesh-and-blood woman. *Henriette II* bears the alternate title *Large Head,* suggesting not only an estrangement from the individuality of the sitter but also an interest in the head as a kind of monument. Matisse even considered the possibility of displaying this bronze on a marble or granite socle.[4] This degree of formal reduction was characteristic of his sculpture in the later 1920s. The reduction of surface incident to a series of taut, swollen curves reflects contemporary taste for a streamlined aesthetic and calls to mind the work of a younger generation of sculptors, such as Jacques Lipchitz; Monod-Fontaine calls this work "the most dated of the three versions."[5]

Matisse's last engagement with this series, in 1929, brought yet another radical shift in his approach. *Henriette III* was based directly on a plaster cast of *Henriette II,* a serial mode of working that is familiar from the *Madeleine* and the *Back* series.[6] With a fresh clay model, cast from the

Henri Matisse, *Henriette I,* 1925. Bronze

Musée départemental Matisse, Le Cateau-Cambrésis; Gift of Maria-Gaetana Matisse (Pontoise), 1999. Cat. 92

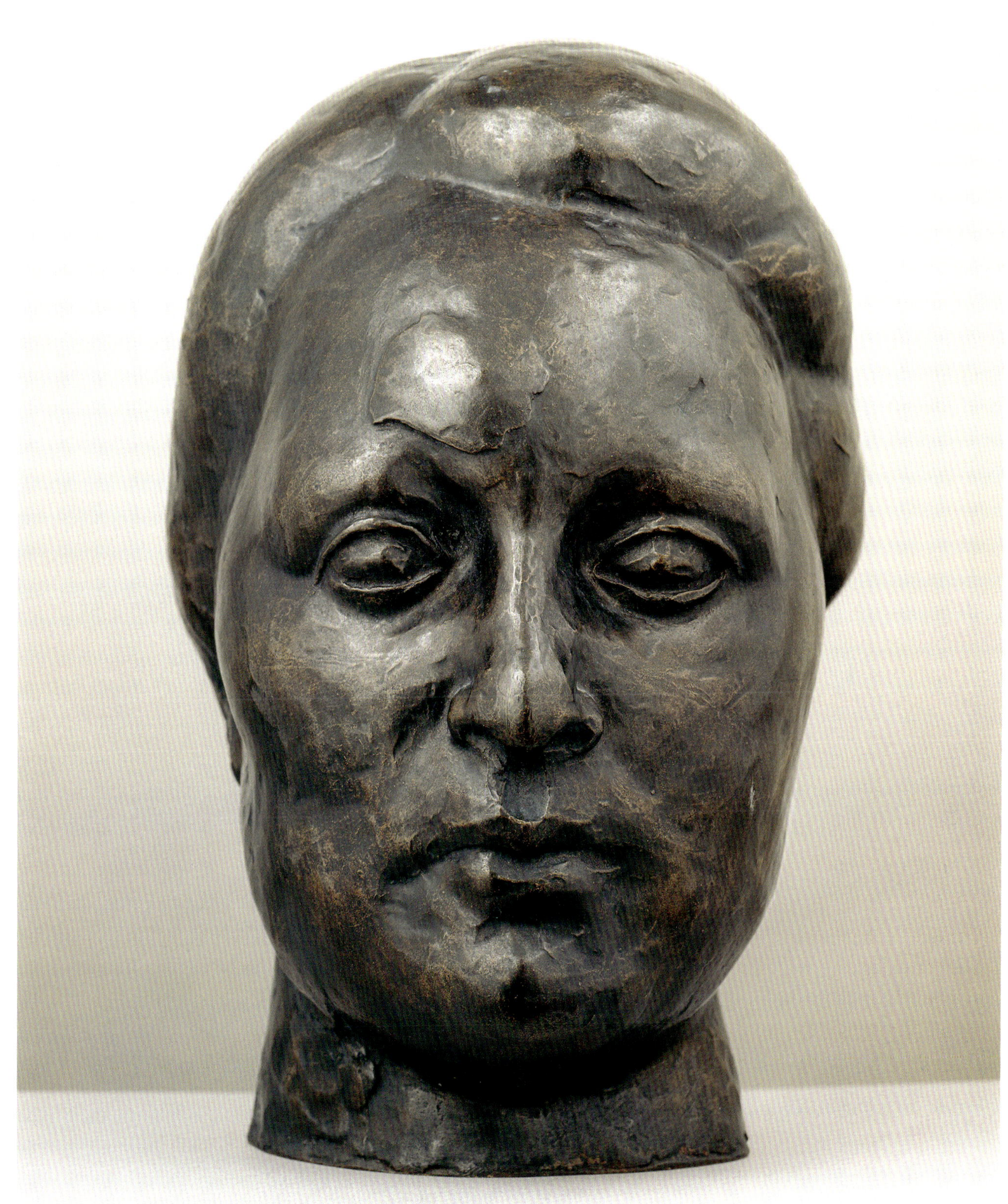

plaster version of the previous sculpture, Matisse set about creating a surface that reflected the touch of sculptor's hands and tools. Whereas the rigorously smooth surface of *Henriette II* had suggested "the heavy coldness of marble," *Henriette III* is unmistakably modeled in clay.[7] As he had in *Jeannette V,* Matisse carves directly into the face, slicing away sections of the chin and jaw. The strong brow of the model becomes a pair of stylized ridges that meet at the bridge of the nose. The eyes are outlined in thin, schematic lines that relate to the linear style he had adopted in his drawings of the period. Darricarrère had ceased modeling for Matisse two years earlier, unable to sustain the physical rigors of the work,[8] and so the changes that he introduced were not, Mezzatesta tells us, "a result of Matisse's direct reaction to the model . . . but rather reflect a reorientation of his own sensibilities. He sought to invigorate the work sculpturally, a process indifferent to the sitter's personality. The large square base which Matisse added to *Henriette III* presents the head in a form reminiscent of medieval head reliquaries and stresses its 'objectness.'"[9]

HMacD

Notes

1. Monod-Fontaine 1984, 38.
2. Elsen 1972, 161.
3. See Ann Boulton's essay in this volume, p. 75.
4. See Matisse, letter to his wife, March 24, 1929, quoted in Duthuit 1997, 386 n.27.
5. Monod-Fontaine 1984, 38.
6. Mezzatesta 1984, 120; see also Boulton.
7. Monod-Fontaine 1984, 38.
8. Spurling 2005, 284, 289–90.
9. Mezzatesta 1984, 122.

Henri Matisse, *Study for Henriette II,* c. 1928
Graphite
Musée départemental Matisse, Le Cateau-Cambrésis,
Gift of Marie Matisse, 1993. Cat. 95

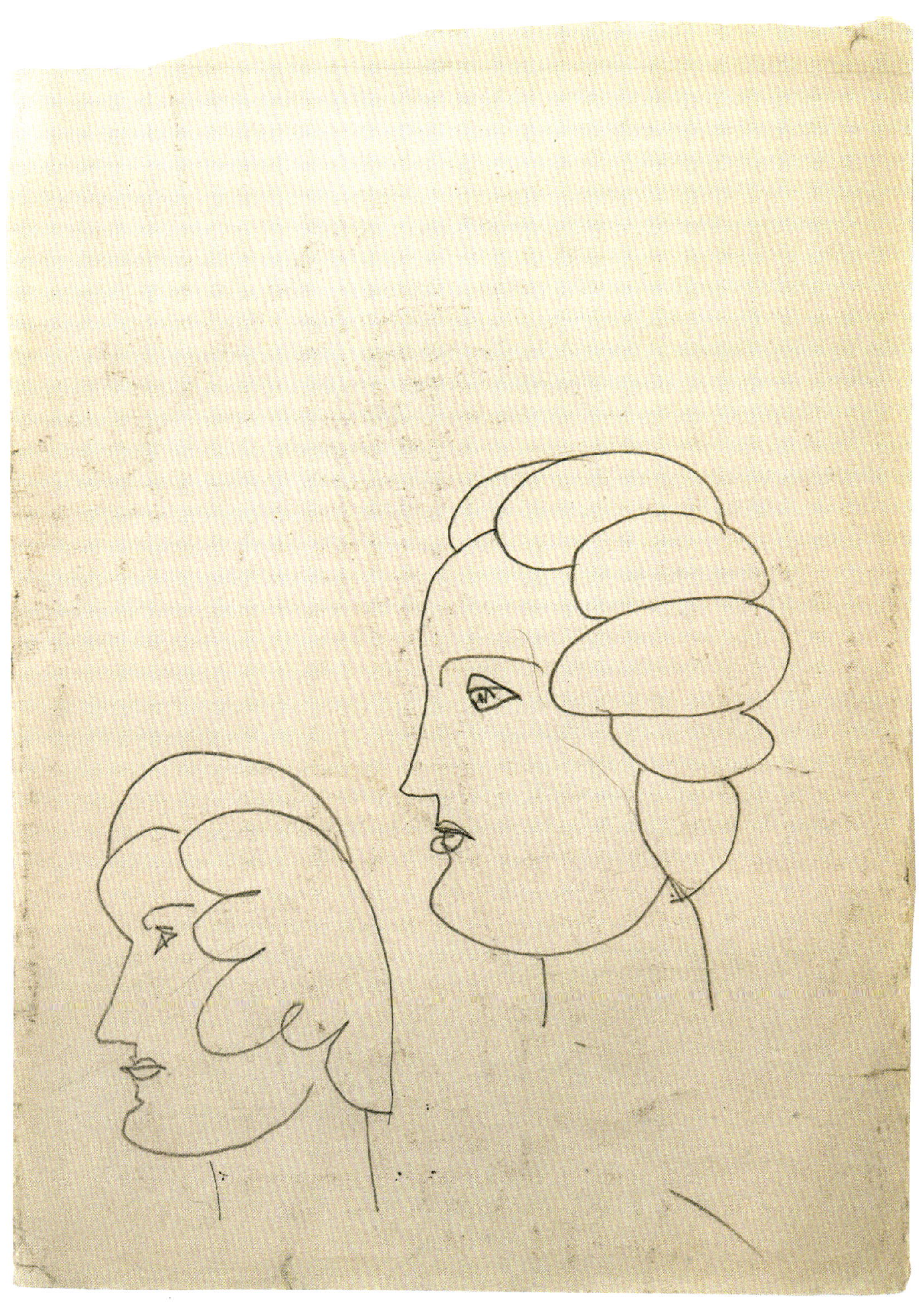

Henri Matisse, *Henriette II,* 1927. Bronze

San Francisco Museum of Modern Art, Bequest of Harriet Lane Levy. Cat. 93

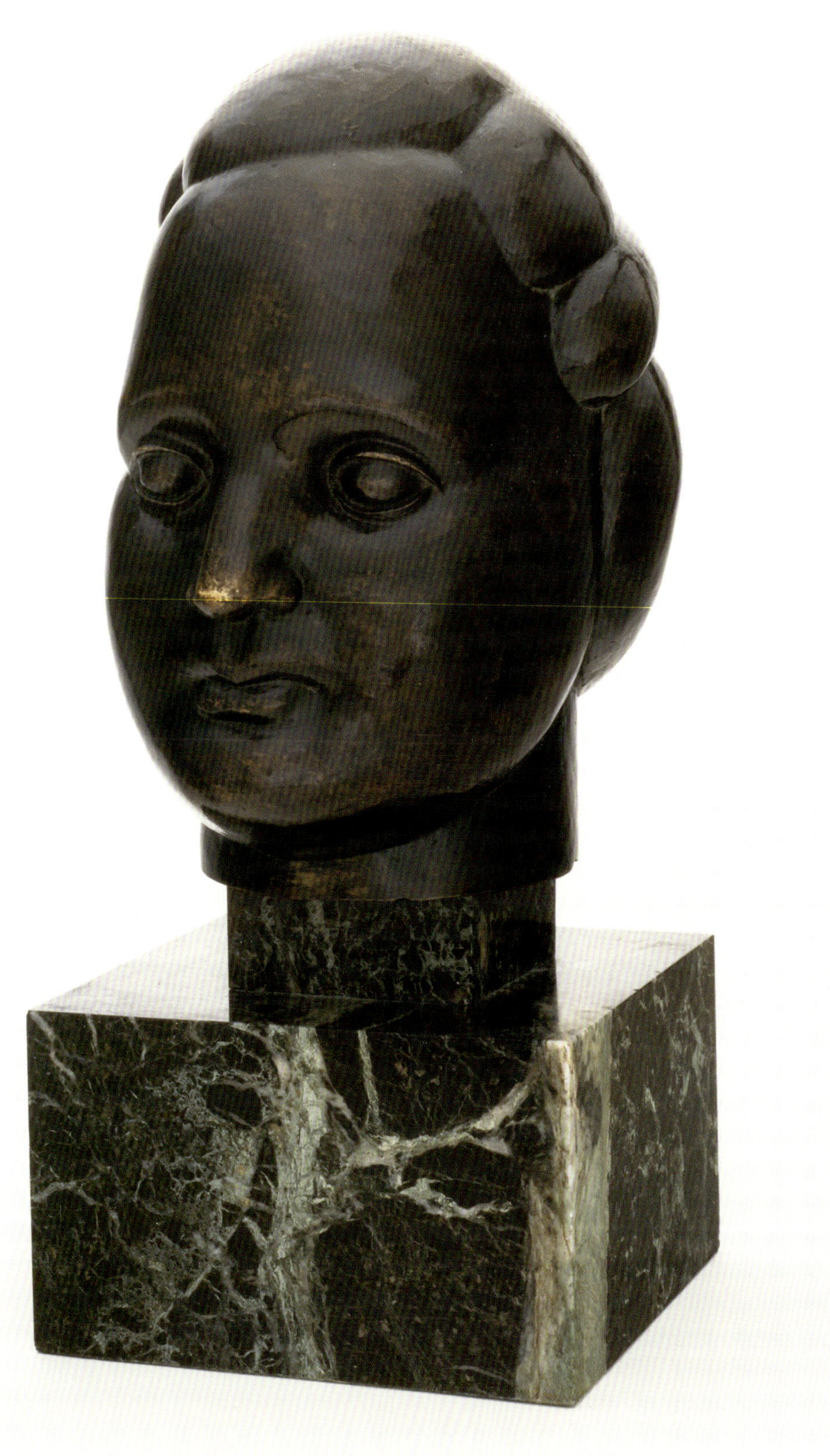

Jacques Lipchitz, *Gertrude Stein,* 1920. Bronze

The Baltimore Museum of Art, The Cone Collection, formed by Dr. Claribel Cone and Miss Etta Cone of Baltimore, Maryland. Cat. 156

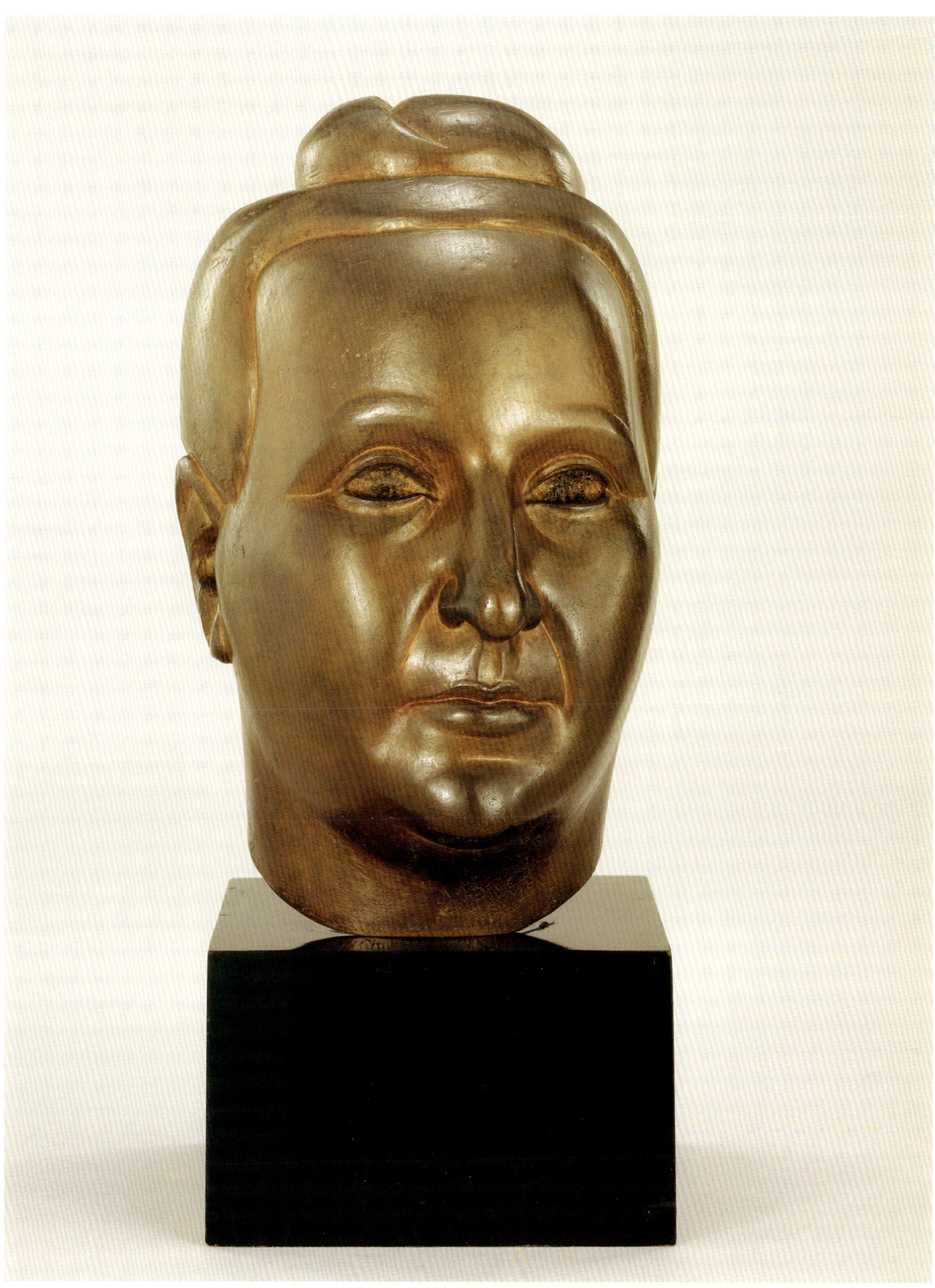

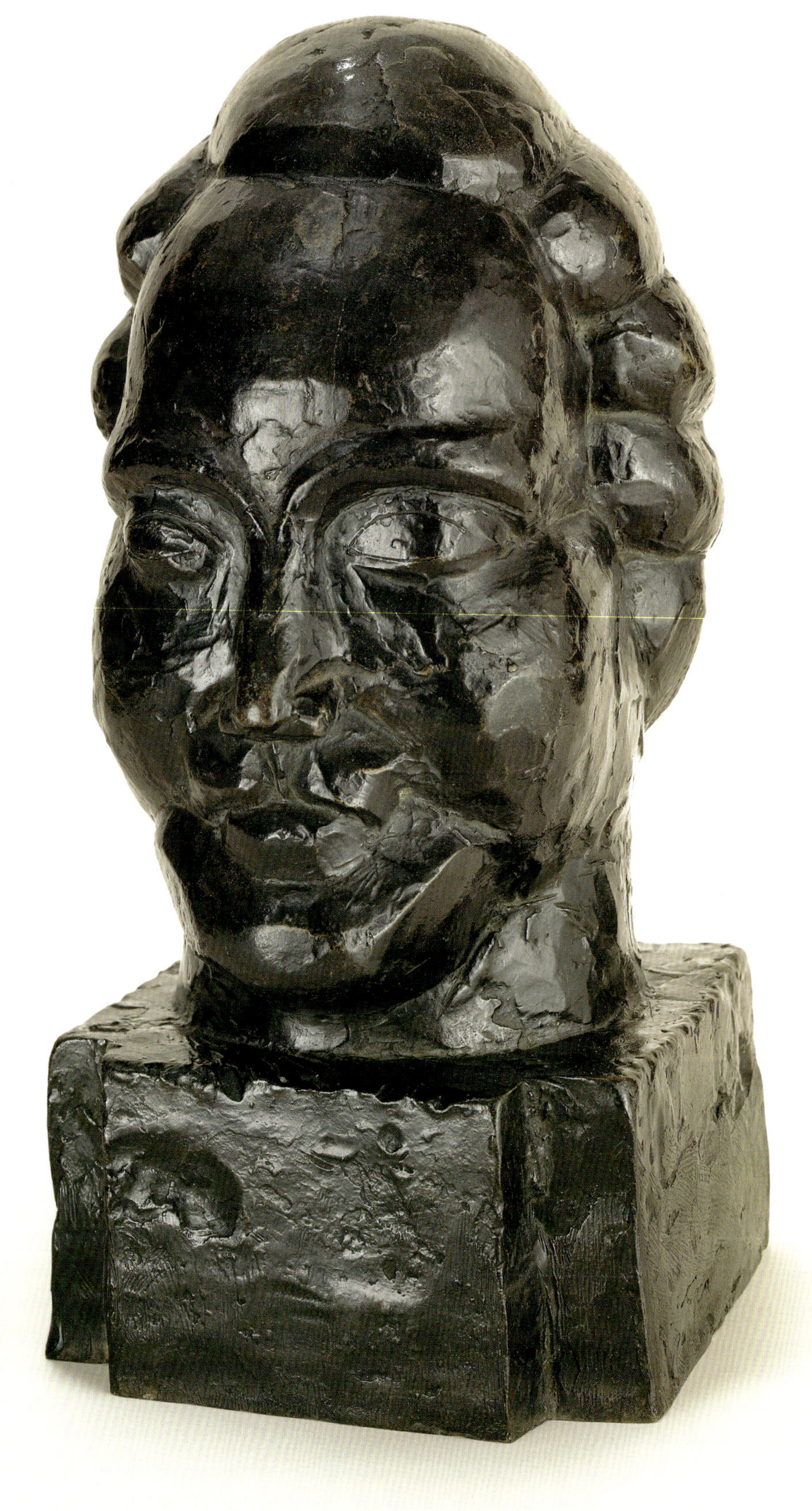

Henri Matisse, *Henriette III,* 1929. Bronze

Hirshhorn Museum and Sculpture Garden, Smithsonian Institution, Washington, D.C.; Gift of Joseph H. Hirshhorn, 1966. Cat. 94

Henri Matisse, *Titine Trovato in a Dress and Hat*,

1934. Oil on canvas

V. Madrigal Collection, New York. Cat. 96

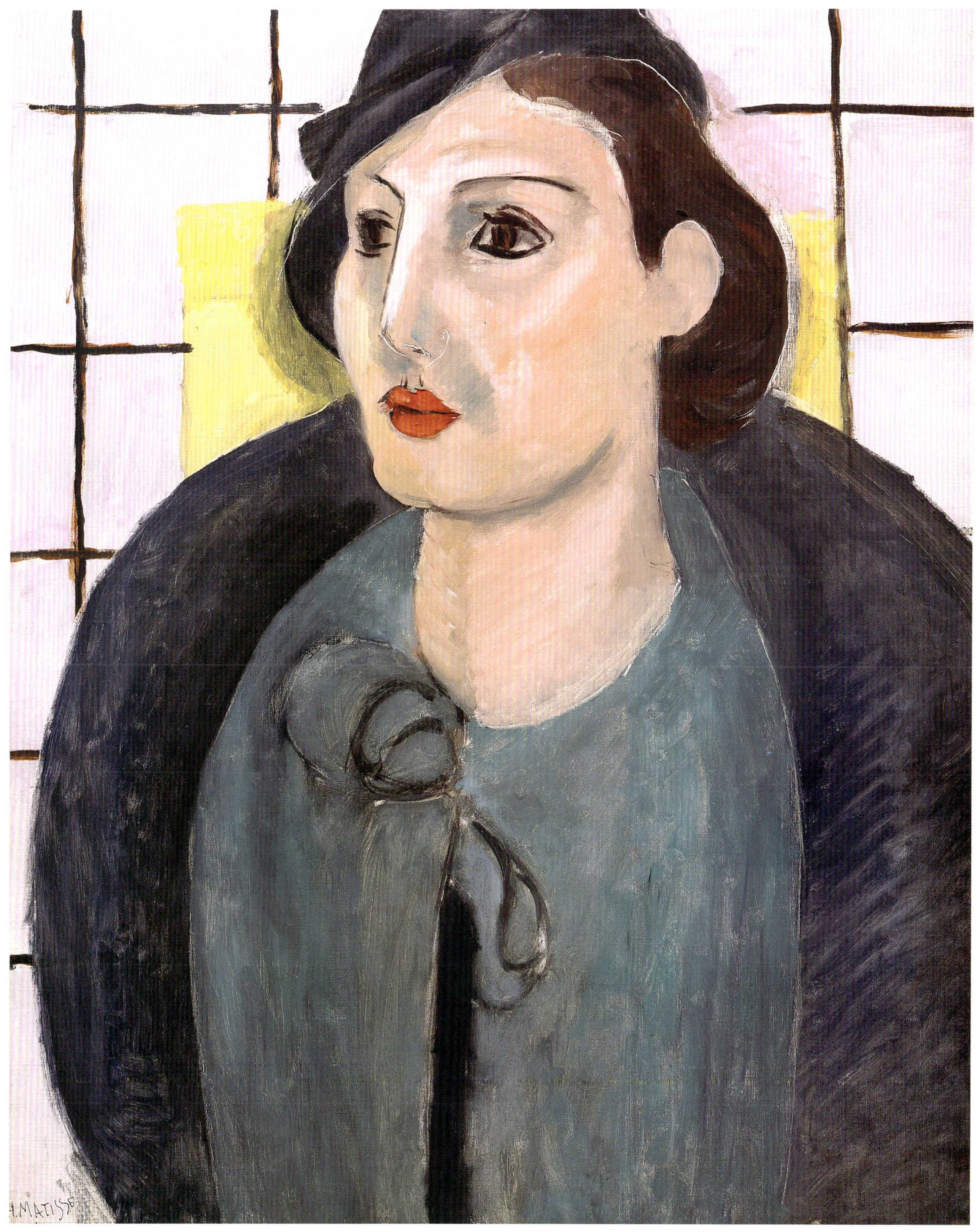

Large Seated Nude

Measuring over thirty inches in height, *Large Seated Nude,* is among Matisse's largest and most ambitious freestanding sculptures.[1] The artist explored variations of the figure's characteristic pose—with one leg raised, the foot curled and protruding from under the other leg, and arms above the head—in drawings, lithographs, a sculpture, and at least three oil paintings. In his *Odalisque with a Tambourine,* Matisse reverses the figure; the proper right leg, rather than the left, is raised and the model is lifting only one arm. A similar reversal in the diminutive sculpture *Small Nude in an Armchair* transforms the sense of detached, Olympian grandeur of *Large Seated Nude* into a more relaxed domestic mood. Comparing the various drawings and lithographically printed sketches that are associated with *Large Seated Nude,* one finds the term *study* inadequate. There is no sense of preparation; Matisse conceived his graphic works as autonomous artwork. This aesthetic independence is well illustrated in the large lithograph *Nude with Blue Cushion.* Matisse fills the entire sheet with a series of forms cascading from left to right and anchored at the top left by the attentive, lively portrait of his model, the young dancer Henriette Darricarrère. As this arrangement is reiterated in clay—and later bronze—we lose much of the figure's individuation but something of Henriette's observant intelligence is preserved in the figure's concentrated posture.

The dating of *Large Seated Nude* has greatly expanded in recent Matisse scholarship. Beginning with Barr's clear date of 1925, the period grew to the somewhat open-ended 1924–1925(?) in Elsen, enlarged to 1923–1925 in Monod-Fontaine and Mezzatesta, and then to 1922–1929 in Duthuit's catalogue raisonné.[2] This amounts to a total of seven years, far exceeding the former record of three years spent completing *The Serf.* It is not inconceivable that the period needs to be backdated further, to 1918. The initial inspiration for the sculpture can be traced in letters Matisse wrote then in which he mentions modeling a sculpture after Michelangelo's figure of *Night*—a copy of which was at the École des Arts décoratifs in Nice.[3] Elsen raises the possibility that an early plaster version of *Large Seated Nude* known from studio photographs may in fact be that sculpture.[4]

Relevant passages from twenty-two letters Matisse wrote to his family and friends regarding *Large Seated Nude* have been assembled in Duthuit. They paint an almost farcical picture of prolonged and arduous struggle. To his wife in 1922: "My work goes on . . . once it is finished, it will look good"; to his wife in 1924: "I am harnessed to my sculpture"; to his wife later in 1924: "I have to finish my nude sculpture . . . it will be towards June 15, the end of June at the latest"; To Sarah Stein in 1926: "The sculpture I have been working on for several years is, I hope, close to being finished"; to his wife in 1927: "the sculpture needs finishing—or to be ditched"; and finally, to his daughter in 1929: "concerning the sculpture . . . have the molding done . . . and wait for me to get back to cast it in bronze."[5]

Our growing understanding of the scope and duration of Matisse's preoccupation with this sculpture calls for a reassessment of its place within his art and, more generally, during the so-called

Henri Matisse, *Large Seated Nude,* 1922–1929

Bronze

The Baltimore Museum of Art, The Cone Collection, formed by Dr. Claribel Cone and Miss Etta Cone of Baltimore, Maryland. Cat. 98

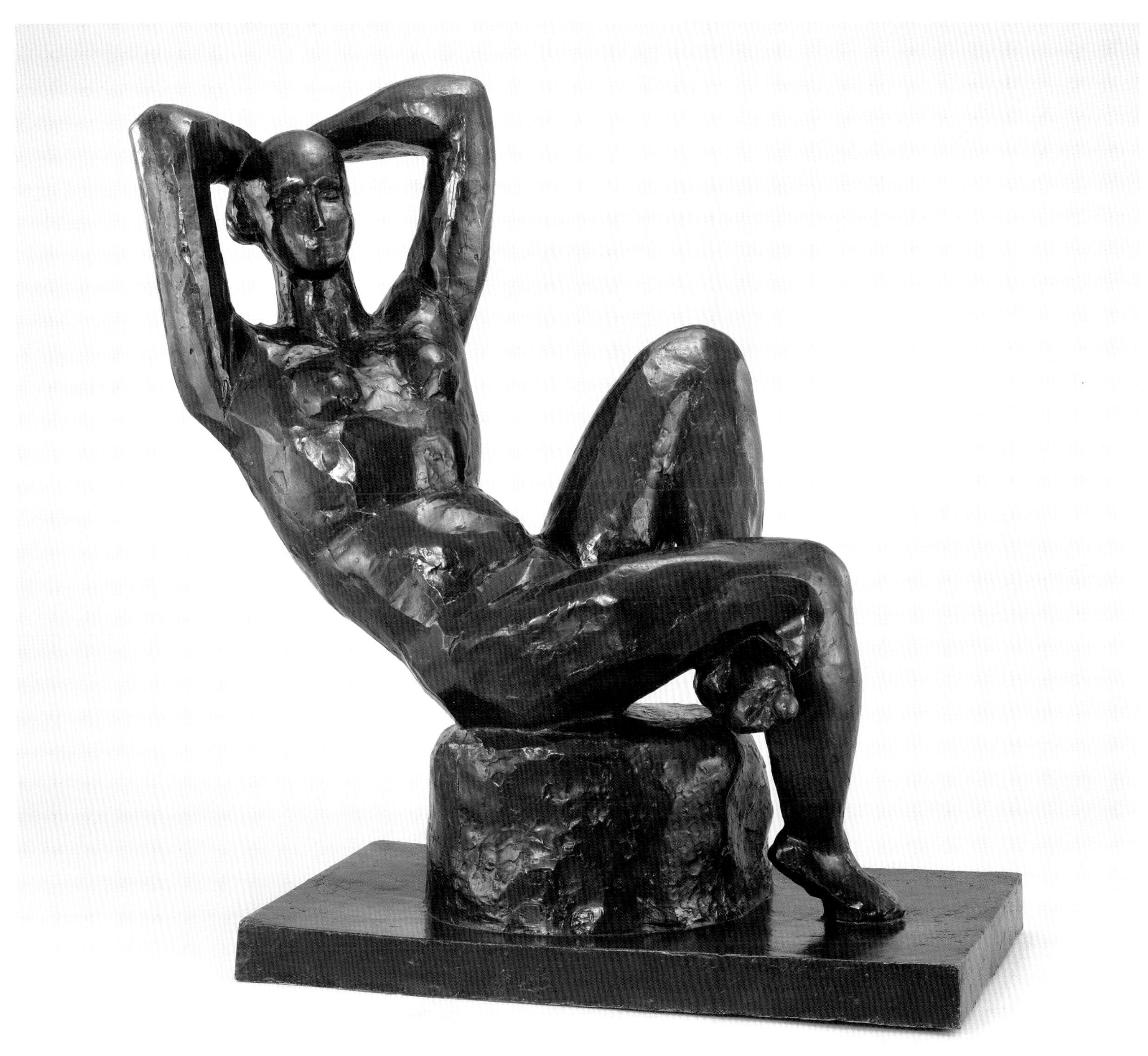

Nice period. Viewed mainly as the product of 1925, *Large Seated Nude* was interpreted as a catalyst helping Matisse find his way back to a formally rigorous, monumental style after a period in which his art was often viewed as lacking those qualities. Barr notes the importance of the work as a marker for larger changes during the second half of the decade, changes that he characterizes as "a reaction against the soft, ingratiating, and comparatively realistic style of the previous five years" and considers the "masculine proportions and vigorous, angular lines" of the sculpture as "far removed from the voluptuous odalisques who precede her."[6] Monod-Fontaine links the "monumental qualities" of *Large Seated Nude* to work from an earlier heroic period, "1910–16," but also credits the sculpture as the source for a renewed "constructed and monumental expression" evident in painted works such as *Decorative Figure on an Ornamental Ground* (1925–1926).[7] While the transformational and catalytic explanations seem plausible, these arguments suffer from the increasing knowledge that Matisse worked on variations of this sculpture throughout the Nice period—even as he produced allegedly "decorative and sensual," "fluid and pearly," "ingratiating" paintings.[8] This knowledge leads one to question Barr's characterization of this as a time of "relaxation in Nice."[9] An alternate way to conceive of *Large Seated Nude* is as a kind of intellectual undercurrent for the entire Nice period from 1918 to 1929. Matisse's constant preoccupation with themes and formal issues related to this project constitute a conceptual framework for his work in many media. The interesting point may not be to differentiate *Large Seated Nude* from the "voluptuous odalisques" that surround her, as Barr wanted to do, but to examine their connections on levels going beyond the aesthetic imperatives of formalist modernism.[10]

OS

Notes

1. The *Backs* are larger but they are bas-reliefs; among his freestanding work only *The Serf* and *Decorative Figure* are comparable in size; Duthuit 1997. The introduction of concepts derived from psychology into discussions of Matisse's interaction with models and the different meanings of the odalisque theme are broadening the context in which we must now consider *Large Seated Nude;* see especially the section beginning with Disguises in Elderfield 1996, 37–51; and chapter three, "Identification with the Model," in Bourguignon 1998, 107–64.

2. Barr 1951, 213; Elsen 1972, 144; Monod-Fontaine 1984, 56; Mezzatesta 1984, 116; and Duthuit 1997.

3. In 1918, Matisse wrote to his friend, the painter Charles Camoin: "I'm drawing *The Night* and modeling it. I'm also studying Michelangelo's *Laurent de Médicis.* I'm hoping to clearly and completely immerse myself in Michelangelo's construction" (Duthuit 1997, 355 n.23). See fig. 42, p. 41, for a photograph of Matisse's studio in which an early plaster of *Large Seated Nude* is seen next to a door on which there is a graphic reproduction of Michelangelo's figure of *Night,* and cat. 104 and 106 respectively, for Matisse's two lithographs *Day* and *Night.* Mezzatesta (1984, 112) observes that these lithographs are "direct postural prototypes for the bronze," but he also notes the differences from Michelangelo's sculptures.

4. On the evidence of various studio photographs Elsen identifies at least two and perhaps three early versions of the sculpture that were either destroyed or radically altered. He does not declare himself definitively regarding the earliest of these having been the one Matisse discusses with Camoin, but raises the possibility. He also discusses the relevance of the closely related sculpture *Small Nude in an Armchair;* Elsen 1972, 146, 148–49; fig. 194.

5. Duthuit 1997, 385–86 n.24.

6. Barr 1951, 213.

7. Monod-Fontaine 1984, 38.

8. Ibid.; Barr 1951, 213.

9. Ibid., 195.

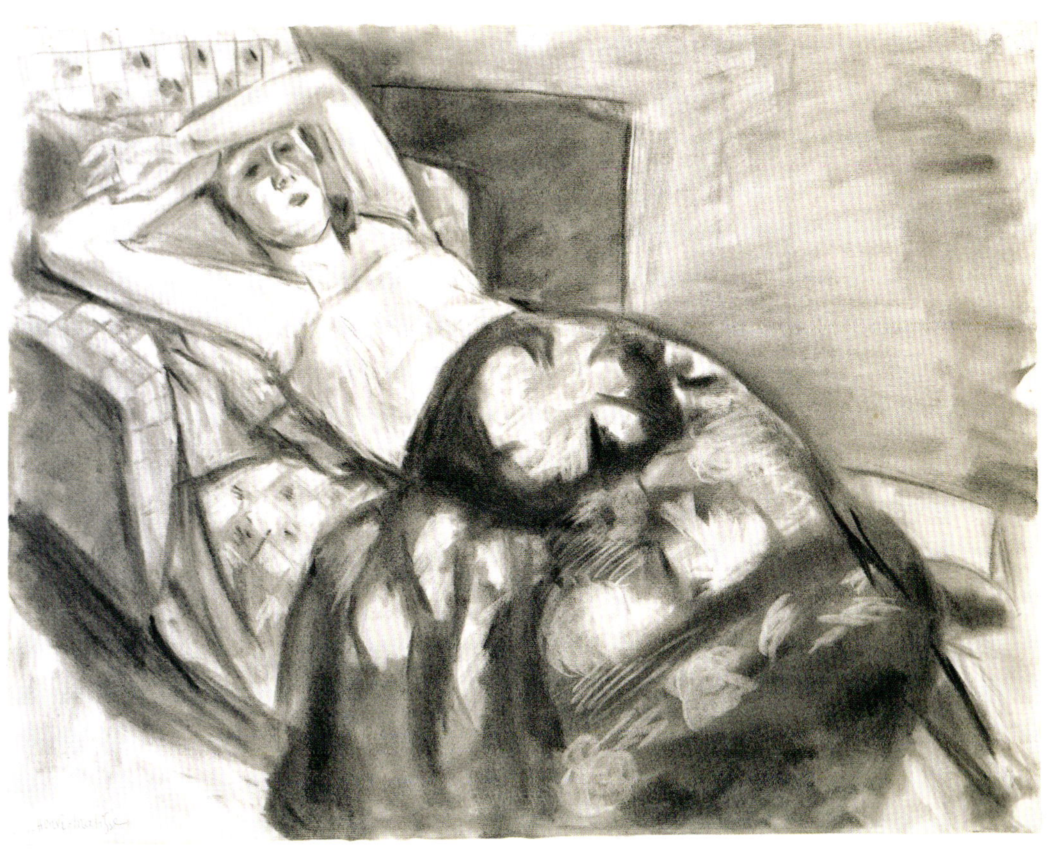

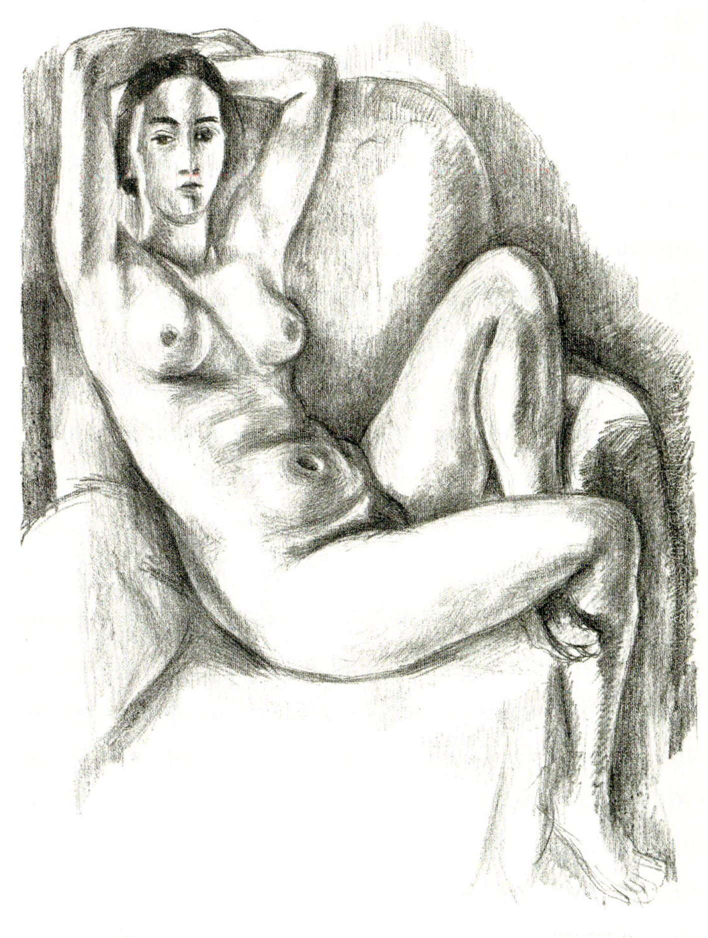

Henri Matisse, *Reclining Model with a Flowered Robe,* c. 1923–1924. Charcoal with stumping and erasing

The Baltimore Museum of Art, The Cone Collection, formed by Dr. Claribel Cone and Miss Etta Cone of Baltimore, Maryland. Cat. 105

Henri Matisse, *Nude with Blue Cushion,* 1924 Crayon transfer lithograph

The Baltimore Museum of Art, The Cone Collection, formed by Dr. Claribel Cone and Miss Etta Cone of Baltimore, Maryland. Cat. 107

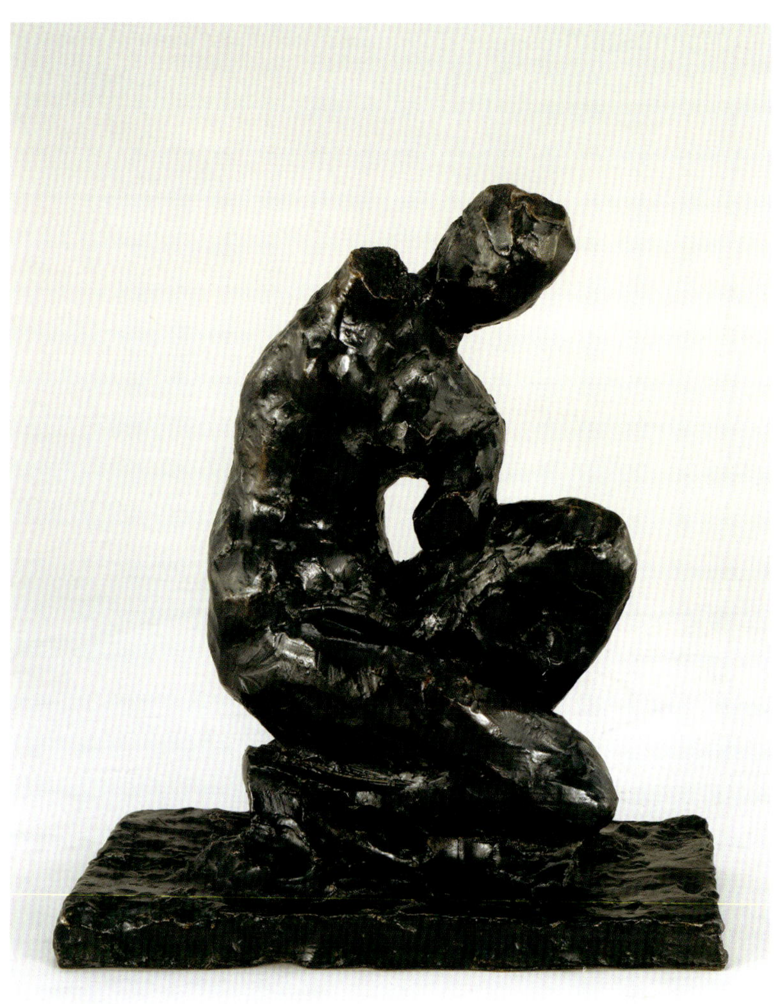

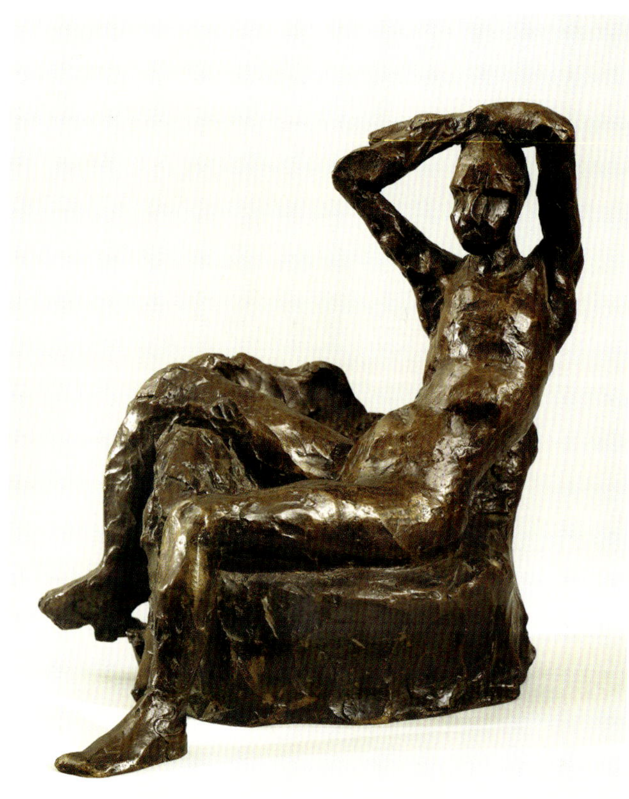

Henri Matisse, *Crouching Venus,* 1918–1919
Bronze

The Baltimore Museum of Art, The Cone Collection, formed by Dr. Claribel Cone and Miss Etta Cone of Baltimore, Maryland. Cat. 97

Henri Matisse, *Small Nude in an Armchair,* 1924
Bronze

Stephen Mazoh. Cat. 100

Henri Matisse, *Odalisque with a Tambourine,* 1925–1926. Oil on canvas

The Museum of Modern Art, New York; The William S. Paley Collection. Cat. 109

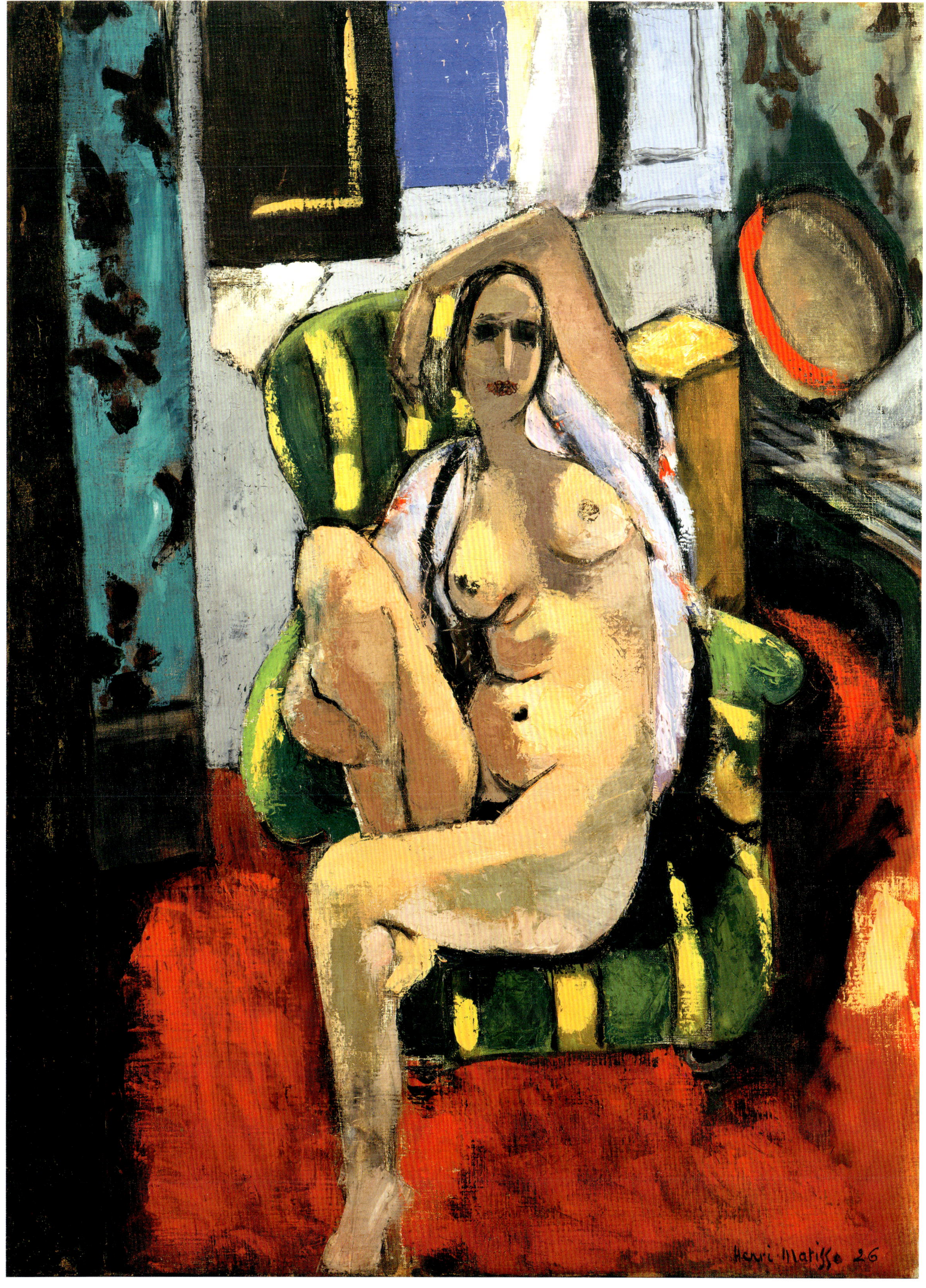
Henri Matisse 26

Henri Matisse, *Large Nude,* 1906. Crayon, brush, and tusche lithograph with scraping

The Baltimore Museum of Art, The Cone Collection, formed by Dr. Claribel Cone and Miss Etta Cone of Baltimore, Maryland. Cat. 101

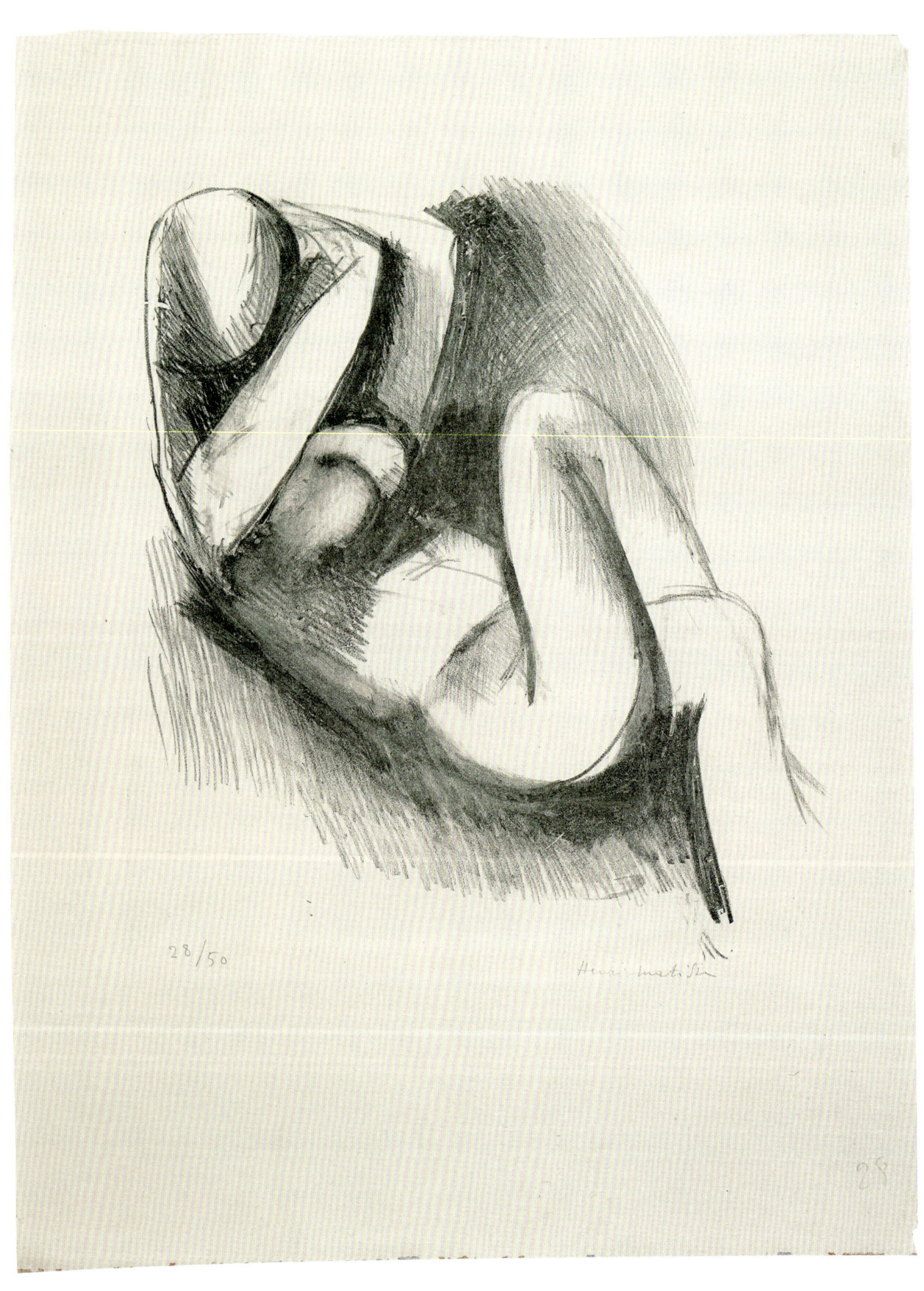

Henri Matisse, *Day,* 1922. Crayon transfer lithograph

The Baltimore Museum of Art, The Cone Collection, formed by Dr. Claribel Cone and Miss Etta Cone of Baltimore, Maryland. Cat. 104

Henri Matisse, *Night,* 1924. Crayon transfer lithograph

The Baltimore Museum of Art, The Cone Collection, formed by Dr. Claribel Cone and Miss Etta Cone of Baltimore, Maryland. Cat. 106

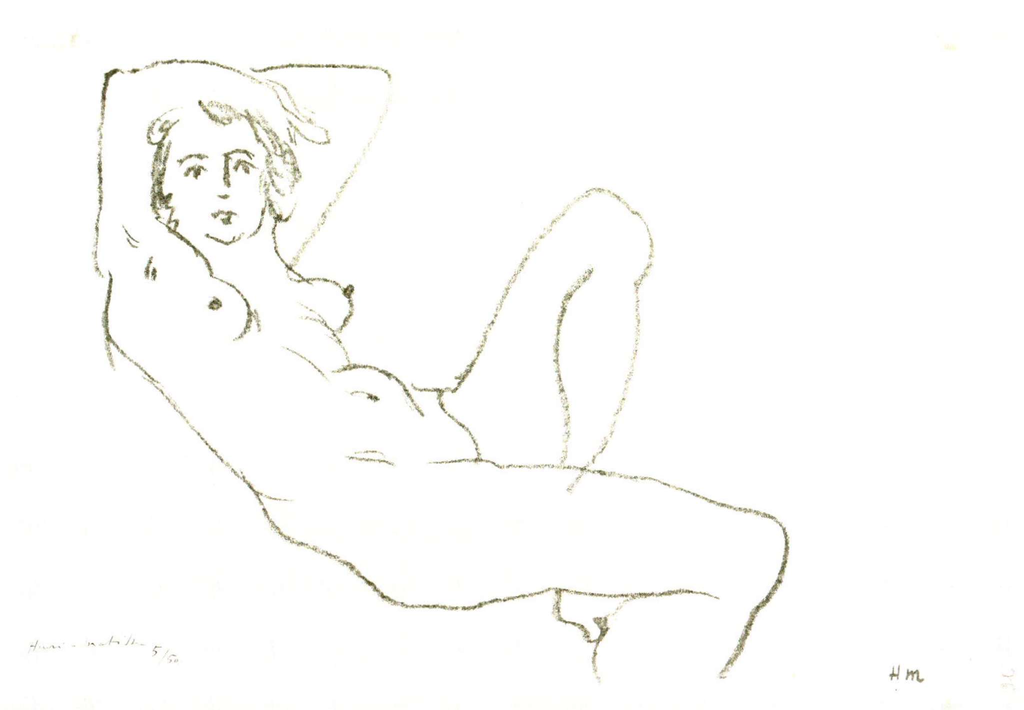

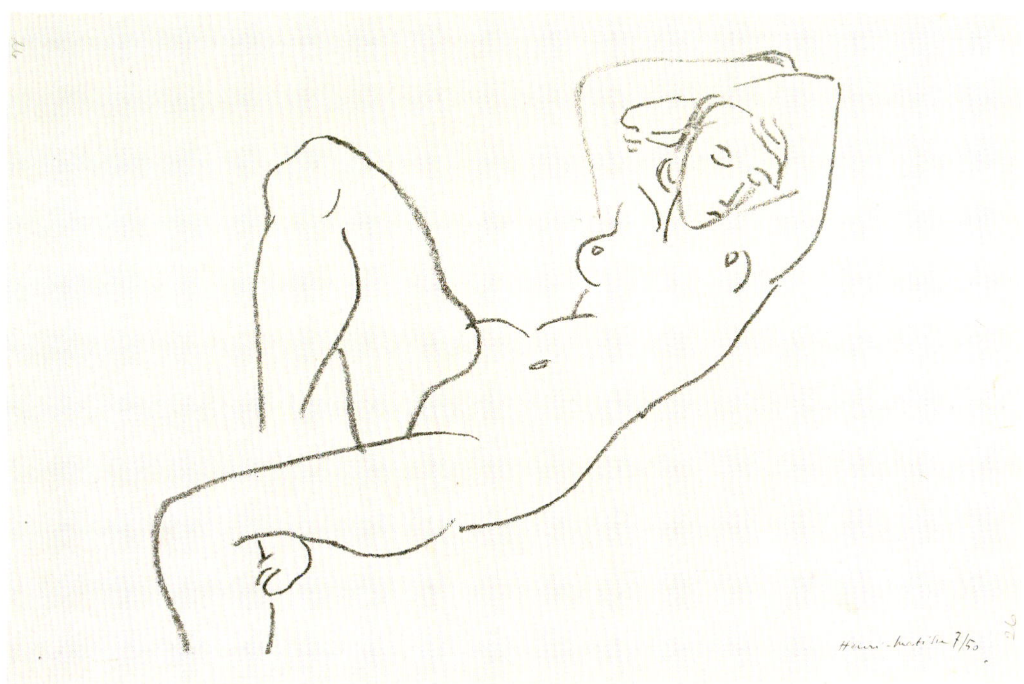

Henri Matisse, *Reclining Nude,* c. 1907–1908
Graphite with stumping

Kunstmuseum Winterthur, Purchase, 1947. Cat. 102

• Not in the exhibition

Henri Matisse, *Study of a Reclining Nude,*
1910–1911. Graphite

Centre Pompidou, Paris; Musée national d'art moderne/
Centre de création industrielle; Gift of Marie Matisse, 1984.
Cat. 103

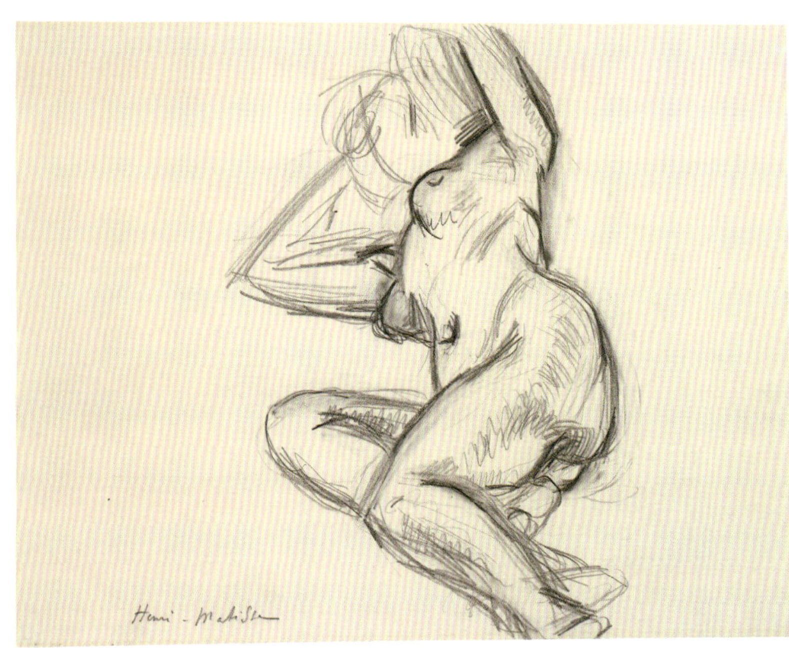

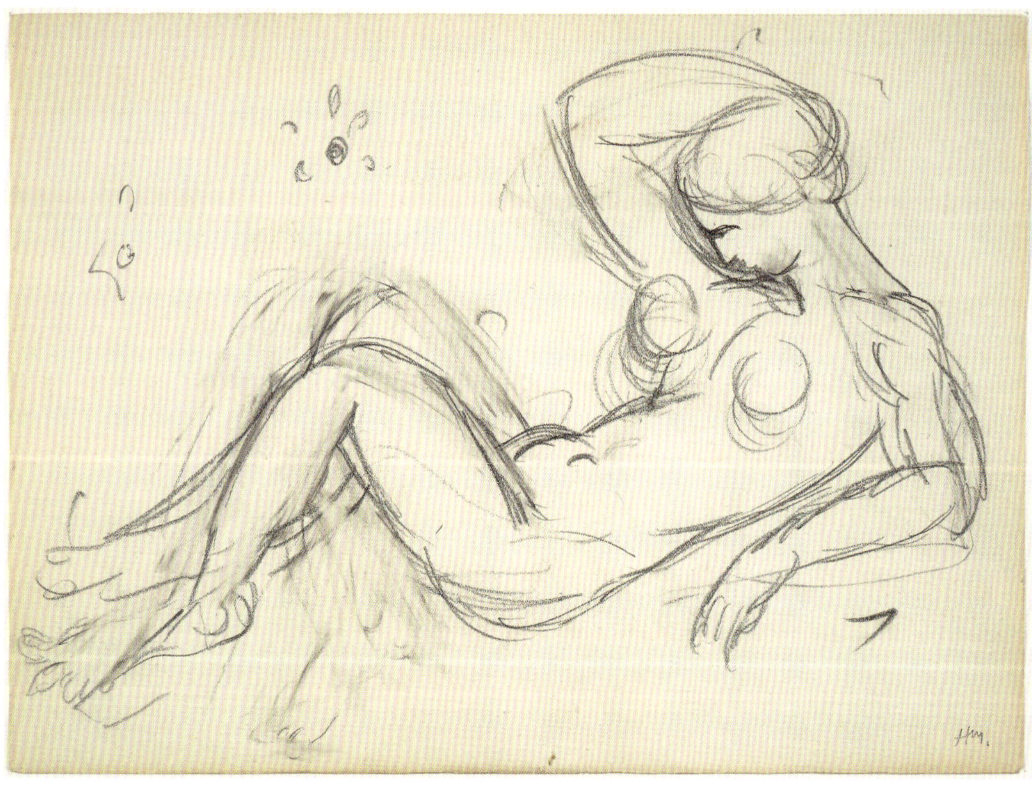

Henri Matisse, *Nude, Legs Crossed,* c. 1925

Pen and ink

Pierre and Maria-Gaetana Matisse Foundation Collection.

Cat. 108

Henri Matisse, *Reclining Nude,* c. 1927–1928

Graphite

Private collection. Cat. 110

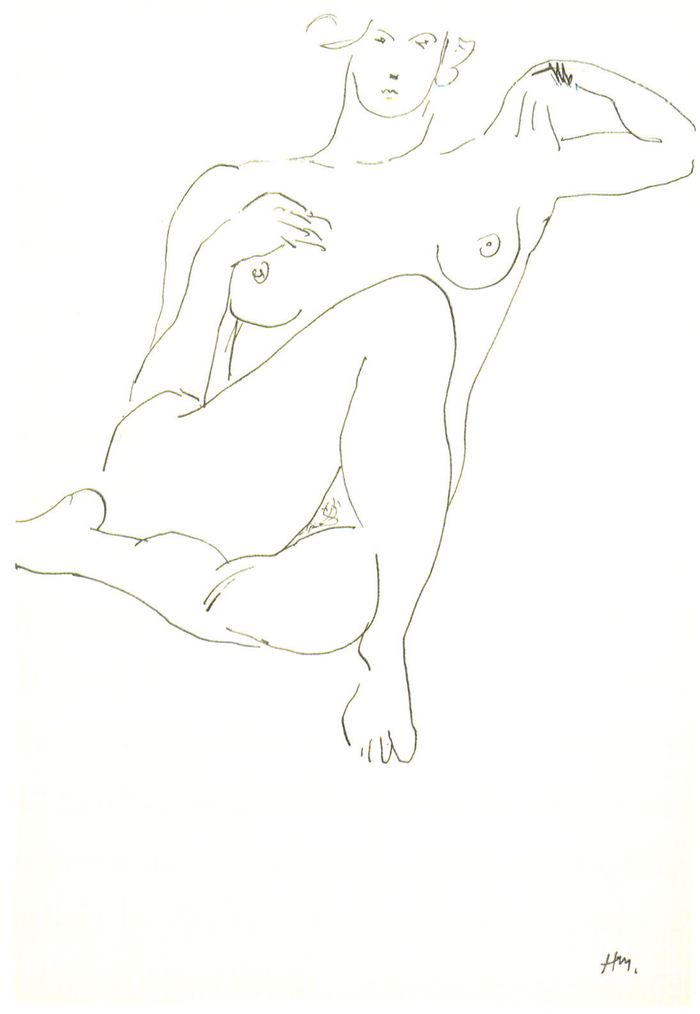

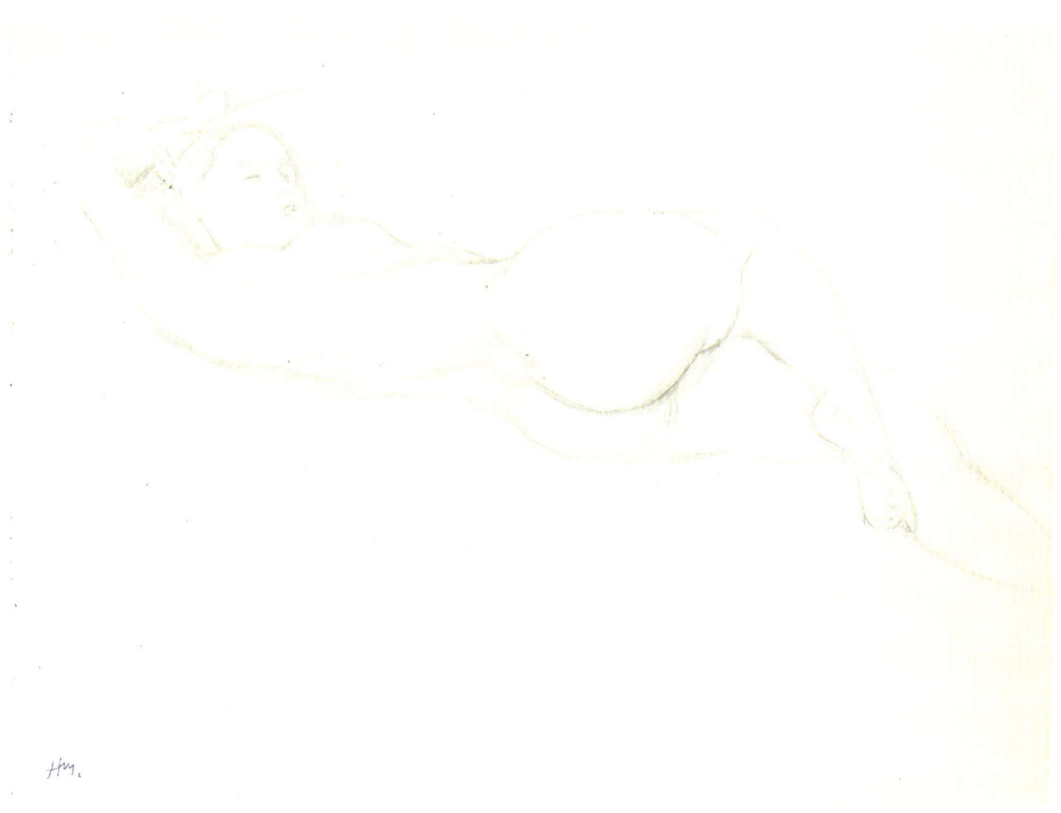

Reclining Nude II and *III*

With *Reclining Nude II* and *Reclining Nude III,* Matisse once again modeled the lounging female nude posed with the characteristic raised arm and thrusting hip—a common art historical archetype. The figure had first appeared in his work twenty-two years earlier in the guise of a classical nymph occupying the center of his fauve painting *Le bonheur de vivre* (fig. 28, p. 29). In 1907 she was forcefully sculpted in *Reclining Nude I (Aurora),* a definitive treatment of the theme that, in terms of raw expressiveness, Matisse would never exceed. When he took up the subject again in the late 1920s, he thoroughly transformed the stylistic handling of the sculpture. To mark his new approach he reversed the posture of the nudes, who now rest on their proper left elbow and face the viewer's left.[1] He eliminated any geometric base, limiting all relational play of forms within the figure's freely interpreted anatomy.[2] A desire to retain hard-edged structural elements, formerly associated with the base, is now expressed by inscribing or cutting into the bodily forms of *Reclining Nude II*—evident in her cubical breasts, flattened planar surfaces, and the decisive, wedge-shaped cuts, especially pronounced in the rear view. The same figure also incorporates sensual curves, and it is the dialogue between these two types of forms that Michael Mezzatesta interprets as a broader "oscillation in these years between the voluptuous and the tectonic . . . a balance between the sensual and the structural."[3] *Reclining Nude II* can itself be viewed as representative of the "tectonic" antipode when compared to its successor, *Reclining Nude III,* which is far smoother, more "voluptuous," and decidedly streamlined —even her breasts have been eliminated as unnecessary formal interruptions. Where the former bears the activating marks of considerable knife work, all traces of such cutting are eliminated from *Reclining Nude III,* with the exception of two furrows in the figure's ample belly. These lines—Monod-Fontaine reads them as folds—serve to emphasize the horizontal flow of the piece and unitize its volumes, rather than to activate the surfaces with discontinuous planar transitions. On the whole, Matisse's surfaces undergo a general simplification and smoothing in this period, as can be seen in the almost glossy *Henriette II* of 1927.

The two sculptures could be viewed as pendants embodying a range of metaphoric oppositions.[4] There is some evidence, however, to suggest that they may be serially linked iterations of a single process. A pair of photographs of Matisse, clearly taken at the same time (he wears the identical vest and tie), depicts the artist sculpting a reclining figure. One photograph is published in Elsen, and the other serves as the cover photo of Monod-Fontaine's book.[5] Elsen identifies the photo as "Matisse modeling *Reclining Nude III,* Nice, 1929"; Monod-Fontaine captions the photograph, "Matisse working on *Reclining Nude II,* 1927."[6] The figure Matisse works on appears to be a version between *Reclining Nude II* and *Reclining Nude III.* The head and neck correspond to the later version while the breasts and most of the body appear closer to its predecessor. The identification of the work in progress in the photographs, however, remains problematic. We know that on some occasions Matisse made piece molds off wet clay models.[7] The advantage of such a method was that he could continue to work the still extant clay model after it had been cast and to transform it—in essence getting two or more sculptures from a single modeling campaign. If the two sculptures were of a similar size, this is what one might surmise is occurring here; the later sculpture, however, is a full three-and-five-eighths inches shorter than *Reclining Nude II.*[8] If Matisse did transform the model, he radically reshaped the clay, cutting it down dramatically. No matter what technique he used, it is safe to conclude that these two works represent sequential stages, at least conceptually, of a single meditation, and perhaps of a single material process.

In 1941, Matisse told Pierre Courthion:

> I took up sculpture because what interested me in painting was a clarification of my ideas. I changed my method, and worked in clay in order to have a rest from painting, in which I had done absolutely all I could for the time being. That is to say that it was done for the purpose of organization, to put order into my feelings and to find a style to suit me. When I found it in sculpture, it helped me in my painting.[9]

This statement is borne out, to a degree, if we compare the *Reclining Nude*s *II* and *III* to his later painting *Large Reclining Nude / The Pink Nude.* After attempting twenty-one variations of the figure's pose, Matisse ends up adopting almost the same S-shaped arrangement of the arms that he had previously explored in the *Reclining Nudes.*[10] The pose of the lower half of the nude differs, being turned away from the viewer; however, the simplified linear drawing of the figure and seamless planar transitions bear stylistic analogies to the smoothed surfaces of *Reclining Nude III.* This sculpture, the last he would produce of this theme—and less satisfying, perhaps, than its precursors—nonetheless played a decisive role in preparing the way for Matisse's later painting style and even for the elegantly contoured decoupages.

OS

Notes

1. This change of direction is discussed in Elsen 1972, 155–57.

2. Matisse always paid great attention to the relationship between his bases and the figures—frequently employing off-centered arrangements as in *Crouching Venus;* just as with his paintings, he did not privilege the figure over any other element in the compositional arrangement but viewed it as integral.

3. Mezzatesta 1984, 124.

4. For Mezzatesta these are abstract opposing principles, the "sensual and the structural," but, given the ease with which ethical and even gender associations are frequently substituted for such terms, they remain metaphorical; other oppositions could be nominated, the interrupted and multiple versus the seamless and unitary.

5. Elsen 1972, 158; Monod-Fontaine 1984.

6. It seems probable that each author dated the photographs in light of the content, as perceived, without independent confirmation from the material history of the photograph itself. The dates match the dates of the sculptures. This practice is methodologically problematic because it creates a false enhancement of the evidentiary value of the photograph. One of these authors is clearly wrong, perhaps both are.

7. Professional *mouleurs* (plaster molders) would differentiate between *bons creux* (piece molding) and *creux perdus* (waste molding) processes. In the former the model survives, in the latter it is washed or broken away and destroyed. Making a *bon creux* mold from a wet clay model is considerably more difficult than from a hardened piece—especially if one has to construct a piece mold; this information comes from conversations with M. Laurent, head molder at the Atelier du moulage (formerly "du Louvre et des musées de France"; now separate).

8. Duthuit 1997, 196, 204.

9. Courthion (1941) 1995, 298 n.11.

10. The twenty-two photographs of all the stages the *Pink Nude* went through are published in Richardson 1985, 136–37.

Henri Matisse, *Reclining Nude II,* 1927. Bronze

The Minneapolis Institute of Arts, Gift of the Dayton-Hudson Corporation. Cat. 112

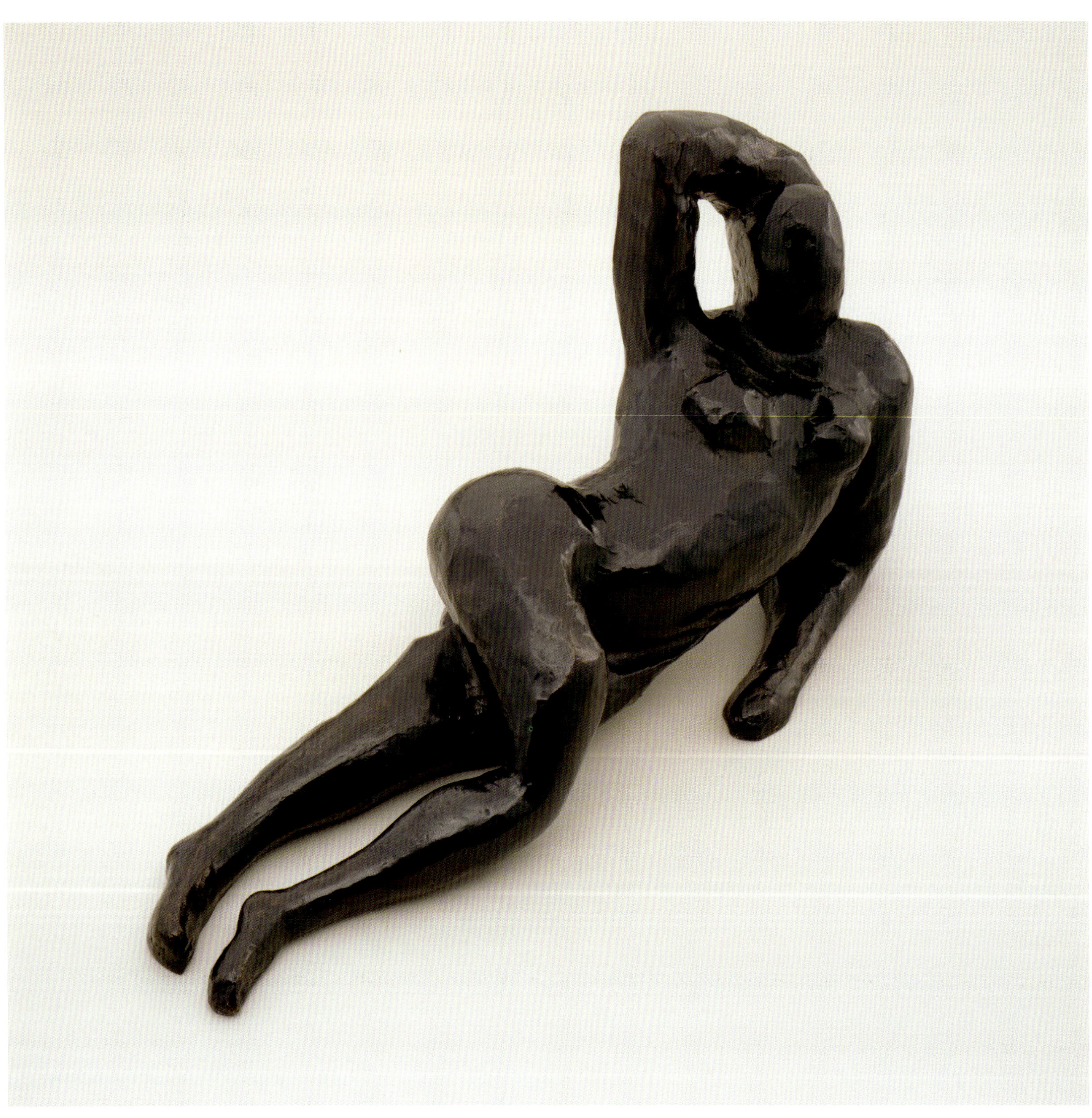

Henri Matisse, *Reclining Nude III*, 1929. Bronze

The Baltimore Museum of Art, The Cone Collection, formed by Dr. Claribel Cone and Miss Etta Cone of Baltimore, Maryland. Cat. 113

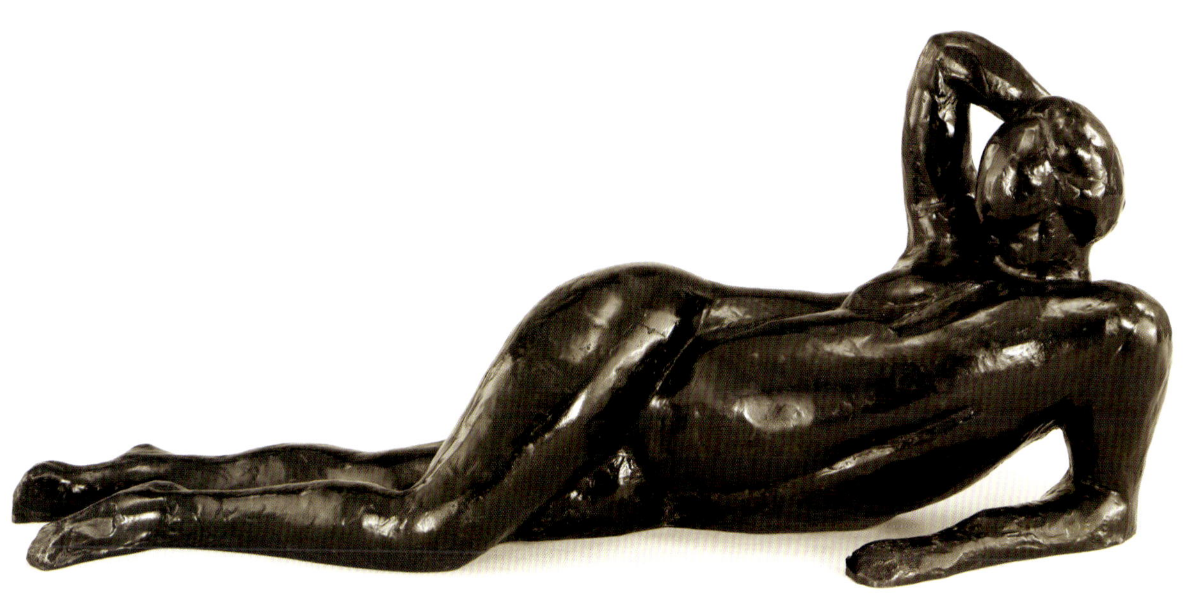

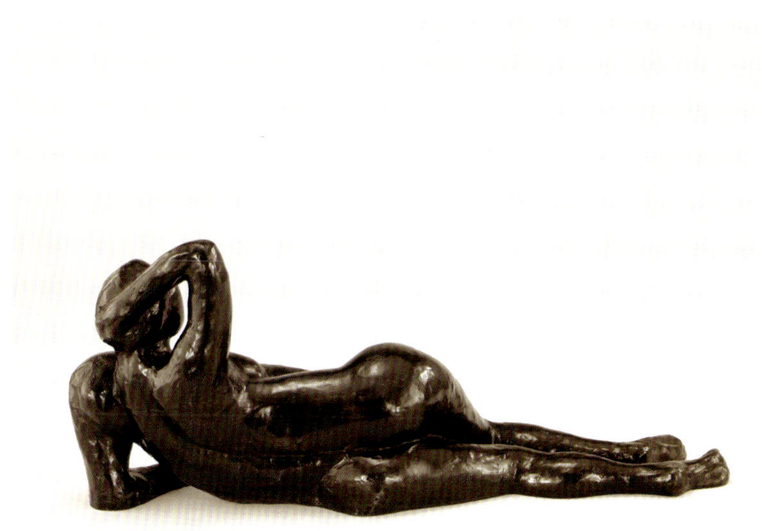

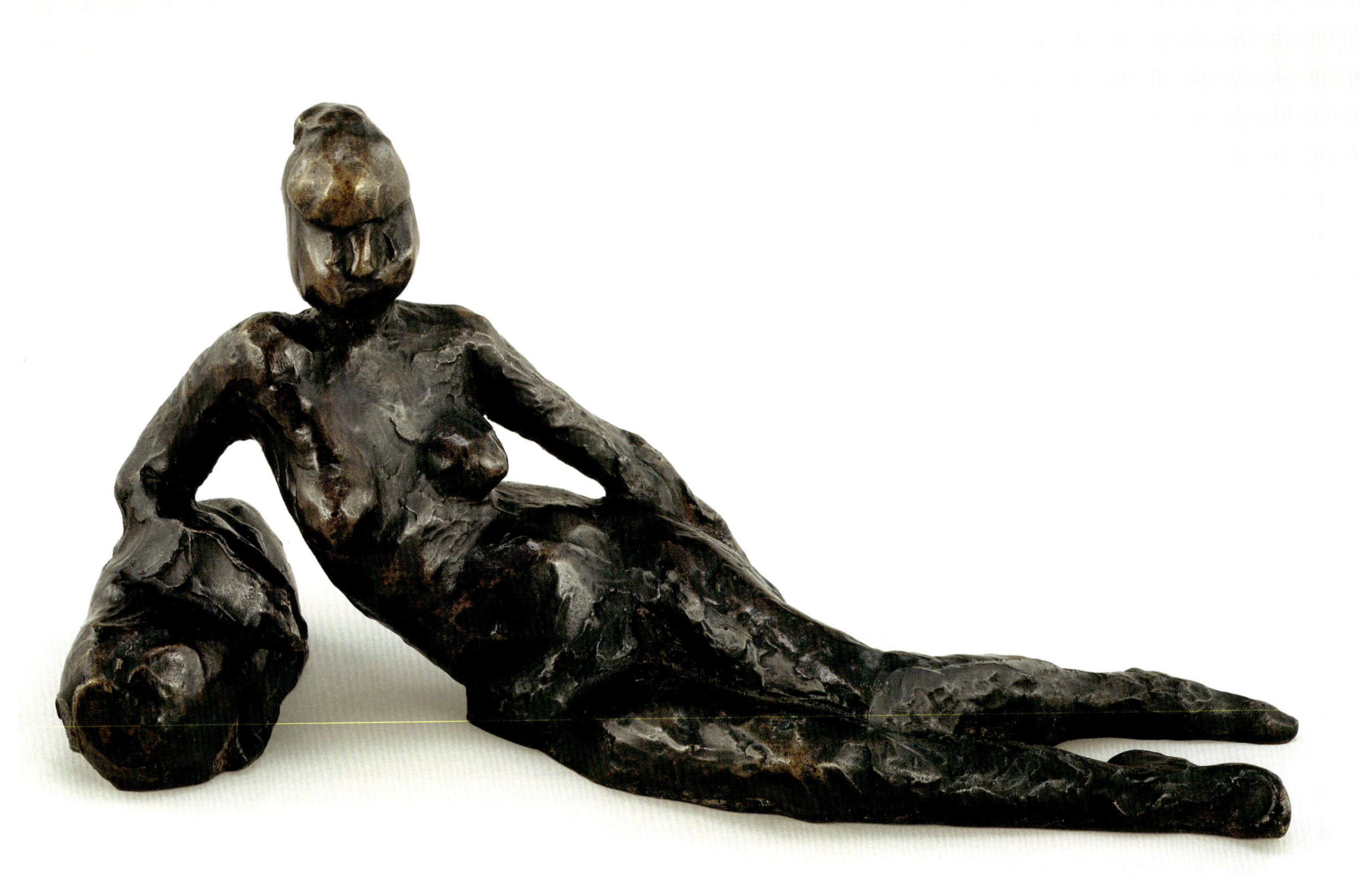

Henri Matisse, *Figure with Cushion,* 1918
Bronze
The Baltimore Museum of Art, The Cone Collection, formed by Dr. Claribel Cone and Miss Etta Cone of Baltimore, Maryland. Cat. 111

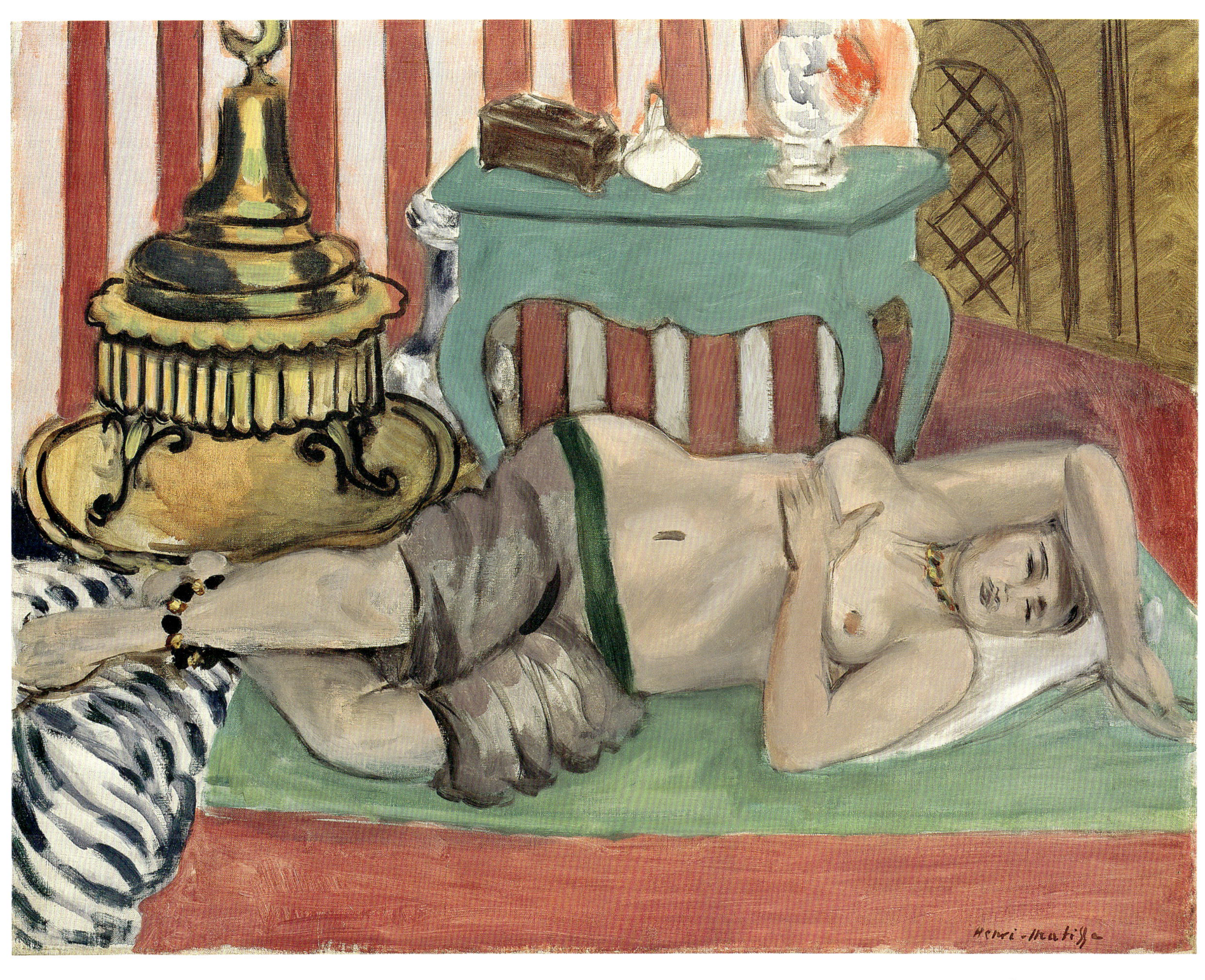

Henri Matisse, *Odalisque with Green Sash,* 1927. Oil on canvas

The Baltimore Museum of Art, The Cone Collection, formed by Dr. Claribel Cone and Miss Etta Cone of Baltimore, Maryland. Cat. 115

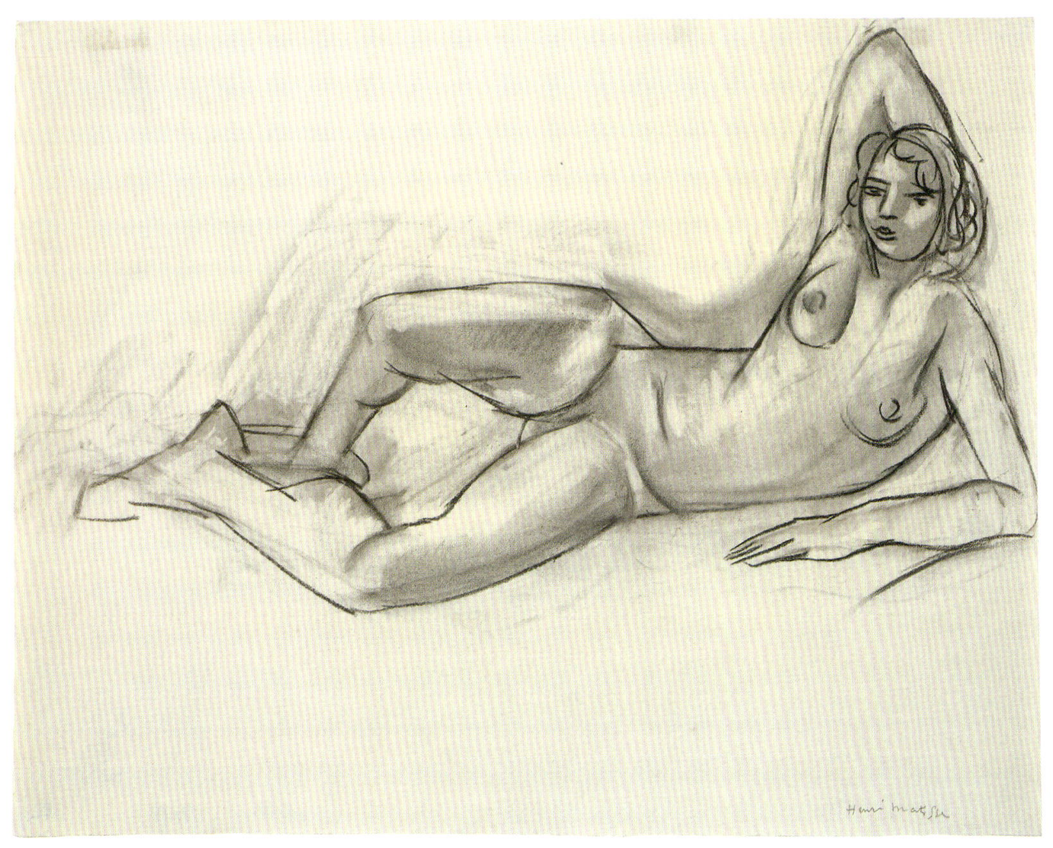

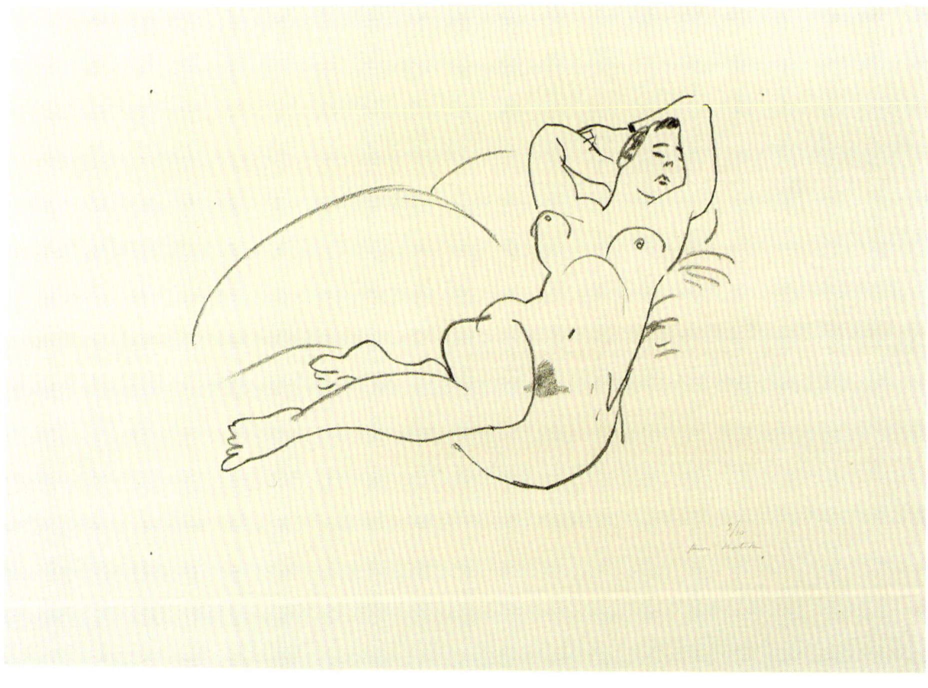

Henri Matisse, *Reclining Nude,* 1929. Charcoal with stumping and erasing

Pierre and Maria-Gaetana Matisse Foundation Collection. Cat. 116

Henri Matisse, *Sleeping Figure,* 1927. Crayon transfer lithograph

The Baltimore Museum of Art, The Cone Collection, formed by Dr. Claribel Cone and Miss Etta Cone of Baltimore, Maryland. Cat. 114

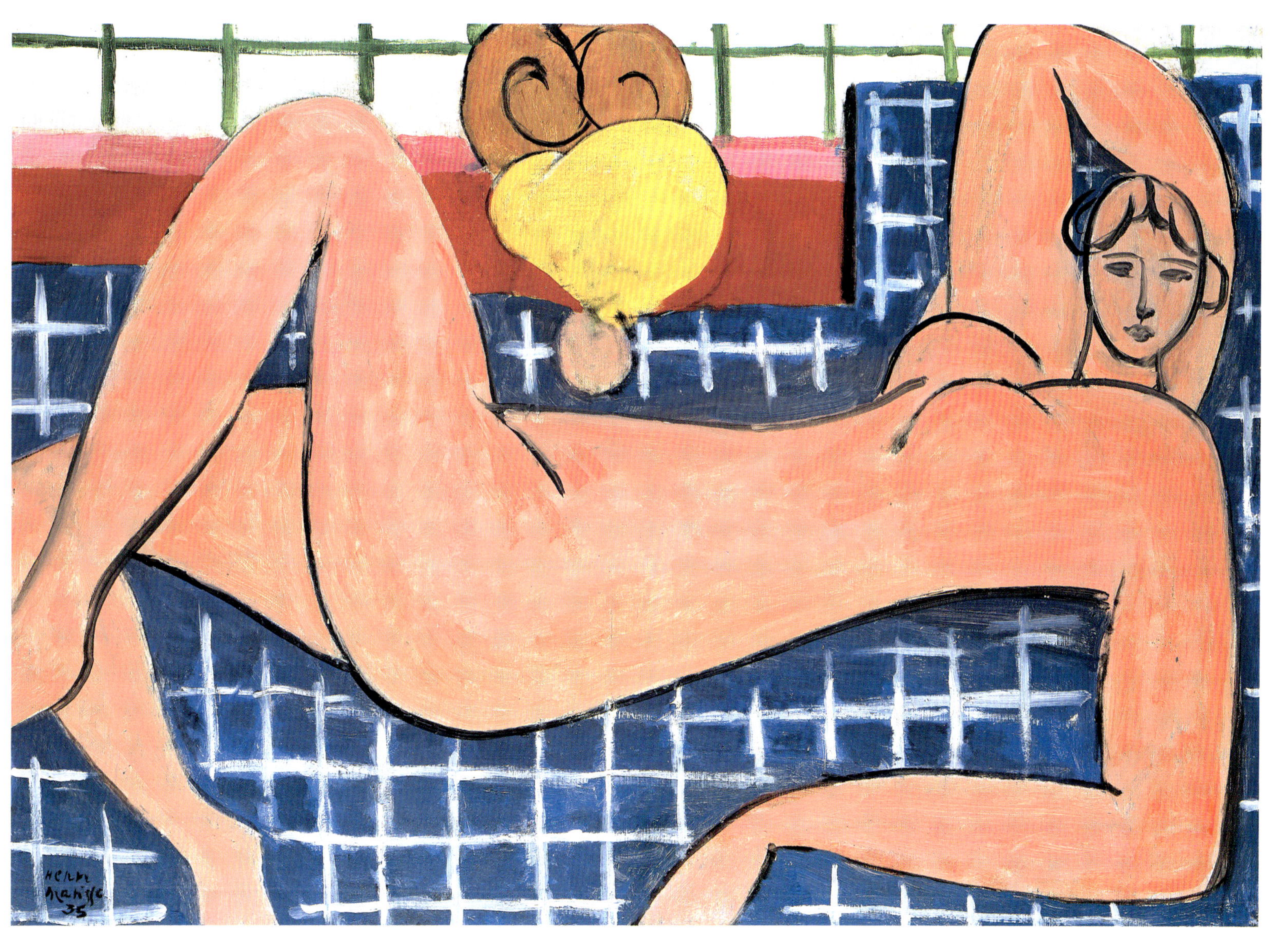

Henri Matisse, *Large Reclining Nude / The Pink Nude,* 1935. Oil on canvas

The Baltimore Museum of Art, The Cone Collection, formed by Dr. Claribel Cone and Miss Etta Cone of Baltimore, Maryland. Cat. 117

Torsos

Matisse's two stylized torsos, *Small Torso* and *Small Thin Torso,* both of 1929, are among his smallest sculptures, each between three and four inches in height. Matisse conceived of these two sculptures in response to a Roman torso he owned, a figure that had been amputated at mid-thigh and worn to a smooth roundness where the missing head and arms had once been. It was perhaps this marble fragment that lay behind Matisse's description of the plenitude that he found in classical sculpture: "full, firm as, say, an egg, and with cylindrically shaped limbs."[1] He even made a partial cast of one of his earlier sculptures, *Standing Nude,* with the lower legs, arms, and head removed, creating a sculptural echo of his heavily eroded classical marble.

Michael Mezzatesta has described the *Small Torso* as "subsuming the form of the female body in that of a phallus."[2] Isabelle Monod-Fontaine instead points to the desire for simplification and generalization implicit in the sculpture. "*Small Torso,*" she writes, "(even more so than *Small Thin Torso*) greatly resembles a polished pebble, a worn or ageless object. Both these sculptures suggest the universality of form which is devoid of any individual particularity that might attract attention."[3] This new priority on stylistic generalization characterized much of Matisse's sculpture of the period, including *Reclining Nude III, Tiari,* and *Henriette II.* Elsen suggests that the two torsos were originally displayed without bases, a presentation that would have greatly enhanced our sense of them as organic objects, sculpted by nature and time rather than by the hand of an artist. Their minute scale and simplified forms remind us of Matisse's dictum that "a sculpture must invite us to handle it as an object. The smaller the sculpture, the greater should be the essentialness of the form."[4]

In the work of many of Matisse's contemporaries we see a similar effort to reduce the form of the torso, the most essential signifier of the human figure, to a generalized state, devoid of individual specificity. Charles Despiau's *Adolescent Girl (Diana)* is, like Matisse's torsos, derived from classical models, a relationship acknowledged by the title, with its reference to the goddess of the hunt, and by the pose, a *contrapposto* borrowed from archaic *korai* figures. In Constantin Brancusi's *Torso of a Young Girl (II)* and Alexander Archipenko's *Torso in Space (Floating Torso),* the human torso is treated as an iconic form with a minimum of surface incident, radically divorced from both classical precedent and anatomical reference. Alberto Giacometti in his *Headless Woman,* like Matisse in his small torsos, retains the conventional markers of gender, but otherwise strips away any signs of individuality and elongates the figure to proportions that alienate it from its human character and recall ancient Etruscan and Egyptian precedents.

Matisse also incorporated the motif of the torso into his collage work. In a print from the *Jazz* portfolio, *Forms,* the simple cut-out figures—shown both as a positive form and as its negative double—retain the truncation of Matisse's classical fragment, legs cut off at mid-thigh and with neither head nor shoulders.

HMacD

Notes

1. Quoted in Schneider 1984, 524.
2. Mezzatesta 1984, 127.
3. Monod-Fontaine 1984, 40.
4. Quoted in Soria 2003, 110.

Henri Matisse, *Small Torso,* 1929. Bronze

Private collection, New York. Cat. 120

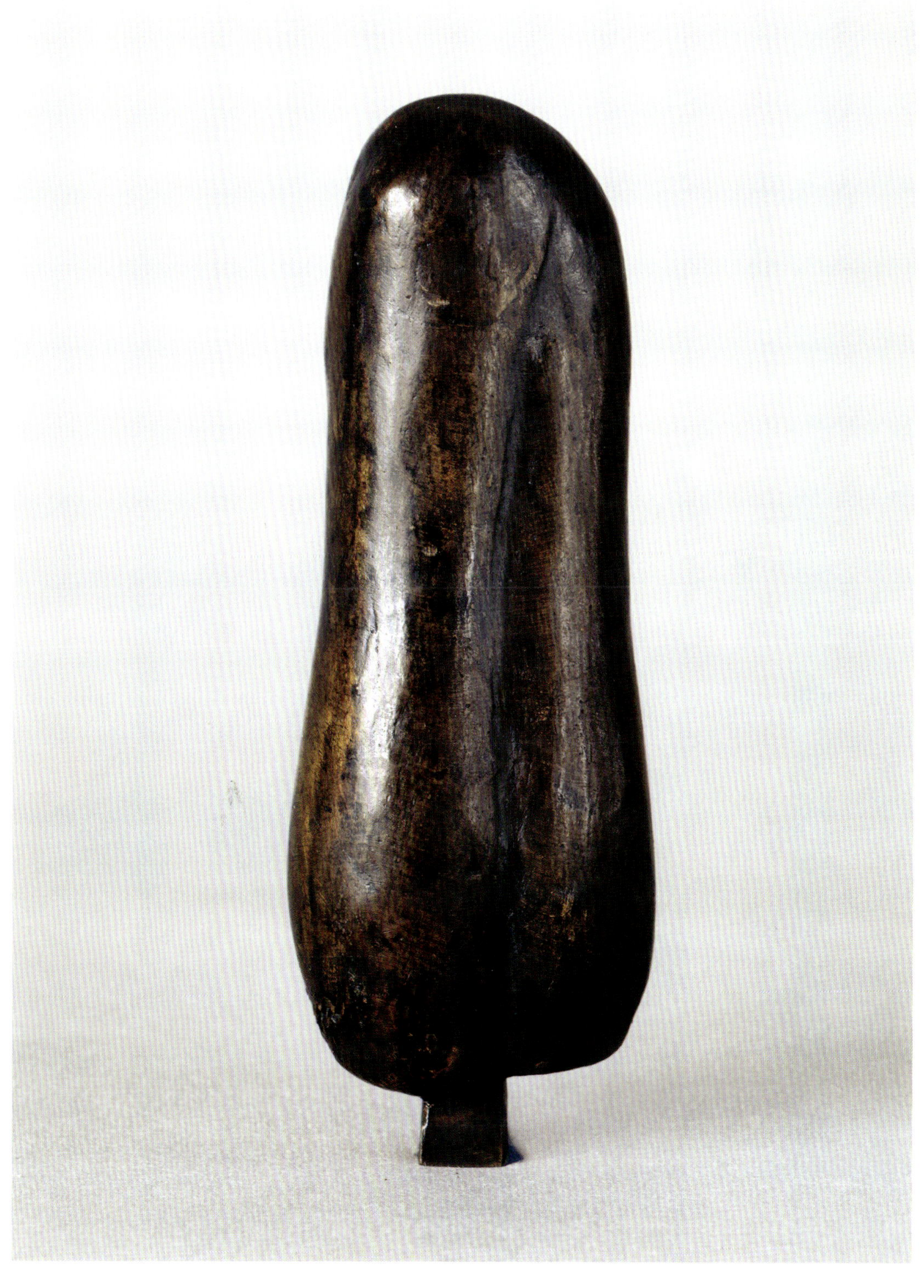

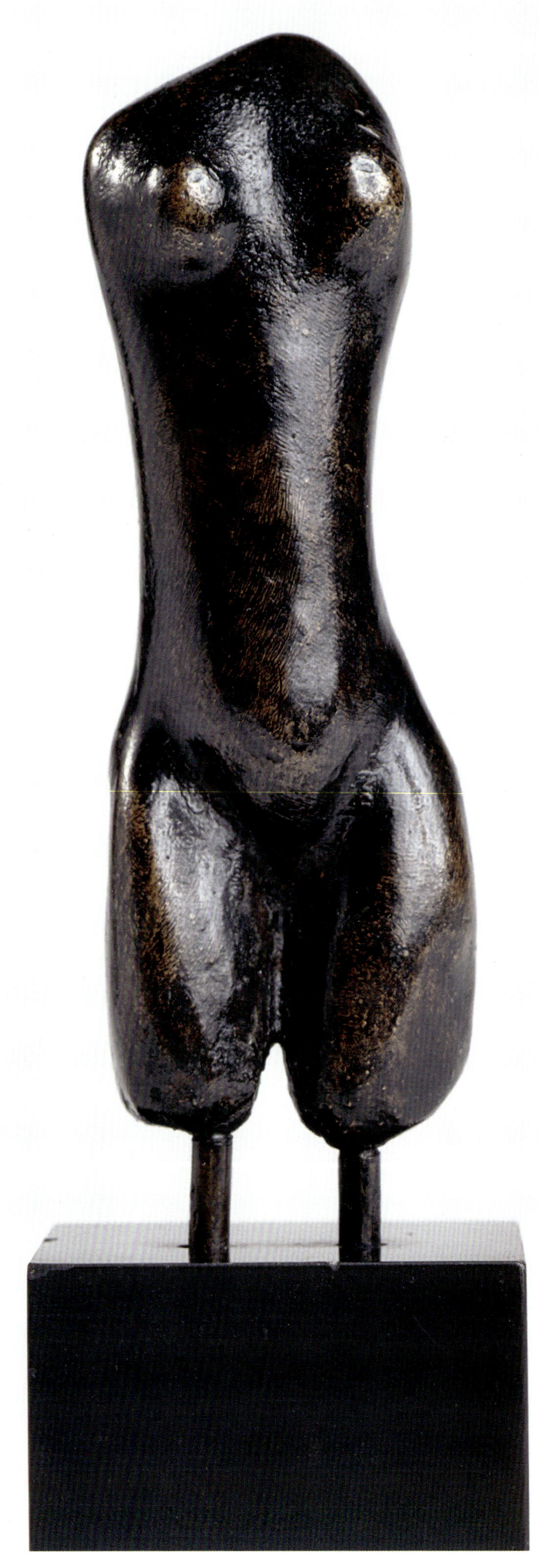

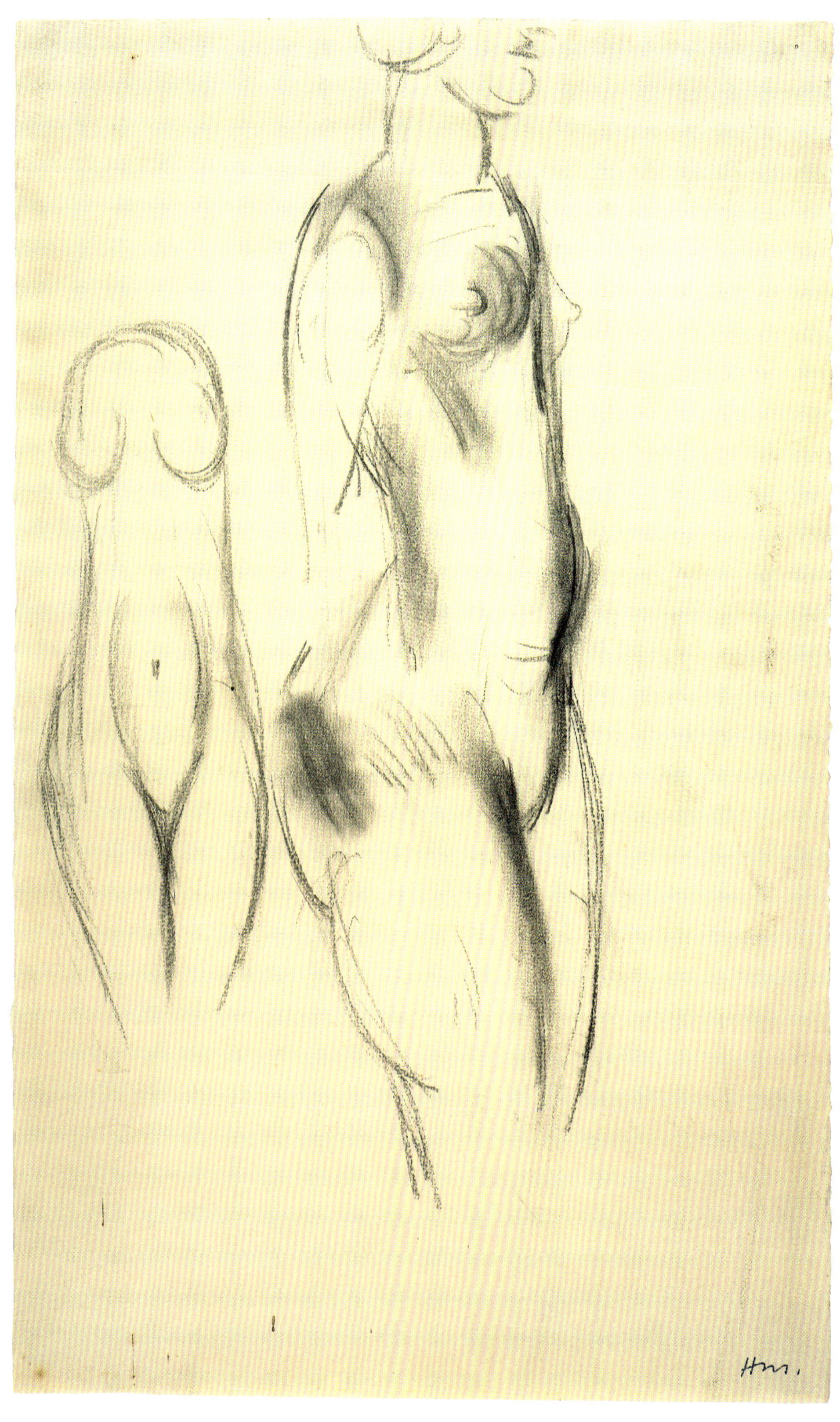

Henri Matisse, *Small Thin Torso,* 1929. Bronze

Direction des Musées de France, Gift of Jean Matisse, on deposit at the Musée Matisse, Nice, 1978. Cat. 119

Henri Matisse, *Studies of a Woman,* 1929

Charcoal with stumping

Pierre and Maria-Gaetana Matisse Foundation Collection. Cat. 121

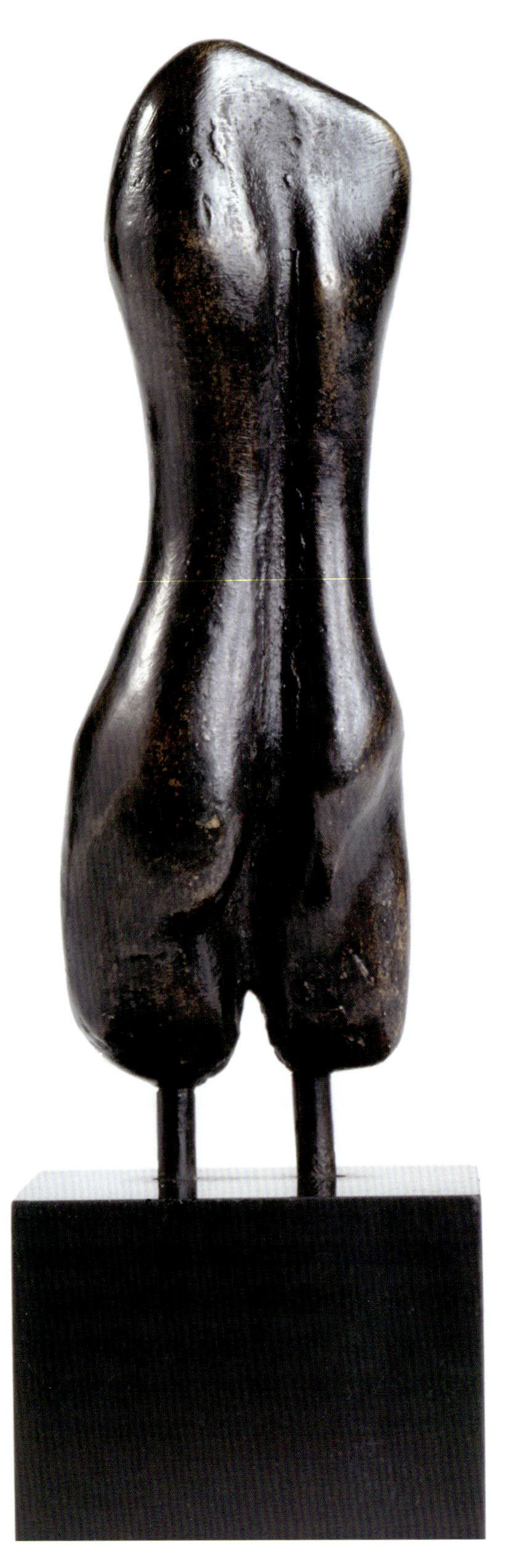

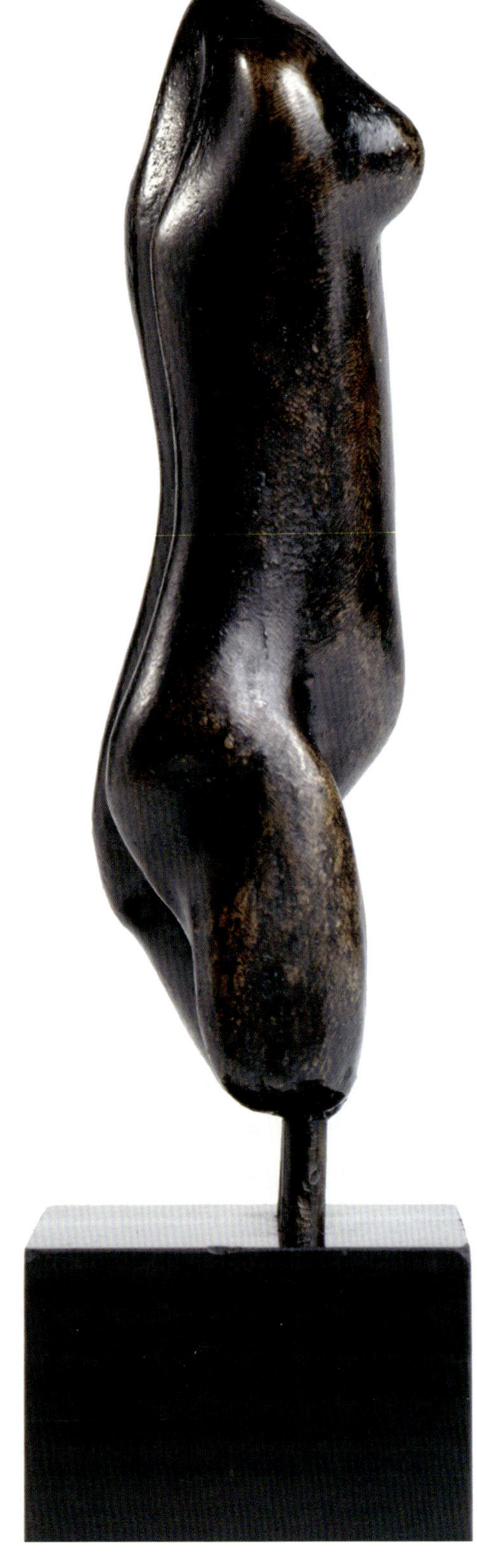

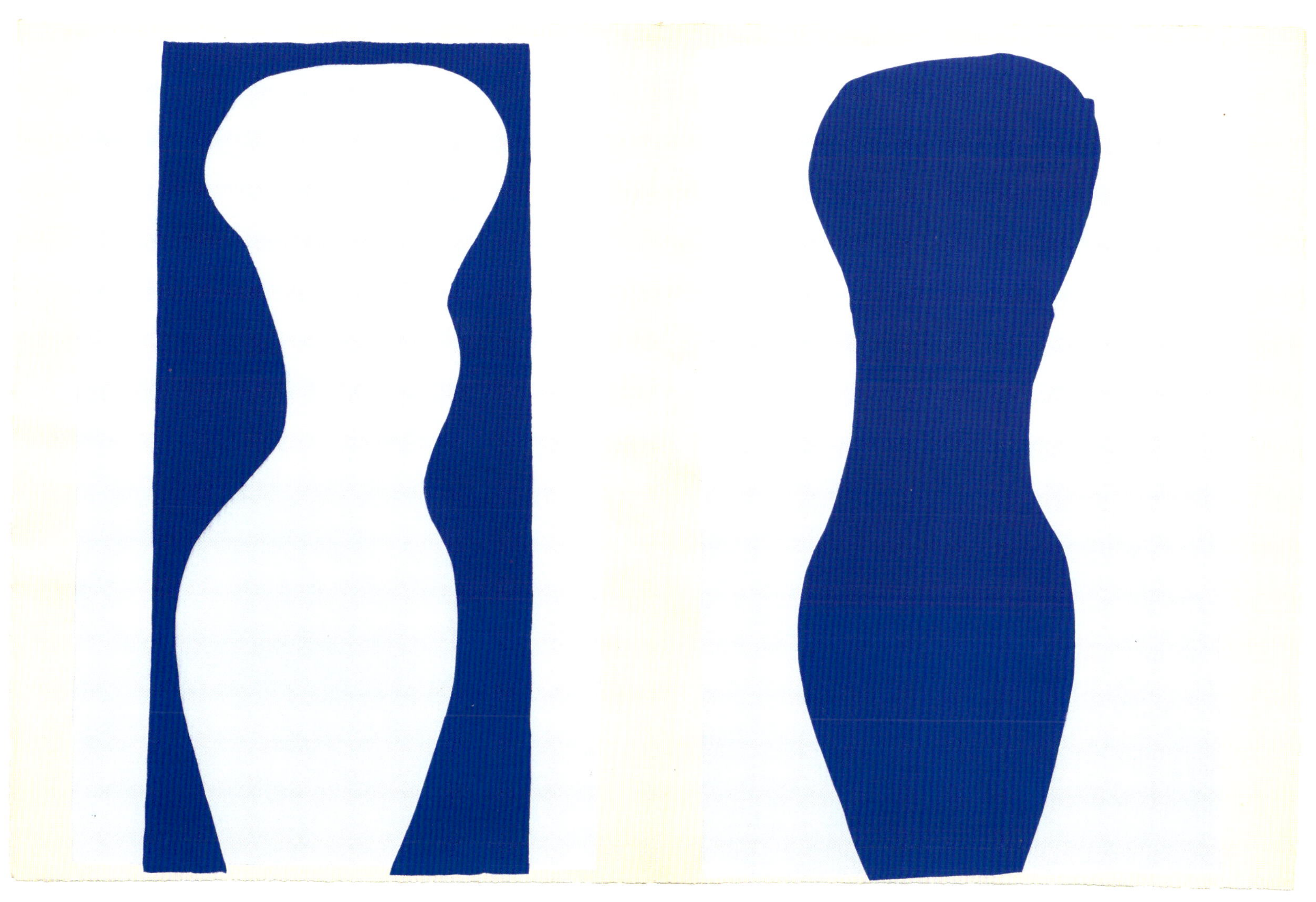

Henri Matisse, *Small Thin Torso,* 1929. Bronze

Direction des Musées de France, Gift of Jean Matisse, on deposit at the Musée Matisse, Nice, 1978. Cat. 119

Henri Matisse, *Forms,* plate IX from *Jazz,* 1947

Hand-printed colored stencil

The Baltimore Museum of Art, The Cone Collection, formed by Dr. Claribel Cone and Miss Etta Cone of Baltimore, Maryland. Cat. 122

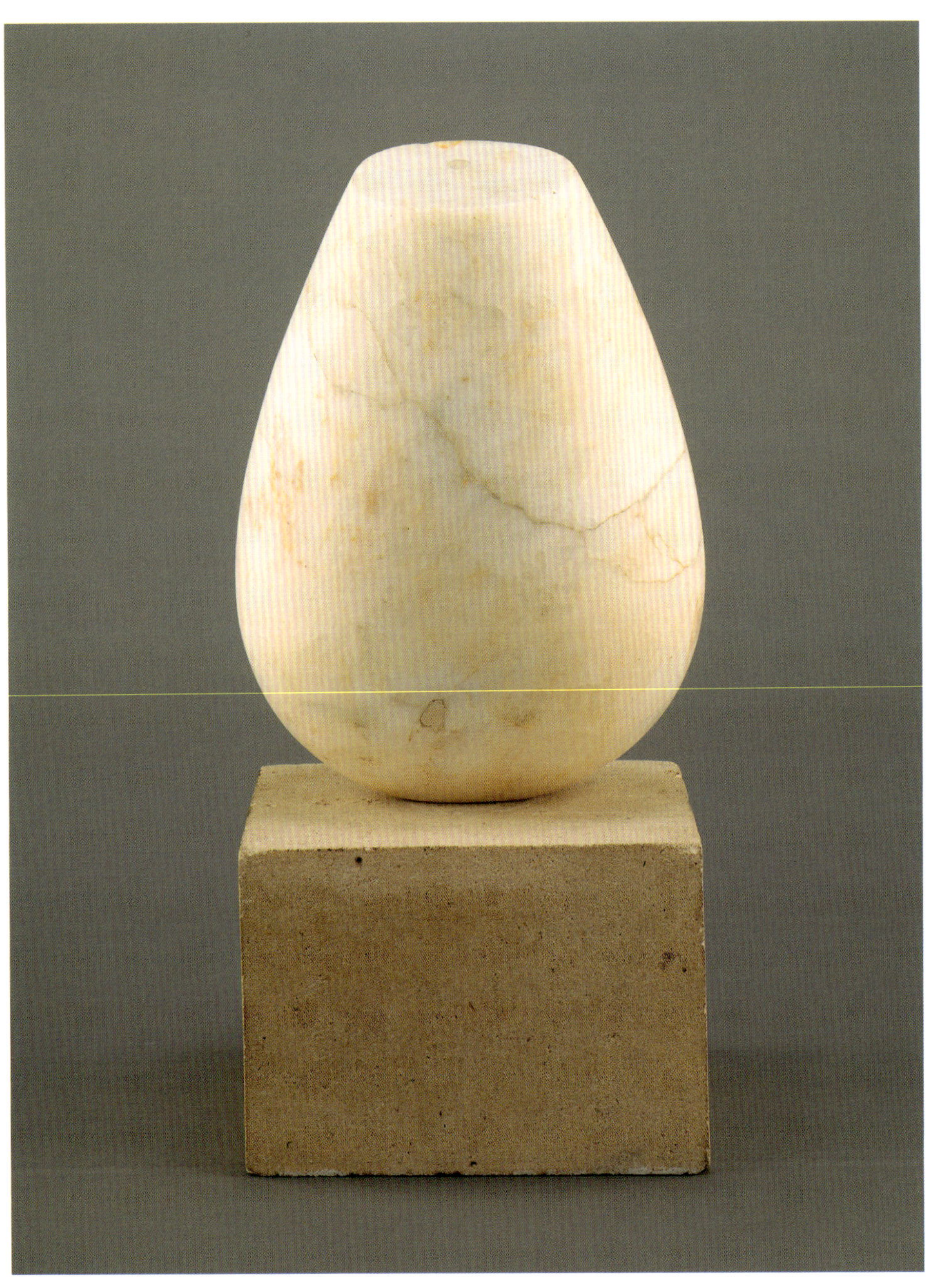

Constantin Brancusi, *Torso of a Young Girl (II),*
c. 1923. White marble on limestone block

Philadelphia Museum of Art, A. E. Gallatin Collection, 1952.
Cat. 148

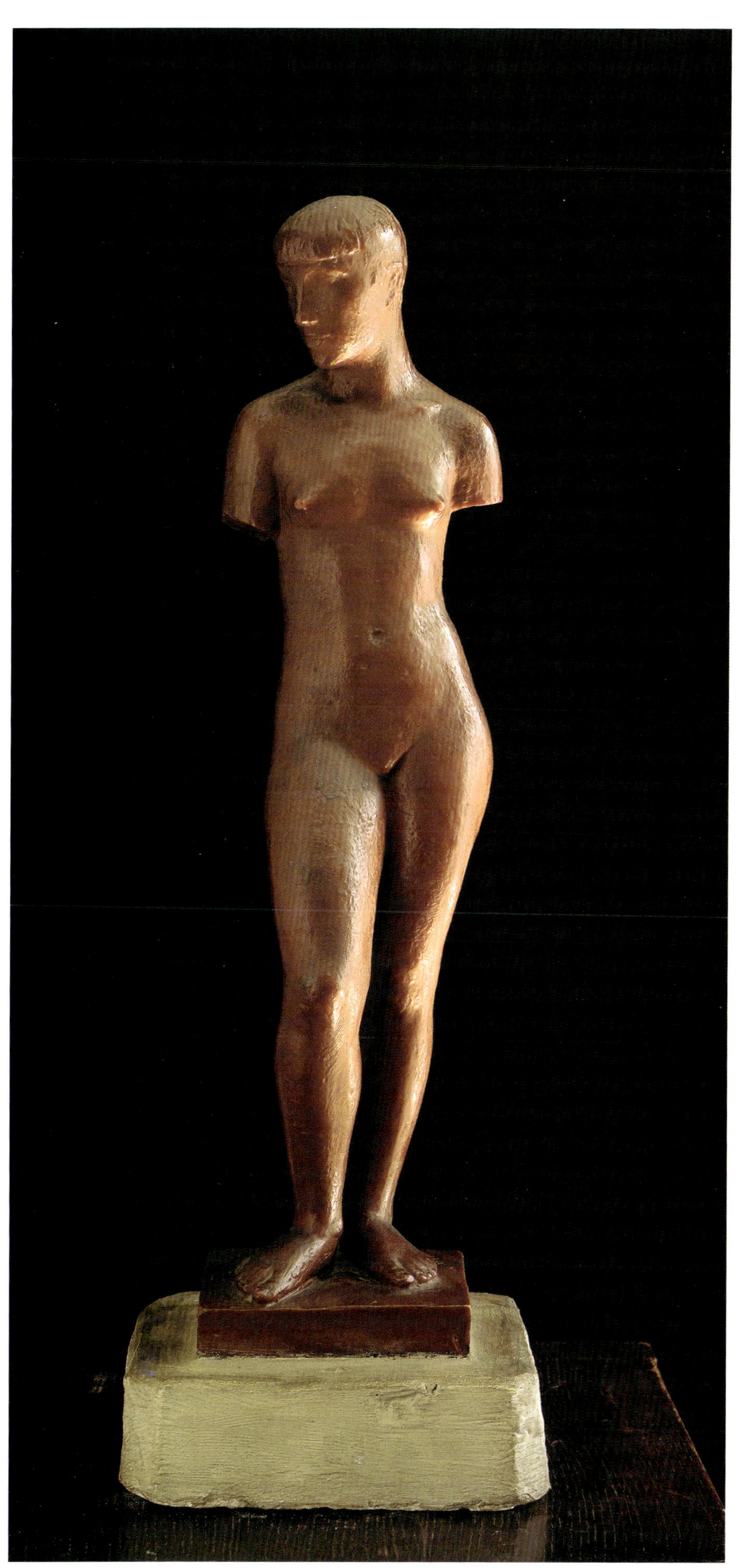

Charles Despiau, *Adolescent Girl (Diana),* 1928
Red wax on plaster base
Charles Janoray, LLC, New York. Cat. 153

Alexander Archipenko, *Torso in Space,* also called *Floating Torso,* 1935. Bronze

Nancy A. Nasher and David J. Haemisegger. Cat. 145

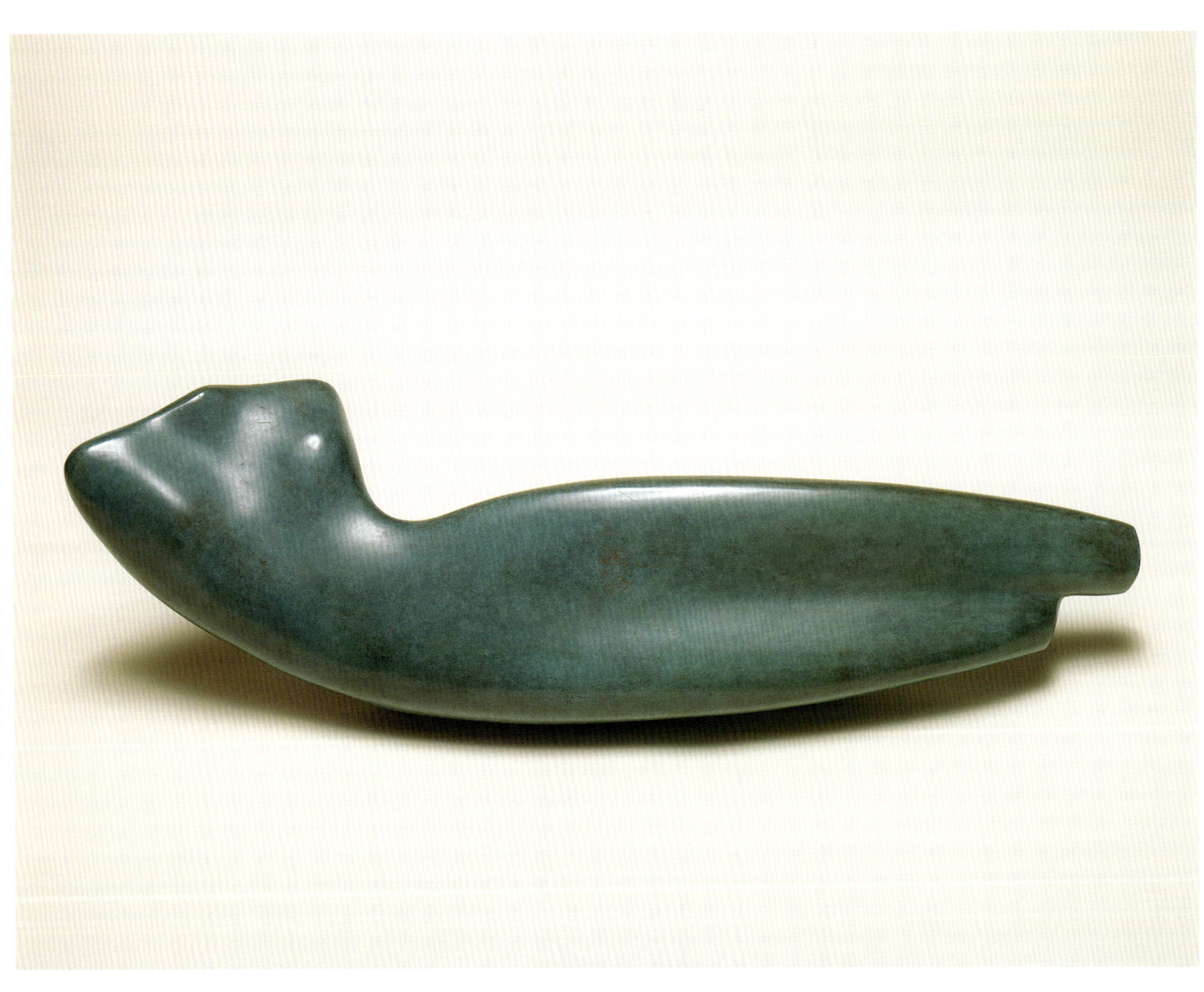

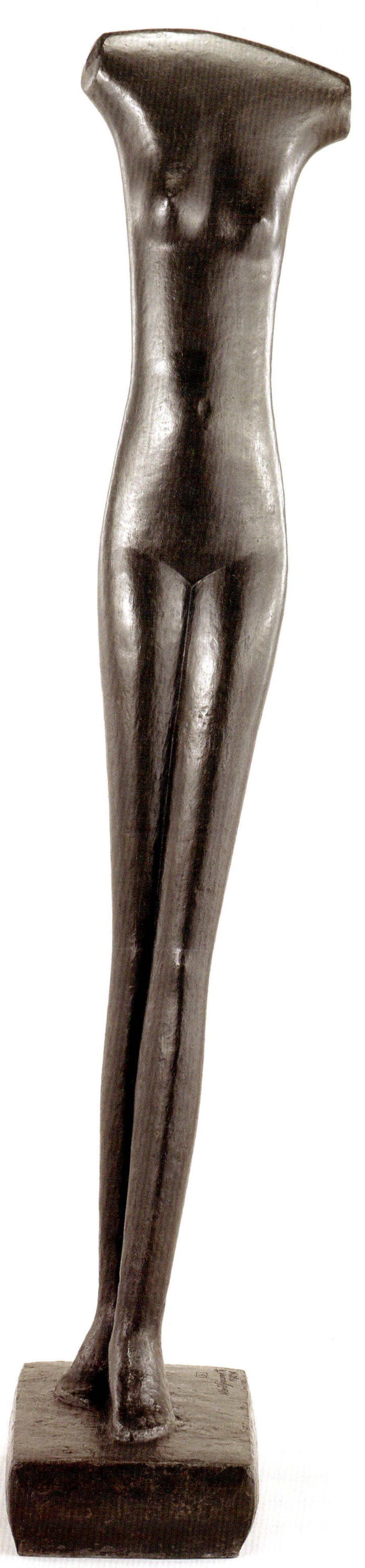

Alberto Giacometti, *Headless Woman,*
1932–1936. Bronze

The Baltimore Museum of Art, Alan and Janet Wurtzburger Collection. Cat. 154

Venus in a Shell

The two bronze versions of *Venus in a Shell* reflect opposing modes of sculptural expression that Matisse explored in other works at the beginning of the 1930s. The smooth surface, rounded volumes, and generalized form of *Venus in a Shell I* reflect the same formal concerns and curvaceous sensuality of works such as *Tiari. Venus in a Shell II* exhibits the rough angularity, carved planar surfaces, and raw physicality seen in *Large Seated Nude.* Similar juxtapositions of refined and coarse treatments of a subject appear in series or complementary compositions throughout his career, beginning with *Madeleine I* and *II* and continuing through *Reclining Nude II* and *III* and the complete series of *Back*s.

Matisse's rendering of the goddess of beauty has its roots in both the poetic and the mundane. Preparatory drawings he made at this time to illustrate the book *Poésies de Stéphane Mallarmé* echo the pose and composition of *Venus in a Shell.* In the drawings, a curvaceous, seated nude with arms above her head emerges from surrounding forms. The oft-noted source for this was a photograph Matisse had taken in Tahiti of a cloud formation that looked to him like a nude woman rising from a billowy source. The artist associated this vision with a poem by Théophile Gautier that described a sculpted cloud against the sky, rising like a nude maiden from the water of a lake and echoing the myth of the birth of Venus, who emerged from the ocean on a clam shell. One also finds this evocation of the birth of Beauty in the painting *The Yellow Dress,* in which Matisse represents his stunning young model as a chaste torso emerging from her billowing gown. Other authors have also pointed out ancient sculptures of the birth of Venus that Matisse may have drawn upon, as well as photographs of one of Matisse's own earlier sculptures, now destroyed, of a reclining Venus on a shell.

For Matisse, this vision of the birth of Beauty also evoked the more quotidian scene of the modern bather. Studies for *Venus in a Shell* recall his earlier drawings of bathing women, such as *The Bath* and *Woman Standing in Tub.* Although executed in response to the *toilette* tradition exemplified by late nineteenth-century artists such as Degas and Toulouse-Lautrec, the drawings depict the bather rising from a curved shell-like basin and represent the artist's first attempts to come to grips with the formal aspects that he tackles in *Venus in a Shell.* The revelation of Degas's sculptures in an exhibition at Galerie A.-A. Hébrard in 1921 may also have provided another source for Matisse's Venus. Many of Degas's depictions of bathing women were included in the exhibition, among them *Seated Woman Wiping Her Left Side,* which also shows a bather rising from a rounded base.

Venus in a Shell II was the last sculpture Matisse modeled until 1949. It was at this point that he began cutting paper shapes with scissors. The cut-outs would become his primary sculptural vehicle for the rest of his life.

JM

Henri Matisse, *Venus in a Shell I,* 1930. Bronze

The Baltimore Museum of Art, The Cone Collection, formed by Dr. Claribel Cone and Miss Etta Cone of Baltimore, Maryland. Cat. 123

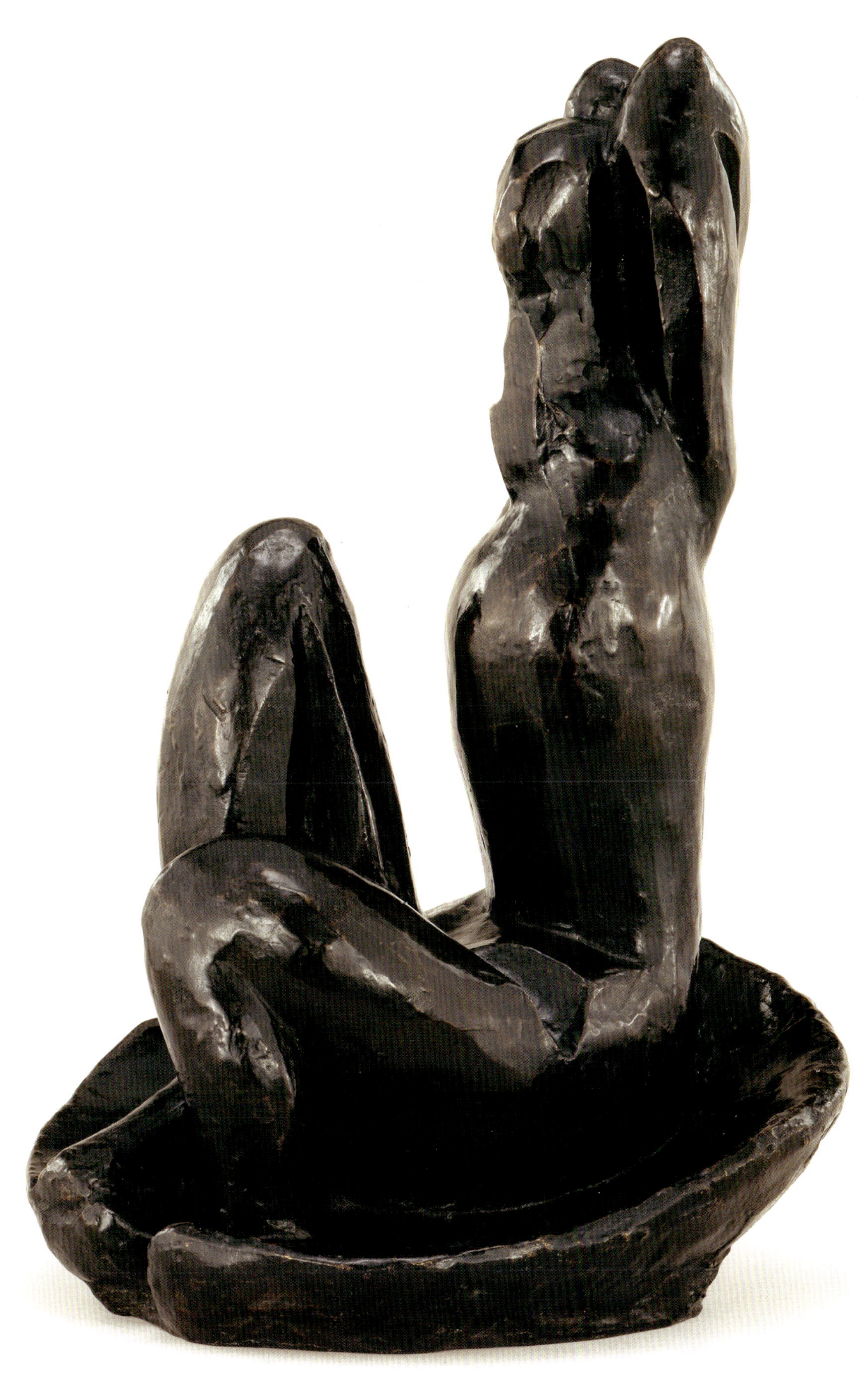

Henri Matisse, *Venus in a Shell I,* 1930. Bronze

The Baltimore Museum of Art, The Cone Collection, formed by Dr. Claribel Cone and Miss Etta Cone of Baltimore, Maryland. Cat. 123

Henri Matisse, *The Yellow Dress,* 1929–1931

Oil on canvas

The Baltimore Museum of Art, The Cone Collection, formed by Dr. Claribel Cone and Miss Etta Cone of Baltimore, Maryland. Cat. 128

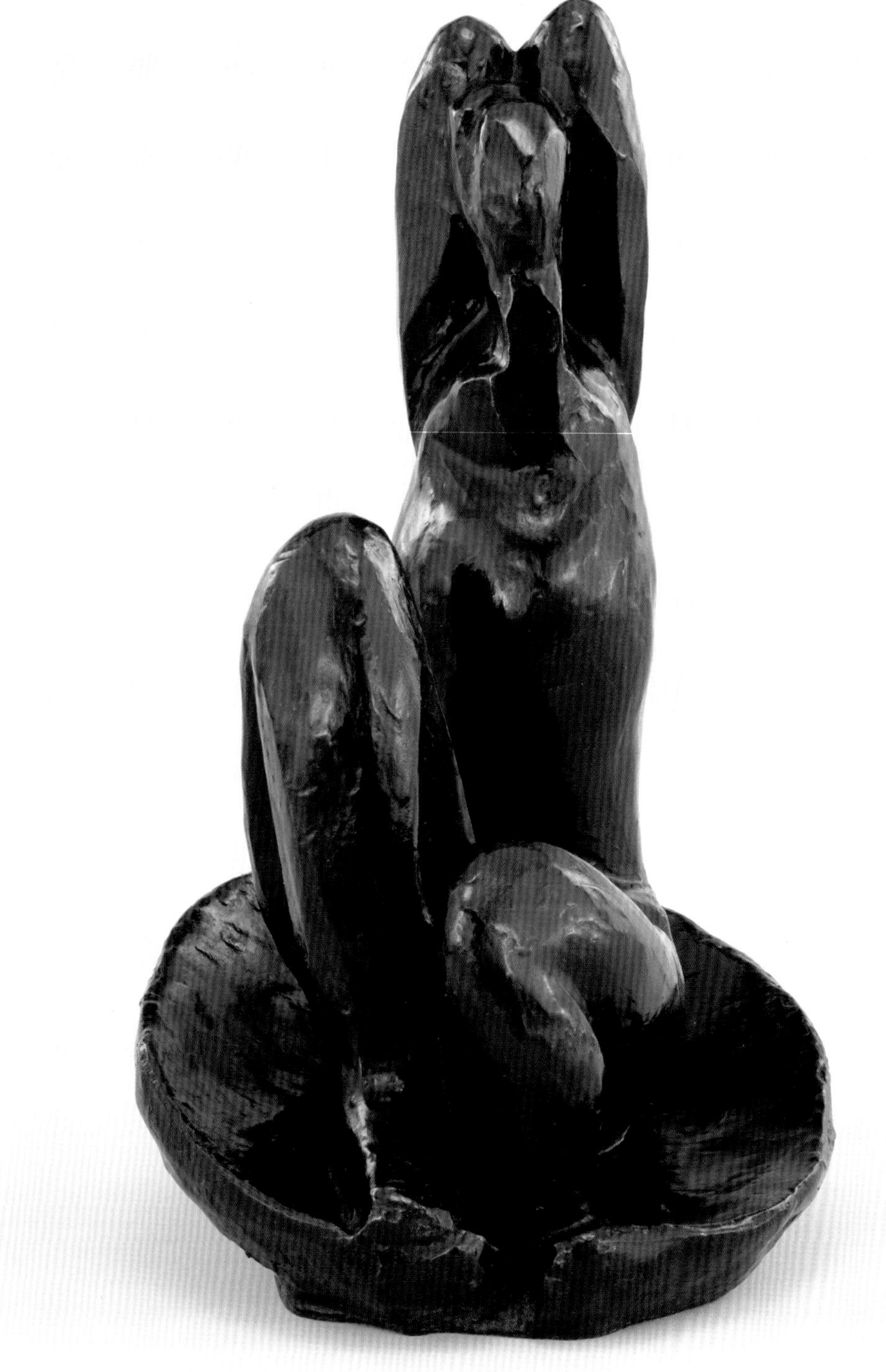

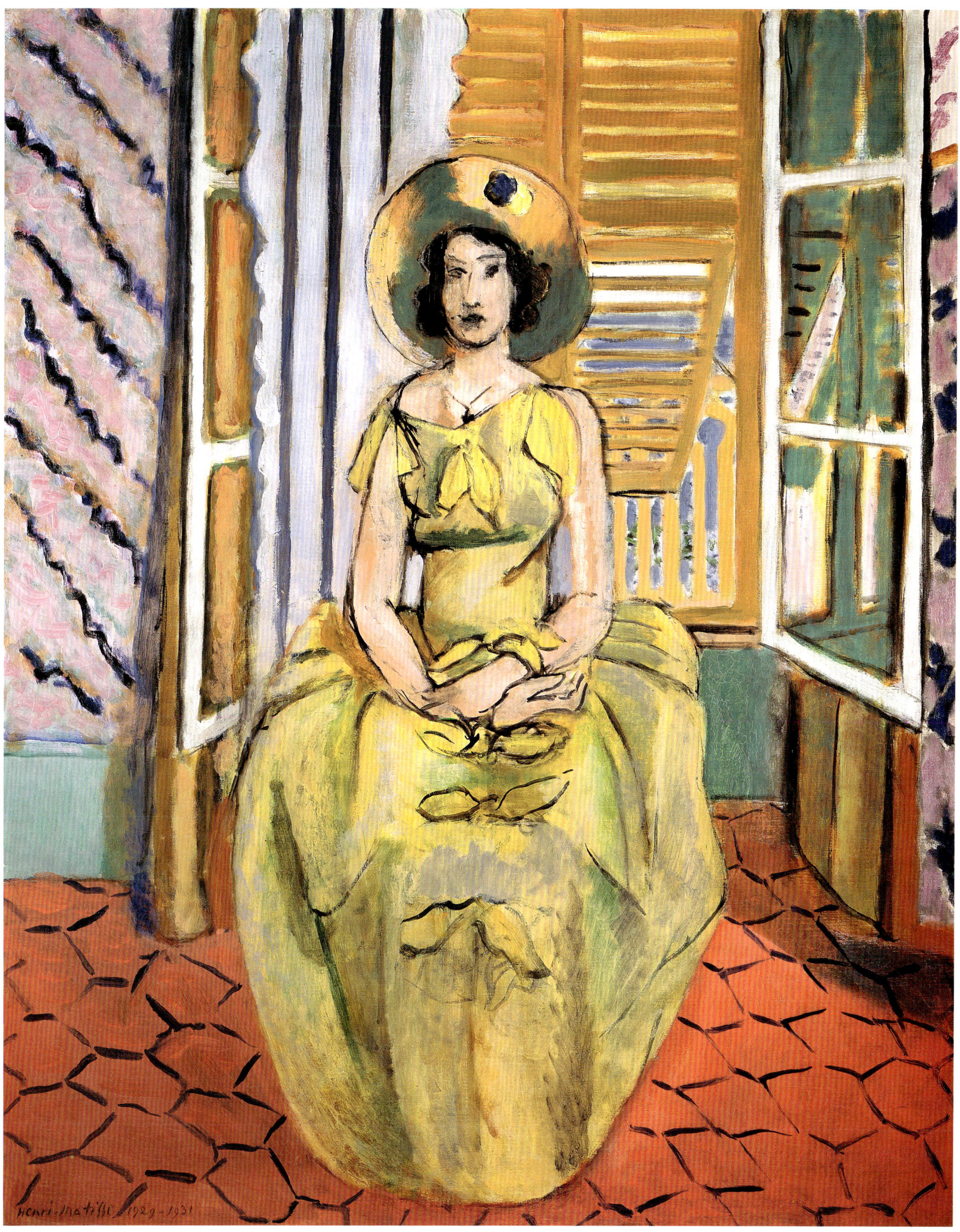
Henri-Matisse 1929-1931

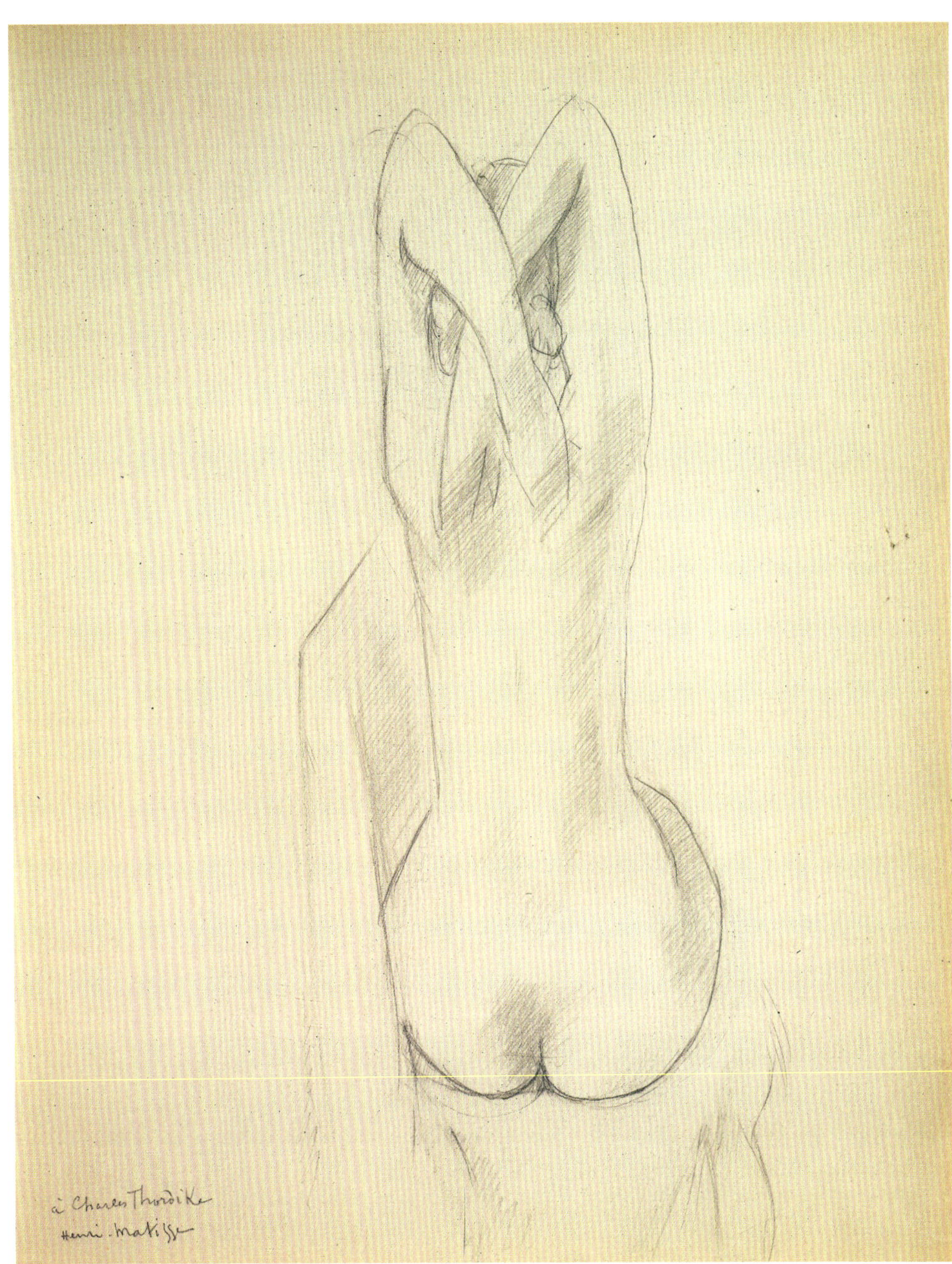

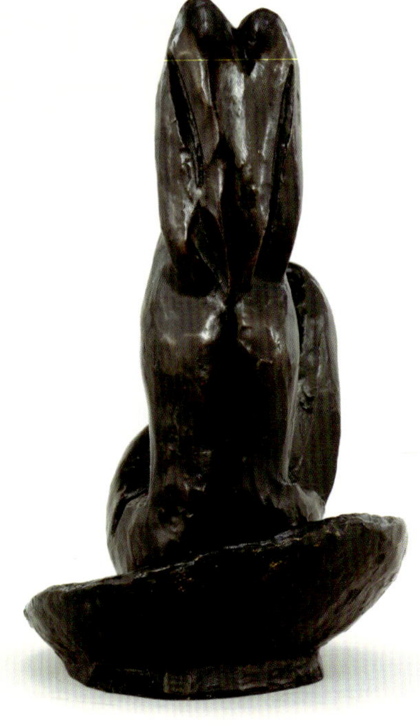

Henri Matisse, *Venus in a Shell I,* 1930. Bronze

The Baltimore Museum of Art, The Cone Collection, formed by Dr. Claribel Cone and Miss Etta Cone of Baltimore, Maryland. Cat. 123

Henri Matisse, *Seated Nude,* c. 1929–1930 Graphite

Mr. and Mrs. Stanley R. Gumberg, Pittsburgh. Cat. 127

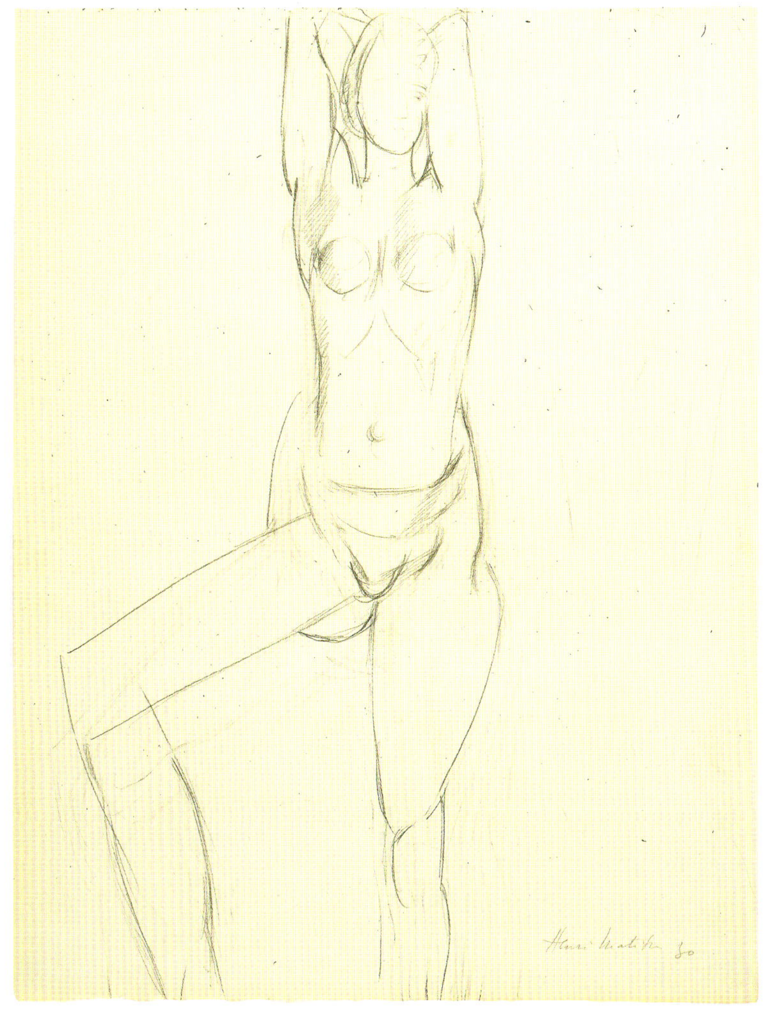

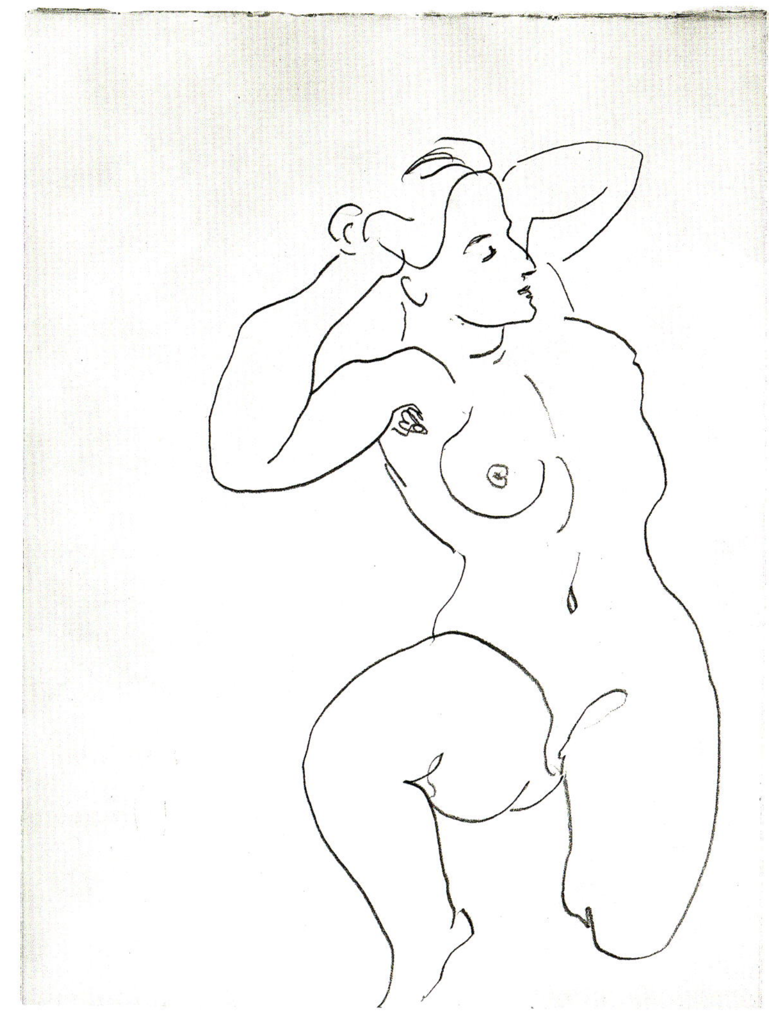

Henri Matisse, *Standing Nude,* 1930. Graphite

Pierre and Maria-Gaetana Matisse Foundation Collection. Cat. 129

Henri Matisse, *Nude with Raised Arms,* 1930–1933. Graphite on imitation vellum paper

Centre Pompidou, Paris; Musée national d'art moderne/ Centre de création industrielle; Gift of Marie Matisse, 1984. Cat. 130

Henri Matisse, Preliminary drawing for *Hommage III,* from *Poésies de Stéphane Mallarmé,* c. 1932. Graphite

The Baltimore Museum of Art, The Cone Collection, formed by Dr. Claribel Cone and Miss Etta Cone of Baltimore, Maryland. Cat. 131

Henri Matisse, *Venus in a Shell II,* 1932. Bronze

Raymond and Patsy Nasher Collection, Dallas. Cat. 124

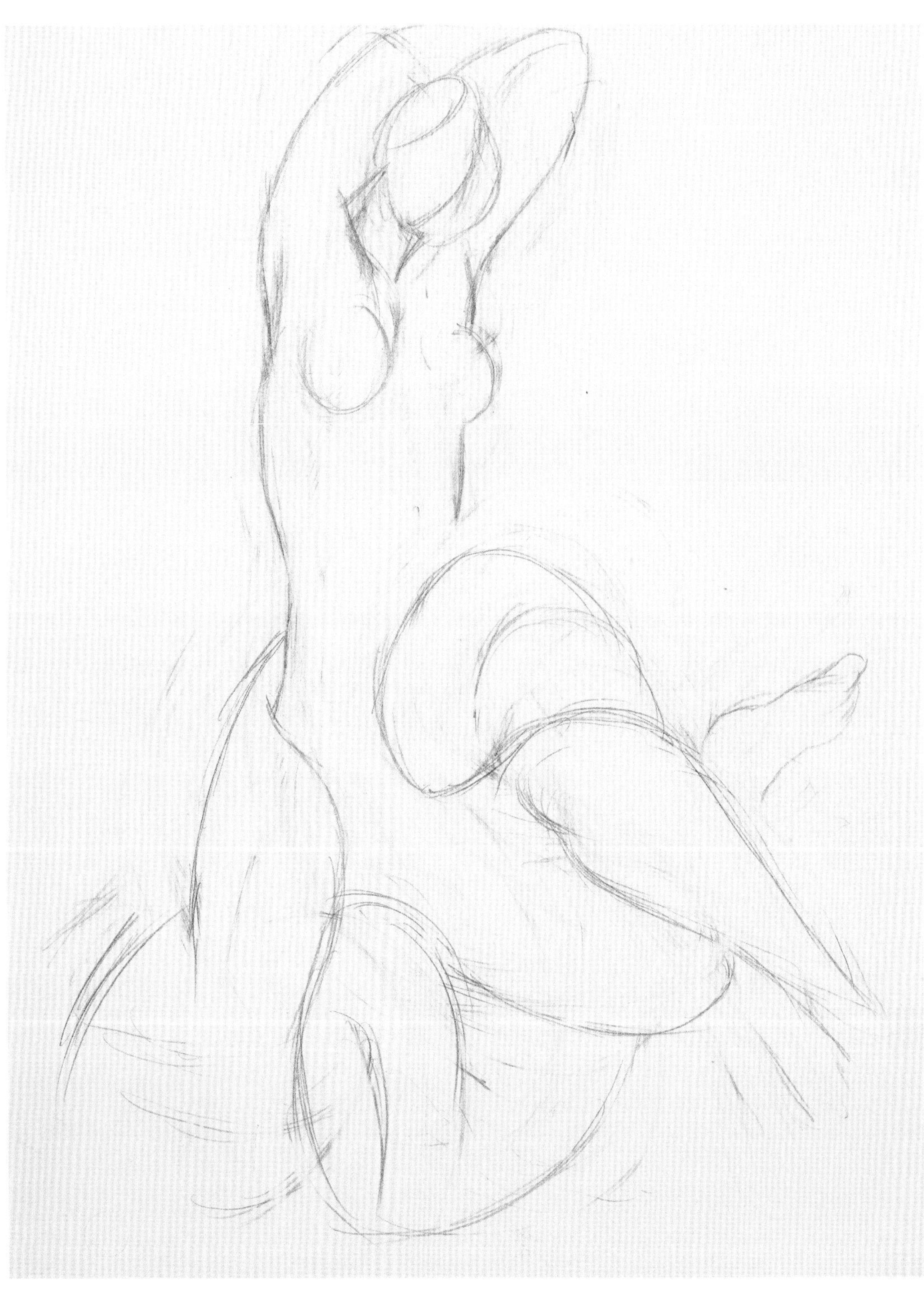

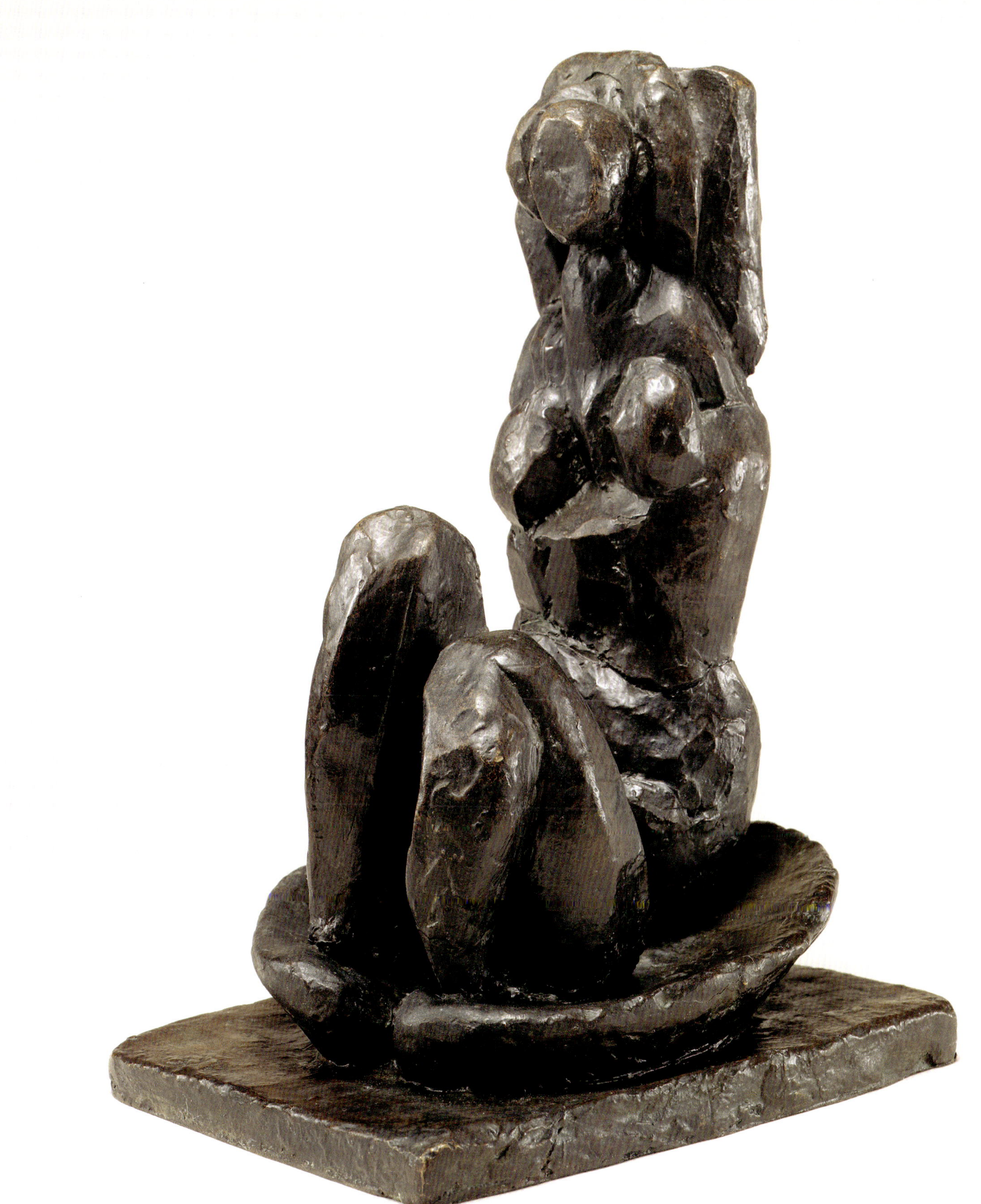

Edgar Degas, *Seated Woman Wiping Her Left Side,* 1900–1905. Bronze

The Detroit Institute of Arts; Gift of Edward E. Rothman.

Cat. 151

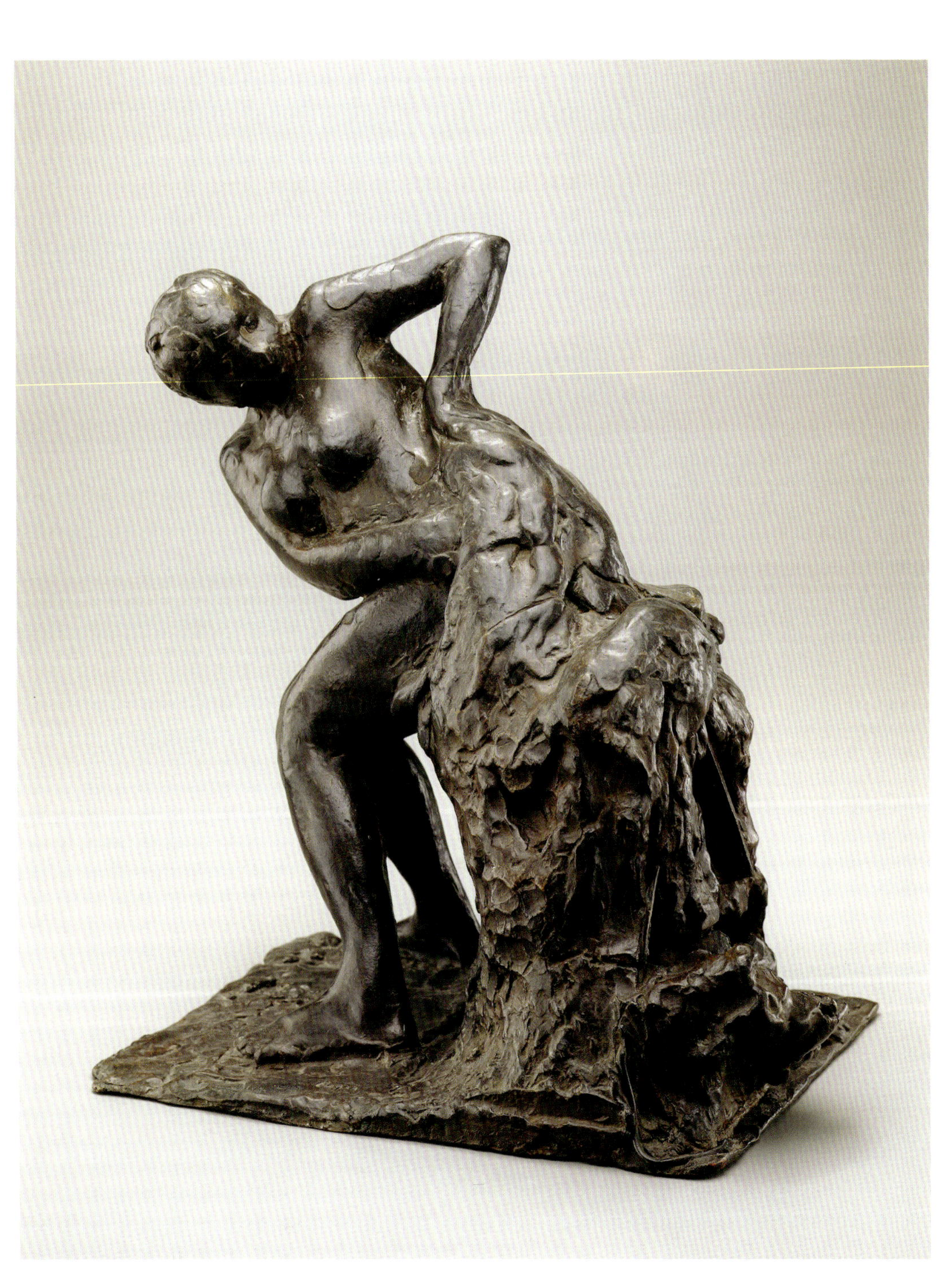

Henri Matisse, *Woman Standing in Tub,* 1905–1906. Pen and india ink

Private collection. Cat. 125

Henri Matisse, *The Bath,* 1905–1906

Pen and india ink

Centre Pompidou, Paris; Musée national d'art moderne/ Centre de création industrielle; Gift of Marie Matisse, 1984. Cat. 126

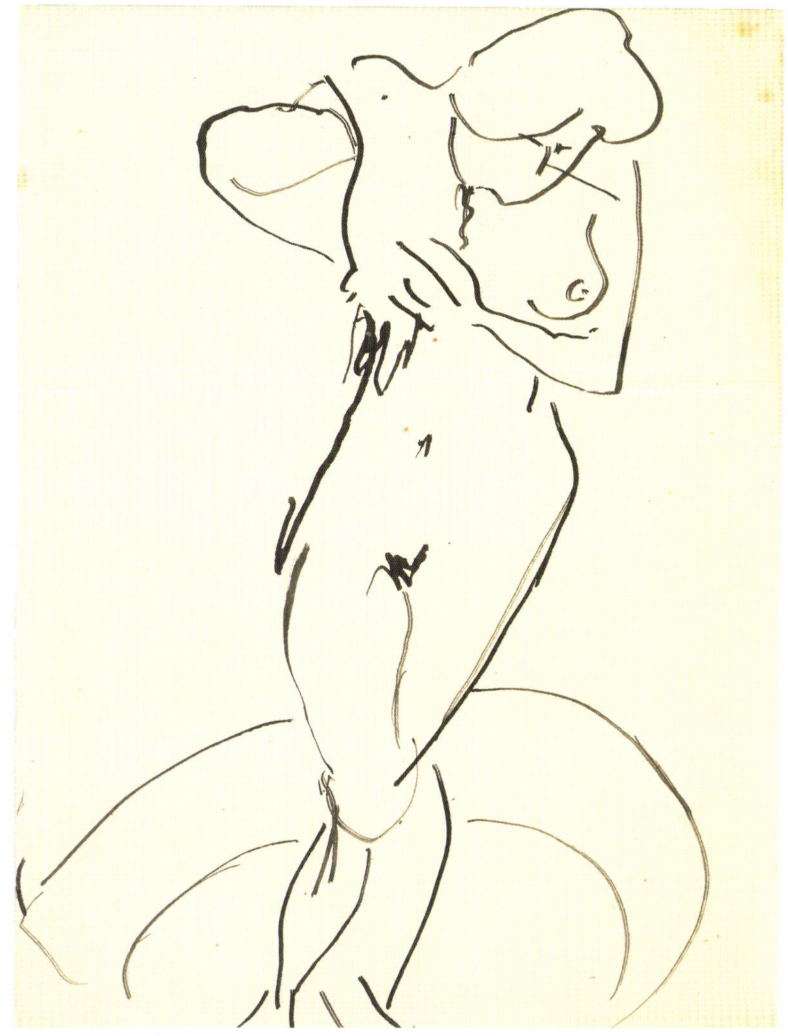

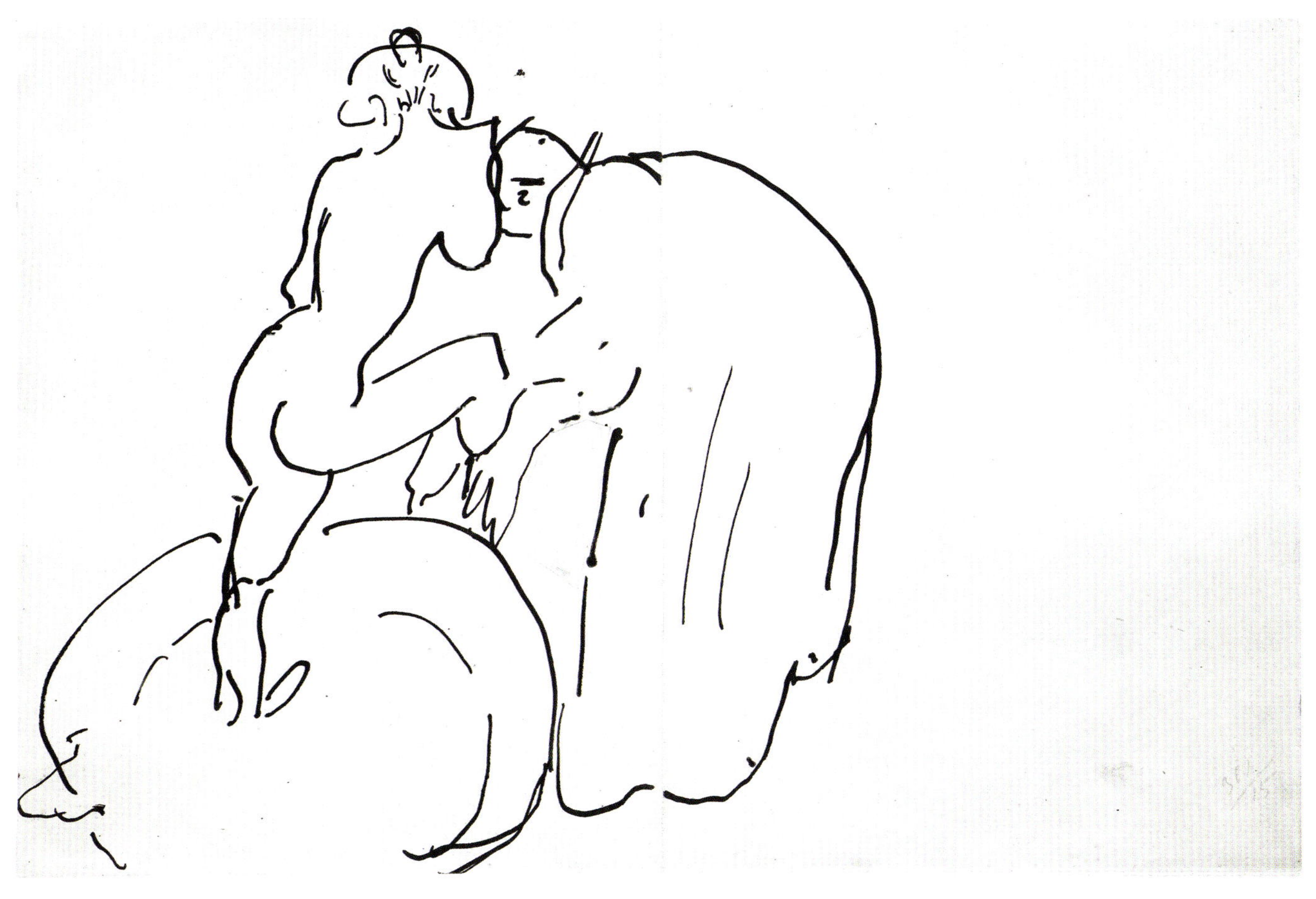

Standing Nude (Katia)

After completing *Venus in a Shell II* in 1932, Matisse ceased to sculpt for more than sixteen years. In 1949, he made two sculptures, the small *Seated Nude, Arm Raised* and the sinuous *Christ* for the altar of the Dominican chapel at Vence. Matisse's last sculptural project was *Standing Nude (Katia),* an erect, symmetrical figure of the type that had interested him more than forty years earlier in works such as *Standing Nude* and *Standing Nude, Arms on Head.* It was a figural motif that he had developed early in his drawings, but it was only in 1950, near the end of his life, that he returned to the subject with a new intensity, sculpting the rather solid figure of a model that he had nicknamed "The Plane Tree" for her supple, statuesque physique.[1] The legs, separated by the slimmest of gaps, and torso of the figure form a rounded column not unlike the trunk of a tree, while the slight spreading around the ankles (the figure has no feet) suggests unseen roots below. The richly articulated surface of the bronze, eloquent in its testimony to the touch of the sculptor, solicits the caress of the viewer.

Photographs show Matisse modeling this sculpture while propped up in bed, as he often worked in his final years, when his health began to fail (fig. 22, p. 22). The sculpture's alternate name, *The Broken Waist,* refers to the conspicuous rupture at the waistline of the figure. According to Ann Boulton, the crack resulted from Matisse's decision to put regular drying clay over an undrying core of plasticine, an oil-based modeling clay. As the outer layer hardened from simple air drying, it contracted and sloughed off from the inner material, resulting in the crack at the waist. Matisse accepted this dramatic technical failure (although it would have been relatively simple to repair the model) and incorporated it into the final work. This had also been his solution in 1909, when a similar accident broke the waist of *Torso without Arms or Head.* In her essay in this catalogue, Ann Boulton discusses Matisse's interest in retaining the traces of process in his sculptures and suggests that he may even have manipulated his materials to generate such apparent accidents.[2]

The upright and symmetrical figure of *Standing Nude (Katia)* continued to interest Matisse after he completed the sculpture and ceased to work at all in clay and bronze. His paper cut-outs, such as the *Standing Blue Nude* of 1952, revisit the motif and dematerialize the solid, treelike figure of the sculpture. The rigid, hieratic standing figure is reduced to five simple shapes, each floating almost independently on a white field. Works such as this suggests the intimate relationship between the cut-outs, collages of paper coated in gouache, and his earlier work in three-dimensional media.

HMacD

Notes

1. Schneider 1984, 548.
2. See Ann Boulton's essay in this volume, p. 73.

Henri Matisse, *Standing Nude (Katia),*
1950. Bronze

Private collection. Cat. 132

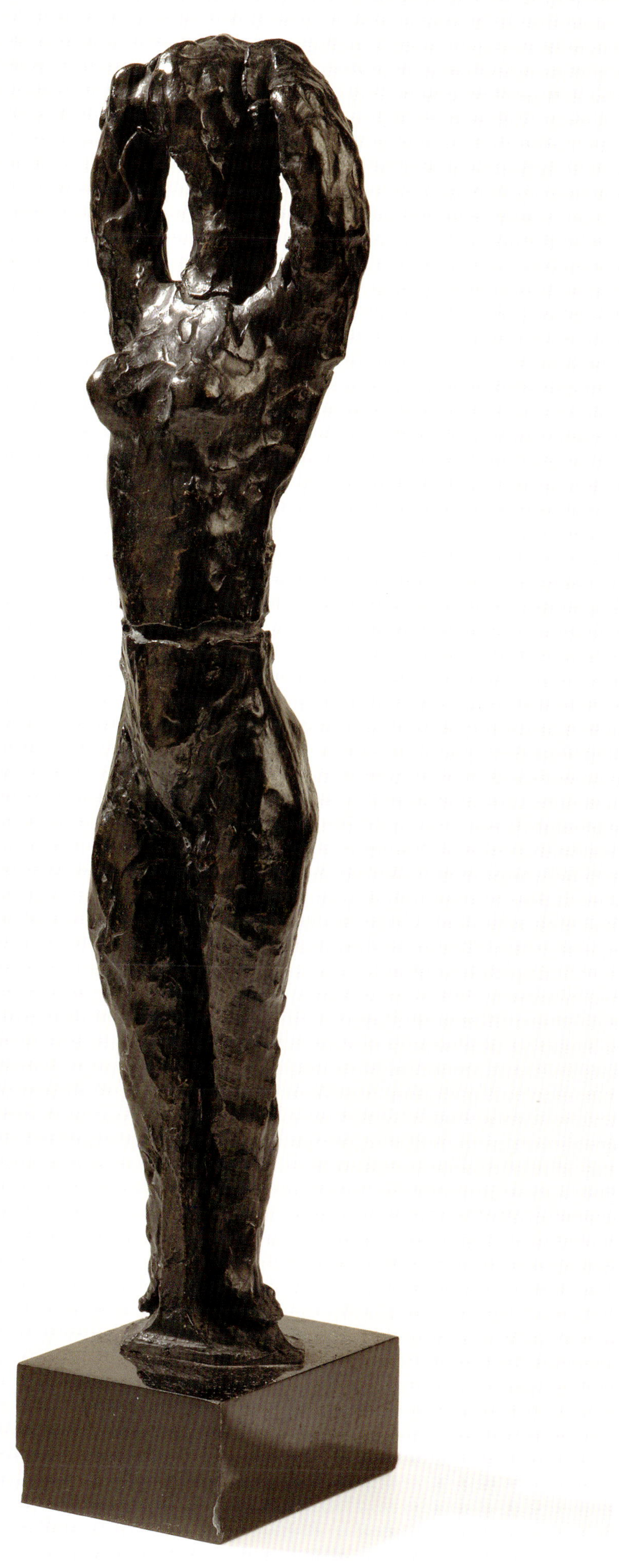

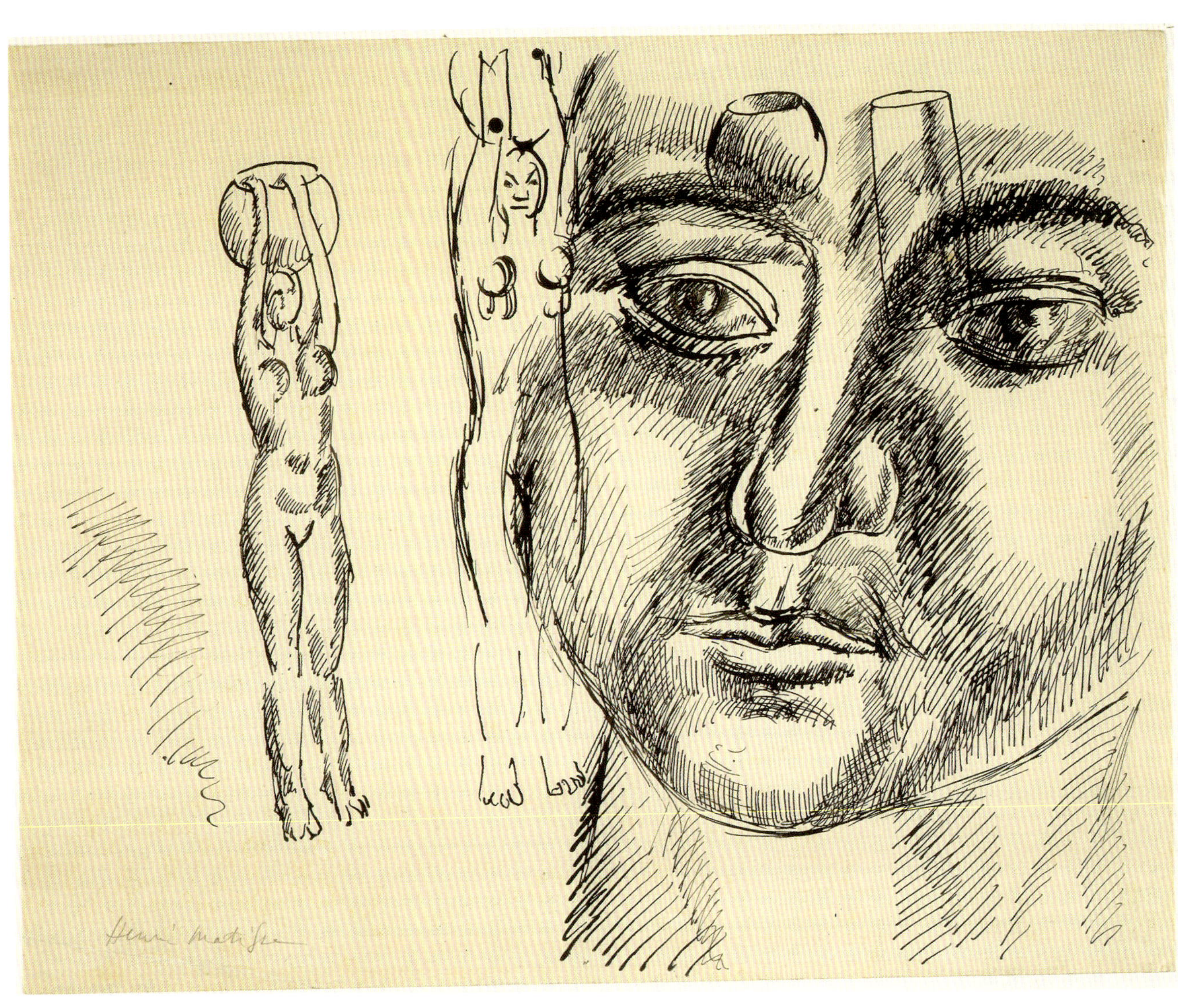

Henri Matisse, *Face and Two Nudes with Gourds,* 1912–1913. Pen and india ink on squared paper

Centre Pompidou, Paris; Musée national d'art moderne/ Centre de création industrielle; Purchased from Marie Matisse, 1984. Cat. 134

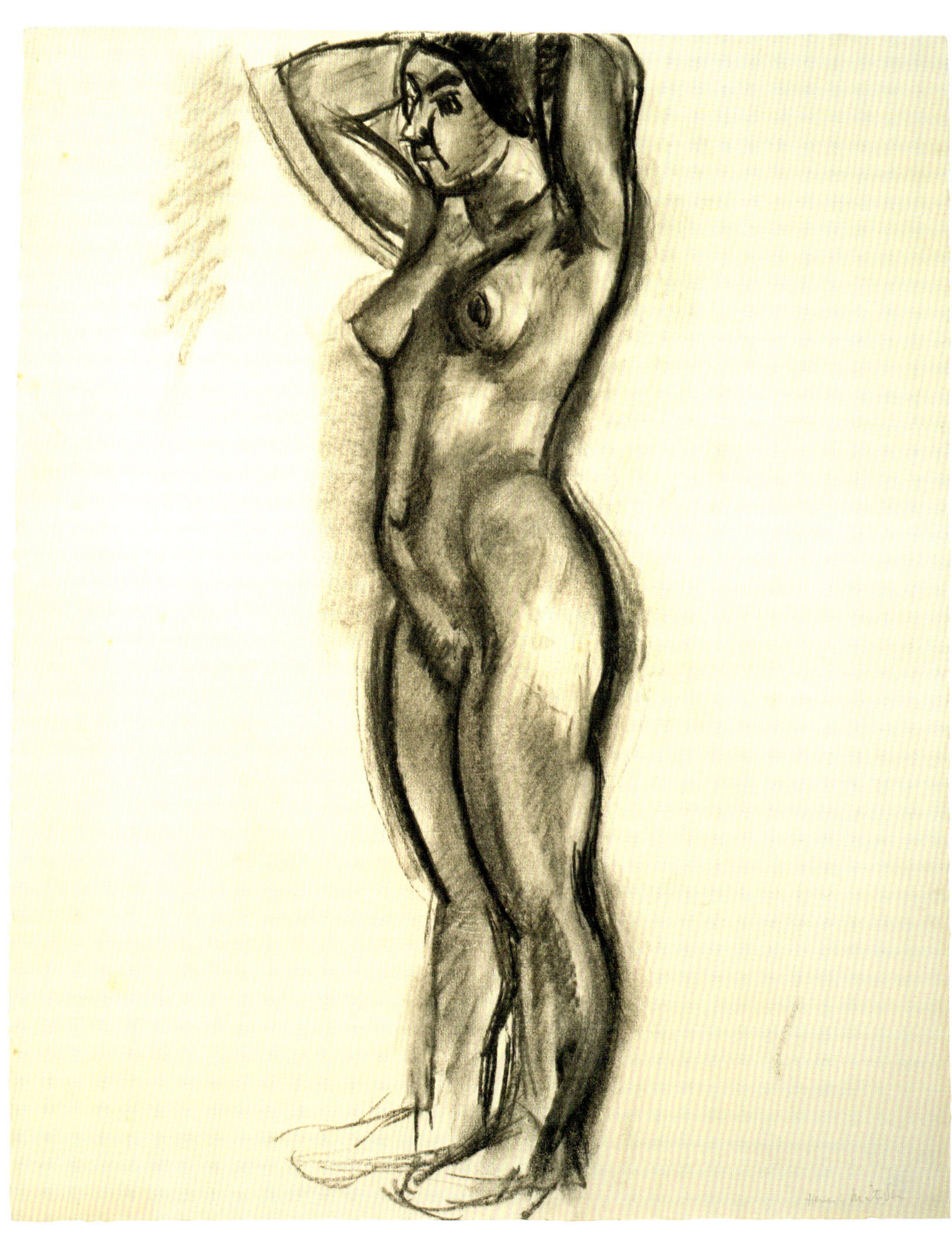

Henri Matisse, *Standing Nude, Seen from the Side,* 1908–1909. Charcoal with stumping
Collection of Gerald and Kathleen Peters. Cat. 133

Henri Matisse, *Figure,* c. 1950. Pen and ink

Pierre and Maria-Gaetana Matisse Foundation Collection.

Cat. 136

Henri Matisse, *Standing Nude, Seen from the Back (Lisette),* c. 1930. Graphite

Pierre and Maria-Gaetana Matisse Foundation Collection.

Cat. 135

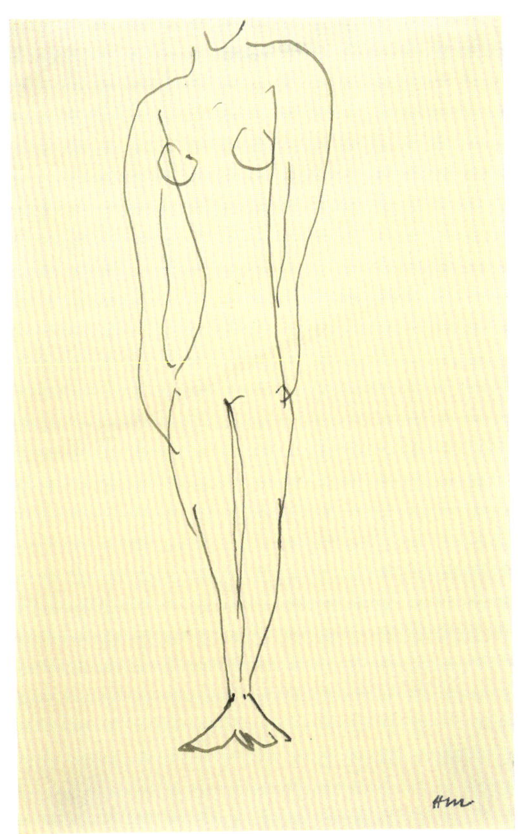

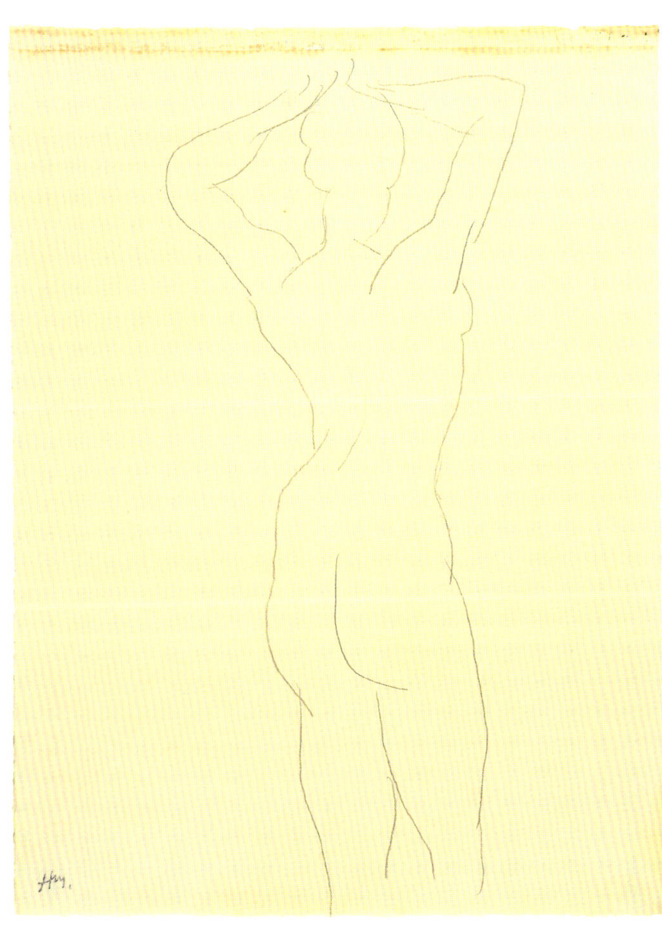

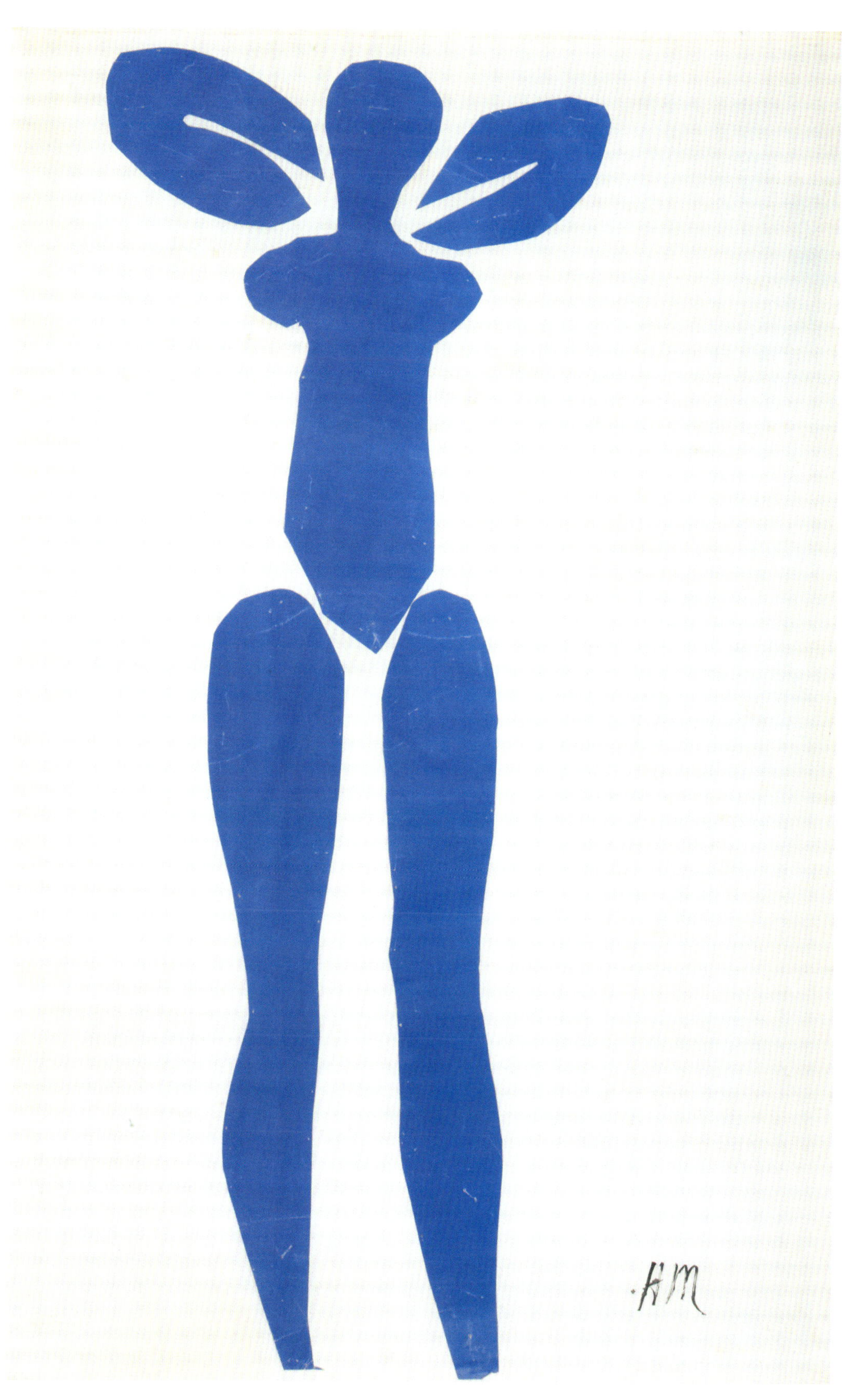

Henri Matisse, *Standing Blue Nude,* 1952
Gouache on paper, cut and pasted
The Metropolitan Museum of Art, New York; The Pierre and Maria-Gaetana Matisse Collection, 2002. Cat. 137

Cut-Outs

Matisse first started using cut-outs in preparing large and complex compositions, such as the murals of *The Dance* (1930–1933) at the Barnes Foundation. By working with paper templates of the pictorial elements, he was able to make myriad adjustments to his compositions before or during the process of painting. Matisse first treated his cut-outs as independent works in 1936, when he made a collage to serve as the cover of an issue of the periodical *Cahiers d'art,* and the medium would continue to play a central role in his work until the end of his life.[1] To make his cut-outs, Matisse used scissors to slice shapes out of heavy paper that had been painted with gouache by his studio assistants. The pigment was applied with a brush, creating a slightly textured, nuanced surface. Matisse then assembled the fragments of gouache-coated paper, often working first on the walls of his studio before pasting the elements to a paper or canvas support. His materials were not traditional sculptural materials but rather the media of painting and drawing: paper, canvas, and paint. "Paper cutouts allow me to draw in colour," he told André Lejard in 1951, a reference to the tension between drawing and color that had preoccupied his work for many decades. "For me, that simplifies matters. Instead of drawing an outline and then adding colour—which means that line and colour modify one another—I can draw directly in colour. . . . The simplification means that the two means of expression become a single means of expression."[2]

The cut-outs enabled Matisse not only to unify his painting and drawing but also to merge his sculptural practice with those other areas of artistic exploration. The intimate relationship between his three-dimensional work and the cut-out collages has long been acknowledged. It was Matisse himself who first drew attention to this connection when he wrote, "cutting straight into color reminds me of the direct carving of the sculptor."[3] The metaphor is striking, for Matisse did very little direct carving, the only extant example being a tree trunk carved with a relief of *The Dance,* and in fact the cut-outs have been described in terms of extremely shallow bas-relief.[4] Michael Anthonioz notes that the French word for scissors, *ciseaux,* is simply the plural of the word for chisel, *ciseau.*[5] Scissors, like the sculptor's chisel, imply direct contact with the material, and it was this action of carving into a mass of pure color that Matisse likened to the action of the sculptor.

The series of four *Blue Nudes* of 1952 was one of Matisse's masterpieces in the medium. Matisse called these works *baigneuses* (bathers), a clear reference to the work of Cézanne, whose images of bathers (cat. 149, p. 165, and fig. 10, p. 9, for example) had been so influential. Like many of Matisse's most inventive sculptures—works such as *Decorative Figure, The Serpentine,* and *Large Seated Nude*—the cut-outs activate their negative space, making it an essential component of the image. In the *Blue Nudes,* Isabelle Monod-Fontaine notes, "it is the empty space between the cut-out pieces that accentuate the joints. It is these gaps that shape the fullness, the swell of the volumes."[6]

In 1943, the publisher Efstratios Tériade persuaded Matisse to collaborate with him on a printed portfolio of cut-outs, which was published in 1947 under the title *Jazz.* Although Matisse was initially displeased with the way that the print medium flattened out much of the texture and modulation of

Henri Matisse, *The Knife Thrower,* plate XV from *Jazz,* 1947. Hand-printed colored stencil

The Baltimore Museum of Art, The Cone Collection, formed by Dr. Claribel Cone and Miss Etta Cone of Baltimore, Maryland. Cat. 142a

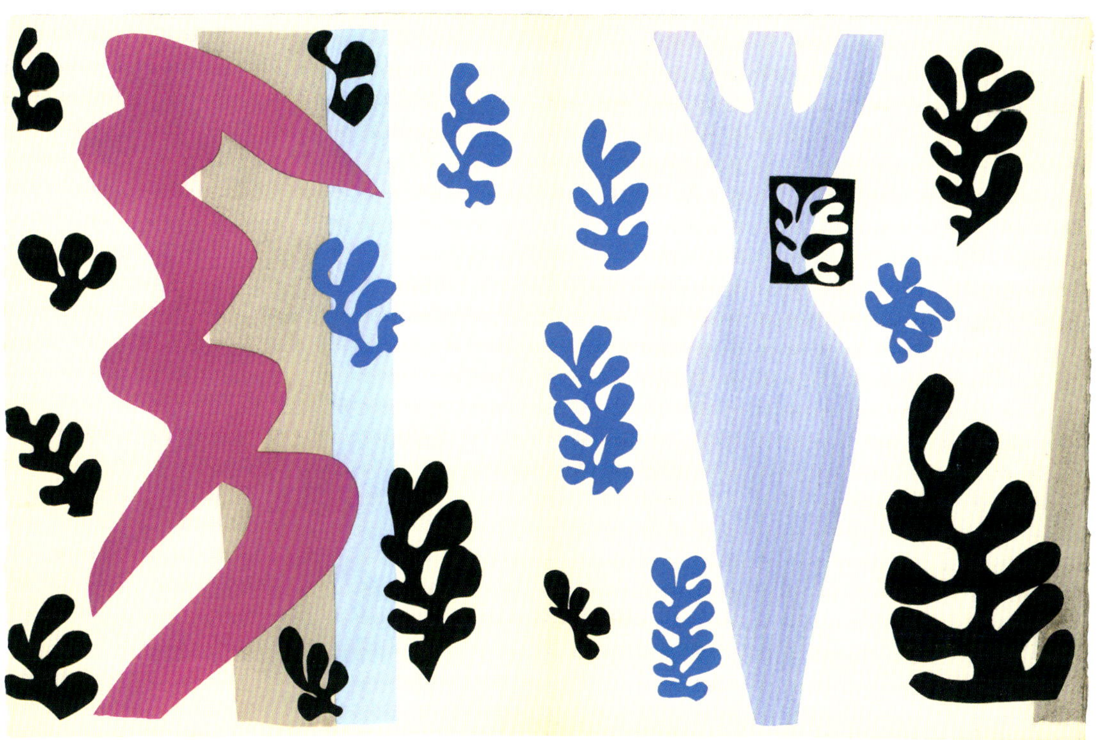

pigment of the cut-outs, the publication was a success and caused what he himself described as "a considerable stir."[7] In 1958, in a special issue of Tériade's periodical *Verve,* dedicated to Matisse's late works, several major cut-outs, including the *Blue Nudes,* were reproduced.[8] The two publications greatly expanded the audience for the cut-outs and have made some of these works, such as *The Fall of Icarus,* the most iconic of Matisse's entire oeuvre.

HMacD

Notes

1. *Cahiers d'art,* 3–5 (1936).
2. Quoted in Guichard-Meili 1983, 54.
3. Quoted in Fourcade 1977, 49.
4. De Barañano 2003, 40.
5. Anthonioz 2002, 53.
6. Monod-Fontaine 2003, 78.
7. Quoted in Guichard-Meili 1983, 50.
8. "Les derniers oeuvres de Matisse," *Verve* 35–36 (1958).

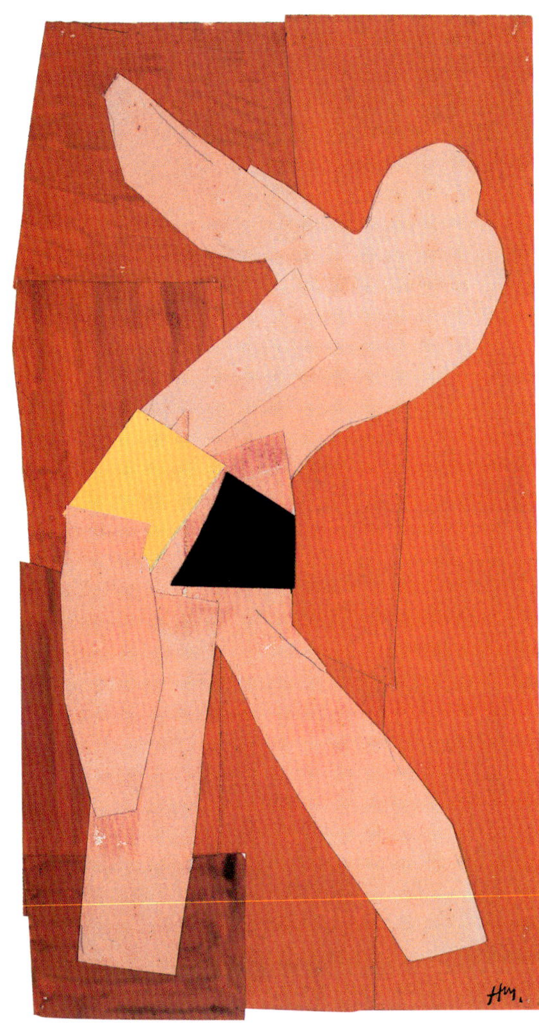

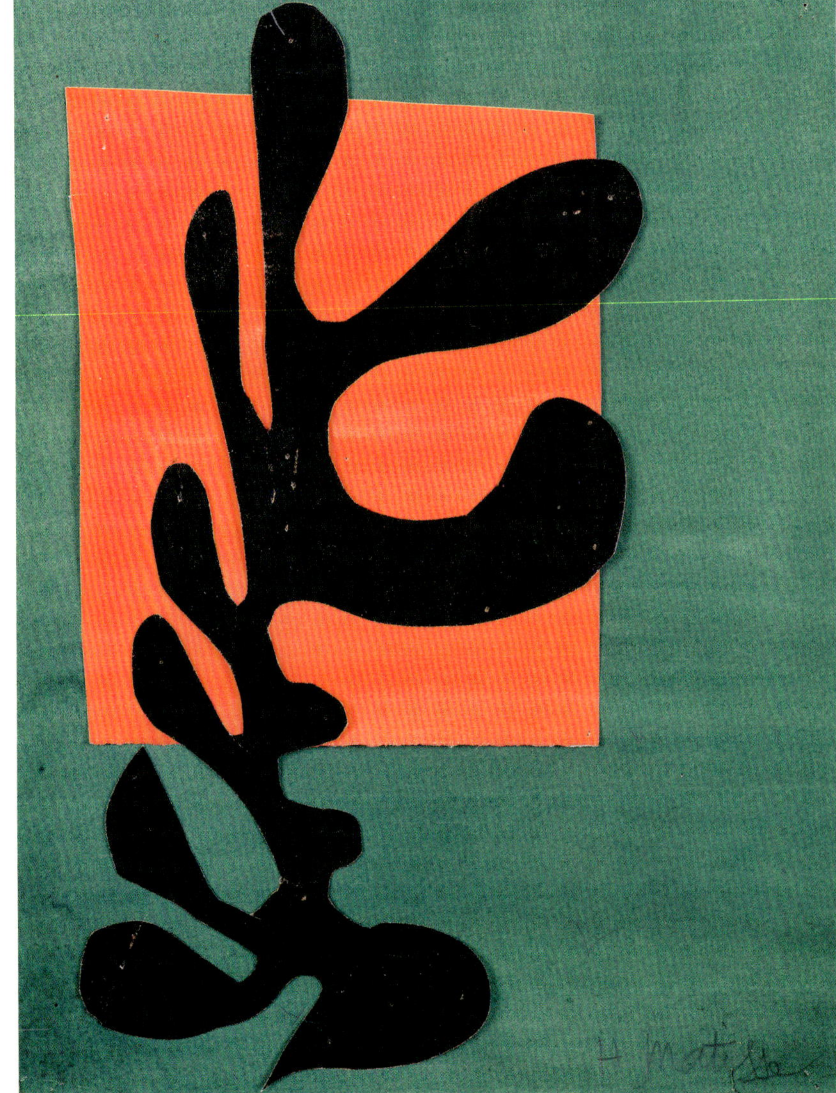

Henri Matisse, *Small Dancer on Red Ground,* 1937–1938. Gouache on paper, cut and pasted

Private collection. Cat. 138

Henri Matisse, *Negro Boxer,* 1947. Gouache on paper, cut and pasted

Private collection, New York. Cat. 139

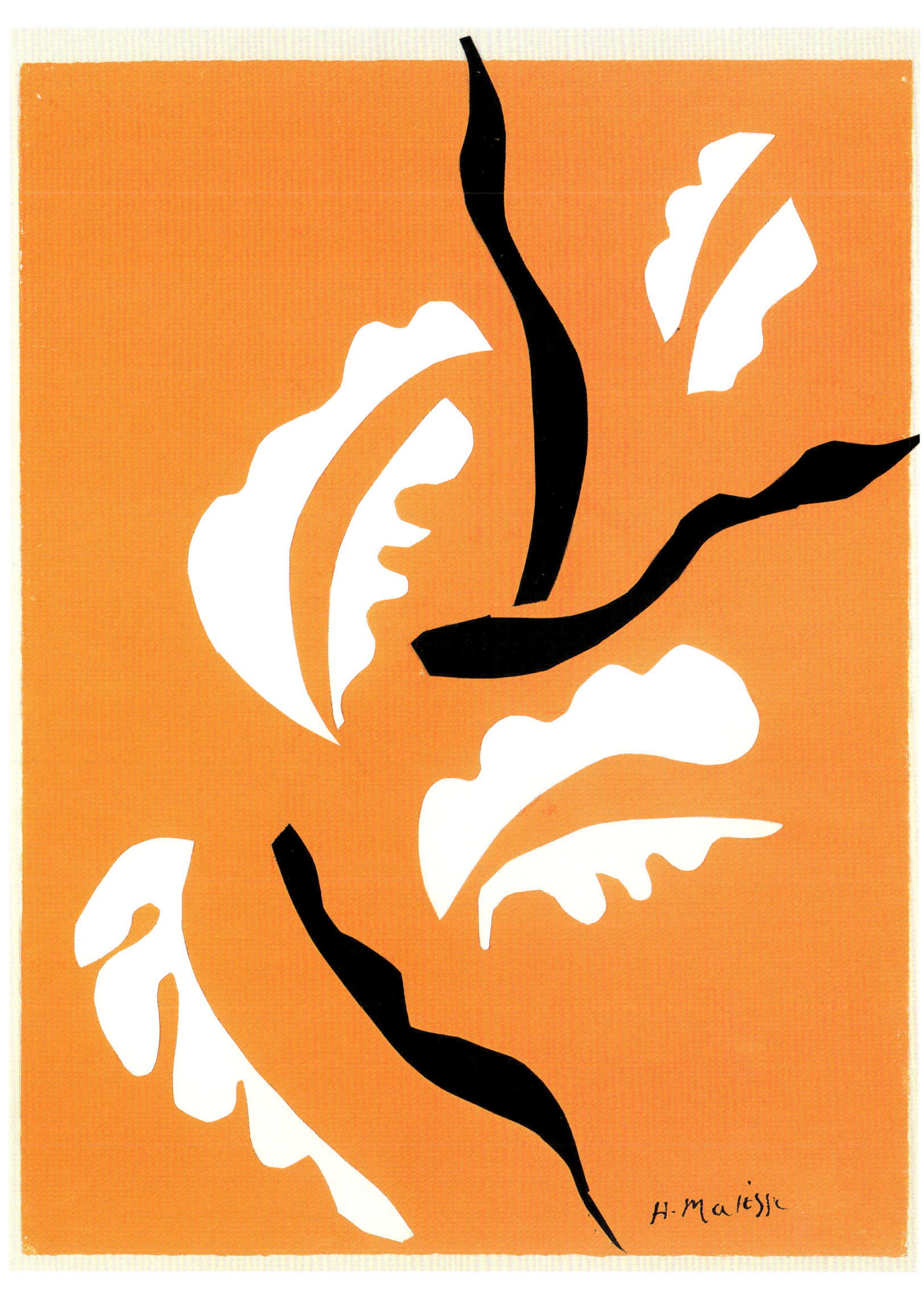

Henri Matisse, *Acrobatic Dancer,* 1949. Gouache on paper, cut and pasted

Pierre and Maria-Gaetana Matisse Foundation Collection.

Cat. 140

Henri Matisse, *Four Studies of an Acrobat,* 1950
Pen and ink

Pierre and Maria-Gaetana Matisse Foundation Collection.
Cat. 144

Henri Matisse, *Acrobat, Study,* 1950. Pen and ink

Pierre and Maria-Gaetana Matisse Foundation Collection.
Cat. 143

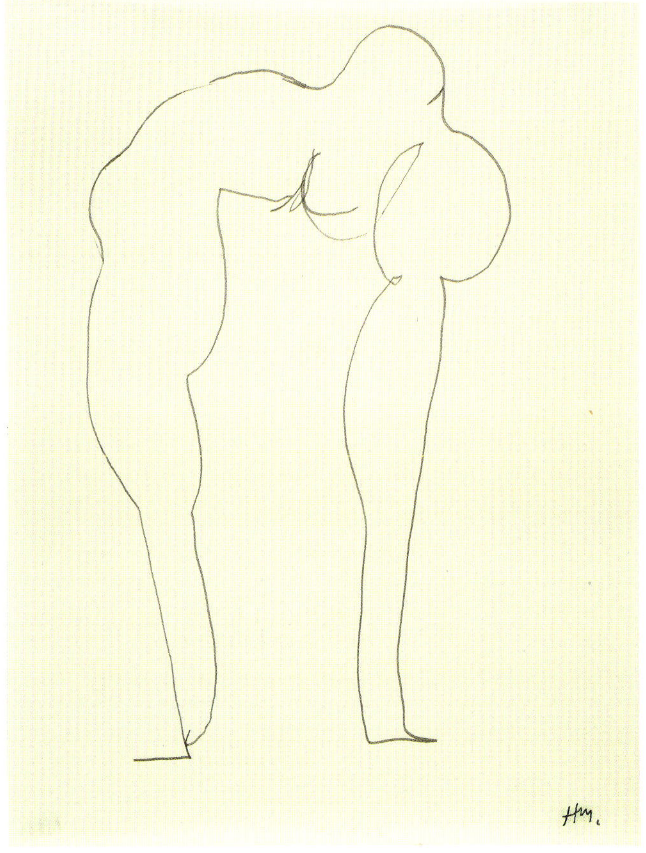

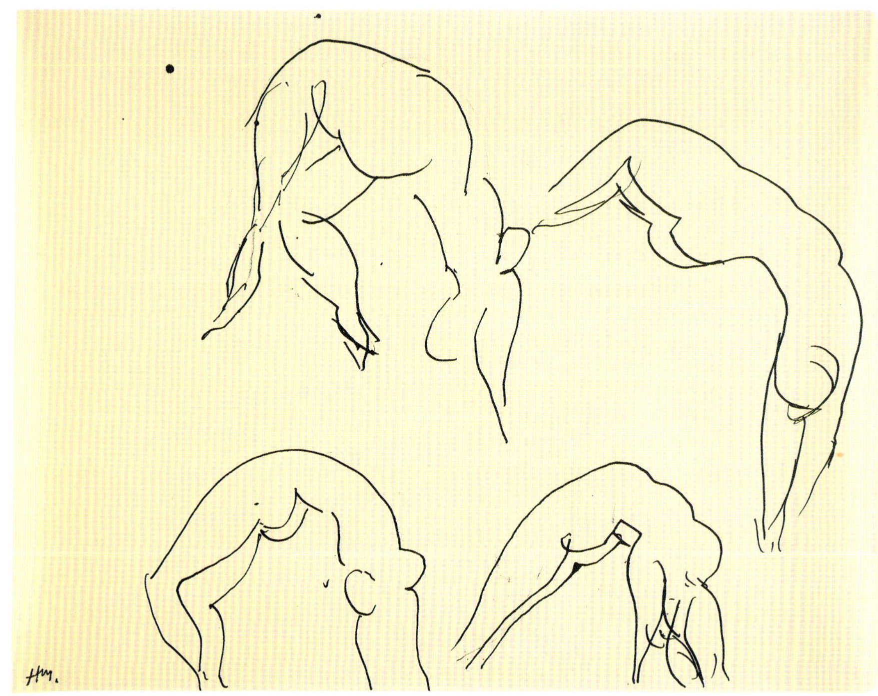

Henri Matisse, *Blue Nude I,* 1952. Gouache on paper, cut and pasted

Fondation Beyeler, Riehen/Basel. Cat. 141

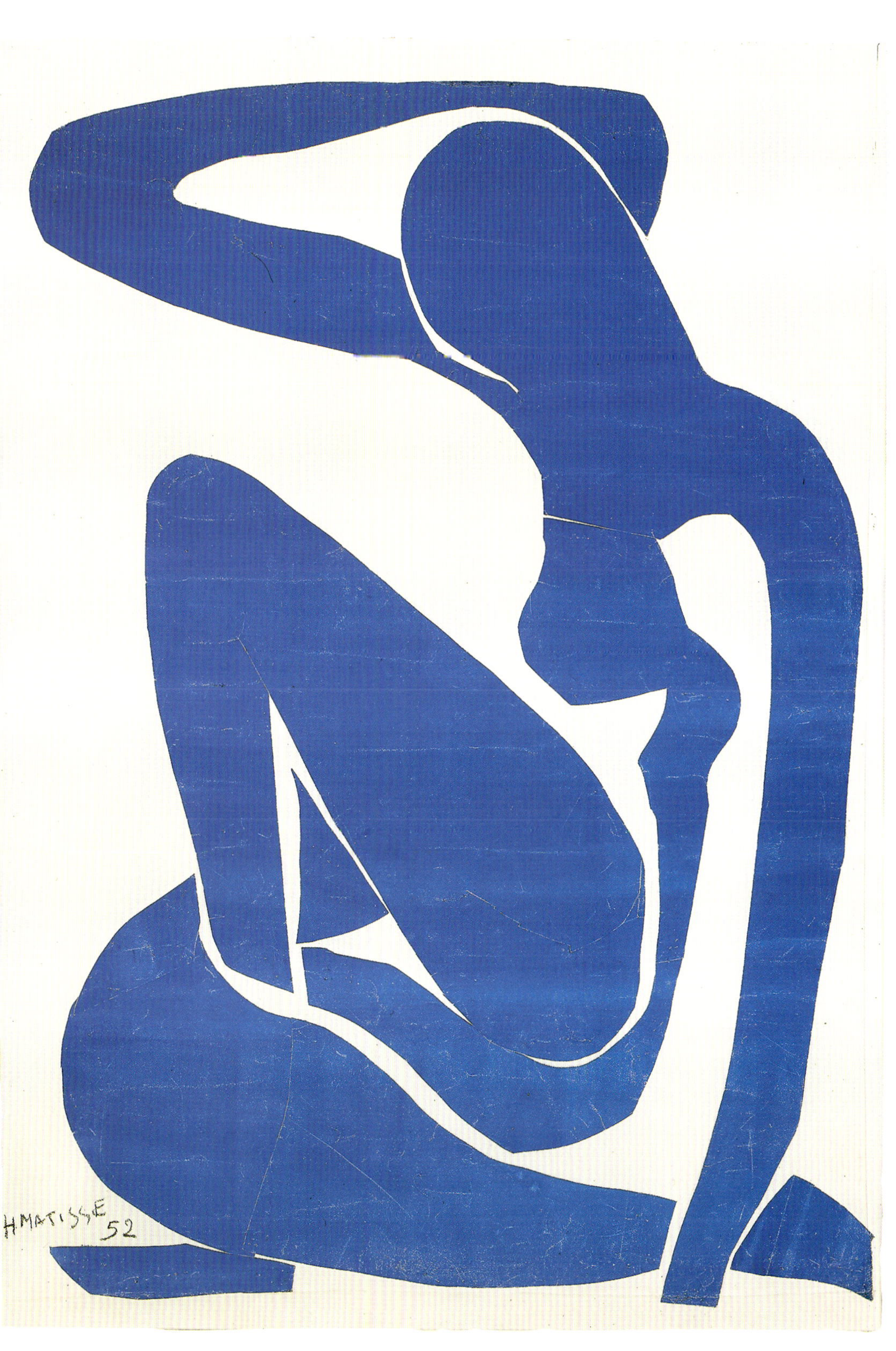

Checklist

1. ***Jaguar Devouring a Hare,*** copy after Barye
1899–1901 (cast 1953), Valsuani
Bronze, lost-wax cast
4/10
Duthuit no. 4
8½ × 23 × 8 in. (21.6 × 58.4 × 20.3 cm)
The Baltimore Museum of Art, Purchase with exchange funds from the Nelson and Juanita Greif Gutman Collection. BMA 1999.3
Pages 101, 102, 105

2. ***Study for Jaguar Devouring a Hare***
c. 1900
Pen and india ink
8⅝ × 13 in. (22 × 33 cm)
Musée départemental Matisse, Le Cateau-Cambrésis, Gift of Marie Matisse, 1982
• San Francisco and Baltimore only
Page 103

3. ***Study for Jaguar Devouring a Hare***
c. 1900
Pen and india ink
8¹¹⁄₁₆ × 13¹⁄₁₆ in. (22.1 × 33.1 cm)
Private collection
• Baltimore only
Page 104

4. ***The Serf***
1900–1903 (cast 1908), Bingen and Costenoble
Bronze, sand cast
2/10
Duthuit no. 6
36⅛ × 11¼ × 13¹⁄₁₆ in. (91.8 × 28.6 × 33.2 cm)
The Baltimore Museum of Art, The Cone Collection, formed by Dr. Claribel Cone and Miss Etta Cone of Baltimore, Maryland. BMA 1950.422
• Baltimore only
Page 266

5. ***The Serf***
1900–1903 (cast c. 1912), F. Costenoble
Bronze, sand cast
5/10
Duthuit no. 6
36⅜ × 13¼ × 12⅜ in. (92.4 × 33.7 × 31.4 cm)
Raymond and Patsy Nasher Collection, Dallas
• Dallas only
Page 266

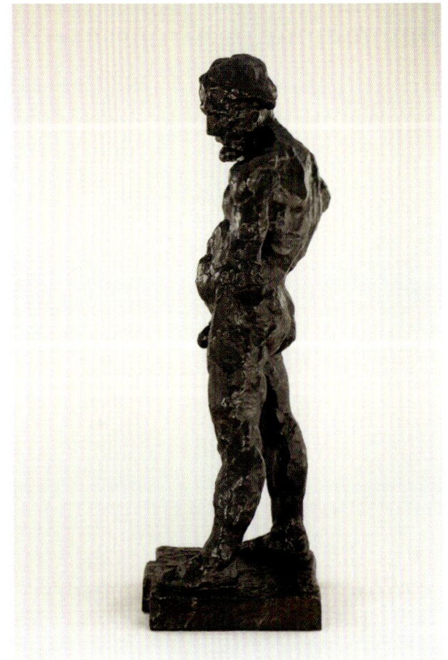

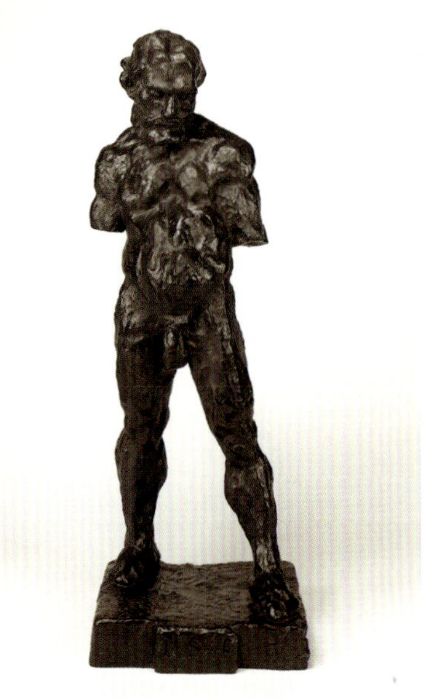

Henri Matisse, ***The Serf,*** 1900–1903. Bronze
The Baltimore Museum of Art, The Cone Collection, formed by Dr. Claribel Cone and Miss Etta Cone of Baltimore, Maryland. Cat. 4

Henri Matisse, ***The Serf,*** 1900–1903. Bronze
Raymond and Patsy Nasher Collection, Dallas. Cat. 5

6. *The Serf*
1900–1903 (cast before 1929), Valsuani
Bronze, lost-wax cast
6/10
Duthuit no. 6
36⅛ × 14⅞ × 13 in. (91.8 × 37.8 × 33.0 cm)
San Francisco Museum of Modern Art, Bequest of Harriet Lane Levy
• San Francisco only
Pages 107, 109

7. *Male Model*
c. 1900
Oil on canvas
39⅛ × 28⅝ in. (99.3 × 72.7 cm)
The Museum of Modern Art, New York; Kay Sage Tanguy and Abby Aldrich Rockefeller Funds, 1975
Page 110

8. *Study for The Serf*
1900
Graphite
10⅝ × 8¼ in. (27 × 21 cm)
Musée départemental Matisse, Le Cateau-Cambrésis; Purchase, 1991
• San Francisco and Baltimore only
Page 113

9. *Male Model*
c. 1900
Pen and ink
12$\frac{5}{16}$ × 10$\frac{7}{16}$ in. (31.3 × 26.5 cm)
Solomon R. Guggenheim Museum, New York; Thannhauser Collection, Gift, Justin K. Thannhauser, 1978
Page 112

10. *Study for The Serf*
1900–1902
Graphite
9$\frac{7}{16}$ × 7½ in. (24.0 × 19.1 cm)
Private collection
• Baltimore only
Page 112

11. *Standing Man, Seen from the Back*
1900–1903
Pen and ink
9$\frac{7}{16}$ × 7½ in. (24.0 × 19.1 cm)
Pierre and Maria-Gaetana Matisse Foundation Collection
Page 113

12. *Madeleine I*
1901 (cast 1925), Valsuani
Bronze, lost-wax cast
3/10
Duthuit no. 8
23¼ × 8¾ × 7⅛ in. (59.1 × 22.2 × 18.1 cm)
The Baltimore Museum of Art, The Cone Collection, formed by Dr. Claribel Cone and Miss Etta Cone of Baltimore, Maryland. BMA 1950.423
• Dallas and Baltimore only
Page 267

13. *Madeleine I*
1901 (cast 1925), Valsuani
Bronze, lost-wax cast
5/10
Duthuit no. 8
21½ × 7⅝ × 6¾ in. (54.6 × 19.4 × 17.2 cm)
San Francisco Museum of Modern Art, Bequest of Harriet Lane Levy
• San Francisco only
Page 115

14. *Madeleine I*
1901 (cast 1903)
Painted plaster
2/4
Duthuit no. 9
23¾ × 9½ × 7½ in. (60.3 × 24.1 × 19.1 cm)
Raymond and Patsy Nasher Collection, Dallas
Page 120

15. *Madeleine II*
1903 (cast 1953), Valsuani
Bronze, lost-wax cast
5/10
Duthuit no. 10
23$\frac{7}{16}$ × 7$\frac{5}{16}$ × 7⅞ in. (59.5 × 18.5 × 20 cm)
Centre Pompidou, Paris; Musée national d'art moderne/Centre de création industrielle; Remittance in lieu of inheritance taxes to the government of France, 1991
Page 119

16. *Standing Model (Nude Study in Blue)*
1899–1900
Oil on canvas
28¾ × 21⅜ in. (73.0 × 54.3 cm)
Tate; Bequeathed by C. Frank Stoop, 1933
Page 117

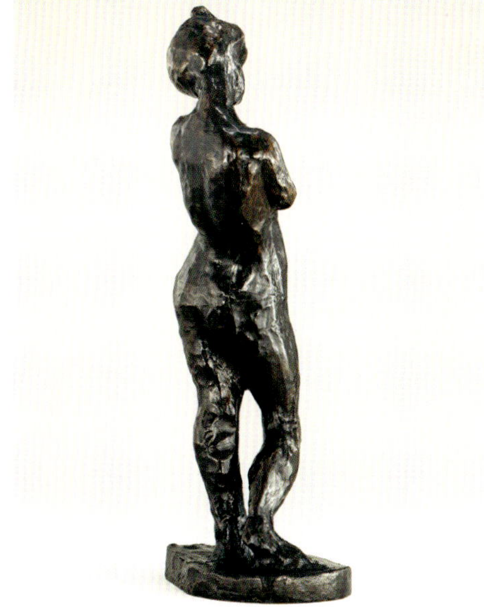

Henri Matisse, *Madeleine I*, 1901. Bronze
The Baltimore Museum of Art, The Cone Collection, formed by Dr. Claribel Cone and Miss Etta Cone of Baltimore, Maryland. Cat. 12

17. *Standing Figure*
1900
Graphite
11⅝ × 9¼ in. (29.5 × 23.5 cm)
Pierre and Maria-Gaetana Matisse Foundation Collection
Page 123

18. *Standing Nude*
c. 1900
Black crayon with stumping
10⅝ × 8 11/16 in. (27 × 22 cm)
Stedelijk Museum, Amsterdam
Page 123

19. *Nude, Seen from the Back, on a Hatched Ground*
1900–1903
Graphite
11 13/16 × 9¼ in. (30.0 × 23.5 cm)
Pierre and Maria-Gaetana Matisse Foundation Collection
Page 122

20. *Study for Madeleine I*
1901
Graphite
11¾ × 9¼ in. (29.9 × 23.5 cm)
The Museum of Modern Art, New York, Gift of Mr. and Mrs. Pierre Matisse in honor and memory of Victor Leventritt
Page 120

21. *Nude, Seen from the Back*
1901–1903
Graphite
11⅝ × 9¼ in. (29.5 × 23.5 cm)
Pierre and Maria-Gaetana Matisse Foundation Collection
Page 122

22. *Study for Madeleine II*
1903
Graphite
11⅝ × 9¼ in. (29.5 × 23.5 cm)
Musée départemental Matisse, Le Cateau-Cambrésis, Gift of Marie Matisse, 1993
• San Francisco and Baltimore only
Page 121

23. *Standing Nude, Seen from the Back*
1903
Graphite with stumping and scraping
9 × 13 in. (22.9 × 33.0 cm)
Dr. and Mrs. Morton Mower
Page 122

24. *Woman Leaning on Her Hands*
1905 (cast 1922), Godard
Bronze, sand cast
5/10
Duthuit no. 17
4⅞ × 9⅜ × 6⅜ in. (12.4 × 23.8 × 16.2 cm)
The Baltimore Museum of Art, The Cone Collection, formed by Dr. Claribel Cone and Miss Etta Cone of Baltimore, Maryland. BMA 1950.424
Pages 127, 128

25. *Thorn Extractor*
1906 (cast 1951), Valsuani
Bronze, lost-wax cast
7/10
Duthuit no. 26
8½ × 5⅞ × 6 in. (21.5 × 14.9 × 15.2 cm)
Collection, Art Gallery of Ontario, Toronto; Gift of Sam and Ayala Zacks, 1970
Page 129

26. *Reclining Nude, Back View*
1905
Pen and ink
8 11/16 × 10⅝ in. (22.1 × 27.0 cm)
Private collection
• Baltimore only
Page 130

27. *Reclining Woman Leaning on Hands*
c. 1905
Graphite
7 9/16 × 9 7/16 in. (19.2 × 24 cm)
Private collection
• Baltimore only
Page 131

28. *Reclining Woman Leaning on Hands*
c. 1905
Graphite
9¼ × 11¾ in. (23.5 × 29.8 cm)
Private collection
• Baltimore only
Page 131

29. *Still Life with a Geranium*
1906
Oil on canvas
38½ × 31½ in. (100.3 × 81.5 cm)
The Art Institute of Chicago, Joseph Winterbotham Collection
Page 126

30. *Reclining Figure with Chemise*
1906 (cast c. 1930), Valsuani
Bronze, lost-wax cast
5/10
Duthuit no. 19
5½ × 11⅞ × 5⅞ in. (14.0 × 30.2 × 14.9 cm)
The Baltimore Museum of Art, Gift of Mr. and Mrs. Albert Lion, Jr. BMA 1955.164
Pages 133, 134

31. *Oil Sketch for The Joy of Life* (*Le bonheur de vivre*)
1905–1906
Oil on canvas
16 × 21½ in. (41.0 × 54.6 cm)
San Francisco Museum of Modern Art, Bequest of Elise S. Haas
Page 135

32. *Standing Nude*
1906 (cast 1951), Valsuani
Bronze, lost-wax cast
0/10
Duthuit no. 20
19 × 5 × 6½ in. (83.0 × 12.7 × 16.5 cm)
The Metropolitan Museum of Art, New York; The Pierre and Maria-Gaetana Matisse Collection, 2002
Pages 137, 140

33. *Standing Nude*
c. 1901
Oil on canvas
17½ × 31 in. (44.5 × 78.7 cm)
Fine Arts Museums of San Francisco, Bequest of Aurelie Henwood to the de Young Museum in memory of Lucille and Gardner Dailey
Page 141

Henri Matisse, *Reclining Nude I (Aurora)*, 1907. Bronze
Raymond and Patsy Nasher Collection, Dallas. Cat. 44

34. *Still Life with Plaster Figure*
1906
Oil on canvas
21¼ × 17¾ in. (54.0 × 45.1 cm)
Yale University Art Gallery, New Haven; Bequest of Mrs. Kate L. Brewster
• Baltimore only
Page 139

35. *Seated Nude with Arms on Head*
1904 (cast c. 1930), Valsuani
Bronze, lost-wax cast
2/10
Duthuit no. 15
13¾ × 6⅜ × 7⅛ in. (34.9 × 16.2 × 18.1 cm)
The Baltimore Museum of Art, The Cone Collection, formed by Dr. Claribel Cone and Miss Etta Cone of Baltimore, Maryland. BMA 1950.431
Pages 148, 149

36. *Standing Nude, Arms on Head*
1906 (cast c. 1950), Valsuani
Bronze, lost-wax cast
3/10
Duthuit no. 22
10¼ × 5¼ × 4¼ in. (26.0 × 13.3 × 10.8 cm)
Raymond and Patsy Nasher Collection, Dallas
Page 144

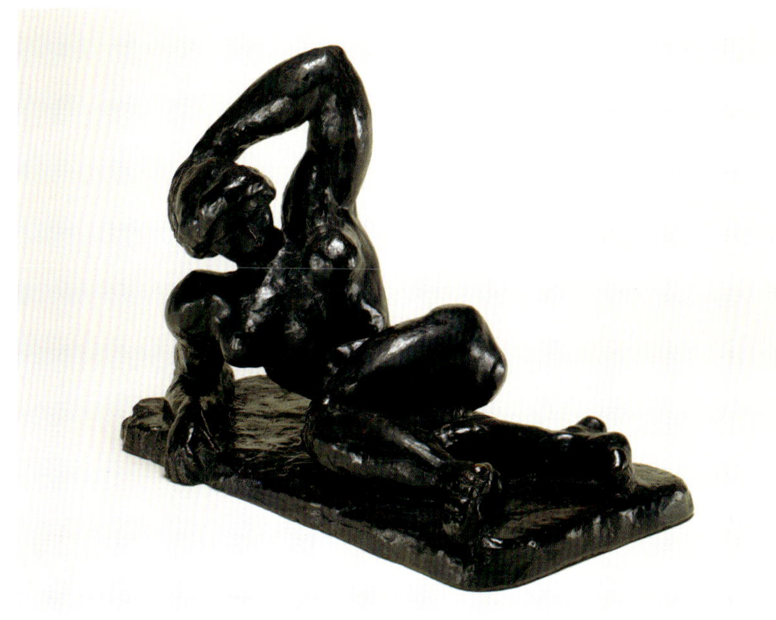

37. *Torso with Head (La Vie)*
1906 (cast c. 1908), Bingen and Costenoble
Bronze, sand cast
2/10
Duthuit no. 23
9⅛ × 4 × 3 in. (23.3 × 10.2 × 7.6 cm)
The Metropolitan Museum of Art, New York; Alfred Stieglitz Collection, 1949
Page 151

38. *Nude*
1904
Graphite
13³⁄₁₆ × 8⅞ in. (33.5 × 22.5 cm)
Pierre and Maria-Gaetana Matisse Foundation Collection
Page 147

39. *Standing Nude*
1905
Charcoal with erasing
24¹³⁄₁₆ × 18½ in. (63 × 47 cm)
Pierre and Maria-Gaetana Matisse Foundation Collection
Page 150

40. *Girl with Ivy in Hair*
1905–1906
Pen and india ink
10⅝ × 8¾ in. (27.0 × 22.2 cm)
Private collection
• Baltimore only
Page 143

41. *Standing Nude, Version 1*
1905–1908
Reed pen and india ink
10⁹⁄₁₆ × 8³⁄₁₆ in. (26.8 × 20.8 cm)
Folkwang Museum, Essen
• Dallas only
Page 145

42. *Standing Nude, Version 2*
1905–1908
Reed pen and india ink
10⁹⁄₁₆ × 8³⁄₁₆ in. (26.8 × 20.8 cm)
Folkwang Museum, Essen
• Dallas only
Page 145

43. *Standing Nude, Version 3*
1905–1908
Reed pen and india ink
10⁹⁄₁₆ × 8⅛ in. (26.8 × 20.6 cm)
Folkwang Museum, Essen
• Dallas only
Page 145

44. *Reclining Nude I (Aurora)*
1907 (cast 1951), Valsuani
Bronze, lost-wax cast
10/10
Duthuit no. 30
13¹⁄₁₆ × 19¾ × 11 in. (33.2 × 50.2 × 27.9 cm)
Raymond and Patsy Nasher Collection, Dallas
• Dallas and San Francisco only
Page 269

45. *Reclining Nude I (Aurora)*
1907 (cast c. 1930), Valsuani
Bronze, lost-wax cast
6/10
Duthuit no. 30
13⁹⁄₁₆ × 19⅝ × 11 in. (34.4 × 49.9 × 27.9 cm)
The Baltimore Museum of Art, The Cone Collection, formed by Dr. Claribel Cone and Miss Etta Cone of Baltimore, Maryland. BMA 1950.429
• Baltimore only
Pages 153, 155, 156

46. ***Blue Nude: Memory of Biskra (Nu bleu: Souvenir de Biskra)***
1907
Oil on canvas
36¼ × 55¼ in. (92.1 × 140.4 cm)
The Baltimore Museum of Art, The Cone Collection, formed by Dr. Claribel Cone and Miss Etta Cone of Baltimore, Maryland. BMA 1950.228
Page 157

47. ***Two Negresses***
1907–1908 (cast c. 1930), Valsuani
Bronze, lost-wax cast
8/10
Duthuit no. 36
18⅜ × 10½ × 7½ in. (46.7 × 26.7 × 19.1 cm)
Raymond and Patsy Nasher Collection, Dallas
Page 159

48. ***The Back I***
1909 (cast 1965), Rudier
Bronze, sand cast
6/10
Duthuit no. 48
75 × 46 × 6½ in. (190.5 × 116.8 × 16.5 cm)
Franklin D. Murphy Sculpture Garden, University of California, Los Angeles; Gift of Michael J. Connell Memorial Fund; Courtesy of the Hammer Museum
Page 162

49. ***The Back II***
1913 (cast 1962), Rudier
Bronze, sand cast
6/10
Duthuit no. 57
75 × 48 × 6¾ in. (190.5 × 121.9 × 17.2 cm)
Franklin D. Murphy Sculpture Garden, University of California, Los Angeles; Gift of the UCLA Art Council Fund; Courtesy of the Hammer Museum
Page 162

50. ***The Back III***
1916–1917 (cast 1964), Rudier
Bronze, sand cast
6/10
Duthuit no. 60
75 × 45 × 6½ in. (190.5 × 114.3 × 16.5 cm)
Franklin D. Murphy Sculpture Garden, University of California, Los Angeles; Gift of the UCLA Art Council through the generosity of Mrs. Robert E. Gross and Mrs. Charles E. Ducommun; Courtesy of the Hammer Museum
Page 163

51. ***The Back IV***
1930 (cast 1965), Rudier
Bronze, sand-cast
6/10
Duthuit no. 77
75 × 45 × 6½ in. (190.5 × 114.3 × 16.5 cm)
Franklin D. Murphy Sculpture Garden, University of California, Los Angeles; Gift of Mr. and Mrs. Sidney F. Brody in honor of the UCLA Art Council; Courtesy of the Hammer Museum
Page 163

52. ***Back Study***
c. 1907–1909
Graphite with stumping
12⅜ × 9½ in. (31.4 × 24.2 cm)
Kunsthaus Zürich, Grafische Sammlung
• Not in the exhibition
Page 166

53. ***Standing Woman Seen from Behind (Study for The Back I)***
1909
Pen and ink
10½ × 8⅝ in. (26.6 × 21.9 cm)
The Museum of Modern Art, New York; Carol Buttenweiser Loeb Memorial Fund
Page 164

54. ***Study of a Model's Back***
1909
Pen and dark brown ink
11⁵⁄₁₆ × 7⁵⁄₁₆ in. (28.8 × 18.6 cm)
National Gallery of Canada, Ottawa; Purchase 1974
Page 164

55. ***Study for The Back II***
1913
Pen and ink
7⅞ × 6⅛ in. (20.0 × 15.7 cm)
The Museum of Modern Art, New York; Gift of Pierre Matisse
Page 167

56. ***Nude, Seen from the Back***
1914–1915
Crayon
24¹³⁄₁₆ × 18¹¹⁄₁₆ in. (63.0 × 47.5 cm)
Pierre and Maria-Gaetana Matisse Foundation Collection
Page 167

57. ***Torso Without Arms or Head***
1909 (cast 1952), Valsuani
Bronze, lost-wax cast
8/10
Duthuit no. 44
9¹¹⁄₁₆ × 2¹¹⁄₁₆ × 2¹¹⁄₁₆ in. (24.6 × 6.8 × 6.8 cm)
Private collection
Page 176

58. ***The Serpentine***
1909 (cast c. 1930), Valsuani
Bronze, lost-wax cast
3/10
Duthuit no. 46
21½ × 11½ × 7½ in. (54.6 × 29.2 × 19.1 cm)
The Baltimore Museum of Art, Gift of a Group of Friends. BMA 1950.93
Pages 170, 172

59. ***The Dance***
1911 (cast c. 1930), Valsuani
Bronze, lost-wax cast
1/10
Duthuit no. 54
16¾ × 7⅛ × 7⅜ in. (42.5 × 18.1 × 18.7 cm)
Hirshhorn Museum and Sculpture Garden, Smithsonian Institution, Washington, D.C.; Gift of Joseph H. Hirshhorn, 1966
Page 174

60. ***Nude***
1908
Pencil
12 × 9¹⁄₁₆ in. (30.5 × 23.0 cm)
The Metropolitan Museum of Art, New York; Alfred Stieglitz Collection, 1949
• Dallas only
Page 171

61. *Bather Leaning against a Tree*
c. 1909
Pen and ink
10½ × 8¼ in. (26.7 × 21.0 cm)
Private collection
Page 171

62. *Study for Dance (II)*
1909–1910
Charcoal with stumping
18⅞ × 25⅝ in. (48 × 63.5 cm)
Musée de Grenoble
• Dallas only
Page 173

63. *Study for The Dance*
1909–1910
Graphite
9 7/16 × 8¼ in. (24 × 21 cm)
Pierre and Maria-Gaetana Matisse Foundation Collection
Page 175

64. *Study for The Dance*
c. 1930–1931
Graphite and pen and ink
12 1/16 × 9 in. (30.7 × 22.8 cm)
Private collection
• Baltimore only
Page 179

65. *Small Crouching Nude without an Arm*
1908 (cast 1922), Godard
Bronze, sand cast
6/10
Duthuit no. 38
5 × 2⅝ × 3⅝ in. (12.7 × 6.1 × 9.2 cm)
The Baltimore Museum of Art, The Cone Collection, formed by Dr. Claribel Cone and Miss Etta Cone of Baltimore, Maryland.
BMA 1950.432
Pages 184, 185

66. *Decorative Figure*
1908 (cast 1930), Valsuani
Bronze, lost-wax cast
2/10
Duthuit no. 41
28⅜ × 20⅜ × 12⅜ in. (72.1 × 51.8 × 31.4 cm)
Raymond and Patsy Nasher Collection, Dallas
Page 181

67. *Seated Nude (Olga)*
1909–1910 (cast 1952), Valsuani
Bronze, lost-wax cast
6/10
Duthuit no. 49
H: 16⅞ in. (43 cm)
Private collection, Courtesy of Ivor Braka, Ltd., London
Page 183

68. *Seated Nude Clasping Her Right Leg*
1918 (cast 1930), Valsuani
Bronze, lost-wax cast
6/10
Duthuit no. 61
9 × 8⅝ × 6 in. (22.9 × 21.9 × 15.2 cm)
The Baltimore Museum of Art, The Cone Collection, formed by Dr. Claribel Cone and Miss Etta Cone of Baltimore, Maryland.
BMA 1950.434
Pages 186, 187

69. *Study, Heads and a Figure*
1909
Reed pen and ink
9⅞ × 12 in. (25.1 × 30.5 cm)
Pierre and Maria-Gaetana Matisse Foundation Collection
Page 187

70. *The Branch of Lilac*
1914
Oil on canvas
57½ × 38 in. (146.1 × 96.5 cm)
The Metropolitan Museum of Art, New York; The Pierre and Maria-Gaetana Matisse Collection, 2002
Page 188

71. *Seated Figure on a Decorative Background*
1925–1927
Charcoal with stumping and erasing
24 3/16 × 19 in. (61.5 × 48.3 cm)
Private collection, New York
• Dallas only
Page 189

72. *Still Life with Statuette by Henri Laurens*
1942
Pen and ink
20¾ × 16 in. (52.7 × 40.6 cm)
Musée Matisse, Nice; Bequest of Madame Henri Matisse, 1960
• Dallas only
Page 191

73. *Small Head with Comb*
1907 (cast 1922), Godard
Bronze, sand cast
6/10
Duthuit no. 33
3 1/16 × 2 3/16 × 2½ in. (7.8 × 5.6 × 6.4 cm)
The Baltimore Museum of Art, The Cone Collection, formed by Dr. Claribel Cone and Miss Etta Cone of Baltimore, Maryland.
BMA 1950.427
Page 194

74. *Head with Necklace*
1907 (cast 1930), Valsuani
Bronze, lost-wax cast
8/10
Duthuit no. 34
5 15/16 × 5⅛ × 4⅜ in. (15.1 × 13.0 × 11.1 cm)
The Baltimore Museum of Art, The Cone Collection, formed by Dr. Claribel Cone and Miss Etta Cone of Baltimore, Maryland.
BMA 1950.428
• Baltimore only
Page 272

75. *Head with Necklace*
1907 (cast 1930), Valsuani
Bronze, lost-wax cast
9/10
Duthuit no. 34
5⅞ × 5⅛ × 3¾ in. (14.9 × 13.0 × 9.5 cm)
Raymond and Patsy Nasher Collection, Dallas
• Dallas and San Francisco only
Page 193

76. *Head with Necklace*
1907 (cast 1906–1908), Bingen and Costenoble
Bronze, sand cast
00/10
Duthuit no. 34
H: 5 9/16 in. (14.1 cm)
Direction des Musées de France, Gift of Jean Matisse, on deposit at Musée Matisse, Nice, 1978.
• Baltimore only
Page 272

77. *Tiari*
1930 (cast c. 1930), Valsuani
Bronze, lost-wax cast
3/10
Duthuit no. 78
8 × 5½ × 5⅛ in. (20.3 × 14.0 × 13.0 cm)
Raymond and Patsy Nasher Collection, Dallas
Page 195

78. *Tiari (with Necklace)*
1930 (cast 1930), Valsuani
Bronze with gold and silver necklace, lost-wax cast
1/10
Duthuit no. 78
8 × 5⅝ × 7⅝ in. (20.3 × 14.3 × 19.4 cm)
The Baltimore Museum of Art, The Cone Collection, formed by Dr. Claribel Cone and Miss Etta Cone of Baltimore, Maryland. BMA 1950.438
Pages 196, 197

79. *Head of a Woman*
c. 1900
Brush and ink
9⁷⁄₁₆ × 7½ in. (24.0 × 19.1 cm)
Pierre and Maria-Gaetana Matisse Foundation Collection
Page 194

80. *Jeannette I*
1910 (cast 1952), Valsuani
Bronze, lost-wax cast
4/10
Duthuit no. 50
12⅞ × 11 × 11 in. (32.7 × 27.9 × 27.9 cm)
Los Angeles County Museum of Art; Gift of the Art Museum Council in memory of Penelope Rigby
• Dallas and San Francisco only
Page 200

81. *Jeannette I*
1910 (cast 1953), Valsuani
Bronze, lost-wax cast
7/10
Duthuit no. 50
13 × 9¼ × 10⅛ in. (33.0 × 23.4 × 25.7 cm)
Hirshhorn Museum and Sculpture Garden, Smithsonian Institution, Washington, D.C., Gift of Joseph H. Hirshhorn, 1966
• Baltimore only
Page 273

82. *Jeannette II*
1910 (cast c. 1930), Valsuani
Bronze, lost-wax cast
5/10
Duthuit no. 51
10½ × 12 × 11 in. (26.7 × 30.5 × 27.9 cm)
Los Angeles County Museum of Art; Gift of the Art Museum Council in memory of Penelope Rigby
• Dallas and San Francisco only
Page 201

83. *Jeannette II*
1910 (cast 1952), Valsuani
Bronze, lost-wax cast
7/10
Duthuit no. 51
10⅜ × 8⅞ × 10¼ in. (26.5 × 22.4 × 26.0 cm)
Hirshhorn Museum and Sculpture Garden, Smithsonian Institution, Washington, D.C., Gift of Joseph H. Hirshhorn, 1966
• Baltimore only
Page 273

84. *Jeannette III*
1911 (cast 1952), Valsuani
Bronze, lost-wax cast
4/10
Duthuit no. 52
23½ × 12 × 12 in. (59.7 × 30.5 × 30.5 cm)
Los Angeles County Museum of Art; Gift of the Art Museum Council in memory of Penelope Rigby
• Dallas and San Francisco only
Page 202

85. *Jeannette III*
1911 (cast 1966), Valsuani
Bronze, lost-wax cast
9/10
Duthuit no. 52
23¾ × 9⅜ × 12⅛ in. (60.2 × 23.7 × 30.6 cm)
Hirshhorn Museum and Sculpture Garden, Smithsonian Institution, Washington, D.C., Gift of the Joseph H. Hirshhorn Foundation, 1972
• Baltimore only
Page 274

86. *Jeannette IV*
1912 (cast 1951), Valsuani
Bronze, lost-wax cast
4/10
Duthuit no. 53
24 × 11 × 11 in. (61.0 × 27.9 × 27.9 cm)
Los Angeles County Museum of Art; Gift of the Art Museum Council in memory of Penelope Rigby
• Dallas and San Francisco only
Page 203

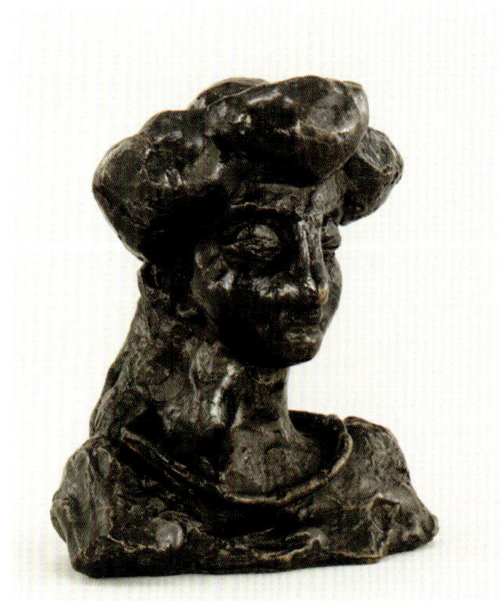

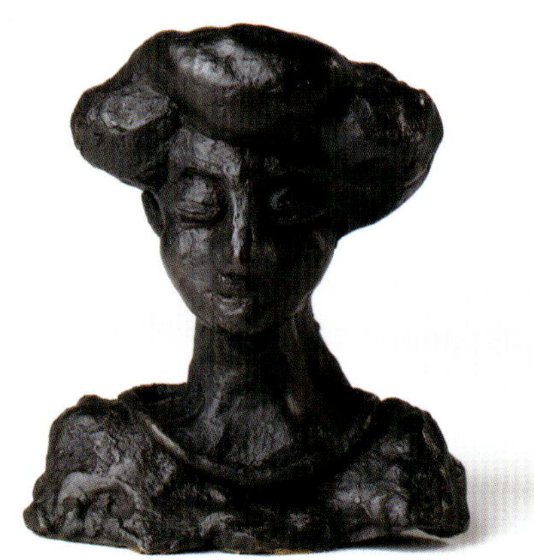

Henri Matisse, ***Head with Necklace,*** 1907. Bronze
The Baltimore Museum of Art, The Cone Collection, formed by Dr. Claribel Cone and Miss Etta Cone of Baltimore, Maryland. Cat. 74

Henri Matisse, ***Head with Necklace,*** 1907. Bronze
Direction des Musées de France, Gift of Jean Matisse, on deposit at Musée Matisse, Nice, 1978. Cat. 76

87. *Jeannette IV*
1911 (cast 1954), Valsuani
Bronze, lost-wax cast
3/10
Duthuit no. 53
24⅛ × 8⅞ × 11⅛ in. (61.2 × 22.5 × 28.1 cm)
Hirshhorn Museum and Sculpture Garden, Smithsonian Institution, Washington, D.C., Gift of Joseph H. Hirshhorn, 1966
• Baltimore only
Page 274

88. *Jeannette V*
1913 (cast 1954), Valsuani
Bronze, lost-wax cast
1/10
Duthuit no. 55
22⅞ × 8½ × 9¼ in. (58.1 × 21.6 × 23.5 cm)
Los Angeles County Museum of Art; Gift of the Art Museum Council in memory of Penelope Rigby
• Dallas and San Francisco only
Page 206

89. *Jeannette V*
1913 (cast 1954), Valsuani
Bronze, lost-wax cast
2/10
Duthuit no. 55
22¾ × 8¼ × 11⅝ in. (57.7 × 20.8 × 29.5 cm)
Hirshhorn Museum and Sculpture Garden, Smithsonian Institution, Washington, D.C., Gift of the Joseph H. Hirshhorn Foundation, 1972
• Baltimore only
Page 274

90. *Portrait of Sarah Stein*
1916
Oil on canvas
28½ × 22¼ in. (72.4 × 56.5 cm)
San Francisco Museum of Modern Art, Sarah and Michael Stein Memorial Collection, Gift of Elise S. Haas
Page 205

91. *The Italian Woman*
1916
Oil on canvas
45 5/16 × 35¼ in. (116.7 × 89.5 cm)
Solomon R. Guggenheim Museum, New York; by exchange, 1982
Page 204

92. *Henriette I*
1925 (cast 1958), Valsuani
Bronze, lost-wax cast
1/10
Duthuit no. 66
11⅝ × 9 1/16 × 7 1/16 in. (29.5 × 23.0 × 18.0 cm)
Musée départemental Matisse, Le Cateau-Cambrésis; Gift of Maria-Gaetana Matisse (Pontoise), 1999
Page 209

93. *Henriette II*
1927 (cast 1929), Valsuani
Bronze, lost-wax cast
6/10
Duthuit no. 70
13 × 9 × 12 in. (33.0 × 22.9 × 30.5 cm)
San Francisco Museum of Modern Art, Bequest of Harriet Lane Levy
Page 212

94. *Henriette III*
1929 (cast 1953), Valsuani
Bronze, lost-wax cast
6/10
Duthuit no. 75
16½ × 8⅜ × 10½ in. (41.8 × 21.2 × 26.6 cm)
Hirshhorn Museum and Sculpture Garden, Smithsonian Institution, Washington, D.C.; Gift of Joseph H. Hirshhorn, 1966
Page 214

95. *Study for Henriette II*
c. 1928
Graphite
9⅛ × 8¼ in. (23.3 × 21.0 cm)
Musée départemental Matisse, Le Cateau-Cambrésis, Gift of Marie Matisse, 1993
• San Francisco and Baltimore only
Page 211

96. *Titine Trovato in a Dress and Hat*
1934
Oil on canvas
28 × 23 in. (71.1 × 58.4 cm)
V. Madrigal Collection, New York
Page 215

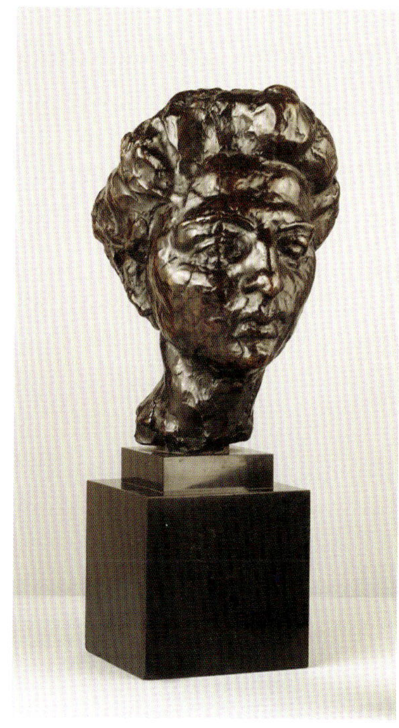

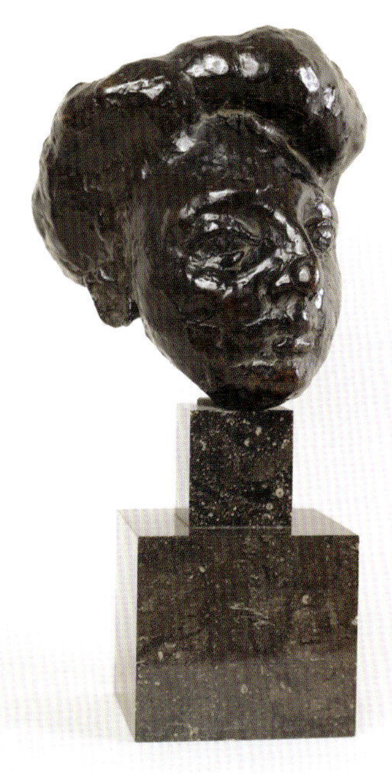

Henri Matisse, *Jeannette I*, 1910. Bronze
Hirshhorn Museum and Sculpture Garden, Smithsonian Institution, Washington, D.C., Gift of Joseph H. Hirshhorn, 1966. Cat. 81

Henri Matisse, *Jeannette II*, 1910. Bronze
Hirshhorn Museum and Sculpture Garden, Smithsonian Institution, Washington, D.C., Gift of Joseph H. Hirshhorn, 1966. Cat. 83

97. *Crouching Venus*
1918–1919 (cast 1930), Valsuani
Bronze, lost-wax cast
6/10
Duthuit no. 63
10⅜ × 9⁷⁄₁₆ × 5⅝ in. (26.4 × 24.0 × 14.3 cm)
The Baltimore Museum of Art, The Cone Collection, formed by Dr. Claribel Cone and Miss Etta Cone of Baltimore, Maryland.
BMA 1950.435
Page 220

98. *Large Seated Nude*
1922–1929 (cast 1930), Valsuani
Bronze, lost-wax cast
7/10
Duthuit no. 64
30³⁄₁₆ × 31⅝ × 14 in. (76.7 × 80.3 × 35.6 cm)
The Baltimore Museum of Art, The Cone Collection, formed by Dr. Claribel Cone and Miss Etta Cone of Baltimore, Maryland.
BMA 1950.436
• Baltimore only
Page 217

99. *Large Seated Nude*
1922–1929 (cast 1952), Valsuani
Bronze, lost-wax cast
9/10
Duthuit no. 64
30½ × 31⅝ × 13⅝ in. (77.5 × 80.3 × 34.6 cm)
Raymond and Patsy Nasher Collection, Dallas
• Dallas and San Francisco only
Page 275

100. *Small Nude in an Armchair*
1924 (cast 1958), Valsuani
Bronze, lost-wax cast
9/10
Duthuit no. 65
9⅛ × 8½ × 6⅝ in. (23.2 × 21.6 × 16.8 cm)
Stephen Mazoh
Page 220

101. *Large Nude*
1906
Crayon, brush, and tusche lithograph with scraping
17¹¹⁄₁₆ × 13⅜ in. (44.9 × 34.0 cm)
The Baltimore Museum of Art, The Cone Collection, formed by Dr. Claribel Cone and Miss Etta Cone of Baltimore, Maryland.
BMA 1950.12.195
Page 222

Henri Matisse, *Jeannette III,* 1911, Bronze
Hirshhorn Museum and Sculpture Garden, Smithsonian Institution, Washington, D.C., Gift of the Joseph H. Hirshhorn Foundation, 1972. Cat. 85

Henri Matisse, *Jeannette IV,* 1911, Bronze
Hirshhorn Museum and Sculpture Garden, Smithsonian Institution, Washington, D.C., Gift of Joseph H. Hirshhorn, 1966. Cat. 87

Henri Matisse, *Jeannette V,* 1913, Bronze
Hirshhorn Museum and Sculpture Garden, Smithsonian Institution, Washington, D.C., Gift of the Joseph H. Hirshhorn Foundation, 1972. Cat. 89

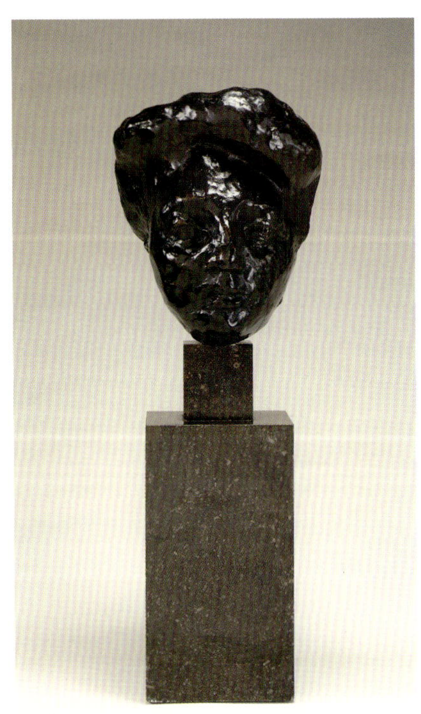

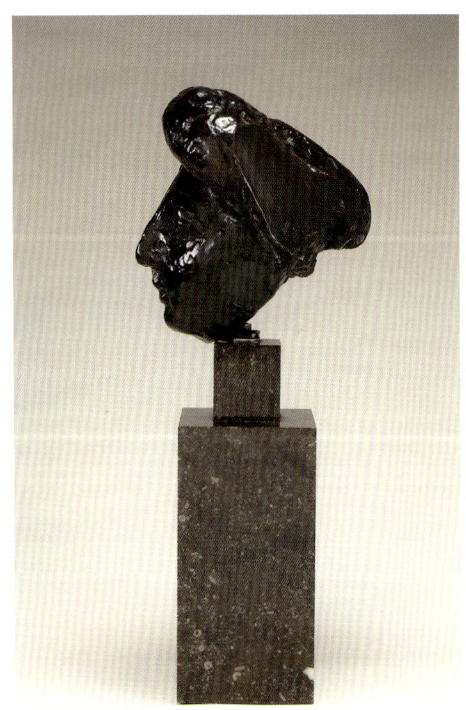

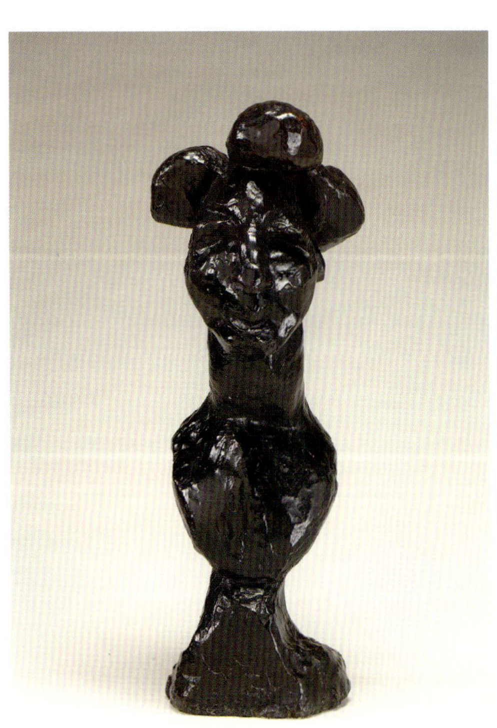

102. *Reclining Nude*
c. 1907–1908
Graphite with stumping
9¼ × 11¹³⁄₁₆ in. (23.5 × 30.0 cm)
Kunstmuseum Winterthur; Purchase, 1947
• Not in the exhibition
Page 224

103. *Study of a Reclining Nude*
1910–1911
Graphite
10¹⁄₁₆ × 13¹⁵⁄₁₆ in. (25.5 × 35.4 cm)
Centre Pompidou, Paris; Musée national d'art moderne/Centre de création industrielle; Gift of Marie Matisse, 1984
• Dallas and San Francisco only
Page 224

104. *Day*
1922
Crayon transfer lithograph
10⅜ × 17¼ in. (28 × 44 cm)
The Baltimore Museum of Art, The Cone Collection, formed by Dr. Claribel Cone and Miss Etta Cone of Baltimore, Maryland. BMA 1950.12.303
Page 223

105. *Reclining Model with a Flowered Robe*
c. 1923–1924
Charcoal with stumping and erasing
18⅞ × 24¾ in. (47.9 × 62.9 cm)
The Baltimore Museum of Art, The Cone Collection, formed by Dr. Claribel Cone and Miss Etta Cone of Baltimore, Maryland. BMA 1950.12.52
Page 219

106. *Night*
1924
Crayon transfer lithograph
10¼ × 17¼ in. (26.0 × 43.8 cm)
The Baltimore Museum of Art, The Cone Collection, formed by Dr. Claribel Cone and Miss Etta Cone of Baltimore, Maryland. BMA 1950.12.302
Page 223

107. *Nude with Blue Cushion*
1924
Crayon transfer lithograph
29¹³⁄₁₆ × 22¹⁄₁₆ in. (75.7 × 56.1 cm)
The Baltimore Museum of Art, The Cone Collection, formed by Dr. Claribel Cone and Miss Etta Cone of Baltimore, Maryland. BMA 1950.12.322
Page 219

108. *Nude, Legs Crossed*
c. 1925
Pen and ink
12¹³⁄₁₆ × 9¹⁄₁₆ in. (32.5 × 23.0 cm)
Pierre and Maria-Gaetana Matisse Foundation Collection
Page 225

109. *Odalisque with a Tambourine*
1925–1926
Oil on canvas
29¼ × 21⅞ in. (74.3 × 55.6 cm)
The Museum of Modern Art, New York; The William S. Paley Collection
Page 221

110. *Reclining Nude*
c. 1927–1928
Graphite
10¹³⁄₁₆ × 15 in. (27.5 × 38.1 cm)
Private collection
• Baltimore only
Page 225

111. *Figure with Cushion*
1918 (cast c. 1925), Valsuani
Bronze, lost-wax cast
2/10
Duthuit no. 62
5¼ × 10½ × 4⅛ in. (13.3 × 26.7 × 10.5 cm)
The Baltimore Museum of Art, The Cone Collection, formed by Dr. Claribel Cone and Miss Etta Cone of Baltimore, Maryland. BMA 1950.433
Page 230

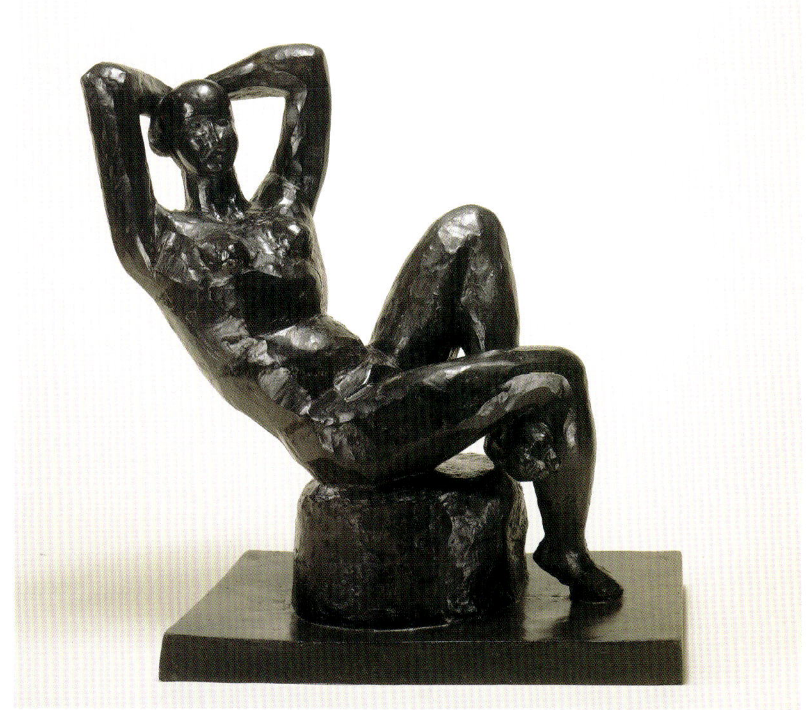

Henri Matisse, ***Large Seated Nude,*** 1922–1929. Bronze
Raymond and Patsy Nasher Collection, Dallas. Cat. 99

112. *Reclining Nude II*
1927 (cast 1948), Valsuani
Bronze, lost-wax cast
8/10
Duthuit no. 69
11¼ × 19¾ × 6 in. (28.6 × 50.2 × 15.2 cm)
The Minneapolis Institute of Arts, Gift of the Dayton-Hudson Corporation
Page 228

113. *Reclining Nude III*
1929 (cast 1929), Valsuani
Bronze, lost-wax cast
5/10
Duthuit no. 71
7⅜ × 18½ × 5¹³⁄₁₆ in. (18.7 × 47.0 × 14.8 cm)
The Baltimore Museum of Art, The Cone Collection, formed by Dr. Claribel Cone and Miss Etta Cone of Baltimore, Maryland. BMA 1950.437
Page 229

114. *Sleeping Figure*
1927
Crayon transfer lithograph
10 × 13½ in. (25.4 × 34.3 cm)
The Baltimore Museum of Art, The Cone Collection, formed by Dr. Claribel Cone and Miss Etta Cone of Baltimore, Maryland. BMA 1950.12.137
Page 232

115. *Odalisque with Green Sash*
1927
Oil on canvas
20 × 25½ in. (50.8 × 64.8 cm)
The Baltimore Museum of Art, The Cone Collection, formed by Dr. Claribel Cone and Miss Etta Cone of Baltimore, Maryland. BMA 1950.253
Page 231

116. *Reclining Nude*
1929
Charcoal with stumping and erasing
18⅞ × 24⁷⁄₁₆ in. (48 × 62 cm)
Pierre and Maria-Gaetana Matisse Foundation Collection
Page 232

117. *Large Reclining Nude / The Pink Nude*
1935
Oil on canvas
26 × 36½ in. (66.0 × 92.7 cm)
The Baltimore Museum of Art, The Cone Collection, formed by Dr. Claribel Cone and Miss Etta Cone of Baltimore, Maryland. BMA 1950.258
Page 233

118. *Small Thin Torso*
1929 (cast 1930), Valsuani
Bronze, lost-wax cast
1/3
Duthuit no. 73
3⅛ in. (7.9 cm)
Private collection
• Baltimore only
Page 276

119. *Small Thin Torso*
1929 (cast 1930), Valsuani
Bronze, lost-wax cast
3/3
Duthuit no. 73
H: 3⅛ in. (8 cm)
Direction des Musées de France, Gift of Jean Matisse, on deposit at the Musée Matisse, Nice, 1978
• Dallas and San Francisco only
Pages 236, 238

120. *Small Torso*
1929 (cast before 1936), Valsuani
Bronze, lost-wax cast
1/10
Duthuit no. 74
3⅞ in. (9.8 cm)
Private collection, New York
Page 235

121. *Studies of a Woman*
1929
Charcoal with stumping
19½ × 12 in. (49.5 × 30.5 cm)
Pierre and Maria-Gaetana Matisse Foundation Collection
Page 237

122. *Forms,* plate IX from *Jazz*
1947
Hand-printed colored stencil
16⅝ × 25⅝ in. (42.2 × 65.1 cm)
The Baltimore Museum of Art, The Cone Collection, formed by Dr. Claribel Cone and Miss Etta Cone of Baltimore, Maryland. BMA 1950.12.745
Page 239

123. *Venus in a Shell I*
1930 (cast 1931), Valsuani
Bronze, lost-wax cast
3/10
Duthuit no. 79
12¹⁄₁₆ × 7 × 8 in. (30.6 × 17.8 × 20.3 cm)
The Baltimore Museum of Art, The Cone Collection, formed by Dr. Claribel Cone and Miss Etta Cone of Baltimore, Maryland. BMA 1950.439
Pages 245, 246, 248

124. *Venus in a Shell II*
1932 (cast 1958), Valsuani
Bronze, lost-wax cast
4/10
Duthuit no. 80
13⅜ × 6⅞ × 9⅛ in. (34.0 × 17.5 × 23.2 cm)
Raymond and Patsy Nasher Collection, Dallas
Page 251

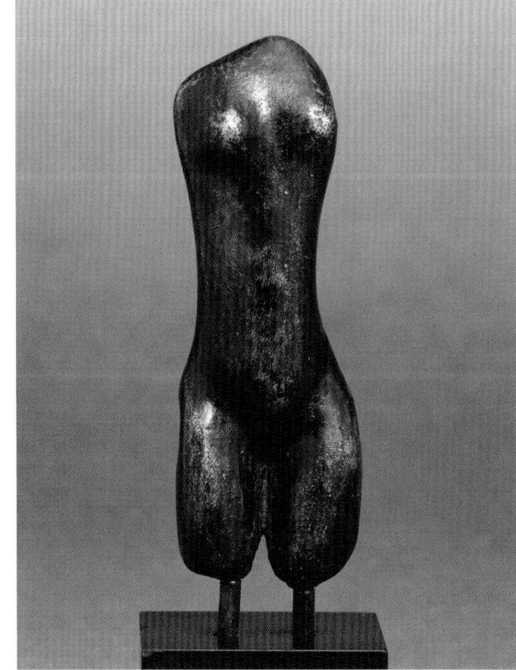

Henri Matisse, *Small Thin Torso,* 1929. Bronze. Private collection. Cat. 118

125. *Woman Standing in Tub*
1905–1906
Pen and india ink
9 15/16 × 7 3/4 in. (25.2 × 19.7 cm)
Private collection
• Baltimore only
Page 253

126. *The Bath*
1905–1906
Pen and india ink
10 5/8 × 16 7/16 in. (26.9 × 41.8 cm)
Centre Pompidou, Paris; Musée national d'art moderne/Centre de création industrielle; Gift of Marie Matisse, 1984
• Dallas and San Francisco only
Page 253

127. *Seated Nude*
c. 1929–1930
Graphite
11 × 8 7/8 in. (28.0 × 22.5 cm)
Mr. and Mrs. Stanley R. Gumberg, Pittsburgh
Page 248

128. *The Yellow Dress*
1929–1931
Oil on canvas
39 1/4 × 31 3/4 in. (99.7 × 80.7 cm)
The Baltimore Museum of Art, The Cone Collection, formed by Dr. Claribel Cone and Miss Etta Cone of Baltimore, Maryland. BMA 1950.256
Page 247

129. *Standing Nude*
1930
Graphite
13 × 10 1/16 in. (33.0 × 25.5 cm)
Pierre and Maria-Gaetana Matisse Foundation Collection
Page 249

130. *Nude with Raised Arms*
1930–1933
Graphite on imitation vellum paper
12 5/8 × 9 3/4 in. (32.1 × 24.7 cm)
Centre Pompidou, Paris; Musée national d'art moderne/Centre de création industrielle; Gift of Marie Matisse, 1984
• Dallas and San Francisco only
Page 249

131. Preliminary drawing for *Hommage III*, from *Poésies de Stéphane Mallarmé*
c. 1932
Graphite
13 × 10 1/8 in. (33.0 × 25.7 cm)
The Baltimore Museum of Art, The Cone Collection, formed by Dr. Claribel Cone and Miss Etta Cone of Baltimore, Maryland. BMA 1950.12.692XV
Page 250

132. *Standing Nude (Katia)*
1950 (cast 1959), Valsuani
Bronze, lost-wax cast
9/10
Duthuit no. 84
17 3/4 × 3 7/16 × 2 3/4 in. (45.1 × 8.7 × 7.0 cm)
Private collection
Page 255

133. *Standing Nude, Seen from the Side*
1908–1909
Charcoal with stumping
21 7/8 × 17 3/4 in. (55.6 × 45.1 cm)
Collection of Gerald and Kathleen Peters
Page 257

134. *Face and Two Nudes with Gourds*
1912–1313
Pen and india ink on squared paper
8 1/8 × 10 1/4 in. (20.6 × 26.0 cm)
Centre Pompidou, Paris; Musée national d'art moderne/Centre de création industrielle; Purchased from Marie Matisse, 1984
• Dallas and San Francisco only
Page 256

135. *Standing Nude, Seen from the Back (Lisette)*
c. 1930
Graphite
12 7/16 × 9 7/16 in. (31.5 × 24.0 cm)
Pierre and Maria-Gaetana Matisse Foundation Collection
Page 258

136. *Figure*
c. 1950
Pen and ink
8 1/4 × 5 5/16 in. (21.0 × 13.5 cm)
Pierre and Maria-Gaetana Matisse Foundation Collection
Page 258

137. *Standing Blue Nude*
1952
Gouache on paper, cut and pasted
44 3/8 × 29 in. (112.7 × 73.7 cm)
The Metropolitan Museum of Art, New York; The Pierre and Maria-Gaetana Matisse Collection, 2002
• Dallas only
Page 259

138. *Small Dancer on Red Ground*
1937–1938
Gouache on paper, cut and pasted
14 9/16 × 7 11/16 in. (37.0 × 19.5 cm)
Private collection
Page 262

139. *Negro Boxer*
1947
Gouache on paper, cut and pasted
12 5/8 × 10 1/16 in. (32.1 × 25.6 cm)
Private collection, New York
• Dallas only
Page 262

140. *Acrobatic Dancer*
1949
Gouache on paper, cut and pasted
20 1/2 × 15 3/4 in. (52 × 40 cm)
Pierre and Maria-Gaetana Matisse Foundation Collection
Page 263

141. *Blue Nude I*
1952
Gouache on paper, cut and pasted
41 3/4 × 30 3/4 × 1 3/16 in. (106 × 78 × 3 cm)
Fondation Beyeler, Riehen/Basel
• Baltimore only
Page 265

142. *Jazz*
Published by Tériade, Paris, 1947
Twenty hand-printed colored stencils with text
Each double sheet: 16⅝ × 25⅝ in. (42.2 × 65.1 cm)
142a. The Baltimore Museum of Art, The Cone Collection, formed by Dr. Claribel Cone and Miss Etta Cone of Baltimore, Maryland. BMA 1950.12.745
• Baltimore and San Francisco only
Page 261
142b. The Raymond and Patsy Nasher Collection, Dallas
• Dallas only
142c. Bridwell Library Special Collections, Perkins School of Theology, Southern Methodist University
• Dallas only

143. *Acrobat, Study*
1950
Pen and ink
10 7/16 × 8¼ in. (26.5 × 21.0 cm)
Pierre and Maria-Gaetana Matisse Foundation Collection
Page 264

144. *Four Studies of an Acrobat*
1950
Pen and ink
13⅜ × 10¼ in. (34 × 26 cm)
Pierre and Maria-Gaetana Matisse Foundation Collection
Page 264

WORKS BY OTHER ARTISTS

145. Alexander Archipenko
Torso in Space, also called *Floating Torso*
1935 (cast 1957–1958)
Bronze
6¾ × 22½ × 5½ in. (17.1 × 57.2 × 14.0 cm)
Nancy A. Nasher and David J. Haemisegger
Page 242

146. Antoine Barye
Jaguar Devouring a Hare
1850 (casting date unknown)
Bronze
17¼ × 19½ × 40 1/16 in. (43.8 × 49.5 × 101.8 cm)
The Baltimore Museum of Art, Purchased in Honor of Stiles Tuttle Colwill on his 50th Birthday with funds contributed by his Friends and Colleagues. BMA 2003.199
Pages 103, 104

147. Emile-Antoine Bourdelle
Large Bacchante
1907
Plaster on a pedestal of sculpted wood
72½ × 20½ × 6¼ in. (184.2 × 52.1 × 15.9 cm)
Dallas Museum of Art, General Acquisitions Fund
Page 178

148. Constantin Brancusi
Torso of a Young Girl (II)
c. 1923
White marble on limestone block
13¾ × 9¾ × 6 in. (34.9 × 24.8 15.2 cm)
Base: 6⅛ × 9 × 8⅞ in. (15.6 × 22.9 × 22.5 cm)
Philadelphia Museum of Art, A. E. Gallatin Collection, 1952
Page 240

149. Paul Cézanne
Three Bathers
c. 1875
Oil on canvas
12 × 13 in. (30.5 × 33.0 cm)
Private collection
Page 165

150. Paul Cézanne
Standing Female Nude
1898–1899
Oil on canvas
36½ × 28 in. (92.7 × 71.1 cm)
Property of a Trust
Page 146

151. Edgar Degas
Seated Woman Wiping her Left Side
1900–1905
Bronze
13½ × 14 × 9 in. (34.3 × 35.6 × 22.9 cm)
The Detroit Institute of Arts, Gift of Edward E. Rothman
• Dallas and San Francisco only
Page 252

152. Edgar Degas
Woman Getting out of the Bath, fragment
1896–1911
Bronze
16⅝ × 6 15/16 × 8 1/16 in. (42.2 × 17.6 × 20.5 cm)
Noortman Master Paintings, Maastricht
Page 177

153. Charles Despiau
Adolescent Girl (Diana)
1928
Red wax on plaster base
28 × 9 × 8 in. (71.1 × 22.9 × 20.3 cm)
Charles Janoray, LLC, New York
Page 241

154. Alberto Giacometti
Headless Woman
1932–1936 (cast c. 1955)
Bronze
57¾ × 9½ × 14¼ in. (146.7 × 24.1 × 36.2 cm)
The Baltimore Museum of Art, Alan and Janet Wurtzburger Collection. BMA 1966.55.9
Page 243

155. Henri Laurens
Little Seated Nude
1932
Terra-cotta
H: 12 13/16 in. (32.5 cm)
Musée Matisse, Nice; formerly Collection of Henri Matisse; Bequest of Madame Henri Matisse, 1960
• Dallas only
Page 191

156. Jacques Lipchitz
Gertrude Stein
1920 (cast before 1948)
Bronze
13 7/16 × 8¼ × 10⅝ in. (34.1 × 21.0 × 27.0 cm)
The Baltimore Museum of Art, The Cone Collection, formed by Dr. Claribel Cone and Miss Etta Cone of Baltimore, Maryland. BMA 1950.396
Page 213

157. Aristide Maillol
Study for La Méditerranée
1902 (cast 1902)
Bronze
6⅛ × 6⅛ × 3 15/16 in. (15.5 × 15.5 × 10.0 cm)
Museum Boijmans Van Beuningen, Rotterdam
Page 190

158. Aristide Maillol
Woman Kneeling Down with One Knee Raised
c. 1926
Etching
12¼ × 15⅛ in. (35.6 × 42.6 cm)
Dallas Museum of Art, Foundation for the Arts Collection, Gift of Mrs. Alfred L. Bromberg
Page 190

159. Aristide Maillol
Hylas disparu dans une fontaine from
The Eclogues of Virgil
Published by Emery Walker for the Cranach Press, London, 1927
Woodcut
$3\frac{15}{16}$ × 3⅝ in. (10.0 × 9.2 cm)
Harry Ransom Center, University of Texas, Austin
Page 190

160. Pablo Picasso
Head of a Woman
1931 (cast 1973)
Bronze
34 × 14⅜ × 19¼ in. (86.4 × 36.5 × 48.9 cm)
Raymond and Patsy Nasher Collection, Dallas
Page 207

161. Pablo Picasso
Two Nudes
1906
Brush and gouache, charcoal, watercolor, and black crayon
$24\frac{13}{16}$ × 18⅞ in. (63 × 48 cm)
The Baltimore Museum of Art, The Cone Collection, formed by Dr. Claribel Cone and Miss Etta Cone of Baltimore, Maryland. BMA 1950.277
• Baltimore only
Page 159

162. Auguste Rodin
Meditation
1885 (cast 1926)
Bronze
29 × 11 × 11 in. (73.7 × 27.9 × 27.9 cm)
Philadelphia Museum of Art, Bequest of Jules E. Mastbaum, 1929
Page 118

163. Auguste Rodin
Jean d'Aire, from the *Burghers of Calais*
1895 (cast early 20th century)
Bronze
81 × 28 × 24 in. (205.7 × 71.1 × 61.0 cm)
Dallas Museum of Art, Given in memory of Louie N. Bromberg and Mina Bromberg by their sister Essie Bromberg Joseph
Page 111

164. Auguste Rodin
Dance Movement Pas de Deux 'B'
c. 1910–1911 (cast 1965)
Bronze
13 × 7⅛ × 5 in. (33.0 × 18.1 × 12.7 cm)
Iris & B. Gerald Cantor Collection
Page 175

165. Edward Steichen
Matisse working on *La Serpentine,*
from *Camera Work*
1909
Photogravure
$11\frac{9}{16}$ × 8 in. (29.4 × 20.3 cm)
The Baltimore Museum of Art, E. Kirkbride Miller Library. BMA MS 2005.30
Page 172

Abbreviated References and Selected Bibliography

Adil and DePhillips 1991

Adil, Carol, and Henry DePhillips. ***Paul Wayland Bartlett and the Art of Patination.*** Wethersfield, Conn.: Paul Wayland Bartlett Society, 1991.

Anthonioz 2002

Anthonioz, Michael. "Painting with Scissors: *Jazz* and *Verve*." In ***Henri Matisse: Drawing with Scissors: Masterpieces from the Late Years,*** edited by Olivier Berggruen and Max Hollein, translated by Paul Anton. Munich and London: Prestel Verlag, 2002.

Apollinaire 1907

Apollinaire, Guillaume. "Knowing Oneself." ***La Phalange*** (November 15, 1907). Reprinted in Barr 1951.

Apollinaire 1913

Apollinaire, Guillaume. "La Vie Artistique." ***L'Intransigent*** 17 (April 1913). Reprinted in ***Chroniques d'art (1902–1918),*** by Guillaume Apollinaire, edited by L.C. Breunig. Paris: Gallimard, 1960.

Aragon 1972

Aragon, Louis. ***Henri Matisse, a Novel.*** New York: Harcourt Brace Jovanovich, 1972.

Aspley, Cowling, and Sharratt 2000

Aspley, Kenneth, Elizabeth Cowling, and Peter Sharratt, eds. ***From Rodin to Giacometti: Sculpture and Literature in France, 1880–1950.*** Amsterdam and Atlanta, Ga.: Rodopi, 2000.

Baldassari 2002

Baldassari, Anne. In ***Matisse Picasso,*** by Elizabeth Cowling et al. Exh. cat. London: Tate Publishing, 2002.

Baligand et al. 1998

Baligand, Françoise, Sylvie Carlier, Isabelle Compin, and Monique Nonnne. ***Henri-Edmond Cross: 1856–1910.*** Paris: Somogy Éditions d'Art, 1998.

Barr 1951

Barr, Alfred, Jr. ***Matisse: His Art and His Public.*** New York: Museum of Modern Art, 1951.

Baudry et al. 1978

Baudry, Marie-Thérèse, et al. ***La Sculpture: Méthode et vocabulaire.*** Paris: Imprimerie national, 1978.

Beale 1975

Beale, Arthur. "A Technical View of Nineteenth-Century Sculpture." In Wasserman 1975.

Beale 1998

Beale, Arthur. "Little Dancer Aged Fourteen: The Search for the Lost Modèle." In ***Degas and the Little Dancer,*** edited by Richard Kendall, 97–108. New Haven, Conn.: Yale University Press, 1998.

Benjamin 1987

Benjamin, Roger. ***Matisse's "Notes of a Painter": Criticism, Theory, and Context, 1891–1908.*** Ann Arbor, Mich.: UMI Research Press, 1987.

Benjamin 1989

Benjamin, Roger. "Recovering Authors: The Modern Copy, Copy Exhibitions, and Matisse." ***Art History*** 12, no. 2 (June 1989): 176–201.

Benjamin 1990

Benjamin, Roger. "Fauves in the Landscape of Criticism: Metaphor and Scandal at the Salon." In Freeman 1990.

Benjamin 1992

Benjamin, Roger. "L'Arabesque dans la modernité: Henri Matisse sculpteur." In Le Nouëne 1992.

Berger and Zutter 1996

Berger, Ursel, and Jörg Zutter. ***Aristide Maillol.*** Paris: Flammarion and Musée des Beaux-Arts, Lausanne, 1996.

Boardingham 1995

Boardingham, Robert. "Cézanne and the 1904 Salon d'Automne: 'Un chef d'une école nouvelle.'" ***Apollo*** 142 (October 1995): 31–39.

Bock 1981

Bock, Catherine C. ***Henri Matisse and Neo-Impressionism, 1898–1908.*** Ann Arbor, Mich.: UMI Research Press, 1981.

Bock-Weiss 1996

Bock-Weiss, Catherine C. *Henry Matisse: A Guide to Research.* New York: Garland, 1996.

Bois 1994

Bois, Yve-Alain. "On Matisse: The Blinding." *October* 68 (spring 1994): 61–121.

Bois 1997

Bois, Yve-Alain. Preface. In Duthuit 1997.

Bois 1998

Bois, Yve-Alain. *Matisse and Picasso.* Paris: Flammarion, 1998.

Bois 1999

Bois, Yve-Alain. *Matisse and Picasso.* Exh. cat. Fort Worth, Tex.: Kimbell Art Museum, 1999.

Bouer 1995

Bouer, Raymond. "Le procès de l'art moderne au Salon d'Automne," *Revue Politique et Littéraire* (November 5, 1905): 605.

Bourguignon 1998

Bourguignon, Katherine M. "'Un Viol De Moi Même': Matisse and the Female Model." PhD diss., University of Pennsylvania, 1998.

Carlson 1971

Carlson, Victor I. *Matisse as a Draughtsman.* Exh. cat. Baltimore, Md.: Baltimore Museum of Art, 1971.

Carrier 1994

Carrier, David. "'You, too, are in Arcadia': The Place of the Spectator in Matisse's Shchukin Triptych." *Word and Image* 10, no. 2 (April–June 1994): 119–37.

Cauman 2000a

Cauman, John. "Henri Matisse, 1908, 1910, and 1912: New Evidence of Life." In *Modern Art and America: Alfred Stieglitz and His New York Galleries,* edited by Sarah Greenough, 83–96. Exh. cat. Washington, D.C.: National Gallery of Art, 2000.

Cauman 2000b

Cauman, John. "Matisse and America, 1905–1933." PhD diss., City University of New York, 2000.

Cellini 1967

Cellini, Benvenuto. *The Treatises of Benvenuto Cellini on Goldsmithing and Sculpture.* New York: Dover, 1967.

Champion and Janoray 2002

Champion, Jean-Loup, and Charles Janoray. *Classical Modernity from Bourdelle to Despiau, 1907–1937.* Exh. cat. New York: Charles Janoray, 2002.

Chappius 1973

Chappuis, Adrien. *The Drawings of Paul Cézanne.* Greenwich, Conn.: New York Graphic Society, 1973.

Charbonnier 1960

Charbonnier, Georges. "Entretien avec Henri Matisse." *Le Monologue du peintre.* 2 vols. Paris: Editions Julliard, 1960. Reprinted in Flam 1995.

Charbonnier n.d.

Charbonnier, Georges. Nine unpublished interviews with Matisse. Typescript. Getty Center for the History of Art and the Humanities, Archives of the History of Art, Santa Monica, Calif. Reprinted in Flam 1995.

Clark 1956

Clark, Kenneth. *The Nude: A Study in the Ideal Form.* New York: Bollingen Foundation and Pantheon Books, 1956.

Claudel 1937

Claudel, Judith. *Maillol: Sa Vie, Son Oeuvre, Ses Idées.* Paris: Grasset, 1937.

Collection Pompidou 1998

La collection du Centre Georges Pompidou, Musée national d'art moderne. *Matisse.* Paris: Centre Georges Pompidou et Réunion des musées nationaux, 1998.

Cooke 1986

Cooke, Lynn. "Paragone Rediscovered: The Painter Sculptor in the Twentieth Century." In *In Tandem: The Painter Sculptor in the Twentieth Century,* 11–42. Whitechapel, London: Whitechapel Art Gallery Foundation, 1986.

Courthion 1941

Courthion, Pierre. "Nine Unpublished Interviews with Matisse," 1941. Getty Center for the History of Art and the Humanities, Archives of the History of Art, Santa Monica, Calif. In Flam 1995.

Courthion n.d. (Matisse Archives)

Courthion, Pierre. *Bavardages: Entretiens avec Courthion.* Typescript. Matisse Archives, Paris.

Courthion n.d. (Getty Center)

Courthion, Pierre. "Conversations avec Henri Matisse." Typescript. Getty Center for the History of Art and the Humanities, Archives of the History of Art, Santa Monica, Calif.

Cowart et al. 1990

Cowart, Jack, Pierre Schneider, John Elderfield, Albert Kostenevich, and Laura Coyle. *Matisse In Morocco: The Paintings and Drawings, 1912–1913.* Exh. cat. Washington, D.C.: National Gallery of Art, 1990.

Cowart and Fourcade 1986

Cowart, Jack, and Dominique Fourcade. *Henri Matisse: The Early Years in Nice, 1916–1930.* New York: Harry N. Abrams, 1986.

Cowling et al. 2002

Cowling, Elizabeth, et al. *Matisse Picasso.* Exh. cat. London: Tate Publishing, 2002.

Dauberville 1995

Dauberville, Guy-Patrice, and Michel Dauberville. *Matisse.* 2 vols. Paris: Editions Bernheim-Jeune, 1995.

De Barañano 2003

De Barañano, Kosme. "Matisse's Sculpture: The Fractal Theory." In Soria 2003.

Diehl 1943

Diehl, Gaston. *Peintres d'aujourd'hui.* Paris: Publications Technique, 1943.

Druet 1906

Galerie Druet. *Exposition Henri Matisse.* March 19–April 7, 1906.

Duthuit 1988

Duthuit, Claude. *Henri Matisse: Catalogue raisonné des ouvrages illustrés établi avec la collaboration de Françoise Garnaud.* Introduction by Jean Guichard-Meili. Paris: Imprimerie Union à Paris, 1988.

Duthuit 1997

Duthuit, Claude, with Wanda de Guébriant. *Henri Matisse: Catalogue raisonné de l'œuvre sculpté.* Preface by Yve-Alain Bois. Paris: Claude Duthuit Éditeur, 1997.

Duthuit-Matisse 1983

Duthuit-Matisse, Marguerite, and Claude Duthuit. *Henri Matisse: Catalogue raisonné de l'œuvre grave établi avec la collaboration de Françoise Gernaud.* 2 vols. Preface by Jean Guichard-Meili. Paris: Imprimerie Union, 1983.

Duval 2000

Duval, Jean Luc. "La Méditerranée: L'Ouverture à la mythologie du désir." In *Aristide Maillol,* edited by Dina Vierny. Berne: Éditions Benteli, 2000.

Eisler n.d.

Eisler, Colin. *Sculptors' Drawings Over Six Centuries, 1400–1950.* New York: Agrinde, n.d.

Elderfield 1972

Elderfield, John. "Matisse Drawings and Sculpture." *Artforum* 11, no. 1 (September 1972): 77–85.

Elderfield 1978a

Elderfield, John. *The Cut-Outs of Henri Matisse.* New York: Braziller, 1978.

Elderfield 1978b

Elderfield, John. *Matisse in the Collection of the Museum of Modern Art.* Exh. cat. New York: Museum of Modern Art, 1978.

Elderfield 1984

Elderfield, John. *The Drawings of Henri Matisse.* Exh. cat. New York: Museum of Modern Art, in association with the Arts Council of Great Britain and Thames and Hudson, 1984.

Elderfield 1992

Elderfield, John. *Henri Matisse: A Retrospective.* Exh. cat. New York: Museum of Modern Art, 1992.

Elderfield 1996

Elderfield, John. *Pleasuring Painting: Matisse's Feminine Representations.* New York: Thames and Hudson, 1996.

Elsen 1972

Elsen, Albert E. *The Sculpture of Henri Matisse.* New York: Harry N. Abrams, 1972.

Elsen 1974

Elsen, Albert. *Origins of Modern Sculpture: Pioneers and Premises.* New York: Braziller, 1974.

Elsen and Varnedoe 1971

Elsen, Albert, and J. Kirk T. Varnedoe. *The Drawings of Rodin.* With contributions by Victoria Thorsen and Elisabeth Chase Geissbuhler. New York, Prager, 1971.

Escholier 1956

Escholier, Raymond. *Matisse, ce vivant.* Paris: Fayard, 1956.

Escholier 1960

Escholier, Raymond. *Matisse: A Portrait of the Artist and the Man.* Translated by Geraldine and H. M. Colvile. New York: Praeger, 1960.

Fernier 1977–1978

Fernier, Robert. *La vie et l'œuvre de Gustave Courbet: Catalogue raisonné.* Geneva: Fondation Wildenstein, 1977–1978.

Flam 1971

Flam, Jack. "Matisse's *Backs* and the Development of His Painting." *Art Journal* 30, no. 4 (summer 1971): 352–61.

Flam 1984

Flam, Jack. "Matisse and the Fauves." In *"Primitivism" in 20th Century Art: Affinity of the Tribal and the Modern,* edited by William Rubin. 2 vols. New York: Museum of Modern Art, Boston, 1984.

Flam 1986

Flam, Jack. *Matisse: The Man and his Art, 1869–1918.* Ithaca, N.Y.: Cornell University Press, 1986.

Flam 1988

Flam, Jack. *Matisse: A Retrospective.* New York: Hugh Lauter Levin, 1988.

Flam 1993

Flam, Jack. *Matisse: Image Into Sign.* Exh. cat. St. Louis, Mo.: Saint Louis Art Museum, 1993.

FLAM 1995
Flam, Jack, ed. *Matisse on Art.* Rev. ed. Berkeley: University of California Press, 1995.

FLAM 1998
Flam, Jack. *Henri Matisse: Sculpture.* Exh. cat. New York: C & M Arts, 1998.

FLAM 2001
Flam, Jack. *Matisse in the Cone Collection: The Poetics of Vision.* Baltimore, Md.: Baltimore Museum of Art, 2001.

FLAM 2003
Flam, Jack. *Matisse and Picasso: The Story of Their Rivalry and Friendship.* Cambridge, Mass.: Westview Press, 2003.

FLETCHER 2003
Fletcher, Valerie. "Process and Technique in Picasso's *Head of a Woman (Fernande).*" In *Picasso: The Cubist Portraits of Fernande Olivier,* edited by Jeffrey Weiss, Valerie J. Fletcher, and Kathryn A. Tuma, 165–92. Exh. cat. Washington, D.C.: National Gallery of Art, 2003.

FOURCADE 1972
Fourcade, Dominique, ed. *Henri Matisse: Écrits et propos sur l'art.* Paris: Hermann, 1972.

FOURCADE 1977
Fourcade, Dominque. "Something Else." In *Henri Matisse: Paper Cut-outs,* edited by Jack Cowart. Exh. cat. New York: Harry N. Abrams, 1977.

FRANZKE 1983
Franzke, Andreas. "Der Mahler Hans Purrmann as Bildhauer." *Pantheon* 41 (January–March 1983): 29–34.

FRASCINA 1993
Frascina, Francis. "Realism and Ideology: An Introduction to Semiotics and Cubism." In *Primitivism, Cubism, Abstraction: The Early Twentieth Century,* by Charles Harrison, Francis Frascina, and Gill Perry, 87–184. London and New Haven: Open University and Yale University Press, 1993.

FREEMAN 1990
Freeman, Judi, ed. *The Fauve Landscape.* Exh. cat. Los Angeles: Los Angeles County Museum of Art, 1990.

FRY 1912
Fry, Roger. "The Grafton Gallery: An Apologia." *The Nation* 9 (November 1912): 249–51. Reprinted in Reed 1996.

GEISSBUHLER 1963
Geissbuhler, Elisabeth Chase. *Rodin: Later Drawings.* With interpretations by Antoine Bourdelle. Boston: Beacon Press, 1963.

GIDE 1905
Gide, André. "Promenade au Salon d'Automne," *Gazette des Beaux-Arts* 34 (December 1905): 475–85.

GIRARD 1993
Girard, Xavier. *Matisse, la danse.* Cahier Henri Matisse, no. 10. Cannes, France: Lamamaison, 1993.

GIRARD AND KUTHY 1990
Girard, Xavier, and Sandor Kuthy. *Henri Matisse, 1869–1954: Skulpturen und Druckgraphik—Sculptures et gravures.* Exh. cat. Bern: Kunstmuseum Bern und Autoren, 1990.

GOLDWATER 1972
Goldwater, Robert. "The Sculpture of Matisse." *Art in America* 60, no. 2 (March–April 1972): 40–45.

GONON 1876
Gonon, Eugène. "Art de la fonte a cire perdue." Paris, 1876. Manuscript. Photocopy in Documentation section, Musée d'Orsay, Paris.

GORDON 1974
Gordon, Donald E. *Modern Art Exhibitions: 1900–1916.* 2 vols. Munich: Prestel Verlag, 1974.

GOWING 1979
Gowing, Lawrence. *Matisse.* New York: Oxford University Press, 1979.

GRAMMONT 1997
Grammont, Claudine, ed. *Correspondance entre Charles Camoin et Henri Matisse: Lettres présentées et annotées par Claudine Grammont.* Lausanne: La Bibliothèque des Arts, 1997.

GRAMMONT 2002
Grammont, Claudine. "L'ecriture des formes: Les fauves et le dessin caricatural." In *Quelque chose de plus que la couleur: Le dessin fauve, 1900–1908.* Exh. cat. Paris: Musées de Marseille, Reunion des musées nationaux, 2002.

GRENDON 1912
Grendon, Felix. "Matisse." *The International* 6 (July 1912): 34–35. Reprinted in *Modern Art and America: Alfred Stieglitz and His New York Galleries,* edited by Sarah Greenough. Exh. cat. Washington, D.C.: National Gallery of Art, 2000.

GROHÉ 2005
Grohé, Stefan. "Body Control: Matisse the Painter Quotes Matisse the Sculptor." In *Henri Matisse: Figure, Color, Space.* Exh. cat. English ed. Osfildern-Ruit, Germany: Hatje Cantz Verlag, 2005.

GUICHARD-MEILI 1983
Guichard-Meili, Jean. *Matisse: Paper Cutouts.* London: Thames and Hudson, 1983.

GUICHARD-MEILI 1986
Guichard-Meili, Jean. *Matisse.* Paris: Somogy, 1986.

Güse 1991

Güse, Ernst-Gerhard. *Henri Matisse: Drawings and Sculpture.* With contributions by Christian Arthaud, Xavier Girard, and Ernst W. Uthemann. Munich: Prestel Verlag, 1991.

Hahnloser 1987

Hahnloser, Margrit. *Matisse: The Graphic Work.* New York: Rizzoli, 1987.

Haviland 1912

Haviland, Paul. "Photo-Secession Notes." *Camera Work* 38 (April 1912): 36–37.

Hepp 1908

Hepp, Pierre. "Le Salon d'Automne." *Gazette des Beaux-Arts* (1 November 1908). Translated and reprinted in Benjamin 1987.

Herbert 1992

Herbert, James D. *Fauve Painting: The Making of Cultural Politics.* New Haven, Conn.: Yale University Press, 1992.

Hocquard and Laupies, 1980

Hocquard, Claude-Nicole, and Lydie Laupies. *La Fonte à cire perdue.* Videocassette. Neyrac Films, 1980; 50 minutes.

Hoffman 1939

Hoffman, Malvina. *Sculpture Inside and Out.* New York: Norton, 1939.

Hoffman 1966

Hoffman, Malvina. *Heads and Tales.* New York: Norton, 1966.

Jazz 1947

Jazz. Paris: Tériade, 1947.

Jianou and Dufet 1965

Jianou, Ionel, and Michel Dufet. *Bourdelle.* Paris: Arted-Editions d'Art, 1965.

Kramer 1966

Kramer, Hilton. "Matisse as Sculptor." *Boston Museum Bulletin* 64, no. 336 (1966): 48–65.

Labrusse and Chassey 2002

Labrusse, Rémi, and Éric de Chassey. *Henri Matisse, Ellsworth Kelly: Plant Drawings.* Corte Madera, Calif.: Gingko Press, 2002.

Lacambre 1999

Lacambre, Geneviève. *Gustave Moreau: Between Epic and Dream.* Paris and Chicago: Réunion des musées nationaux and Art Institute of Chicago, in association with Princeton University Press, 1999.

Lacombe, Debonliez, and Malepeyr 1979

Lacombe, M. S., M. M. G. Debonliez, and F. Malepeyre. *Nouveau manuel complet du bronzage des metaux et du plâtre.* 1887. Reprint, Paris: Chez Leonce Laget, 1979.

Lebon 2003

Lebon, Élisabeth. *Dictionnaire des fondeurs de bronze d'art: France, 1890–1950.* Perth, Australia: Marjon, 2003.

Legg 1972

Legg, Alicia. *The Sculpture of Matisse.* Exh. cat. New York: Museum of Modern Art, 1972.

Le Marchant 1989

Le Marchant, Michael. *Bourdelle Evolution.* London and New York: Bruton Gallery, 1989.

Le Nouëne et al. 1992

Le Nouëne, Patrick, et al. *De Matisse à aujourd'hui: La sculpture du XXe siècle dans les collections des Musées et du Fonds Régional d'Art Contemporain du Nord-Pas-de-Calais.* Calais, France: Association des Conservateurs des Musées du Nord-Pas-de-Calais, 1992.

Lie 2003

Lie, Henry. "Technical Features in Rosso's Work." In *Medardo Rosso: Second Impressions,* edited by Harry Cooper and Sharon Hecker, 69–93. Exh. cat. New Haven, Conn.: Yale University Press 2003.

Loffredo 1989

Loffredo, François-Raphael. "L'inventaire après décès d'Antoine-Louis Barye (1769–1875)." *Documents sur la sculpture française et Répertoire de fondeurs du XIX siècle.* Vol. 30. Archives de l'Art français, Société de l'Histoire de l'Art français. Nogent-le-Roi, France: Librairie des Arts et Métiers-Editions, 1989.

Lorquin 1994

Bertrand Lorquin, *Aristide Maillol.* Geneva: Editions d'Art Albert Skira, 1994.

Lorquin 2002

Lorquin, Bertrand. "I seek to express the impalpable." In *Aristide Maillol,* by Kosme De Barañano, Michael Peppiatt, and Bertrand Lorquin. Exh. cat. Valencia, Spain: Institut Valencià d'Art Modern, 2002.

Martin 2000

Martin, Graham Dunstan. "Proprioception, Mental Imagery and Sculpture." In Aspley, Cowling, and Sharratt 2000.

Marx 1908

Marx, Roger "Le Vernissage du Salon d'Automne." *Chronique des arts* 10 (October 1908). Translated and reprinted in Benjamin 1987.

Maryon 1971

Maryon, Herbert. *Metalwork and Enameling.* New York: Dover, 1971.

Mathiey 1984

Pierre-Louis, Mathiey, ed. *L'Assembleur des rêves: Écrits complets de Gustave Moreau.* Paris: Bibliothèque Artistique et Littéraire, 1984.

Matisse 1908

Matisse, Henri. "Notes d'un peintre." *La Grande Revue* 2, no. 24 (December 25, 1908): 731–45. Reprinted in Flam 1995.

See also Purmann 1960

Mattusch 1996

Mattusch, Carol. *The Fire of Hephaistos.* Cambridge, Mass.: Harvard University Art Museums, 1996.

Meier-Graefe 1923

Meier-Graefe, Julius. *Degas.* Translated by J. Holroyd-Reece. New York: Knopf, 1923.

Mezzatesta 1984

Mezzatesta, Michael P. *Henri Matisse, Sculptor, Painter: A Formal Analysis of Selected Works.* Exh. cat. Fort Worth, Tex.: Kimball Art Museum, 1984.

Michaelides 1958

Michaelides, Claude. "900° centigrades." *L'Œil,* no. 46 (October 1958).

Michel 1931

Michel, Jacques. *Coloration des metaux.* Paris: Desforges, Girardot et Cie, 1931.

Millard 1976

Millard, Charles W. *The Sculpture of Edgar Degas.* Princeton, N.J.: Princeton University Press, 1976.

Mitchell 1916

Mitchell, William Donald. *The Art of the Bronze Founder.* New York: Gibbs and Van Vleck 1916.

Monod-Fontaine 1984

Monod-Fontaine, Isabelle. *The Sculpture of Henri Matisse.* Exh. cat. London: Arts Council of Great Britain and Thames and Hudson, 1984.

Monod-Fontaine 2003

Monod-Fontaine, Isabelle. "Matisse: Painter Sculptor." In Soria 2003.

Monod-Fontaine, Baldassari, and Laugier 1989

Monod-Fontaine, Isabelle, Anne Baldassari, and Claude Laugier. *Œuvres de Henri Matisse.* Paris: Centre George Pompidou, Collections du Musée national d'art moderne, 1989.

Nash 1987

Nash, Steven A., ed. *A Century of Modern Sculpture: The Patsy and Raymond Nasher Collection.* Dallas: Dallas Museum of Art, 1987.

Neff 1975

Neff, John. "Matisse and Decoration: The Shchukin Panels." *Art in America* 63, no. 4 (July–August 1975): 38–48.

Nochlin 1993

Nochlin, Linda. "'Matisse' and Its Other." *Art in America* 81, no. 5 (May 1993): 88–97.

O'Brian 1999

O'Brian, John. *Ruthless Hedonism: The American Reception of Matisse.* Chicago: University of Chicago Press, 1999.

Oppler 1976

Oppler, Ellen C. *Fauvism Reexamined.* New York & London: Garland, 1976.

Pinet 2001

Pinet, Hélène. "Eugène Druet, homme-orchestre et gardien du temple." In *Rodin en 1900: L'exposition de l'Alma,* edited by Claudie Jurdin and Hélène Pinet, 275–95. Exh. cat. Paris: Musée du Luxembourg, 2001.

Pullen 2003

Pullen, Derek. "Gelatin Molds: Rosso's Open Secret." In *Medardo Rosso: Second Impressions,* edited by Harry Cooper and Sharon Hecker, 96–102. Exh. cat. New Haven: Yale University Press 2003.

Purrmann 1960

Matisse, Henri. *Farbe und Gleichnis: Gesammelte Schriften. Mit den Erinnerungen von Hans Purrmann.* Zurich: Arche, 1955; Frankfurt and Hamburg, 1960.

Puy 1939

Puy, Jean. "Souvenirs." *Le Point* 4, no. 21 (July 1939): 112–33.

Rama 1988

Rama, Jean-Pierre, with Jacques Berthelot. *Le bronze d'art et ses techniques.* Dourdan, France: Éditions H. Vial, 1988.

Reed 1996

Reed, Christopher, ed. *A Roger Fry Reader.* Chicago and London: University of Chicago Press, 1996.

Reff 1976

Reff, Theodore. "Matisse: Meditations on a Statuette and Goldfish." *Arts Magazine* 51, no. 3 (November 1976): 109–15.

Renoir 1962

Renoir, Jean. *Pierre-Auguste Renoir, mon père.* Boston: Little Brown, 1962.

Rewald 1996

Rewald, John. *The Paintings of Paul Cézanne: A Catalogue Raisonné.* 2 vols. New York: Harry N. Abrams, 1996.

Richardson 1985

Richardson, Brenda. *Dr. Claribel & Miss Etta: The Cone Collection of The Baltimore Museum of Art.* Baltimore, Md.: Baltimore Museum of Art, 1985.

Rodin 1981

Rodin: The Gates of Hell. Iris and B. Gerald Cantor Center for the Visual Arts at Stanford University. Videocassette. Kultur, 1981; 53 minutes.

Rosenthal 1956
Rosenthal, Gertrude. "Matisse's Reclining Figures: A Theme and Its Variations." ***Baltimore Museum of Art News*** (February 1956).

Russell 1999
Russell, John. ***Matisse: Father and Son.*** New York: Harry N. Abrams, 1999.

Saint-Hilaire 1905
Saint-Hilaire, Jules de. "Le Salon d'Automne." ***Journal des Arts*** 11 (November 1905). Translated and reprinted in Wright 2004.

Schapiro 1932
Schapiro, Meyer. "Matisse and Impressionism: A Review of Matisse at the Museum of Modern Art, New York, November 1931." ***Androcles 1*** (February 1, 1932): 21–36.

Schlesser 2005
Schlesser, Thomas. "Le fonds Druet-Vizzavona." ***La Gazette de l'Hotel Biron,*** no. 51 (May 2005).

Schneider 1972
Schneider, Pierre. "Matisse's Sculpture: The Invisible Revolution." ***Art News*** 71, no. 1 (March 1972): 22–25.

Schneider 1984
Schneider, Pierre. ***Matisse.*** Translated by Michael Taylor and Bridget Stevens Romer. New York: Rizzoli, 1984.

Schneider, Cowart, and Coyle 1990
Schneider, Pierre, Jack Cowart, and Laura Coyle. "Appendix 2: Triptychs, Triads and Trios: Groups of Three in Matisse's Paintings of the Moroccan Period." In ***Matisse in Morocco: The Paintings and Drawings, 1912–1913,*** edited by Jack Cowart et al., 270–74. Exh. cat. Washington, D.C.: National Gallery of Art, 1990.

Serrano and Grammont 2002
Serrano, Véronique, and Claudine Grammont. ***Quelque chose de plus que la couleur: Le dessin fauve, 1900–1908.*** Exh. cat. Marseille: Musée Cantini Marseille, 2002.

Shapiro 1985
Shapiro, Michael. ***Bronze Casting and American Sculpture, 1850–1900.*** Newark, Del.: University of Delaware Press 1985.

Shiff 1984
Shiff, Richard. ***Cézanne and the End of Impressionism: A Study of the Theory, Technique, and Critical Evaluation of Modern Art.*** Chicago: University of Chicago Press, 1984.

Shiff 1995
Shiff, Richard. "Imitation of Matisse." In Turner and Benjamin 1995.

Simonds 1886
Simonds, George. "Artistic Bronze Casting." ***Scientific American Supplement*** 21, no. 553 (January–June 1886): 8504.

Smith 1981
Smith, Cyril Stanley. ***A Search for Structure.*** Boston: MIT Press, 1981.

Soria 2003
Soria, Martine, ed. ***Henri Matisse.*** Exh. cat. Valencia, Spain: Institut Valencià d'Art Modern, 2003.

Spurling 1998
Spurling, Hilary. ***The Unknown Matisse: A Life of Henri Matisse—The Early Years, 1869–1908.*** New York: Knopf, 1998.

Spurling 2005a
Spurling, Hilary. ***Matisse the Master: A Life of Henri Matisse—The Conquest of Colour, 1909–1954.*** New York: Knopf, 2005.

Spurling 2005b
Spurling, Hilary. "Matisse's Pajamas." ***New York Review of Books*** 52, no. 13 (August 11, 2005): 33–36.

Stein 1908
Sarah Stein, "Notes." 1908. Reprinted in Flam 1995.

Stein 1933
Stein, Gertrude. ***The Autobiography of Alice B. Toklas.*** New York: Harcourt, Brace, 1933.

Steinberg 1972
Steinberg, Leo. ***Other Criteria: Confrontations with Twentieth-Century Art.*** London: Oxford University Press, 1972.

Steinberg 1978
Steinberg, Leo. "Resisting Cézanne: Picasso's 'Three Women.'" ***Art in America*** 66, no. 6 (November–December 1978): 14–33.

Sykora 2005
Sykora, Katharina. "At Second Glance: Henri Matisse and Photography." In ***Henri Matisse: Figure, Color, Space.*** Exh. cat. English edition. Osfildern-Ruit, Germany: Hatje Cantz Verlag, 2005.

Szymusiak 1993
Szymusiak, Dominique. ***Matisse: Sculpture—dessins, dialogue.*** Exh. cat. Le Cateau-Cambrésis, France: Musée Matisse, 1993.

Tancock 1976
Tancock, John L. ***The Sculpture of Auguste Rodin.*** Coll. cat. Philadelphia: David R. Godine and Philadelphia Museum of Art, 1976.

THEOPHILUS 1963
Theophilus. *On Divers Arts.* Chicago: University of Chicago Press, 1963.

THIEBAULT N.D.
Thiebault archives. "Fonte à cire perdue: Procédés Italiens-Japonais." Paris: Musée d'Orsay, Documentation section, Thiebault file. n.d. [after 1927].

TRAPP 1962
Trapp, Frank Anderson. "The Atelier Gustave Moreau." *Art Journal* 32, no. 2 (winter 1962–1963): 92–95.

TUCKER 1969A
Tucker, William. ***Henri Matisse, 1869–1954: Sculpture.*** London: Waddington, 1969.

TUCKER 1969B
Tucker, William. "The Sculpture of Matisse." *Studio International* 178, no. 913 (July/August 1969): 25–28.

TUCKER 1974A
Tucker, William. *Early Modern Sculpture: Rodin, Degas, Matisse, Brancusi, Picasso, González.* New York: Oxford University Press, 1974.

TUCKER 1974B
Tucker, William. *The Language of Sculpture.* London: Thames and Hudson, 1974.

TUCKER 1975
Tucker, William. "Matisse's Sculpture: The Grasped and the Seen." *Art in America* 63 (July–August 1975): 62–68.

TURNER AND BENJAMIN 1996
Turner, Caroline, and Roger Benjamin, eds. *Matisse.* Exh. cat. Brisbane, Australia: Queensland Art Gallery and Art Exhibitions Australia Ltd., 1995.

UCLA 1966
UCLA Art Council. *Henri Matisse: Retrospective, 1966.* Texts by Jean Leymarie, Herbert Read, and Williams S. Lieberman. Berkeley: University of California Press, 1966.

VARENNE 1937
Varenne, Gaston. *Antoine Bourdelle, par lui-même.* Paris: Fasquelle, 1937.

VARNEDOE 1981
Varnedoe, Kirk. "Rodin's Drawings." In *Rodin Rediscovered,* edited by Albert Elsen, 153–89. Exh. cat. Washington, D.C.: National Gallery of Art, 1981.

VAUXCELLES 1904
Vauxcelles, Louis. "Le Salon d'Automne." *Gil Blas* (October 14, 1904). Reprinted in Flam 1988.

VAUXCELLES 1905A
Vauxcelles, Louis. "La fonte à cire perdue." *Art et Décoration* 8 (1905): 195.

VAUXCELLES 1905B
Vauxcelles, Louis. "Le Salon d'Automne." *Gil Blas* 17 (October 1905). Reprinted in Flam 1988.

VAUXCELLES 1908
Vauxcelles, Louis. "Le Salon d'Automne." *Gil Blas,* 30 (October 1908). Reprinted in Benjamin 1987.

VERDET 1952
Verdet, André. *Prestiges de Matisse: Précedé de visite à Matisse, Entretiens avec Matisse.* Paris: Émile Paul, 1952.

VERVE 1958
"Les derniers œuvres de Matisse." *Verve* 35–36 (1958).

VIERNY AND LORQUIN 1995
Vierny, Dina, and Bertrand Lorquin. *Maillol: La passion du bronze.* Paris: Fondation Dina Vierny–Musée Maillol, 1995.

WASSERMAN 1975
Wasserman, Jeanne. *Metamorphoses in Nineteenth-Century Sculpture.* Cambridge, Mass.: Fogg Art Museum, Harvard University, 1975.

WERTH 1990
Werth, Margaret. "Engendering Imaginary Modernism: Henri Matisse's *Bonheur de vivre.*" *Genders,* no. 9 (fall 1990): 49–74.

WRIGHT 2004
Wright, Alastair. *Matisse and the Subject of Modernism.* Princeton, N.J.: Princeton University Press, 2004.

Index

Notes: References in this catalogue to specific casts of sculpture and to other works not easily distinguishable have been annotated with the names of the holder. The following abbreviations have been used: BMA = Baltimore Museum of Art; DMA = Dallas Museum of Art; Guggenheim = Solomon R. Guggenheim Museum, New York; Hirshhorn = Hirshhorn Museum and Sculpture Garden, Smithsonian Institution; LACMA = Los Angeles County Museum of Art; MOMA = Museum of Modern Art, New York; Nasher = the Nasher Sculpture Center, Dallas; SFMOMA = Museum of Modern Art, San Francisco.

Page references in *italics* denote illustrations; page references in ***boldface italics*** denote plates.

Photography and Copyright Credits

All works by Henri Matisse: © 2007 Succession H. Matisse, Paris/Artists Rights Society (ARS), New York

© 2007 Estate of Alexander Archipenko/Artists Rights Society (ARS), New York: cat. 145

Photo Archives Matisse, Paris—All rights reserved: fig. 2, 9, 15, 36, 38, 45, 51, 53, 62, 63, 69; pp. 16, 48, 98–99; endsheets

The Art Institute of Chicago: cat. 29

© 2007 Artists Rights Society (ARS), New York/ADAGP, Paris: Constantin Brancusi: cat. 148; Alberto Giacometti: cat. 154; Henri Laurens: cat. 155; Aristide Maillol: fig. 21; cat. 157–59

Photograph © reproduced with the Permission of The Barnes Foundation, All Rights Reserved: fig. 28 (BF 719)

Photographie Jean Bernard ©: fig. 5, 26, 31; cat. 76, 119

Philip Bernard: cat. 8, 22, 95

Bibliothèque Kandinsky, Centre Pompidou, Musée national d'art moderne, Paris: p. 26

Ben Blackwell: cat. 6, 13, 31

Ann Boulton: fig. 66, 72, 79, 83, 86

Christopher Burke, New York: cat. 11, 17, 19, 21, 38, 39, 56, 63, 69, 79, 108, 116, 121, 129, 135, 136, 140, 143, 144

CNAC/MNAM/Dist. Réunion des musées nationaux/Art Resource, N.Y.: cat. 15, 103, 126, 130, 134

The Condé Nast Publications Inc. (*Vanity Fair*), New York: fig. 7

Guy-Patrice et Michel Dauberville, *Matisse* (Paris: Bernheim Jeune, 1995), vol. 1, pp. 86, 88–90, 174 (for fig. 59, 57, 58, 56, 48, respectively)

© The Detroit Institute of Arts: cat. 151

Ted Dillard Photography: cat. 132

D. R.: fig. 67; cat. 2

Ali Elai: cat. 57

Lee Ewing: fig. 17

Courtesy of Galerie Bernheim-Jeune, Paris: fig. 48, 56–59

George Eastman House: fig. 71; p. xvi

Courtesy of the Research Library, Getty Research Institute, Los Angeles: fig. 74

Tom Haartsen: cat. 157

David Heald, Courtesy of the Nasher Sculpture Center: front cover; fig. 23; cat. 14, 36, 44, 47, 66, 75, 77, 99, 124, 145, 160, 275

Mitro Hood: fig. 16, 18, 20, 24, 29, 30, 32–35, 39, 40, 43, 44 a–d, 46, 47, 80, 84; cat. 1, 4, 12, 24, 30, 35, 45, 58, 65, 68, 73, 74, 78, 97, 98, 111, 113, 122, 123, 142, 146, 154, 156

C. Jean: fig. 55

Tom Jenkins: fig. 1, 8, 12, 68; cat. 5

Dmitri Kessel for *Life Magazine*, © Getty Images: fig. 22

Florian Kleinefenn: cat. 92

Howard Matthew Korn: cat. 23

Ellen Lebenski, Courtesy of PaceWildenstein, New York: cat. 96

Erich Lessing/Art Resources, NY: fig. 10

© 2003 The Metropolitan Museum of Art: cat. 32, 37, 60, 70, 137 (inv. 2002.456.116, 49.70.222, 49.70.8, 2002.456.4, 2002.456.58, respectively)

Philippe Migeat: cat. 15, 134

Photographie © Musée de Grenoble: cat. 62

Musée national d'art moderne, Centre Georges Pompidou, Paris: fig. 41

2005 © Museum Associates/LACMA: cat. 80, 82, 84, 86, 88

Digital image © The Museum of Modern Art, New York/Licensed by SCALA/Art Resource, N.Y.: fig. 3, 6, 13, 42; cat. 7, 20, 53, 55, 109; back cover

National Gallery of Art, Washington, D.C., image © Board of Trustees: fig. 17

© National Gallery of Canada: cat. 54

© Photothèque des musées de la Ville de Paris/cliché Pierrain: fig. 10

© 2007 Estate of Pablo Picasso/Artists Rights Society (ARS), New York: cat. 160, 161

Réunion des musées nationaux/Art Resource, NY: fig. 55

José A. Sanchez Jr.: fig. 19; cat. 46, 101, 104–107, 114, 115, 117, 128, 131, 150, 161, 165

Lee Stalsworth: cat. 59, 81, 83, 85, 87, 89, 94, 273, 274

The Sussse Fondeur Archive, fig. 77; p. 74

Tate London 2006: fig. 37; cat. 16

Thannhauser Records, Zentralarchiv des internationalen Kunsthandels, Cologne; A77/X: fig. 64

© V&A Images: fig. 14

Ville de Nice, Musée Matisse/Nathalie Lavarenne: fig. 78

Ville de Nice, Service photographique: cat. 72, 155

Photography by Robert Wedermeyer: cat. 48–51

Graydon Wood: cat. 148

Library of Congress Cataloging-in-Publication Data
Kosinski, Dorothy M.
Matisse : painter as sculptor / Dorothy Kosinski, Jay McKean Fisher, Steven Nash ; essays by Ann Boulton, Oliver Shell ; contributions by Heather MacDonald, Jed Morse, Oliver Shell.
p. cm.
Published in conjunction with the exhibition held at the Dallas Museum of Art and Nasher Sculpture Center, Jan. 21–Apr. 29, 2007; San Francisco Museum of Modern Art, June 9–Sept. 16, 2007; and Baltimore Museum of Art, Oct. 28, 2007–Feb. 3, 2008.
Includes bibliographical references and index.
ISBN 10: 0-300-11541-5 (hardcover : alk. paper)
ISBN 13: 978-0-300-11541-3 (hardcover : alk. paper)
1. Matisse, Henri, 1869–1954—Exhibitions. I. Fisher, Jay McKean, 1949–. II. Nash, Steven A., 1944–. III. Matisse, Henri, 1869–1954. IV. Dallas Museum of Art. V. Title.
NB553.M39A4 2006
730.92—dc22 2006027506

Front cover: Henri Matisse, *Large Seated Nude,* 1922–1929. Cat. 99
Back cover: Henri Matisse, *Odalisque with a Tambourine,* 1925–1926. Cat. 109
Endsheets: Matisse in his apartment in Paris, boulevard de Montparnasse, with a group of his sculptures, c. 1946
Page ii: Henri Matisse, *Blue Nude: Memory of Biskra,* 1907. Cat. 46
Page iii: Henri Matisse, *Reclining Nude I (Aurora),* 1907. Cat. 44
Frontispiece: Henri Matisse, *The Dance,* 1911. Cat. 59
Page vi: Henri Matisse, *Still Life with a Geranium,* 1906. Cat. 29
Page xvi: Alvin Langdon Coburn, Matisse in his studio at Issy-les-Moulineaux, May 1913, at work on *The Back II*
Page 16: Pierre Matisse, photograph of Matisse and Aristide Maillol in Maillol's studio
Page 26: Hélène Adnant, Matisse in his studio in Nice, working on cut-outs, 1952; in the background, *Two Negresses* in an early state
Page 48: Matisse working on *Large Seated Nude,* c. 1925
Page 72: The Susse Foundry, Arcueil, France, c. 1980–1981, with castings of Henri Matisse's *The Back I–IV,* center
Pages 98–99: Group of Matisse's sculptures in the artist's apartment in Paris, boulevard de Montparnasse, c. 1946

Dallas Museum of Art
Dorothy Kosinski, Senior Curator of Painting and Sculpture and The Barbara Thomas Lemmon Curator of European Art
Heather MacDonald, The Lillian and James H. Clark Assistant Curator of European Painting and Sculpture
Tamara Wootton-Bonner, Director of Exhibitions and Publications
Eric Zeidler, Publications Assistant
Laura Bruck, McDermott Curatorial Intern

The Baltimore Museum of Art
Jay McKean Fisher, Deputy Director of Curatorial Affairs and Senior Curator of Prints, Drawings, and Photographs
Oliver Shell, Assistant Curator of European Painting and Sculpture
Ann Boulton, Objects Conservator
Michelle Boardman, Director of Creative Services
Mitro Hood, Senior Photographer
Chelsey Moore, Publications Coordinator

Nasher Sculpture Center
Steven Nash, Director
Jed Morse, Assistant Curator
Jennifer Ritchie, Head of Registration and Rights & Reproductions

Published in association with Yale University Press
P.O. Box 209040
302 Temple Street
New Haven, Connecticut 06520-9040
www.yalebooks.com

Edited by Frances Bowles
Proofread by Melissa Duffes
Designed by Jeff Wincapaw
Typeset by Marissa Meyer in Le Monde Sans
Color separations by iocolor, Seattle
Produced by Marquand Books, Inc., Seattle
www.marquand.com
Printed and bound in China by C&C Offset Printing Co., Ltd.

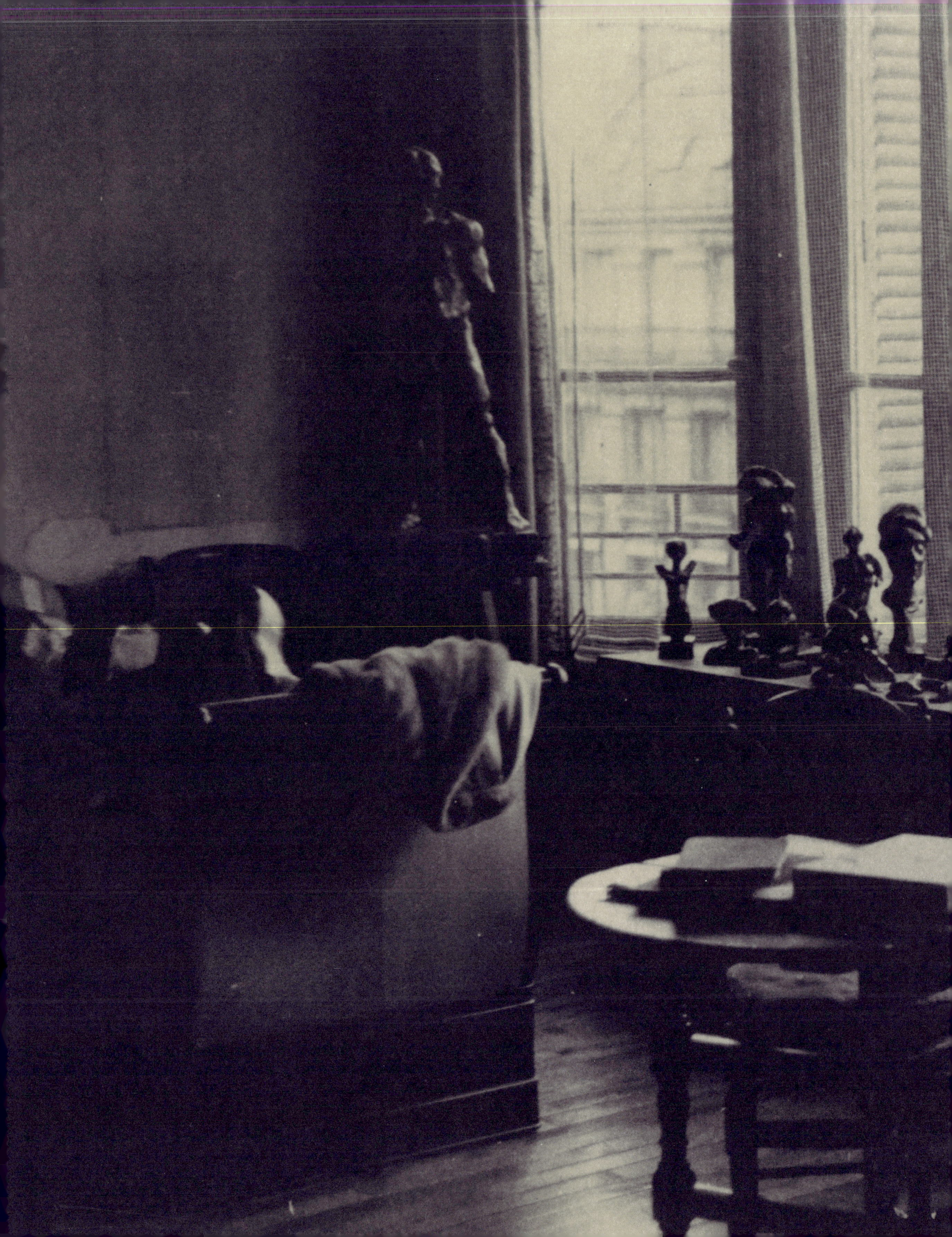